D1610018

The Edinburgh History of Education in Scotland

The Edinburgh History of Education in Scotland

Edited by Robert Anderson, Mark Freeman and Lindsay Paterson

EDINBURGH
University Press

© editorial matter and organisation Robert Anderson,
Mark Freeman and Lindsay Paterson, 2015
© the chapters, their several authors, 2015

Edinburgh University Press Ltd
The Tun – Holyrood Road
12 (2f) Jackson's Entry
Edinburgh EH8 8PJ
www.euppublishing.com

Typeset in 10/12 Goudy Old Style by
Servis Filmsetting Ltd, Stockport, Cheshire,
printed and bound in Great Britain by
CPI Group (UK) Ltd, Croydon CR0 4YY

A CIP record for this book is available from the British Library

ISBN 978 0 7486 7915 7 (hardback)
ISBN 978 0 7486 7916 4 (webready PDF)
ISBN 978 0 7486 7917 1 (epub)

Contents

Figures and Tables

Figures

Tables

Acknowledgements

The editors are grateful to the contributors to this volume, to our copy-editor Anna Stevenson, and to John Watson and Ellie Bush at Edinburgh University Press for their encouragement, assistance and forbearance. We also acknowledge a research workshop grant awarded to Mark Freeman in 2011 by the Royal Society of Edinburgh. Many of the contributors to this volume presented papers at a conference in October 2011, held at the Royal Society of Edinburgh, that was supported by this grant.

Permission for the use of illustrations as figures has been kindly given as follows:

Figure 4.1: British Library
Figure 4.2: University of Aberdeen
Figures 15.1 and 15.2: SCRAN
Figures 17.1 and 17.2: Bòrd na Gàidhlig

Editors' Introduction

Robert Anderson, Mark Freeman and Lindsay Paterson

Scholarly work on the history of Scottish education has developed significantly in the past four decades. The contributors to this book draw upon the best of it, presenting new ways of interpreting Scotland's educational history since the Middle Ages, and casting new light on long-established debates about its significance. The book is not intended to be a comprehensive account, but rather to distil good-quality recent research. Nevertheless, so active has the field become that the essays brought together here provide a broad picture of Scottish education in the periods which it covers. All the chapters were written specially for this volume, and all the authors are authorities in the fields about which they write. They cover topics ranging from the origins of the Scottish universities, through the development of parish schooling in the Reformation, through the reforms of the nineteenth century, to the radical extension of educational participation during the twentieth century. It is hoped that the broad coverage will appeal to the general reader interested in Scottish history and to students studying the history or current development of Scottish education.

Discussion of the history of Scottish education invariably comes round to the question of myth – the supposedly long-standing belief that the country's education system has been of high quality, has been nationally distinctive and has consisted for a long time of educational institutions that are accessible to social groups which would have had more limited opportunities in other countries. The contrast traditionally drawn is most often with England, especially in the twentieth century, but in the long period of educational development from the Reformation to at least the middle of the nineteenth century Scotland's educational distinction was thought to be notable on a much wider stage, epitomising what Anderson and Wallace in their chapter call the Calvinist stereotype of 'the "metaphysical" Scot, a lover of argument and speculation, always inclined to see issues in terms of abstract principle'. That potentially complacent national belief was then challenged from early in the twentieth century, first of all – in the 1920s and earlier – by educational outsiders such as the radical teacher A. S. Neill, and later by mainstream opinion, such as by social historians and social scientists between the 1960s and the 1980s.[1] Many of the authors here address the question of myth, but they also have moved on from it in a manner that has become evident in scholarship only since the 1980s. Partly this is because, as David Northcroft notes, 'an anti-myth to replace the officially cherished one' is no less a myth than what it denounces, but the main reason is that careful scholarship has given a better understanding than hitherto of the extent to which the myths of open access and of intellectualism rest on actual experience. We have come to understand, too, the ways in which myth can be invoked in public debate, as a way in which national identity can shape politics. Beliefs about Scottish education have thus contributed to national self-definition as Scotland has moved from being a fairly content partner in the Union to acquiring a large amount of political self-government.

There are common themes that give substance to the perennial concerns about whether Scottish education is distinctive, and indeed none of the contributors here is particularly preoccupied with the question of distinctiveness: that is another development of recent decades, a greater inclination than in the previous half-century to interpret Scottish education in the context of its own social development rather than primarily by comparison with elsewhere. The old theme of how wide opportunity was still features strongly, but equally prominent is attention to contemporary discourse about that question. The key Act of 1872 – which laid the basis of a modern national system of schooling – 'may indeed be seen', McDermid argues in her chapter, 'as an attempt to revive the Presbyterian educational tradition by seeking to ensure common provision across the country', so that this was new only because the agency of national provision had become the state in place of the churches. In debates about nineteenth-century university reform, Anderson and Wallace point out, 'it was widely agreed that the openness of the universities to all citizens was a national principle to be valued and defended'. The emerging towns of the eighteenth century, Moore notes, kept fees low so that a full elementary curriculum would be accessible to poor families. Fifteenth-century schooling made 'some attempt to provide for poor scholars', in the words of Ewan. The principle of accessibility then may be found to be sufficiently consistent to provide the myth with a basis in tradition, even if not perhaps strongly enough to make tradition into what Northcroft calls 'chronicle'.

The tradition was thus not absent, though perhaps exiguous. The same might be said of other ways in which the national system had inclinations towards the universal. Though girls did not have equal access until well into the twentieth century, there were probably, writes Moore – even in the early modern period – 'some schools where girls were educated . . . Girls may have been taught along with boys in some reading schools'. Girls might receive education from convent schools, one of the many ways – Holmes points out – in which pre-Reformation education was better than the reformers were willing to accept. That in turn depended on there being nuns who, as Curran notes, were well-educated and who had access to libraries of the same kind of quality (though not as extensive) as monks. The immediate precursor to twentieth-century emancipation was in the slow growth in the nineteenth century of girls 'taking higher subjects, including Latin and mathematics' (McDermid), and the willingness of some teachers to provide classes for girls, aided – as Moore notes – by teachers' then having much greater freedom than their successors to recruit pupils directly into individual classes, even when they were not enrolled for a whole programme of study in what would later be called a school.

In contrast to many other countries in the modern period, moreover, Scottish rural education outside the Highlands was of high quality, and so – as noted by Cameron and by Stevenson – the rural poor were generally quite well provided for. So good were the schools of the North-East – aided by the Dick bequest which raised teachers' salaries in return for their undertaking further study – that the counties in a broad arc from Moray round to Kincardine became the core repository of the whole national myth. But the situation in the Gaelic-speaking districts after the seventeenth century was not nearly so commendable, because the language barrier was not properly addressed (or even thought about educationally) until well into the twentieth century: as Cameron, and O'Hanlon and Paterson, explain, even using Gaelic as a route to learning English was only poorly understood in the nineteenth century, and any idea that Gaelic itself might be a pedagogically worthwhile medium was largely absent until after the Second World War. This contrasts with the flourishing of Gaelic scholarship in the medieval period, as noted in the chapters by Hammond and Curran, which had legacies well into the sixteenth century (Holmes and Ewan).

Accessibility is, though, not the most strongly recurrent theme in this collection. More prominent, in fact, is the authors' agreement that some version of liberal education has retained a status in Scotland quite consistently. The concept of liberal education – as Sheldon Rothblatt has observed[2] – is so protean that it has been adapted to multitudinous programmes, but a common theme has been an ethical ideal, and an eschewing of directly practical immediate purposes. Linking with the theme of open access has also been a further principle that liberal education was not to be reserved to an elite: 'in other countries', Anderson and Wallace observe, 'the classics were the preserve of the social elite; in Scotland they were open to the people'. As in many European countries, the classical ideal was nourished in the medieval monasteries, the secluded learning in which is described by Curran as serving rules of how to live well: 'the cloister area', where contemplation and meditation would be focused, 'was a peaceful haven from the outside world, a symbol of heavenly paradise, a carefully planned centre of the community'. The ideal then gradually reached into the wider society, through the graduates of the medieval universities who served what Hammond calls the 'increasingly secular bureaucracies' of the medieval court. The notion that the mind, reared on good thoughts, might gain ethical strength from contemplative reading, was then strong enough to survive the turmoil of Reformation. Holmes's chapter takes as one of its main themes the persistence of a humanist idea of education through the Reformation period, a stronger continuity than is usually supposed, a sharing of 'a common Latin humanist culture': in consequence, 'the first educational programme of the Scottish Protestant Reformers was . . . in its shape and emphasis on grammar very close to Catholic humanist reform'. Ewan links this to a civic purpose, Scotland's most recurrent version of the ethical concerns that liberal education raises: there was a 'stress on education and classical learning, as well as the ideal of responsible citizenship and service to the state'. The parish schools finally established properly by the Act of 1696 aimed to provide what Bischof calls a 'liberal curriculum'. The Enlightenment was liberal not only in the most obvious way, at the elite level of the universities (Allan), but also through school textbooks (Moore). Moreover, if the Reformation was as much about educational continuity as about disruption, the Enlightenment started the process of making the religious tradition secular, rather than abolishing it. The Scottish Enlightenment practice of tolerant education was as crucial in its way to the evolution of liberal ways of thinking as were Adam Smith's more obviously important ideas. As Allan puts it,

> that [the atheist] Hume was . . . able to prosper, to publish, to live freely and indeed be a good friend of many of the younger and more liberal-minded clergy and academics of his day is another strong indication of just how intellectually tolerant parts of Scottish society were becoming by the middle years of the eighteenth century.

In the nineteenth century, the Dick bequest's insistence on advanced education for the teachers whom it paid not only established an academic liberal curriculum as the core of the schools in the North-East (as Northcroft notes), but also contributed to reform of the education of teachers throughout Scotland, through such writers as S. S. Laurie (professor of education at Edinburgh University – the first such post in the English-speaking world) aided by the churches, as Stevenson notes: 'it was the Presbyterian churches who continually tried to resist the anglicising influence of their paymasters, the Privy Council, and uphold the Scottish tradition of a broad school curriculum and raise standards through their teacher training colleges'. The school boards after 1872 maintained the tradition at local level: as McDermid puts it, they 'saw it as their duty to preserve the meritocratic tradition by providing a liberal education and a uniform curriculum taught by qualified teachers'.

The main impetus to maintain the liberal tradition in the twentieth century came through the increasing importance of the professions – what Harold Perkin has called the rise of professional society,[3] and which Anderson and Wallace here describe as meaning that 'careers in the expanding middle class came to depend on examinations and formal qualifications'. Placing liberal education at the heart of professional education had a long history in Scotland, notably in the education of ministers and lawyers. As Finlay notes of the law, 'at the summit of the profession, there was great respect for learning, and much weight was placed on the intellectual world of civilian study and classical literature'. Anderson and Wallace point out that the Scottish university tradition had long seen a grounding in liberal studies as necessary for the professions: 'the purpose of the [under-graduate curriculum] was to give a general liberal education, complete in itself but also as a foundation for the professional faculties of law and divinity'. This conception then became the touchstone of liberal education in the twentieth century, what George Davie called (in 1961) the 'democratic intellect'. Paterson, though acknowledging the effect of the idea of a liberal education in twentieth-century policy, notes that enabling wide access to it was much more a matter of the expansion and new definition of secondary schooling than of the universities where Davie directs his main attention. Indeed, the development of adult education in the early twentieth century (as outlined by Sutherland) had an important social impact that Davie ignores. By this time, moreover – in a more firmly democratic age – citizenship could be exercised directly by students themselves while they were studying and not merely as a consequence later: students' becoming political activists, even well before the 1960s, was, as Macdonald puts it, 'when the elitism of the "democratic intellect" felt the full force of democracy in real time and not in the abstract'. Perhaps the main political effect of that stronger democratic assertiveness has been the emergence of a consensus by the end of the century that Scotland should have its own parliament, and – as Humes explains – educational debates, often invoking history, have been prominent in its deliberations.

Part of the general process of the growth of professional education was the growing professionalism of school teaching itself. By the eve of the First World War – in McDermid's words – 'the majority of teachers employed by boards in Scotland held certificates from training colleges, compared to under half of those working for school boards in England'. There was a growth of expertise in pedagogy and in its contributory disciplines of psychology and child development, culminating in the first half of the century in the remarkable episode of what Lawn and Deary call the Scottish School of Educational Research, under the guidance of Godfrey Thomson at Edinburgh University. Teachers throughout the land were recruited as a field force to test psychometrically in 1932 every child born in 1921 and attending a school in Scotland. The exercise was repeated in 1947, with effects on the development of Scottish educational research which lasted until the end of the century, although by then the education of teachers had become once more much less academic.

In these interlinked currents of thought in Scottish education – widening access to a predominantly liberal curriculum – Scottish distinctiveness could at most be described as being pioneering, because such developments have spread now globally. International connections are a further recurrent theme in this collection. There has often been emulation of England, though, as McDermid puts it, English influences 'did not mean passively following English policy and practice'. The Enlightenment, Allan points out, 'open[ed] up . . . the Scottish universities to a much broader non-Scottish clientele'. But there had always been external contacts, for example in the seventeenth-century legal connections with Dutch law (Finlay), or in what, for the twelfth and thirteenth centuries,

Hammond describes as '"Europeanisation", spurred on by a centralising hier-archical church establishment, increasingly intertwined royal and aristocratic classes across Western Europe with common cultural touchstones, and an expan-sive monetising commercial economy'. In the late nineteenth century – to which the rhetoric about anglicisation has often referred (following George Davie's writing) – German examples were at least as important as English: in the words of Anderson and Wallace, 'German universities were now setting the pace in science and scholarship for the whole of Europe'. In any case, the effects were in both directions. Nineteenth-century universities in England were founded on Scottish models (as were eighteenth- and seventeenth-century universities in the USA), drawing sometimes also on distinctive Scottish traditions in adult educa-tion, as Sutherland notes. In the twentieth century, the Scottish contribution to international educational research through Thomson's school was, as Lawn and Deary explain, highly distinctive.

At the same time as sharing in – and occasionally leading – international developments, Scottish education has also been one of the defining features of Scottish identity. Educational politics has often had an effect on Scottish politics generally. One little-noticed example is the role of women in governing educa-tion: as elsewhere in Britain, McDermid notes, because women could be elected to the school boards established by the 1872 Act, 'education was a key area where women could achieve a measure of status and authority, and the work they did on school boards set an important precedent for women holding public office'. In a quite different era, the educational controversies of the 1980s contributed to the wider campaigning for some measure of Scottish self-government. The effect of educational concerns on national identity is, moreover, wider than these specifically political topics, important though they are. The mid-nineteenth-century debates about creating a national system were partly debates about the place of education in national identity in a secular age. The slightly later debates about the distinctiveness (or otherwise) of Scottish university education – debates which have never subsequently gone away – revealed the variety of forms which Scottish national identity might take: as Anderson and Wallace say, 'this [variety] allowed the Scottish universities to develop on authentically national lines within the unionist political system'.

The papers collected in this book thus raise perennial concerns about Scotland, and concerns that transcend national boundaries. The focus of this book is historical, and it does not supersede two other collections of recent schol-arly writing about Scottish education: the volume on education edited by Heather Holmes in the 'Scottish Life and Society' series published by the European Ethnological Research Centre and the four editions of *Scottish Education* pub-lished by Edinburgh University Press since 1999.[4] The historical approach of the present volume is needed for a full understanding of the present, and comple-ments other disciplinary approaches from which readers of these two collections will profit. Each chapter here also includes a select bibliography of further reading that would provide an introduction to further investigation of its topic.

The many new ways of thinking about Scotland which have developed in the past four decades have now shaped Scottish identity and, through that, Scottish politics. As the country experiments with constantly evolving types and amounts of autonomy, the legacy of educational history will continue to be a rich source of ideas. At the same time, the educational dilemmas which have faced Scotland are instances of debates that affect education in many other places. The difficulties of widening of access, the meaning of liberal education, the roles of ethics and religion and politics: as discussed by the contributors to this book, these and similar problems offer some ways of thinking about the nature of education that are relevant far beyond Scotland's own path.

Notes

1. See, for example: Christopher Harvie, *No Gods and Precious Few Heroes*, 1st edn (Edinburgh University Press, 1981); R. A. Houston, *Scottish Literacy and the Scottish Identity: Illiteracy and Society in Scotland and Northern England 1600–1800* (Cambridge University Press, 1985); Walter M. Humes, *The Leadership Class in Scottish Education* (John Donald, 1986); W. M. Humes and H. M. Paterson (eds), *Scottish Culture and Scottish Education* (John Donald, 1983); James G. Kellas, *Modern Scotland* (Pall Mall Press, 1968), pp. 76–100; T. C. Smout, *A Century of the Scottish People* (Collins, 1986), pp. 209–30.
2. Sheldon Rothblatt, *Tradition and Change in English Liberal Education* (Faber & Faber, 1976), pp. 195–206.
3. Harold Perkin, *The Rise of Professional Society* (Routledge, 1989).
4. Heather Holmes (ed.), *Institutions of Scotland: Education*, Scottish Life and Society: A Compendium of Scottish Ethnology, vol. 11 (Tuckwell Press, 2000); T. G. K. Bryce, W. M. Humes, D. Gillies and A. Kennedy (eds), *Scottish Education*, 4th edn (Edinburgh University Press, 2013).

I

Education in Scotland from 1000 to 1300

Matthew Hammond

Across Europe in the middle ages, education was the preserve of the church, and schooling was run by clerics, from ad hoc provision under the local priest to formally organised monastic, cathedral and burgh schools.[1] By the thirteenth century, there were burgeoning communities of scholars in a few places scattered across Europe and England (but not in Scotland) which eventually became known as universities. The first priority of any school was the teaching of Latin, the language of the Vulgate Bible and, just as importantly, the international language of ecclesiastical, as well as increasingly secular, bureaucracies. Being literate meant being able to read and write Latin. In some times and places, moreover, some students also achieved literacy in vernaculars like Gaelic, French and English.

Education before 1100

There are very few surviving written texts from Scotland before the twelfth century and these have come down to us in later copies. However, wherever churchmen went, so did literacy and learning, and important monastic centres like Iona were also focal points for authorship and manuscript production. Pictland, which covered much of modern Scotland north of the Forth, and its successor, the kingdom of Alba, were home to important religious houses; however, due to the failure of any textual evidence to survive from these sites, our main evidence of literacy in Pictland comes from stone inscriptions.[2]

Although the names and locations of specific teachers and schools in Scotland do not begin to appear until around 1100, it is still possible to glean a hint of the nature of learning before this time from stories about famous learned churchmen. The first comes from the late-tenth-century *Life* of St Cathróe, who was born in east central Scotland around 900 and spent his ecclesiastical career in continental Europe, eventually as abbot of Metz in Lorraine. Cathróe, member of a royal dynasty, studied at Armagh in Ireland, a major church which was the centre of the cult of St Patrick. There, he 'explored from end to end the school of Wisdom', studies which, according to his hagiographer at least, included rhetoric, philosophy, mathematics and astronomy. Returning to Scotland, he was enticed to act as an instructor to students there. 'The Scots have many thousand teachers', wrote the hagiographer, 'but not many fathers'.[3] The importance of Ireland as a centre of learning is moreover suggested by the story, recorded in Latin poetry, of the Welshman Sulien, bishop of St David's in the 1070s and 1080s. Scion of a great ecclesiastical dynasty, Sulien first studied in Wales and then set out to continue his education in Ireland. Blown off course to 'Albania' (Scotland north of the Forth), he studied the seven liberal arts for five years there, before spending the next decade in Ireland.[4] While we should be wary of reading too much detail into these stories, they do at the very least suggest there were teachers and schools in Scotland in the tenth and eleventh centuries.

It is important to keep in mind that when contemporaries mentioned 'Scotland' in stories like these, the land to which they were referring was much smaller than modern Scotland. *Albania* or *Scotia* in Latin referred only to the lands north of the Forth-Clyde isthmus, and sometimes only to those between the Firth of Forth and the River Spey. The realm ruled over by the kings of Scots before the reign of Alexander III (1249–86) was a collection of distinct lands, with varying types of relationship to the king, characterised by different languages and customs, legal and political traditions, and social and economic ties. The largely English-speaking rump of Northumbria, referred to as Lothian, the formerly Welsh-speaking kingdom of Strathclyde and the Hiberno-Norse region of Galloway were not thought of as part of 'Scotland' until the thirteenth century.[5] The kingdom's core region in the eleventh and twelfth centuries was to be found in the east central counties of Fife, Perthshire and Angus, and it is from here that the lion's share of our evidence survives.

Literacy and Schools in Scotland North of the Forth

The first centre of learning it is now possible to discern is Abernethy in south-east Perthshire, the place where Máel Coluim (Malcolm) III met William the Conqueror in 1072. We have striking visual confirmation of its prominence in the late eleventh century in the form of the remarkable free-standing round tower there. Recent scholarship has demonstrated that Abernethy was an important locus for high-status intellectual activity and manuscript production at this time. One likely output was a version of the Pictish king-list which included a short foundation narrative of Abernethy, composed in the reign of King Máel Coluim (1058–93). Furthermore, Thomas Clancy has argued convincingly that this was the location for the production of both the Latin recension of the ninth-century *Historia Brittonum* ('History of the Britons') which attributed the work to 'Nennius' as well as its Gaelic-language translation, the *Lebor Bretnach*, suggesting the existence of scholars working at a high level in both languages. Both the scribe of the Latin recension, one Euben (Owain or Ywein), and its recipient, Samuel, are named. Samuel is called '*infans magistri mei*', 'the child of my master', one Beulan the priest.[6] As with the poem on Sulien's mention of 'fathers', this reference appears to suggest a figurative father-son relationship for the teacher and pupil, a conception that was further applied in the term *mac léginn*, 'son of learning', to refer to a student. A number of Abernethy clerics appeared as witnesses to a gift of land around 1100 by a member of the royal family to the house of *céli Dé* (Culdees, or 'clients of God', an Irish ascetic religious order) at St Serf's on Loch Leven. Among them was the apparent son (Máel Snechta) of the master (Beólán) who had ordered the transcription and translation of the *Historia Brittonum*. Also among the Abernethy contingent of c. 1100 was one Berbeadh, 'rector of the schools of Abernethy', demonstrating that learning went hand in hand with literacy there.[7]

Nearby in Fife the main church centre was St Andrews, seat of Scotland's premier bishop and a focus for pilgrimage, and home to secular clerics, a house of *céli Dé* and, from the middle of the 1140s, an Augustinian cathedral chapter. It is likely that as the kingdom's principal bishop's see, some provision for education had long been available; this is also implied by a foundation account of c. 1100 which makes mention of Master Samuel and his forebears and successors. The Latin term *magister* later came to be used by clerics who had studied at the *studia generalia* (later university), but before this, it may have referred to very learned men more generally. The suggestion that there was a long line of masters at St Andrews certainly bolsters the notion that Master Samuel was a schoolmaster.[8] Eadmer of Canterbury, at least, commented on the presence of scholars (*scholastici*) there in the 1120s.[9]

A century after Eadmer, schools run by Gaelic-speaking *literati* still existed. In or about 1212, Master Samuel's successor, Master Patrick, held the title 'master of the schools of the city of St Andrews'.[10] Between 1210 and 1225, Macbeth, *rex scolarum* ('king of the schools') of Dunblane, and Máel Domnaig, holder of the same office in Muthill, had some of their customary renders in kind converted to a cash payment by the bishop of Dunblane. Around the same time, the cathedral chapter of Dunkeld was still receiving income 'for the use of the *macleins* and *scolocs*'.[11] It is due to a major dispute over revenue that we know about Master Patrick, because the attempts of the cathedral priory to restrict the ancient customary renders of the 'poor scholars' led to the case being referred to Rome and the three papal judges delegate deciding in the scholars' favour. This was probably due to the good offices of their superior, Master Laurence of Thornton, archdeacon of St Andrews. Laurence also held the title of *fer léginn* ('man of learning'), which helps explain why Laurence was so deeply involved in the case. The charter also makes clear that a residence in the city was set aside for the *fer léginn*, and that the renders in grain and cheese were to be delivered there on Martinmas. There was evidently a great deal of distrust between the schools (or the bishop's *familia*) and the priory, because both the *fer léginn* and the prior were to have servants present at the collection of the renders to ensure their quality was good enough for market. Laurence was evidently a man of both cunning and power, because in addition to his servant (as *fer léginn*) checking the quality of the renders, he was also empowered as archdeacon to compel the priory to pay if they failed to do so.[12]

The *fer léginn* was the highest office associated with education found in church establishments across Gaelic Ireland and Scotland. It has been rendered in English with the Latinate term 'lector', but translates literally as 'man of reading or learning'. That the powerful archdeacon of St Andrews held the office in the early thirteenth century gives some sense of its importance. Evidence for a few individuals of this rank in Scotland survives, but must surely be only the tip of an iceberg that once existed. The first mention to survive is Domongart, *fer léginn* of Turriff, a monastery in Buchan, who witnessed a record of a gift to the church of Deer in 1131×32.[13] In 1164, the Annals of Ulster record the existence of Dub Síde, *fer léginn* of Iona, a monastic site whose enduring link to the cult of St Columba (Columcille) suggests that it may have continued to play a part in literacy and learning in the Hebrides at this period.[14] In the early fourteenth century, there was a 'rector of the schools' at Inverness called Master *Felanus*. This name has been interpreted by modern scholars as a garbling of *ferlanus*, the latinisation of *fer léginn*, but it is also possible that this is simply the Gaelic personal name Fáelán.[15] Placename evidence also suggests the existence of a *fer léginn* at Aberdeen.[16] These examples are useful reminders that, although most of our little surviving evidence comes from the east-central core of 'Scotland', similar arrangements must have existed at important churches across Gaelic-speaking regions. It would appear that the *fer léginn* was sometimes a man of great reputation who drew particularly talented students to his school from far and wide; it was probably this figure to which the *Life* of St Cathróe referred when it lamented the scarcity of 'fathers' in 'Scotland'. In 1169, Ruaidrí Ua Conchobair, king of Ireland, endowed the position of *fer léginn* in Armagh to support the instruction of students from Ireland and Scotland. The *fer léginn*, Flann Ua Gormáin (d. 1174), had studied for twenty-one years in England and France before returning to Ireland to run the schools there for the following two decades.[17]

There were a number of terms used in the sources to refer to the students. The *fer léginn* was contrasted in Irish sources with the *mac léginn*, literally meaning 'son of reading or learning'. These are the *macleins* to whom the bishop of Dunkeld owed financial support. In most of our (Latin) sources, however, the students are called by a Latin word. The charters relating to schools at Dunblane and Muthill refer to *scolastici*, whereas the St Andrews agreement of c. 1212 mentions *pauperes scolares*, 'poor scholars'. The Dunkeld provision, however, was for '*Macleins et Scoloccorum*'. *Scolóc* was a word which originally described a scholar or student, but by this time had come to refer broadly to a kind of peasant living on land owned by the bishop. In some cases, as at Ellon in Aberdeenshire, these men evidently retained some duties in staffing the churches, and it is just possible that in the Dunkeld case they still refer to some sort of student, but this must remain unsettled.[18]

Between the experienced 'man of learning' and the youthful 'son of learning', we find the rank of cleric who must have done most of the actual teaching. A number of terms were used to describe these educators. Berbeadh in c. 1100 was called 'rector of the schools', while Macbeth and Máel Domnaig in 1210×25 were 'king of the schools'. Within the same group we must place Master Samuel (c. 1100) and Master Patrick, 'master of the schools of the city of St Andrews' (c. 1212), who clearly worked below the level of the *fer léginn*, Archdeacon Laurence. It is also possible, though not proven, that Beán, 'master of Dunblane' in the 1190s, was a schoolmaster.[19] 'Rector' and 'king' of the schools are translations into Latin of the Gaelic word *toisech*, meaning 'leader'. This is confirmed by the Gaelic notes in the Book of Kells, where a *toisech* of the students is found alongside the *fer léginn*.[20] The choice of one of these terms by a scribe writing in Latin was arbitrary; whereas the leader of the schools of St Andrews around 1212 was 'master', in 1285 Master John Scot of Monethy was 'rector' of the schools there.[21]

What did the students who attended schools such as these go on to do with their lives? Dauvit Broun has identified elite Gaelic *literati* who maintained their high status until some time in the reign of Alexander II (1214–49). The majority of these scholars would have gone on to become churchmen of one sort or another, perhaps priests, living in a community as *céli Dé* or canons, or chaplains or clerks. This knowledge has left only a shadow of its former written output, but their expertise in Gaelic survives in property records in the Book of Deer from c. 1150, in the seal of King Máel Coluim IV (1153–65), in some early charters of Inchaffray Abbey, and in various royal genealogies and king-lists.[22] The genealogy was compiled and recited at the royal inauguration by a high-status individual called the *ollamh ríg*, the King's Poet, who we see in action in accounts of the inauguration of Alexander III in 1249. Genealogy and praise poetry required a high level of education at that time, and many famous churchmen also composed such literature.[23] The Gaelic educated class also included a figure called the *brithem* or *judex* ('judge'). In addition to holding important judicial and administrative duties, these judges comprised a class of legal experts who acted as repositories of the law and may have even drafted new legislation.[24] 'By the second half of the thirteenth century, however', according to Broun, 'Gaelic clerics had all but disappeared, the *judices* had decisively lost status, and the King's Poet had performed his last inauguration'.[25] Gaelic was superseded as the language of power in the Lowlands by, first, Latin and French, and eventually English (or Scots), and the character of schools like those at St Andrews gradually changed.

The twelfth and thirteenth centuries were a period of 'Europeanisation', spurred on by a centralising hierarchical church establishment, increasingly intertwined royal and aristocratic classes across western Europe with common cultural touchstones, and an expansive monetising commercial economy. These developments were encouraged by the kings of Scots, and reformist monasteries staffed by monks and canons regular were deeply involved in all three dimensions of this project. Kings and other power players encouraged the growth of towns licensed with special trading privileges, and it is in these burghs that we find what were likely the biggest schools in the central middle ages. In places where older church establishments and quasi-urban settlement probably predated the burgh, such as Perth, it is possible that the schools already existed; where burghs were created on greenfield sites, like Ayr, the schools must have been new. As was common elsewhere, authority over many of these schools was given by the king or bishop to a monastic house, and it is due to the accident of the survival of the records of some of these monasteries that we know anything at all about these schools.

From Dunfermline Abbey we have two charters of Bishop Robert of St Andrews, probably dating to late in his episcopate (1127–59). One confirms to the abbey a number of things 'which pertain to the episcopal right', including 'the churches of Perth and Stirling and the schools and all the other things belonging to them', suggesting that the schools lay under the immediate authority of the parish churches. There must have been some argument about the nature of this authority, because Bishop Robert issued a second charter specifically reminding people of his gift of 'the schools of Perth and Stirling and all schools which belong to the abbey', which he wished to be 'preserved unimpaired'.[26] Whether Dunfermline had other schools or merely hoped to acquire some is unclear, but the schools (along, perhaps, with the fees paid by the students) were obviously important enough to the abbey for them to complain to the bishop. The churches of Stirling and Perth had been given by King David I to Dunfermline Abbey, without mention of the schools, and it is possible that the schools had attempted to assert independent status against the abbey's claims.[27] In any event, as a daughter-house of the Benedictine cathedral chapter at Canterbury, Dunfermline would have been in direct contact with an advanced centre of learning in the twelfth century. Outside of the cathedral cities, it seems that the control of schools was often – perhaps usually – in the hands of monasteries. For example, between 1218 and 1225, Bishop Gregory of Brechin granted licence to establish schools in the burgh of Dundee to the monks of Lindores Abbey.[28]

Schools in Southern Scotland

Before the mid-thirteenth century, the Scottish kingdom south of the Forth-Clyde line comprised a collection of lands including Lothian, Teviotdale, Strathclyde and Galloway. Welsh as a vernacular had probably disappeared by the twelfth century, and Gaelic and English were the main spoken tongues, with French and Flemish being spoken by many twelfth-century immigrants. It is likely that, as in 'Scotland proper', there would have been schools based at major church settlements. As the seat of a bishopric, Glasgow must have provided some level of education. In Galloway, at Kirkcudbright, there was some kind of school, because when Aelred of Rievaulx visited in the 1160s he encountered some scholars there, according to Reginald of Durham.[29] Obvious candidates for schools would have been other churches with Cuthbertine dedications, like Old Melrose and Edinburgh. It is possible that many English-speaking subjects of the king of Scots may have been drawn to the centre of Cuthbert's cult, Durham, which was staffed by Benedictine monks from 1083. Before the twelfth century, boys were educated in the cathedral itself, but from that point there was a fee-paying grammar school in the city, which was called 'the school of liberal arts' in 1229.[30] Given the extensive cross-border ties of family and lordship at this time, the schools that existed at Norham, Carlisle and Hexham may have also attracted students, but this is not to imply that there were not similar schools north of the Tweed.[31]

As with 'Scotland proper', the major new monasteries south of the Forth were given control over the larger schools. Bishop Herbert of Glasgow (1147–64) gave the churches and schools of Roxburgh to Kelso Abbey.[32] In 1241, the rector of the schools of Roxburgh was one Master Thomas.[33] It has been suggested, but must remain conjectural, that the gift by King David I to Holyrood Abbey of the church of St Cuthbert of Edinburgh also included the schools under their authority.[34] A papal bull of 1187 stated that the schools of Linlithgow were under the jurisdiction of the priory of St Andrews.[35] We know from mentions of their masters that there were also schools in Ayr and Berwick-upon-Tweed by the 1230s.[36] In 1184, Pope Lucius III prohibited anyone – presumably canons of Dryburgh Abbey – from restraining the masters of the schools in the parish of Lanark and other parishes, suggesting a possible interest by the abbeys in rural schools.[37]

Nicholas Orme, expert on medieval schools in England, has warned against reading patterns into the accidental survival of mentions of schools.[38] We must be particularly careful around the issues of schools in the countryside and the question of lay education. The chance survival of the case of Matilda, widow of Richard of Lincoln, is instructive. A landholder in Roxburghshire, she surrendered her lands in Mow on the condition that the monks rebuild 'better and more appropriate schools' in the poor house on the land, at least partly for the benefit of her son William.[39] This mention is remarkable because it implies that there were sometimes schools in more rural settings which religious houses were expected to staff. In this case, the implication is that there had been 'schools' (contemporary sources almost always use the plural) previously that Matilda had deemed inappropriate. Furthermore, there is no indication that William was to follow a career in the church; it would appear that she simply wanted him to get an education. It quite possible that lay literacy was much more widespread in the central middle ages than the (mostly church) records suggest. A thirteenth-century account of the miracles of St Margaret, queen of Scotland, includes a story in which a nobleman 'sent for his Psalter' and 'read the psalms for a long time' without any indication that this was unusual.[40]

Occasionally, masters of schools were either respected or well-connected enough to be enlisted as papal judges-delegate. In canon law cases under the pope's jurisdiction, it was common for the papal *curia* to empanel three clergy-men to adjudicate. Bishops, archdeacons and members of cathedral clergy were often selected, as were abbots, priors and their underlings, but occasionally, masters of schools were appointed. Clerics from one part of the kingdom were often selected to hear cases in another region, for obvious reasons. Master Adam of Perth, master of the schools of Perth, acted alongside the archdeacons of Dunkeld and Dunblane dealing with a dispute over the chapel of Prestwick in Ayrshire. The master of the schools of Berwick was appointed alongside the archdeacon and dean of Lothian in a matter regarding Dundrennan Abbey in Galloway. Alternatively, however, masters may have been chosen sometimes because of local knowledge. Alan, master of the schools of Ayr, dealt with disputes regarding Paisley Abbey's claims in Old Kilpatrick parish, Dunbartonshire. Master John, rector of the schools of St Andrews, acted alongside Ralph, prior of the Isle of May, in a case dealing with Inverkeithing in Fife. Sometimes the judge delegates themselves delegated the work to commissaries who were likely seen as both competent and available; schoolmasters seem to have fitted the bill. Such at least was the case for masters of schools of Berwick in 1279 and of Aberdeen in 1282.[41]

Secular Cathedral Schools

In Scotland, the surviving evidence suggests that most schools in towns (presumably grammar schools open to the fee-paying public) and apparently some rural schools were under the authority of religious houses of monks and canons of various orders. The obvious exception to this pattern were the schools run by the secular cathedrals.[42] The thirteenth-century constitutions of the chapters of Moray (1212) and Aberdeen (1256) placed the authority for the schooling of the choirboys with the precentor (sometimes called the cantor or chanter).[43] The Aberdeen statutes stipulated that four boys were to attend the choir at the discretion of the precentor; however, the duty of ensuring the boys' attendance rested with the master of the schools of Aberdeen, a figure who appears in the charter record in 1282. The 1215 Fourth Lateran Council in Rome had called for bishops and chapters to endow masters in order to teach grammar to clerks, although these edicts were often not followed to the letter.[44] In England, it was common for secular cathedrals to support a public grammar school in addition to the precentor's song school. The likelihood of this scenario in Aberdeen is bolstered by the fact that Thomas of Benham, 'rector of the schools of Aberdeen' in 1263, later became the cathedral's chancellor.[45] In England, schoolmasters in secular cathedrals often became chancellors whose teaching duties were limited to giving lectures in canon law or theology.[46] The Moray statutes tasked the chancellor with directing the schools in theology, although this was apparently not the case in Aberdeen. Based on the usage at Lincoln cathedral, the Moray statutes allowed the chancellor broad authority over schools in the diocese, and it seems likely that other Scottish chancellors had similar rights. Glasgow's chancellor clearly could appoint the master of the grammar school in the fifteenth century; the chapter there included a precentor by 1221 and a chancellor by 1258.[47] Smaller cathedral establishments also filled these positions in the thirteenth century, with that of precentor usually preceding that of chancellor. Precentors were appointed at Aberdeen (by 1244), Brechin (by 1246), Caithness (by 1275), Dunblane (filled by the abbot of Inchaffray by about 1240), Dunkeld (by 1221), Glasgow (by 1221), Moray (by 1230) and at Ross (by 1255); chancellors were appointed at Aberdeen (by 1240), Brechin (by 1343), Caithness (by 1275), Dunblane (by 1296), Dunkeld (by 1287), Glasgow (by 1288), Moray (by 1221) and at Ross (by 1223).[48] As we have seen, authority over the schools in St Andrews remained with the *fer léginn*, perhaps merged with the duties of the archdeacon, and the cathedral did not get a chancellor until the mid-fifteenth century.[49]

Although we know very little about the music schools run by the precentors in the cathedrals, they have left us ample written evidence of the impressive quality of their work. Several cathedral establishments evidently created or collected manuscripts of plainchant offices for saints venerated in Scotland, including Saints Kentigern, Cuthbert, Brigid, Thomas of Canterbury, Machutus and likely Ninian. Gerald of Wales commented on the high quality of music in Scotland, and this is certainly borne out by what we know of religious chant, in particular as regards the development of polyphony. St Andrews was the location for the production in the second quarter of the thirteenth century of the manuscript known now as W_1, in which a sophisticated new Parisian polyphonic chant was adopted and then built upon with two new Office responsories for the feast of St Andrew. Interest in polyphony was not confined to St Andrews: a Dominican friar named Jeronimus of Moray composed several key texts on polyphony in Paris between 1272 and 1304.[50]

Higher Studies

It is clear that many Scottish schools were working to a relatively high level in various fields, but many students left the kingdom to further their studies abroad. There were centres of higher learning across Europe in the twelfth and thirteenth centuries which had grown up around cathedral and monastic establishments, and, increasingly, around the private schools that were rapidly proliferating. These eventually acquired more formal structures and became known as universities (although many such schools never made it that far). At burgeoning centres of learning like Paris, scholars could attain the status of *magister* ('master') and a further proficiency in the seven liberal arts. The *trivium* was seen as the more important component, including within it the essential linguistic skills of grammar, rhetoric and logic; the *quadrivium* (arithmetic, geometry, music, astronomy) often received less attention. More ambitious scholars could then specialise in the higher studies of theology, canon or civil law, or medicine. Bologna was the unrivalled centre for the study of law, and Paris had a high reputation for theology and logic.[51] That so many inhabitants of Scotland went on to study in such places is testament to the quality of the education they received at home.

Medical doctors were among the most likely to have studied at university (or *studium generale*). The *People of Medieval Scotland 1093–1314* database reveals twenty physicians prior to 1300 documented in Scottish charters; all but one of these is also called 'master' in the charters. The earliest of these on record may be Master Thomas, an episcopal clerk at St Andrews from the 1150s. Many of these medical doctors were also clerks or canons attached to bishops and other ecclesiastical prelates, but others were in the service of kings and nobles. King William employed Master Martin as a physician in the 1190s, when he is known to have suffered from serious illness, but Martin seems to have been replaced by a Master Nicholas from the early 1200s. Master Ness (Ramsay?) was given the title of 'physician of the lord king' while in the service of Alexander II. Magnates also sometimes employed medical doctors: a Master Clement appears to have been a physician and chaplain for the constables Richard and William de Morville. A Master Anthony Lombard was in the patronage of Alexander Stewart and appears to have abandoned his vocation in order to become a knight. Not infrequently, these men benefited from the largesse of their wealthy patrons, acquiring landed estates, presumably for producing the desired results.[52]

Study at an institution of higher learning was increasingly seen by the thirteenth century as desirable for those wishing to follow a career in the secular church establishment. The majority of the 678 people in the *People of Medieval Scotland* database to use the title 'master' would have fallen into this category. The bishop of St Andrews had clerks who were masters from the 1150s, while there were cathedral canons of Glasgow and Dunkeld in the 1160s who had undertaken higher studies. There were masters in all the dioceses south of Inverness by 1200, and in some places they made up the majority of canons and dignitaries.[53] It was not unusual for bishops to be masters. William Malveisin, bishop of Glasgow (1199–1202) and bishop of St Andrews (1202–38) may have studied at Paris but probably did not gain a degree. His successors at St Andrews, David of Bernham (1239–53), Abel of Gullane (1254), Gamelin (1255–71), William Wishart (1271–79), William Fraser (1279–97) and William of Lamberton (1297–1328) were all *magistri* (masters). At Dunkeld, Bishops John Scot (1183–1203), John of Leicester (1211–14), Richard of Inverkeithing (1250–72) and Robert de Stuteville (1273–82) had all attended universities. Clement, bishop of Dunblane (1233–58), was one of the first Dominican friars in Scotland and undertook a major reorganisation of the diocese.[54] Masters were ubiquitous in the cathedral chapters, as deans and subdeans, precentors and succentors, chancellors, treasurers and simply as canons. Seventy-five masters were explicitly identified as bishops' clerks and twelve as bishops' chaplains, although the numbers may have been higher. A great number of masters were associated with their parish churches, either as rectors, *personae* or vicars, although in many cases these would have been benefices to supply them with income.

Little is known about the places and courses of study associated with these men, but it would have been seen as advantageous for archdeacons and officials to have an understanding of canon law, for chancellors to be trained in theology and for precentors, with their authority over the music schools, to have at least some grounding in the *quadrivium*. It was common for archdeacons to have undertaken higher studies, and both the long-serving Laurence of Thornton (archdeacon and official of St Andrews, 1209–1238×40) and his brother Adam were masters. At some point Adam picked up the moniker 'Ovid', indicating his love of classical literature.[55] In the thirteenth century, there is seldom a distinction made in personal titles between masters of arts and those who had attained doctorates in fields such as law or theology, although in 1274 an Abraham, professor of law, is found in Fife, perhaps working for St Andrews, and John of Tinwald, professor of civil law, set his seal to a charter in 1294. Master William of Eaglesham, clerk of Bishop William Lamberton, was a professor of decrees and later became archdeacon, and later William Frere, archdeacon of Lothian, was a regent in decrees.[56]

There was much cross-fertilisation between the king's household and the dioceses. Many university graduates also found careers in the royal administration; at least twenty-seven royal clerks in this period were masters. Matthew Scot, who probably studied and/or taught at Paris, was a chancellor of Alexander II; under his son Alexander III the future bishops Gamelin, Richard of Inverkeithing, William Wishart and William Fraser were all chancellor; they were succeeded by the master Thomas de Chartres. Many other masters were clerks to heads of religious houses or lay magnates.

As might be expected, people who made it to university generally came from privileged and well-connected backgrounds. Many masters were nephews and other relatives of bishops, archdeacons and other prelates. The sons of the aristocracy, especially younger sons who did not stand to inherit, made up a large number of Scottish graduates. These included members of the Avenel, del Bois, Bruce, Campbell, Carrick, Chartres, Glencarnie, Hay, Keith, Kennedy, Lincoln, Lindsay, Lockhart, Lovell, Maule, Merlay, Montfort, Montgomery, Murray, de Ros, St Martin, Vaux and Wallace families. At the same time, many people gave up their family name upon entering a career in the church, which is why the backgrounds of many masters are poorly understood. Many masters are known from the names of the churches they held as benefices, the cathedral cities which were their homes or, particularly while they were studying out of the kingdom, were simply called 'Scot' or 'of Scotland'. At Bologna in the 1260s and 1270s, for example, we find Henry Scot and Peter, Robert and Thomas 'of Scotland'.[57]

Students at the universities were divided into 'nations'. The faculty of arts at Paris had four 'nations' – France, Picardy, Normandy and England. In addition to Scots, the English nation at Paris included Germans and a number of other European nationalities. In Oxford, the divide was between 'Southerners' (southern England, Wales and Ireland) and 'Northerners' (northern England and Scotland). This system was scrapped in 1274 due to constant conflict.[58] Violence was a distinct possibility for students abroad, but the case of Gilbert of Dunfermline, who was murdered without provocation by the townspeople of Oxford in 1248, was perhaps an extreme one.[59] Peter Scot and Roger Scot were indicted for being involved in an attack on the papal legate Otto at Osney Abbey in 1238. Simon Scot, a student at Bologna in 1235, was banished for attacking Hugh the Englishman at his lodgings.[60] Finding suitable accommodation was evidently a constant challenge for Scots students abroad, and one of the advantages of the endowed colleges for students was that food was subsidised. Balliol College, Oxford, was founded in the 1260s by John Balliol, father of King John of Scotland (1292–6), apparently as part of a penance imposed upon him by the bishop of Durham, and the foundation was formalised by a charter of Lady Dervorguilla of Galloway, his widow, in 1282. Around this time, the Melrose chronicler commented that scholars staying at Balliol College got eight pence weekly for their common table, while the bishop of Bath's house offered students twelve.[61]

The difficulties of financing a university education are evident from the surviving 'student letters home' of Master William de Bernham, nephew of Bishop David de Bernham and probable son of a mayor of Berwick-upon-Tweed, in the 1250s. The texts of eighteen letters and fragments of his expense accounts survive. He wrote to his mother, his uncle, his nephew and various friends and clerics.[62] Despite his family's wealth and connections, William struggled to maintain a steady income while pursuing his studies at Paris and Oxford. Scholars were typically funded through holding benefices, but the collection of the revenues while William was out of the country proved a major hurdle. Bernham sent letters of attorney to his chaplain at Inchture in Perthshire before obtaining the services of the neighbouring vicar of Longforgan to help in collecting the rents. 'Don't accept a penny', William instructed the vicar, 'unless it is monetised [current] silver, or, if you must, weighed silver, but charge a [commission] on exchange'. William was still able to set aside some of the income for his brother and mother, and was evidently able to afford wine, mustard, bread, soup and other items, although he did have to pawn his books to afford a trip to the papal *curia*, in order to litigate against (Master) Peter Ramsay, bishop of Aberdeen's, claims to a pension of sixty marks from his church of Inchture.[63] Financing a university education, it seems, was far from straightforward in the thirteenth century.

William's letters also reveal something of his network of personal relationships, suggesting that the kingdom's intellectual elites must have formed small cliques while abroad. William's friends included William Wishart, future bishop of St Andrews, and prominent Scottish churchman Adam of Makerstoun. We should not be surprised that William de Bernham's associates were deeply embedded in the church establishment at St Andrews, where his uncle was bishop from 1239 to 1253. In 1250, we find Makerstoun and Wishart, described as provost and *céli Dé* of St Andrews, with five of their fellow '*céli Dé* acting as canons', engaged in a major dispute with the cathedral priory. Just as Master Laurence of Thornton took on the role of *fer léginn*, the best-educated and best-connected men of letters in Scotland were now made *céli Dé* (and Laurence's own brother Adam Ovid had also been associated with the *céli Dé* in 1220).[64] And while the older institutions at St Andrews and across Scotland were undergoing a metamorphosis, this does not mean that they had lost their connection to the past. Alongside Makerstoun and Wishart in 1250 was their fellow *céli Dé*, Master Richard Vairement. A native of Vermand in Picardy who came to Scotland with Queen Marie de Coucy, Richard evidently formed a deep connection with the history of his adopted homeland while in St Andrews. For Richard Vairement was the first great historian of Scotland. Using Geoffrey of Monmouth's *History of the Kings of Britain* and a few short origin accounts and king-lists, Richard created the first narrative of Scottish history from the ancient past to the accession of King Máel Coluim III in 1058, and the foundation for the later chronicles of

John of Fordun and Walter Bower.[65] Vairement symbolises nicely the spirit of the age, with the birth of a new Scotland emerging from the marriage of the Gaelic and the francophone European. And yet he also brings us full circle to where we began, to Abernethy nearly two centuries earlier, to a place of schools and culdees, of masters and learning, and a place of writing history.

Appendix

Table 1.1   Table of known masters and superiors of schools in Scotland, 1100–1315

c. 1100	Berbeadh, rector of the schools of Abernethy	PoMS, no. 3385*
c. 1100	Master Samuel (St Andrews)	
1131×1132	Domongart, *fer léginn* of Turriff	PoMS, no. 6222
1164	Dub Síde, *fer léginn* of Iona	
1210×1225	Macbeth, 'king' of the schools of Dunblane	PoMS, no. 3446
1210×1225	Máel Domnaig, 'king' of the schools of Muthill	PoMS, no. 3459
1211×1213	Master Patrick, master of the schools of the city of St Andrews	PoMS, no. 8385
1211×1213	Master Laurence of Thornton, archdeacon and *fer léginn* of St Andrews	PoMS, no. 835
1210	Master Adam of Perth, master of the schools of Perth	PoMS, no. 3058
1230, 1232	—, master of the schools of Berwick-upon-Tweed	PoMS, no. 7397
1232–1234	Alan, master of the schools of Ayr	PoMS, no. 3760
1233	Master John, rector of the schools of St Andrews	PoMS, no. 3310
1241	Master Thomas, rector of the schools of Roxburgh	PoMS, no. 5761
1243	—, master of the schools of Berwick-upon-Tweed	PoMS, no. 7397
1263	Master Thomas of Benham, rector of the schools of Aberdeen	PoMS, no. 3173
1279	—, rector of the schools of Berwick	PoMS, no. 7397
1282	—, master of the schools of Aberdeen	PoMs, no. 8374
1285	Master John Scott of Monethy, rector of the schools (of St Andrews)	PoMS, no. 5178
c. 1315	Master *Felanus*, rector of the schools of Inverness	

* Individuals appearing in the *People of Medieval Scotland 1093–1314* database (www.poms.ac.uk) are given their unique PoMS number.

Notes

1. I would like to thank first and foremost Simon Taylor for sharing with me his unpublished 2012 paper 'Teaching and learning in St Andrews before the university's foundation'; thanks are also due to Elizabeth Boyle, Dauvit Broun, John Reuben Davies, Nick Evans, Alice Taylor, Eystein Thanisch and Alex Woolf.
2. See Katherine Forsyth, 'Literacy in Pictland', in Huw Pryce (ed.), *Literacy in Medieval Celtic Societies* (Cambridge University Press, 1998), pp. 39–61.
3. David Dumville, 'St Cathróe of Metz and the hagiography of exoticism', in John Carey, Máire Herbert and Pádraig Ó Riain (eds), *Saints and Scholars: Studies*

in Irish Hagiography (Four Courts Press, 2001), pp. 172–88. For text, see Alan Orr Anderson, *Early Sources of Scottish History* A.D. *500 to 1286*, 2 vols (Oliver and Boyd, 1922), i, pp. 431–43. Quotations on p. 437.

4. Michael Lapidge, 'The Welsh-Latin poetry of Sulien's family', *Studia Celtica* 8 (1973), 68–106 (poem at 80–8); John Reuben Davies, 'Aspects of church reform in Wales', in C. P. Lewis (ed.), *Anglo-Norman Studies XXX. Proceedings of the Battle Conference 2007* (Boydell and Brewer, 2008), pp. 85–99.

5. Dauvit Broun, 'Defining Scotland and the Scots before the Wars of Independence', in Dauvit Broun, Richard Finlay and Michael Lynch (eds), *Image and Identity: The Making and Re-making of Scotland Through the Ages* (Edinburgh University Press, 1998), pp. 4–17.

6. Thomas Owen Clancy, 'Scotland, the "Nennian" recension of the *Historia Brittonum*, and the *Lebor Bretnach*', in Simon Taylor (ed.), *Kings, Clerics and Chronicles in Scotland, 500–1297. Essays in Honour of Marjorie Ogilvie Anderson* (Four Courts Press, 2000), pp. 87–107.

7. Cosmo Innes (ed.), *Liber Cartarum Prioratus Sancti Andree in Scotia* [henceforth: *St Andrews Liber*] (Bannatyne Club, 1840). The property records were first written in Gaelic but survive in a thirteenth-century Latin translation copied into the priory of St Andrews' cartulary. A critical edition of the text will appear in Simon Taylor, *The Place-Names of Kinross* (Shaun Tyas, forthcoming).

8. Simon Taylor with Gilbert Márkus, *The Place-Names of Fife*, 5 vols (Shaun Tyas, 2006–12), iii, pp. 412–14. I am grateful to Simon Taylor for this suggestion. It is possible, but purely conjectural, that Master Samuel is to be identified with Samuel 'child' of Beulan the priest in Abernethy.

9. Alan Orr Anderson, *Scottish Annals from English Chroniclers* A.D. *500 to 1286* (Paul Watkins, 1991), p. 142.

10. *St Andrews Liber*, pp. 316–18. A translation and discussion appears in Taylor, *Place-Names of Fife*, iii, pp. 418–20.

11. John Dowden (ed.), *The Chartulary of Lindores Abbey* (Scottish History Society, 1903), nos 33, 34, 46, 47. It is possible that Macbeth, 'king of the schools of Dunblane', was the same person as the Macbeth the priest who was at Dunblane in the 1190s. See Amanda Beam et al., *The People of Medieval Scotland, 1093–1314* [henceforth: PoMS] (PoMS, 2012). Available at www.poms.ac.uk (accessed 26 July 2014), record no. 2734.

12. Taylor, *Place-Names of Fife*, iii, pp. 418–20.

13. Katherine Forsyth, Dauvit Broun and Thomas Clancy, 'The property records: Text and translation', in Katherine Forsyth (ed.), *Studies on the Book of Deer* (Four Courts Press, 2008), pp. 131–44.

14. Anderson, *Early Sources*, ii, p. 253.

15. William Fraser, *The Chiefs of Grant* (n.p., 1883), p. 258; G. W. S. Barrow, 'The lost Gàidhealtachd', in G. W. S. Barrow, *Scotland and its Neighbours in the Middle Ages* (Hambledon, 1992), p. 123; D. E. R. Watt, *A Biographical Dictionary of Scottish Graduates* (Clarendon Press, 1977), p. 187.

16. Cosmo Innes (ed.), *Registrum Episcopatus Aberdonensis* [henceforth: *Aberdeen Reg.*], 2 vols (Spalding and Maitland Clubs, 1845), i, pp. 5, 11. I am grateful to Simon Taylor for this suggestion based on the lands of *Pethferlen* or *Petenderleyn* in Old Machar parish.

17. Anderson, *Early Sources*, ii, p. 267; Dauvit Broun, *The Irish Identity of the Kingdom of the Scots* (Boydell and Brewer, 1999), pp. 2–3.

18. Taylor, *Place-Names of Fife*, v, pp. 485–9.

19. William Fraser (ed.), *Registrum Monasterii S. Marie de Cambuskenneth* (Grampian Club, 1872), no. 122.
20. Máire Herbert, 'Charter material from Kells', in Felicity O'Mahony (ed.), *The Book of Kells: Proceedings of a Conference at Trinity College, Dublin, 6–9 September 1992* (Trinity College, 1994), pp. 60–77; Taylor, *Place-Names of Fife*, v, pp. 618–19.
21. Cosmo Innes (ed.), *Registrum Sancte Marie de Neubotle* (Bannatyne Club, 1849), no. 59.
22. Dauvit Broun, 'Gaelic literacy in eastern Scotland between 1124 and 1249', in Pryce (ed.), *Literacy in Medieval Celtic Societies*, pp. 183–201.
23. John Bannerman, 'The King's Poet and the inauguration of Alexander III', *Scottish Historical Review* 68 (1989), 120–49. The term 'coronation' cannot be used to describe this event, as a crown was not used before 1329.
24. G. W. S. Barrow, 'The judex', in G. W. S. Barrow, *The Kingdom of the Scots*, 2nd edn (Edinburgh University Press, 2003), pp. 57–67; Alice Taylor, *The Shape of the State in Medieval Scotland* (Oxford University Press, forthcoming). I am grateful to Dr Taylor for sharing unpublished material.
25. Broun, 'Gaelic literacy', p. 197.
26. Cosmo Innes (ed.), *Registrum de Dunfermelyn* [henceforth: *Dunfermline Reg.*] (Bannatyne Club, 1842), nos 92, 96; translation from Norman Shead, *Scottish Episcopal Acta, vol. 1* (Scottish History Society, forthcoming). I am grateful to Mr Shead for sharing unpublished material with me.
27. G. W. S. Barrow, *Regesta Regum Scottorum*, i, *Acts of Malcolm IV* (Edinburgh University Press, 1960), no. 118.
28. W. B. D. D. Turnbull (ed.), *Liber Sancte Marie de Lundoris* (Abbotsford Club, 1841), no. 15; John Edgar, *History of Early Scottish Education* (James Thin, 1883), p. 81.
29. J. Raine (ed.), *Reginaldi monachi Dunelmensis libellus de admirandis beati Cuthberti virtutibus* (Surtees Society, 1835), p. 179.
30. Nicholas Orme, 'The schools and schoolmasters of Durham, 1100–1539', *Archaeologia Aeliana*, 5th series, vol. 39 (2010), 289–305.
31. Nicholas Orme, *Medieval Schools from Roman Britain to Renaissance England* (Yale University Press, 2006), pp. 346–72; see also G. G. Coulton, *Scottish Abbeys and Social Life* (Cambridge University Press, 1933), pp. 184–6.
32. Cosmo Innes, *Liber Sancte Marie de Calchou* [henceforth: *Kelso Liber*], 2 vols (Bannatyne Club, 1846), ii, no. 413.
33. Ibid., no. 239.
34. Joseph Robertson, 'On scholastic offices in the Scottish church in the twelfth and thirteenth centuries', in John Stuart (ed.), *Miscellany of the Spalding Club* (Spalding Club, 1852), pp. 56–77; G. W. S. Barrow (ed.), *The Charters of King David I: King of Scots, 1124–53 and of His Son Henry Earl of Northumberland* (Boydell and Brewer, 1999), no. 147.
35. *St Andrews Liber*, pp. 62–7.
36. Cosmo Innes (ed.), *Registrum monasterii de Passelet* (Maitland Club, 1832), pp. 164–75; Cosmo Innes (ed.), *Registrum Episcopatus Glasguensis*, 2 vols (Bannatyne and Maitland Clubs, 1843), nos 160, 166.
37. William Fraser (ed.), *Liber Sancte Marie de Dryburgh* (Bannatyne Club, 1847), no. 249.
38. Orme, *Medieval Schools*, p. 189.
39. *Kelso Liber*, no. 173.
40. Robert Bartlett (ed.), *The Miracles of Saint Aebbe of Coldingham and Saint Margaret of Scotland* (Clarendon Press, 2003), pp. xlvii, 102–3.

41. Paul C. Ferguson, *Medieval Papal Representatives in Scotland: Legates, Nuncios, and Judges-Delegate, 1125–1286* (Stair Society, 1997), pp. 207–68, case nos 30, 53, 57, 85, 86, 87, 153, 154.
42. All but St Andrews and Whithorn had secular chapters.
43. Cosmo Innes (ed.), *Registrum Episcopatus Moraviensis* (Bannatyne Club, 1837), nos 48, 49; *Aberdeen Reg.*, ii, pp. 38–50. For translations of the statutes, see Isobel Woods Preece, *Our Awin Scottis Use: Music in the Scottish Church up to 1603* (Universities of Glasgow and Aberdeen, 2000), pp. 325–42. In England, the teaching duties were delegated to the succentor (or subchanter). Orme, *Medieval Schools*, p. 191.
44. Orme, *Medieval Schools*, p. 202.
45. Cosmo Innes and Patrick Chalmers (eds), *Liber Sancte Thome de Aberbrothoc*, 2 vols (Bannatyne Club, 1848–56), no. 254. What is perhaps odd here is that the four choirboys in Aberdeen appear to have been attending the grammar school, rather than (in addition to?) the music school.
46. Orme, *Medieval Schools*, pp. 81–3, 164.
47. Robertson, 'On scholastic offices', p. 70.
48. D. E. R. Watt and A. L. Murray, *Fasti Ecclesiae Scoticanae Medii Aevi Ad Annum 1638*, revised edn (Scottish Record Society, 2003).
49. Some English dioceses maintained control in the hands of the archdeacon. Orme, *Medieval Schools*, p. 198.
50. Warwick Edwards, 'Chant in Anglo-French Scotland' and 'Polyphony in thirteenth-century Scotland', in Preece, *Our Awin Scottis Use*, pp. 201–71.
51. Hilde de Ridder-Symoens (ed.), *A History of the University in Europe, vol. 1. Universities in the Middle Ages* (Cambridge University Press, 1992), pp. 47–55; Robert Bartlett, *England under the Norman and Angevin Kings 1075–1225* (Clarendon Press, 2000), pp. 508–9.
52. Beam et al., PoMS.
53. Norman Shead, 'Compassed about with so great a cloud: The witnesses of Scottish episcopal *Acta* before *ca* 1250', *Scottish Historical Review* 86 (2007), 159–75.
54. Watt, *Graduates*, passim.
55. Ibid., p. 436.
56. *Dunfermline Reg.*, no. 207; Liber Cartarum Sancte Crucis, ed. Cosmo Innes (Bannatyne Club, 1840), no. 91B; *St Andrews Liber*, p. 120; Joseph Bain (ed.), *Calendar of Documents Relating to Scotland*, 5 vols (HMSO, 1881–8), ii, no. 1709.
57. Watt, *Graduates*, pp. 484–91.
58. Ridder-Symoens (ed.), *History of the University*, pp. 114–15.
59. Watt, *Graduates*, p. 165.
60. Ibid., p. 490.
61. Amanda Beam, *The Balliol Dynasty 1210–1364* (John Donald, 2008), pp. 66–7; Anderson, *Early Sources*, p. 664.
62. N. R. Ker and W. A. Pantin, 'Letters of a Scottish student at Paris and Oxford c. 1250', in H. E. Salter et al. (eds), *Oxford Formularies* (Oxford Historical Society, 1942), ii, pp. 472–91.
63. A. A. M. Duncan, *Scotland. The Making of the Kingdom* (Mercat Press, 1975), pp. 303–4; Watt, *Graduates*, pp. 44–6. Translation is Duncan's.
64. G. W. S. Barrow, 'The clergy at St Andrews', in Barrow, *Kingdom of the Scots*, pp. 187–202.
65. Dauvit Broun, *Scottish Independence and the Idea of Britain* (Edinburgh University Press, 2007), pp. 258–63; Watt, *Graduates*, pp. 559–60.

Bibliography

Beam, Amanda, John Bradley, Dauvit Broun, John Reuben Davies, Matthew Hammond and Michele Pasin (with others), *The People of Medieval Scotland, 1093–1314* (PoMS, 2012). Available at www.poms.ac.uk (accessed 26 July 2014).

Broun, Dauvit, 'Gaelic literacy in eastern Scotland between 1124 and 1249', in Huw Pryce (ed.), *Literacy in Medieval Celtic Societies* (Cambridge University Press, 1998), pp. 183–201.

Clancy, Thomas Owen, 'Scotland, the "Nennian" recension of the *Historia Brittonum*, and the *Lebor Bretnach*', in Simon Taylor (ed.), *Kings, Clerics and Chronicles in Scotland, 500–1297. Essays in Honour of Marjorie Ogilvie Anderson* (Four Courts Press, 2000), pp. 87–107.

Ker, N. R. and W. A. Pantin, 'Letters of a Scottish student at Paris and Oxford c. 1250', in H. E. Salter, W. A. Pantin and H. G. Richardson (eds), *Formularies which Bear on the History of Oxford, c. 1204–1420*, 2 vols (Oxford Historical Society, 1942), ii, pp. 472–91.

Orme, Nicholas, *Medieval Schools from Roman Britain to Renaissance England* (Yale University Press, 2006).

Ridder-Symoens, Hilde de (ed.), *A History of the University in Europe, vol. 1. Universities in the Middle Ages* (gen. ed. Walter Rüegg) (Cambridge University Press, 1992).

Robertson, Joseph, 'On scholastic offices in the Scottish church in the twelfth and thirteenth centuries', in John Stuart (ed.), *Miscellany of the Spalding Club Volume Five* (Spalding Club, 1852), pp. 56–77.

Taylor, Simon, with Gilbert Márkus, *The Place-Names of Fife*, 5 vols (Shaun Tyas, 2006–12).

Watt, D. E. R., *A Biographical Dictionary of Scottish Graduates* (Clarendon Press, 1977).

Watt, D. E. R., 'Scottish student life abroad in the fourteenth century', *Scottish Historical Review* 59 (1980), 3–21.

2

'Through the Keyhole of the Monastic Library Door'[1]: Learning and Education in Scottish Medieval Monasteries

Kimm Curran

we intend to establish a school for the Lord's service . . . Never swerving from his instructions, but faithfully observing his teaching in the monastery until death . . .[2]

Life in the medieval period was ritualised by religion and the church; these rituals were learned and practised alongside skills necessary to live life or gain employment. Literacy, learning and education were not the same as what we recognise as such today, and most members of society in medieval Scotland could not read or write, including those who became monks, canons or nuns. Formal education, going to school or university for example, was not a part of life or indeed understood by the majority of the population.[3] University education or schooling may have been chosen by the clergy, those training for priesthood, monks or canons, or by the nobility, gentry or middling classes; some monasteries were in charge of schools near the precincts of the monastic community and would sometimes take in members to educate. James Clark has challenged the notion that the role of monastic schools was insignificant in the development of pre-Reformation education; this notion overlooks the progressive, active engagement in learning and education that monks, canons and nuns provided secular society.[4]

Monasteries were active in their engagement with secular society and schooling but what this education consisted of in medieval Scotland is uncertain. As was the case elsewhere in Europe, lay individuals were sent to monastic establishments by their families to learn instruction in letters, religion such as basic Latin prayers, reading or life skills, good manners (for men, women, boys and girls) and embroidery or sewing (for women). There were members of the laity in the nunneries of Haddington, Elcho and Aberdour and we can assume that they were sent to these places for an education and received instruction from the nuns.[5] It should be recognised that it was those who could afford it who sent members of their families to monastic schools, or to board in monasteries, for education. We have very little understanding of the role monastic schools played in medieval

Scotland and even less evidence of which monasteries had schools, bar a handful of references. We can assume, however, that they functioned much like monastic schools elsewhere.[6]

With this in mind, this chapter will discuss what we know and understand of the learned rituals and practices within the monastery, and the learning undertaken by communities of cloistered monks, canons and nuns. Monastic education is often misunderstood, and a close examination of the rules governing orders of monks, canons and nuns shows the importance of books, reading and learning in a community. Further discussion focuses on the practical issues surrounding learning in the monastery, the places where books were stored, including monastic libraries, spaces within monasteries for learning as well as the practical literacy that was needed for a monastery to function in the world.

Learning within the Monastery

Monasteries were ordered by structures dictated in the monastic rule: the head of house was not only the governor of his/her flock but also a teacher.[7] The monks and nuns were advised to follow the teaching of the Rule, under the watchful eye of their head of house or others chosen for this task.[8] Obedience to the head of house was vital as this individual was the 'master [who] gives instructions to the disciple[s]'.[9] The Rule set out to instruct the members of the community with the head of house and the Rule itself as the 'teachers'; St Benedict set out his Rule as instructions to 'observe teaching' and the monastery was set up to establish a 'school for the Lord's service'.[10] A monastery as a community of monks, canons or nuns was a school, a place where religious instruction, the teaching of scripture and examples of good works were part of daily life. In the prologue to his Rule, Benedict writes: 'Listen carefully . . . to the master's instructions and attend to them with the ear of your heart'.[11] The structure and routine for a life of community living was laid out carefully in the Rule – it was designed to be used as a simple guide to order daily life, look after the inhabitants of the monastery, maintain discipline and provide instruction for the pursuit of a life dedicated to God and salvation. Monastic life was therefore set apart by its community living and commitment to a life of shared devotion, private prayer and work.

The conception of the monastery as a school with the head of house and Rule as 'teachers' gives us an understanding of how monastic houses were dedicated in their devotion to God. The teachings of God and his disciples were disseminated through readings, and the Rule is explicit in the readings that monks should undertake on a daily basis. For this to be fulfilled, there was an expectation that monks, canons and nuns were somewhat literate (both reading and writing) upon entry to the community as it would be necessary for the reading of scripture outlined in the Rule, for tasks such as performing the liturgy, for private study and reading, and for keeping accurate community records. How literacy was measured is not certain, and the extent of literacy and learning opportunities prior to entry is not fully understood, especially for women.[12]

If one entered a community one would be welcomed as a novice with a probationary period before committing to the monastic life, as 'transition [into this life] . . . could be extremely difficult'.[13] The novice was clothed in what the community provided – cowl, tunic (habit), sandals, shoes, belt and handkerchief – and issued with a knife, needle, stylus and writing tablet.[14] Thus, from entry into the monastic community even as a noviciate, tools for writing were provided. Although private property on entry to a monastery was not allowed – all personal articles became common possessions of the monastery[15] – the fact that part of the 'habit' of the novice included a writing tablet and stylus indicates the importance of the ability to write.

Learning took place in the cloister and was designed to teach the young monks, canons and nuns the customs of the house, as well as the Latin language, which would enable them to take part in services of choir and altar. They were taught the practical matters of rules of order, behaviour and duties required of them as well as the customs of the community. This was their 'training' and was usually done by the novice master or mistress. The process of learning was by rote – of daily offices, prayers, hymns and psalms. Full profession into the order could take place once the novice was capable of following religious life without supervision, having learnt the Rule and daily offices.[16]

In the Rule of St Benedict there are examples of scripture to read (Old and New Testament) and explanation of those texts; there was also reading listed by the Catholic fathers. Depending on the season, time of day or activity, readings were generally dictated by the Rule[17] and silence was only broken by reading aloud.[18] Speech was permitted when reading aloud for the community and specifically during meals where individuals were chosen to read from scripture or other liturgical texts. The understanding that monks or nuns may have difficulty in reading was mentioned in the Rule as 'no one is to read unless he [sic] is able to benefit the hearers'.[19] This suggests that a wide range of individuals with different levels of literacy could be accommodated in the religious life: lack of literacy was acknowledged in monastic rules, which allowed for the variety and understanding of individual circumstances.

The monastic community's rituals were based around close reading of scripture and the Rule of the order, and can be divided into three types: liturgical devotion, or the *Opus Dei*; reading and contemplation, or *lecto divinia*; and manual labour. The day was structured around the seven Canonical hours, and celebrated in the church. Daily life was punctuated by the ringing of a bell to call the community to the offices of the day and to meetings: Lauds at dawn; Prime at 6am which was the prayer for the beginning of the day; Terce at 9am; Sext at 12 noon (sixth hour of the day); Nones at 3pm (ninth hour of the day); Vespers at dusk; the office of Compline, which brought day to a close; and lastly the night offices of Vigils (at midnight) and Nocturns at the hours of 9pm, midnight and 3am. At these various points in the day, individuals would be saying a number of psalms as dictated by the Rule, and these would have been learnt, memorised and read.[20]

Monastic rules show that private study and meditation were important alongside individual learning, and monks, canons and nuns would receive a book from the library at Lent, in particular, and read it for a short period each day.[21] There were senior members of the community who looked after others to see that they were reading during this time, and that those who were not engaged in study, or were unable to study, were assigned to other work such as assisting with manual duties. Devotion to reading and prayer was an important part of Lent.[22] The use of books in the liturgical calendar is outlined in the *Ancient Uses of the Cistercian Order*. For example, the day after the Mass of St Thomas of Becket, held during Christmas week, the monks took 'leisure for reading for one to two hours';[23] and nine Sundays before Easter, Septuagesima, until Lent was when books were distributed for Lenten reading.[24] At the first Sunday of Lent, the cantor or cantoress brought the books which were to be given out to the chapter room, placing them in front of the abbot's or abbess's seat. The cantor or cantoress was responsible for the choir books, correcting mistakes in choir and assigning readings, and was in charge of the *armarium* (a part of the monastery where books and vestments were kept). Books that were given out to read during Lent were returned each night to the book cupboard; this was strictly regulated by the cantor or cantoress. The duties of this office were important: the cantor or cantoress taught reading and singing, was the librarian and was in charge of correcting and annotating the monastery's liturgical books; he or she played the role of being in charge of the library, the liturgy and education of new entrants.[25]

The community gathered every day to read and meditate: *lectio divina*. Texts were to be read slowly, so that the words could be studied carefully and their meanings meditated upon. The *lectio divina* required mindfulness and attentive recollection, and concentrated on the reading of texts. The reading of scripture and other texts led to inward contemplation, reflection, self-awareness and focus. Daily reading was done alone and in silence and usually took place in cloister or dormitory. During the daily office, private meditation was encouraged; indeed, it was essential, forming the core of monastic life. Silence was important as it allowed for this meditation and the concentration needed for monks, canons and nuns to memorise texts with accuracy and in full. Mary Carruthers has empha-sised the skill and dedication needed to memorise texts and to form awareness of scripture, which involved different techniques from those usually employed today. Monks, canon and nuns used techniques common in the art of 'forming memory': the practice was ordered and structured, sometimes taking visual cues from the texts themselves, and using colour and pictures – blue and red ink to set apart lines of text, for example – as well as going over the subject again in one's mind for accuracy in recall. These became the basic methods for reading, and for meditating on scripture and keeping it secure within one's memory.[26] Reading an assigned book from start to finish during Lent was also useful, encouraging meditation on sacred texts 'and inscribing [them] in the body and in the soul'.[27]

The cloister area was a peaceful haven from the outside world, a symbol of heavenly paradise, a carefully planned centre of the community.[28] The

Augustinian Rule for nuns, for example, emphasises this by stating that sisters live together with 'one heart and one soul seeking God'.[29] As the cloister was a contemplative place, it brought the community together in prayer, work and study. For this purpose, cloister areas had benches or seats for the monks, canons or nuns to read and to contemplate their reading; they may have had assigned seats. The reconstruction of the cloister for Iona Nunnery, the remains of the internal cloister area at Inchcolm and the area below the cloister arches at Melrose Abbey all show the seating and arrangements that were made for use of the space for contemplation.[30]

The Archaeology of Learning

The storage of books in Scottish monasteries has not been widely discussed amongst scholars although books and the storage of these important items – whether used by the monks, canons or nuns for learning or for the recording of practical information for the monastery, or made for wider distribution to the outside world – was an important part of the monastic milieu. When building a monastery and designing spaces for books, for example, the cost of building shelving, rooms and spaces and identifying those spaces would have been significant. Cloisters often were not present at the foundation of a religious house and would have taken years to build and design, and perhaps this is why book storage and libraries are rarely mentioned; it would have been assumed that these were part of the accepted plan for a religious house throughout its development.

The book cupboard, or *armarium*, would be near the sacristy at the eastern portion of the cloister near the north-eastern entrance to the nave, between the church and chapter house; but books may have been kept in one small area in the sacristy or cloister depending on the space and size of the monastic house.[31] An alcove or closet in the cloister wall near the entrance to the church would function as a storage space or could have a moveable wooden book cupboard. Book crannies or shelves were often built into the monastic cloister walls. Evidence of these has been found in European houses and we can assume that Scottish houses also had them. Two surviving plans of Scottish monasteries indicate where the book storage space or library might have been located. At Dryburgh Abbey and Sweetheart Abbey, the layout of the monastic buildings varied, but both had libraries or an *armarium* outlined on the plans. The plan of Dryburgh shows the library and vestry at the eastern portion of the cloister, with entrance ways to this location; at the entrance to the nave from the north doorway, there is what appears to be a storage cupboard built into the wall and this could very well have been used for shelving books. Sweetheart Abbey's plan also indicates the library's location in the eastern part of the cloister, and Glenluce Abbey's shows a storage cupboard very similar to that of Dryburgh.[32] The location of libraries and storage for books are in the same position as that of many continental houses and would be in the cloister area.[33] However, we must acknowledge that not all monasteries were laid out in the same way and smaller houses may not have had large areas set aside for libraries.

It was not until a comparatively late period that a few of the larger houses provided a special room or building for the library. Cistercians were encouraged by the General Chapter to organise and maintain large libraries, and Kinloss Abbey's rebuilding of a library away from the eastern cloister area is one example of this. At the excavation of Pluscarden Abbey, evidence was found of a library at the south end of the refectory – an unusual place for a library, which would normally be at the east range of the cloister – indicating the necessity and desire for these larger spaces for the storage of books.[34] Some houses in England had large and valuable libraries: Titchfield was one example: in c.1400 there was a special apartment for the library opening out of the cloister. Other houses such as the Cistercian houses of Buildwas in Shropshire, Croxton Abbey in Staffordshire, the Benedictine house of Ramsay Abbey in Huntington and the Augustinian Canons of Leicester also had large documented library collections; the Cistercian abbeys of Tintern and Byland both had separate areas set aside for their libraries. Many books survive from the nunneries of Crabtree, Campsee Ash, Barking and Syon, which suggests the presence of libraries.

Books

Books were an important part of daily life and were essential for learning and education within the monastery.[35] Liturgical books formed the staple of the monastic library, and houses had varied collections of them, as well as texts from the church fathers, calendars, breviaries, missals and books of hours. Collections of texts for an entire community do not survive but we do have pieces, fragments and in some cases whole manuscripts. Psalters are the most numerous: there are examples from Coupar Angus, Blantyre, Ardchatton, Sweetheart, Inchmaholme, Culross, Kinloss and elsewhere.[36] The surviving psalter from the nunneries of Iona and Sciennes, the Constitutions of Order at Sciennes, the English Bible at Elcho and a possible missal fragment from Lincluden are all further examples of evidence that convents of nuns in Scotland had books too, though in smaller numbers than male houses. These should not be overlooked in studies of monasticism and literacy in Scotland. The discovery of book clasps at the excavation of the nunnery at Elcho also provides evidence of a literate culture among religious women in Scotland.[37]

In addition to the great libraries of the cathedral canons of St Andrews, the monasteries of Culross, Deer, Scone, Cambuskenneth, Melrose, Dryburgh and Kinloss also had libraries, as well as books that were owned or used by individual monks and canons. The library at Kinloss was refounded and enhanced in the late fifteenth century by Abbot Thomas Chrystal and his successor, Abbot Robert Reid. The influence from continental scholars is well known, and Kinloss had a scholarly visitor, Giovanni Ferreri, who was a major influence on the rejuvenation of learning there. The number of individual books that survive from Kinloss is greater than other monastic houses of the enclosed orders; this is due to careful planning and preservation on the part of the community and/or its influential patrons and supporters.

The individual ownership of books by monks, canons and nuns was discouraged: as noted above, upon entry to monastic life books and other possessions were to be donated to the community. There is evidence, however, of book ownership within monasteries by individuals; it is uncertain whether these books were brought to the monastery and given to the library.[38] The widespread ownership of books emphasises that they were important for learning in the monastic community, and the acquisition of books by communities and individuals from patrons, scholars or family members shows the permeable nature of the cloister and the continued exchange between the religious and the secular worlds.

Other books were also found in monasteries. Accounts, records, deeds and ledgers were kept and drawn up, and were essential for good governance and estate management. Records of lands and deeds, and account books of food and necessities coming in and out of the house, were needed for practical and legal reasons, and show the day-to-day workings of monasteries. The surviving cellaress account from Syon Abbey, the ledger book of Vale Abbey and the cartularies of some of Scotland's monasteries show the importance of good governance and business acumen, and the skills that were necessary to keep religious houses running. Some of this record-keeping may have been done by employees of the monastery, such as a bailie or a notary, or by the monks, canons or nuns themselves. For these documents to be prepared, monks, canons or nuns had to have some practical literacy, including the ability to write and understand basic Latin and vernacular, sometimes French, which was common. An entry in the *Accounts of Thirds of Benefice* for the convent of Haddington records that the teinds (tithes) of the Nungait were set in feu to John Young, writer, but it is not clear whether Young's relationship with the convent was one of employee, boarder, friend or patron.[39] Monks and canons as scribes were found at Kinloss, Newbattle, Dunfermline and Pittenween, and Culross had a scriptorium producing books for profit; monks were also found as notaries at the monasteries of Melrose, Lindores, Culross, Coupar Angus and Dunfermline. Walter Bower's *Scotichronicon* was created and written at Inchcolm Abbey and is one of the best-known histories of Scotland that survive today, while books such as Blind Harry's *Wallace* and Barbour's *Bruce* were also copied in monasteries.

Signatures of semi-literate monks and nuns survive on feu charters and precepts of sasine (documents relating to the holding and transfer of property) from the later middle ages. Mark Dilworth claims that nuns in Scotland could not write, but there is plenty of evidence to the contrary. Some nuns may have been unable to write their full name, but this was also true of monks.[40] In fact, the literacy of nuns has been the subject of some debate in recent historiography.[41] The issue remains controversial, partly due to the limited survival of records that were kept by or for nuns, and also to the uncertainty as to the provisions for acquiring literacy that were available to women prior to entering religious life. Most monks, canons and nuns came to this life with some degree of literacy or learning, but this is only part of the picture. It is possible that they learnt to read and write in the monastery in order to perform specific duties such as keeping accounts, but we still lack understanding of what was necessary for office-holders to learn, and what was learnt by those who were not chosen for offices in monasteries.

The survival of records for religious houses in Scotland is piecemeal. During the sixteenth century, many records and books were destroyed by English invaders and reformers. In some cases parchment or paper from monasteries was reused elsewhere, by burghs for example. Sweetheart Abbey's books were burned in the 1600s, and in 1559 Lindores Abbey was overthrown by reformers who burned books and vestments.[42] However, evidence of learning and education in monasteries can also be found in visual and material sources.

Visual Literacy and the Fabric of the Monastery

Material images and writing may have been strategically placed throughout the monastic house in areas such as the chapter house, cloister, altars, churches and chapels, as well as in warming houses and the refectory. Imagery took the form of monumental sculpture, wall paintings and scriptural depictions, monastic seals and floor tiles; it served a liturgical function, enhanced monastic activity and reinforced moral lessons.[43] Images acted as reminders of important events from scripture, such as the Passion of Christ, or inspired devotion to saints and martyrs. Other visual imagery could be simply decorative and sometimes heraldic, linking the religious house to its patrons, or serving as a reminder of individuals in the institutional memory of the house, such as an important abbot or prioress. For example, the carved shield at the south-west pier crossing of Jedburgh Abbey depicts Abbot Thomas Cranston (1484–1501), and the carved shield of Abbot John Hall (1478–9) is in the south aisle of the choir.[44] Both were reminders of the abbey's identity: the canons saw these shields daily, and this contributed to their own remembrance and understanding of the institution, and reinforced its collective memory.

Monumental sculpture fragments, wall paintings and writing survive, albeit in small quantities, for Scotland's religious houses, and these have been given fairly little attention beyond architectural analysis. Melrose Abbey has one of the best collections of surviving sculpture in Scotland; figures, animals and foliage decorate doorways, ceilings and columns throughout. The figure of the fat monk or pig playing bagpipes may symbolise gluttony and could be linked to a text in the monastic library: John Cassian's *Institutes*, in which the author outlines the rules of morality, especially the eight vices.[45] Angels and saints are also depicted throughout monastic houses: the south doorway at Melrose and the chancel ceiling both have carved saints and angels, while the north transept has the carved figure of St Peter.[46] The vaulted ceiling and bosses in the chapter house at Glenluce also depict angels, saints and heraldic imagery;[47] Jedburgh Abbey has corbels with carved faces depicting angels or possibly a monk;[48] and the sacristy of Crossraguel has a head of a saint or Christ (Figure 2.1) squirrels (Figure 2.2), lions and a green man.

These carefully placed images served a purpose in that they were seen when

Figure 2.1 The sacristy of Crossraguel: head of saint or Jesus. Copyright the author.

people were processing into the church, and thus reminded the community of sermons and moral lessons. Marking the entrance ways could also serve as a transition place – individuals could contemplate the visual messages carved on the entrance (such as the figures of the apostles) and learn from them. Walkways with sculptured tiles could also be important; many were decorative but some had representations of

Figure 2.2 The sacristy of Crossraguel: squirrels. Copyright the author.

lions, heraldic designs, scripture and representations of martyrs such as Catherine's wheel: the floor tiles from the nunnery of North Berwick, Melrose Abbey, Glenluce and Newbattle hold such designs.[49] Visual images such as these were an extension of the monastic *lectio divina* and served an 'exegetical' function.[50]

Roberta Gilchrist has remarked that architectural internal fittings served another purpose: symbolism and iconography held meaning particular to a religious house, especially female religious houses of nuns, and were linked to their spirituality and identity.[51] Surviving fragments of internal fittings and material culture from Scotland's nunneries are rare – with the exception of Iona – making it difficult to make general assumptions about female religious houses. Some of the carved corbels from the nave that survive from the nunnery of Iona depict a human head (possibly a male saint), an animal head with oak leaves, an angel with a scroll, a rosette and the Annunciation. For the nuns, the symbolism in these figures would be learnt and understood. The male saints could be St John the Baptist, St John the Evangelist or St Augustine. Oak leaves were common foliage motifs with a particular meaning: examples of the oak-covered green man, for example, a sign of divinity, are found throughout Scotland in this period. The angel with the scroll was a particular reference to scripture (Revelations 10: 1–11), where the mighty angel came down from heaven; and the rosette is a symbol of Marian imagery. Iona's other sculptures also reveal moral messages and provide evidence of learning within the monastic setting: figures with snakes adorn the capitals of nave arcades, representing renewal or destruction, along with an unusual sheela-na-gig on the outer wall of the refectory as a protection to ward off evil spirits.[52]

Visual images would remind individuals and the community of memories within certain locations, images in religious texts or particular individuals, and would foster a deeper understanding of religious life and the space in which monks, canons and nuns lived. Pluscarden Abbey's wall paintings are an example of religious symbolism that would have been learnt, internalised and contemplated. The Lady Chapel has a fifteenth-century painting of a female figure in the chancel archway, and in the covered walkway between the chapter house and transept there sits a painted figure of a female saint, possibly Mary, adorning the wall.[53] Mary was important to Pluscarden as the abbey was dedicated to her alongside St Andrew and St John. The abbey of Inchcolm also has a painted mural on the south wall of the choir as well as an inscription in the warming house and chapter house.[54] A preliminary evaluation of the writing in the warming house seems to indicate that these were morally and spiritually encouraging phrases that may suggest that the canons had a library and drew upon lessons within books held there.[55] This further illustrates the link between the internal memorisation and learning of scriptures, psalms and texts, and the visual representations of the *lectio* which were encapsulated within the architecture and spaces of monastic houses.

Conclusions

The monastery itself was a school where members passed days learning to serve both God and their peers by way of obedience and humility. Monastic education drew on the understanding of routines and rules followed within and by enclosed monastic communities. These routines and rules grounded monks, canons and nuns in the learning of scripture and in the monastic way of life, as well as providing the awareness and skills necessary for the day-to-day running of the monastery. Learning was multifaceted, with books and visual imagery serving dual purposes of grounding the community in the *lectio divina* but also reinforcing this with visual prompts placed in spaces and places throughout the monastic complex in the form of sculpture, wall paintings and the like. The idea of the monastery as a 'school', together with the evidence of books, libraries and visual culture, indicates that Scotland's religious houses were significant contributors to education, not only for the monks, canons and nuns who lived in them, but also for the population more widely.

Notes

1. Joan Greatrex, 'The scope of learning within the cloisters of the English cathedral priories in the later Middle Ages', in George Ferzoco and Carolyn Muessig (eds), *Medieval Monastic Education* (Leicester University Press, 2000), p. 52.
2. Timothy Fry (trans.), *Rule of St. Benedict in English* [henceforth: *RB*] (Liturgical Press, 1982), prologue.

3. For literacy and schooling in this period see John Durkan, 'Education in the century of the Reformation', *Innes Review* 10 (1959), 67–90. Schools were set up for clerks and for training for specific occupations. Some monks and friars went to university further afield.

4. James G. Clark, 'Monasteries and secular education in late medieval England', in Janet Burton and Karen Stöber (eds), *Monasteries and Society in the British Isles* (Boydell and Brewer, 2008), pp. 145–67.

5. Nunneries would also take in young boys to be educated as boarders. Nicholas Orme, *Medieval Schools from Roman Britain to Renaissance England* (Yale University Press, 2006), p. 285. For Haddington, Elcho and Aberdour, see Durkan, 'Education in the century of the Reformation', 90.

6. Orme, *Medieval Schools*, pp. 255–88. See also Clark, 'Monasteries and secular education', pp. 145–67.

7. *RB*, Chapter 2.

8. Ibid., Chapter 3.

9. Ibid., Chapter 5.

10. Ibid., prologue.

11. Ibid., prologue.

12. Veronica O'Mara, 'The late medieval nun and her scribal activity: A complicated quest', in Virginia Blanton, Veronica O'Mara and Patricia Stoop (eds), *Nuns' Literacies in Medieval Europe: The Hull Dialogue* (Brephols, 2013), p. 73.

13. Julie Kerr, *Life in the Medieval Cloister* (Continuum, 2009), p. 30.

14. *RB*, Chapter 55.

15. Ibid., Chapter 36.

16. Orme, *Medieval Schools*, p. 266.

17. *RB*, Chapters 9–13, 17, 18, 38, 42, 47–9.

18. Ibid., Chapter 42.

19. Ibid., Chapter 47.

20. For a detailed account of daily life in the cloister, see Kerr, *Life in the Medieval Cloister*, pp. 17–42.

21. In the mid-thirteenth century, the Cistercian General Chapter encouraged facilities to be set up so that every monk could study theology all year round in their houses. However, it is unclear how far this was realised. Later, monks and canons were encouraged to go to university. See Orme, *Medieval Schools*, pp. 267–70, and Matthew Hammond's chapter in this volume.

22. *RB*, Chapters 48–9.

23. *Ancient Uses of the Cistercian Order: Ecclesiastica Officia* [henceforth: EO] (Guadalupe Trappist Publications, 1998), Chapters 5.30–5.36.

24. Ibid., Chapters 11.2–11.6.

25. Susan Boynton, 'Training for the liturgy as a form of monastic education', in Ferzoco and Muessig (eds), *Medieval Monastic Education*, pp. 9–16.

26. Mary Carruthers, *The Book of Memory: A Study of Memory in Medieval Culture*, 2nd edn (Cambridge University Press, 2008), pp. 99–152.

27. Ibid., p. 112.

28. Dennis B. Gallagher, 'The planning of Augustinian monasteries in Scotland', in Martin Locock (ed.), *Meaningful Architecture: Social Interpretations of Buildings* (Ashgate, 1994), p. 170.

29. George Lawless, *Augustine of Hippo and his Monastic Rule* (Clarendon Press, 1987), Chapter 1: 2.

30. Iona Nunnery, canmore.rcahms.gov.uk: SC370794; Inchcolm Abbey, canmore.

rcahms.gov.uk: SC1104657; Melrose Abbey, canmore.rcahms.gov.uk: SC1291560 and SC129120 (all accessed 26 July 2014).
31. *EO*, Chapter 15.
32. Dryburgh Abbey, canmore.rcahms.gov.uk: SC1207716 and DP027705 (plan); SC798809 and SC1207647 (cupboard and view to the north entrance of cloister); Glenluce Abbey, canmore.rcahms.gov.uk: SC1207002 (view of chapter house, cloister range from the west). For Sweetheart Abbey, see www.ancient-egypt.co.uk/Cistercians/Sweetheart/index.htm (all accessed 26 July 2014).
33. Terryl N. Kinder, *Cistercian Europe: Architecture of Contemplation* (William B. Eerdmans, 2002), pp. 133–6, 173–4, 243–5, 342–3.
34. Pluscarden Abbey, canmore.rcahms.gov.uk: SC1201697 (accessed 26 July 2014).
35. Greatrex, 'Scope of learning', p. 41.
36. Stephen Mark Holmes, 'Catalogue of liturgical books and fragments in Scotland before 1560', *Innes Review* 63 (2012), 127–212. See also David McRoberts, 'Catalogue of Scottish medieval liturgical books and fragments', *Innes Review* 3 (1952), 49–63.
37. National Library of Scotland, Iona Psalter, MS 10000 and Psalter of Marion Crawford, MS GB.En 8.f17h; Will of Euphemia Leslie and book clasps finds, in *Pitmiddle Village and Elcho Nunnery, Research and Excavation at Tayside* (Perthshire Society of Natural Science, 1988). See also the seminal work on women and book ownership, David N. Bell, *What Nuns Read* (Cistercian Publications, 1995), and Paul Lee, *Nunneries, Learning and Spirituality in Late Medieval English Society* (Boydell and Brewer, 2001).
38. For list of books by individual owners, see John Durkan and Anthony Ross, 'Early Scottish libraries', *Innes Review* 9 (1958), 66–163; for nuns, see note 37 above.
39. James Kirk (ed.), *The Books of Assumption of the Thirds of Benefices: Scottish Ecclesiastical Rentals at the Reformation* (Oxford University Press, 1995), p. 178.
40. Mark Dilworth, *Scottish Monasteries in the Later Middle Ages* (Edinburgh University Press, 1995), p. 64; See also Kimm Curran, 'Religious women and their communities in late medieval Scotland' (unpublished PhD dissertation, University of Glasgow, 2005), Chapters 3–5.
41. Blanton et al. (eds), *Nuns' Literacies*; Mary Erler, *Reading and Writing during the Dissolution: Monks, Friars and Nuns, 1538–1558* (Oxford University Press, 2013).
42. David McRoberts, 'Material destruction caused by the Scottish Reformation', *Innes Review* 10 (1959), 126–72.
43. Miriam Gill, 'The role of images in monastic education: The evidence from wall painting in late medieval England', in Ferzoco and Muessig (eds), *Medieval Monastic Education*, pp. 115–35.
44. Jedburgh Abbey, canmore.rcahms.gov.uk: SC1202291 and SC1202294.
45. Melrose Abbey, canmore.rcahms.gov.uk: SC1291196 (pig) and SC12208293 (monk).
46. Melrose Abbey, canmore.rcahms.gov.uk: SC1260713 (chancel); SCC1263609 (north transept); SC1291200 (south doorway).
47. Glenluce Abbey, canmore.rcahms.gov.uk: DP026501.
48. Jedburgh Abbey, canmore.rcahms.gov.uk: SC1202288 (all in notes 44 to 48 accessed 26 July 2014).
49. Christopher Norton, 'Medieval floor tiles in Scotland', in John Higgit (ed.), *Medieval Art and Architecture of the Diocese of St Andrews* (British Archaeological Association, 1994), pp. 137–73.
50. Gill, 'Role of images', p. 115.
51. Roberta Gilchrist, *Gender and Material Culture: The Archaeology of Religious Women* (Routledge, 1994), pp. 140–2.

52. Iona Nunnery, canmore.rcahms.gov.uk: SC366543 (human head); SC366542 (animal with oak); SC366541 (angel with scroll); SC366540 (rosette); SC366539 (Annunciation); SC369632 and SC369630 (snaked capitals); SC366554 (sheela-na-gig). A sheela-na-gig is a grotesque figure of a naked woman with an exaggeratedly large vulva.
53. Pluscarden Abbey, canmore.rcahms.gov.uk: SC1203577 (Lady Chapel); SC1201732 (saint).
54. Inchcolm, canmore.rcahms.gov.uk: SC1209650 and SC1209681 (text); SC1209635 (mural) (all in notes 52 to 54 accessed 26 July 2014).
55. John Reuben Davies, Richard Sharpe and Simon Taylor, 'Comforting sentences from the warming room at Inchcolm Abbey', *Innes Review* 63 (2012), 260–6.

Bibliography

Bell, David N., *What Nuns Read* (Cistercian Publications, 1995).
Blanton, Virginia, Veronica O'Mara and Patricia Stoop (eds), *Nuns' Literacies in Medieval Europe: The Hull Dialogue* (Brepols, 2013).
Clark, James G. (ed.), *The Culture of Medieval English Monasticism* (Boydell and Brewer, 2007).
Ferzoco, George and Carolyn Muessig (eds), *Medieval Monastic Education* (Leicester University Press, 2000).
Gilchrist, Roberta, *Gender and Material Culture: The Archaeology of Religious Women* (Routledge, 1994).
Orme, Nicholas, *Medieval Schools from Roman Britain to Renaissance England* (Yale University Press, 2006).

3

Schooling in the Towns, c. 1400–c. 1560

Elizabeth Ewan

In till [into] Dunde Wallace to scule thai send
Quhill [until] he of witt [learning] full worthily was kend [known].

The Wallace, lines 155–6[1]

This is how the late-fifteenth-century poet Hary, known as Blind Harry, described the boyhood education of William Wallace to his audience. Records suggest that there was at least one school in Dundee from the mid-thirteenth century; there certainly was one by 1434. Whether Wallace did in fact attend school in Dundee in the late thirteenth century is less important than that Harry's audience found such a statement believable, and also commendable. However, lest his hero be thought to be too bookish, Harry went on to reassure them that once Wallace had finished his schooling, he went on to many feats of prowess.

Harry's description reflects the ambivalence of many in his courtly audience about book-learning, which was generally felt to be of less importance than the military and chivalric skills taught to noble youths. However, lay attitudes to education were beginning to change in the later middle ages, even among the nobles. The fifteenth century in Scotland, as elsewhere in Europe, saw a rising trend in lay literacy, stimulated partly by government demand for educated servants of the crown, partly by growing commerce and partly by the development of new ways of thinking about the world. In Scotland, the practical effects of this change in attitude were probably felt first in the schools situated in its towns. It was in this period that townspeople sought increased control over urban schools, schools which had earlier been governed by the church.

The Study of Late Medieval Urban Education

There has been interest in medieval schools since at least the mid-nineteenth century. In 1840, the Maitland Club published some parliamentary records from 1496 to 1696 concerning schools, as well as payments for schooling from town common good funds. John Edgar in 1898 devoted most of his study of early

Scottish education to the period before 1560, illustrating that the sources were more numerous than many had thought. Much of his material on urban schools was drawn from James Grant's 1876 study of the burgh schools of Scotland, of which Part One dealt with the pre-Reformation period. James Scotland's 1969 book on education also included material on medieval schools.[2] The study of this period specifically, however, was developed, almost single-handedly, by John Durkan in a series of articles on the medieval and early modern periods, beginning in the 1950s. Durkan continued making material available, publishing documents and lists of schools and schoolmasters, culled from a wide range of sources. Although his large-scale work was still in typescript when he died, it was edited and published by the Scottish History Society in 2013 as *Scottish Schools and Schoolmasters*. Not only does it summarise a lifetime of work on the topic, but it also updates and supplements his earlier work.[3]

Material on medieval town schools also appeared in regional and local studies such as J. C. Jessop's *Education in Angus* (1931), and a recent history of Aberdeen. Individual schools traced their origins to as early a period as possible. Local traditions also exist. In Montrose it was believed that the school was founded by Robert Bruce, based on an ambiguous reference in the Exchequer Rolls of 1329 to a payment to David of Montrose *in auxilium ad scolas* (in help to the schools). Reporting on this tradition, however, the careful Jessop commented 'though this would be of interest we cannot justify the claim of such slender evidence'.[4]

Early education has been considered in relation to other topics, particularly religion and politics. The state of the schools has been seen by some as reflecting the strength or weakness of the pre-Reformation church. Medieval education has also figured in discussions of the growth of the state in late medieval Scotland, as historians have pointed to the increasing need of the crown for educated laymen as well as churchmen to staff the growing bureaucracy of government. Studies of literacy, especially those examining the cherished idea of Scotland's unusually high literacy rate before the twentieth century, have also considered education, although as several historians have pointed out schooling and literacy are not necessarily connected. Education has also been studied within the context of intellectual and literary developments such as the growth of humanism and the development of an educated lay reading public. One branch of early education, the song schools, has been important to the historians of music who have recently done so much to recover Scotland's medieval musical heritage. Outside Scotland, education has been an important part of studies of the family and childhood. This is a field which has only recently developed in Scotland for the medieval and early modern period, but the role of schools will doubtless play an important part of future work in the field. Recent work on the ways in which education moulds gender identities, particularly masculinity, suggests new avenues of exploration for Scottish historians.[5]

The Late Medieval Context, c. 1400–c. 1560

Education both reflects and helps shape the society of which it is a part. The fifteenth and sixteenth centuries witnessed many changes in Scottish society and politics. As royal authority increased and as state bureaucracy grew, there was a growing need for educated men to act as administrators and record keepers. From the time of James I onwards, the crown took a lively interest in education. The fifteenth century also saw the establishment of three universities in Scotland. In 1496, what is often known as the Education Act was passed, requiring all barons and freeholders to send their sons and heirs to school in order to learn Latin and then law. This Act is sometimes seen as the start of the movement for universal education in Scotland and credited with beginning the establishment of schools in every parish. It might more accurately be seen as 'the first positive intervention by the state in Scottish education'.[6] Its main purpose was to ensure a supply of educated nobles and lairds who could fill government positions and dispense justice fairly in the localities, although it does not appear to have been very successful in the short term. Rather than establishing new schools, the Act of 1496 rested on an assumption that such schools existed. Jenny Wormald has argued that literacy rates among laymen were increasing in the fifteenth century, in Scotland as elsewhere in Europe, and that this led to 'a massive and even revolutionary change in the value-judgements of a whole society'. The Act reflected this new mindset. The royal licence which gave permission to establish the first printing press in Scotland in 1507 was intended to put literacy and education at the service of the state.[7]

In Scottish towns, as the population gradually recovered from the losses from plague in the fourteenth century, local government began to grow and take on new responsibilities. New needs for record-keeping developed as craft guilds started to form incorporated bodies, with their own rules and regulations. Overseas merchants participated in new methods of book-keeping and commercial transactions that were spreading through Europe and which relied on written records. All of these factors increased the interest of towns in education and schools.

The period also saw the rise of humanism, with its stress on education and classical learning, as well as the ideal of responsible citizenship and service to the state. The universities were perhaps the first to feel its influence but the schoolmasters who had been trained in those universities were soon bringing humanist ideas to bear on the curricula of the schools as well. Education was also seen as a way in which to bring about reform from within to the Catholic Church, which was faced with the growing threat of Protestantism in the mid-sixteenth century. A series of reforming church councils from 1549 placed new stress on the importance of educating clergy to become effective preachers and meet the religious needs of their congregations. Although this programme of Catholic reform was ended by the Reformation of 1559–60, the importance of education was not. The late middle ages had set the precedent for the central role of education in religious life which the Protestant reformers would attempt to implement.

Schools in Towns

The first schools established in Scottish towns in the twelfth century were those associated with church institutions, cathedrals, parish churches or religious houses. Scottish schools differed little from those throughout medieval Christendom. Their main purpose was to produce men to serve the church; many early schools were song schools providing training for the choristers and clergy in the sung liturgy of the church. They focused on singing, reading and sometimes writing, and the rudiments of Latin. In some towns, more advanced training in Latin grammar was provided by grammar schools. This was especially true in towns with cathedrals which modelled their constitutions on those of English cathedrals. The 1256 constitutions for St Machar's Cathedral in Old Aberdeen followed those of Salisbury which required the cantor to provide musical instruction for the choristers, and the chancellor to be master of the scholars associated with the cathedral, to whom he would teach grammar and logic. In Glasgow the sub-chantor was in charge of the song school, which was governed by the bishop's official. No one was to hold a grammar school in Glasgow and teach grammar to scholars or rudiments to youths without the licence of the chancellor. At Elgin Cathedral, which based its constitutions on those of Lincoln Cathedral, the chancellor claimed jurisdiction over all the schools in the diocese.[8] Schools were also included in grants of lands and churches to abbeys. Holyrood had in its jurisdiction the schools of Canongate and Edinburgh, while Dunfermline Abbey had control of the schools in Perth and Stirling, as well as in its own town of Dunfermline.[9] John Durkan has suggested that indirect evidence of schools can be found in the existence of almonries or hospitals where scholars from outside the town, as well as novices, would have boarded. Dunfermline's school, located at the abbey gate, probably started as an almonry school. The abbot provided a house for the schoolmaster and arranged for the board of poor scholars. He retained the right to appoint the Dunfermline schoolmaster throughout the pre-Reformation period. The noted composer John Angus was precentor of the abbey church in 1552, probably responsible for the song school, and principal almoner after the Reformation.[10]

Education was also provided by the collegiate churches which were established from the mid-fifteenth century onwards, many of them in towns. The foundation charters of some such collegiate churches specified teaching as one of the responsibilities of the prebendaries. At Biggar in 1545 the first of the eight prebendaries was to be master of the song school and instruct the four boys of the college in singing, descant and the organ, while the second prebendary was to be master of the grammar school.[11] Some collegiate churches had provisions to teach other boys as well as the choristers. A number of towns acquired collegiate status for their parish churches in the later fifteenth and sixteenth centuries; often one or more chaplaincies in these churches was reserved for a priest who also served as schoolmaster. Even towns without collegiate churches often had chaplaincies to support their schoolmasters.

Grammar schools generally recruited from song schools or more informal reading schools which educated boys to age seven or eight, although sometimes one school combined the functions of song and grammar schools. The Act of 1496 expected boys to attend for three years 'to obtain perfect Latin'. Not all grammar schools were the same. Some educated boys for longer periods and to a more advanced standard. Some concentrated more on practical Latin, others provided more study of rhetoric and classical literature. Some differences may have been due to demand. Tradesmen and merchants probably wanted basic Latin for commercial purposes and appreciated the shorter courses offered by schoolmasters such as Adam Mure in Edinburgh who offered to prepare boys in three years (suggesting that, despite the 1496 Act, this was not the norm in Edinburgh).[12]

The establishment of Scottish universities may have encouraged more grammar schools, although in St Andrews itself the number appears to have been cut to one by the arts faculty.[13] The grammar schools prepared boys for university, which they usually entered at the age of fifteen or sixteen, although some were as young as thirteen or fourteen. In the university towns, schoolmasters might participate in university teaching or examinations as well, while some transferred permanently to the university. Although the universities taught advanced subjects, in some ways the transition from grammar school to university may not have been that great:

> all the universities were collegiate in their way of life. They formed a community which studied, lived, ate and worshipped in common. Strict discipline was enforced, covering students' dress and recreation as well as academic matters, and the atmosphere was essentially that of a school.[14]

The support of clerical schoolmasters through the endowment of altars was particularly appropriate as the masters, especially those of song schools, were expected to participate in liturgical activities. Similar endowments supported clerical masters of grammar schools. Sometimes altars were specifically designated for this purpose. Chaplains themselves sometimes initiated the foundation of schools. In 1542, Sir David Bowman, a prebendary of the collegiate church of Crail, founded a grammar school there. He retained patronage of the appointment for life, but after his death patronage was to pass to the town. The pattern of patronage of an altar passing to the town after the founder's death was common in late medieval towns. This may have happened in Peebles, which has the earliest recorded example of a town appointment of a schoolmaster without presentation to a church official, in 1464.[15]

Clerical schoolmasters were usually appointed for life, perhaps reflecting the chaplaincies which supported the positions. As positions began to be filled by laymen, however, there was some experimentation with shorter terms. The Ayr grammar schoolmaster Mr William Nechay was only appointed for one year in 1551, while the new Aberdeen master appointed in 1550 served during the town's will. These shorter terms made it easier to dismiss unsatisfactory masters. In 1555, the schoolmaster of Peebles agreed that if he was absent from teaching the children for four days without licence, he would lose the balance of his fees and be discharged from his post immediately.[16]

Arrangements for the payment of teachers varied. If no chaplaincy was available, they might be given a fixed pension until they could be presented to one. This arrangement did not work for lay teachers, however. They were more likely to receive a fixed yearly sum, although some towns experimented with other ways of providing for them through voluntary contributions or assigning annual rents from particular properties. A town might change arrangements between appointments. In 1556, the new Peebles schoolmaster was given a pension and the town also paid for a chamber with chimney, closet and necessaries, except furnishing, but his successor had to provide his own chamber. In 1559, Peebles also offered the incentive of higher payment if the master taught more diligently, which in the town's eyes would result in the children acquiring more wisdom.[17] Masters were sometimes aided by one or more assistants, usually known as doctors. In some schools, the master was responsible for their pay, in others the town provided an income or pupils paid a separate lesser fee to the doctor. Both clerical and lay teachers might supplement their income with fees paid by individual students as well as bursaries for poor scholars. In 1559, Haddington paid its new schoolmaster Mr Robert Dormont 24 merks yearly, while he was to receive 12d fee from every bairn, and his assistant was to receive 4d per child. The town would also find him a chamber and a schoolhouse free of rent.[18]

Schools were not always physical buildings. Some classes were held in churches, others in public buildings such as the tolbooth and some even in teachers' homes. The lack of purpose-built schoolhouses or endowments for such was lamented by Ninian Winzet who taught school in Linlithgow in the 1550s; he saw it as a sign of a general lack of commitment to education in Scotland. However, many towns did try to provide and maintain schoolhouses, either renting premises or erecting new buildings themselves.

Urban schools were usually established by a religious institution but maintained by the town. Church and town often shared responsibilities for the upkeep of the parish church, with the town taking on more and more responsibility; arrangements for schools followed a similar pattern. In cathedral towns such as Glasgow the chancellor was often in charge of the school; while the town might be allowed to present a candidate, it was the chancellor who had the final say in admitting him to the position. Generally the division of responsibilities was agreed between the religious and lay authorities, but, as townspeople took an increasing interest in the education of their children, conflicts might occur.

In Aberdeen, the first reference to a named schoolmaster occurs in 1418 when the town presented John Homyll as master of the schools to the chancellor of the cathedral for approval. In 1509, however, it took full responsibility for appointing John Marshall to the post. The chancellor and the town contested the right to appoint the master several times during the sixteenth century, but the town usually won its point. When Marshall said in 1523 that he held his post from the chancellor, he was forced to ask the town's pardon. By 1529, the town council was referring to 'their' grammar school and 'their' bairns. In 1550, the town, having made its point, appointed the new master but presented him to the chancellor to be admitted.[19]

The existence of schools other than song and grammar schools is harder to trace, but their presence is noted in the various attempts by masters of the song and grammar schools to maintain their monopoly on education in the town. The masters were mainly concerned with competing schools of the same type, and some ordinances specified those schools which were exempt, usually English or reading schools. These other schools provided rudimentary education, often preparing boys to enter the more advanced grammar schools. In Stirling in 1557, David Ellis was only allowed to teach bairns under the age of seven, except those who had still to learn reading, writing and arithmetic. Not all such schools taught writing. In 1520, the Edinburgh town authorities ordained that schools other than the high school (the grammar school) were only allowed to teach 'the grace book, primer and plain Donat' – the prayer book, an elementary reader and the *Ars Minor* of Donatus, the basic Latin grammar.[20] There was no mention of writing. Such schools were often run by unofficial ('adventure') schoolmasters and schoolmistresses. These schools were freer of town regulations than the official schools and did not have to follow set curricula.

There were some schools where girls were educated, but the evidence is sparse. Girls may have been taught along with boys in some reading schools. There were also schools run by women. In 1499, a visitation of plague in Edinburgh led to all schools being shut down, including those run by women. Some education may also have been provided by female religious houses, although the extent of this has been debated. Haddington Priory, for example, housed a royal princess in the late fifteenth century but it is not clear whether it also provided an education – many of the nuns were unable to sign their names in the sixteenth century.[21] Sciennes Priory, established in Edinburgh in the early sixteenth century, had a much stronger record of literacy, and may have contributed to educating girls from Edinburgh and the surrounding area. While the dangers of equating literacy and education have been mentioned above, it is perhaps noteworthy that the earliest signature of a middling-status woman, that of Katherine Bray of Dunfermline in 1493, is found in a town. Her brother could also sign his name;[22] if Katherine did not learn to write at home, she may well have attended a reading school with him.

Curriculum

Almost nothing is known of the curriculum of the more informal schools, but song schools and grammar schools followed a curriculum familiar throughout Europe. Training boys for the church, early schools focused on music, reading and Latin. In a period when most reading was done aloud, singing and reading were closely related. Singing encouraged clear and correct pronunciation of words rather than mumbling. The rudiments of Latin grammar were taught in the song schools, with the more advanced grammar required by those seeking a higher career in the church or entrance to university being taught at the grammar schools.

Instruction in basic reading followed the European system of providing an alphabet and perhaps Roman numerals on cheap tablets or hornbooks, then having students read and learn by heart Latin prayers and psalms collected together in a primer. A grace book also contained pieces of verse, perhaps longer than the materials in the primer. Rudimentary Latin grammar was taught with the help of grammars such as that of Aelius Donatus, the standard schoolbook used throughout Europe for centuries.[23] Books were expensive; as elsewhere, it was common to make use of the service books of the nearby church for reading practice for the students. Those mentioned in the 1507 licence for printing were probably also intended as schoolbooks; Donatus may have become cheaper and more accessible in the early sixteenth century as it was one of the first books printed after the establishment of the first Scottish printing press. Printing probably made works in the vernacular more accessible as well, although the impact of the press should not be exaggerated.

Records of the music curriculum of song schools are fragmentary but the quality of music which survives suggests high standards. Plainsong or chant dominated in the earlier period, but by the later fifteenth and sixteenth centuries, polyphony was becoming the style of choice for composers and teachers. Not all contemporaries approved – Robert Richardson, an Augustinian canon, complained in 1530 that over-emphasis on music, especially polyphony, led to neglect of the education of novices and boys and of Bible study.[24] A bond between the town of Inverness and its new song schoolmaster James Affleck in 1538 shows the type of teaching offered there. Fees were four shillings for plain singing and pricked singing (music read from a score), eight shillings for descant and sixteen shillings for counterpoint, playing the organ and faburden (improvised polyphony). There are some indications as to how polyphony was taught, thanks to the survival of what are known as the 'Inverness fragments' containing three and four part faburden. Affleck was also expected to teach the organ. However, his skills as an organist were not quite up to par as he was not to begin instructing pupils immediately, but to continue his studies in Elgin for another six months or even longer until he could read music by sight.[25] Singing and instrumental music were valued by laypeople as well as churchmen. In 1496, a contract between the town of Aberdeen and their song schoolmaster Robert Huchoson stipulated that he was to teach *burgesses' sons* to sing and play the organ. Lay demands for specific skills probably had some influence on how teaching was carried out in urban schools.

The requirements for entrance to St Leonard's College in the early sixteenth century give an idea of the knowledge students were expected to acquire in grammar school. They had to have finished at least the first and second parts of grammar, know the greater part of the syntax section, know plainsong and be able to write, although writing was omitted in the original statutes. Some knowledge of poetry and rhetoric was also expected, although since these were not taught in all Latin schools, the principal could order remedial classes for those students lacking such background.[26]

The school curriculum also reflected the changing intellectual currents of the time. The Inverness fragments include parts of a printed Latin grammar, possibly that of Alexander de Villa Dei, including maxims intended to encourage an elegant style of speaking. In the sixteenth century, under the influence of humanism, the focus on medieval Latin and logic in the medieval schools began to be replaced by a new emphasis on classical Latin and other languages, rhetoric and elegant diction, as put forward in works such as Lorenzo Valla's *Elegantiae*. The influence of Valla and of new European grammars was increasingly felt in Scotland and can be seen in John Vaus, master of the grammar school at Aberdeen in 1520 and humanist at King's College, Aberdeen. Vaus wrote his own grammar, *Rudimenta puerorum in artem grammaticalem*, which was published in Paris in 1522 and went through another two editions before the Reformation. The grammar of the Flemish John Despauterius, which also paid some attention to rhetoric, became the leading grammar in Scottish grammar schools from the 1540s.[27] The emphasis on rhetoric can be seen in practice in Linlithgow in the 1550s where Ninian Winzet 'proponed almost daily some theme, argument, or sentence, of which he caused them [his students] to make orison or epistle, in Latin tongue'.[28] The emphasis on classical languages can be seen in the statutes for the Old Aberdeen grammar school which date from around 1553, although they may have been in use as early as the 1530s. Students were to converse only in Latin, Greek, Hebrew, French or Gaelic (suggesting the presence of students from the Highlands). They received lessons on Terence, Virgil and Cicero as models for writing and speaking. There was a teacher of Greek in Montrose from at least 1534; one of his pupils was the noted reformer Andrew Melville.[29]

Despite the emphasis on classical languages, there was also an increasing role for the vernacular in education. From the later fifteenth century, burgh records were usually kept in Scots rather than in Latin, suggesting that the vernacular had achieved a new respectability as a language of record. Vaus's grammar was partly in Scots. The skills of reading and writing in the vernacular appealed to urban parents who were not planning a clerical career for their sons. In 1556, Ayr Council ordered that pupils 'be lairned bay the Inglis and Latyne at the optioun and pleasure of the parents'.[30]

In 1559, a special licence was granted to William Nyddry to print works for the better instruction of schoolchildren in grammar. The list of works provides a snapshot of those books which were regarded as the best educational texts of the period. Several were in Scots, for use in schools where Latin was not taught and in grammar schools which also encouraged the study of vernacular. There were texts for learning Latin and Greek and possibly Hebrew, as well as extracts from classical texts. One text which seems to have had an underlying political message in the Scotland of Mary of Guise was 'Ane A B C for Scottismen to rede the French toung with an exhortatioun to the nobles of Scotland to favour their ald freindis'. Befitting a humanist education, there was also 'Ane regiment for educatioun of young gentillmen in literature and virtuous exercitioun'.[31] Schools were expected to teach good behaviour and morals as part of the education of the pupils. The ideals of civic humanism may have strengthened this component of the curriculum. In 1544, the Aberdeen master was ordered to teach science, manners, writing and other such virtues, while the new schoolmaster in Dundee, Thomas MacGibbon, was to teach oratory, poetry, grammar and moral letters but also 'gude manners and cumlie order'.[32]

Teachers

When Mr John Homyll was made master of the schools in Aberdeen in 1418, he was examined for his sufficient qualifications, and found to be a man of good life, praiseworthy and honest conversation, great skill in literature and learning generally, and holding a well-deserved degree (which he had received from St Andrews in 1415, making him one of the first Scottish schoolmasters to have earned his degree in his own country). Teachers were to be skilled in their subjects, but also to be of blameless life and reputation.[33]

As clergy, most schoolteachers, if not graduates, were identified by the honorific Dominus, which in the vocative form Domine is the origin of 'dominie'. The clerical character of the profession has caused problems for historians in identifying early schoolmasters as many designated themselves as clerics rather than as schoolmasters. For example, Gavin Ros of Ayr is known to many medieval historians as a notary public, but less well known is the fact that he was also a schoolmaster, as this is not mentioned in his protocols.[34] Lists of masters and doctors provide names from as early as the thirteenth century for St Andrews, Perth, Roxburgh, Aberdeen and Ayr, and in the fourteenth century Cupar and Haddington. As more names appear in the fourteenth and fifteenth centuries, many include the title 'Master', indicating that they were university graduates. In the later fifteenth and sixteenth centuries, perhaps reflecting the rising status of literacy in society at large, more laymen became schoolmasters. The change can be seen at Perth – the grammar school was taught by clerics for most of the first half of the sixteenth century, but then by Andrew Simson, a layman. Simson became part of the burgess community, marrying a burgess daughter and entering the guild. Mr Thomas McGibbon, master of the Dundee grammar school in the 1550s, was married; his wife contributed to the family income through selling ale. The process was not one-way, however: in Aberdeen the lay schoolmaster Mr Hew Munro was succeeded in 1550 by a cleric, Mr James Chalmer.[35]

Masters rarely spent their entire time in teaching. Song schoolmasters were often the organists for the church. Several masters also worked as notaries. Some of these men fell short of the moral standards required of teachers. John Sowtare who was created a notary in 1526 was prosecuted for keeping an illegal school in Dundee in 1566 and was hanged in 1580 for abusing his office of notary.[36] Some schoolmasters were also appointed as parish clerks, while others served as royal customs officers.[37]

One of Mr John Homyll's qualifications was that he was 'of good life'. As those who were charged with inculcating good morals and manners in their charges, teachers were held to a high standard of morality themselves. The 1542 foundation of Crail grammar school required teachers to be priests 'of proved learning and blameless life'. Mr John Bowman and his successors were not to be gamblers, card players, drunkards or nightwalkers, nor were they to have a housekeeper or a public concubine.[38] Occasionally masters left accounts of their experiences. Ninian Winzet of Linlithgow later commented on how much he had enjoyed teaching there and how he had been privileged to teach 'humane children of happy ingynis [genius, cleverness]', modestly adding that they were more able to learn than he was to teach as his erudition was but small. However, he also bemoaned the lack of respect for teachers and education, as he felt that schoolmasters should rank in importance second only to the clergy and ministers of justice.[39]

The books of a number of schoolmasters still survive. At least one master, John Brown of Crail, passed on one of his books to a pupil, suggesting a close friendship between teacher and student.[40] In 1539, the Linlithgow schoolmaster Mr James Browne attempted to protect his students from what he saw as unreasonable demands and loss of time from study. The schoolmaster was maintained by the chaplainry of All Saints which required certain religious observances by the master and scholars. Browne complained that the curate was exceeding these obligations in demanding the bairns enter the kirk on festival days for mass and evensong and sit down on 'cauld stanis' when they should have been learning their lessons. His comment that this was harming the reputation of the curate in the minds of his parishioners suggests that the scholars' parents also saw the value of Browne's teaching and their children's education.[41] Some pupils have left comments about their teachers. James Melville said of Mr Thomas Andersone, his uncle's teacher in Montrose in the 1550s, that he was 'esteimed the best maister in his tyme, whowbeit nocht the maist lernit', while David Hume of Godscroft recalled of Perth schoolmaster Andrew Simson in the 1540s and 1550s that he could strike terror into his pupils but might also allow innocent fun.[42]

Students

One of the cherished, but debated, ideas about Scottish education is its openness to students of all social ranks.[43] There was some attempt to provide for poor scholars. Bursaries were provided for some poor students, and occasionally payments were made for the expenses of individual poor scholars. Churches often arranged that poor students should be educated for free, with some of them being boarded in the hospitals or almonries, while those who were wealthier were expected to pay fees. It was not uncommon for lairds to send their sons to a town school to receive the benefits of a grammar school education, and the 1496 Education Act encouraged such initiatives. It seems unlikely, however, that many peasants' sons would sit beside the scions of the nobility in the classroom, given the fact that educational provision was still restricted to relatively few.

Few first-hand accounts of school life exist for the period, but there are some surviving letters written to his parents by Patrick Waus of Barnbarroch who was at school in Musselburgh in the 1540s. From these letters we learn something of his studies, which included Caesar and Sallust as well as the New Testament, and the fact that he bought books in Edinburgh. Like students throughout the centuries, he complained to his parents that he was short of money – he told his mother that he was 'verie scant' of shirts and neckcloths and reminded her that she had promised to send some shoes. He sent his father a copy of an account showing how he had spent his money, including three pounds for three pairs of blue hose, suggesting there may have been a school uniform. He enjoyed recreation and seems to have been an energetic but possibly careless archer as he complained to his father that he was 'verie scant' of arrows.[44]

The statutes of the grammar school of Old Aberdeen set out a typical day for a scholar. On entering the school in the morning, he knelt and saluted Christ and the Virgin Mary. Work began at 7 a.m. with parsing, at the end of which the master entered and either rebuked or physically punished those who failed. The schoolmaster then addressed all the classes at 8 a.m. Breakfast followed. At 10.00 there were individual classes by the undermasters until 11 or 11.30 at which point poor scholars were allowed to go into town, followed shortly afterwards by town boys going home. For advanced students, there was a lecture by the master on Terence, Virgil or Cicero until noon and then the midday meal. Individual classes began again at 2.00 with doctors present to correct bad Latin, mark mistakes and deal with any idlers. At 4.00 the boys went over the work done that day with their instructors. If nature called, the boys were allowed to go out in pairs, carrying some sort of token or symbol, but no more than one pair was allowed to leave the classroom at a time. The master could inspect any of the classes at any time. From 5.00 to 6.00 there were evening disputations, and thereafter all the scholars sang the psalms.

Total silence was ordained for elementary pupils and beginners for the first year (of apparently three), while older pupils could converse only in Latin, Greek, Hebrew, French or Gaelic, not in the vernacular, except with those who did not know Latin. All were to learn the 'table of confession' (perhaps the articles of the creed) and some arithmetic. Each boy was to carry his own ruler (perhaps meaning all his school supplies). No outsiders were to enter the college, and no boy studying grammar was to associate with anyone doing logic.

Schoolboy misconduct was also covered. Property could not be bartered, bought or sold without the knowledge of the headmaster or his assistant. A certain amount of gambling on games was permitted, but no one was allowed to stake books, money, clothes or food on the outcome. Older boys were allowed to stake shoelaces or pins. Dice playing was prohibited, and all games were to be played within sight of the undermasters, not privately. Fighting was prohibited, even if it was to avenge a wrong. Older boys leading younger boys into any of these faults would be doubly punished as not only did they do wrong but they also corrupted others. Other offences included disobedience, lateness in the morning, ignorance of assigned work, moving from place to place without adequate reason, running around the school, talking during lectures, lateness returning from meals, wasting time if allowed to leave the room, long absences from the lecture room and the catch-all 'mischief'.

Keeping order among rambunctious pupils was a necessary requirement for a schoolmaster. In Dundee in 1558, masters and doctors of schools were to see that scholars and servants did not play, cry or dispute during preaching. Occasionally students were led astray by their teachers. When Dave Anderson, doctor in the grammar school of Aberdeen, was assaulted in the kirk by Gilbert Kintore, he retaliated by fetching his pupils to attack Kintore.[45] A more constructive way of controlling schoolboy energies was sport. Patrick Vaus lost his arrows at archery in Musselburgh in the 1540s, but there were other forms of physical activity for schoolboys as well, including golf, football and tennis. The students of the grammar school of Perth practised their archery on the South Inch of Perth, probably at 'Scholars' Knoll'.[46] There was also licensed disorder. In December, it was traditional for schoolboys to elect a 'boy bishop'. He presided over revels and also collected money from door to door for the festivities. Some boy bishops even importuned the king for money. In Aberdeen, the town authorities, looking for a way to pay their lay schoolmaster one year, ordered that he should also collect contributions door to door in December along with the boy bishop.[47]

Other Forms of Education

Most histories of education have focused on schools, but education could also take other forms. The most formalised of these was apprenticeship. Edgar's study of early education included a chapter on 'artistic, industrial, technical education'. As a recent study of the locksmith craft in sixteenth- to eighteenth-century Edinburgh points out, 'Apprenticeship was a hands-on practical education, which served both the parties involved. The master got help and the apprentices got skills, food, clothing and shelter.'[48] In some respects, this was not so different from the way in which smaller song schools might function – the pupils learnt music skills but also assisted their teacher in his responsibility to provide the music for the church services. Apprenticeship differed in that apprentices were older, probably usually entering about the age of thirteen or fourteen and, at least by the later middle ages, often subject to a written contract.

Apprentices become easier to trace as crafts began to become incorporated in the late fifteenth century. The seals of cause (letters of incorporation) establishing the various craft guilds in Edinburgh between 1473 and 1523 frequently mention apprenticeship. Lengths of apprenticeship varied, with seven years for the goldsmiths but five for the cordiners, although a cordiner then had to serve a further three years with a craftsman for his 'meat and fee'. These lengths of apprenticeship were not always adhered to. In towns without incorporated crafts, it was the burgh court which regulated apprentices – some sixteenth-century contracts can be found in the manuscript burgh court records and more may yet be discovered. Just as many entering formal schooling did not complete their studies, the same was true of apprentices. Even those who did finish might not become masters in the town. There were many more apprentices in the Edinburgh locksmith trade from 1550 to 1750 than incoming masters. This was not necessarily to the detriment of the trade as a whole. Many apprentices came from outside the town and, after their apprenticeship, probably returned home to set up as a master there.[49]

For girls, the most common equivalent to formal schooling was domestic service, although rather than paying an employer to take them on, they received wages. They were also more likely to have short-term contracts and move between employers. Most girls remained in service until marriage, although some servants set up business on their own. As adolescent boys learnt the skills of their chosen craft, girls learnt the skills they needed to run a household after marriage. Like boys, many female domestic servants came from outside the town.

Coming of the Reformation

In 1553, a dispute broke out in Dundee over the control of its grammar school. Upset that Thomas MacGibbon was apparently allowing discussion of reformed ideas in his school, in 1553 the abbot of Lindores, who had the right to appoint the grammar schoolmaster, tried to counter his influence by appointing another master. This master then appointed substitutes who established rival schools to take away MacGibbon's pupils. The town council, however, supported MacGibbon, as well as their song schoolmaster Richard Barclay, and tried to suppress their rivals in 1555 by forbidding any other schools to teach grammar, English or singing. The council also fined at least thirty families who did not send their children to the town grammar school in 1556. The abbot appealed to the church court which ordered the council to allow the rival schools, under pain of excommunication. The council appealed to the pope and was granted temporary absolution from cursing. The action was then taken to a civil court where it was still pending when the Reformation finally ended the power of the abbot of Lindores.[50]

It is not clear how much of a role religion played in this dispute. The town may have been more concerned with its rights over its school than any religious issues. However, even if MacGibbon was not Protestant himself, the fact that he allowed open discussion of Reformation principles shows the power of schools as inculcators of new ideas as well as skills. It was the Scottish grammar schools which educated most of the men who established the Protestant Reformation in their country. The town schools also had the easiest access to the heretical Protestant books which were coming into Scotland, despite attempts to prohibit their import. As schools became increasingly secularised and literacy made churchmen less crucial, criticism of the church in these schools may have grown, with pupils being influenced by their teachers. John Row reported that 300 pupils of Andrew Simson in Perth hissed at a friar's sermon in 1556. The role of the schools in preparing the ground for the Reformation is one which deserves further investigation.[51] But recent work on the Reformation has emphasised that while there were changes, there were also continuities. Although some masters were forced to leave their schools with the change in religion, others converted and remained in post. Similar daily routines continued, although religious texts changed. Latin continued to be important, despite the new importance of the vernacular as the language of scripture and liturgy. And in some respects, it was schools, or at least schoolboys, which held on longest to certain older traditions. The last word belongs to them. Although they could no longer elect a boy bishop in December, they had not forgotten the time of revelry completely. In 1569, the Aberdeen authorities received a formal letter of complaint written in Latin by the pupils of the grammar school, requesting the restitution of their accustomed Christmas holiday. Perhaps impressed by their Latin, the council granted them two weeks off school.[52]

Acknowledgement

This chapter is dedicated to the memory of my own teacher and mentor, G. W. S. Barrow, who first suggested this topic to his new postgraduate student thirty years ago, but who died just before she could show him that she had finally taken his advice.

Notes

1. Blind Harry, *The Wallace*, ed. Anne McKim (Canongate Classics, 2003), lines 155–6.
2. 'Acts of the Parliament and of the Privy Council of Scotland Relative to the Establishing and Maintaining of Schools from the Year MCCCCXCVI to the Year MDCXVI', *Miscellany of the Maitland Club*, vol. 2, part 1 (Maitland Club, 1840), pp. 1–50; James Edgar, *History of Early Scottish Education* (James Thin, 1883); James Grant, *History of the Burgh Schools of Scotland* (William Collins, Sons & Co., 1876); James Scotland, *The History of Scottish Education*, 2 vols (University of London Press, 1969).
3. John Durkan, *Scottish Schools and Schoolmasters, 1560–1633*, ed. and rev. Jamie Reid-Baxter (Scottish History Society, 2013). I am very grateful to Jamie Reid-Baxter for allowing me to see the typescript version of the work ahead of publication. Durkan's updated list of urban schools adds the French and Trinity schools in Edinburgh and a school in Kirkintilloch to the list of pre-Reformation schools in 'Education in the century of the Reformation', *Innes Review* 10 (1959), 90. Several of Durkan's articles are referenced below.
4. J. C. Jessop, *Education in Angus: An Historical Survey of Education up to the Act of 1872 From Original and Contemporary Sources* (University of London Press, 1931), p. 6. Other works are Shona Vance, 'Schooling the people', in E. Patricia Dennison, David Ditchburn and Michael Lynch (eds), *Aberdeen before 1800. A New History* (Tuckwell Press, 2002), pp. 309–26; William C. A. Ross, *The Royal High School*, 2nd edn (Oliver and Boyd, 1949); John Strawhorn, *750 Years of a Scottish School. Ayr Academy 1233–1983* (Alloway Publishing, 1983); Edward Smart, *History of Perth Academy* (Milne, Tannahill and Methven, 1932); Brian R. W. Lockhart, *The Town School. A History of the High School of Glasgow* (John Donald, 2010).
5. Shulamith Shahar, *Childhood in the Middle Ages* (Routledge, 1990), esp. Chapter 11; Nicholas Orme, *Medieval Children* (Yale University Press, 2002), Chapter 7; Ruth Mazo Karras, *From Boys to Men. Formations of Masculinity in Late Medieval Europe* (University of Pennsylvania Press, 2003).

6. Donald Withrington, 'Church and state in Scottish education before 1872', in Heather Holmes (ed.), *Institutions of Scotland: Education*, Scottish Life and Society: A Compendium of Scottish Ethnology, vol. 11 (Tuckwell Press, 2000), p. 47.

7. Jenny Wormald, *Court, Kirk and Community 1470–1625* (Edinburgh University Press, 1992), pp. 68–71.

8. Jessop, *Angus*, pp. 25–6; Vance, 'Schooling the people', p. 309; Grant, *Burgh Schools*, p. 19; John Durkan, 'Early song schools in Scotland', in *Notis Musycall*, ed. Gordon Munro (Musica Scotland Trust, 2005), p. 125; Durkan, *Schools*, p. 7.

9. Grant, *Burgh Schools*, pp. 4, 22–4; Durkan, *Schools*, pp. 9–10.

10. Durkan, 'Song schools', pp. 125–6; John Durkan, 'Care of the poor: Pre-Reformation hospitals', *Innes Review* 10 (1959), 268–80; Jamie Reid-Baxter, Michael Lynch and E. Patricia Dennison, *Jhone Angus Monk of Dunfermline & Scottish Reformation Music* (Doublebridge Press, 2011), p. 71.

11. Jessop, *Angus*, pp. 29–30.

12. Durkan, *Schools*, pp. 36–9; Durkan, 'Education: The laying of fresh foundations', in John MacQueen (ed.), *Humanism in Renaissance Scotland* (Edinburgh University Press, 1990), p. 131. For similar patterns in Europe, see Shahar, *Childhood*, pp. 187–8.

13. Durkan, *Schools*, p. 27.

14. R. D. Anderson, 'Scottish universities', in Holmes (ed.), *Institutions of Scotland*, pp. 155–6.

15. Edgar, *Early Education*, pp. 113–14.

16. Grant, *Burgh Schools*, pp. 42–3.

17. William Chambers (ed.), *Charters and Documents Relating to the Burgh of Peebles* (Scottish Burgh Records Society, 1872), pp. 233, 243, 257.

18. Scotland, *History*, vol. 1, p. 19.

19. Vance, 'Schooling the people', p. 311; Edgar, *Early Education*, pp. 114–15.

20. Durkan, *Schools*, p. 38; *Extracts from the Records of the Burgh of Edinburgh (1403–1718)*, eds James D. Marwick, Marguerite Wood, Robert Kerr Hannay and Helen Armet, 14 vols (Scottish Burgh Records Society, 1869–1967), pp. 193–4.

21. Rosalind Marshall, *Virgins and Viragos* (Collins, 1983), pp. 55–7. On women's signatures, see also Margaret Sanderson, *A Kindly Place? Living in Sixteenth-Century Scotland* (Tuckwell Press, 2002), Chapter 9.

22. Erskine Beveridge (ed.), *The Burgh Records of Dunfermline* (William Brown, 1917), p. 55.

23. Very similar methods were used elsewhere. See Nicholas Orme, *English Schools in the Middle Ages* (Methuen and Co, Ltd, 1973), pp. 60–3; Shahar, *Childhood*, p. 189.

24. Durkan, *Schools*, p. 35; Durkan, 'Fresh foundations', p. 125.

25. Athol L. Murray, 'The parish clerk and song school of Inverness, 1538–9', *Innes Review* 58(1) (spring 2007), 107–15 – the bond is transcribed in the article; Stephen Allenson, 'The Inverness fragments: Music from a pre-Reformation Scottish parish church and school', *Music and Letters* 70(1) (February 1989), 1–45. For another similar bond in Linlithgow, see Durkan, 'Education in the century of the Reformation', 89.

26. Durkan, *Schools*, p. 41.

27. Allenson, 'Fragments', 16; Durkan, 'Fresh foundations', p. 131; David Murray, 'Some early grammars and other school books in use in Scotland, more particularly those printed at or relating to Scotland', *Proceedings of the Royal Philosophical Society of Glasgow* 36 (1904–5), pp. 5–6; Durkan, *Schools*, pp. 100–2.

28. Ninian Winzet, *Certane Tractatis for Reformatioun of Doctryne and Maneris in Scotland* (Maitland Club, 1835 [1562]), p. 27.

29. Durkan, *Schools*, pp. 84–5; Grant, *Burgh Schools*, pp. 47–8. The statutes are given in English translation in Edgar, *Early Education*, pp. 122–4.
30. Strawhorn, *Ayr*, p. 10; Chambers (ed.), *Peebles Charters and Documents*, p. 257.
31. Murray, 'Some early grammars', pp. 4–5.
32. Grant, *Burgh Schools*, p. 46; Durkan, *Schools*, p. 40.
33. John Stuart (ed.), *Extracts from the Council Register of the Burgh of Aberdeen 1398–1570* (Spalding Club, 1844), pp. 4–5; Durkan, *Schools*, pp. 28–9.
34. Durkan, *Schools*, pp. 3, 31; Durkan, 'Education in the century of the Reformation', p. 89 prints the contract by which Ros was appointed schoolmaster.
35. Mary Verschuur, *Politics or Religion? The Reformation in Perth 1540–1570* (Dunedin Academic Press, 2006), p. 30; Dundee City Archives, Dundee Burgh Court Register 1554–8, fo. 168v; Stuart (ed.), *Aberdeen Extracts*, pp. 276–7.
36. John Durkan, 'The early Scottish notary', in Ian B. Cowan and Duncan Shaw (eds), *The Renaissance and Reformation in Scotland* (Scottish Academic Press, 1983), pp. 23, 27, 36.
37. Murray, 'Parish clerk'; Grant, *Burgh Schools*, p. 11.
38. Grant, *Burgh Schools*, p. 25.
39. Winzet, *Certane Tractatis*, pp. 25–7.
40. John Durkan and Anthony Ross, *Early Scottish Libraries* (John S. Burn and Sons, 1961), p. 79.
41. Durkan, *Schools*, pp. 31–2.
42. James Melville's diary quoted in Jessop, *Angus*, p. 37; Durkan, 'Fresh foundations', p. 137.
43. Robert Anderson, 'In search of the "lad of parts": The mythical history of Scottish education', *History Workshop* 19 (spring 1985), 82–104.
44. Robert Vans Agnew (ed.), *Correspondence of Sir Patrick Waus of Barnbarroch, Knight* (Ayr and Galloway Archaeological Association, 1887), pp. 2–6.
45. Jessop, *Angus*, p. 167; Stuart (ed.), *Aberdeen Extracts*, pp. 265–6 (misdated as 1549 instead of 1550).
46. Smart, *Perth Academy*, p. 6.
47. David McRoberts, 'The boy bishop', *Innes Review* 19(1) (spring 1968), 80–2.
48. Aaron M. Allen, *The Locksmith Craft in Early Modern Edinburgh* (Society of Antiquaries of Scotland, 2007), p. 31.
49. Ibid., pp. 8, 10, 11, 31–2. For England, see Ilana Krausman Ben-Amos, *Adolescence and Youth in Early Modern England* (Yale University Press, 1994), pp. 86, 92–3, 133. For Europe, see Shahar, *Childhood*, pp. 226–9, 232–6.
50. Durkan, *Schools*, pp. 40–1.
51. Wormald, *Court, Kirk and Community*, p. 108; Durkan, *Schools*, p. 103; see also Durkan's list of post-Reformation schoolmasters on pp. 229–382 for those who were in post before 1560.
52. Vance, 'Schooling the people', p. 314; Stuart (ed.), *Aberdeen Extracts*, p. 366.

Bibliography

Agnew, Robert Vans (ed.), *Correspondence of Sir Patrick Waus of Barnbarroch, Knight* (Ayr and Galloway Archaeological Association, 1887).
Durkan, John, 'Education in the century of the Reformation', *Innes Review* 10 (1959), 67–90.
Durkan, John, 'Education: The laying of fresh foundations', in John MacQueen (ed.), *Humanism in Renaissance Scotland* (Edinburgh University Press, 1990), pp. 123–60.

Durkan, John, 'Early song schools in Scotland', in Gordon Munro (ed.), *Notis Musycall. Essays in Honour of Kenneth Elliott* (Musica Scotland Trust, 2005), pp. 125–32.

Durkan, John, *Scottish Schools and Schoolmasters, 1560–1633*, ed. and rev. Jamie Reid-Baxter (Scottish History Society, 2013).

Edgar, James, *History of Early Scottish Education* (James Thin, 1883).

Grant, James, *History of the Burgh Schools of Scotland* (William Collins, Sons & Co., 1876).

Lockhart, Brian R. W., *The Town School. A History of the High School of Glasgow* (John Donald, 2010).

Murray, Athol L., 'The parish clerk and song school of Inverness', *Innes Review* 58(1) (spring 2007), 107–15.

Vance, Shona, 'Schooling the people', in E. Patricia Dennison, David Ditchburn and Michael Lynch (eds), *Aberdeen Before 1800: A New History* (Tuckwell Press, 2002), pp. 309–26.

4

Education in the Century of Reformation

Stephen Mark Holmes

It is a commonplace that 'the Scottish Reformation' of 1560, with its desire to enable people to read the Bible in their own language, led to the establishment of a system of education available to the whole nation, rooted in an extensive network of parish schools and headed by a unique system of universities. First Minister Alex Salmond reflected this view at a conference in 2010 to mark the Reformation's 450th anniversary:

> The educational climate established by the Reformation has been vital to the development of the society we know today. The *First Book of Discipline* of 1560 led to the Act for Settling of Schools of 1696 in the Scottish Parliament and culminated in the establishment of Scotland's free, universal education system. I believe that Scotland's greatest invention, from which all the other inventions sprang, is public education.[1]

This chapter will challenge this view by investigating the history of education in Scotland in the 'long sixteenth century' and by rejecting the remnants of sectarian historiography in order to understand 'the Scottish Reformation' not as the Protestant revolution of 1560 but as a series of movements of church reform, both Catholic and Protestant, during this whole period.

A Long Century of Reformation

The problem with the traditional interpretation is that it is rooted in an understanding of 'the Scottish Reformation' which was created by the Protestant victors in the revolution of 1559–60.[2] They used the term 'Reformation' for this revolution in the same way as one might use a royal or pontifical reign; for example the Dysart notary Henry Young dated a protocol of July 1564, '*Anno Reformationis ecclesie Jesus Christi in Scotis quinto*' ('the fifth year of the Reformation of the Church of Jesus Christ among the Scots').[3] The same use is found in 1560 in the *First Book of Discipline* (also known as the *Buik of Reformatioun*), which gave a blueprint for the future of education in Scotland, and it was applied to history in the title of John Knox's *History of the Reformation of Religioun within the Realme of Scotland* (1587). Catholic Scots, however, rejected this use: the schoolmaster-priest Ninian Winzet wrote in 1563 of 'the new impietie callit by sum the Reformatioun of the Protestantis', which was a 'praetendit reformatioun', and in 1581 the controversialist Nicol Burne spoke of the 'deformation', its 'deformed religione' and 'the reformation (as the Ministeris callis it) of that deformit kirk in Scotland'.[4] 'Reformation' was thus a disputed term. It was also not the sole property of the Protestants but was a key concept in the strong Catholic reform movements before 1560 being used, for example, in the 1540 Act of the Scottish Parliament 'for reforming kirks and kirkmen', in the legislation for reformation of morals and teaching in the Scottish Provincial Councils of 1549–58 and in the reform programmes of Archbishop Hamilton and the bishops of Aberdeen.

Catholic and Protestant reform movements shared a concern for education and, while scholars have moved away from partisan denominational views of religion in sixteenth-century Scotland, the use of the term 'the Scottish Reformation' solely for the Protestant revolution of 1559–60 is an unwitting way of maintaining prejudice. It is thus best to call the events of 1559–60 'the Scottish Protestant Reformation' and to use 'the Scottish Reformation' (or 'Reformations') for a series of movements of church reform in the long sixteenth century which stretched from the activity of reforming bishops such as Kennedy and Elphinstone in the fifteenth century to the reforms under James VI and Charles I and the religious wars of the late 1630s. This enables one to escape stark binary views of this period (Catholic/Protestant; Presbyterian/Episcopalian) and it reveals hidden continuities, in education even more than in religion.

Schools

The first two books to be published by a Scottish publisher were schoolbooks, a Latin vocabulary (1505) and a liturgical commentary on the Sarum sequences (1506), both printed in Rouen by Pierre Violette for the Edinburgh bookseller Androw Myllar.[5] This shows the importance of education in this period and the two main aspects of pre-university education throughout this period, language and religion. The language was primarily Latin because, despite the growth of vernacular literature, Latin retained cultural dominance even after the move to vernacular in public worship in 1560.

Legislation for pre-university education

One way of studying education in Scotland is to examine its institutional regulation. A 1496 Act of Parliament required barons and freeholders of substance to put their eldest sons to school from the age of eight or nine until the grammar school had ensured that they had 'perfite latyne' and could proceed to study the arts and law at university. This was to provide for good governance of the realm and was an aspiration rather than a description but it does show that schools were not only of importance to the church. Education was, however, central to Catholic reform as seen in the legislation of the fifth Lateran Council (1512–17), encouraging grammar schools to teach the commandments, creed,

Expolitio Sequentiarum

Figure 4.1 Woodcut from the 1506 *Expositio Sequentiarum*. With permission of British Library, C.35.c.6.

hymns and psalms, and of the Council of Trent (1545–63), encouraging education in grammar and scripture in churches and monasteries.[6] This was repeated in the reform programme of the 1549 Scottish Provincial Council under the heading 'Concerning reformation in the matter of instruction', which required each benefice to fund a grammar master to prepare poor scholars for the study of scripture; education by parish clergy was also ordered by the 1552 Provincial Council.[7]

Protestant and Catholic reformers shared this concern. The section 'For the Schollis' in the *First Book of Discipline* followed the Catholic councils in calling for every parish to provide education by a grammar schoolmaster in towns and by the reader or minister in the country. Its language recalls the 1549 Council and the 1496 Act but it also drew on the work of the reformed educationalists Jean Sturm (1507–89) at Strasbourg and Claude Baduel (d. 1561) at Nîmes and Geneva. Even its desire for arts colleges teaching 'the tongues' (Latin, Greek and Hebrew) in notable towns, designed to replace the traditional university arts course for those over fifteen, recalled the Parisian 'Royal Trilingual College' which was imitated in the 1550s by Mary of Guise and Bishop Robert Reid (d. 1558) in their plans for lectureships and a college in Edinburgh. The curriculum outlined in the *First Book of Discipline*, while it included 'the tongues', was the traditional one of reading, catechism, Latin grammar and philosophy, something which remained constant as reflected in a 1616 Act of the Privy Council which desired that 'the youth may be taught at the least to write and to read and be catechised and instructed in the grounds of religion'. The religion to be taught was reformed in content but was divided up like Catholic catechesis into commandments, creed, prayer and sacraments. The first educational programme of the Scottish Protestant reformers was thus in its shape and emphasis on grammar very close to Catholic humanist reform.

The *First Book of Discipline*, like the Provincial Councils, presented an ideal. The 1616 Act, ratified by parliament in 1633, and followed by Acts in 1646 and 1696, ordered that a school be established in every parish, thus showing its provisions had still not been implemented by the end of that century. The Acts of the General Assemblies did however demonstrate a continuing concern with education as part of the mission of the church by legislating to divert teinds to schools (1562 – teind is the Scots word for tithe, a tenth of produce given as a tax to the church); exclude Catholic teachers (1563, 1569); support poor scholars (1563, 1572); and improve education in the dioceses of Moray, Dunkeld and Caithness (1563, 1571, 1573, 1574). The Presbyterian General Assembly of 1638 continued this interest, legislating for the establishment of country schools. Parliament shared this concern, passing an Act in 1579 to re-erect song schools in the burghs on the basis of old collegiate foundations, 'for instruction of the youth in the art of music and singing, which is almost decayed and shall shortly decay unless timely remedy be provided'.

In the Scottish Gàidhealtachd, the area of Gaelic speech and culture, education was to be in Scots (English) as well as Latin. The 1616 Act of the Privy

Council ordered that the use of Scots 'be universally planted' and Gaelic be abolished and removed. This followed the 1609 Statutes of Icolmkill (Iona) drawn up by Andrew Knox, bishop of the Isles, and signed by local chiefs, which promised that gentlemen and yeomen would send their eldest son or daughter to a school in the Lowlands to be educated until they could speak, read and write Scots.

An institutional concern with education was common to Catholic and Protestant reformers, bishops and Presbyterians, but it remained concerned with ideals. There is little evidence about what actually happened in pre-university education in Scotland in this period but the research of John Durkan (1914–2006) and comparison with elsewhere in Europe enables its outlines to be established.

Types of school

Scottish schools were broadly divided by curriculum into 'elementary schools' and 'grammar schools', although some had elements of both ('grammar school' was a contemporary term, but 'elementary school' is a modern term conveniently covering a variety of schools teaching basic reading and song). Another place of education was the household of nobles and lairds who often employed a chaplain as a pedagogue for their children. Concerning the numbers of schools, Durkan lists 107 schools in Scotland before 1560 of which thirty-six were song schools, forty-three grammar schools and thirteen associated with monasteries. New forms of evidence enabled him to list about 800 schools in Scotland between 1560 and 1633 of which over 500 were parochial and many of the others were probably continuations of the traditional laird's chaplain's schools, and he also lists about a hundred more schools from the period between 1634 and 1660.[8] With over a thousand parishes, this confirms the evidence of legislation that the ideal of a school in each parish took a long time to be achieved.

ELEMENTARY SCHOOLS

Elementary schools before 1560 were of various types but in general pupils began at the age of about seven learning the alphabet in order to read liturgical Latin (proved by the Latin contractions and prayers included with printed alphabets). There is little evidence from Scotland but Kate Van Orden's study of sixteenth-century French sources shows that religion and the Latin liturgy were central to the curriculum as pupils learnt how to read and sing plainsong and memorised psalms, Latin prayers and liturgical texts.[9] At Dumbarton the chaplain of the Rood altar taught choirboys and burgesses' sons the psalter and singing before they went on to the grammar school taught by the chaplain of St Peter's altar.[10]

Latin liturgical books were the first textbooks but from the thirteenth century special Latin prayer books called primers, books of hours and grace books came to be used to help children read. In 1520, Edinburgh Burgh Council decided that schools other than the High School were only permitted to teach 'grace book, prymar and plane donatt', the last being basic grammar from the Ars Minor of the fourth-century grammarian Aelius Donatus.[11] By the sixteenth century many elementary schools taught in Scots, as is shown by the vernacular version of the

Ars Minor produced by John Vaus (c. 1484–c. 1539), grammarian at Aberdeen University, but they still provided a grounding for a Latin education at the grammar school. An example of elementary education is provided in the autobiography of James Melville (1556–1614), the nephew of the Protestant reformer Andrew Melville (1545–1622), who began his education at home with the grace book at the age of five in 1561, and went to school two years later with the local minister, William Gray. He and the other boys learnt their catechism, prayers and passages from the Bible, then worked at the rudiments of Latin and French, learning vocabulary and pronunciation, then basic Latin grammar using books by the English grammarians Lily and Linacre together with texts by Erasmus, Virgil, Horace and Cicero.[12]

SONG SCHOOLS

Although the term 'song school' was used in England before 1300 for elementary schools, in Scotland it generally denoted a specialised school providing advanced musical and liturgical education for choristers attached to cathedrals, monasteries and collegiate churches. Such schools were designed to supply the developing musical needs of the Renaissance church and the boys' education was ordered to the liturgy, for example the choristers at Restalrig collegiate church 'should daily, when they are able to be free from choir, practise their work in the song school'.[13] Although the Scottish theologian John Mair (1467–1550) complained of low standards in singing among the clergy, the surviving works of the composer Robert Carver show that Scottish musical education could produce music as good as anywhere else in Europe and some paper fragments of musical exercises from the song school of Inverness demonstrate a more practical competence.[14] The education included Latin; for example at Lochwinnoch song school the choristers were to be taught the first two books of the grammar of Alexandre de Villedieu, and when a place had two schools, students in the song schools could move on to the local grammar school when their voice broke, as prescribed at the collegiate church of Our Lady in Glasgow and St Nicholas, Aberdeen.[15]

After the Protestant Reformation the future of song schools was in doubt with the move from the complex polyphony of the Latin liturgy to the congregational singing of vernacular metrical psalms. Singing was, however, an important part of James Melville's education and some song schools did continue as vernacular reading schools with a musical slant. These enabled boys to sing harmonised metrical religious texts in church such as those in the part books written by Thomas Wode of St Andrews and in the 1635 psalter. After James VI's attempt to reinstate song schools on a civic basis in 1579 we find Andrew Stewart appointed to the song school at Ayr in 1583 and obliged to teach the boys music theory, singing, 'to read and write Inglis' and to lead their singing 'the four partis of musik' in church on Sundays.[16] A manuscript, *The Art of Music collectit out of all antient doctouris of musick* (c. 1580), containing a mixture of Gregorian chant, Catholic polyphony and part settings of metrical psalms, may have been a result of this revival.[17] Parish song schoolmasters often acted as precentors in church;

Stirling Burgh Council in 1621 ordered seats to be constructed under the pulpit for the master of the song school and his bairns, and they also taught choral and instrumental music for use outside church. Liturgical reform under James VI and Charles I encouraged the revival of song schools, and Durkan argues that between 1560 and 1638 song schools 'were more numerous than has perhaps been appreciated hitherto'.[18]

GRAMMAR SCHOOLS

The grammar school was concerned with the study of Latin, to which reading and song were merely introductions, and its purpose was to enable boys to speak and write Latin fluently. Scotland was part of a common Latin learnt culture in Western Europe which remained after the Protestant Reformation. The works of European humanist grammarians were used in Scotland, and Scottish humanists such as Florence Wilson of Elgin (d. c. 1551) and George Buchanan (1506–82) published grammar works on the continent. There is also some evidence towards the end of our period that Greek and even Hebrew, usually university subjects, were taught in grammar schools. Both languages were taught by Patrick Balfour in Elgin in 1566 and basic notes on both are found in James Carmichael's 1587 Latin grammar; Greek is also noted as part of the curriculum at Banff in 1588 and Haddington in 1591.

Religion was as important as grammar in the grammar school, and liturgical and catechetical texts were central to the curriculum. Before 1560, the hymnal (hymns from the office), sequentiary and lectionary (sequences and readings from mass) were studied alongside classical poetry. Only one copy of the Ars Minor survives from pre-1560 Scotland, in a volume owned by Mathias Moncur of Dundee, but it is bound with a commentary on the hymns and sequences and a Latin lectionary.[19] Two other school commentaries on liturgical poetry have survived and study of their contents reveals that they were largely concerned with grammar but also had a spiritual purpose and contained allegorical commentary.[20] Moncur's lectionary was annotated so that it could be used with the Book of Common Prayer which suggests that such liturgical books continued to be used in schools after 1560 together with the vernacular psalter in the Book of Common Order and new Latin versions such as Buchanan's Paraphrases. Reformed catechisms were also used in schools, primarily Calvin's in the Book of Common Order but also Patrick Adamson's Catechismus Latino Carmine (1572, 1581); Robert Pont's Parvus Catechismus (1573); John Craig's A Short Summe of the Whole Catechisme (1581) and Ane Forme of Examination before the Communion (1592); and the Latin and vernacular versions of the Heidelberg Catechism printed by Robert Waldegrave (Edinburgh, 1591).

James Melville's diary gives an idea of the grammar school curriculum. After five years' elementary education he went to school at Montrose in 1569 where he went through the rudiments again for a year, after which he studied the syntax of Despauterius (Joannes de Spouter, d. 1520) and continued his study of Calvin's catechism and the psalter. Two years later, he went up to St Andrews where his grammar was so deficient he needed remedial classes. Apart from the choice of religious texts his education was substantially the same as that before 1560. A description of a school day in the second quarter of the sixteenth century is given in the statutes of King's College grammar school, Aberdeen, found in the 1553 Paris printing of Vaus's grammar. The school day began at 7 a.m. with the saying of a prayer inspired by Erasmus followed by parsing, at 8 the master addressed all the classes; there then followed a break and at 10 a.m. individual classes were taught by teaching assistants known as doctors. At about 11 a.m. the master then held a class on Terence, Virgil or Cicero for some of the pupils; this was followed by lunch and then lessons in different classes at 2 p.m. From 5 to 6 p.m. there were disputations and then final prayers and psalms were sung. The course lasted for three years.[21]

Together with classical authors and religious texts, grammar books were central to the curriculum. As well as using Donatus and humanist grammarians such as Despauterius, Scotland produced its own Latin grammars. Vaus published a number of grammar books including his Scots Donatus's *Ars Minor* and his own *Rudimenta puerorum in artem grammaticam* (Paris, 1522). In 1568, Alexander Hepburn, schoolmaster in Dundee and later bishop of Ross, published a grammar in Antwerp based on Despauterius. Hepburn encouraged the idea of a 'national grammar' which was developed in discussions led by Buchanan under the Regent Morton in 1575. This failed but the idea was revived by the Privy Council in 1593, and in 1607 parliament issued a commission to Chancellor Seton to produce a standard national grammar. Alexander Hume, a friend of Andrew Melville who became master of the trilingual school at Prestonpans, responded by publishing his *Grammatica nova* (1612) which propounded a new approach to education, rejecting the methods of both Despauterius and the French educationalist Ramus (Pierre de la Ramée, 1515–72). Hume also failed to attract support and the disputes continued until 1633 when the Convention of Royal Burghs approved the Latin grammar of David Wedderburn (1579–1646) of Aberdeen to be used in the whole Kingdom. The discussions and publications about grammar in this period reveal a lively interest in pedagogy and Latin culture.

Other types of education

In addition to the grammar, elementary and song schools there were other types of pre-university education in Scotland during this period; for example a French school is noted in Edinburgh in 1556 and Durkan notes six writing schools in Aberdeen, Ayr, Dumfries, Dunfermline, Edinburgh and Glasgow. Before 1560, the religious orders educated their members and often other boys or girls. At Kinloss Abbey in Moray, Abbot Robert Reid and the Piedmontese humanist Giovanni Ferrerio established a full programme of humanist formation.[22] There is little evidence of the involvement of nuns in education but the Franciscan nuns of Aberdour were given permission in 1487 to instruct young girls in letters and 'good arts' and girls were taught at the Cistercian convents of Elcho and Haddington. In the houses of the rich, pedagogues were common whose curricula would have varied greatly. One example is found in the expenses in 1600 and 1602 of Andrew Dalrymple, who taught the young John Stewart at Newmilns. He purchased the Heidelberg Catechism, select epistles of Cicero, the grammars of Despauterius, Ramus and Buchanan, Buchanan's psalm paraphrases and Ovid's *Metamorphoses*.[23] Women were not excluded from this domestic education as is revealed by the sophisticated poetry of Elizabeth Melville, Lady Culross (c. 1582–1640).[24]

In the Gàidhealtachd of the Highlands and Islands there was a distinct educational system taught by the learned orders. Classical Gaelic schools which taught bardic verse, harping, piping, *seanchus* (history and genealogy), law, medicine and other skills have left little trace in Scotland, although courts of chiefs were centres of education and some from the Gàidhealtachd travelled to Ireland for education.[25] The book of James MacGregor, Dean of Lismore, and the Beaton medical manuscripts in the National Library of Scotland show that Latin was as important as Gaelic in this educational milieu. MacGregor's book also contains items in Scots and there were increased connections with Lowlands culture in this period and attempts to promote Scots, as found in the Statutes of Iona. Some boys were sent away for their education as in the case of the children of Sir Ruari Mór McLeod whom he visited at school in Glasgow in 1582.[26] There were also some grammar schools in or near the Gaelic-speaking areas as at Tain, Inverness and the Chanonry of Ross, and religious houses provided education; the heir of Lord Lovat was educated at Beauly Priory whose novices were sent in 1541 to the humanist centre of Kinloss. Protestant bishops were keen to establish parish schools in the Highlands and Islands and Durkan's research shows that this bore fruit, for example at Dornoch (1585), Kiltearn (1612), Kilberry (1617), Inveraray (1619), Kilmichael Glassary and Lochhead (1629).

Another type of education was the formation of clergy. Grammar schools played an important role in this; the 1575 General Assembly called them 'the fountain from which ministers must flow', and for most clergy before 1560 they provided their highest education. A survey of the Scottish clergy using the evidence in Charles Haws, *Scottish Parish Clergy at the Reformation, 1540–1574* (Scottish Record Society, 1972) shows that while 82 per cent of senior clergy were graduates (100 per cent in the diocese of Aberdeen, a result of Bishop Elphinstone's reform), the vast majority of vicars, chaplains and unbeneficed clergy were not. This does not mean that they were ill-educated. The charge of clerical illiteracy, repeated by Catholic and Protestant reformers, has been challenged for Europe in general by Leonard Boyle and for pre-1560 Scotland by Mark Dilworth and John Durkan who concluded that 'there is little evidence of ignorant clerics'.[27] Non-graduate clergy generally learnt their ministry through a form of apprenticeship with a priest and some worked as teachers or parish clerks between leaving grammar school in their mid-teens and attaining the age for ordination. In addition to Latin for the liturgy, ordinands would need to know prayers, various administrative documents, how to celebrate the sacraments, basic theology, the basic moral theology needed to hear confessions and competence in liturgical chant. This curriculum is found in the *Examen ordinandorum* of the Franciscan Johann Wild (1497–1554), of which two copies survive from Scotland, and was tested by the archdeacon before ordination, as Archibald Hay noted in his *Panegyricus*.[28]

Schoolmasters

All schoolmasters before 1560 were clerics in the sense of being literate and having benefit of clergy, although not all were in major orders and some were married, such as Andrew Simpson at Perth in the 1550s. Most schools were attached to churches, with the parish clerk frequently teaching in the parish school as specified, for example, in the appointment of Jacob Afflek as parish clerk of Inverness in 1539.[29] The schoolmaster, called a regent in university grammar schools, could employ teaching assistants (doctors) who often added to their income by acting as notaries or scribes. The masters of grammar schools were in theory subject to the chancellor of the diocese (in St Andrews and Galloway the archdeacon) or to the superior of a local monastery but by the sixteenth century the local council had often assumed control of burgh schools although there were still disputes such as that between Dundee Burgh Council and Lindores Abbey described in Elizabeth Ewan's chapter. Many teachers were chaplains and their title 'Dominus' (vocative, 'Domine') survived in the Scots word for schoolmaster, 'dominie'. Where women are recorded as teaching, as in Edinburgh in 1499, it is to be presumed that it was an elementary (dame) school of which there were likely many more than the eleven that Durkan has found noted in written records. Few schools were like the grammar schools of Glasgow, Elgin and Dumfries which had a dedicated schoolhouse and pupils may have been taught in the choir of the church to which the school was attached or in the private houses of clerics. Durkan notes that parish schools were almost always held '*apud ecclesiam*/at the kirk', although at Fintry the school was held 'at the bridge' until 1641.[30] Durkan's researches have shown much mobility by schoolmasters, possibly because of the limited reward and the desire for preferment, although the profession retained distinguished men such as the poet Robert Henryson at Dunfermline and the controversialist Ninian Winzet at Linlithgow.

John Durkan said of the revolution of 1559–60, 'as far as schools are concerned, there is no observable change in many places' but it did affect the lives of some schoolmasters.[31] Some Catholics were dismissed such as Winzet in 1561 and John Henderson at Aberdeen in 1569, but others retained their jobs, like William Robertson who was still teaching at Edinburgh High School in the late 1570s and Ninian Dalzell, schoolmaster of Dumfries until 1587. Private Catholic education survived in the Catholic houses as in the case of the 'papist or atheist' Stephen Bannatyne who was teaching the children of Alexander Seton, Lord Urquhart in 1593. While many of the ecclesiastical posts and institutions that supported education disappeared after 1560 some of the benefices remained as sources of income. Burgh schoolmasters were paid by the burgh and parish schoolmasters usually by the heritors, but in general the pupils' parents also had to pay for their education. Schoolmasters sometimes supplemented their income by acting as reader, precentor or session clerk as in the case of Francis Peirson, schoolmaster of Cupar Angus in 1613, who was to teach, lead the psalms in the kirk and be scribe to the kirk session.[32]

Universities

In the fifteenth and sixteenth centuries six universities were founded in Scotland, three Catholic foundations and three Protestant. All were closely associated with reform movements in the church. Many of their early records have been published and our understanding of them and their place in Scotland and Latin Europe has been extended by the research of, amongst others, Ronald Cant and James Cameron on St Andrews, Leslie Macfarlane and David Stevenson on Aberdeen, John Durkan and James Kirk on Glasgow, Michael Lynch on Edinburgh and Steven Reid on the universities after 1560. This work has shown the importance of Catholic reform movements in the ancient foundations and put into context the traditional emphasis on the importance of Andrew Melville in the period of Protestant ascendency thus allowing the importance of town councils, the crown and bishops to be appreciated, although much work remains to be done. While the revolution of 1559–60 changed the religious aspect of the universities, much of their life and teaching remained unchanged; as Reid notes at the conclusion of his study, 'continuity is one of the most significant findings of this work'.[33]

The first foundations and church reform

After grammar school, boys could go on to a university, a *studium generale* which taught the arts course that in its turn enabled students to enter the higher faculties of medicine, law and theology. The university was an ecclesiastical institution integrated into the framework of Latin Christendom; its members had clerical status and by virtue of its papal bull it could confer degrees and the *licentia ubique docendi*, permission to teach at any other university. While a university was ordered around intellectual pursuits, the Christian religion was at its heart, symbolised by the central place of theology and the physical importance of college chapels.

Before 1410, Scottish students had to leave the kingdom for a university education, as seen in Donald Watt's *Biographical Dictionary of Scottish Graduates to A.D. 1410* (Clarendon Press, 1977), but in that year some graduates, mainly from Paris, began teaching at St Andrews. This development was encouraged by Bishop Henry Wardlaw and the university was established in 1413 by bulls of Benedict XIII, an antipope only recognised in Scotland, Sicily and Spain. Allegiance to different popes may explain why the Scottish masters returned home but the foundation was also a response to a desire for church reform. The foundation bull said that the new university was to be 'an impregnable rampart of doctors and masters to resist heresy'. Wardlaw himself was concerned with reform and the repression of heresy and many of its early members, such as the

Scottish inquisitor Laurence of Lindores, played an important part in the church. The university constitution was based on those of Orléans and Paris and the main faculties were those of arts and theology although there is also evidence of teaching both laws (canon and civil) and, occasionally, medicine. There is also mention of a College of St John with a chapel and a pedagogy for the arts faculty. In 1450, Bishop James Kennedy founded a college at St Andrews dedicated to the Holy Saviour (Saint Salvator) with a fine chapel and provision for elaborate choral worship to support education in arts and theology and to pray for the founder and his kin. The bull of foundation notes that it was founded for the reform of the church and the overthrowing of heresy. The following year, the University of Glasgow was established by Bishop William Turnbull with a papal bull from Nicholas V. The University of Aberdeen was founded by Bishop William Elphinstone in 1495 with a bull of Pope Alexander VI. It was closely integrated with Elphinstone's reform movement and also with continental humanism. Hector Boece, who studied with his friend Erasmus at the Collège de Montaigu, was its first principal.

Teaching at the Scottish universities followed standard European models. The arts courses at St Andrews and Glasgow were based on that of Paris and centred on Aristotle and commentaries on his texts. The system of 'regenting' meant that one teacher or regent took the student through the whole four-year arts curriculum, of which the first eighteen months led to the baccalaureate and the remainder to the Masters degree and the licence. Students usually matriculated between the ages of fourteen and sixteen and were formed in Aristotelian logic before moving on to natural philosophy, astronomy, mathematics, ethics and metaphysics, all based on Aristotle. Teaching involved both lectures on the text and disputations, formal debates which required logical proof rather than rhetorical persuasion. Theology was the most important of the higher faculties although law (canon and civil) was more often the foundation of a clerical career, as in the cases of Wardlaw, Kennedy, Turnbull and Elphinstone. Theology was taught primarily from two books, the Bible and the *Sentences* of Peter Lombard, and the methods of teaching involved hearing and delivering theological commentary on these books, listening to and taking part in disputations, and hearing and delivering sermons. The length of the course leading to a doctorate at Paris was fourteen years, but this was reduced to about ten at St Andrews, and Elphinstone established a reduced course of six years at Aberdeen to produce an educated clergy for his reform movement. In the law faculties canonists studied the various parts of the *corpus iuris canonici* together with commentaries, and civilists studied what was to be called in the sixteenth century the *corpus iuris civilis*, the collection of legal texts issued by the Emperor Justinian in the sixth century. In addition to lectures and disputations law students had practical experience from attending local courts. Practical work was also a small part of the medical curriculum, although faculties of medicine were not properly established until later despite the continued existence of a chair in medicine at Aberdeen.

Catholic and Protestant Reformation and the universities to 1574

If the fifteenth-century foundations were influenced by a desire for church reform, rival Catholic and Protestant visions of Reformation played an important role in the life of the universities in the next century although there was a remarkable continuity in the arts curriculum.

St Leonard's College, St Andrews, originally called the 'College of Poor Clerks', had been founded in 1512 by Archbishop Alexander Stewart, a pupil of Erasmus, and the Augustinian prior James Hepburn in the tradition of Catholic humanist reform. When in the 1520s some of its members became interested in the evangelical ideas of Martin Luther, this provoked a reaction from Archbishop James Beaton. He burnt Patrick Hamilton, a student who had studied at Marburg, outside St Salvator's in 1528 and his fellow student Henry Forrest was executed for heresy in 1533. The next foundation at St Andrews was the 'College of St Mary of the Assumption', established by Archbishop Beaton as part of his Catholic reform programme to ensure a well-educated secular clergy. Beaton's nephew, the Parisian humanist Archibald Hay who became principal of St Mary's in 1546, argued for the college to adopt a radically humanist programme including poetry, history and the study of Plato with an emphasis on the study of the tongues. These plans ended with the murder of Archibald's cousin, Cardinal David Beaton, in 1546 and Hay's own death the following year but the college was refounded in the mid-1550s as a key part of the moderate Catholic reform programme of Archbishop John Hamilton. He added to the college buildings erected by the Beatons and his plan for the foundation followed that of the school of divinity at Bonn established by the Catholic reformer Archbishop Hermann von Wied. Catholic reform had been part of the purpose of Aberdeen University from its foundation. It was in advance of St Andrews with a strong humanist element to the curriculum designed by Hector Boece, William Hay and John Vaus who had all studied at Paris, and there is also evidence of the study of Greek. This is also found in the courses taught under Ferrerio at Kinloss whose abbot, Robert Reid, appointed Edward Henryson in 1556 to give lectures on Greek in Edinburgh. There were thus strong elements of religious and intellectual reform in the Scottish universities before 1560.

Apart from the centre of Catholic reform at St Mary's, St Andrews, there was a decline in numbers at the Scottish universities in the decade before 1560. This was the background for the university reform plan in the *First Book of Discipline* which was probably authored by two St Andrews Catholic reformers who joined the Protestants in 1559–60, John Douglas (c. 1500–74) and the Augustinian John Winram (c. 1492–1582). This plan was rooted in the constitutions of St Leonard's and St Mary's and influenced by the Academy set up at Geneva by Calvin in 1558. It emphasised scriptural languages and advocated having three colleges at St Andrews and two at Glasgow and Aberdeen respectively, with the first college in each city fulfilling the role of a town arts college. The aim was to establish the new reformed faith and supply learned ministers and elders for the parishes; the General Assembly, however, largely ignored this scheme although in 1583 it did order visitations of the universities. In their desire for an educated clergy and the reform of university education on humanist lines, Protestant reformers followed closely the priorities of the Catholic reform movements in which many of them had grown up.

At St Andrews the adoption of Protestantism in 1559 led to a period of confusion in the university – in that year the matriculation register notes that 'on account of the religious conflict . . . very few scholars came to this university'.[34] Although some university staff such as the provost of St Salvator's, William Cranston, remained Catholic and left the city, and a Catholic faction remained at St Mary's under Hamilton patronage, most adopted the new religion. A key figure who did was John Douglas, provost of St Mary's from 1547 to 1574, where he had led Archbishop Hamilton's humanist Catholic refoundation from 1555. Although George Buchanan made some proposals for reform in 1563 the curriculum at St Andrews remained much the same, with its focus on Aristotle and neglect of Greek and Hebrew, and so the reforms of the *First Book of Discipline* were not implemented. One of the reformers noted of the statutes of the theology faculty that they were 'in part unchanged and in part better reformed to the rule of the Word of God'.[35] The main change in theology was the removal of the study of Lombard's *Sentences* and concentration on the Bible. At Aberdeen the university remained Catholic until 1569 when the Regent Moray purged it of those who would not sign the *Confession of Faith* and installed Protestants in the faculty. This was defended in an oration by Moray's chaplain, George Hay, which proposed a new humanist curriculum. In fact, Aberdeen had a noble humanist tradition, Catholic masters remained in some subjects, mass continued to be said and the Catholic bishop Gordon remained chancellor until his death in 1577. Glasgow University remained in a poor state after 1560, and in 1573 the city council, possibly inspired by the Protestant academies on the continent, offered to refound it although there was little impact until the *Nova erectio* of 1577. Apart from the departure of Roman Catholics and the removal of the *Sentences*, the universities were remarkable for educational continuity in this period of change.

The Melvillian interlude and Protestant foundations: 1574–1606

In his 2011 book *Humanism and Calvinism*, Steven Reid noted that 'the Universities in the 1560s and early 1570s were stuck between reformation and reform' but a new impetus and a controversial new educational programme were provided by Andrew Melville, who returned from Geneva in 1574 imbued with a potent mix of Calvinist Presbyterianism, humanism and Ramist educationalist ideas.[36] Ramus rejected scholastic Aristotelianism and developed a pragmatic educational method which privileged dialectic or logic and claimed to be able to teach all subjects by proceeding from the general to the particular, thus producing systematic tables of knowledge. This gave Melville an efficient way of delivering his new emphasis on reading Aristotle in Greek, humanist subjects such as history and chronology, the biblical languages and Calvinist theology. Reid has, however, demonstrated that Melville's influence has been overemphasised.

Melville directed a Protestant refoundation of the University of Glasgow between 1574 and 1580, institutionally authorised in the *Nova erectio* of 1577, of which he said he had brought 'the matters of Rome, Jerusalem, Greece and Athens to the Glaswegian desert', but it went through difficulties following his departure.[37] In 1578, a commission that included the archbishops of St Andrews and Glasgow (Patrick Adamson and James Boyd), the bishop of Aberdeen, Andrew Melville and, later, George Buchanan was set up to reform the universities and purge them of Roman Catholicism. While they did not draw up plans for Aberdeen they did produce radical plans for St Andrews which were close to Melville's reform at Glasgow. The reform at St Andrews began in 1579; the 'Nova fundatio' proposed for Aberdeen by the General Assembly in 1583, however, did not succeed due to Melville's association with radical religious reform in the church.

In the St Andrews 'New Foundation', St Mary's was to be a purely theological college teaching scripture in the original languages, a Calvinist 'anti-seminary' in reaction to the continental Jesuit colleges. St Salvator's and St Leonard's would be arts colleges with an emphasis on Greek texts, and the regenting system would be abolished in favour of specialist professors. Melville's responsibility for this plan is, however, usually overemphasised; his enemies Boyd and Adamson, both reputable scholars, also influenced it. Reid notes that the visitation of the university in 1588 revealed that Melville's reform programme had largely failed, because of internal opposition and church politics, although there was some engagement with Ramism. It did, however, flourish to an extent between 1590 and 1597 while Melville was rector as well as principal of St Mary's. Some idea of teaching at St Andrews during this period can be found from the St Leonard's College 'Orator's Book' which contains essays and poetry in Latin and Greek by senior arts students from the first half of the 1590s.[38] Its contents show no evidence of Ramism, however, although its influence is found in the seven extant St Andrews theological theses from 1595 to 1602. Evidence from Melville's last decade at St Andrews, 1597–1606, suggests that while his Ramist-Presbyterian-Calvinist influence continued at St Mary's, the other colleges were anti-Ramist and returned to older ways of reading Aristotle, although there was perhaps more use of the Greek texts, as shown in extant arts theses from around 1600.

In addition to the attempts to reform the ancient universities associated with Andrew Melville, the last two decades of the sixteenth century saw three new Protestant arts colleges set up at Edinburgh (1583), Fraserburgh (1592) and New Aberdeen (Marischal College, 1593). Local secular authorities took the lead in these foundations (the burgh council and local Protestant magnates) and all were approved by the royal government just as previous foundations were founded by bishops and approved by popes. This local involvement was also paralleled in Glasgow where the council asserted its right of supervision over the university from the last decades of the sixteenth century. Each new foundation taught arts and theology and Edinburgh and Marischal flourished, developing teaching in other disciplines. They were part of a growth in such colleges, both Catholic and Protestant, in the second half of the sixteenth century as seen in the Genevan Academy (1558). While 'Melvillian' ideas of Presbyterian educational reform played a role in these new foundations, Reid's study concluded that the 'pragmatic needs of the local community' were dominant.

Edinburgh University has its roots in the 1558 bequest of 8,000 merks by Bishop Robert Reid to found a college in Edinburgh with schools for grammar, arts, and civil and canon law. After many difficulties James VI issued a foundation charter in 1582 and the college was opened on the site of the Kirk o'Field in October 1583. The research of Michael Lynch has shown that while radical Presbyterian ministers played a role in the foundation, it was a town council purged of radical members which established the 'tounis college' with the remit of teaching the youth of the city. The first principal, Robert Rollock, had studied under the Melvilles at St Mary's, St Andrews and employed the Ramist method in teaching but Steven Reid's study of published theses at Edinburgh from 1596 shows a decidedly anti-Ramist spirit among the regents after Rollock's death. The 1628 statutes and earlier eyewitness accounts of teaching do, however, show that Ramist methods were used in the early stages of arts teaching before moving on to the study of Aristotle in Greek. First-year students improved their grammar school Latin and began basic Greek using classical texts and the New Testament. After an annual examination reviewing the previous year, second years worked at their Greek with an emphasis on rhetoric and logic, moving on from Ramus to Porphyry and Aristotle. Third years continued logic and Greek and began Hebrew, ending with a study of human anatomy. The fourth year studied astronomy and Aristotle's *De anima*, and reviewed the entire course for the graduation disputations. The study of theology continued throughout, beginning with the catechism and including controversial topics. The method of instruction included much repetition and memorisation and weekly practice at disputation and rhetoric. This emphasis on praxis, characteristic of Ramist pragmatism, was important as the aim was to train ministers, lawyers and administrators.

Marischal College, Aberdeen was founded in April 1593 by the Presbyterian George Keith, fifth Earl Marischal, who had studied under Beza in France and Geneva and was a proponent of the curriculum favoured by Melville. The new foundation can be seen as a Presbyterian and Melvillian rival to King's, but it was also a response to the desire for education in the rapidly expanding burgh of New Aberdeen which was developing a Protestant identity. Further north another Protestant magnate, Sir Alexander Fraser, got permission in 1592 to establish a burgh of barony to be called Fraserburgh and establish a university there. The project was ratified by parliament in 1597, buildings were begun and a regent and graduate from Edinburgh, Charles Ferme, was given the local church of Philorth and in 1600 appointed as principal. When Ferme was imprisoned between 1605 and 1608 for attending the illegal General Assembly the college collapsed and the attempt decisively failed when Fraser got into trouble for debt in 1613, although in 1647 King's College, Aberdeen temporarily moved there because of plague. This was the high point of the interest in establishing Protestant arts colleges, influenced by Melvillian ideas, to give a practical Protestant education for local boys.

Episcopal and royal reform, 1606–1638

The influence of Andrew Melville was thus limited and a different sort of university reform associated with royal and episcopal authority followed Melville's removal from the scene in 1606. Steven Reid's research has shown that the arts curriculum in this period reverted to being largely Aristotelian using Latin scholastic commentators such as Thomas Aquinas and Cardinal Cajetan. The study of the Greek text as encouraged by Melville was maintained but without the interest in Ramism, which was roundly condemned in some St Andrews theses and would not return until the 1640s. The seventeenth century also saw a revival of interest in all the universities in metaphysics, a breaking down of the strict division between philosophy and theology, and a renewed interest, especially at St Andrews, in Plato.

King James VI had a particular interest in the reform of St Andrews. Melvillians were removed from St Mary's, the 'New Foundation' of 1579 was dismantled (except at St Mary's) and there was a reassertion of the pre-1560 collegiate system which was ratified by the formal parliamentary revocation of the 'New Foundation' in 1621. After the Union of the Crowns, King James ensured that St Andrews conformed to Oxford and Cambridge in ceremonies and organisation. The local bishop also took a prominent role in this reform. In 1605, Archbishop Gledstanes of St Andrews was made chancellor of the university, restoring the archbishop's ex-officio role, and he did much to promote the university. In 1611, he began the project to build a central university library and restored the faculty of divinity which had lapsed in 1560, a significant renewal of the original structure of the university. His work was continued after his death in 1615 by Archbishop Spottiswoode, who established a new theology curriculum and in 1616 restored the degrees of bachelor and doctor in divinity. This was part of a set of royal Articles of Reform which established St Mary's as the principal divinity school of the kingdom. A royal visit to St Andrews in 1617 was a great success during which King James took part in public disputations and gave funds to complete the library. In the same year more Articles were issued as part of the king's plan to reform all the universities of Britain, for example extending the duration of the arts curriculum, reforming university ceremonies in line with England and restoring the liturgical life of the university. The buildings of all the colleges were restored and extended in this period, a sign that the university was flourishing. Charles I continued his father's support for university reform. St Mary's had used the English form of Morning and Evening Prayer from 1623, and in 1633, when the *Book of Common Prayer* was published in Scotland, the king instructed Archbishop Spottiswoode to ensure that it was used in St Salvator's chapel (previously St Salvator's and St Mary's worshipped on

Sundays in the parish church of Holy Trinity whereas St Leonard's continued to use its old chapel). The use of the prayer book was extended to all the universities in 1634, thus restoring dignified worship to the heart of university life.

At Glasgow a visitation ordered by the Privy Council in 1613 resulted in a purge of religious radicals including the principal, Patrick Sharpe. Melville's *Nova erectio* continued as the constitutional foundation of the university but his influence diminished. In 1617, the king, noticing the university's poverty, made a major benefaction of the churches of Kilbride and Renfrew thus nearly doubling its income. This new flourishing of the university resulted in a major rebuilding of the college which began in 1631. At King's Aberdeen, Elphinstone's original foundation was officially restored in 1619 although novel ideas had never been accepted. Apart from two attempts by the General Assembly in 1593 and parliament in 1597, there was no significant reform until the work of Bishop Patrick Forbes of Corse (1564–1635), called the 'second founder' of King's, who was sent by King James on a visitation of the two universities in Aberdeen in 1617. From 1618, he improved the library and buildings at King's, increased endowments, restored the higher degrees and introduced a printing press. In 1620, he established a chair of theology to which his son John, one of the greatest theologians of his time, was appointed and the college became an important centre of theological study. John Forbes of Corse (1593–1648) was one of a number of distinguished Aberdonian theologians known as the 'Aberdeen doctors' who opposed the 1638 Covenant which marked the end of this royal and episcopal university reform.

While the crown and bishops took an interest in the ancient foundations and ratified their endowments, the local councils consolidated their interest in the new colleges at Edinburgh and Aberdeen. Compared to the ancient universities, these new foundations also received a great increase in endowments in this period, both from the councils and from individual donors. Between 1615 and 1618, Edinburgh Council spent over £9,000 on new buildings including a library and individuals supported the establishment of a chair of divinity in 1620. Aberdeen Town Council granted funds for a library in 1609 and proper accommodation for students in the burgh kirk in 1612. Individuals also provided generous benefactions including six bursaries and a chair in mathematics endowed by the Aberdonian scientist Duncan Liddell (1561–1613) who had studied under Tycho Brahe. Marischal maintained one aspect of the Melvillian system in eschewing regenting in favour of specialised professors, something adopted by the other universities from the 1620s.

The development of the Scottish universities from the first episcopal foundations in the fifteenth century to the royal and episcopal reforms of the early seventeenth was one of the great success stories of Scottish intellectual history. In general the major reform plans, whether of the *First Book of Discipline* or Andrew Melville, had little impact and reform was effected locally in an evolutionary way. Interventions from the government had more effect, such as the visitations of Aberdeen in 1569 and the 1570s, St Andrews in the 1570s and 1588, and

Figure 4.2 Bishop Patrick Forbes of Corse. With permission of University of Aberdeen.

Glasgow in 1602 and 1614, and local government and episcopal authority was effective in the early seventeenth century.

Conclusions on Education in General

The period of the Scottish Reformations, a series of church reform movements, both Catholic and Protestant, during the 'long sixteenth century' which shared a common Latin humanist culture, was thus very fruitful for the development of education in Scotland. The gradual creation of a network of parochial schools, for example, was inspired by the decrees of Catholic reform councils in Italy and Scotland and continued by the reformed church after 1560 with the support of the royal government. Likewise the universities and colleges established in the fifteenth and sixteenth centuries by reforming bishops continued after the Protestant Reformation and were joined by other foundations, always in close touch with developments elsewhere in Europe. Apart from the fragile reforms of Andrew Melville and necessary changes to the theology curriculum, this development was predominantly marked by continuity. Little is known of education in the Gàidhealtachd or of elementary and practical education, but throughout this period Scottish education at all levels continued to be influenced by church reform movements and the secular authorities and to be an integral part of Latin education in Western Europe as a whole. The traditional sectarian narrative of the decisive nature of the Protestant Reformation of 1560 for Scottish education and the centrality of Andrew Melville in the reform of the Scottish universities thus needs to be discarded and a new narrative constructed based on the research used in this chapter.

Notes

1. Available at http://www.scotland.gov.uk/News/Releases/2010/11/03101638 (accessed 12 May 2014).
2. For the historiography of the Scottish Reformation, see Stephen Mark Holmes, 'Historiography of the Scottish Reformation: The Catholics fight back?', in Peter D. Clarke and Charlotte Methuen (eds), *Studies in Church History 49: The Church on its Past* (Boydell and Brewer, 2013), pp. 98–311.
3. National Records of Scotland, B21/1/2, fo. 25.
4. Ninian Winzet, *Certain Tractates*, ed. J. K. Hewison (Scottish Text Society, 1888–90), pp. 55, 67; *Catholic Tractates of the Sixteenth Century 1573–1600*, ed. T. G. Law (Scottish Text Society, 1901), pp. 169, 167.
5. One copy of each is extant: John Garland, *Multorum vocabulorum . . . interpretatio* (Paris, Bibliothèque Nationale de France, RES P-X-16); *Expositio Sequentiarum* (London, British Library, C.35.c.6).
6. Norman Tanner, *Decrees of the Ecumenical Councils* (Georgetown University Press, 1990), pp. 621, 668.
7. David Patrick, *Statutes of the Scottish Church 1225–1559* (Scottish History Society, 1907), pp. 98–100, 143–8.
8. John Durkan, 'Education in the century of the Reformation', in David McRoberts (ed.), *Essays on the Scottish Reformation 1513–1625* (Burns, 1962), p. 168; John Durkan, *Scottish Schools and Schoolmasters, 1560–1633*, ed. and rev. Jamie Reid-Baxter (Scottish History Society, 2013), pp. 229–392.
9. Kate Van Orden, 'Children's voices: Singing and literacy in sixteenth-century France', *Early Music History* 25 (2006), 209–56.
10. Durkan, 'Education', p. 164.
11. *Extracts from the Records of the Burgh of Edinburgh (1403–1718)*, eds James D. Marwick, Marguerite Wood, Robert Kerr Hannay and Helen Armet, 14 vols (Scottish Burgh Records Society, 1869–1967), vol. 1, p. 194.

12. *The Autobiography and Diary of Mr James Melville*, ed. Robert Pitcairn (Wodrow Society, 1842).

13. 'Pueri . . . quotidie cum a choro vacare poterunt cantacionis scholis operam exhibeant', *Charters of . . . Collegiate Churches in Midlothian*, ed. David Laing (The Bannatyne Club, 1861), p. 286; Durkan, 'Education', p. 146.

14. Edinburgh, National Library of Scotland, Acc.11218.6.1.H-L; Stephen Allenson, 'The Inverness fragments: Music from a pre-Reformation Scottish parish church and school', *Music and Letters* 70(1) (February 1989), 1–45; Athol L. Murray, 'The parish clerk and song school of Inverness, 1538–9', *Innes Review* 58(1) (spring 2007), 107–15.

15. *Registrum Episcopatus Glasguensis*, ed. Cosmo Innes, 2 vols (Maitland Club, 1843), vol. 2, pp. 509–14. *Liber collegii nostre Domine: Registrum ecclesie B.V. Marie et S. Anne . . . Glasguensis . . .*, ed. Joseph Robertson (Maitland Club, 1846), pp. 43–4; *Cartularium ecclesiae Sancti Nicholai Aberdonensis*, ed. James Cooper, 2 vols (New Spalding Club, 1888–92), vol. 1, pp. 509–10.

16. Durkan, *Scottish Schools*, pp. 152–3.

17. Ibid., p. 158.

18. Ibid., p. 165.

19. The commentary and lectionary were edited by the Dutch grammarian Torrentinus (Edinburgh University Library, RB.S.501/5).

20. Myllar's 1506 commentary on the Sarum sequences and a sixteenth-century *Expositio hymnorum* printed at Rouen owned by the Scot John Abercromby (Edinburgh, New College Library, tVK 74 EXP).

21. John Stuart (ed.), *Miscellany of the Spalding Club* (Spalding Club, 1852), pp. 5, 397–402.

22. John Durkan, 'Giovanni Ferrerio, humanist: His influence in sixteenth-century Scotland', in Keith Robbins (ed.), *Religion and Humanism, Studies in Church History* 17 (Blackwell, 1981), pp. 181–94; Stephen Holmes, 'The meaning of history: A dedicatory letter from Giovanni Ferrerio to Abbot Robert Reid at the start of his *Historia Abbatum de Kynlos*', *Reformation and Renaissance Review* 10(1) (2008), 89–116.

23. Durkan, *Scottish Schools*, p. 94.

24. *Poems of Elizabeth Melville, Lady Culross*, ed. Jamie Reid-Baxter (Solsequium, 2010).

25. Fiona MacDonald, *Missions to the Gaels* (John Donald, 2006), p. 1.

26. Durkan, *Scottish Schools*, p. 191.

27. Leonard E. Boyle, 'Aspects of clerical education in fourteenth-century England', in Leonard E. Boyle, *Pastoral Care, Clerical Education and Canon Law, 1200–1400* (Variorum, 1981), pp. 19–32; Mark Dilworth, 'Literacy of pre-Reformation monks', *Innes Review* 24 (1973), 71–2; Durkan, *Scottish Schools*, p. 37.

28. Edinburgh University Library, Dd.6.4. and Aberdeen University Library, pi.2382. Nau. Hay, *Panegyricus* (Jérôme de Gourmont, 1540), f o. 34v.

29. Murray, 'Parish clerk'.

30. Durkan, *Scottish Schools*, p. 182.

31. Ibid., p. 75.

32. Ibid., p. 179.

33. Stephen Reid, *Humanism and Calvinism: Andrew Melville and the Universities of Scotland 1560–1625* (Ashgate, 2011), p. 270.

34. *Early Records of the University of St Andrews*, ed. James M. Anderson (Scottish History Society, 1926), pp. 266–7.

35. Reid, *Humanism and Calvinism*, p. 37.

36. Ibid., p. 48. For Ramism see Steven J. Reid and Emma Annette Wilson (eds), *Ramus, Pedagogy and the Liberal Arts: Ramism in Britain and the Wider World* (Ashgate, 2011).
37. Reid, *Humanism and Calvinism*, p. 107.
38. St Andrews University Library, UYSL320.

Bibliography

Bannerman, John, 'Literacy in the Highlands', in Ian B. Cowan and Duncan Shaw (eds), *The Renaissance and Reformation in Scotland* (Scottish Academic Press, 1983), pp. 214–35.

Durkan, John, 'Education in the century of the Reformation', in David McRoberts (ed.), *Essays on the Scottish Reformation 1513–1625* (Burns, 1962), pp. 145–68.

Durkan, John, 'Early song schools in Scotland', in Gordon Munro (ed.), *Notis Musycall. Essays in Honour of Kenneth Elliott* (Musica Scotica Trust, 2005), pp. 125–32.

Durkan, John, *Scottish Schools and Schoolmasters, 1560–1633*, ed. and rev. Jamie Reid-Baxter (Scottish History Society, 2013).

Durkan, John and James Kirk, *The University of Glasgow 1451–1577* (University of Glasgow Press, 1977).

Macfarlane, Leslie J., *William Elphinstone and the Kingdom of Scotland 1431–1514: The Struggle for Order* (Aberdeen University Press, 1985).

Orme, Nicholas, *Medieval Schools from Roman Britain to Renaissance England* (Yale University Press, 2006).

Reid, Stephen, *Humanism and Calvinism: Andrew Melville and the Universities of Scotland 1560–1625* (Ashgate, 2011).

Stevenson, David, *King's College, Aberdeen, 1560–1641: From Protestant Reformation to Covenanting Revolution* (Aberdeen University Press, 1990).

Watt, D. E. R., 'Education in the Highlands in the Middle Ages', in L. Maclean (ed.), *The Middle Ages in the Highlands* (Inverness Field Club, 1981).

5

Urban Schooling in Seventeenth- and Eighteenth-century Scotland

Lindy Moore

The Urban Background

The period between 1600 and 1800 was a time of enormous political, religious, economic, social and cultural change in Scotland. Urban areas, where probably less than a tenth of the population lived at the beginning of the period, were particularly affected by the military violence, dearths, epidemics and ensuing swings in population and economic prosperity that marked a period of civil war, military occupation and religious fanaticism, the loss of the royal court in 1603, the impact of Union with England and Wales in 1707 and the two Jacobite rebellions of 1715 and 1745. Following a period of relative prosperity for the first forty years of the seventeenth century, between 1644 and 1649 up to a fifth of the entire urban population of Scotland was lost in war and epidemics. Aberdeen and Dundee were sacked in 1644 and Dundee again in 1651. The plague arrived in Aberdeen as the army left, killing one in five in New Aberdeen. Dundee was in debt, its trading opportunities further reduced by storm damage to the harbour. Glasgow was effectively bankrupt at one point, and a third of the town was damaged in the great fire of 1652. Many of the smaller towns were similarly affected. Economic development was restricted in the second half of the seventeenth century by the expense of quartering troops, debt payments, restrictive English navigation laws and the disastrous Darien colonisation project which led to the estimated loss of a quarter of Scotland's entire liquid assets.[1] Successive bad harvests from 1695 to 1699 resulted in an almost national famine at a time when few towns had any reserves left to cushion the crisis for the poor. Once again, epidemic diseases linked to malnutrition caused deaths, the birth rate fell, people migrated away and the population of Scotland dropped by about 15 per cent.[2] Although different towns were differently affected and there were wide regional variations, with some settlements even benefiting from the misfortunes of others, not surprisingly the overall impact affected urban development throughout the country. The towns, even the royal burghs, were small compared with those of continental Europe. With only some 3 per cent of its population living in towns of over 10,000 inhabitants, Scotland was one of the least urbanised of the Western European territories in the early seventeenth century.[3] Not until the mid-eighteenth century did the town population start growing rapidly, more rapidly than anywhere else in Europe, and this rapid urbanisation was exacerbated by additional social dislocation as the centre of economic activity shifted from the east to the west of Lowland Scotland. By 1800, a quarter of the population lived in towns; Scotland had become highly urbanised.

Towns were distinguished from rural areas by a more varied and hierarchical occupational structure and some form of corporate governance. The burghal system had a focus for civic identity in its notion of 'the common good' based on the collective assets of the burgh, and public schooling formed a part of this. In their capacity as administrative, political, legal, religious and trading centres, urban environments created a quantity of written and printed materials and supported a higher concentration of the gentry and families from the expanding middling ranks, factors which led to a greater availability and higher standard of schooling. The disparity in the respective sign-literacy rates (inhabitants' ability to write their signature) of urban and rural areas was a reflection of their differing literary and cultural environments, although how influential schools were in this is still to be determined.[4]

Seventeenth-century Schooling

At the beginning of the seventeenth century the disruption to the educational system which had resulted from the Reformation was only beginning to be resolved. The General Assembly of the Church of Scotland continued its efforts to retain or recover from the nobility some of the endowments and church lands which the Reformation fathers had intended should be used to fund the educational system. Meanwhile the church actively supported education which it saw as central to the furtherance of Presbyterianism. In 1595, the General Assembly ordered every presbytery to work with the local magistrates to augment the stipends of grammar schoolmasters, while in 1641 it petitioned parliament to erect and maintain schools in all burghs and other 'considerable places'.[5] Glasgow Town Council might speak confidently of the value to both God and the town of having a grammar school, but in practice the council encountered considerable difficulty in finding the means to repair and enlarge the school building in 1600, eventually using money left to Glasgow University.[6] The town councils were still struggling with a lack of funds and the problem was about to get much worse. Unlike England, very little of what was given in educational endowments or 'mortifications' was for the benefit of schools and much of what was given was subsequently lost. The widespread financial losses of the mid-seventeenth century affected the trading abilities of Scottish burghs and as endowment funds from private individuals entrusted to the councils were not held separately they were particularly at risk. Glasgow Town Council temporarily bankrupted Hutchesons' Hospital.[7] Aberdeen Town Council borrowed money it could never realistically hope to pay back and by 1646 the city owed about £77,000 to its mortifications alone: 'the haill moneyes mortified to our colledge and schooles . . . and other pious uses'.[8] By 1695, the burgh owed £92,392 to its charitable trusts. Here, and in other towns, the legacy of debt, sometimes combined with mismanagement or the promotion of personal interest by the self-electing clique of merchants and guild burgesses who formed the burgh councils, was to last into the eighteenth century.

Nevertheless, recent scholarship has suggested that despite its small, poor and divided population, schooling was more widely available in Scotland during the difficult seventeenth century than was previously believed. Some 800 schools are known to have been in existence, chiefly in the Lowlands, before 1633. These included grammar (Latin), song, writing, vernacular and French schools, as well as a handful of schools taught by women – 'woman schools'.[9] In the absence of adequate church funds there was no means of ensuring the permanency of rural schools and so the famous Education Acts of 1616, 1633, 1646–61 and 1696 were passed, legislating for, and later enforcing, a national network of parish schools 'to landward', that is, outside burgh boundaries. Meanwhile, the burghs were expected to support grammar schools where boys could learn Latin and from 1579 were legally required to support music schools, but there was no official obligation for them to make provision for elementary or vernacular schooling, or any taxation source specifically allocated to enable them to do so. An early form of approved schooling was provided by the precentors, or readers. These men formed the front line of the church of the Reformation and were paid by the church to lead the psalm-singing and give Bible readings several times a week to the townspeople, but they might have their meagre salaries supplemented if they also ran schools to teach the psalms, catechism and basic reading to children. If an assistant master, usually called a 'doctor', was appointed to teach the younger children in the grammar school to read Scots (or 'Inglis') or to write, funding for his post was often jointly supported by the town and the local kirk session. Officially appointed grammar and music school teachers, always men, had usually attended university and while some might not have stayed on to graduate, others were hoping to become church ministers, a better paid occupation with a higher status. Assistant masters, especially poorly paid, were particularly notorious birds of passage. But even men of status could struggle financially, as the string of peti-tions to town councils for salary increases testifies: a year after the schoolmaster of Dumfries burgh school died in 1652 the kirk session arranged a special collection for his distressed children, and when an able burgh-salaried Inverness mathemat-ics teacher died in 1753 his widow petitioned to be put on poor relief as she was destitute.[10]

Women, who were invariably paid at a lower rate than men in every occu-pation, faced even greater difficulties. As private (adventure) teachers, they struggled to survive. But 'woman schools', although usually lumped together as a category, could vary considerably in terms of the social status of the school-mistress and her scholars, the subjects that she personally taught and the other school subjects that might be available in connection with the school. Women teachers are most often located teaching basic literacy and the catechism to a handful of children. But even reading literacy, however minimal, was a skill most individuals, particularly women, did not have in the early seventeenth century. Women were also specialist teachers of various kinds of needlework and cookery, combined in more elite individuals with the teaching of (civil) manners or the polite accomplishments,[11] and from at least the mid-seventeenth century various burgh councils actively recruited and paid gentlewomen schoolmistresses to teach the daughters of the gentry and the middling ranks and enhance the culture of their towns. In the early eighteenth century it was expected that such schoolmistresses would be expert in practical housewifery subjects such as working stockings, lace-making, 'white and coloured seam' (needlework), washing and dressing (ironing) linens, preparing meat and household cleaning, as well as hearing their pupils read the essential sacred texts.[12] But it was sufficiently uncommon for a woman to teach writing, arithmetic or church music for the directors of the endowed Merchant Maiden Hospital in Edinburgh to prescribe in 1718 that if a suitably proficient woman could not be obtained to teach the girls these subjects, a male teacher should be employed.

Up until the 1720s or 1730s, town councils and magistrates strenuously tried to regulate the schooling in their burghs, firstly to ensure that only those whose teaching qualifications, moral rectitude and religious convictions were known and approved by the civic authorities and the kirk session were permitted to teach (licensed) and secondly to control the number of teachers in the town. As part of every burgh teacher's income came from pupils' fees (scollage), a charge which all pupils had to pay or have paid on their behalf, councils tried (not always successfully) to suppress private teachers in order to ensure that the officially appointed burgh teachers earned a sufficient income to encourage them to stay in post. Private teachers were allowed if they were offering specialist teaching in subjects such as the 'art of writing' (calligraphy), French or sewing. More contentiously, permission might be given for those who were effectively providing elementary or kindergarten teaching for children up to the age of seven or eight, where young girls and boys learnt the alphabet, catechism, proverbs and psalms by heart. These vernacular schools were the most likely to compete with the official schools for pupils and therefore, depending on the size of the available school age population, town councils passed local acts enforcing compulsory attendance at the grammar/burgh school, either on all the children in the town, or on all children over the age of about seven, or on all boys, or all boys over the age of seven. Some of the larger towns introduced an alternative gendered segregation by sending girls and infants who wished to learn either reading or writing to the music school. The arrangements are not always clearly indicated and were seldom permanent. Ambivalence about the position of girls was illustrated by Dumfries Council in 1660 when it complained that parents were damaging the town school by sending their children to small private schools locally and ordered that all the inhabitants should instead put their children, 'especially lads', to the official school.[13] Many, perhaps most, parents were doubtful about the value of literacy for girls: in 1618, Paisley Town Council had to order that no bairns were 'to be put to the sewing schuill till they can red perfytlie', a process which was expected to take about two years.[14] Sewing defined femininity, and was as inevitable a subject for girls of all sections of society as Latin was for boys of the nobility and middling ranks.

Latin was seen as the basis of all learning: 'the ground of all liberall artis and scienceis' as the Privy Council expressed it in 1593.[15] Grammar schools provided a concentrated diet of Latin as the basis for progress to the universities and the professions. A scholarly education was seen as being both grammatical and moral. Boys (aged about eight to twelve) learnt the grammar, verse and rhetoric of the principal tongues, particularly Latin, and optimistically, but rarely in practice, the scriptural languages of Greek and Hebrew. Learning grammar was in itself seen as a moral exercise, but in addition, through these languages and through the study of humanist authors, the scholars would, in theory, gain moral training, both spiritual from an acquaintance with scripture and its summation in sacred teaching, and social, based on the learning of civil manners, a civility which included behaviour relating to bodily functions, social manners and regard for others.

Following a sharp decline in music education after the Reformation, James VI passed an Act in 1579 which required 'maist speciall' burghs to erect song schools, to enable the continuation of teaching through music. Music education had moved from ecclesiastical to civic control by the seventeenth century and its availability and standard became a point of civic concern as each town wished to consider itself 'maist speciall'. At least twenty new music schools opened between 1584 and 1633, several with the assistance of small royal endowments, while other burghs arranged for the teaching of church music in their grammar schools.[16] The role of church music had changed after the Reformation; whereas previously trained professional choirs had sung complex polyphonic music in Latin while the congregation listened, under Presbyterianism the congregation were expected to join in the singing as an act of worship. Psalm singing was 'an essential component of reformed worship, and a recognised form of dissemination of doctrine and channelling of emotion'.[17] Hence the significance attached to the precentor's ability in singing each line first for the congregation to follow ('raising the psalmes').

When the new town music schools opened they catered for secular as well as sacred music and followed the new Western European fashion for instrumental music. As the high fees for instrumental music indicate, the schools were used by children of the gentry, although probably not those whose families were closet Catholics, who tended to employ private tutors or pedagogues. The Restoration of the monarchy in 1660 and the return of Episcopalianism brought new demands which most of the music schools were, by then, unable to satisfy, given the lack of any career structure or provision for the advanced training of musicians. In the 1670s Aberdeen, Edinburgh and Glasgow were prepared to offer relatively high salaries for good music masters and at Stirling in 1699 it was considered that the lack of a public music teacher 'hinders many of the gentrie from sending their childring to be here educat, to the noe small prejudice of this burgh'.[18] As a secular musical culture developed in the eighteenth-century towns music masters found more profit in private schools than in the burgh music schools with their fee restrictions, and most of the publicly funded music schools closed or completed their long transformation into 'English' or 'writing and arithmetic' schools. The legal requirement for the establishment of song schools had in effect provided a town school where the memorising of psalms, reading and writing could conveniently be taught and by the 1660s, arithmetic was usually included also. Increasingly, an ability to teach these subjects became the chief condition of appointment for the music master and by the early eighteenth century the General Assembly of the Church of Scotland had conceded the reversal of educational priorities. Nevertheless the kirk could sometimes assert pressure where it traditionally contributed part of the teacher's salary, resulting in polymath appointments. In 1761, for example, Stirling Council appointed a precentor, music master, writing master, arithmetic master and teacher of book-keeping, all in the one individual. The burgh writing and arithmetic school (sometimes referred to as the mathematical school) was the successor of the town's old music school and it was not until 1791 that it was specifically decided that the postholder should not also teach church music or hold a precentorship.[19]

Pedagogies

Most learning was based on memorising, from that of young children learning their ABC, Lord's Prayer, *Shorter Catechism*,[20] proverbs and psalms, to older pupils learning lists of words to spell or pronounce, or grammar school boys learning the rules for Latin grammar (in Latin). Question and answer formats, lists, verse mnemonics, music and, for those who could write, copying texts might be used as learning aides. The youngest children often learnt from a hornbook, which consisted of a page displaying the alphabet, a prayer and perhaps numerals, which was pasted onto a wooden frame and covered with a transparent sheet of horn to protect it from grubby fingers. The traditional method of learning to read was by endless repetition and memorising, with pupils matching the text against what they had memorised and repeated. This method meant that the ability to read might be quite superficial, the text acting more as a prompt for material that had already been memorised. In 1705, Kirkcaldy Council's regulations for its grammar school required that 'such as learne English get frequent lessons in reading print and bills', an indication that this was not necessarily the usual practice and it remained quite common to 'learn to read by the ear and memory only' in the eighteenth century.[21] Scotland was not unusual among the countries of Western Europe in its use of the catechism as a teaching material or, more precisely, in using schools to teach the catechism. Nor was there 'a' catechism. A number were published at a variety of educational levels from infant readers through to those with theological notes for the use of university students and adults, available in both Latin and English and in some cases as dual-language texts. Catechisms were also bound in collections with other sacred texts such as the proverbs of Solomon or the psalms and extra quantities of the first pages were printed, some destined for hornbooks. These were the schoolbooks of the vernacular schools.

The cultural turn in historical analysis, focusing on the ways in which meaning is created and distributed through social and economic practices and beliefs, has encouraged scholarship on the use of material artefacts, textbooks and contemporary educational discourse to discover the pedagogical methods and social interactions that took place in the schoolroom and the ideologies that lay behind them. Thus early-eighteenth-century changes in long-established teaching methods can be seen in the context of a moralising elite of pedagogic writers in Western Europe who developed 'an increasing belief in the moral and intellectual weakness of childhood' and hence the need for simplified texts and learning methods.[22] Initiatives in teaching methods might occur anywhere, but were most often introduced by urban schoolmasters, who also followed the vogue for writing school textbooks to illustrate teaching methods and advertise their own schools. In the early eighteenth century a number of new 'easy' Latin grammars were published, the 'easiness' being that the numerous grammatical rules scholars had to learn by heart were given in English or in a dual-language text instead of solely in Latin. Several of the textbooks also included references to the corresponding English grammar in footnotes. This raised the profile of English to that of a structured language rather than merely a vulgar tongue and teachers of English began to claim new pedagogic skills.

Aberdeen magistrates set up a school 'for teaching, grammatically, the English language' in 1672, prohibiting any other 'unqualified' teachers. By the beginning of the eighteenth century a new method of teaching children to read was being introduced, which replaced the crude form of word recognition from verbal repetition with a system of breaking words up into syllables. One Edinburgh master advertised that he could teach children over the age of six who could not read any English, to read Latin in eight or nine months.[23] This did not mean the children would understand what they read; indeed, an exercise used by some teachers was for pupils to practise reading aloud nonsense words. If 'syllabication' was one 'new method' of instruction, teaching English 'grammatically', based on the format of Latin grammars, was another. In 1769, the Ayr English master had a 'class learning English grammar, which is a branch almost new'.[24] A third 'new method' of teaching English involved the collation of extracts, initially from the *Spectator* and the French author Charles Rollin, and later including works by Scottish Enlightenment philosophers in school textbooks for reading and recitation. Introduced in 1737, in English and Latin, by John Warden, a private Edinburgh schoolmaster, various literary collections were published throughout the eighteenth century and into the early nineteenth. These constituted an important change of emphasis from sacred to secular texts as the school literature of the more advanced English pupils, as well as introducing Enlightenment authors as part of the adoption of university *belles-lettres* by schools.

Such reading collections may not always have achieved their intended purpose. While the barriers to literacy facing urban Gaelic-speaking Highlanders are obvious, the difficulties facing monoglot Scots-speaking children were also considerable. No one explained the English vocabulary to George Combe, the eight-year-old son of an Edinburgh brewer, with the result that: '[a]n English book was as unintelligible to me after I could pronounce and spell the words of it as was a Latin book before I had learned the rudiments of that language'.[25] The many polite spelling books of the period, with their emphasis on an 'English' pronunciation, were irrelevant for the majority of Scottish children.

Initially writing had been a skill needed only by ecclesiastical clerks and it was taught as an 'art', but as schooling became secularised and reading and writing spread to the wider population a distinction developed between everyday handwriting and the calligraphic script which was used for formal and legal documents and official certificates. Specialist writing masters taught a variety of different hands for use in different contexts, including the most common, secretarial, and the new italic hand popular with elite women. In the early seventeenth century writing masters were rare in Scotland and, like other later teachers with specialist skills such as mathematics or dancing, they were often peripatetic, but from the mid-century most towns either licensed or employed someone who could teach the subject. Writing was taught by copying, and this was also its main function. Pupils, students and apprentices of all ages did a great deal of copying, creating their own personalised commonplace books for later reference in subjects such as arithmetic, music and cookery, or keeping religious, legal or medical extracts, or noting literary quotations to reuse later in their own correspondence or writing. Writing masters probably kept the expensive published copybooks for their own reference and provided hand-copied examples to be used in the classes, possibly protected by a transparent sheet as a kind of hornbook.[26] During a discussion about the Glasgow writing master's salary in 1738, it was reported that whereas boys were formerly fourteen or fifteen before they started learning to write, they now began when they were seven or eight.[27] It remained quite common for girls (if they were taught writing at all) to learn in their teens, and some individuals learnt to write as adults. Writing masters usually also taught arithmetic or 'accounts', subjects which were mainly taught by rote and by copying down examples for future reference. Hutchesons' Hospital school even bound the boys' handwritten arithmetic books for them. Composition skills were traditionally taught in the grammar schools through Latin themes, but in the mid-eighteenth century they began to appear in the schooling of elite girls in English. Demainbray, an Edinburgh schoolmaster from England, set his female pupils a weekly letter-writing task to teach them the skill of 'juggling the formulaic polite demands of compliments with the expression of genuine emotion and sympathy' appropriate for elite members of polite society.[28] By the 1760s and 1770s, it was becoming more common for pupils of the middling ranks who were learning English grammar to be given compositional exercises in correspondence writing.

Schooling the Poor

Two kinds of poor people could be found in the burghs. Some lived there and had residential rights to some support in case of destitution, while others were from 'landward', outside the town boundary, and did not. The former category was sub-divided between the 'corporate poor' who were from the middling ranks – burgesses and guildsmen in the form of the wealthier merchants and craftsmen (and those gentry with town houses and professionals, including teachers, who might be given honorary status as burgesses) who were 'freemen', and the remaining two-thirds of the burgh population who were 'unfree', the common poor. Most of the mutual benefits and educational endowments of the burgh were for the corporate poor, designed to ensure that people of the middling ranks retained their status within the burgh even if they fell into poverty, so that the social hierarchy ordained by God would be preserved. Educational endowments donated in the seventeenth century often gave priority to individuals with the family surname, a practice which could be almost the equivalent of setting up a family trust. However, in marked contrast to England, very few of these 'mortifications' were left for schools, with the exception of a handful of large endowments which provided for the maintenance of needy children who were to be boarded, fed and clothed as well as educated. These residential or boarding schools (known as 'hospitals'), which required substantial buildings, were also intended for children from the urban merchant or trades guilds. The children admitted might come from poor, even destitute, families but they were connected to the middling ranks, not the town's poor, and certainly not the rural or 'landward' poor. The Edinburgh hospital schools included George Heriot's Hospital (founded 1624, opened in 1659), two Edinburgh endowments for girls, initiated by bequests from Mary Erskine, a druggist's widow and herself a merchant, the Merchant Maiden (1696) and Trades Maiden (1704), and George Watson's (1734). Another large seventeenth-century endowment was Hutchesons' Hospital in Glasgow (1648), while Robert Gordon's Hospital was founded in Aberdeen in 1732 and opened in 1750. The educational position of these hospital schools for the urban middling ranks is not easily defined for the eighteenth century. They were managed by councillors, ministers and merchants who were part of the influential urban patronage network, yet quite small pupil numbers were involved – there were about 390 places in total at the end of the eighteenth century – and the schools have been described as being 'at once in the city, and yet not entirely of it'.[29]

With these few exceptions, early ideas about helping the poor were on an individual, personal scale, assuming a static community and small numbers. Rather than providing hospital or boarding schools, the traditional arrangement was for bursaries or payments which allowed poor children to get appropriate schooling at the existing town schools. One example was the Stirling Merchant Guild which by the early eighteenth century was supporting the education of the sons and daughters of indigent guild members at the town-supported English school, writing and arithmetic school, and sewing school, with a few boys going on to the grammar school. Guildry curriculum regulations drawn up in 1813 indicated the ideal that had been aimed at for most of the eighteenth century. Boys and girls should start their schooling when they were about six, study at the English school for up to four years and beginning writing in their last year, when they would be about nine years old. At ten they were to go to the writing and arithmetic school (which in many towns might be in the same building or even the same schoolroom, but was probably under a separate master or assistant) where they should study for another two years, but the girls would also 'be put to sewing', and so would have about half as much time learning writing and arithmetic as the boys.[30]

In practice, children often started school at an earlier age, causing disruption to classes, or when they were much older, so that they were behind others of a comparable age, or they left and then returned later for a different subject. Complaints by the Dundee Presbytery in 1768 that parents often indulged their children by changing masters were echoed elsewhere.[31] The Stirling Guild committee of 1813 also found there was a high rate of absenteeism by pupils, even when they were being funded. In the seventeenth century, urban and church authorities made strenuous attempts to ensure compulsory school attendance, but the frequent repetition of such efforts in itself indicates their relative failure despite the threat or imposition of fines or imprisonment for recalcitrant parents. The school attendance of most children, even if they did not come from families officially considered 'poor', was short and spasmodic. Of those at Cupar burgh school between 1774 and 1788, half were in school for a year or less. Only a fifth stayed for more than three years, and many of these missed one or more 'quarter'. Girls, in particular, attended very sporadically.[32] An inquiry into elementary educational provision in Edinburgh in 1758 found twenty-four schools taught by men of which four or five were charging higher rates and two were free charity schools.[33] Another six schools were taught by women. The male teachers had an average of thirty pupils, the women fifteen, giving a maximum of 800 pupils and leaving an estimated two-thirds of the children in the city not attending any school. Some of the children might continue to be educated during their absence from school; learning at home and at school was an interwoven experience for all ages and social groups. But most children of non-burgess families would leave school when they were seven or eight, and the short and erratic school attendances meant many children would never get beyond learning to read, and even that not well.

The town public schools were intended for a manageable and relatively static population. But when severe dearth or civil war resulted in whole localities of out-dwellers being reduced to begging and drawn to the urban areas, the towns were unable to cope. The first charity school in Edinburgh opened in 1699 and, supported by various bequests, it continued, managed by the town council, into the nineteenth century. Establishing corporate schools specifically for the poor was problematic. When Edinburgh Town Council established four 'English' schools in 1759, the first provision by the burgh for elementary education, these were quickly adopted by the middling ranks of the city, while the three working charity or free schools set up under the Society in Scotland for Propagating Christian Knowledge at the same time closed after ten years because of lack of funds. Charity workhouses were established, but most support for charity schooling came instead from private individuals from the urban middling ranks who established a variety of educational institutions in increasing numbers in the Scottish towns in the second half of the eighteenth century. In these schools, as in the charity workhouses, the children of the destitute labouring poor and child-vagabonds without a family were put under a work ethic rather than a learning ethic and closely supervised. This was a new attitude in Scotland, although similar urban responses to the unmanageable influx of labouring poor and perceived threat to civic order had occurred in parts of mainland Europe at a much earlier date. By the end of the eighteenth century, a wide variety of privately run free or charity schools had come into existence including the first Sunday schools and schools for religious and linguistic minorities such as Methodists and Gaelic-speaking urban Highlanders. They did not, however, include the 'schools of industry' for girls run by committees of philanthropic middle-class women which were prevalent in England; these did not appear in Scotland until the early nineteenth century.

Eighteenth-century Schooling

Regardless of hard times for the poor, the Scottish landowning and professional classes had become more affluent by the 1690s and each town was eager to attract them to increase its revenue. Consequently a wider range of private teachers skilled in the polite and performative arts which would become popular in Georgian Britain were licensed by the towns. French, Italian, fencing and dancing schools appeared in Edinburgh. Glasgow competed for music and French masters, Dundee licensed a dancing and fencing master from Perth, while the Inverness music master's clientele consisted of 'gentlemen's children from the country'. Keen to attract the gentlemen's daughters also, towns such as Glasgow, Stirling, Cupar, Irvine and Forres looked for gentlewomen to educate 'young gentlewomen' or wealthy 'burgessis daughteris'.

By the 1720s, a change of attitude regarding more academic subjects was also becoming evident: town councils were accepting rather than opposing private schools while, at the same time, instead of hiring or licensing private teachers, they began to attach teachers of new subjects to the towns' own schools. By this date it was the normal arrangement to have town-funded English and 'writing and arithmetic' teachers. The arrangements could vary, however, in terms of both the hierarchy of authority and the physical location of the schools, which, depending on the availability and durability of suitable buildings, might often be multi-site schools, becoming known collectively as the burgh's 'public schools'. Schools and teachers were split up or combined in myriad patterns as town councils tried to deal economically with changing school populations and the available accommodation. It was not until the end of the eighteenth century that such arrangements had much to do with meeting the demand for new subjects, although they might have implications for girls' access to classes. In the period of severe inflation during the early eighteenth century town authorities continued to insist that the school fees for reading, writing, arithmetic, Latin and basic sewing remained sufficiently low to be affordable by the less wealthy families. The 'public hours' at which these core subjects were to be taught were prescribed by the town councils to ensure they were given priority, but schoolmasters were permitted, or increasingly encouraged, to give classes in extra subjects 'privately' in the early morning, evening or during the prolonged lunchtime. This arrangement extended the range of middle-class subjects available in a town and it augmented the salaries of the burgh teachers as they were permitted to charge fees at higher rates for such teaching. School subjects which were useful for commerce and fed into the perceived attributes of polite society were the most popular. These included English grammar (so-called to distinguish it from the Latin grammar of the grammar schools), composition, French and geography, the last appearing in various forms in mathematics, navigation, classics, book-keeping and 'the globes' (astronomical and terrestrial).[34] Attending various teachers at their schools or homes for the different subjects was called going to the schools, or going to classes. A reference to the 'disagreeable necessity of strolling from school to school at the expiration of almost every hour' appeared in an advertisement for a private academy in Glasgow in 1762[35] and it was the continuance of this practice by upper-middle-class Edinburgh girls which led to the founding of the influential Scottish Institution for the Education of Young Ladies in 1834. Attendance at individual classes also occurred in England, but either this has been under-researched or the practice was more widespread in Scotland.

For children coming to school from outside the town, boarding was almost inevitable given the logistics of terrain and travel, but it remained relatively small-scale and personal. Scholars often boarded in the town with relatives or in lodgings, but it could be a valuable source of income for teachers. In the 1760s, the Irvine burgh school rector (headmaster) had from twenty to twenty-six boarders, many of them from the West Indies and American colonies,[36] an example, too, of the way in which Scotland's involvement in British imperialism and slavery supported Scottish education (as did the substantial financial assistance received from Scotsmen in the West Indies and India towards new 'academy' schools such as Inverness, Fordyce, Fortrose and Tain). Boarding arrangements could also produce the anomaly, still evident in the nineteenth century, of both public and private schools where boys boarded but girls were also pupils. In contrast, some of the provincial burgh-funded sewing schools which provided boarding facilities for girls struggled to survive, although in the late eighteenth century Edinburgh's numerous private boarding schools for young ladies, offering fancy work and music in addition to the ubiquitous sewing, became increasingly popular.

The Academy Movement

Concern as to whether a humanist classical education provided the most appropriate skills for improving the economy and commerce of the country was evident even in the seventeenth century and by 1700 included the Presbyterian Church – more usually considered a drag on innovation. Presbyteries in the west of Scotland expressed concern that schools were wasting pupils' time on Latin and recommended other subjects which would be more useful for trade such as (modern) geography, history or geometry.[37] To attract students to Edinburgh when the university lacked a law or medical faculty, the town council started licensing private teachers, who could make their money by training surgeons' apprentices and law clerks in subjects such as anatomy, botany, chemistry, Scots law and civil law.[38] In 1704, one teacher was offering classes in law, mathematics, grammar, logic and rhetoric, history and philology, while in 1734, a merchant recently returned from Rotterdam, who taught book-keeping, gave a free lecture on 'the education and qualities requisite in a perfect merchant'.[39]

In 1727 two undergraduate candidates were examined for the post of doctor at Ayr grammar school. Over a three-day period they were tested on their writing, Greek, Latin, book-keeping, arithmetic and navigation.[40] Two years later, John Mair (who gained the appointment only as the second choice) asked the town council to purchase maps and globes as these were 'highly necessary for forming the man of business' and in 1735, he persuaded the council that the boys studying Latin were disadvantaged by their ignorance of geography.[41] Mair subsequently published textbooks on book-keeping, arithmetic, geography, ancient history and Latin, all of which went through a number of editions. In 1746, he became rector of the school, which was then divided into three departments, classical, English and mathematical, the last including arithmetic, book-keeping, geometry, navigation, surveying, algebra and 'other parts of mathematical sciences and parts of natural philosophy' (physics).[42] The school was thus a publicly run institution which included all the post-elementary education available in the locality. In 1761, Mair was headhunted as co-rector of Perth Academy. Unlike Ayr burgh school, Perth Academy was not a metamorphosis of an existing school, but an entirely new institution which the town council opened in 1762, intending that it should exist alongside the grammar school as an Academy for literature and the sciences, based (in name as well as philosophy) on the model of the private dissenting academies in England. The literary department which was intended to introduce the *belles-lettres* was not a success and the co-rector resigned after the first year, but the academy continued as a successful science school to the end of the century.[43]

Perth Academy's new two-year science curriculum challenged the universities (although with some university students aged only twelve or thirteen this was hardly difficult) but although the academy was highly influential, it had few direct imitators except in its name. Without substantial funding it was difficult to start and maintain a new institution of this standard. Dundee Academy collapsed within a few years (1786–92) and only restarted in 1802 due to a fortuitous endowment. Private academies varied in quality and were often mainly elementary in standard, but some were run by graduate teachers capable of secondary or university-level teaching. Their existence in the cities enabled the town grammar schools to continue on a largely unchanged classics-based curriculum. Apart from at Perth, Dundee and Inverness Academies, the standard of mathematics and science was generally low. At the end of the century, one critic alleged that 'In the different public schools and academies . . . the mathematics are taught in an easy and popular manner, adapted to the object of these institutions'.[44] Inverness Academy originated out of the concept of providing an alternative, more technically orientated education based in the Highlands than the universities offered and some expensive teaching apparatus was bought.[45] But, like a number of the other burgh schools or 'academies' which were reorganised or created from the 1780s onwards, Inverness actually followed the example of Ayr in 1746 more closely, with a variety of subject options in various departments ranging from physics and mathematics to basic literacy. Similarly, Banff Academy, reorganised by the influential educationalist George Chapman, consisted of six departments in the 1790s. It became a matter of civic pride as much as pedagogical innovation, that a new, suitable building should be provided to accommodate all the schools or departments together, a development which continued into the nineteenth century.[46] Town councils usually lacked the finance for such a project and called on local private subscribers for assistance, but in most cases the academy remained a community school (albeit one intended for the middling and gentry classes), with either total or influential representation by the town councillors on the controlling body.

The 'academy movement' was not only about reforming the subjects taught, but was also an attempt to provide a more coherent overall curriculum. This was largely vitiated by the virtually autonomous status of the masters of the various departments or 'schools', and the financial difficulties of both the teachers and the civic authorities, which resulted in competition for pupils. Thus despite the influence of the academy movement, few pupils followed any recognised post-elementary curriculum. Boys aiming at university followed a fairly standard Latin syllabus, but what their other subjects consisted of and where they studied them could vary enormously depending on which private classes they attended. The genuinely science-oriented academies provided a syllabus (two years at Perth and three at Dundee) but had to arrange for most of the subjects to be available individually also, to attract sufficient pupils.

As most children who progressed beyond basic literacy took subjects in a piecemeal 'cafeteria' or module fashion, this meant that although girls and boys might coincidentally learn together in the same school or classroom for a few months, there was no recognisable 'co-educational' syllabus, nor indeed was there a universally accepted academic curriculum for girls. Nevertheless, the traditional ad hoc schooling arrangements could also work to girls' advantage. In Edinburgh, Glasgow and Aberdeen, where there were plenty of alternatives, girls were excluded from the cities' grammar schools, as they were also from Fortrose and Banff Academies. But in some provincial towns such as Perth, Stirling, Inverness and Ayr, even though the new curriculum was specifically planned to provide boys in the reorganised burgh academies with an alternative to, or preparation for, university study as a seemingly masculine space, arrangements might also be made for girls to attend classes for post-literacy subjects such as French, English grammar, composition, geography, drawing or dancing.

Conclusion

The cultural turn in the history of education places schooling within a broader social context. Each individual's personal development had various aspects of learning embedded within it. But schooling was only one facet of the educational process, and for many individuals, especially the poorest, it was of relatively minor importance. For others, particularly the elite, it was crucial. Insightful research has shown, *inter alia*, how specific social groups, such as the Highland gentry and the Scottish female elite, used urban educational facilities, including schools, to promote and retain their social status and how families used the apparently chaotic choice available in carefully selected ways to differentiate the requirements of their children by gender and family order, in anticipation of their future social roles. The earnest theological *raison d'être* of seventeenth-century schooling, when virtually all vernacular schoolbooks were religious texts, became diffused during the eighteenth century. From the end of the seventeenth century there was an increasing emphasis on trade and commerce which led towns to encourage specialist teachers in the useful sciences and to promote education itself as an economic and community asset. The locality that achieved this above all others was Edinburgh, whose attraction as a centre of education made it difficult for provincial towns to compete. Nevertheless, developments in educational provision in the later eighteenth century, particularly the academy movement, 'testified to the strength of the provincial urban commitment to "improvement and learning"'.[47]

Recent scholarship on seventeenth- and eighteenth-century Scotland has explored a variety of related issues which have still to be fully incorporated into the history of schooling, such as literacy levels and patterns, changing attitudes to childhood and pedagogic artefacts, the relationship between schools and the universities (complex and ever-changing with respect to both the curricula and the staff, sometimes competitive, sometimes supplementary or in partnership), the dissemination of Enlightenment ideas through school textbooks, educational tracts and libraries, the geographical networks of educational subjects and the role of urban educational institutions as motivators and indicators of the development of polite society and Enlightenment ideology in provincial Scotland.

Schooling should also be seen within a sociological framework. It influenced and was influenced by contemporary and competing ideologies and practices, religious, political, economic and cultural. It was affected by the macropolitics of the state and the church, the micropolitics of local communities and by the desire of middle-ranking Scots to become part of the British imperial project. It was strongly gendered. The educational system of legislation and administration through the town councils, kirk sessions and guilds was male-only. Men determined the provision of schooling, the curriculum and the selection of teachers, even when they decided to establish or support schools taught by women. Urban schooling was also strongly classed; everyone was to be educated, but the system was never intended to produce equality of opportunity; schooling was streamed initially according to burgh status, later according to wealth. Yet if urban schooling was not markedly democratic or co-educational in the seventeenth and eighteenth centuries, it could also have been much more socially divisive than it was, and credit must be given for the provision that was achieved despite enormous political, religious and economic difficulties.

Notes

1. Gordon Jackson, 'Glasgow in transition, c. 1660–c. 1740', in T. M. Devine and Gordon Jackson (eds), *Glasgow. Volume I: Beginnings to 1830* (Manchester University Press, 1995), pp. 63–105.
2. Karen J. Cullen, Christopher A. Whatley and Mary Young, 'Battered but unbowed – Dundee during the seventeenth century', in Charles McKean, Bob Harris and Christopher A. Whatley (eds), *Dundee: Renaissance to Enlightenment* (Dundee University Press, 2009), pp. 57–83; Gordon DesBrisay, '"The Civill Warrs Did Overrun All": Aberdeen, 1630–1690', in E. Patricia Dennison, David Ditchburn and Michael Lynch (eds), *Aberdeen Before 1800: A New History* (Tuckwell Press, 2002), pp. 238–66.
3. T. M. Devine, 'Urbanisation', in T. M. Devine and Rosalind Mitchison (eds), *People and Society in Scotland, Vol. I: 1760–1830* (John Donald, 1988), p. 28.
4. R. A. Houston, *Scottish Literacy and the Scottish Identity: Illiteracy and Society in Scotland and Northern England 1600–1800* (Cambridge University Press, 1985), pp. 45–54, 61–2.
5. James Grant, *History of the Burgh and Parish Schools of Scotland. Vol 1. Burgh Schools* (William Collins, Sons & Co., 1876), p. 80; James Scotland, *The History of Scottish Education*, vol. 1 (University of London Press, 1969), p. 50.
6. Brian R. W. Lockhart, *The Town School: A History of the High School of Glasgow* (John Donald, 2010), p. 20.
7. A. D. Dunlop, *Hutchesons' Grammar: The History of a Glasgow School* (Hutchesons' Educational Trust, 1992), pp. 13–14.
8. DesBrisay, '"Civill Warrs Did Overrun All"', p. 264.
9. John Durkan, *Scottish Schools and Schoolmasters 1560–1633*, ed. and rev. Jamie Reid-Baxter (Scottish History Society, 2013), p. 203. I am grateful to Dr Reid-Baxter and Dr John McCallum for permitting me to see a pre-publication copy.
10. G. W. Shirley, 'Fragmentary notices of the burgh school of Dumfries', *Dumfriesshire and Galloway Natural History & Antiquarian Society Transactions and Journal of Proceedings 1936–1938*, 3rd series, vol. 21 (1939), pp. 133–4; Robert Preece, *Song School, Town School, Comprehensive: A History of Inverness Royal Academy* (For the Right Reasons, 2011), p. 37.
11. R. A. Houston, 'Literacy, education and the culture of print in Enlightenment Edinburgh', *History* 78 (1993), 386–7.

12. Margaret K. B. Sommerville, *The Merchant Maiden Hospital of the City of Edinburgh* (Former Pupils' Guild of the Mary Erskine School for Girls, 1970), p. 121.
13. Shirley, 'Fragmentary notices', p. 143.
14. Grant, *History of the Burgh and Parish Schools*, pp. 527–8.
15. Durkan, *Scottish Schools and Schoolmasters*, p. 172.
16. Gordon Munro, '"Sang schwylls" and "Music schools": Music education in Scotland, 1560–1650', in Susan Forscher Weiss, Russell E. Murray Jr. and Cynthia J. Cyrus (eds), *Music Education in the Middle Ages and the Renaissance* (Indiana University Press, 2010), pp. 65–83.
17. Shona Maclean Vance, 'Godly citizens and civic unrest: Tensions in schooling in Aberdeen in the era of the Reformation', *European Review of History* 7(1) (2000), 126.
18. Gordon James Munro, 'Scottish church music and musicians, 1500–1700' (unpublished PhD dissertation, University of Glasgow, 1999), vol. 1, 104–5, 174–5.
19. Stirling Council Archives, Stirling Town Council Minutes, B66/21/11, 24 August 1761; B66/21/14, 4 April 1791.
20. Approved by the Church of Scotland in 1648, with 107 questions and answers it was short and easy only compared with the *Larger Catechism*.
21. James M. Beale, *A History of the Burgh and Parochial Schools of Fife*, ed. Donald J. Withrington (Scottish Council for Research in Education, 1983), pp. 206–8; Alexander Law, 'Scottish schoolbooks of the eighteenth and nineteenth centuries', *Studies in Scottish Literature* 18(1) (1983), 15.
22. Craig Beveridge, 'Childhood and society in eighteenth-century Scotland', in John Dwyer, Roger A. Mason and Alexander Murdoch (eds), *New Perspectives on the Politics and Culture of Early Modern Scotland* (John Donald, n.d. [1982]), p. 266.
23. Alexander Law, *Education in Edinburgh in the Eighteenth Century* (University of London Press, 1965), pp. 194–5.
24. Grant, *History of the Burgh and Parish Schools*, p. 392.
25. Charles Gibbon, *The Life of George Combe: Author of 'The Constitution of Man'*, 2 vols (Macmillan, 1878), vol. 1, p. 9.
26. Illustrated in Donald J. Withrington, *Going to School* (National Museums of Scotland, 1997), p. 24.
27. Jackson, 'Glasgow in transition', p. 91.
28. Katharine Glover, *Elite Women and Polite Society in Eighteenth-Century Scotland* (Boydell and Brewer, 2011), pp. 24–5.
29. Law, *Education in Edinburgh*, p. 143.
30. W. B. Cook and David B. Morris (eds), *The Stirling Guildry Book: Extracts from the Records of the Merchant Guild of Stirling, A.D. 1592–1846* (Glasgow Stirlingshire & Sons of the Rock Society, 1916), 15 March 1739, 2 June 1813.
31. J. W. W. Stephenson, *Education in the Burgh of Dundee in the Eighteenth Century: Related Mainly from Contemporary Manuscripts* ([Scottish Council for Research in Education], [1973]), p. 28.
32. Paula Martin, *Cupar: The History of a Small Scottish Town* (Birlinn, 2006), pp. 127–9.
33. Law, *Education in Edinburgh*, pp. 224–5.
34. Charles W. J. Withers, *Geography, Science and National Identity: Scotland since 1520* (Cambridge University Press, 2001), pp. 134–6.
35. Donald J. Withrington, 'Education and society in the eighteenth century', in Nicholas T. Phillipson and Rosalind Mitchison (eds), *Scotland in the Age of Improvement: Essays in Scottish History in the Eighteenth Century* (Edinburgh University Press, 1970), p. 197.
36. Scotland, *History of Scottish Education*, vol. 1, p. 128.

37. Withrington, 'Education and society', pp. 170–4.
38. Nicholas Phillipson, 'The making of an enlightened university', in Robert D. Anderson, Michael Lynch and Nicholas Phillipson (eds), *The University of Edinburgh: An Illustrated History* (Edinburgh University Press, 2003), pp. 59–60.
39. Ibid., p. 60; Houston, 'Literacy, education and the culture of print', 385.
40. Grant, *History of the Burgh Schools*, pp. 219–20.
41. Withrington, 'Education and society', p. 170; Grant, *History of the Burgh Schools*, p. 396.
42. Withrington, 'Education and society', pp. 176–7.
43. Grant, *History of the Burgh Schools*, pp. 115–16, 118–19.
44. Alex D. D. Craik and Alonso D. Roberts, 'Mathematics teaching, teachers and students at St Andrews University, 1765–1858', *History of Universities* 24 (2009), 251.
45. Preece, *Song School*, pp. 49–52, 69–70.
46. Bob Harris, 'The Enlightenment, towns and urban society in Scotland, c.1760–1820', *English Historical Review* 126 (2011), 1114–15.
47. Bob Harris, 'Cultural change in provincial Scottish towns, c.1700–1820', *Historical Journal* 54 (2011), 119.

Bibliography

Beale, James M., *A History of the Burgh and Parochial Schools of Fife*, ed. Donald J. Withrington (Scottish Council for Research in Education, 1983).

Durkan, John, *Scottish Schools and Schoolmasters, 1560–1633*, ed. and rev. Jamie Reid-Baxter (Scottish History Society, 2013).

Grant, James, *History of the Burgh and Parish Schools of Scotland. Vol 1. Burgh Schools* (William Collins, Sons & Co., 1876).

Law, Alexander, *Education in Edinburgh in the Eighteenth Century* (University of London Press, 1965).

Moore, Lindy, 'The value of feminine culture: Community involvement in the provision of schooling for girls in eighteenth-century Scotland', in Katie Barclay and Deborah Simonton (eds), *Women in Eighteenth-Century Scotland: Intimate, Intellectual and Public Lives* (Ashgate, 2013), pp. 97–114.

Moore, Terrence O., 'Textbooks', in Stephen W. Brown and Warren McDougall (eds), *The Edinburgh History of the Book in Scotland. Vol. 2: Enlightenment and Expansion 1707–1800* (Edinburgh University Press, 2012), pp. 310–14.

Munro, Gordon, '"Sang schwylls" and "Music schools": Music education in Scotland 1560–1650', in Susan Forscher Weiss, Russell E. Murray, Jr. and Cynthia J. Cyrus (eds), *Music Education in the Middle Ages and the Renaissance* (Indiana University Press, 2010), pp. 65–83.

Nenadic, Stana, *Lairds and Luxury: The Highland Gentry in Eighteenth-Century Scotland* (John Donald, 2007), Chapter 2.

Vance, Shona, 'Schooling the people', in E. Patricia Dennison, David Ditchburn and Michael Lynch (eds), *Aberdeen Before 1800: A New History* (Tuckwell Press, 2002), pp. 309–26.

Withrington, Donald J., 'Education and society in the eighteenth century', in Nicholas T. Phillipson and Rosalind Mitchison (eds), *Scotland in the Age of Improvement: Essays in Scottish History in the Eighteenth Century* (Edinburgh University Press, 1970), pp. 169–99.

6

The Universities and the Scottish Enlightenment

David Allan

One phenomenon above all others is now recognised as having marked out Scotland's first post-Union century: this is, of course, the Scottish Enlightenment. A brilliant concentration of cultural and intellectual activity starting in the 1720s or 1730s and running through until at least the late 1780s, it encompassed the enduring legacies of leading philosophers of consciousness and behaviour like David Hume and Thomas Reid and pioneering theorists of human society such as Adam Smith and Adam Ferguson. It also, however, took in the more ephemeral work of numerous lesser lights, the wider community of scholars and scientists alongside whom those great original minds lived and worked. The result, an extraordinary phase during which Scotland was recognised as exerting genuinely international cultural influence, even appeared to substantiate Voltaire's famous observation in 1762, not itself offered without a hint of sarcasm, that 'it is an admirable effect of the progress of the human mind, that at this day we receive from Scotland rules of taste in all the arts from Epic poetry to gardening'.[1] For understandable reasons it has been in this singular context of widely recognised collective impact by Scottish intellectuals that the contemporary history of the country's five universities has principally been approached. Modern scholarship has accordingly expended much effort in exploring the major publications and characteristic inquiries of the most prominent members of the Enlightenment professoriate – Reid in Aberdeen, Smith's teacher Francis Hutcheson in Glasgow, Ferguson and his successor Dugald Stewart at Edinburgh, and so forth – as they strove to push back the very frontiers of knowledge and understanding and to impart their distinctive ideas and arguments to an audience not only inside but also far beyond Scotland. Successful attempts have also been made, as we shall see, to recover significant aspects of the peculiar academic environments that nurtured and sustained such an innovative and influential group of thinkers. Unfortunately, however, this has not been the only function performed by the universities in the continuing search for a better appreciation of the origins and nature of the Scottish Enlightenment. For the natural desire to establish a fixed baseline against which the magnitude of its literary, philosophical and scientific achievements can be properly measured has meant that the state of Scotland's academic institutions two or three generations earlier – and especially some of the controversies in which they were embroiled before and after the start of the eighteenth century – has also proved an inevitable focus for scholarly attention.

From Darkness into Light

An inescapable element in the traditional historiography of the Scottish Enlightenment's first emergence – one might be tempted to say its mythology – has always been the fact that as recently as 1690 the universities were clearly subjected to what can only be described as systematic purges. These were undertaken by the government and the kirk following the deposition of the Catholic King James VII of Scotland and II of England, and, in what in England at least became known as the Glorious Revolution, the installation of the Protestant co-sovereigns William and Mary in his place. Commissions were established by the Scots Parliament in the summer of 1690 to visit each academic institution with the explicit task of rooting out ('rabbling' in the vernacular) those professors who might be unsympathetic to the new revolutionary order. In practice not merely brazen Jacobitism – support for the ousted James – but also anything less than strict adherence to the Calvinist theology insisted upon by the triumphant Presbyterian party in the kirk could get a Scottish university teacher into the most severe professional difficulty. At Edinburgh, for example, the victims were as high-profile as could be: Principal Alexander Monro was thrown out of his post, John Strachan lost his position as professor of divinity and John Drummond and Thomas Burnet, who taught humanity (that is, Latin) and philosophy respectively, were also deprived. At Glasgow, too, Principal James Fall, the holder of the chair of divinity James Wemyss and William Blair, a third professor, were all quickly jettisoned. In St Andrews, where the university community had issued a disastrously ill-timed proclamation in favour of the old king only shortly before the arrival of the new, almost the entire professoriate was eventually culled. Seven of the eight academic staff, who as a group attempted an unabashed public defence before the commissioners while wearing full academic dress, were replaced by more reliable individuals who could be trusted not to espouse what their inquisitors had denounced as the 'dangerous and pernicious tenets' of their predecessors.[2] Only in Aberdeen, where the defiant professors benefited from well-dug-in local backing for the Jacobite interest, was the academic purge substantially resisted: in the event the professor of divinity at King's College, the combative James Garden, was the sole ejectee, and even then the process took seven long years to complete because the offender and his allies gamely contested the decision.

As well as the forced expulsion of teaching staff on ideological grounds in the aftermath of the Revolution, an exercise that was actually repeated once more following the rebellion of 1715 (Aberdeen, still a notorious hotbed of Jacobite zeal, being particularly badly affected second time around), historians have readily identified in the prevailing culture of the Scottish universities in this era an ingrained hostility to intellectual freedom that appears not merely in stark contrast to the subsequent Enlightenment but actively inimical to its potential emergence. In particular, great significance has traditionally been vested in the totemic case of one Edinburgh undergraduate, Thomas Aikenhead. A student with notably idiosyncratic opinions, he was prosecuted for blasphemy and duly convicted and executed in the Scottish capital in January 1697, acquiring in the process the unwanted distinction of being Britain's last blasphemer to suffer capital punishment. The kind of views, and not least the flippant tone, which got Aikenhead into such deep water can easily be ascertained from the official deposition (or Scots law indictment) made against him:

> That . . . the prisoner had repeatedly maintained, in conversation, that theology was a rhapsody of ill-invented nonsense, patched up partly of the moral doctrines of philosophers, and partly of poetical fictions and extravagant chimeras: that he ridiculed the holy scriptures, calling the Old Testament Ezra's fables, in profane allusion to Aesop's fables; that he railed on Christ, saying, he had learned magic in Egypt, which enabled him to perform those *pranks* which were called miracles: that he called the New Testament the history of the imposter Christ: that he said Moses was the better artist, and the better politician; and he preferred Mahomet to Christ: *that the holy scriptures were stuffed with such madness, nonsense, and contradiction, that he admired the stupidity of the world in being so long deluded by them*: that he rejected the mystery of the Trinity, as unworthy of refutation; and scoffed at the incarnation of Christ . . .[3]

Importantly, the problem was not that these claims were necessarily clear harbingers of the coming Enlightenment – though some parts, like the apparent anti-Trinitarianism, arguably were, and several aspects of Aikenhead's reported comments do hint at a robustly sceptical disposition and a certain inquisitiveness about the potential intellectual fruitfulness of comparative religion that would have been largely unexceptional in Scotland a century later. It was more that they challenged and openly mocked the rigidly Calvinist beliefs and language which following the Revolution held the universities in their thrall. Aikenhead was definitely unlucky to be the victim of some thoroughly unpleasant tensions in wider Scottish society at a point in time when the newly installed Presbyterian authorities, still in the same intolerant and suspicious frame of mind which had inspired the recent professorial purges, were especially anxious about the threat posed by deviant beliefs, perceived or real. Personal animosity from some of Aikenhead's student contemporaries also probably helped the fatal accusations first see the light of day and then be sufficiently supported by damning witness testimony as to secure a conviction which would subsequently be upheld even on appeal. Yet these peculiar circumstantial factors have not made this case any less emblematic of the profoundly unenlightened approach to intellectual liberty and freedom of speech in and around Scotland's universities on the verge of the eighteenth century.

Another arraignment of an alleged purveyor of unsound theological views in the groves of academe – this time with non-lethal consequences though the defendant again suffered serious loss – has also attracted predictable interest from historians seeking to demarcate the early boundaries of the Scottish Enlightenment. The victim this time was John Simson, professor of divinity at Glasgow, who in many ways looks even more like a precocious but persecuted proto-Enlightenment figure than Thomas Aikenhead. Simson's approach as a theologian and teacher was certainly progressive: for example, he allowed students to discuss and debate ideas openly in his classes in what we would now think of as a seminar format (a daring and, it turned out, unwise departure in early-eighteenth-century Scotland where monologue and dictation were the preferred methods for inculcating dogmatic Calvinist precision in the next generation of ministers). Simson's doctrinal position was no less perplexing, clearly pushing at the boundaries of Presbyterian orthodoxy by emphasising the power of human reason and the benevolence of God in matters of salvation. Together these features of his work in the university led to repeated accusations by devout local clergy that what they took to be Simson's creative attempts to move Calvinist doctrine in a seemingly Arian direction – in short, questioning the divinity of Christ – represented a grave danger to tender young minds. The kirk duly investigated, though at the first time of asking, in 1717, Simson, who made no bones about his views and was openly contemptuous of his inquisitors but also benefited from friends in high places, was able to get away with a warning as to his future conduct. The zealous, however, predictably kept him in their sights and after a decade of further pressure he was finally removed from teaching, specifically, in a chilling echo of the Aikenhead case, for purportedly maintaining 'damnable doctrines' in relation to the Trinity, and therefore for being, in effect, a heretic.[4] Again, the forces of darkness rather than of Enlightenment, even in the second quarter of the new century, appeared to retain control of what could be taught, and also of who would be allowed to teach, in Scotland's universities.

Yet this emphasis on purges and prosecutions, melodramatic though the resulting narrative invariably becomes, is only part of the picture and not necessarily the most significant aspect if we want to take the true measure of the Scottish universities in the early years of the eighteenth century. To start with, there is actually a much more encouraging late-seventeenth-century context that provides less of a contrast with the subsequent Enlightenment and which helpfully challenges the conventional emphasis on the sacking of doctrinally suspect theologians and the hanging of tactless undergraduates. Even in the 1680s, indeed, there were interesting developments that do seem to foreshadow the eighteenth-century achievements of the Scottish universities. For example, the associated academic infrastructure, as we would doubtless now call it, was already measurably improving in this period. The country's first genuine research library, the Advocates Library in Edinburgh, of which seventy years later both Ferguson and Hume would briefly serve as librarians, was founded. So too was the Royal College of Physicians, which in the coming generations would be a foundation of Scotland's, especially Edinburgh's, international reputation as a centre for medical excellence. In the same vein a Physic Garden also started up in the capital as a focus for pharmacological botany, while in 1685 the first professorship of medicine at the University of Edinburgh was created. The man who became King James VII, when still Duke of York and actually resident in Scotland in the early 1680s, also established two significant new official academic positions that gave a platform to public intellectuals, the Historiographer-Royal in 1681 and the Geographer-Royal in 1682, both royal appointments clearly intended to reward and dignify exponents of these important scholarly disciplines. And one of the greatest intellectual achievements in Scotland's history also first saw the light of day early in the same decade: the *Institutions of the Laws of Scotland*, published in 1681 by Sir James Dalrymple, Viscount Stair, which, fusing the Roman law inheritance with the latest European thinking within the natural jurisprudential tradition, became and remains the definitive philosophical treatment of Scots law understood as merely the local expression of 'the Law of all Rational Creatures'.[5] Seen in this rather different perspective, therefore, the close of the seventeenth century appears less a time of unremitting gloom in Scotland than one of enveloping darkness pierced by several brilliant shafts of light: to refine the hackneyed metaphor of luminescence which was first used during the eighteenth century itself and has been in common usage ever since, the Scottish scene at this point, in the generation or two immediately before the Enlightenment proper spread its wider illumination, is actually characterised by the starkest contrasts of intense light and deep shade, appearing much more like a striking *chiaroscuro* composition by Caravaggio than a uniformly black canvas.

Other changes from around the turn of the eighteenth century, entirely within the confines of the universities themselves, can also be understood as harbingers of the Scottish Enlightenment soon to come. One of both symbolic and practical importance was the decision by each of the five universities in turn to alter the relationship between individual staff members and the teaching of specific academic disciplines. Hitherto, although Scottish professors had invariably held chairs in named subjects (professor of Greek, professor of logic, and so forth), each group of newly arrived first-year undergraduate students had been assigned a dedicated teacher called a 'regent' who would take them through the entire standard four-year arts degree course, covering each subject in turn himself. But during the first half of the eighteenth century, this system, which clearly did not rely on the instructor being a specialist in most of what he taught, was replaced by the familiar modern regime in which professors teach only the discipline in which they have been specifically trained. At Edinburgh from 1708, Glasgow by 1727 and somewhat later elsewhere, regenting was abolished, ensuring that undergraduates were for the first time taught by men who might be, and often were, active contributors to the development of their own disciplines. This meant that when students attended Glasgow between 1751 and 1763, for example, and took moral philosophy, as they were required to do, it was Smith, the professor of moral philosophy and a leading contemporary thinker in the field whose ideas were moving the subject towards legal studies in one direction and towards what we would think of as economics in the other, to whom they were directly exposed. It is easy to see why this essentially organisational change has come to be viewed as an important intellectual precondition for the elevated status and prestige of a Scottish university education by the second half of the eighteenth century. After all, it deliberately placed susceptible adolescent minds – most undergraduates were in their early to mid-teens at this juncture – in immediate contact with men who were experts in the relevant discipline and in not a few cases also strongly committed to pushing back its boundaries.

Again rather cutting against the grain of an established narrative dominated by dismal stories like the persecutions of Aikenhead and Simson, the end of the seventeenth century and the start of the eighteenth also saw significant developments in the intellectual content of university teaching that clearly do look in retrospect like early signs of the subsequent Enlightenment. Professors of mathematics, for example, had been appointed at St Andrews in 1669 and at Edinburgh in 1674, in both cases in the person of the gifted Aberdonian scholar James Gregory, who had picked up radical ideas about Galilean science at Padua and may even have discovered the infinitesimal calculus independently of Newton and Leibniz. More importantly, the undergraduate curriculum in science and mathematics was being steadily modernised. The traditional scholastic natural philosophy based on Aristotle's *Physica* and Sacrobosco's *De Sphaera* steadily gave way to topics drawn from modern observational and experimental science: Lord Bacon's inductive methodology, Sir Robert Boyle's pioneering work on the air pump and the remarkable mechanical philosophy of René Descartes all began to crop up, tellingly, in Scottish students' graduation theses through the later seventeenth century, paving the way for Newton's laws of motion and theory of gravitation also to appear by as early as 1690. But science was not the only academic field where ideas that would be critical to the Enlightenment were starting to establish themselves in the preceding period. In the moral philosophy curriculum, in many ways the centrepiece of a Scottish undergraduate degree at this time, new influences were starting to make themselves felt. A particularly important milestone was the introduction of modern textbooks in natural law written by the Dutch jurist Hugo Grotius and the German philosopher Samuel Pufendorf. The latter's work was adopted especially early at Glasgow by the professor of moral philosophy Gershom Carmichael. Carmichael's pupil and successor Hutcheson, widely seen today as the founder of the Scottish Enlightenment's philosophical tradition, also used the natural lawyers, Pufendorf above all, in his classes, which, breaking with convention, he also delivered in English rather than in Latin. The innovative philosophical sources Hutcheson used gave his teaching a new dimension, emphasising that we are social creatures endowed by our Creator not just with the power of reason but also with instinctive sociability and an in-built 'moral Sense natural to us' which guides us in our daily conduct.[6] This increasingly secular and decidedly optimistic account of human nature and of man's proper place in the world had become an accepted part of the moral philosophy curriculum by the 1730s – interestingly in Hutcheson's case in the same university in which Simson had less than a decade earlier been successfully silenced by narrow-minded clerical enemies angered by his unorthodox theological teaching. And the successful and largely unchallenged importation of natural jurisprudence into the syllabus would lead on in the next few decades to the development of the social sciences of sociology, anthropology and economics by Hutcheson's pupil and successor Smith at Glasgow and by other admirers like Ferguson and later Stewart at Edinburgh.

The Triumph of Liberty

For all these reasons we should probably think of the universities by the 1740s, as the Scottish Enlightenment decisively emerged to view, not as engaged in a sudden dramatic escape from a totally benighted past but rather as building more selectively on some crucial foundations that had already been laid over the previous sixty or even eighty years while also finally rejecting other legacies, still potent even in the relatively recent past, which it was now at last accepted had been both harmful and retrograde. Central to this process was clearly a shift in attitudes towards intellectual inquiry as such which cannot sensibly be distinguished from wider developments in Scottish culture and Scottish society at this time. As it happens, the nature and the proximate causes of this changing outlook can be reasonably easily identified. For what characterised Scottish intellectual life by mid-century was a growing openness to new ideas and to speculation, even to what contemporaries called 'free thinking' (meaning potentially difficult philosophical and theological arguments in particular), that would definitely not have been possible in the time of Aikenhead back in the 1690s. It was this, for example, that allowed the increasingly secularised moral philosophy of Hutcheson, disseminated by teaching and publication between the 1720s and his death in the 1740s, to become so influential among educated Scots both inside the universities and out. After all, these were in many ways subversive ideas, certainly in relation to the pre-existing Calvinist world-view, and were rightly seen by orthodox-minded clergymen as forming an integral part of the new thinking that we would today want to call the Enlightenment, with its trademark optimism about the human understanding of a mechanical and material universe, explicable in terms of natural forces, designed and watched over by a benevolent Creator-God and inhabited by sociable and well-meaning creatures.

If we want to see how normal these innovative philosophical notions had become in the universities by the 1750s, how worried about this development were the more doctrinaire, old-fashioned clergy, but also how increasingly limited were their options for resisting it, we can do no better than inspect a satirical counter-blast penned by John Witherspoon, later President of the College of New Jersey (today Princeton University) and a signatory of the Declaration of Independence, but at this time merely an anxiously conservative cleric from Paisley in the west of Scotland. This text beautifully captures the core philosophical tenets of the Enlightenment by presenting them in the form of a modern religious creed, as though all of the most progressive trainee clergymen coming through the Scottish universities would now be comfortable reciting them:

> I believe in the beauty and comely proportions of Dame Nature, and in almighty Fate, her only parent and guardian, for it hath been most graciously obliged (blessed be its name,) to make us all very good.
>
> I believe that the universe is a huge machine, wound up from everlasting by necessity, and consisting of an infinite number of links and chains, each in a progressive motion towards the zenith of perfection, and meridian of glory; that I myself am a little glorious piece of clockwork, a wheel within a wheel, or rather a pendalum [sic] in this grand machine, swinging hither and thither by the different impulses of fate and destiny; that my soul (if I have any) is an imperceptible bundle of exceeding minute corpuscles, much smaller than the finest Holland sand; and that certain persons, in a very eminent station, are nothing else but a huge collection of necessary agents, who can do nothing at all.
>
> I believe that there is no ill in the universe, nor any such thing as virtue absolutely considered; that those things vulgarly called sins, are only errors in the judgment, and foils to set off the beauty of nature, or patches to adorn her face; that the whole race of intelligent beings, even the devils themselves, (if there are any,) shall finally be happy; so that Judas Iscariot is by this time a glorified saint, and it is good for him that he hath been born.
>
> In fine, I believe in the divinity of L. S———, the saintship of Marcus Antoninus, the perspicuity and sublimity of A———e, and the perpetual duration of Mr. H———n's works, notwithstanding their present tendency to oblivion. Amen.[7]

This parody of Enlightenment truisms is, then, a measure of just how far Scotland, its intellectual culture and its academic life had come in the sixty years since Aikenhead's public hanging: satire such as this, rather than the rope, was now the most effective weapon available to disgruntled religious traditionalists like Witherspoon troubled by the creative new thinking that swirled threateningly around them.

There is also plenty of other evidence that a more tolerant intellectual environment had emerged inside and outside the universities by the middle years of the century. A strong indication of changed attitudes was the failure of two famous attempts by elements in the kirk to censure two Scottish philosophers, neither of them a professor but both of them closely engaged with the philosophical debates underway in the universities, for their 'free thinking'. In 1755, the initial target was Lord Kames, the kind of eighteenth-century man for whom one really needs a list in order to do justice to his many different roles – senior judge, legal philosopher, historian, writer on education, literary theorist, art critic, landowner, agricultural improver, raconteur, wit, claret drinker (including, notoriously, when sitting in judgment in his own court). It was Kames' recently published *Essays on the Principles of Morality and Natural Religion* (1751) that led to attempts to have him excommunicated for heresy – essentially he had taken too deterministic a view of human agency and so had clearly trespassed onto probably the most hotly disputed theological terrain for traditional Calvinist doctrine. What is most significant about the controversy, however, is not that Kames was challenged but that he had felt able to publish his opinions in the first place and that his opponents in Scotland's Established Church then failed to carry the day with their attempt to punish him for his temerity.

The second illustrative case has broadly the same implications. This involved Hume, the greatest living Scottish philosopher, whose religious doubts and waspishly anti-clerical sentiments were already well-known. In 1755–6 he too was the subject of an attempt by orthodox clergymen to have him censured by the kirk and this too fizzled out embarrassingly. Of course, by this time Hume himself had actually failed to be appointed to the chair of moral philosophy at Edinburgh in 1744 when the successful candidate had turned out to be an undistinguished man who just happened to be the nephew of the leader of Edinburgh's town council in whose gift appointments at the university lay; and we know that it was the local clergy who, in a hostile statement to the councillors, effectively blackballed Hume's candidacy with a deathly phrase – 'On account of his principles', meaning, of course, his provocative philosophical claims.[8] Appointing an atheist to teach philosophy in a Scottish university, and thus to be responsible for educating the next generation of Presbyterian clergymen on questions of morality and metaphysics, was still understandably too much for the kirk and its defenders to bear at this time. Yet that Hume was otherwise able to prosper, to publish, to live freely and indeed be a good friend of many of the younger and more liberal-minded clergy and academics of his day is another strong indication of just how intellectually tolerant parts of Scottish society were becoming by the middle years of the eighteenth century.

The proximate cause of this transformation in attitudes, with religiously motivated disputes becoming increasingly confined to questions of theology and church government which in any case progressively mattered less and less to non-clerical thinkers and teachers with much broader philosophical preoccupations, is also clear enough. The umbilical connection between the Scottish universities and the kirk means that growing intellectual freedom for academic and scholarly endeavour can be explained directly by changes in the internal character of the Established Church. By 1771, the Scottish novelist and former Glasgow medical student Tobias Smollett could write the following in his last great novel, *Humphry Clinker*: 'the kirk of Scotland, so long reproached with fanaticism and canting, abounds at present with ministers celebrated for their learning, and respectable for their moderation'.[9] The change to which Smollett was alluding had several roots but probably the most important had been the slow but relentless effect of the parliamentary union with England in 1707. It was this that subjected the kirk to Westminster legislation such as the Toleration Act of 1712 which effectively ended the official persecution of non-Presbyterian Protestants in Scotland, forcing the ruling Presbyterian party to accept unprecedented religious diversity whether they liked it or not. Legislation quickly imposed from

London – unpopular with many Presbyterians at the time it has to be said – also allowed Scottish landowners and town councils to appoint their own preferred candidates as parish clergymen which in many cases meant the insertion of more easy-going clerics with a liberal education and a talent for genteel conversation, especially with the lay elite, in place of the rough-tongued Calvinist demagogues previously favoured by many ordinary parishioners. The resulting gradual change of clerical personnel, which eventually saw important Enlightenment figures like the Edinburgh-educated dramatist and historian John Home inducted at Athelstaneford in East Lothian and the gossipy diarist Alexander 'Jupiter' Carlyle, another admiring former Glasgow student of Hutcheson's, installed at nearby Inveresk, evidently altered the internal culture of the kirk in striking ways. Instead of the traditional Scottish style of preaching, proverbially comprising thunderous denunciations of immorality from the pulpit which substantial numbers of the people in the pews actually seemed to like, this new breed of minister, polite and scholarly in equal measure, came to be known as Moderates – not least because they tended to have flexible theological opinions as well as exhibiting a far greater tolerance of difference and dissent in others. Their sermons, too, rather than hurling down fire and brimstone onto the heads of the congregation for two or three hours every Sunday, tended more often to amount to what James Boswell, with his well-known ambivalence about the strict Calvinist doctrines in which he had been steeped, half-mocked as mere 'comfortable answers'.[10]

The reign of the Moderate party in the kirk, which continued until well into the nineteenth century, had numerous implications for the nature of the Scottish universities through their golden age. At its worst, the Moderate hegemony, and the battle to ensure that jobs in the more prestigious parishes and in the universities fell into the hands of suitably progressive men of enlightened views rather than those of blinkered old-school zealots, made academic life even more nepotistic than it would otherwise have been. At Edinburgh, notwithstanding the official function of the town council in making appointments, the Moderate clergy, having captured the institution by mid-century, were determined not to relax their grip. Under William Robertson, their recognised leader who also secured the position of principal of the university in 1762, it was dominated by intellectually distinguished sympathisers. One was Ferguson, unkindly known as 'Bute's Ferguson' because he had previously served as tutor to the sons of the first Scottish Prime Minister: a former army chaplain who had actually renounced his clerical vocation in order to pursue a career as a man of letters, Ferguson was initially maintained by his powerful friends in the chair of natural philosophy until such time as the more suitable professorship of moral philosophy could be procured.[11] Another beneficiary was Hugh Blair, a prominent local clergyman in the capital but also Edinburgh's professor of rhetoric and Scotland's leading literary critic. Later the same nexus of overlapping personal connections between congenial men of known reliability yielded up Dugald Stewart, Ferguson's pupil and successor as professor of moral philosophy from 1785 and subsequently the great publicist of Scottish Enlightenment ideas (not least through the pages of the Edinburgh-based *Encyclopaedia Britannica* and his biographies of Smith, Robertson and Reid). Stewart was the son of another professor, Matthew, who had succeeded Newton's great disciple Colin Maclaurin in the mathematics chair in 1747 (a position Dugald himself would initially fill following his father's retirement in 1775) and had earlier studied under Hutcheson at Glasgow. It was St Andrews, however, by some distance the smallest and most enclosed of Scotland's academic communities, which, uniting the kirk, the professoriate and the political authorities in what disgusted Evangelicals regarded as an unholy Trinity of corruption, witnessed the worst excesses of Moderatism. Indeed under Principal George Hill, leader of the party after Robertson's retirement in 1780 as well as the controlling influence in the University of St Andrews between 1791 and his death in 1819, six of the thirteen professors were at one stage members of his own extended family. The joke that went the rounds at the time, long remembered locally, was that every Sunday morning in chapel the principal would presumably favour a reading from Psalm 121: 'I lift up mine eyes unto the hills, from whence cometh my help'.[12]

The Universities and the World

If Moderatism was deplorably incestuous, however, it was also undoubtedly beneficial to intellectual freedom in Scotland's universities. For it helped to underwrite the transformation in attitudes towards speculative thinking that definitively separated the age of Aikenhead from that of Hume. It was, after all, the Moderates in the kirk, shrewdly led by Robertson, who were able to prevent the more militant clergy clipping the wings of Kames and Hume in the mid-1750s. It was also the Moderates who, with their commitment to modern educational practices, drove through many of the more interesting and forward-looking changes that now took place in the universities, especially in the moral philosophy curriculum. We have already noted some of the related intellectual developments that were happening and to which scholars still look back today – Smith's work on economics, Ferguson's early explorations in sociology, and so forth, which were pushing the traditional syllabus in all sorts of interesting directions. But in addition whole new academic disciplines were being carved out in Scotland after 1750, and not least again by professors who were also Moderate clergymen. For example, Blair at Edinburgh and his colleague (and cousin) Robert Watson, professor of rhetoric and eventually principal at St Andrews, were busy shifting the focus of their subject from its traditional humanist emphasis on the spoken word in pulpit and courtroom oratory to what we would now recognise as literary criticism, concentrating instead therefore on the use of language in written texts: indeed, one of the more ironic achievements of the Scottish universities in the first century after the Union was effectively the invention of nothing less than English literature as an academic subject. History too featured increasingly in the university curriculum, with dedicated professors like William Wight at Glasgow, Alexander Fraser Tytler at Edinburgh and Hugh Cleghorn at St Andrews offering lecture courses in subjects like 'universal history' or 'general history' by the second half of the century.

Medicine was an especially important aspect of academic provision, especially at Glasgow and Edinburgh, for the wider reputation of the universities. The latter had acquired a proper medical school in 1726, Scotland's first, and, linked to other institutions in the city like the Physic Garden, the Royal Colleges of Surgeons and Physicians and the new Royal Infirmary which served as a teaching hospital from 1729, this provided the basis for the university's rapidly growing profile in medical research and education. So widely recognised was its work in the broad fields of science and medicine that by the late 1780s Thomas Jefferson, no mean judge of intellectual distinction, was able to declare that 'no place in the world can pretend to a competition with Edinburgh'.[13] This eminence did not, however, rest on infrastructure alone: individuals, in the form of distinguished professors, also brought lustre to academic medicine in the Scottish capital. Ferguson's cousin Joseph Black was the chemist who first explained the phenomenon of latent heat and also became the first man to isolate carbon dioxide (or 'fixed air' as it was known in his day). But it was as an educator, as professor of medicine first at Glasgow and then at Edinburgh, that he exercised the greatest influence. His contemporary William Cullen, who made advances as a physicist in the development of artificial refrigeration and then published widely in physiology and the classification of diseases, also made the same professional journey between the two great medical schools of Glasgow and Edinburgh and ended up recognised as a founder of modern chemistry. Even here, however, blatant nepotism was in evidence, as three successive men called Alexander Monro – father, son and grandson, and distinguished in the vocabulary of the classically trained academic community of the time as *primus, secundus* and *tertius* – held the Edinburgh chair of anatomy for 126 years until as late as 1846. It was even said that all three used the same lecture notes, literally handed down with the job, and that consequently, in the early nineteenth century, students of the third incumbent would actually hear him at the appropriate moment in the course intone the profoundly incongruous words 'When I was a student at Leiden in 1719'.[14] Attending *tertius*'s classes, which were definitely not to his liking, may well have helped change the mind of one scientifically minded young English student about pursuing an orthodox career in medicine – a most peculiar instance of a Scottish university education having truly seminal consequences: 'I dislike him & his Lectures so much', wrote Charles Darwin to his sister in 1826, 'that I cannot speak with decency about them'.[15] But there can be no doubt that the seemingly interminable Monro hegemony, for all Darwin's distaste for the lecturing performances of the last of the trio, did lend Edinburgh medicine genuine intellectual substance throughout this period. All were recognised by their contemporaries as scholars and scientists as well as teachers. *Primus*, for example, added significantly to the understanding of the structure of the bones, while *secundus* did major work on the nervous system and identified the part of the brain still known as the foramen of Monro. Even *tertius*, trading on the hallowed family name, published a number of influential anatomical texts.

Medicine, more than any other academic field, was also what allowed the

Scottish universities in the second half of the eighteenth century to become increasingly cosmopolitan institutions, particularly in their student intakes. Already by the 1760s the anatomy theatre at Edinburgh needed to be rebuilt to accommodate additional spectators, now drawn not just from Scotland but also from Ireland and England, and with other students coming from as far afield as America, Russia, Scandinavia and Portugal. By the turn of the nineteenth century hundreds of American doctors had also been trained in Scotland's universities and not a few of them became involved in the American Revolutionary War. Jefferson's praise for an Edinburgh scientific education in particular has already been mentioned, but Benjamin Franklin was as impressed by the sheer breadth of academic excellence that was attracting more and more students to Scotland, writing in 1771 that Edinburgh possessed 'a set of as truly great Men, Professors of the several Branches of Knowledge, as have ever appeared in any Age or Country'.[16] Because of this widening student catchment by the end of the eighteenth century, there is much that could be said about the posthumous impact of the Scottish Enlightenment deep into the nineteenth, mediated through its universities to the future leaders, innovators and opinion-formers of British society. The roll call of eminent non-Scottish alumni includes many talented medical men whose primary achievements came in other areas, like Peter Mark Roget, the notable lexicographer and scientist from a Swiss background who graduated MD at Edinburgh in 1798 and went on to play a prominent role in the intellectual life of both Manchester and London, and his friend and contemporary the progressive educationist George Birkbeck, whose family were actually Yorkshire Quakers. As importantly, some of the English physicians who trained at Edinburgh in the early years of the nineteenth century, like Thomas Addison from Newcastle upon Tyne, who discovered the degenerative disease of the adrenal glands that still bears his name, and Thomas Hodgkin from London, who was the first to describe the eponymous lymphoma, went on to secure permanent places in medical history. Edinburgh also educated some of the great mid-Victorian statesmen like Lord John Russell and Lord Palmerston, both of them Prime Minister twice, and other heavyweight politicians like the third Marquess of Lansdowne, who served as Home Secretary and Chancellor of the Exchequer and sat in Cabinet for nearly half a century: as young blue-blooded aristocrats, all three men had been despatched north by ambitious parents to imbibe the arts curriculum and learn moral philosophy at the feet of the incomparable Stewart.

This opening up of the Scottish universities to a much broader non-Scottish clientele is an interesting feature of the period not least because these institutions had always hitherto been, and would actually long remain (as they still are to an extent even today), markedly regionalised in their domestic recruitment patterns, certainly much more so than the two ancient English universities. Glasgow, for instance, tended to take more of its Scottish students from the west coast like Smollett and from Ulster like the young Hutcheson whose Presbyterian family had strong Scottish roots. For its part Edinburgh recruited more of its Scottish matriculants from the south-east of the country like Hume, Robertson and Blair, as well as, in a later generation, the future literary giant of the nineteenth century, Walter Scott, who hailed from the Borders. St Andrews, meanwhile, performed the same function in Fife, Angus and Perthshire, with recruits like the young Ferguson and also James Wilson, the latter from the nearby village of Ceres but later a citizen of Philadelphia and a prominent signatory of the Declaration of Independence, while the Aberdeen colleges drew particularly heavily from the North-East and the Highlands, educating promising students from their own hinterland like the future philosophers Reid and James Beattie and the young poet and literary fraudster James Macpherson. One striking oddity of the universities through their golden age was therefore that, particularly in Glasgow and Edinburgh, they were becoming perceptibly much more internationalised because of their growing fame even as they also never stopped playing their traditional local roles. At Glasgow, for example, in the late 1760s and early 1770s, a remarkable 28 per cent of matriculants actually came from outside the country, a large proportion of them medical students.[17] Intriguingly the proportion of non-Scots at Glasgow is almost exactly the same today, nearly two-and-a-half centuries later, at a little over 28 per cent in academic year 2010–11.[18] Allowing for the facts that today's non-Scots more often come from outside the British Isles and even from outside Europe than they did in the late eighteenth century and that fewer are now pursuing a medical education, it is nonetheless a striking thought that, because of the reputation it had earned in the era of the Scottish Enlightenment, the country's second-largest university was statistically almost as successful in recruiting students from outside Scotland as it is in our own time, in an age that we normally like to imagine is distinguished by unprecedented globalisation and unparalleled multiculturalism.

This is also an important reason why the Scottish student population as a whole, another measure of the universities' success in many accounts, probably trebled through the eighteenth century from around 1,000 to about 3,000 individuals at any one time.[19] Edinburgh grew most, from a student body of around 400 to more like 1,400, and its expansion and financial position even justified in 1789 the building of what was then called New College on South Bridge, today known as Old College.[20] St Andrews, however, had grave problems through the same period: with its early-seventeenth-century heyday long behind it, the institution, in its isolated semi-rural location, shorn of its significant link to the country's principal archdiocese by the Revolution of 1690 and also without any of the newly fashionable medical training to offer, struggled to recruit students (or for that matter high-flying staff); and, indeed, in 1747 what even its own professors felt it necessary to call 'This sinking, though once flourishing University' was forced to implement the merger of two of its historic colleges, St Leonard's and St Salvator's, to create the United College, and, in desperate need of cash, to sell off almost all of the historic site of the former.[21] The fate of the country's oldest university in this period is thus an important reminder that the narrative of glittering academic success in Scotland in the age of the Enlightenment is once again less straightforward than the conventional historiography, dominated by the themes of protean intellectual achievement and institutional expansion, has sometimes implied.

Remembering the Golden Age

One last piece of contemporary witness testimony affirms the extraordinary vigour and academic excellence of the Scottish universities as a whole in the age of the Scottish Enlightenment. It comes from the memoirs of Lord Cockburn, a distinguished judge and politician of the first half of the nineteenth century who was an undergraduate at Edinburgh in the 1790s, slightly after Scott and shortly before Lansdowne. Fifty years later, when looking back on his own youth, Cockburn described the impact that his university experience had had upon him. Interestingly he placed the emphasis not just on the formal teaching (although that was important: he had warm words for several of his old professors, particularly Stewart's exhilarating lectures) but also on the active involvement in extra-curricular student discussion and debating societies that marked out the intensely aspirational intellectual culture of the universities of the period. Here is what Cockburn claimed:

> These institutions, which when ill-managed are the hot-beds of conceit and petulance, and when managed tolerably well are powerfully productive of thought, of talent, and even of modesty, were in full operation at this time in the College of Edinburgh. It was a discussing age.

One of these societies, of which he was a member, he recalled:

> met in Playfair's class room, which was then the great receptacle of youthful philosophers and orators. There were more essays read, and more speeches delivered, by ambitious lads, in that little shabby place, than in all Scotland . . . No part of my training did me so much good . . . It was here that I got my first notions of composition and debate, and that delightful feeling of free doubting and independent discussion, so necessary for the expansion and manliness of young minds.[22]

Even allowing for the understandable nostalgia of old age, if even half of what Henry Cockburn claimed had been experienced by students like his younger self at Edinburgh at the end of the eighteenth century was true, we can be sure that this was a very different era indeed from that in which Thomas Aikenhead, almost exactly one hundred years earlier, had lived and spoken and died. And it was, more than anything else, as the Scottish universities' transformation had amply proven, an age of Enlightenment.

Notes

1. Voltaire, *Philosophical Letters*, trans. Ernest Dilworth (Macmillan, 1961), p. 25.
2. Ronald G. Cant, *The University of St Andrews: A Short History* (Oliver and Boyd, 1946), p. 77.

3. *Celebrated Trials and Remarkable Cases of Criminal Jurisprudence from the Earliest Records to the Year 1825* [ed. George Henry Borrow], 6 vols (Knight & Lacey, 1825), vol. 3, p. 268.
4. Anne Skoczylas, *Mr Simson's Knotty Case: Divinity, Politics and Due Process in Early Eighteenth-Century Scotland* (McGill-Queens University Press, 2001), p. 304.
5. James, Viscount Stair, *The Institutions of the Laws of Scotland*, 2nd edn (Heirs of Andrew Anderson, 1693), p. 2.
6. Francis Hutcheson, *An Inquiry into the Original of Our Ideas of Beauty and Virtue. . .*, 3rd edn (R. Ware et al., 1753), p. 219.
7. *The Works of John Witherspoon, D.D. . . .*, 9 vols (Ogle & Aikman, 1804–5), vol. 6, pp. 185–6.
8. Alexander Broadie, *A History of Scottish Philosophy* (Edinburgh University Press, 2009), p. 148.
9. Tobias Smollett, *The Expedition of Humphry Clinker* (S. Doig, 1811), p. 260.
10. Marvin B. Becker, *The Emergence of Civil Society in the Eighteenth Century: A Privileged Moment in the History of England, Scotland and France* (Indiana University Press, 1994), p. 154.
11. David Kettler, *The Social and Political Thought of Adam Ferguson* (Ohio State University Press, 1965), p. 55.
12. Bruce Lenman, 'From the Union of 1707 to the franchise reform of 1832', in R. A. Houston and W. W. J. Knox (eds), *The New Penguin History of Scotland* (Allen Lane, 2001), pp. 276–354 (quotation at p. 309).
13. *Papers of Thomas Jefferson*, ed. Julian P. Boyd, 33 vols [to date] (Princeton University Press, 1950–), vol. 15, p. 204.
14. Arturo Castiglioni, *A History of Medicine*, ed. and trans. E. B. Krumbhaar, 2nd edn (Alfred A. Knopf, 1947), p. 594.
15. Keith Thomson, *The Young Charles Darwin* (Yale University Press, 2009), p. 35.
16. Stanley Finger, *Doctor Franklin's Medicine* (University of Pennsylvania Press, 2006), p. 142.
17. R. A. Houston, *Scottish Literacy and the Scottish Identity: Illiteracy and Society in Scotland and Northern England, 1600–1800* (Cambridge University Press, 1985), p. 245.
18. Taken from 'HE students at the Scottish universities, 2010–11: Institution by domicile'. Available at https://heidi.hesa.ac.uk (accessed 21 December 2012).
19. David Allan, *Scotland in the Eighteenth Century: Union and Enlightenment* (Longman, 2002), p. 122.
20. Roger Emerson, *Academic Patronage in the Scottish Enlightenment: Glasgow, Edinburgh and St Andrews Universities* (Edinburgh University Press, 2008), p. 211.
21. Cant, *St Andrews*, p. 88.
22. Henry Cockburn, *Memorials of His Time* (A. & C. Black, 1856), p. 27.

Bibliography

Cant, Ronald G., 'The Scottish universities and Scottish society in the eighteenth century', *Studies on Voltaire and the Eighteenth Century* 58 (1967), 1953–66.
Cant, Ronald G., 'The origins of the Enlightenment in Scotland: The universities', in R. H. Campbell and Andrew S. Skinner (eds), *The Origins and Nature of the Scottish Enlightenment* (John Donald, 1982), pp. 42–64.
Crawford, Robert (ed.), *The Scottish Invention of English Literature* (Cambridge University Press, 1998).

Emerson, Roger L., 'Scottish universities in the eighteenth century, 1690–1800', *Studies on Voltaire and the Eighteenth Century* 167 (1977), 453–74.

Emerson, Roger L., *Professors, Patronage and Politics: The Aberdeen Universities in the Eighteenth Century* (Aberdeen University Press, 1993).

Emerson, Roger L., *Academic Patronage in the Scottish Enlightenment: Glasgow, Edinburgh and St Andrews Universities* (Edinburgh University Press, 2008).

Sher, Richard B., *Church and University in the Scottish Enlightenment* (Edinburgh University Press, 1985).

7

Legal Education, 1650–1850

John Finlay

Introduction

This chapter outlines the history of legal education in Scotland with particular focus on the period 1650–1850 and the contrasting but complementary educational history of the two branches of the legal profession. Practising lawyers, as well as learning a body of substantive rules and principles, needed training in how to apply their theoretical knowledge by using court procedure or preparing documents capable of achieving desired legal effects.

From the sixteenth century, two branches of the profession began to develop. In Scotland's supreme courts, the Court of Session and High Court of Justiciary, advocates enjoyed a monopoly right of audience while their clerks (and, later, writers to the session) took responsibility for managing legal actions. The lower branch of the profession consisted of writers and procurators in the inferior courts, principally the local sheriff, burgh and commissary courts, across the country. In Edinburgh, some writers acted as agents in the management of Court of Session cases without formal licence until, from 1754, the lords of session began formally to admit 'agents or solicitors' to manage cases in their court and, like the Faculty of Advocates and the Society of Writers to the Signet, these men formed themselves into a society which became the Society of Solicitors to the Supreme Courts. Similarly, in the inferior courts, local societies of practitioners also emerged and these bodies all had an influence on educational standards within the profession.

Writers to the signet had a slightly ambivalent position. Some of them managed legal actions but not all. As members of the College of Justice in Edinburgh, they enjoyed privileges along with members of the Faculty of Advocates which set them apart from those who practised in the inferior courts. At the same time, they dominated the art of conveyancing (the transferring of interests in land) and were entitled to draft documents under the signet which were used generally in legal practice across the country. These activities involved them in correspondence with local writers. Despite the individual wealth of some writers to the signet, by the later seventeenth century it was the Faculty of Advocates which conceived of itself as an exclusive and elite body whose members alone constituted the upper branch of the profession. By 1700, the advocates were increasingly marked out by their distinctive and expensive university training.

The dichotomy between academic learning and the transmission of practical knowledge lies at the heart of legal education and reflects the different approach taken in each branch of the profession. At one extreme lay the employment of counsel in the supreme courts, who relied on rhetorical skills in oral debate and wrote reasoned arguments which drew liberally from texts and commentaries on Roman law as well as sources of Scots law. Local writers and notaries, in the course of their business in the inferior courts, or in drafting documents or managing funds, needed procedural knowledge and book-keeping skills alongside an understanding of substantive Scots law. The difference lay in status and in the worlds they inhabited. Advocates, writers and agents in the rarefied atmosphere of the Court of Session needed a higher level of training from those practising in the more mundane, but still quite complex, world of the local inferior courts.

Medieval University Education

Scots were attracted to the late medieval continental universities which offered them an education in civil (Roman) law and canon law. Teaching in both subjects was organised around textual exegesis. In the case of civil law, the key texts were the *Digest*, a large compilation of updated classical texts which was promulgated by the emperor Justinian in AD 533, and the *Institutes*, a short introductory text intended for use in the universities of Justinian's empire. Roman law teaching therefore revolved around fixed texts, later known as the *Corpus Iuris Civilis* (which included also Justinian's *Codex*, a collection of late Roman legislation).

In contrast, canon law, the law of the Western church, was still developing. An important text was Gratian's *Decretum*, produced and revised early in the twelfth century, which helped to make sense of some of the key sources of early church law. The authors known as Gratian provided a rational basis for discriminating between the canons (or laws) of the various early church councils, the patristic fathers, papal decretals (or letters) and other sources of authority. With the aid of the *Decretum*, it was possible to develop a methodology for studying canon law in the universities and, as the papacy reached the zenith of its power in the thirteenth century, new decretals and canons of important church councils were added to the body of canon law.

Similar techniques were used in teaching civil law, canon law and theology, although there were some important differences. At the centre was the lecture, where texts of law were explained to students and scholarly glosses on those texts (some of which predated the universities) were discussed. A gloss was generally a marginal or interlinear addition, perhaps defining a word, raising a query or providing a cross-reference. Collections of glosses (a collection was known as an *apparatus*), carrying the authority of some respected figure, were influential in teaching. Eventually, by 1240, a standard gloss on the texts of civil law had been written, by the jurist Accursius, containing authoritative definitions. This was used thereafter in the production of more extensive treatises discussing aspects of the law at greater length. The sources of canon law were also glossed; these glosses were collected into *apparatus* and discussed in the universities as new collections of canons and decretals were compiled.

Lectures in civil law followed the order of the texts, explaining the meaning of each in turn. The professor would advance from a basic literal discussion of what the terms meant, to a more detailed analysis of their significance (*sensus*) and, going beyond mere exegesis, give his own opinion (*sententia*) on the wider importance of the text in terms of other texts and the law generally.[1] The professor gave the ordinary lectures (*lectiones ordinaria*). For this purpose legal texts were split into a number of points (*puncta*), with each one to be covered in a separate lecture. Less important points were discussed by bachelors (advanced students) in extraordinary lectures (*lectiones extraordinaria*), the reading of which was a requirement of graduation.

Repetitiones were special lectures on certain laws or doctrines which were considered a suitable starting point for a wider discussion of matters not touched upon in the ordinary lectures. A *repetitio* generally ended in a debate between the professor and his more advanced students. This might be based on a *quaestio*, a question drawn from the texts that was open to dispute, and the students would present opposing arguments to which the professor provided answers.[2] Learning law in the medieval universities was not a passive experience. An important form of practical exercise was the *disputatio* which also typically took the form of a *quaestio*. The difference between a *quaestio* in a *disputatio*, as compared to a *repetitio*, was that in the former the subject matter could not derive directly from the texts: having to be either invented or drawn from real life, it provided an exercise in legal reasoning that stood quite separate to an exegesis from the texts.[3] The *disputatio* made demands on the student's ability to think logically and to understand and reconcile legal authorities; he had to grasp the legal significance of a problem, identify and understand the relevant legal texts and exercise his judgment in applying them in order to propose a solution. The educational aim of the *disputatio*, like the moot in the English Inns of Court, was to initiate students in the relevant form of reasoning used by those practising in the courts.

The methodology of university teaching created what legal historians refer to as legal science. It developed an awareness of dealing with the sources of the *ius commune*, a term generally translated as 'the learned law' to differentiate it from the English idea of a common law in the territorial sense of a law common to the subjects of a particular kingdom. Although the nuances of the term are still debated, the *ius commune* reflected a common inheritance, the principles and ideas of the Roman law, which were influential in developing canon law and the legal procedure of both church and secular courts. This internationalisation of legal studies was of profound importance because, as we shall see, continental ideas, about law and legal education, permeated the Scottish experience for centuries.

Foreign Educational Influences

By the fifteenth century, Scots had long favoured French universities, especially Orléans, for legal education. This is clear from its popularity amongst the general procurators licensed to appear in the College of Justice at its foundation in Edinburgh in 1532. A Scot, William Barclay (1546–1608), even became professor of law at Angers in the seventeenth century. Scots did study law elsewhere, including Louvain and Italian and German universities. For example, the late-sixteenth-century figures Sir James Balfour and Sir John Skene both studied in Wittenberg. Thomas Craig (d. 1608), the best-known Scots advocate of his age, studied at the University of Paris. Craig's fame primarily rests on a treatise, printed under the title *Jus Feudale* in 1655, which influenced the thinking of generations of Scots lawyers. Craig and Skene fell firmly within a legal humanist tradition, characterised by an historical and philological approach to the sources and language of law, associated so strongly with sixteenth-century legal scholarship in France that it is described as the *mos gallicus*.[4] In contemporary Scottish legal literature, examples of French influence can be traced. By the 1670s, however, it was the Dutch universities, following in the same humanistic tradition, which began to emerge as the favoured destination for Scots students.

France and the Netherlands were favoured because Scotland's own universities never enjoyed sufficient financial endowments to sustain the teaching of law. Efforts were certainly made in St Andrews, Glasgow and King's College, Aberdeen, to provide such teaching. In Glasgow, this had failed before 1577, while in Aberdeen the posts of canonist and civilist were abolished at the end of the sixteenth century. St Andrews, apparently in the strongest position to continue offering legal education, ceased to teach law in the seventeenth century. A civilist (i.e. a teacher of Roman law) was again appointed regularly from 1619 in Aberdeen but actual teaching was intermittent and apparently never extended beyond the elementary level of Justinian's *Institutes*.[5]

Money was also a factor in explaining why Dutch education became attractive to Scots in the later seventeenth century. Through innovations in teaching, Scottish students typically needed to spend no more than a year or two at a Dutch university. This was facilitated by the introduction of *compendia*, elementary student texts which were criticised by scholars, most famously Gerard Noodt at Utrecht in 1684, for the damage they inflicted on traditional Roman law studies. The German Johannes Bockelman introduced the first such work, his *Compendium Institutionum*, at Leiden where he became professor of law in 1670, and the genre quickly developed, providing students with a manual containing the essential principles and texts of Roman law.[6] Foreign study was sometimes followed by a further period of travel, perhaps experiencing the courts in London, Paris or further afield. Charles McDouall, son of Patrick McDouall of Crichen WS, is not untypical. In 1730, aged twenty, he matriculated at Leiden. By June 1732, he was in London, en route for Paris, to commence a tour of France.

Returning to Scotland in January 1733, he petitioned for entry to the Faculty of Advocates the following June and was admitted in January 1734.[7]

Personal correspondence presents a vivid picture of the experiences of Scottish students in the Netherlands. Legal education was often generational and an aspiring law student, before setting out, might receive advice from his father, uncle or a family friend. This would help him identify which legal commentaries to acquire and which professors to attend. Accessing the Dutch book market was important due to the relative difficulty in obtaining texts in Scotland, and educational and learned literature from those teaching in Dutch universities had a long-lasting influence on Scottish legal thought.

Professors in the Netherlands traditionally gave a prescribed number of public lectures (*praelectiones*). These were on the sources of Roman law and they followed a traditional pattern and order. Students did not have to pay to attend these lectures but they did pay to attend private colleges (*collegia privata*) which, by 1700, had become the dominant form of instruction. Taught in small groups, colleges allowed more direct contact with the professor and covered in greater depth particular areas of law. As professors drew much of their income from fees for the colleges they offered, it was in their interests to make the content as relevant as possible to legal practice. Thus alongside colleges in civil law there might be offered also colleges in feudal law, criminal law, natural law (particularly Grotius) and aspects of legal procedure.[8]

Scottish students focused on Roman law and natural law, although they also sought to learn languages and to engage in gentlemanly pursuits. Nor did they neglect other aspects of law. In January 1700, Colin Campbell, studying at Utrecht, mentioned in a letter to his father, the laird of Barcaldine, the relevance of his studies in feudal law:

> I have just now a College on the feuds for now in vacans we have none on the Civil Law but I still continue my private studies. I find the feuds to be very usefull for Scotland; and that it not only agrees with those holdings that have the name of it, but with the others especially in the highlands.[9]

A professor's success depended on his reputation, influenced by his written work but also by word of mouth. The noted natural lawyer Jean Barbeyrac had few students because, 'through grimace and loss of teeth', they found him difficult to follow. Kenneth Mackenzie attended a college in law given by Antonius Schulting, successor to the celebrated Johannes Voet, and a college in history taught by Pieter Burman. However, he eschewed the class on Grotius given by Philippus Reinhardus Vitriarus, referring to the seventy-two year old as having 'turned perfectly dotard'.[10]

The Faculty of Advocates and Legal Education

The interest of practising advocates in the educational standards of their Faculty was very important in developing legal education and was demonstrated in several ways. First, the Faculty was heavily involved in agitating for the foundation of a chair in law in Scotland, with pressure building towards the end of the seventeenth century. Secondly, the foundation of the Advocates Library, formally opened in 1689, saw the creation of a useful learning resource for anyone connected to a member of the bar. Individual advocates, of course, also owned their own libraries and manuscripts which they might make available to others. Recently admitted advocates were often nominated by the Faculty to act for the poor, gaining experience in pro bono causes.

The demand for domestic legal education, as an alternative to the expense of studying abroad, led to formal courses being offered, on a private basis, by members of the bar. Alexander Drummond advertised classes from 1699; John Cunningham, who died in 1710, was perhaps the most successful but it was his contemporary, John Spotswood, because of his publications, who is best known.[11] Spotswood, like Cunningham, had studied at Leiden and that experience influenced his own teaching. For Scots law he used Sir George Mackenzie of Rosehaugh's *Institutions of the Law of Scotland* (1684) as a working text and produced his own edition of that work, along with works which he himself authored on procedure and legal styles. In teaching civil law, he relied on Bockelmann's *Compendium*.

Once chairs in law were founded in Scotland, it was from the membership of the Faculty of Advocates that they were filled (except for Charles Areskine, appointed to the new regius chair of Public Law and the Law of Nature and Nations in 1707, who entered the Faculty in 1711 but probably never taught law). It has been suggested that Spotswood ceased teaching civil law after James Craig became the first professor of civil law in the University of Edinburgh in 1710, and that he may have given up teaching Scots law after Alexander Bayne was appointed to a new chair in Scots law at Edinburgh in 1722. That is not to say that private teaching entirely disappeared. The best known of the later private teachers was John Wright, whose admission to the Faculty in 1783 was controversial because of his low social status and advanced age.

The most important collective involvement of the Faculty in legal education was in the admission process. In 1664, the Faculty appointed members as examiners of new intrants for the first time, with the first recorded public examination taking place that year. By the end of the seventeenth century, there were two modes of admission to the Faculty and these are reflected in the petition for entry of Aeneas Macpherson in 1683. He noted that there

> hes beine always tua wayes of entering to bee Advocats in this Kingdome one
> by going abroad and studying the civil and common lawes (i.e. the *ius commune*)
> and another by long attendance on this House and studying the Municipall Law
> of the Nation.[12]

Entry by petition, involving private and public examinations on civil law, was regarded as the ordinary and more honourable route into the Faculty compared to the extraordinary procedure of entry by bill which, from 1688, meant an examination by the lords of session concerning a candidate's knowledge of 'the styles, the forme of process, and of the principles of our law'. From 1692, candi-dates entering by bill were remitted for examination to the dean and Faculty of Advocates (as, from 1664, had been candidates entering by examination in civil law) and, from 1696, they were to undergo a private and public trial on Scots law. In fact, entry by trial on civil law became the norm from the 1690s and was soon universally adopted. It was not until 1750 that all candidates formally had to undergo examination in Scots law.

In 1760, the Faculty, considering that it concerned their honour to have members who were 'versant in every part of Polite Literature', recommended candidates to study the law of nature and nations upon which, from 1762, the private 'examinators' were recommended to examine them. This was followed in November 1768 by a resolution recommending that students be examined on the 'history and Antiquities of the Roman Law'. These requirements echo the idea of lawyers as well-grounded Romanists which can be found, for instance, in Lord Bankton's *Institute of the Law of Scotland* published in the 1750s:

> Not only natural endowments, a liberal education, and a knowledge of the law of this country, and of the stile and forms of securities, are necessary to accom-plish an advocate; but likewise a competent theory of the civil law, which is in effect a transcript of the law of nature and nations, is requisite to complete his character; especially, since our law is, in a great measure, founded on the civil law.[13]

The public lesson or speech on civil law traditionally made by candidates to the judges and Faculty was abolished in 1814. Committees of the Faculty, how-ever, continued to issue reports on legal education. In 1817, for example, it was recommended that from 1819 candidates for the bar produce certificates of two years' attendance at a class of civil law, prior to their Faculty examination in the subject, and of one year's attendance at a Scots law class. In 1829, a Faculty committee recommended that every candidate for admission attend a course of lectures in conveyancing, such as that recently established in Edinburgh, while reiterating the need for 'a sufficient preparatory education in classical and other branches of liberal study', by which they meant studying for at least four years at university before commencing legal study. The Faculty's admission regulations were changed in 1854 but there was still a strong emphasis on general education as well as knowledge of civil and Scots law. A candidate was deemed to satisfy the first requirement if he held an MA from a Scottish university or some equivalent degree. If he did not, then he would be examined in Latin, Greek (or a further two alternative languages), ethical and metaphysical philosophy, and logic (or mathematics).[14]

Domestic Teaching

The early history of law teaching at the universities of Edinburgh and Glasgow has been given much attention in recent years and only a summary can be given here. Once it began, with the foundation of the first chair at Edinburgh in 1707, progress was rapid. By 1722, chairs existed in public law and the law of nature and nations (1707), civil law (1710), universal history (1719) and Scots law (1722). In Glasgow, the regius chair was created in 1713 with its holder, William Forbes, entitled to teach civil, feudal, canon and Scots law.

These chairs did not cause an immediate shift in the orientation of legal study. Students still travelled to the Netherlands in significant numbers and initially relatively few were attracted to Edinburgh or Glasgow. Over time, however, these chairs attracted increasing numbers of students. William Wallace, professor of Scots law at Edinburgh, reached a peak in 1766–7, with fifty-two students, although he often had significantly fewer.[15] The chairs in law should not be seen in isolation. Students, as noted above, were also expected to attend classes in universal history. The professors of moral philosophy also attracted law students. At Glasgow, Francis Hutcheson and Adam Smith covered important aspects of legal philosophy in a spontaneous style of lecturing which also became characteristic of Smith's student, John Millar, who took the regius chair in law at Glasgow in 1761.

The effort of attracting students led to a measure of innovation, especially in Glasgow which suffered through being so remote from the Court of Session. Hercules Lindsay (d. 1761) began to teach the course on Justinian's *Institutes* at Glasgow in English. His successor, Millar, also taught his course on the *Digest* in English, to the disapproval of the Faculty of Advocates. Students were examined in Latin, because the Faculty's exam was conducted in Latin, but by teaching in English, Millar permitted himself a much freer style of elucidation.

The method of teaching generally adopted by the professors was described by Bayne who followed that of his own teacher, Spotswoode. They worked through a text, by dictation, with the lecturer explaining its meaning and extending it by reference to later judicial decisions and the works of other authors (Stair's lengthy treatise being an obvious source in lectures on Scots law). Mackenzie's *Institutions* was used by Bayne who published his own notes on municipal law by way of supplement to it while, in Glasgow, William Forbes published his own *Institutions* (in two volumes, 1722, 1730). Students were to memorise essential rules and principles and would be examined regularly by the professor on their understanding of the earlier lectures. Lord Kames later criticised this form of teaching as simply 'heaping' facts upon the student without discernment or method, leading the recipients to accept them passively and unthinkingly so that 'they husband their reasoning faculty, as if it would rust by exercise'. Those teaching domestic law in the vernacular followed established methodologies in the traditional teaching of Roman law. The familiar format of 'persons, things and actions' had been adopted for 'institutional' texts. These vernacular works, expounding national law, have been identified as a distinct genre of literature across Europe, often associated, as in Scotland, with actual or intended university teaching. Devising alternative bases for structuring courses in domestic law was unnecessary and more likely to confuse students than help them.[16]

John Millar's extemporary style seems to have been one reason for his popularity, as the size of his classes was considerably larger than that of his pre-decessors. He did not dictate his lectures but worked from a scheme of notes in which he had arranged his main topics. His curriculum is known in detail from student notes, printed outlines and other sources and it is clear that he was responsive to the perceived needs of his students, offering classes in a range of subjects even including English law. Like their Dutch counterparts, and follow-ing the abolition of the system of regents, Scots professors supplemented their salaries by generating fee income and Millar prospered through offering a range of courses. He taught separate classes on the *Institutes*, the *Digest*, Scots private law, Scots public law (or 'Lectures on Government') and, in the 1790s, a course on English law. Like other Scots professors and private teachers, he advertised his teaching in the newspapers. Those who lacked distinction tended to attract small numbers of students. David Hume's appointment at Edinburgh in 1786 increased student attendance after William Wallace's numbers had fallen away; likewise, John Wilde, also in Edinburgh, attracted many more students when appointed in 1792 than had his predecessor Robert Dick.[17]

Literature

Domestic legal education required a literature capable of supporting it. This, like earlier texts of use by novices finding their way in Scots law, was produced from the profession itself. An important type of literature which circulated in manuscript was known as *practicks*. This consisted of collections of court deci-sions or digests of legal rules gathered together alphabetically under titles. They were associated with leading fifteenth- and sixteenth-century figures, including Sir James Balfour and Thomas Hope. Thomas Craig's *Jus Feudale* (written about 1600 and published in 1655) was a more comprehensive work which dealt his-torically with the principles of feudal law as understood in Scotland; Sir James Stair's *Institutions of the Law of Scotland* (written in the 1650s but first published in 1681) was an extensive philosophical treatise on Scots law, excluding crimi-nal law, while Sir George Mackenzie's *Institutions of the Law of Scotland* was a short work which fits more neatly into a European tradition of 'institutional' or educational legal works.[18]

Mackenzie's work, the most elementary, was specifically written with the education of young lawyers in mind and, as we have seen, it was used by private teachers. Spotswood published an edition with notes and also ventured into publishing his own works, such as his *Introduction to the Knowledge of the Stile of Writs* (Edinburgh, 1711), which he used in teaching. Alexander Bayne in Edinburgh also supplemented Mackenzie with notes which he published while William Forbes wrote his own *Institutions*. The most notable eighteenth-century publications were by the Edinburgh professors John Erskine, whose *Principles* (1764) and posthumous *Institutes* (1773) became standard educational texts, and David Hume, who published a treatise on criminal law in 1797.

From 1765, the professor of Scots law in Edinburgh had his own box for receiving papers in the Court of Session.[19] He was thus provided with copies of written legal arguments, a useful resource for teaching purposes alongside the briefer reported decisions of the court. Novice advocates themselves continued to learn much through observing the lords in action and through personal attachment to an established practitioner or experience in a writer's chamber. In the latter case, this would not normally involve a formal apprenticeship, although a few eighteenth-century advocates, including Henry Home and Allan Maconochie, seem to have been apprentices to writers to the signet as part of their preparation for the bar.

Writers

Writers and procurators traditionally learned through apprenticeship.[20] Some apprenticeships were more specialised than others. Admiralty practitioners, for instance, required to understand a body of law and practice that was significantly different from that encountered by most lawyers. Writers to the signet in the Court of Session had a particular expertise in conveyancing and enjoyed the exclusive right to draft certain papers under the signet, including those initiating and incidental to actions heard in the Court of Session. The learning experience of all writers and procurators, while similar in outline, varied in detail because the regulations of inferior courts were determined by judges locally. Even in the sheriff courts, despite the drafting of a common set of regulations by sheriff-deputes in 1748, procedural variations soon developed between sheriffdoms.

Many magistrates and sheriffs remitted the examination of candidates for admission to practise as procurators to a committee of existing practitioners in their court. These lawyers often formed societies, the largest and most notable being the Society of Advocates in Aberdeen, the Faculty of Procurators in Glasgow and the Society of Solicitors at Law in Edinburgh. Such societies effectively claimed a veto on the admission of candidates by asserting the right to reject them on the basis of their poor education or character. Such vetoes were challenged, sometimes successfully, in the Court of Session and other restrictive practices, such as rules insisting on the admission to a court only of those trained by an existing procurator, rather than a lawyer elsewhere, were also questioned.

Societies of lawyers carefully regulated and recorded apprenticeships. The WS Society held visitations to writers' chambers to ensure that proper practices were being followed. In 1772, it even required its members to provide information about proposed new apprentices, including details of their education, before making agreements with them. Such apprentices had to be at least fifteen years old, the same age as required by the Glasgow Faculty in its regulations in 1797. At Aberdeen, from 1792, apprenticeships had to endure for at least five years and it was provided in 1794 that no candidate be admitted a member of the Society of Advocates if aged below twenty-one or over forty. An upper age limit, which the Faculty of Advocates considered in 1785 but did not introduce, was thought to preserve respectability because older candidates may have dallied with other professions or contracted improper 'habits of Life'.[21]

Good general knowledge and, in particular, proficiency in Latin was expected of new apprentices. From June 1781, the WS Society raised expectation by requiring its apprentices to have attended two years of university classes in subjects other than law. Evidence of 'equal good education' under private tutors was initially accepted as an equivalent, but this option was removed from 1783. In Aberdeen, according to the 1799 regulations of the Society of Advocates, anyone intending to enter an apprenticeship had to certify that he had studied Latin 'under some master of character' for at least four years and had spent two sessions at a university. George Forbes, son of a local tailor, produced evidence in 1793 that he had studied five years of Latin at the local grammar school before attending 'the Mathematical class of the Marrishall [sic] College two sessions'. The Glasgow Faculty of Procurators required new apprentices to have 'studied the Latin Language in a public school or university, or with a private teacher, for at least four years'.[22]

When it came to legal training, the indentures signed between master and apprentice (or the latter's father or curators) are normally vague as to precisely what knowledge the master was expected to impart. An example is the indenture agreed in 1762 between the Perth writer James Richardson and Robert Stewart of Gairth in which James obliged himself to instruct Robert 'in the whole branches of the said vocation of writeing in sofar as he knows the same himself and the said Robert Stewart is willing & able to learn'. As an apprentice was bound to keep his master's secrets, so the master was bound, in the language commonly employed, to conceal nothing of the 'Art of and Vocation of writing' insofar as the apprentice was capable of understanding it. In the case of procurators, whose training was weighted heavily towards knowledge of legal procedure or 'form of process', attendance in the courts was an absolute requirement. The sheriff-depute of Edinburgh in 1765 demanded that new procurators in his court, before their admission, had served a three-year apprenticeship followed by a further three years' attendance on the court, a total of six years of learning and observation of practice.[23]

Examinations

Candidates for admission as procurators were normally remitted by the judge for examination of their knowledge by existing procurators. These followed a similar pattern but reflected local variation in court procedure. The Society of Solicitors at Law in Edinburgh, incorporated by royal charter in 1780, consisted of practitioners in Edinburgh's inferior courts. It required new members, such as Robert Tennent who entered in 1791, 'to undergo a private trial upon his knowledge of Stiles, Form of Proces and Principles of the Law and Scotland'.[24] The Aberdeen Society of Advocates, in its regulations in 1799, similarly required a committee of its number to 'take trial of the Candidates knowledge in the Municipal Laws, Form of Process before the Courts at Aberdeen, and Conveyancing'. New notaries public petitioned the lords of council and were examined, although not rigorously, on their notarial skills.[25]

Nothing is known of the detailed content of examinations until 1793. In that year, following a three-year apprenticeship, James Clark was examined by a committee of procurators in Dumfries and a minute of their meeting survives.[26] Clark produced a class ticket, signed by Professor David Hume in Edinburgh, indicating he had attended the Scots law class for one session. He claimed to have read four treatises on Scots law (Erskine's *Institutes* and *Principles*, Forbes' *Institutes* and Stair's *Institutions of the Law of Scotland*), together with a book on styles and another on conveyancing. He was then asked forty-eight questions on substantive law and legal procedure. These questions mainly related to evidence and procedure, natural points of emphasis in the training of court procurators. Clark was asked nothing about important aspects of property law, including leases and rights in security, or about the law of contract or bankruptcy proceedings. These were the province of the writer, rather than the procurator.

The regulations of the Glasgow Faculty provide some detail as to the conduct of examinations. The committee of examiners (a quorum being three), in examining the candidate's knowledge of legal styles, procedure and the principles of law, used Erskine's *Institutes of the Law of Scotland*, with 'each examinator being obliged to examine upon at least one different title of the text, besides being at liberty to put other pertinent questions'.[27] The candidate having withdrawn, the examiners would decide, by majority if need be, whether to report him qualified to undertake a further public examination. The format of the public examination, in the commissary court, was the same. All Faculty members in attendance had the right to vote on admission and the dean, if necessary, exercised a casting vote.

Examination papers from the nineteenth century confirm the durability of these educational trends. Local societies developed their own syllabi for apprentices and instituted annual examinations to take place at the end of each year of the apprenticeship.[28] Aside from this hands-on learning, university attendance at law classes was generally expected by the mid-nineteenth century but that had been a feature, and in the case of the WS Society, a requirement, since the middle of the eighteenth century.

University Training

WS Society members in 1753 expressed the view that it was to

> the honour and character of the Society that those who intend to follow the business of writing to the signet be trained up by a regular Education in the knowledge of the stile of writes and of the Laws of the country.[29]

To that end, they instituted a new regulation requiring

> that every Candidate for the office of Clerk to the Signet shall attend two Colleges either of the Civil or Scots law, or one of each, and shall produce a certificate from the professors of his due attendance to the commissioners before he can be admitted to trial; excepting those whose Indentures are already current or expired.[30]

This was a novelty. No previous regulation had required university attendance of any kind by writers (also known as clerks) to the signet, although the regulation came only three years after the Faculty of Advocates had required its intrants to be examined in Scots law.

In 1773, the keeper of the signet approached the professor of Scots law in Edinburgh, William Wallace, asking whether he would be prepared, in addition to his lectures on Scots law, to set aside an hour each week to examine those intending to become writers to the signet and also whether he would 'hold a College on Stiles'. The Scots law class cost three guineas and an additional sum of two guineas to cover the separate class on styles was thought appropriate. Wallace was willing but a WS Society committee, having considered the matter, rejected the idea. Apart from the additional cost, they did so

> because they considered it to be the duty of Writers to the Signet to instruct their apprentices in the several Branches of their Business, and to use all necessary means by practice, prelection and examination, to discharge their duty to their apprentices; and as the knowledge of stiles, and the framing of Deeds and securities are their proper Province, the Regulation proposed, would, in their apprehension, import an acknowledgement of their incapacity, or of a want of inclination, to do their duty.[31]

Lectures in conveyancing, under the auspices of the Society itself and without the co-operation of the university, only began in the 1790s, with Robert Bell WS the first lecturer.

Petitions for admission as procurators in Aberdeen commissary court, from 1722 to the early nineteenth century, do not include claims of attendance at university law classes until the 1790s. The difficulty of such attendance was recognised by the Society of Advocates in 1786, when it declared its desire to see the introduction of law classes in Aberdeen to avoid the expense of young men having to travel south for such education.[32] If such classes were introduced, the members resolved to apply to the judges in the local courts to have an act introduced making it necessary for every candidate seeking admission as a procurator to produce 'a Certificate of his having regularly attended for one year any Scots law class that may be established in this City or in some other university'.[33] In the absence of classes at Aberdeen, apprentices often headed to Edinburgh. An example is Arthur Dingwall Fordyce who was admitted in March 1794. He had attended the civil and Scots law classes at the University of Edinburgh and had also spent time working in the chamber of a writer to the signet.[34]

From the later eighteenth century, many seeking admission as procurators in the sheriff courts claimed to have attended university classes in Scots law. The Dumfries writer John Bushby, for example, claimed to have attended a session of lectures in Scots law at the University of Edinburgh in 1761–2.[35] Alexander Laing, in unsuccessfully pressing for his right to be admitted as a procurator before the courts in Aberdeen in 1780 (he was refused on grounds of character), produced notarial copies of certificates, from Professors Wallace and Dick in the

University of Edinburgh, 'of his having attended each of these Gentlemen thro a course of Lectures'.[36] Robert Davidson, successor to John Millar as holder of the chair of civil law in the University of Glasgow, primarily catered in his teaching to those who intended to enter the local Faculty of Procurators. He covered the basic principles of Scots Law, and rudiments of legal styles, and there was clearly a market for this. Davidson's lack of ambition and talent, however, affected his income, rendering his appointment, as he admitted in 1809, 'inferior in value to many parish churches'.[37]

Able professors, however, continued to attract students eager to join the lower branch of the profession. In his petition for admission as a procurator before the court of the sheriff of Forfarshire in 1834, Robert Kilgour stated that he had

> attended the lectures delivered by George Joseph Bell Esquire Professor of Scotch Law in the Edinburgh University during the session 1828/9; and likewise those on Conveyancing by Macvey Napier Esquire, during session 1829/30. The class tickets of these two Professors with relative certificates are herewith produced.[38]

Kilgour exemplifies the desire of many intending local procurators to spend part of their time working in Edinburgh as apprentices (in his case, as a clerk to James Burness WS), or as an advocate's clerk, to gain familiarity with Court of Session practice.

Conveyancing

Founding a chair in conveyancing proved to be a difficult process. In 1793, the WS Society appointed Robert Bell as its own lecturer in that subject and made overtures for the foundation of a university chair. This suggestion was opposed by the Faculty of Advocates. Petitions by candidates for entry to the WS Society included certificates of attendance at Bell's lectures alongside those in the class of Scots law. It was not until 1824 that a university chair in conveyancing was created and Macvey Napier, who had lectured for the WS Society since 1816, was appointed. Napier was not a distinguished practitioner but his lecturing style made him popular and his classes were thought more useful than those of his contemporary, the professor of Scots law, George Joseph Bell.[39] In Glasgow, the chair of conveyancing, established in 1861, was similarly linked to the profession through the encouragement of the Faculty of Procurators. The Faculty, like the WS Society in Edinburgh, had earlier introduced its own lecturer in conveyancing.[40] At the university, Allan Maconochie, appointed regius professor in the 1840s, taught Scots law as well as Roman law and included conveyancing in his course.[41] By the middle of the nineteenth century, writers to the signet had typically studied classes in conveyancing, Scots law and an elementary course in civil law.

Centralisation

The admission requirements for sheriff court procurators were centrally defined by the lords of session only in 1825. The lords, by Act of Sederunt, confirmed that a WS, or member of the SSC Society, or anyone who had served three years as an apprentice to either of these, had the same right to practise in any sheriff court as any procurator admitted there or his apprentice. Moreover, they required that a sheriff court procurator must be at least 'twenty one years of age and be regularly admitted by the sheriff, without prejudice to the legal rights of Chartered Bodies' (i.e. the recognised legal societies).[42] This preserved the education requirements expressed in the regulations of lawyers' societies. As well as including detailed prescriptions of legal knowledge to be met by new members, these regulations had also defined the standards of general education expected of those seeking entry as apprentices.

The Procurators' (Scotland) Act 1865 was a further limited step towards centralisation. It created a new General Council of Procurators with the power to introduce a uniform standard of qualification for those seeking to practise in the sheriff courts. In 1866, the Council drafted regulations governing common examinations to be held up to three times per year in Edinburgh, Glasgow and Aberdeen.[43] Applicants were required to have attended university classes in Scots law and conveyancing. This, however, did not remove the right of legal societies to impose entrance examinations on those seeking to become apprentices and to oblige them to undertake a curriculum of legal study with examinations at the end of each year of apprenticeship.

The Law Agents (Scotland) Act 1873 brought uniformity by effectively eliminating the role of local societies. The Act's provisions regulated admission as a law agent and specified a five-year apprenticeship (three years for graduates and certain other categories of person), a common examination and a minimum age of twenty-one. Admission was by petition to the Court of Session, and the lords of session in December 1873 laid down a detailed prescription of the topics to be examined under the heads of general knowledge and law.[44] The examination for admission was to be taken in Edinburgh, on a remit from the court. There was also an entrance examination for apprentices to law agents, unless they were graduates or otherwise exempt. This examination could be taken in Edinburgh, Glasgow, Aberdeen or Dundee; it was partly oral and partly written, and the focus was on English, arithmetic and elementary Latin.

Conclusion

By the time of university reform, and reforms to the legal profession, in the 1860s and 1870s, university classes in law and conveyancing were fully established.[45] Edinburgh's Law Faculty had six professors by 1862, including one in constitutional history and another in medical jurisprudence and police. A few intending lawyers still ventured abroad, especially to Germany where a small number of influential men, particularly future university professors, studied Roman law in the nineteenth century.[46] But a period of study at a Scottish university had long been the norm for both the upper and lower branches of the profession.

University education, however, is not the whole story. The most fundamental feature of legal education has been the necessary engagement of the profession in transmitting knowledge of Scots law from one generation to the next. This has had many aspects. In individual terms, it certainly included the professor, drawn from the bar, teaching law in the university, but it also encompassed the apprentice-master in his writing chamber and the practising advocate encouraging his younger colleagues. Collectively, legal societies determined their own educational requirements, came to establish written syllabi and appointed examiners from their number to ensure that standards were met. This engagement brought with it a professional ethos and a practical orientation in legal studies. At the summit of the profession, there was great respect for learning, and much weight was placed on the intellectual world of civilian study and classical literature. There was a breadth of engagement in learning which can make eighteenth-century arguments a joy to read. Yet, even for Edinburgh advocates, the law also functioned through the daily grind of familiarity with legal styles, court procedure, statutory requirements and the basic principles of the law of Scotland. Successful lawyers at all levels required a mix of substantive legal knowledge and practical skills which ranged from drafting to speaking and procedural strategising.

The close relationship between legal education and legal literature was an important feature which reflected and reinforced the development of Scots law itself. That literature ranged from institutional works on Scots law written by judges and university professors to practical style books and manuals for law agents written by practising law agents. In early modern Scotland men were often described as being 'bred to the Profession of the Law'. Entering legal practice was a cultural as much as an educational experience and lawyers were trained in ways of thinking and habits of behaviour intended to bring them into a professional fold. It was a conservative culture but one which nonetheless saw a great deal of development between the earliest involvement of the Faculty of Advocates in education in the 1660s to widespread university attendance seen at all levels of the profession in the nineteenth century.

Acknowledgements

The author wishes to thank the Arts and Humanities Research Council for funding which permitted him the time to write this chapter and the librarians in the Signet Library and the Royal Faculty of Procurators for access to manuscripts in their care.

Notes

1. See Antonio García y García, 'The faculties of law', in Hilde de Ridder-Symoens (ed.), *A History of the University in Europe, volume 1: Universities in the Middle Ages* (Cambridge University Press, 1992), p. 398; O. F. Robinson, T. D. Fergus and W. M. Gordon, *European Legal History* (Butterworths, 2000), pp. 45–7.
2. Kees Bezemer, *What Jacques Saw: Thirteenth Century France through the Eyes of Jacques de Révigny, Professor of Law at Orléans* (Klostermann, 1997), p. 53.
3. C. H. Bezemer, *Les Répétitions de Jacques de Révigny* (Universitaire Pers Leiden, 1987), pp. 23–4.

4. John W. Cairns, Hector L. MacQueen and David Fergus, 'Legal humanism and the history of Scots Law', in J. MacQueen (ed.), *Humanism in Renaissance Scotland* (Edinburgh University Press, 1990), p. 48.

5. See John W. Cairns, 'Academic feud, bloodfeud, and William Welwood: Legal education in St Andrews, 1560–1611, Part I', *Edinburgh Law Review* 2 (1998), 163–4. The office of canonist at Aberdeen, likewise revived, lapsed later in the later seventeenth century: see John W. Cairns, 'Lawyers, law professors, and localities: The universities of Aberdeen, 1680–1750', *Northern Ireland Legal Quarterly* 46 (1995), 304–31; Michael C. Meston, 'The civilists of Aberdeen: 1494–1995', *Juridical Review* (1995), 157.

6. John W. Cairns, 'Importing our lawyers from Holland: Netherlands influences on Scots law and lawyers in the eighteenth century', in Grant G. Simpson (ed.), *Scotland and the Low Countries, 1124–1994* (Tuckwell Press, 1996), pp. 136–53; Kees Van Strien and Margreet Ahsmann, 'Scottish law students in Leiden at the end of the seventeenth century: The correspondence of John Clerk 1694–1697', *Lias* 19 (1992), 271–330; 20 (1993), 1–65; Feenstra, Robert, 'Scottish-Dutch legal relations in the seventeenth and eighteenth centuries', in T. C. Smout (ed.), *Scotland and Europe, 1200–1850* (John Donald, 1986), pp. 128–42; Esther Mijers, *'News from the Republick of Letters': Scottish Students, Charles Mackie and the United Provinces, 1650–1750* (Brill, 2012).

7. National Records of Scotland [henceforth: NRS], GD10/1421/2/96, 102; CS1/12 fo. 22r.

8. Margreet Ahsmann, 'Teaching the *ius hodiernum*: Legal education of advocates in the Northern Netherlands (1575–1800)', *Tijdschrift voor Rechtsgeschiedenis* 65 (1997), 448.

9. NRS, GD112/39/181/3.

10. NRS, GD26/13/613/2; National Library of Scotland [henceforth: NLS], MS 1209, fo. 14; Robert Feenstra and C. J. D. Waal, *Seventeenth-century Leyden Law Professors and their Influence on the Development of the Civil Law* (North Holland Publishing, 1975), p. 12n.

11. John W. Cairns, 'John Spotswood, Professor of Law: A preliminary sketch', in William M. Gordon (ed.), *Miscellany III* (Stair Society, 1992), pp. 131–59.

12. NRS, CS1/8, fo. 41v. See the sources discussed in John Finlay, *The Community of the College of Justice* (Edinburgh University Press, 2012), Chapter 5.

13. A. Macdouall, Lord Bankton, *An Institute of the Law of Scotland*, 3 vols (Edinburgh, 1751–3; repr. Stair Society, 1993–5), IV, 3.9.

14. NLS, FR 5, fo. 163; FR 6, fo. 387; FR 8, fo. 347.

15. John W. Cairns, '"Famous as a school for law, as Edinburgh . . . for medicine": Legal education in Glasgow, 1761–1801', in Andrew Hook and Richard B. Sher (eds), *The Glasgow Enlightenment* (Tuckwell Press, 1995), p. 149.

16. See generally J. W. Cairns, 'Rhetoric, language, and Roman law: Legal education and improvement in eighteenth-century Scotland', *Law and History Review* 9 (1991), 31–57.

17. Cairns, 'Famous as a school for law', pp. 138–9, 149.

18. See John. W. Cairns, 'Institutional writings in Scotland reconsidered', *Journal of Legal History* 4 (1983), 76–117.

19. NRS, CS1/15, fo. 16r; CS1/17, fo. 170v.

20. A writer was a law agent, effectively managing business (dealing with finances, uplifting rents, drafting deeds, managing legal actions) for his client; a procurator was employed to present cases in court and formally admitted by the relevant judge for

that purpose. The two vocations were not mutually exclusive and many procurators were also notaries.

21. Signet Library [henceforth: SL], 'WS Sederunt book, 1750–84', fos 245, 371; Royal Faculty of Procurators in Glasgow [henceforth: RFPG], 'Sederunt book, 1761–1796', fo. 44; ACAA, D528/2/2, entries dated 4 and 14 Mar. 1794; NLS, FR339r/23(iii). The 1851 regulations for apprentices to the WS Society are published as an appendix to John H. Begg, A Treatise on the Law of Scotland relating to Law Agents (Bell and Bradfute, 1873), pp. 515–17.

22. SL, 'WS Sederunt book, 1750–84', fos 371, 407–8; Aberdeen City and Aberdeenshire Archives [henceforth: ACAA], D528/2/2, entries dated 19 Jun. 1799 (reg. xv); 6 Jun. 1793; RFPG, 'Sederunt book, 1761–1796', fo. 44 (see also vol. 1, fo. 193).

23. NRS, GD1/53/31, GD236/2/214; Edinburgh Central Library, 'Register of the Society of Procurators of Edinburgh', fo. 15.

24. Ibid., fo. 37.

25. ACAA, D528/2/2, entry dated 19 Jun. 1799 (reg. xxiii); on notaries, J. Finlay, The Admission Register of Notaries Public in Scotland, 2 vols (Scottish Record Society, 2012), vol. 1, pp. 4–6.

26. Hector McKechnie, 'An eighteenth-century Dumfries procurators' examination', Juridical Review 43 (1931), 337–48; NRS, GD165/box5/5/8.

27. RFPG, 'Sederunt book, 1796–1832', fo. 48.

28. Journal of Jurisprudence, 1869, pp. 182–6; Begg, Law Agents, pp. 518–19.

29. SL, 'WS Sederunt book, 1750–84', fo. 36.

30. Ibid., fo. 37.

31. Ibid., fo. 261.

32. The Faculty of Advocates used the same argument in the seventeenth century about university attendance abroad.

33. ACAA, D528/2/1, entry dated 4 Oct. 1786.

34. NRS, SC47/17/1.

35. John Finlay, 'Pettyfoggers, regulation, and local courts in early modern Scotland', Scottish Historical Review 87 (2008), 50–1.

36. NRS, CS230/L/3/1.

37. Glasgow City archive, TD219/6/414; see, generally, John W. Cairns, 'From "speculative" to "practical" legal education: The decline of the Glasgow Law School, 1801–1830', Tijdschrift voor Rechtsgeschiedenis 62 (1994), 331–56.

38. NRS, SC47/17/1, petition dated 21 Jul. 1834.

39. John W. Cairns and Hector L. MacQueen, Learning and the Law: A Short History of Edinburgh Law School (Edinburgh University Law Faculty, 2006).

40. RFPG, 'Sederunt book 1796–1832', fo. 331.

41. David M. Walker, A History of the School of Law (Glasgow University School of Law, 1990), p. 40.

42. NRS, CS1/23, fo. 112. This act was substantially repeated in 1839: NRS, CS1/26, fo. 88.

43. Anon., 'The education of Scotch lawyers', Journal of Jurisprudence 13 (1869), 179–86.

44. NRS, CS1/30, fos 465–7.

45. See A. Paterson, 'Legal education' and John W. Cairns, 'History of the Faculty of Advocates to 1900', in Thomas Smith and R. Black (eds), Stair Memorial Encyclopaedia (Butterworths, 1987–present), vol. 13, and Anon., 'Education of Scotch lawyers', 124–31, 177–87.

46. Alan F. Rodger, 'Scottish advocates in the nineteenth century: The German connection', Law Quarterly Review 110 (1994), 563–91.

Bibliography

A series of articles by John W. Cairns is essential in understanding the history of Scottish legal education, but only a few can be cited here:

Cairns, John W., 'Rhetoric, language, and Roman law: Legal education and improvement in eighteenth-century Scotland', *Law and History Review* 9 (1991), 31–58.

Cairns, John W., 'The origins of the Glasgow Law School: The professors of the civil law 1714–61', in Peter Birks (ed.), *The Life of the Law* (Hambledon Press, 1991), pp. 151–94.

Cairns, John W., 'Historical introduction', in Kenneth Reid and Reinhard Zimmermann (eds), *A History of Private Law in Scotland*, 2 vols (Oxford University Press, 2000), vol. 1, pp. 14–184.

Cairns, John W., 'The origins of the Edinburgh Law School: The Union of 1707 and the Regius Chair', *Edinburgh Law Review* 11 (2007), 300–48.

Cairns, John W., *Enlightenment, Legal Education, and Critique* (Edinburgh University Press, 2014) is a new collection of essays which may prove more accessible for the general reader.

Cairns, John W. and Hector L. MacQueen, *Learning the Law: A Short History of Edinburgh Law School* (Edinburgh University Law Faculty, 2006).

Macfarlane, Leslie J., *William Elphinstone and the Kingdom of Scotland: The Struggle for Order, 1431–1514* (Aberdeen University Press, 1985, repr. 1995).

Mijers, Esther, *'News from the Republick of Letters': Scottish Students, Charles Mackie and the United Provinces, 1650–1750* (Brill, 2012).

Robinson, Olivia F., David Fergus and William M. Gordon, *European Legal History* (Butterworths, 2000).

Van Strien, Kees and Margreet Ahsmann, 'Scottish law students in Leiden at the end of the seventeenth century: The correspondence of John Clerk 1694–1697', *Lias* 19 (1992), 271–330; 20 (1993), 1–65.

Walker, David M., *A History of the School of Law* (Glasgow University School of Law, 1990).

8

Scottish Schooling in the Denominational Era

John Stevenson

Certain issues emerged as Scottish school education developed in the nineteenth century. The most important of these were how to make adequate provision for a growing and increasingly industrialised population; who should be responsible for its provision and management; and what place religious instruction should have in the curriculum. Concern about the delivery of religious instruction was part of a broader discussion on the relationship of education and public morality. Many thought that depravity and the rising crime rate were due to the lack of education. That religion should assume such a place of importance was inevitable given the long association of church and education and the considerable powers granted to the Church of Scotland by post-Reformation legislation to supervise and inspect parish schools. This was a legacy which the church jealously guarded. In other areas of public life there were moves to deal with issues such as poor law relief and public health through boards at national and local level, and changes in the system of parish education might have followed a similar pattern but resistance, mainly from the Church of Scotland (known as the Established Church after the Disruption in 1843) but also from other denominations, prolonged this outcome. Progress was also hindered by the absence of a political party strong enough to take forward Scottish educational interests in Westminster. Some of the educational issues raised in the mid-nineteenth century are still matters of contention today, in particular the teaching of religious and moral education, and the place of faith schools.

Emerging Needs and Responses

In 1818, a House of Commons committee chaired by Whig MP Henry Brougham was appointed to report on 'charitable establishments for education in Great Britain'. This report highlighted the inadequacy of the parish school system in Scotland. Brougham's enquiry recorded 942 parish schools and 2,222 'ordinary day-schools', mostly adventure schools[1] which were often a poor substitute in terms of curriculum and standards of teaching. In almost every county in Scotland twice as many children were attending adventure schools as attended parish schools.[2] The results also showed that in many areas attendance was erratic and that many more schools were needed, particularly in the Highlands and Islands and in those places where only Gaelic was spoken. For some children it was too far to travel to the nearest parish school. In the rural districts many had to work on the crofts and farms in the summer and were only free to attend school in the winter. There was also the problem of providing education for the growing population in the new industrial towns of central Scotland where the parish system did not apply. The consequence, as Brougham's enquiry had shown, was the unregulated and haphazard growth of schools which had come into existence in an attempt to cater for the educational needs of the country.

In addition to the burgh schools and grammar schools, some of which predated the Reformation, there were subscription and endowed schools supported by individuals or public bodies. The Dick Bequest contributed to the salaries of schoolmasters in the counties of Aberdeen and Moray.[3] Charity schools in the Highlands were provided by the Society in Scotland for Propagating Christian Knowledge (SSPCK),[4] and the Gaelic School Society. Sessional schools and Sunday schools were financed and managed by the Kirk Sessions of individual congregations, often in deprived urban areas. Schools of industry for girls offered spinning and sewing, and schools were funded by the owners of mills and factories for the children of their workers. In the Glasgow Gorbals parish there was no parish school but twenty-nine other day schools and eleven evening schools taught by thirty different teachers. Fourteen belonged to the Established Church and among the others were Baptists, Methodists, a member of the Relief Church and a Roman Catholic. Of these eight had never attended a university and others only for a year or two.[5] In contrast the majority of teachers in the parish schools had had a university education. According to James Scotland, 'in 1827, when nine hundred and six parishes had schools . . . over four hundred had schoolmasters with a four-year university education'.[6] Though the academic standards in many of the adventure schools was low, these schools did provide a basic training in reading and writing which many of the poor would not otherwise have had.

During the 1820s, the situation became even more complex as different religious denominations started their own schools. The Relief Church and other dissenting churches were establishing schools. A parliamentary survey conducted in 1826 showed that in Beith twice as many scholars attended a school founded by dissenters as attended the parish school and in Dalkeith there were ten private schools run by dissenters.[7] C. G. Brown has calculated that by 1826, 38 per cent of the Scottish people were dissenters.[8] The Catholic Schools Society had been formed in 1817 and by 1824 there were Catholic schools in Glasgow, Blantyre and Paisley. Even with these additional schools many hundreds of children were still without education. The introduction to Brougham's report stated that while opportunities for education were expanding, the number of children attending schools showed no increase. It was its reliance on Brougham's findings that ultimately led to a decision by the Church of Scotland's General Assembly in 1825 to appoint a committee to supervise the building and staffing of its own schools. These 'Assembly schools', set up at first in the Highlands and Islands, but eventually throughout the whole country, were managed by a Committee on Education and financed mainly from congregational givings. This scheme not only provided additional schooling, it also helped to strengthen the church's influence and control of education in the face of rival denominations. In establishing its own schools, the church saw itself as supplementing an existing system of national education for which it had statutory managerial responsibility. In its published statistics the church often included parish schools as 'Church of Scotland schools'. The *First Book of Discipline* had laid down that ministers should regularly visit and examine parish schools. From that time parliamentary and General Assembly Acts had confirmed the statutory right of presbyterial inspection of schools and the scrutiny of schoolmasters on their appointment. By seeking to ensure that presbyteries fulfilled this role the church hoped to advance school education.

The church also realised that it could make better provision for schooling by ensuring that teachers received practical training and in 1826 it decided that for this teachers should attend the sessional school in Edinburgh which had first opened its doors in 1813 in Leith Wynd under the guidance of John Wood, an Episcopalian lawyer. In 1835, the church took over Wood's sessional school as the church's Normal Seminary in Edinburgh.[9] Inspired by the work of Thomas Chalmers, David Stow formed the Glasgow Infant School Society in 1828 and six years later George Lewis reconstituted the Infant School Society as the Glasgow Educational Society. In 1837, this body erected a new normal school at Dundas Vale. Through its say in the appointment of schoolmasters and through its teacher training the church exerted a considerable influence on education. Many Church of Scotland schools followed a curriculum similar to that offered in parish schools. In addition to the 3Rs the curriculum might include Latin and often Greek, and in some places modern languages, although the uptake of an available subject varied depending on what scholars could afford and on the teacher's ability. The small settlement of Barvas on the island of Lewis, for example, could boast of an Assembly school offering Gaelic, English, writing, arithmetic, mathematics, Latin and Greek.[10]

The Limitations of the Church's Provision

By 1834 it was clear that the General Assembly's contribution of eighty-six schools had only touched the surface of Scotland's problem. The church's Education Committee estimated that it required approximately £8,600 for the 384 schools still needed in the Highlands and Islands. Facing what was more or less a moratorium on its own schools' programme due to lack of finance, the church decided to petition the House of Commons for finance to establish schools in the Highland parishes where the government had recently allocated £50,000 to build forty-three new churches, aptly called 'Parliamentary Churches'. This move was opposed by the growing body of seceders who were demanding an end to all connection with the state and to the system of patronage.[11] The Edinburgh

Figure 8.1 Old School House, Morningside, Edinburgh. Established as a subscription school in 1823 and used until 1892. Pupils who lived some distance from the school came on horseback and tethered their horses in the land beside the school. The lane became known as Cuddy Lane and the school as the Cuddy School. Copyright the author, courtesy of Altarmotive Films, Edinburgh.

Voluntary Church Association was set up in 1833 to further this cause. The same dissenting voice was now heard in burgh councils. Until then burgh councils and the presbyteries had worked together jointly examining burgh schools, but with the passing of the Burgh Reform Act in 1833 councils became more representative of a broad range of the middle class, including dissenters and radicals critical of the church and less willing to work with it.

As the inadequacies of the educational system grew more apparent, there was increased agitation in many quarters for changes to be made. The debates surrounding the extension of the franchise and the system of patronage stimulated discussion on the role the general public, particularly the middle class, might play in public affairs. McCaffrey has argued that religion was a 'determining line along which political allegiances split. The Church [of Scotland] was suspected of being opposed to further reform . . . to those outside of it, radicalism in religion almost always went with radicalism in politics'.[12] At the end of May 1834, a letter appeared in the *Scotsman* which pointed to daily complaints about the neglect of parish schoolmasters in the discharge of their duties and suggested a radical reform of the method of appointing and removing them and giving a greater say to families and the local community. This would have meant a diminution of the church's influence. In defence of the existing system and in support of the church, in June 1834 J. C. Colquhoun, MP for Dunbartonshire, brought a Bill to the House of Commons to increase the government's provision for Scottish parish schools. The sum he asked for was excessive and the Bill was thrown out but that year Scotland received £10,000 as its share of a parliamentary grant for national education. Parliament simultaneously ordered a further enquiry into the state of schooling in Scotland.[13] The returns to this survey estimated that 236,325 children, 9.64 per cent of the population of 2,452,000, were attending school in Scotland in 1834 compared with 9.00 per cent in England and Wales in 1833.[14] This survey also showed that there were four times as many schools outside the parish system and four times as many scholars attending these schools. The figure of 9.64 per cent of the population, however, concealed the real problem. At that time the average percentage of the population between 0 and 14 was 37 per cent or 907,240 children.[15] The report's estimate of 236,325 meant that only approximately 26 per cent of children attended school. The church's Education Committee claimed that in 1835 in the Highlands and Islands alone, 80,000 were unable to read or write.[16] The 1834 survey also showed that in 916 out of 1,047 parish schools and in 2,285 out of 3,995 schools outside the parish system, children were attending without reference to the religious persuasion of their parents. In nearly every case parents chose to send their children to schools which offered the best education or were geographically convenient. The Established Church and the Free Church of Scotland would later claim that their schools were not in the strict sense 'denominational' since they were open to children irrespective of their religious background and that parents were free to withdraw their children if they objected to the religious instruction given.

Further support for the extension of the parish school system through the medium of the national church came from the *Scottish Guardian* newspaper and from the Glasgow Educational Society which was founded in 1834. It was a report on the proceedings of a meeting of this Society which formed the basis of George Lewis's pamphlet, *Scotland a Half-Educated Nation, Both in the Quantity and Quality of her Educational Institutions*. Lewis claimed that Scottish education was suffering from the lack of qualified teachers belonging to the Established Church and from the want of adequate government funding.[17] Hardship and deprivation in the expanding industrial towns raised the question of how the needs of the poor could be met. Within the church there was an upsurge of evangelicalism which regarded education as an important tool in combating some of the social evils of the time. Men such as Thomas Chalmers and David Stow believed that in the struggle with poverty, schools run by Christian schoolmasters were the answer and that the government should help to provide additional parish schools supervised by the Established Church. William Hanna, Chalmers' biographer, quotes Chalmers as saying, 'it is education, and that only, wherein the whole positive efficiency lies for a permanent amelioration in the state of the lower orders'.[18]

How far the social and moral problems of this time could be laid at the door of the inadequate provision of school education is difficult to determine. The approach of the church reflected the two traditional strands which ran through Scottish education. On the one hand there were those who saw the purpose of education as not only providing a 'godly upbringing' but also as equipping the youth to earn a livelihood and be an asset to the nation. Here the emphasis was on the academic as much as the spiritual. On the other hand there were many who regarded education more as a tool to influence and shape moral and social behaviour.

The Rise of Denominational Schooling

In 1836, and again in 1837, further government grants of £10,000 were made for the erection of schoolhouses and for the education of the children from the poorer classes in the densely populated Scottish towns. A substantial proportion of this went towards the upkeep of sessional schools. Aware of the increasing demands on its funds, in 1838 the government commissioned yet another survey of Scottish schooling. This survey showed a further growth in the number of schools, particularly denominational schools. Catholic schools were on the increase throughout the country. Wherever Irish immigrants settled in large numbers a Catholic school was established. In 1835, a day and boarding school for higher education was opened in a convent in Edinburgh. In 1836, Bishop James Gillis (1802–64, Vicar Apostolic of the Eastern District of Scotland) brought the Ursuline Sisters from France to Edinburgh, the first of many religious communities which would be brought to Scotland to support Catholic school education.

By the mid-1830s there were some 350 schools belonging to Relief and Secession Churches[19] and in 1838 the Episcopal Church Society of Scotland was set up to help establish Scottish Episcopal Church schools. Private and subscription schools were also multiplying. In 1838, the trustees of George Heriot's School, founded in 1659 by bequest of the royal goldsmith George Heriot, opened the first of twenty free schools in Edinburgh educating several thousand pupils across the city.[20] In 1837, the School Accommodation Society of Greenock was set up to meet the educational needs of the considerable population of poor Highlanders living there, and on the Moray Firth the Society of the Respectable Inhabitants of Nairn helped with the education of the fishing population of that town. In Glasgow a growing number of schools were supported by commercial businesses. Messrs Denniston, Buchanan and Company, for example, provided a school and a schoolhouse and a salary of £20 for a teacher in the parish of Stanley, and at Catrine in Ayrshire James Finlay and Company paid £50 to a teacher to hold an evening school for young folks who were employed at their cotton mill during the day and a further £20 to educate those whose working hours had been curtailed by the Factory Regulation Act.

Unable to provide sufficient funding for more schools from church contributions, the church's Education Committee decided to concentrate on two objectives, both of which meant obtaining government finance. One was to persuade the government to grant assistance for establishing schools in the densely populated areas of the Lowlands and in the new parishes of the Parliamentary

Churches in the Highlands. The other was to extend teacher training in its normal schools.

Many presbyteries now expressed fears that increased government funding would mean greater control and threaten the church's authority in school education. These fears were strengthened by the disputes over the appointment of parish ministers that had arisen since the passing by the General Assembly of the Veto Act 1834, which gave congregations the right to reject a minister nominated by the patron.[21] These disputes had raised the whole issue of the extent of the Established Church's jurisdiction in relation to the civil authorities. If the state could intervene as it had done in the appointments to the parishes of Auchterarder and Lethendy (1837–8), how far might it, as paymaster, seek to dictate policy and appointments in schooling? In 1837, there was a flurry of overtures from presbyteries calling on the General Assembly to secure the church's traditional rights over the control of schooling in Scotland but it was now too late to turn the clock back. In May 1838, the Highland Schools Act (an 'Act to Facilitate the Foundation and Endowment of Additional Schools in Scotland') was passed with the government allocating grants and laying down the salary scales for teachers in schools in the new Highland parishes.

The government was now confronted with the educational needs of four countries, Scotland, England, Wales and Ireland, where the involvement of religious interests complicated the situation. It was not just a matter of finding and allocating funding: it was a question of how appropriate it was to use taxpayers' money to support church bodies which were responsible for schools and which had a particular interest in religious instruction. Henry Cockburn recorded in his *Journal* that dissenters who had petitioned against the 1838 government grant to Highland schools had done everything to make it unpopular, 'all because these schools are put under the presbyteries of the Church'.[22] Non-conformists and Secessionists in Scotland, and in Wales the Congregationalists and schools supported by the British and Foreign Society, feared that the extension of state aid would lead to greater control of education by the state and by the Established Churches. In April 1839, with increasing demands being made on its resources the government decided to set up a new Privy Council committee, the Committee of Council on Education. This committee would now be responsible for the allocation of grants for school education, and would insist on inspecting all schools in receipt of government funding. The new Council stated that inspectors would have no powers to interfere with religious instruction or the management and discipline of a school but this reassurance did not allay the Church of Scotland's anxieties.

In the summer of 1840, the church's Education Committee, intent on improving the quality of education, wrote to the Committee of Council asking for financial help to erect a new normal school building in Edinburgh and for a grant to cover its maintenance. The Committee of Council agreed to this provided the church would take over the running of the Glasgow Educational Society's normal school at Dundas Vale which was heavily in debt. This was agreed with the right of government inspection secured. While these negotiations were going on the dispute over patronage came to a head and in 1843, 450 ministers belonging to the Established Church of Scotland walked out of the General Assembly. These and about half the lay membership of the Church of Scotland left to form the Free Church of Scotland. The effect of the Disruption on the Established Church's educational scheme was greater than it cared to admit. It lost the use of the schools and schoolmasters' houses which had been provided by those heritors who joined the Free Church. Half of the teachers in Assembly schools left voluntarily or were dismissed when they went over to the Free Church, and the church lost its right to examine more than 300 others who were sympathetic to Free Church principles.[23] Perhaps most seriously of all the Disruption weakened the kirk's claim to be the national church with statutory oversight of parish schools. In spite of these difficulties the church opened its new normal school in Edinburgh in May 1845.

In February 1845, Her Majesty's Inspector John Gibson produced a highly critical report on the state of Scottish schools. It made reference to the fact that the Established Church's aims for extending the provision of school education lay far beyond its means and there was still a dire shortage of schools and resources, especially in small and scattered rural communities. By 1849, however, in spite of fierce competition from the Free Church, the Established Church had increased its Assembly schools from 146 before the Disruption to 208, fifty-eight of these in Lowland parishes.[24]

Increasing Government Control

Scottish school education now entered a period of uncertainty which would continue until the 1872 Education Act. Increasing dependence on government funding left the traditional character of Scottish education exposed to the anglicising influence of the Privy Council which attempted to apply regulations for inspections and grants to a system of education which had no equivalent in England. In 1849, the feelings of the Established Church were embodied in the Acts of Assembly in the form of a 'Protest, Declaration, and Testimony on the subject of National Education'. It was claimed that in Scotland elementary education was not regarded as just for the poor. It had long been the tradition that the sons (and daughters) of the poor could attend, at least in principle if not always in practice, the same schools as the sons of the gentry, and it had been the ideal of the Protestant reformers that all who were able should be given the chance of a university education. The curriculum in many parish and Assembly schools was not limited to teaching the three Rs but included Latin and Greek so that it was at least possible for the village school to prepare a boy for university. This was a system, therefore, which required teachers themselves to be well-educated. Guaranteed a basic income and accommodation by law, the Scottish schoolmaster had a professional status not shared by his counterpart in England.

The differences between the Scottish and English systems of school education were not always taken into account by the Privy Council. For example, the attempt to shape the duration and nature of normal school courses to replicate teacher training in England failed to take account of the fact that in Scotland the duration of students' courses could not be fixed, since this was often determined by the teaching posts that had to be filled when the need arose. Again when the government introduced a new regulation stating that teachers' salaries would be augmented by the government equivalent to what they were being paid from voluntary subscriptions or local funds, it was ruled that because heritors were legally bound to pay parish schoolmasters' salaries these could not be regarded as voluntary contributions and so could not qualify for the proportional addition. It would appear that the broad comprehensive curriculum covered in normal schools in Scotland was out of step with what was expected of their counterparts in England. In a letter to the Committee of Council in 1854, Henry Moseley, HMI of Schools, insisted that government grants to normal schools were 'expressly for the promotion of elementary education' and there was no time set aside for languages such as French or Latin nor for practical subjects such as agriculture and female domestic skills.[25] In 1864, the Committee of Council's proposals to pay grants not to schools but to individual children, depending on attendance and on their proficiency in the three Rs, were framed from recommendations of the Newcastle Commission in England. This 'Revised Code' with its payment by results was suspended in Scotland until 1872 but individual inspection of the three Rs was implemented.

In 1850, as criticisms of the way education was developing mounted, the National Education Association of Scotland was set up with a view to supporting a new national system of education. It claimed that the supervision of parish schools by the Established Church was defective and argued that state-funded education should be made available freely to everyone, with local boards taking over from heritors and presbyteries and with qualified teachers being appointed irrespective of their religious views. The High School in Edinburgh was held up as an example of what could be achieved:

> In the High School of Edinburgh we have an example of a national unsectarian school in full operation. The local board of patrons consists of men of all sects and parties; the teachers belong to the Episcopalian, Presbyterian, and Dissenting denominations; but this occasions no unfriendly feelings among either teachers or taught, nor has it ever been objected to by the parents of the pupils.[26]

Members of the Free Church were also scathing in their condemnation of the Established Church's management of parish schools and its unwillingness to relinquish its control, and the government's apparent acceptance of the denominational system was denounced by the United Presbyterians. Noting the increasing popularity of the Liberal party at this time, C. G. Brown has concluded that

> social and economic change was the begetter of ecclesiastical schism ... it was those who believed in the social values of the new economically-liberal

society, but who felt the landowning classes' authoritarian grip on the established Church was a denial of such 'democracy', who sought self-determination
and justice in a dissenting meeting house.[27]

The belief that Scottish interests were being neglected at Westminster led to the
formation in 1853 of the National Association for the Vindication of Scottish
Rights. According to J. D. Myers, 'the education controversy was an important
manifestation and an integral part of the mid-century upsurge of Scottish nationalist feeling'.[28]

The question of the government subsidising education was now further complicated by the number of denominations seeking funding for their own schools.
The Scottish Episcopal Church Society had been founded by Dean Ramsay in
1838 to help find financial support for schools and by 1850 there were about
thirty-six Episcopal Church schools. The majority of Scottish Episcopal Church
schools had a greater number of non-Episcopalian pupils but some were exclusively Episcopalian and had been established as centres for proselytising. In 1850,
a training college was set up in Edinburgh and in 1852 there was an appeal
to the government for aid and for an inspector sympathetic to Episcopalian
beliefs. Immediately after the Disruption the Free Church, in a bid to outdo the
Established Church, set itself the goal of developing its own national system, and
by 1850 it had over 650 elementary schools, including thirty-three female industrial schools, seven grammar Schools and two normal schools, one in Edinburgh
(Moray House) and one established by David Stow in Cowcaddens Street in
Glasgow.[29] In 1847, the United Secession Church and the Relief Church came
together to form the United Presbyterian Church, and proceeded to build up the
network of schools already set up by the seceders. The Great Famine of 1845–7
brought even more Irish Catholics to Scotland with the consequent need for
more schools. In 1847, a Catholic Poor Schools Committee was formed and as a
result of pressure from Catholic bodies in England and Scotland the government
agreed that Catholic schools could receive parliamentary grants on the condition that schools receiving grants should be open to government inspection.
Inspectors, who would inspect only secular subjects, had to be approved by the
Catholic Poor Schools Committee. Building grants could not be used where
schools were also used for church purposes, a common practice in that impoverished denomination. That same year a United Industrial School for destitute
and neglected children was set up in Edinburgh. This, in response to Thomas
Guthrie's Ragged School, was interdenominational and was managed by a committee of Catholics and Protestants. It divided religious from secular education
and arranged separate religious instruction for Catholics and Protestants. It was
described by Bishop Gillis as 'an interesting experiment to test the application of
a principle which might soon come before the country at large as a basis for a general system of education'.[30] The 1851 Census records the existence of thirty-two
Catholic schools. The main Presbyterian churches saw the increasing number of
Roman Catholic schools as a threat to the Protestant tradition in Scotland and,

Figure 8.2 Dating from around 1618, Moray House is the oldest Edinburgh University building still in use. From 1848, it was a Free Church normal school used for teacher training. It is now part of the school of education. Copyright the author, courtesy of Altarmotive Films, Edinburgh.

in spite of all their claims to be non-sectarian, in their debates and reports there was an increasingly sectarian attitude towards Roman Catholics.

Towards a New National System

The 1851 Census, while admitting that its statistics for Scotland were incomplete, showed that there were eighty-eight burgh schools and 937 parish schools. Under the category of 'schools supported in any degree by religious bodies', it estimated that there were 914 Established Church schools, 719 Free Church schools, sixty-one schools supported by the United Presbyterian Church, thirty-eight by the Episcopal Church and thirty-two by the Roman Catholic Church.[31] Just three years later the number of Free Church schools had risen to 768 and Episcopalian schools had almost doubled.[32] With the increasing fragmentation and duplication of schooling it became clear that some kind of rationalisation was necessary. In 1848, Lord Melgund, Liberal MP for Greenock, had written a pamphlet in support of a national system of education in Scotland and attacking the Privy Council's financial policy which he maintained only encouraged costly competition and fostered sectarianism. Melgund believed that in Scotland, unlike in England, a national system already existed in all but name. In his view all that was needed was to abolish the Established Church's traditional monopoly of the jurisdiction and superintendence of parish schools. Those agitating for reform made much of the number of children not attending school and blamed this for the immoral state of the nation. Lord Melgund, introducing his Bill in 1850, a 'Bill to Reform and Extend the School Establishment of Scotland', quoted a figure of 180,000 children not at school. W. M. Hetherington, minister of Free St Paul's, Edinburgh, calculated in 1850 that 500,000 children were unprovided for by parish schools and, even taking into account all the non-parochial schools, there still remained at least 200,000 children between the ages of six and fifteen for whom there was no means of education. He noted the 'rapidly advancing tide of intemperance, immorality and crime . . . and increasing instances of juvenile depravity' and laid this at the door of the deficient educational system.[33] This was more of an invective against the Established Church than an accurate estimate of school attendance. School attendance was always notoriously difficult to calcu-late and could vary depending on what was considered school age (three to fifteen or five to fifteen years), what time of day and what time of year the attendance was taken and whether part-time attendance and evening classes were counted.[34]

Melgund's Bill and another similar one brought forward in 1851 were both rejected by the Commons, the latter losing by only thirteen votes. Over the next twenty years some eight Bills on school education in Scotland were con-sidered and rejected by parliament and the various denominations. All proposed changes would have transferred powers traditionally held by the heritors and the Established Church to a national board and locally elected committees and dif-fered mainly in the proposed constituency of a central board and in the conces-sions made with regard to the delivery of religious instruction.

The United Presbyterian Church held the view that the whole system of giving grants to the different denominations to run their schools perpetuated sectarian animosity and that education should be supported solely from voluntary contributions with religious instruction being given not by schools, but by par-ents and the church. Attempts were made to win over the secular lobby and the United Presbyterians by stating that religious instruction would be only given at certain agreed times so that Catholic and dissenting parents who objected could opt out. The Established Church argued that to have religious instruction taught only at stated times and not as part of the compulsory curriculum would create a secular system of education which, indeed, was the ultimate objective of many wishing to bring about reform. It resisted any proposal that would have threat-ened its supervision of parish schools. The Free Church was set on undermining the power and position of the Established Church, but was itself divided as to the suggested proposals. Led by Robert Candlish, the majority of ministers in the Free Church General Assembly believed that with the help of government fund-ing they should maintain the Free Church's own school education programme. Others, like James Begg and Thomas Guthrie, believed that, having left the Established Church at the Disruption on the principle that there should be no state interference in ecclesiastical matters, the church should not be depend-ent on state funding for its schools and training colleges. Begg denounced the existing government scheme as an 'indiscriminate endowment of denominations where even Popery came in for its share'.[35] For Begg nothing short of a fully developed scheme of national education would suffice.

While both the parish schools and the denominational schools in Scotland had a long history of inclusiveness, it would appear that the growing strength of the Roman Catholic Church made the Established Church and the Free Church even more determined to ensure that, whatever the outcome of the national education debate, Scottish schools would be Presbyterian schools and that teaching from the Authorised Version of the Bible and the Shorter Catechism would continue to be the main thrust of religious instruction. Naturally the Roman Catholic Church took great exception to this stance. A letter written by Bishop James Gillis to the Lord Provost of Edinburgh in 1854 made the Roman Catholic position clear with regard to school education:

> We never can, and never will send our children to a school of which the master is not a Catholic . . . and in which secular, as well as religious instruction, is not imparted to the scholars, in the unmistakeable and untrammeled spirit of Catholic teaching . . . History never can be taught fairly to a Catholic child by a Protestant teacher . . . [36]

The Roman Catholic Church was opposed to any legislation which, to satisfy the secular lobby and the United Presbyterians, treated religious instruction as a subject outwith the curriculum rather than as an integral part of a child's education.

It is clear that anyone attempting to reform Scottish education was faced with the impossible task of trying to accommodate the views of the different denominations and their supporters in parliament. While Moncreiff had had the support of the Scottish burghs and the Liberal middle class, events in England were making the task of reforming Scottish education more difficult. Scottish Bills were often defeated by an English vote, with Conservative MPs and Roman Catholics voting against them. In 1855, during Palmerston's Whig government, proposals to promote the establishment of new schools outwith the control of the Church of England were brought forward. These attempts at change failed but they alarmed the English establishment where there was an even greater resistance to reform. MPs south of the border who wanted to protect the Church of England's privileged position with regard to its schools, were not going to vote for a change to the Scottish system and so weaken their own case. It is no wonder that the National Association for the Vindication of Scottish Rights argued that Scottish interests were being neglected at Westminster.[37]

A New National System Established

Although the efforts of Melgund and Moncreiff had failed, support for the view that the existing system of education should be replaced by a national non-denominational system continued to grow and in 1864 a royal commission was set up under the chairmanship of the Duke of Argyll to inquire into schooling in Scotland and to suggest how educational provision could be improved.

The commissioners found that overall the burgh schools in Scotland were in a satisfactory condition and superior to the majority of the English grammar schools, and that elementary education was on the whole better than had been anticipated.[38] A survey of the professions and occupations of the fathers of 882 of the students in the Latin, Greek and mathematics classes in the Scottish universities showed that that while 31 per cent of the students came from professional backgrounds, 18 per cent came from agricultural backgrounds and 16 per cent from artisan and labouring backgrounds.[39] The commission believed that the defects of the Scottish system were the want of proper organisation and of supervision by some competent central authority.

The recommendations and the Bill following the Commission's enquiry divided the churches and the country. Opposition came from diverse quarters. The proposals that new state-supported schools should be built and managed alongside existing parish and denominational schools, and that a Central Board could declare a denominational school unnecessary, were viewed by the Established Church as a policy which would lead to the eventual dismantling of the parish system. The introduction of a conscience clause, giving parents the right to withdraw their children from any religious teaching and making religious instruction no longer subject to government inspection, pleased only the dissenters and the secularists. A proposal that the Revised Code, which had been suspended in May 1864, with its emphasis on the examination of children in the 3Rs and payment by results, should be fully implemented was seen as further undermining the character of Scottish schooling. The creation of a Scotch Department of the Privy Council to oversee the inspection of schools went some way towards distancing Scottish education from the influence of the London-based Privy Council but it did not go far enough to satisfy those who were concerned about the erosion of the Scottish educational tradition and who argued that Scottish schools should be administered by a Scottish Board of Education based in Edinburgh. The Educational Institute of Scotland[40] and the Committee of Parochial Schoolmasters both agreed that with its parish schools Scotland already had a national system of education and argued that a Scottish Board of Education based in Edinburgh should have sole control of education including the inspection of schools and the distribution of parliamentary grants to schools. They were also in favour of religious instruction remaining in the curriculum. The directors of the Edinburgh Apprentice School Association objected to the Bill on the grounds that it made no provision of aid for evening classes which provided educational opportunities for manual workers. Firms who had invested money in education wanted the schools erected and maintained by them to remain as they were. On the other hand, a substantial majority in the Established Church would now have agreed with the proposed changes had the place of religious instruction been secured. One opponent of retaining religious education claimed that using the Bible as a textbook had little to do with moral education and that 'whisky and the Catechism were the two greatest curses of Scotland'.[41]

In the end Argyll's plans were thwarted by his fellow peers. The Duke of

Marlborough, speaking for the Scottish landed gentry, objected to the reduced influence of heritors on local school committees. The Earl of Denbigh, speaking on behalf of the Roman Catholics in Scotland, argued that the Bill had been drawn up by Presbyterians for the benefit of Presbyterians and that it threatened the continuation of the Episcopalian and Catholic schools. The Bill's rejection by the Lords, however, was more than just an expression of political or religious animosity. Moves to change the English system were now well advanced and those who opposed this were concerned about the effect any success in introducing changes to Scotland might have on English opinion. As it happened, a year later Parliament passed a Bill introduced by W. E. Forster which more or less took English elementary schools in the direction which Argyll had wanted for Scotland. With this the reform of the Scottish system was now inevitable and there were signs that the Free Church and the Established Church might co-operate. In 1867, the Moderator of the General Assembly of the Established Church had called for the reunion of all Scottish Presbyterians, and by 1870 there was widespread support for the abolition of patronage.

In 1871, George Young, recently appointed as Lord Advocate, took up the cause of reforming Scottish education. After a first abortive attempt in 1871 his 'Bill to Extend and Amend the Provisions of the Law of Scotland on the Subject of Education' eventually passed and the Education (Scotland) Act 1872 became law. The historic role of the heritors and the churches was abolished, with the management of schools becoming the responsibility of locally elected school boards in every parish and burgh. A temporary Board of Education was set up in Edinburgh but the real power still lay with the Scotch Education Department (SED) in London. For the time being, existing denominational schools which were deemed to be efficiently meeting the needs of a parish would continue to receive government grants except for building purposes. In future parliamentary grants would be given only to denominational schools which the SED deemed necessary to meet the religious beliefs of parents. Roman Catholic and Episcopalian schools fell into this category. The 1872 Act did not outlaw denominational schools, but the fact that schools throughout the land would now be rate-supported made the continuation of Presbyterian Church schools impractical. Congregations could not have expected members to pay for schools through their rates and also contribute to the upkeep of church schools. By the 1880s, the Presbyterian churches and most voluntary bodies had transferred the majority of their schools to the new school boards. Teacher training colleges, however, remained under church control until 1907.

As for religious instruction, Young's proposal was that school boards would decide whether or not it should be provided. This idea was objected to by the Established Church and the Free Church, which both held out for the statutory provision of religious instruction rather than have it left to the prejudices of school boards. After a number of amendments in the House of Lords, Young finally agreed to include in the preamble a clause stating that:

> Whereas it has been the custom in the public schools of Scotland to give instruc-
> tion in religion to children whose parents did not object to the instruction so
> given, but with liberty to parents without forfeiting any of the other advantages
> of the schools, to elect that their children should not receive such instruction,
> and it is expedient that the managers of public schools shall be at liberty to
> continue the said custom: Be it therefore enacted . . .

Two sections of the Act qualified this, stipulating that no parliamentary grant
would be made for providing religious instruction and confirming the right of
parents to withdraw children from religious instruction and religious observance,
which would be given at the beginning or end of the school day.[42] While at
the time this amendment did not guarantee that religious instruction would be
taught according to the 'use and wont' of Scottish schools, the principle would
thereafter be enshrined in future Education Acts. After 1872, the Presbyterian
churches continued to influence school education through their representatives
on school boards and through the content of religious instruction. In 1878, a
report by Her Majesty's Inspectorate claimed that 'the mass of the Scotch people
are Presbyterians, and for these the national schools may be said to exist . . . the
public schools are to all intents and purposes denominational schools. Public
and Presbyterian are practically interchangeable terms'.[43] The Catholic authorities, and the Episcopalians for the most part, refused to transfer their schools to
the new school boards, which they regarded as a threat to their denominational
status and religious character since the church would have had no control over
the curriculum and religious education and secular education would be delivered
separately. Without building grants or grants for religious education Catholic
schools were left to struggle as best they could until the 1918 Education Act. In
the face of Protestant antagonism the Catholic Church canvassed strongly for
seats on the new school boards to which as ratepayers they were entitled.[44] On
the eve of the passing of the 1872 Act the Catholic community represented up
to a third of the population of the industrial towns around Glasgow. In cities like
Glasgow two-thirds of Catholic children did not attend school and there was a
dire shortage of teachers. The Act did nothing to help this desperate situation;
instead its discrimination sowed the seeds of future sectarianism.

Conclusion

It can be argued that the intransigence of the churches and denominational
rivalry had a disastrous effect on Scottish education by preventing the establishment of a national system for almost thirty years. On the other hand Scottish
education in the mid-nineteenth century would have been much poorer had it
not been for the contribution of the churches to teacher training and school provision. Inefficient as the Church of Scotland's superintendence of schools may
have been, it was, nevertheless, the pioneer of school inspection and vocal in its
demands for higher salaries for schoolmasters.

The influence of the denominations on Scottish education was outstanding.

The parliamentary survey carried out in 1854 had calculated that there were almost 5,000 schools in Scotland. Of these 2,035 schools were noted as having a connection with the Established Church (177 Assembly schools and including parish schools, female schools, sessional and subscription schools) and 768 claimed an association with the Free Church. There were fifty-four United Presbyterian schools, sixty-eight Scottish Episcopal schools and thirty-eight Catholic schools.[45] By 1872, the Free Church claimed responsibility for 585 schools (439 congregational schools, ninety-two side schools, fifty-one missionary schools and three grammar schools) while the Established Church report showed it as having 436 schools (218 Assembly schools, eighty-seven female schools and 131 sewing schools).[46] Throughout this period the churches encouraged voluntary associations and individual subscribers to add to the stock of schools. For example, by 1854 the Ladies' Associations in Edinburgh and Glasgow were supporting twenty-two Free Church schools in the Highlands and in 1862 the Duke of Sutherland agreed to support five spinning schools at Established Church schools on his estates and make land available for teaching agriculture.[47]

As for the cost of education, Withrington estimated that in Scotland only 15 per cent of all school expenditure came from government funding (£20,427 in 1854) while 10 per cent came from the churches for their schemes, 21 per cent from heritors and tenants, 33 per cent from fees and the rest from private subscriptions and donations – 'the Scottish system was emphatically and crucially community-led and community-funded'.[48]

It was the Presbyterian churches that continually tried to resist the anglicising influence of their paymasters, the Privy Council, and uphold the Scottish tradition of a broad school curriculum and raise standards through their teacher training colleges. The report to the 1869 Established Church General Assembly noted that in parish schools, in spite of the influence of the Revised Code with its emphasis on elementary subjects, the number learning Latin and Greek showed a tendency to increase rather than the reverse and that there was a marked increase in the numbers learning French and German. In scattered rural areas and in dense urban areas the churches, through their mission schools and session schools, did their best to meet the needs of the poor as well as the middle classes. The Argyll commission agreed that, unlike the situation in England, the mass of the Scottish population in the rural districts had received a good basic education. T. M. Devine identified an improvement in Scottish education in the 1860s and concluded that 'when compulsion took place in Scotland after the 1872 Act it was likely to result in consolidation and some improvement in an ongoing process rather than a radical reform leading to dramatic changes in educational performance'.[49]

That George Young succeeded where Moncreiff and Argyll had failed was mainly due to changes in the electorate and in the churches. The Representation of the People (Scotland) Act 1868 brought an unprecedented extension of the franchise to all householders and effectively gave the vote to the working classes. In the following election in Scotland fifty-three out of sixty MPs elected were Liberals giving Young the majority he needed to succeed with the 1872 Act.

The passing of this Act, which saw control of education move from the church to the state, was partly due to the changing nature and relationships of the Presbyterian churches in Scotland. The Free Church and the Established Church had been willing to sacrifice their schools in order to safeguard the position of religious instruction. Altogether in the churches there was now less acrimonious competition, less interest in denominational self-preservation and more interest in reunion. There were conversations between the Free Church and the United Presbyterians. These churches would come together as the United Free Church in 1900. The Kirk was willing to surrender patronage for good and there were indications that it was becoming more open to theological questioning and less thirled to the Westminster Confession. All these moves produced a climate of opinion which made the 1872 Act more acceptable to the Presbyterian churches and to the country.

Notes

1. Schools set up and taught by individuals as a 'venture' and at their own risk and paid for out of pupils' fees.
2. British Parliamentary Papers, A Digest of Parochial Returns made to the Select Committee appointed to inquire into the Education of the Poor (1818), 3 vols (Irish University Press, 1968), vol. III, pp. 224–5.
3. James Dick (1743–1828) bequeathed £113,787 to encourage the learning and efficiency of parish schoolmasters. See the chapters by David Northcroft and Christopher R. Bischof in this volume.
4. The SSPCK was founded in 1709. In 1825, it claimed that it maintained some 300 schools.
5. PP 1826, vol. XVIII, Parochial Education in Scotland. Returns to an Address of the Honourable House of Commons, dated March 30th, 1825.
6. James Scotland, The History of Scottish Education, 2 vols (University of London Press, 1969), vol. II, p. 191.
7. PP 1826, vol. XVIII, Parochial Education in Scotland.
8. Callum G. Brown, 'Religion and social change', in T. M. Devine and Rosalind Mitchison (eds), People and Society in Scotland, Vol. I: 1760–1830 (John Donald, 1988), p. 151.
9. Established Church of Scotland: Report of the Committee of the General Assembly for Increasing the Means of Education and Religious Instruction in Scotland Particularly in the Highlands and Islands [henceforth: ECR], 1837, p. 29. Normal schools were the forerunners of teacher training colleges.
10. National Archives of Scotland, CH1/2/152, Assembly Papers 1830, Schedule Respecting the Examination of Schools, Presbytery of Lewis.
11. Under the existing system patrons, usually local landowners, nominated ministers to parish churches. They could then be inducted by the presbytery irrespective of the wishes of the congregation and overriding the congregation's right to call.
12. John F. McCaffrey, Scotland in the Nineteenth Century (Macmillan Press, 1998), p. 51.
13. PP 1837, vol. XLVII, Education enquiry. Abstract of answers and returns, dated 9th July 1834, Scotland.
14. PP 1837, vol. XLVII. This enquiry used returns supplied in 1831 and updated them in 1834 to take account of the population increase and defective or missing returns.

15. Michael Flinn (ed.), *Scottish Population History from the 17th Century to the 1930s* (Cambridge University Press, 1977), p. 321.
16. *ECR*, 1835, pp. 23–4.
17. *Scotland a Half-Educated Nation, Both in the Quantity and Quality of her Educational Institutions by the Editor of the 'Scottish Guardian'* (William Collins, 1834), pp. 44–53, 77–9.
18. William Hanna, *Memoirs of the Life and Writings of Thomas Chalmers*, 4 vols (Sutherland and Knox, 1851), vol. III, p. 305.
19. George S. Pryde, *Scotland from 1603 to the Present Day* (Thomas Nelson and Sons, 1962), p. 268.
20. Brian R. W. Lockhart, *Jinglin' Geordie's Legacy* (Tuckwell Press, 2003), pp. 115–17, 320.
21. The legality of the Veto Act was questioned by the civil courts. It was argued that it encroached on the civil rights of the patron and the nominee.
22. Henry Cockburn, *Journal of Henry Cockburn 1831–1854*, 2 vols (Edmonston and Douglas, 1874), vol. I, p. 170.
23. Numbers vary depending on the statistics provided by the denominations. See *ECR*, 1844, p. 10; *General Assembly of Free Church of Scotland Reports and Proceedings* [henceforth: GAFC], 1843, p. 64; 1844, p. 167.
24. *ECR*, 1849.
25. *ECR*, 1855, Appendix IV: *Correspondence*, p. 50.
26. Anon., *Report of a Public Meeting Held on 9 April 1850 in Edinburgh with a View to Forming an Association for the Support and Prosecution of a National System of Education*: New College Library Edinburgh, Special Collections, Ref. Y.g.2/5, p. 17.
27. Callum G. Brown, *The People in the Pews, Religion and Society in Scotland since 1780*, Studies in Scottish Economic and Social History, no. 3 (Economic and Social History Society of Scotland, 1993), p. 29.
28. J. D. Myers, 'Scottish nationalism and the antecedents of the 1872 Education Act', *Scottish Educational Studies* 4 (1972), 73–92.
29. GAFC, 1850.
30. Peter Mackie, 'The foundation of the industrial school of Edinburgh: "A bold experiment"', *Innes Review* 39 (1988), 144.
31. British Parliamentary Papers 1851, *Census of Great Britain Population*, 11 (Irish University Press, 1970), pp. 36–8.
32. PP 1854, vol. LIX, *Abstract of Returns Relating to Population, Number of Schools Etc. in Each of the Counties, Cities and Burghs*.
33. W. M. Hetherington, *National Education in Scotland Viewed in Its Present Condition*, 2nd edn (Johnstone and Hunter, 1850), pp. 5–7.
34. R. D. Anderson, *Education and the Scottish People 1750–1918* (Clarendon Press, 1995), pp. 101–7.
35. James Begg, *National Education for Scotland Practically Considered* (Johnstone and Hunter, 1850), p. 33.
36. Rt Rev. Bishop Gillis, *A Letter to the Rt. Hon. Duncan Maclaren* (Marsh and Beattie, 1854), pp. 6, 12.
37. George W. T. Omond, *The Lord Advocates of Scotland from the Close of the Fifteenth Century to the Passing of the Reform Bill, Second Series 1834–1880* (Andrew Melrose, 1914), p. 185.
38. *Education Commission, Third Report, Burgh and Middle Class Schools*, 2 vols (Thomas Constable for H. M. Stationery Office, 1868), vol. 1, p. xi.
39. Ibid., pp. 237–42.

40. See Christopher R. Bischof's chapter for an account of the formation and early history of the Educational Institute of Scotland.
41. Anon., *Suggestions for the Administration of the Privy Council Grant for Education in Scotland* (John Maclaren, 1870), p. 18.
42. Education (Scotland) Act 1872, 35 & 36 Vict., Preamble and sections 67 and 68.
43. Scottish Education Department, *Memorandum with Regard to the Provision made for Religious Instruction in Schools in Scotland*, Cmd. 6426 (H.M. Stationery Office, 1943), pp. 6–7.
44. After the first election of the new school boards, out of 5,662 elected 1,450 were clergymen; among them were 744 Church of Scotland ministers, 453 Free Church, 146 United Presbyterians and thrty-eight Roman Catholics. James M. Roxburgh, *The School Board of Glasgow 1873–1919* (University of London Press, 1971), pp. 13–28.
45. See note 32.
46. GAFC, 1872 and ECR, 1872.
47. ECR, 1862, pp. 20–1 and GAFC, 1854, p. 81.
48. D. J. Withrington, 'Church and state in Scottish education before 1872', in Heather Holmes (ed.), *Institutions of Scotland: Education*, Scottish Life and Society: A Compendium of Scottish Ethnology, vol. 11 (Tuckwell Press, 2000), p. 63.
49. T. M. Devine, *The Scottish Nation 1700–2000* (Penguin Books, 2000), p. 394.

Bibliography

Anderson, R. D., *Education and the Scottish People 1750–1918* (Clarendon Press, 1995).
Brown, Stewart J., *Thomas Chalmers and the Godly Commonwealth in Scotland* (Oxford University Press, 1982).
Fitzpatrick, T. A. O., 'Catholic education', in Heather Holmes (ed.), *Institutions of Scotland: Education*, Scottish Life and Society: A Compendium of Scottish Ethnology, vol. 11 (Tuckwell Press, 2000), pp. 435–55.
Jones, Gareth Elwyn and Gordon W. Roderick, *A History of Education in Wales* (University of Wales Press, 2003).
Law, Andrew, *Edinburgh Schools of the Nineteenth Century* (n.p., 1995).
McKinney, Stephen J., *Faith Schools in the Twenty-First Century* (Dunedin Academic Press, 2008).
Scotland, James, *The History of Scottish Education*, 2 vols (University of London Press, 1969).
Stevenson, John, *Fulfilling a Vision* (Pickwick Publications, 2012).
Vaughan, Geraldine, '"Papists looking after the education of our Protestant children": Catholics and Protestants on western Scottish school boards 1872–1918', *Innes Review* 63 (2012), 30–47.
White, Gavin, *The Scottish Episcopal Church. A New History* (General Synod of the Scottish Episcopal Church, 1998).
Withrington, Donald J., '"Scotland a Half-Educated Nation" in 1834? Reliable critique or persuasive polemic?', in Walter M. Humes and Hamish M. Paterson (eds), *Scottish Culture and Scottish Education 1800–1980* (John Donald, 1983), pp. 55–74.
Withrington, Donald J., 'Church and state in Scottish education before 1872', in Heather Holmes (ed.), *Institutions of Scotland: Education*, Scottish Life and Society: A Compendium of Scottish Ethnology, vol. 11 (Tuckwell Press, 2000), pp. 47–64.

9

Education in Rural Scotland, 1696–1872

Ewen A. Cameron

Rural Scotland was central to the parochial education system which operated between 1696 and the introduction of compulsory education in 1872. The system was conceived when Scotland was largely a rural society and encountered difficulties in the nineteenth century, by which time Scotland had experienced rapid and intense processes of industrialisation and urbanisation. The idealised history of the Scottish education system that was so prominent in the nineteenth century was largely located in rural areas. There is a further issue to be considered – the place of the education system in the Highlands and the way in which it attempted to cope with demanding physical and geographical challenges. In addition, there was the issue of delivering education – largely thought of in English – to a population that was predominantly Gaelic speaking.

The educational history of rural Scotland, both Highland and Lowland, has attracted historiographical attention but there is scope for original work. This chapter will deal with three areas: the place of rural Lowland Scotland in the development of the history of Scottish education; the debate over educational provision and linguistic issues in the Highlands; and the initial effect of the 1872 Act on rural Scotland (a story continued in the chapter in this volume by O'Hanlon and Paterson). The overall theme of the chapter will be an attempt to try to integrate the history of Scottish education with the principal historical forces affecting rural Scotland in the period between 1696 and 1872. Although it has become orthodox to argue that there has been a revolution in Scottish historiography in the years since the late 1960s, and there have been remarkable advances, the topic of education is one where critical works based on considerable depth of empirical research can be found going back to the early part of the twentieth century. To reach a full understanding of even a specialised topic such as education in rural society these have to be read alongside works of a more general, idealistic or even polemical nature.

The Rural Lowlands

In his important but neglected study of early-nineteenth-century Scotland, Laurance J. Saunders pays particular attention to the educational developments that were central to his thesis of an emergent Scottish democracy. He argues that the parish school after 1696 was both an 'equalising' and a 'selective' agency but he noted that in 'country districts' the 'equalising' elements of its mission were most prominent because of the broad social spectrum of those who attended. In the 'remoter country parishes' the 'children of the local middle class would still attend the parish school all the time and the children of the smaller gentry at least some of the time'. This created a demand, in Saunders' view, for a broad curriculum.[1] This emphasis on 'democracy' in rural Scotland is striking. Most accounts of the Scottish countryside have emphasised the overwhelming power of the landowner and the authoritarian nature of social relations. An older account still places even greater stress on the role of the school in rural society and its capacity for delivering social and moral benefits:

> The history of rural education in Scotland has been marked by gradual developments towards a social ideal. The experiments which have been attempted in the Scottish rural school during a period of nearly two hundred years, from the eighteenth century to the present time, have been inspired by the ideal of establishing a relationship between the school and the community, and progress is characterised by a gradual increase in effort towards the utilisation of environment as a basis for education.[2]

This view of the superiority of Scottish schools was not confined to chauvinistic Scottish historians; writing about the eighteenth century, Lawrence Stone asserted that 'Scotland enjoyed the largest elementary educational system . . . in Europe'.[3] Until more critical work by Anderson and Houston in the 1980s and 1990s this was the framework in which Scottish educational history was written.

The provision of schools in rural Scotland was established by the Act of the Scottish Parliament of 1696 entitled the 'Act for Settling of Schools'. This legislation had the avowedly political object of entrenching the Presbyterian regime of 1689 and provided for the settlement of a school in every parish 'not already provided'. It imposed duties on the heritors (landowners) and ministers of the parish to provide accommodation for school and schoolmaster and to pay the latter a salary of between 100 and 200 merks (between £5 and £10 sterling, prior to the Union of 1707 Scotland having its own currency). This money was to be raised by a property tax levied on both owners and tenants.[4] This Act itself was the subject of idealisation by some of the earliest contributors to an academic historiography of Scotland. The Act was held to show the activity of the parliament in the years before its abolition in 1707 and the centrality of education to Scottish legislative activity, as well as the way in which it provided a contrast to Scotland's general late-seventeenth-century backwardness, a condition which was taken for granted in an uncritical way. This served to exalt the education system as the 'glory of Scotland'.[5] This system remained in place, essentially, until 1872, although some of the monetary values, and terms and conditions were updated in 1803. The structure imposed in 1696 meant that the landowner and Established Church clergyman were responsible for the provision of education in each parish. Where the heritors were active and conscientious, and the clergyman interested in education, this system could work well but there was much scope for difficulty if these conditions were absent. In some areas of Scotland the absence of resident landowners caused problems. In Glasserton parish, in Wigtownshire, the presence of a dilatory landowner, Sir William Maxwell, meant that there was a controversy over the appointment of a schoolmaster that ran from 1715 to 1751.[6] There were problems in areas where the Presbyterian settlement had not taken hold very firmly. This was most notable in parts of the North-East of Scotland where non-juring Episcopalians had Jacobite sympathies and the level of conformity to the Presbyterian kirk was low. One educational historian of this area argues that the result was 'little or no improvement in the educational system of Angus' in the late seventeenth and early eighteenth century.[7]

In other areas of Scotland the effect of the outcome of the Jacobite risings was different. In the aftermath of the rising of 1745–6 the lands of many Jacobite proprietors were forfeited to the state. The Commission established to run these estates recognised that education was a potential medium of encouraging political conformity and were active in establishing schools. These have been seen by some critics merely as agencies of anti-Gaelic cultural vandalism. Other historians have noted the way in which the Commission worked with the Board of Manufactures, another state agency attempting to inculcate the ideology of commercialism and improvement. Together they operated to provide schools that would include in their curriculum craft skills relevant to the new industries, such as textiles, that it was hoped would help to modernise these areas.[8] Further, the records of the Commission contain many petitions from tenants drawing attention to deficiencies in educational provision. In many cases these point to the difficulty of attending the parochial schools, or those provided by the Society in Scotland for Propagating Christian Knowledge (SSPCK), because of their geographical position or the fact that transhumance took the children away from proximity to the schools. Many of these petitions came from the tenants of the estate formerly belonging to Robertson of Strowan in Highland Perthshire.[9] Even if one approaches these petitions critically and with an awareness that the tenantry were keen to demonstrate that they shared the objectives of the Commission, they are still significant. They tell us something about the nature of schooling in rural areas in the middle of the eighteenth century, especially the way in which the parochial schools were part of a system which included other agencies, especially the SSPCK and private adventure schools. In areas such as border counties like Jedburgh, where Presbyterian dissent was strong, there were schools designed to cater for children of members of the Relief Church and the other secessions from the Church of Scotland in the eighteenth century. Private adventure schools designed to fill geographical or religious gaps left by the parochial system were an important part of the network of schools in rural areas in the eighteenth century.[10]

Despite this complex picture the image given in the Statistical Accounts is of a system which was running smoothly. While it has been suggested that these ministers' accounts were disinterested, it does seem relevant to note that they were at the heart of the system that they were describing and that this may have coloured their thoughts. Further, many ministers of the Established Church owed their positions to landowning patrons among the heritors with whom they worked to administer the schools in their parish, another potential reason to read this source carefully. For this reason there are many very bland accounts of schooling in the essays written by parish ministers for Sir John Sinclair of Ulbster's great enterprise.[11] Occasionally, however, this valuable source throws up stimulating material. The minister of Auchtertool in Fife penned a remarkable essay ranging well beyond the standard account of educational provision in his rural parish. He was critical of 'gentlemen of landed property' for their neglect and parsimony in the matter of schoolmasters' salaries and went on to argue in elegant prose that a good education system staffed by well-paid and highly qualified teachers could help to advance the population's 'happiness and best interests, both in this world, and that which is to come . . .'. Further, it would 'make the nation less apt to be misled or convulsed, by designing and seditious men . . .'.[12]

So much for general attitudes towards schooling as a result of changes in Scottish history in the eighteenth century; what did the system deliver for those who experienced it and what were the results? This has been the subject of extensive debate in recent years between those who take an optimistic view of the effect of education on the population and critics who argue that if a comparative focus is adopted then Scotland looks less exceptional than was suggested by Lawrence Stone. This debate has focused on the levels of literacy of the Scottish population in the eighteenth and nineteenth centuries. Scottish literacy studies lack the sources available to those working on other countries as until the introduction of compulsory civil registration in 1855 there were relatively few occasions on which signatures had to be recorded. Nevertheless, the orthodoxy was that literacy in Scotland was relatively high, perhaps approaching 90 per cent for adult males at the turn of the nineteenth century, according to Stone. The absence of conventional sources has led to ingenious analysis of other materials. In an important paper Smout drew attention to the popular religious revival which took place at Cambuslang in Lanarkshire in 1742. The local minister, William MacCulloch, was petitioned by some of his parishioners to preach on 'spiritual regeneration'. This stimulated an extraordinary outburst of evangelical activity; in July and August two outdoor communions were addressed by George Whitfield and mass conversions took place. The event is an important one in the history of popular religious awakening in the Atlantic world but the sources which it generated are also important for the historian of literacy. MacCulloch recorded the testimony of 110 individuals who participated in the revival and this material reveals important information about their literacy. Smout rightly hedged his conclusions with caveats, especially the lack of clarity about the way in which these individuals were selected. Nevertheless, he concluded that in this sample the ability to read was universal among both women (who predominate in the group of 110) and men. The ability to write, on the other hand, was much lower: 11 per cent for the women and 60 per cent for the men. Smout argued that the evidence revealed a society where the link between reading and writing was tenuous and that the link between literacy and schooling may not have been as firm as formerly assumed. Some of the Cambuslang testimony records cases of men and women learning to read later in life, often at the hands of employers. The evidence also seems to point to a widespread expectation that reading skills were general but that writing skills were more limited as they were less useful.[13]

The debate on literacy in this period was taken forward by Houston in the early 1980s. He presented a much less positive picture of literacy and education in Scotland in the eighteenth and early nineteenth centuries. In the absence of marriage records he used a range of other sources including court depositions and tax records to measure the extent of literacy in Scotland. He estimated that illiteracy levels stood at around 35 per cent in the middle of the eighteenth century, compared to around 40 per cent for England and 36 per cent in northern England. He examined the Highlands separately and estimated that illiteracy levels were much higher there.

> This suggests that the rise to nearly universal literacy which we can see in Scotland during the 1850s must have come at some stage during the later eighteenth or early nineteenth century. At the same time we have seen that the contrast between Lowland Scotland and northern England is not as marked as we might expect from some of the balder assertions about Scotland's educational superiority.[14]

His principal methodological advance was to compare the Scottish experience with that of northern England and, in later publications, with continental Europe.[15] Houston has been criticised for placing too much emphasis on writing as a sign of literacy, whereas the separate skill of reading was perhaps more widespread, and it has been suggested that the evidence of ability to sign is not entirely secure evidence of ability to write fluently and extensively.[16]

There is more certainty about literacy after 1855 once compulsory registration was introduced. The evidence from this source indicates that Scotland had fairly high literacy levels and was over 95 per cent for both men and women by the end of the century. This represents a very steep improvement in the levels of female literacy and would seem to indicate that a long process was in train. There is, however, considerable regional variation in this bald statistic. Information about literacy in the 1860s, although still based on ability to sign, indicates that there was a gap between urban industrial areas, where attendance at school, especially that of boys, was relatively low, and 'mainland rural districts' where attendance was better and literacy levels higher. Apart from the special case of Edinburgh, these districts had the highest level of literacy in the country, at

92 per cent for men and 85 per cent for women (the figures for Edinburgh were 96 per cent and 91 per cent). Even within this broad category there are stark differences between northern counties such as Inverness, Ross and Sutherland and wealthier areas in the south-east of Scotland. Areas of the south-west also had lower levels of literacy because of relatively high levels of Irish immigration. Figures from 1869 show that the literacy of Roman Catholic married couples, at 54 per cent for men and 38 per cent for women, were much lower than the 93 per cent and 83 per cent for couples married in the Established Church. Although contemporaries interpreted this as a cultural, religious and racial distinction, the matter can be analysed according to more objective factors. The dominance of Scottish education by the Presbyterian churches – the denominational battles in the aftermath of the Disruption were keen and highly visible in rural areas – did not create a comfortable atmosphere. As Anderson has pointed out, 'The Irish did not bring a tradition of universal literacy with them, and their problems were compounded by poverty, large families, concentration in unskilled and casual employment and reluctance to use Protestant schools'.[17]

Indeed, over the course of the nineteenth century a contrast began to emerge between three broad educational zones in Scotland. The first was the urban industrial areas, where the pressure of the need to earn drew children, especially boys, away from school at a relatively early age. The second encompassed the west Highlands and Islands where there were continuing economic and social difficulties, including a major subsistence crisis in the 1840s, as well as cultural and linguistic distinctions. The third zone was the rural Lowland areas which showed the highest levels of literacy as well as extensive and diverse provision of school accommodation. In most of the seventeen counties defined as rural Lowland country districts surveyed by the Argyll Commission in the late 1860s, the ratio of scholars to the population of children aged between three and fifteen ranged between 1:1.4 in Stirling to 1:2.4 in Roxburgh, with most counties clustered in a range between 1:1.5 and 1:1.8. This compares with the figures for an industrial area like Glasgow where the figure in Bridgeton in the east end of the city was 1:3.9 and the majority of these would have been younger children.[18] In rural areas, although there was seasonal variation in the levels of attendance, as labour demands on older children were significant, there was a greater chance of scholars staying in school until a later age.

Within the rural Lowland country districts, to use the language of the Argyll Commission, one area which stood out further was the North-East of Scotland. The evidence of that Commission notes the very high proportion of teachers in the county of Aberdeen who held university degrees. This was a direct result of the Dick Bequest (for which, see also the chapters by Northcroft and by Bischof in this volume). In a classic example of the effect of the relationship between Scotland and the empire, a West India merchant, James Dick, left approximately £115,000 in 1828 to assist the parochial schoolmasters of the rural counties of Aberdeen, Banff and Moray. The money was used to supplement the salary of the parochial schoolmaster on the condition of his passing a series of stringent academic and pedagogical tests and the results of regular inspection of his school. Indeed, Simon Laurie, the first professor of education at the University of Edinburgh, was the inspector on behalf of the Trustees from 1856 to 1890. Although the role of private endowments was quite common in Scottish education, the Dick Bequest was on a very large scale and had significant effects. By the 1870s, the average salary of recipients of Dick awards was, at around £150, double the national average. The place of Latin in the curriculum was stronger in these counties than elsewhere in Scotland and the connections between the parish schools and the universities in Aberdeen were powerful. Nevertheless, the provision of support from the Bequest was dependent on the heritors' carrying out their duties effectively, as it was designed to be a supplement to their contribution. This endowment made a real difference to the quality of education in one part of rural Scotland but it also helped to bolster the myth of the Scottish parochial tradition. Laurie's reports contain anecdotes of the discovery of learning in unpropitious circumstances, such as the lad called from the turnip field to be tested during one of his impromptu inspections who took the classical texts in his hands covered in the soil of the field in which he was working and performed with distinction.[19]

As we move into the nineteenth century the source material improves markedly on the eighteenth-century picture and we can produce a more nuanced picture of education in rural areas. In contrast to the rather unsystematic comments in the *Old Statistical Accounts* of the 1790s the ministers charged with producing the material for its successor in the 1830s and 1840s were given specific instructions to present information about education. Although some of the same caveats about the relationship between the clergy and the Established Church continue to apply, especially in rural areas, the *New Statistical Account* is a better source than its predecessor. There is more information about the extent of provision, the nature of the schools, the content of the curricula and the attitude of the population towards education. Very often these accounts demonstrate the diversity of schooling in Lowland rural parishes and the way in which the parochial schools were supplemented by private adventure institutions. In one fairly remote parish in the North-East of Scotland there were seven schools in addition to the parochial school. These were often specialised, sometimes teaching sewing to girls for example. In remote areas parents sometimes clubbed together to hire a teacher in the winter months and divided the cost amongst them. By the late 1830s and 1840s when the *New Statistical Account* was compiled there is evidence of attitudes not present in the 1790s. In Glasserton, Wigtownshire, the minister noted that the children of the poor were educated free at the parish school and that there were charitable endowments to support this activity. He could not resist concluding with the comment that the 'habit of receiving assistance diminishes exertion; and the habit of receiving charity destroys the spirit of independence'.[20]

The parish minister of Gamrie in Banffshire alluded to an important theme when he reported:

There is a female school in MacDuff, with a house and moderate endowment, for the useful and common branches of female education, such as reading, sewing, knitting, &c; and one at Gardenstown, not endowed. It would be a great benefit to this part of the country, if the parochial system were extended, and made to embrace female as well as male education.[21]

The nineteenth century saw greater segregation of the genders at school than had been the case in the eighteenth century. Girls were rarely admitted to the curriculum designed for university entrance and they were debarred from professional careers. The result was that other forms of education emerged for girls.[22] These were often patronised by the aristocratic families such as the Roxburghes at Kelso.[23] Female industrial schools were also numerous and often located in rural or semi-rural locations, teaching needlework and sewing. These skills were not only a domestic virtue but also a potential source of income for women. Buried in the Parochial and Burgh Schoolmasters Act of 1861, which raised teachers' salary limits, was a provision for the appointment of female teachers to provide 'industrial and household training'.[24] There is some evidence that this provided a means by which education could be expanded in remote rural locations where it was difficult to attract well-qualified male teachers. Nevertheless, there was a widespread worry that the education provided by such teachers was inferior. For girls, however, the exposure to a curriculum related to domestic tasks and to skills likely to be of benefit in the workplace was evidence of the increasingly gendered nature of education in Scotland in the years before the 1872 Act.[25]

The relationship between the schools and the heritors continued to be a defining feature of the nineteenth-century experience. This was profoundly affected by wider developments in Scotland in the nineteenth century. Where the relationship with the leading landowners was strong they could be a force for good in the education system. This was clearly the case on the Breadalbane estate in Perthshire and Argyll where the third marquis, an unusual member of the Scottish aristocracy in terms of his interest in evangelical religion and support for the Free Church, was often appealed to on a variety of counts. In 1835, William Armstrong, the schoolmaster at Kenmore, asked Breadalbane for an extension to his accommodation in order to facilitate his taking in of boarders. This was something which was often done by the clergy as well. One of the most significant intellectuals of nineteenth-century Scotland, the controversial Biblical scholar William Robertson Smith, received his entire 'school' education at the hands of his father in the Manse of Keig in Aberdeenshire. Armstrong's plea to the landlord was couched in the necessary deferential terms and he was keen to emphasise that he was well catered for and that his wife taught 'young misses in the different branches of female education'. Nevertheless, the direction of the petition emphasised the extent to which the development of schooling in the area was in the hands of the landowner. This interesting document also serves as a reminder that the rich records of landed estates are an important source for the historian of education before 1872.[26]

An intriguing document from the Breadalbane muniments serves to draw attention to another significant event in Scottish history which had important educational implications. In 1844, a group of tenants from Lochearnhead sent a petition to the marquis pointing out that the majority of the population of the district had left the Established Church at the Disruption of 1843 and that the local parochial schoolmaster had been dismissed for also adhering to the newly established Free Church. They were

> apprehensive lest the school accommodation, which they humbly conceive had been granted by the munificence of the late Marquess for their benefit, may be conferred on a residuary teacher [that is, one belonging to the Church of Scotland], and that they shall be thus deprived of the use of them.[27]

The division of the Church of Scotland in May 1843 and the creation of the Free Church of Scotland had important educational implications, as this petition implies. The tenants of Lochearnhead were fortunate in that their landlord was one of the few to support the Free Church. In other areas of Scotland hostility towards the new denomination took the form of denial of sites for church buildings in a small number of highly publicised cases. Landlord denial of sites for schools may have been more numerous. As far as education is concerned the effect of the Disruption is multifaceted. Some of its effects led to problems, not least the migration of many parochial schoolmasters to the pulpits of the Free Church, causing difficulties in the supply of qualified men to the parish schools, although the numbers were probably much smaller than claimed by the Free Church. The Free Church also claimed that nearly 400 teachers in schools of various kinds were expelled from their posts on account of their adherence to the new denomination. On the other hand the Free Church of Scotland was a remarkable institution determined to see itself, and be seen by society, as an alternative national church, not merely yet another dissenting sect. This manifested itself in a desire to match the Established Church in all its activities, including the provision of schools. There was significant controversy within the Free Church on the matter, between those who argued for an essentially sectarian scheme and those who argued that energy should be invested in campaigning to reform the parochial system by abolishing religious tests for schoolmasters' posts. The former party won out in 1850. Money was raised from within the Free Church community and work began to provide a system of schools. This development had a significant effect in the Highlands and other rural areas of Scotland where the new church was well supported. Great care has to be taken in dealing with this matter, however. The Free Church of Scotland was a propaganda machine of considerable sophistication and so when we read that by the 1850s there were over 700 Free Church schools across Scotland the figure should not be taken at face value. Many of these schools, perhaps up to 25 per cent of them, were probably in existence before the Disruption as private adventure schools. Further, the 1851 Census showed that the Church of Scotland had over 900 schools and that there were over 2,000 schools with no church connection at all. Nevertheless, the provision of an extra several hundred schools, many of them in rural areas, was a significant addition to the network in the middle of the century.[28]

The crucial nature of the relationship between the heritor and the schools and the continuing effects of the Disruption is underlined by an extremely carefully worded Memorial of a general meeting of parochial schoolmasters which convened in Edinburgh in 1853 and lauded the role of the heritors in supporting the education system:

> That the arrangement which places the Election in the hands of the Landed Proprietors, who have so large a stake in the Country and so deep an interest in the hands of the Established Church, having a fixed and permanent standard of faith and doctrine, has secured the appointment of teachers of sound constitutional and religious principles; and that a change in the system which would place the Election and Management in the hands of parties without property and without the requisite education, would produce a totally different class of Teachers, and a totally different kind of teaching – and could not fail to give an impetus to the democratic element in this country of which past history affords no parallel.[29]

The fear of a secular education system was palpable from this document which began with an assertion of the original objective of the Scottish education system as being to provide for the inhabitants of the rural districts.

The context for this document was the threat, as they saw it, of state intervention and the erosion of the position of the landowner and the Established Church of Scotland in the political debate over Scottish education that intensified in the years after the Disruption of the Church of Scotland.

Education in the Gaelic-speaking Areas

Another major area of debate among historians of education in rural Scotland has been a set of issues concerned with the Highlands. Very negative attitudes to Gaelic had been formed in the seventeenth century and can be seen in the Statutes of Iona and the 1616 Act, both of which assumed that the Gaelic language was not suitable for the task of education. This was engrained by the time of the 1696 Act which, like its 1872 successor, did not mention Gaelic. The lack of printed material in Gaelic was another obstacle to the establishment of an educational culture in that language. A series of important developments came in the period from the restoration of Presbyterianism in the Church of Scotland in 1689, through to the founding in Edinburgh in 1709 of the SSPCK. These events set the pattern for the remainder of the period down to the setting up of the Edinburgh Gaelic Schools Society in 1811.

Among the founders of the SSPCK was James Kirkwood who had been an advocate of using Gaelic texts to inculcate literacy and religious ideas but this was not carried through into the SSPCK, which remained strongly opposed in theory and practice to the use of Gaelic in its growing network of schools.[30] A distinctive element in the Scottish Highland context, in contrast to Wales and

Ireland, was the lack of availability of the Bible in Gaelic. The New Testament was not published in Gaelic until 1767 and the whole Bible only in 1801.[31] The SSPCK has been identified as the key agency working against the Gaelic language in the eighteenth century. Others have seen it as struggling against the backwardness of the Highland people and the difficulty of extending educational values into a peripheral region.[32] Until 1825, the formal policy of the SSPCK was, indeed, firmly against the use of Gaelic in its schools, although there was a growing recognition that in order to achieve the aim of spreading English some limited use of Gaelic was necessary. The SSPCK and other agencies saw their role as the transformation of the Gael through a combined process of educational and evangelical activity. Initial reluctance to countenance the use of Gaelic to effect this improvement was modified around 1760 when it was recognised that the use of English with very young children who arrived in school with no facility in that language was counterproductive. The use of Gaelic reading as a means of inculcating literacy in English was adopted in 1826. The overall significance of the SSPCK was that it was a vital agency in the project of anglicising and evangelising the Highlands in the interests of political conformity, a project which long pre-dated the Jacobite rebellion of 1745–6.[33]

The late eighteenth and early nineteenth centuries saw not only the continuing marginalisation of Gaelic but also the creation of crofting communities with their necessity for temporary migration to maintain living standards. This was particularly important after 1815 when economic depression in the key industries reduced opportunities for crofter wage-earning to supplement incomes and provide cash to pay rents. There is much evidence in the *Statistical Accounts* concerning the negative effect of temporary migration on Gaelic. Contact with the Lowlands deepened the perception that Gaelic was inimical to economic progress and improvement. A growing demand for English in Highland schools, and the use of Gaelic as an elementary teaching tool, was the result. The end, the promotion of English, remained the same, however. The SSPCK saw its role as one supplementary to the parochial system. It did not plant schools in areas where there was a parochial school. Amongst other reasons for this was an unwillingness to let the heritors off the hook by reliance on the Society. At the peak of its activity in the 1780s the SSPCK had around 180 schools with a population of 10,500 pupils. The curriculum was basic – it did not include Latin or mathematics – accommodation was poor and the teachers were often not well qualified. The schools were concentrated in the south and east Highlands rather than in the crofting communities of the north and west.[34] The records of the SSPCK, although they have to be handled very carefully indeed as they are so ideologically laden, are an extremely rich source for the educational history of the north of Scotland.

It should be added that although much of the historiography concerned with this agency has been concerned with its role in the Gaelic areas it also planted schools in the North-East and other non-Gaelic areas such as Caithness, Orkney and Shetland. Even in these areas, however, there were still religious and political objectives in the education that was being provided. This is clear from the periodic reports of inspections of the schools. For example, in 1830 a report from the Forest of Birse noted:

> Before the new school was established the glens were filled with Roman Catholics and only three persons could read and had bibles. It is only 36 years since the school commenced and now there is only one Roman Catholic in the district and there is not an individual that cannot read nor a family in which the bible is not to be found . . . I left this school with a very favourable impression of its utility, and with every reason to believe that the great objects of the society have been there fully attained.[35]

The attitude of the SSPCK towards the Gaelic language was closely connected to its religious objectives. This comes through very clearly from much of the extensive documentation in the archive of the Society. In 1830, one of its inspectors remarked, 'The Gaelic language in the Highlands constitutes a peculiar obstacle in the way of religious education', but went on to note the difficulties caused by parochial schoolmasters' remaining ignorant of that language even when it was the only one spoken by the majority of the younger children in their schools. He also noted the complex attitude of the population towards Gaelic in schools in that, in his view, they did not perceive Gaelic as the language of education and sent their children to school in order that they should learn English.[36] This, of course, was the view of an SSPCK agent and does not take account of the effect of at least a century of denigration and negative attitudes towards Gaelic as well as the results of a long period of interaction with the Lowlands of Scotland through temporary migration and other commercial activities, such as herring fishing, the black cattle trade and military recruitment. The issues surrounding the place of Gaelic in the educational curriculum of Highland schools would continue to be controversial in the aftermath of the 1872 Act, as we shall see, and, indeed, well into the twentieth century. (See also the chapter by O'Hanlon and Paterson in the present volume.)

Another key issue which has been debated by historians of education in the Highlands is the extent of provision of schools in the area. In much writing on the subject it was taken for granted that the effect of the 1696 Act was limited in the Highlands due to the poverty of the region, including the indigence of the heritors, as well as difficulties associated with the rugged terrain, the dispersed population and the problem of recruiting teachers to work in the area. Houston's study of literacy concluded that 'through neglect, poverty, language and geography the literacy of the Highlands lagged far behind the rest of Scotland until the late nineteenth century'. Withers, in his history of Gaelic, argued that the 1696 Act was of limited effect in the Highlands outside certain favoured areas such as Argyll. He goes on to make the important point that the problem was exacerbated by the 'denial of Gaelic's place within education' and that this had its roots not in the 1696 Act but much earlier, perhaps in the Statutes of Iona in 1609.[37] A counter-argument was put forward by Withrington who, in a series of publications from the 1960s to the late 1980s, argued that there was a tendency to underestimate the provision of education in the Highlands. He suggested that the views of Withers, Houston and, indeed, earlier writers such as Henry Grey Graham rested on a misreading of sources emanating from the SSPCK and a neglect of attention towards other agencies that supplied schools to the region. He suggested that the tendency to underestimate the number of schools in the Highlands stems from an SSPCK document of 1755 which did not accord the title 'parochial school' to establishments where the master was paid less than the minimum salary according to the 1696 Act. In many places, however, the heritors made the decision to try to overcome problems of physical geography militating against school attendance by setting up two schools and paying a lower stipend. Withrington reworked a series of statistical returns to suggest that if one takes into account charity schools, endowed schools and adventure schools the provision in the Highlands was not so meagre and that the levels of attendance did not compare too badly to other areas of Scotland in 1818. The ratio of scholars to the population as a whole for the Highlands was 1:9.9 compared to 1:12 in the North-East, 1:9.6 in Fife and the Lothians and 1:8.53 in the Borders. He found it surprising that the industrial areas of the west of Scotland had the best ratio at 1:7.6. By 1834, the picture had changed and the North-East (1:8.6), Fife and the Lothians (1:6.5) and the Borders (1:6.9) emerged in a stronger position but, according to Withrington, the Highland ratio of scholars to population of 1:8 met 'contemporary expectations' of a country's educational responsibilities.[38]

As well as the SSPCK, the Gaelic Schools Societies, especially that of Edinburgh, played a huge role in extending provision and inculcating Gaelic literacy in the nineteenth century. This important organisation shared with the SSPCK an evangelical outlook and emphasised the importance of literacy as a means of being able to read scripture, the Bible being available in Gaelic from 1801. The development of reading skills in Gaelic was also important as they promoted comprehension of the text being read rather than the very doubtful educational value of being able to 'read' a passage in a poorly understood language.[39] More research is required on this issue, perhaps relating the Highland experience to a wider comparative framework, but this debate suggests that generalisations about Highland educational backwardness have to be treated with considerable caution. Over the course of the nineteenth century there was a very significant expansion of teaching and learning in Gaelic in schools in the Highlands. Even if the ultimate objective was the inculcation of literacy in English, the contrast with the eighteenth-century picture is striking. It is this direction of development that makes the intervention of the state in 1872 so controversial from a Gaelic point of view. Although the 1872 Act was important in terms of funding and quality control, its permissiveness in curricular matters means that a caricature of its substance was allowed to grow in the later nineteenth and twentieth centuries.

The Voluntary Eviction Act of the Future?

The effect of the 1872 Act on Highland schooling has been a further area of debate among historians of education in the Highlands. Among many writers attempting to counter perceived anti-Gaelic views there is a consensus that the Education (Scotland) Act of 1872 was harmful to Gaelic. The Act's creation of the Scottish Education Department (SED), it is held, led to policies inimical to Gaelic in the education system and damaging to its social status.[40] Indeed, the neglect of Gaelic in this statute is a totemic event in Gaelic culture, as evidenced by Ruaridh MacThòmais's poem 'Ceud bliadhna san sgoil' (A hundred years in school) which recounts the survival of Gaeldom despite, as he saw it, the best efforts of the state education system since 1872. The absence of any mention of Gaelic in the provisions of the 1872 Act has been taken as evidence that the language was neglected in official circles but it also suggests that there was little organised pressure on behalf of the language. A further point is that the 1872 Act had little to say about the content of the curriculum and so the absence of reference to Gaelic is not especially significant. The perceived gaps in the 1872 Act, however, gave the nascent lobby on behalf of the language, such as the Gaelic Society of Inverness (formed in 1871), a focus for its work.[41] The Act was concerned with educational administration rather than curricular issues. The latter were dealt with in annual Education Codes produced by the Scotch Education Department (as it was known when it was set up in 1872).

One of the problems in the late nineteenth century was a lack of reliable information on the demand for Gaelic education. Although the educational administration was no longer in the hands of the churches, the clergy remained an important influence on the new elected school boards. Few of them advocated Gaelic teaching. The value of land in the Highlands meant that it generated very low rates of income to fund services such as education. The result was that the facilities were poor and it was difficult to attract highly qualified and motivated teachers. This, however, was not a new problem in Highland education. The poverty of the crofting communities, the relative improvement in the economy since the famine of the 1840s notwithstanding, meant that scholars' attendance was irregular and this reduced the fee income that partly funded teachers' salaries. A further problem was the difficulty of recruiting teachers who were able to teach Gaelic, a consequence of minimal provision for the language in the universities and teacher training (or 'normal') colleges. With these problems in mind the Privy Council investigated the matter. This revealed that there was some demand for Gaelic teaching in the insular areas. The majority of school boards supported a special grant for Gaelic teaching and, surprisingly, only fourteen boards admitted difficulty in recruiting teachers who were able to give lessons in Gaelic.[42] This was seen by many as a surprisingly positive response from the school boards in the Highlands. Only very minimal concessions were granted by the government in the aftermath of this exercise. Gaelic was recognised by the Education Code but its teaching was not funded by any special grant until it was made a 'specific subject' in 1885. This meant that teachers had to deliver the other standard areas of the curriculum, the subjects which would interest the Inspectorate, before they could turn to Gaelic.

The further educational consequences of these debates are investigated in the chapter by O'Hanlon and Paterson in the present volume, but – despite the advent of greater state involvement through the new SED – it might be noted as a sign of continuity with the mid-Victorian preference for minimal government that it is striking that responsibility for implementing this modest change was devolved to the school boards. Power was devolved to the ratepayers who funded the school boards and who elected their members. This was quite a broad electorate, much wider than that for parliamentary elections, and was based on a £4 franchise qualification that included women. This provided an opportunity for Gaelic activists to populate the school boards and bring pressure to bear by that route.[43] This was not easy. School boards included representatives of estate management as well as the clergy, and so there was a challenge for a crofter with, before 1886, an insecure tenancy to seek election. One particular issue arose in the Catholic areas of South Uist and Barra where the school board was dominated by Protestants. It was not, however, until after the Crofters Act of 1886 that a challenge to this position was mounted and even then it was the local priest, Fr Allan McDonald, who put himself forward for election in order to move towards a more representative body with greater sympathy for the appointment of Catholic teachers.[44]

Conclusion

The range of agencies which worked to deliver education in Scotland in the eighteenth and nineteenth centuries had particular challenges to face in rural Scotland. The geographical and cultural issues were at their most acute in the Highlands but schooling in areas of Lowland Scotland, such as the south-west, was far from straightforward. The pace of social and economic change in rural Lowland Scotland in the eighteenth century was rapid and at times overtook older patterns of educational provision. Despite the emphasis on the parochial schools in the legislation and in the image of Scottish education there was a very wide range of schools in the rural areas. Alongside the parish schools were private adventure schools, charity schools (especially those of the SSPCK and the Edinburgh Gaelic Schools Society), General Assembly schools, those provided by religious denominations other than the Church of Scotland (especially the Free Church after 1843) as well as industrial schools aimed at girls and often supported by leading landowners. The integration of Scottish educational history with wider narratives is important. This is perhaps especially so in the Highlands, where most of the educational decision making came from outside the area, and where attitudes to the Gaelic language and the economy and society of the region drove the direction of educational development. Despite these difficulties rural Scotland was the source of much of the mythical history of Scottish education as well as of evidence of the most effective functioning of the system. This was especially so in the North-East of Scotland where the support for the parochial system from the Dick Bequest and the presence of two universities in Aberdeen meant that there was some chance that the ideal could be observed in tangible form.

Notes

1. Laurance J. Saunders, *Scottish Democracy, 1815–1840: The Social and Intellectual Background* (Oliver and Boyd, 1950), pp. 242, 288.
2. John Mason, *A History of Scottish Experiments in Rural Education From the Eighteenth Century to the Present Day* (University of London Press, 1935), p. vii.
3. Lawrence Stone, 'Literacy and education in England 1640–1900', *Past and Present* 42 (February 1969), 69–139.
4. Acts of the Parliaments of Scotland, x, 63, c.26; see Records of the Parliaments of Scotland, available at http://rps.ac.uk/trans/1696/9/144 (accessed 6 October 2014).
5. Edith E. B. Thompson, *The Parliament of Scotland, 1690–1702* (Oxford University Press, c. 1929), pp. 144–6.
6. J. A. Russell, *Education in Wigtownshire, 1560–1970* (Galloway Gazette Press, 1971), pp. 25–6; James Scotland, *The History of Scottish Education*, 2 vols (University of London Press, 1969), vol. i, p. 60.
7. J. C. Jessop, *Education in Angus: An Historical Survey of Education up to the Act of 1872 From Original and Contemporary Sources* (University of London Press, 1931), pp. 77, 84.
8. John Lorne Campbell, *Gaelic in Scottish Education and Life: Past, Present and Future* (Edinburgh, 1950), pp. 50–6; Mason, *Scottish Experiments in Rural Education*, pp. vii, 12–22, 39–49, 63.
9. National Records of Scotland [henceforth: NRS], E783/63/1–9; these petitions cover the period from 1759 to 1782. Most of the forfeited estates were returned to their former owners in 1784.
10. Robert T. D. Glaister, 'Rural private teachers in 18th-century Scotland', *Journal of Educational Administration and History* 23 (1991), 49–61.
11. For a fairly representative sample see *Old Statistical Account* [henceforth: OSA], i, p. 256 (Kirkmaiden); iii, pp. 196–7 (Dirleton); iv, p. 241 (Barrie); xiv, p. 523 (Auchterhouse). Available at http://edina.ac.uk.ezproxy.is.ed.ac.uk/stat-acc-scot (accessed 6 October 2014).
12. OSA, vii, pp. 117–18 (Auchtertool, Fife).
13. T. C. Smout, 'Born again at Cambuslang: New evidence on popular religion and literacy in eighteenth-century Scotland', *Past and Present* 97 (November 1982), 114–27. For the text of the testimonies as recorded by the minister, see Keith Edward Beebe (ed.), *The McCulloch Examinations of the Cambuslang Revival (1742)*, 2 vols, Scottish History Society, sixth series (Woodbridge, 2013), vols 5–6.
14. R. A. Houston, *Scottish Literacy and the Scottish Identity: Illiteracy and Society in Scotland and Northern England 1600–1800* (Cambridge University Press, 1985), p. 56.
15. R. A. Houston, 'Scottish education and literacy, 1600–1800: An international perspective', in T. M. Devine (ed.), *Improvement and Enlightenment* (John Donald, 1988), pp. 43–61.
16. Anderson, *Education and the Scottish People*, pp. 15–16.
17. Ibid., pp. 15–16.

18. *Education Commission (Scotland). Statistical Report on the State of Education in the Lowland Country Districts of Scotland* (1867), p. 10; *Report on the State of Education in Glasgow* (1867), p. 17.

19. Marjorie Cruickshank, 'The Dick Bequest: The effect of a famous nineteenth-century endowment on parish schools of North East Scotland', *History of Education Quarterly* 5 (1965), 153–65.

20 See *New Statistical Account* [henceforth: NSA] ii, pp. 169–71 (Yester); iv, p. 413 (Eskdalemuir); iv, p. 51 (Glasserton); vi, pp. 368–9 (Biggar); ix, p. 555 (Kilmany); xii, p. 783 (Glenmuick, Tullich, Glengairn). Available at http://edina.ac.uk.ezproxy.is.ed.ac.uk/stat-acc-scot (accessed 6 October 2014).

21. NSA, xiii, pp. 293–4 (Gamrie).

22. Lindy Moore, 'Invisible scholars: Girls learning Latin and mathematics in the elementary public schools of Scotland before 1872', *History of Education* 13 (1984), 121–37; Lindy Moore, 'Educating for the "women's sphere": Domestic training versus intellectual discipline', in Esther Brietenbach and Eleanor Gordon (eds), *Out of Bounds: Women and Scottish Society, 1800–1945* (Edinburgh University Press, 1992), pp. 10–41.

23. NSA, iii, p. 340 (Kelso).

24. Anderson, *Education and the Scottish People*, pp. 81–4, 312.

25. Jane McDermid, 'Gender, national identity and the Royal (Argyll) Commission of Inquiry into Scottish education (1864–1867)', *Journal of Educational Administration and History* 38 (2006), 249–62.

26. NRS, GD112/11/10/3/18, Memorial of William Armstrong, Schoolmaster of Kenmore, 13 Jun. 1835; Donald J. Withrington, 'The school in the Free Church manse at Keig', in William Johnstone (ed.), *William Robertson Smith: Essays in Reassessment* (Sheffield Academic Press, 1995), pp. 41–9.

27. NRS, GD112/11/10/8a/42, Representation and Petition of the undersigned Inhabitants of the District of Lochearnhead being Heads of Families, 1844.

28. Donald J. Withrington, 'Adrift among the reefs of conflicting ideals? Education and the Free Church, 1843–55', in Stewart J. Brown and Michael Fry (eds), *Scotland in the Age of Disruption* (Edinburgh University Press, 1993), pp. 79–97; Donald J. Withrington, 'The Free Church educational scheme, 1843–50', *Records of the Scottish Church History Society* 15 (1964), pp. 103–15.

29. NRS, GD46/12/104, Memorial of the Committee Appointed by a General Meeting of the parochial Schoolmasters of Scotland, 15 Sep. 1853.

30. Victor E. Durkacz, 'The source of the language problem in Scottish education, 1688–1709', *Scottish Historical Review* 57 (1978), 28–39.

31. Donald Meek, 'The Gaelic Bible', in David F. Wright (ed.), *The Bible in Scottish Life and Literature* (The Saint Andrew Press, 1988), pp. 9–23.

32. Campbell, *Gaelic in Scottish Education and Life*, pp. 60–2; John Mason, 'Scottish charity schools of the eighteenth century', *Scottish Historical Review* 33 (1954), 1–13.

33. Victor E. Durkacz, *The Decline of the Celtic Languages: A Study of Linguistic and Cultural Conflict in Scotland, Wales and Ireland from the Reformation to the Twentieth Century* (John Donald, 1983), pp. 96–122.

34. Charles W. J. Withers, *Gaelic Scotland: The Transformation of a Culture Region* (Routledge, 1988), pp. 122–36.

35. NRS, GD95/14/23, Report of Visitation of Schools, 11 May 1830 (Forest of Birse, 26 Apr. 1830).

36. NRS, GD95/9/4, Journal of A Visit to the Schools of the Society in Scotland for Propagating Christian Knowledge by Patrick Butter, 1826.

37. Houston, *Scottish Literacy*, pp. 82–3; Charles W. J. Withers, *Gaelic in Scotland, 1698–1981: The Geographical History of a Language* (John Donald, 1984), p. 117.
38. Donald J. Withrington, 'The SPCK and Highland schools in the mid-eighteenth century', *Scottish Historical Review* 41 (1962), 89–99; Donald J. Withrington, 'Schooling, literacy and society', in T. M. Devine and Rosalind Mitchison (eds), *People and Society in Scotland, Vol. I: 1760–1830* (John Donald, 1988), pp. 163–87.
39. Durkacz, *The Decline of the Celtic Languages*, pp. 123–33, 163–4.
40. Campbell, *Gaelic in Scottish Education and Life*, p. 46; Kenneth MacKinnon, *Gaelic: A Past and Future Prospect* (Saltire Society, 1991), pp. 74–6.
41. 'Introduction', *Transactions of the Gaelic Society of Inverness* [henceforth: *TGSI*] 1 (1871–2), p. xi.
42. 'Gaelic in Highland schools', *TGSI* 7 (1877–8), pp. 11–18.
43. 'Great Celtic demonstration', *TGSI* 7 (1877–8), pp. 229.
44. John Lorne Campbell, *Fr Allan McDonald of Eriskay, 1859–1905: Priest, Poet, and Folklorist* (Oliver and Boyd, 1954), pp. 10–11; Roger Hutchison, *Father Allan: The Life and Legacy of a Hebridean Priest* (Birlinn, 2010), pp. 96–100.

Bibliography

Campbell, John Lorne, *Gaelic in Scottish Education and Life: Past, Present and Future* (W. and A. K. Johnston, 1950).

Cruickshank, Marjorie, 'The Dick Bequest: The effect of a famous nineteenth-century endowment on parish schools of North East Scotland', *History of Education Quarterly* 5 (1965), 153–65.

Durkacz, Victor Edward, *The Decline of the Celtic Languages: A Study of Linguistic and Cultural Conflict in Scotland, Wales and Ireland from the Reformation to the Twentieth Century* (John Donald, 1983).

Houston, R. A., *Scottish Literacy and the Scottish Identity: Illiteracy and Society in Scotland and Northern England 1600–1800* (Cambridge University Press, 1985).

Mason, John, *A History of Scottish Experiments in Rural Education From the Eighteenth Century to the Present Day* (University of London Press, 1935).

McDermid, Jane, 'Gender, national identity and the Royal (Argyll) Commission of Inquiry into Scottish education (1864–1867)', *Journal of Educational Administration and History* 38 (2006), 249–62.

Saunders, Laurance J., *Scottish Democracy, 1815–1840: The Social and Intellectual Background* (Oliver and Boyd, 1950).

Smout, T. C., 'Born again at Cambuslang: New evidence on popular religion and literacy in eighteenth-century Scotland', *Past and Present* 97 (November 1982), 114–27.

Withers, Charles W. J., *Gaelic Scotland: The Transformation of a Culture Region* (Routledge, 1988).

Withrington, Donald J., 'Schooling, literacy and society', in T. M. Devine and Rosalind Mitchison (eds), *People and Society in Scotland, Volume I, 1760–1830* (John Donald, 1988), pp. 163–87.

10

A' Yon Skweelin:
The North-East, a Regional Study

David Northcroft

Sir Henry Craik, once head of our Education Department, said Scotland was the best educated country in the world and the North-East counties were the best educated counties in it.[1]

In 1953, a young Englishwoman called Joan Cantlie Stewart bought a semi-derelict cottage in the remote Strathdon settlement of Corgarff. There, in her own stark and beautiful glen, she worked to restore the house and, some 1,400 feet above sea level, to adjoin it with a garden cut out as a verdant ledge on the hard eastern face of the Cairngorms. She became part of the community, raised her children there, sent her son to the local school and ended up teaching in the junior secondary school that lay a twenty-five-minute bicycle ride away down the valley. In 1973, she returned to the south and a quarter of a century later, she published the story of her life in that place and called it *Pine Trees and the Sky*. The section which deals with her educational experiences there she entitled 'Scholars'.[2]

In it, the personal incidents – her son Hughie's first day at school when he came home convinced that the strange Doric tongue of the children in the playground (but never in the classroom) must be 'French' or the efforts of the district's kirk minister, naturally a regular visitor to the school, to teach the lads cricket on 'the only flat field in the parish' – merge easily into general comment and historical explanation. Thus, the end of year prizegiving 'would have pleased the founder of Scottish education, John Knox' because it had been his vision to erect a school in every country parish so that the people might be trained in useful skills and strive for high learning; the fine herds of Aberdeen Angus in the fields all around are seen as a tribute to 'the high standard of universal education that turned the northern Scots into the finest cattle breeders in Britain'. She recalls the time when all the schools of Aberdeenshire 'but two' taught Greek. Where once children brought peats to fire the classroom stove, the 'loons' of the 1960s stacked firewood in the shed and the 'quinies' laid out the tables for dinnertime.

And in that little local place, Mrs McIntyre, the parish schoolmistress, continued to impart a teaching that was 'traditional and of high standard' and was 'impossible to match in any infant or primary school further south'. 'Both children and parents knew they had a teacher who upheld the finest traditions of the school dominie'. During her own spells in the classroom, the author found her pupils to be so 'courteous and self-disciplined' that they 'equated favourably with private rather than public education in England'. But then, the conclusion pounces, 'the English regard education as a means to an end whereas the Scots believe in it as an end in itself'.

The statement is characteristic of a chapter that begins in individual venture and ends as a general commentary which seeks to join her specific experiences to the history of a nation. There was nothing new in this. Here, in a work of North-East domestic reminiscence, published at the very end of the twentieth century, is evidence that the collective belief in the supremacy of the region's educational traditions still carried sufficient power to suffuse the personal account with the incantatory force of a familiar national faith.

In a few paragraphs, Mrs Stewart has gathered together the standard tropes of a genre of regional recall, one which proudly stretches back into the early years of the preceding century. They are all there: the homage to Knox and his *Book of Discipline*; the allusions to 'loons and quinies' and their latter-day 'dominie'; the elevation of the annual prizegiving into a celebration of the nation's adherence to scholarly rigour; the setting of the homely detail into an elemental landscape of rock and hill and testing climate; the laudatory references to the efficient workings of a predominantly agrarian economy as the fruits of native wit and educated endeavour; the self-congratulatory comparisons to the half-hearted English system, here regarded not simply as a matter of systemic inferiority but also of ingrained character; the elevation of daily labour – the peats and the firewood – into an exemplary self-sufficiency. All will be familiar to those who have read within the biographies, literature, commentary and parish histories that range along the 'Local Studies' shelf of any of the region's public libraries.

Above all, there is the urge to place the North-East in particular within the larger narrative of the Scottish educational project. It is this blending of the personal instance with the national myth, so that the localised happening combines with an idealised history which holds them together in the collective memory that sums up the North-East educational tradition. In this, *Pine Trees and the Sky* points to where the driving power of that heritage lies. It is not that the region's parish schools have been different from those elsewhere in Scotland: it is that they are its idealised representation. In their daily excellence and in their fidelity to the national ideal, they, more than any other grouping of counties, sum up its deepest values.

The Dick Bequest

Until the early decades of the nineteenth century, education in the North-East had progressed to an extent that was little different from that in any other predominantly Lowland part of Scotland.[3] This meant that when the government embarked on its nationwide survey of provision in 1834, every parish could demonstrate evidence that it maintained a public school, complete with its properly lettered and salaried master.

Joan Stewart's Strathdon, for example, supported a parochial school that had a total roll of ninety-eight pupils, in the charge of one 'instructor' who drew an annual stipend of £28, plus parental fees of £10. In return, he offered a syllabus which, in addition to 'reading, writing, arithmetic, mathematics, English grammar', ran to 'the elements of Latin'.[4]

However, in the year before this investigation reported, a significant development occurred, one which was to advance the state of North-East schooling beyond that which was available elsewhere in Scotland. This was the Dick Bequest, whereby handsome grants were to be made to each of those parish schoolmasters throughout the counties of Aberdeenshire, Banffshire and Moray who had achieved university-level qualifications and who could demonstrate 'diligence' in their work. The scheme was operated through a series of demanding teacher examinations, covering such subjects as English grammar and the Classics, and of regular inspections. These visitations yielded a voluminous series of Reports, firstly under the authorship of Professor Allan Menzies, and then that of Professor Simon Laurie, both of Edinburgh University (Laurie later held its first chair in education). These works constituted influential advocacies of the importance of high scholarship and thoroughgoing methodology.

James Dick was a native of Forres who made his fortune in the West Indies; his action was made as grateful acknowledgement for the sound education he had received at his local school. Soon afterwards, in 1846, his generosity was matched by a second far-reaching bequest: that of Dr John Milne, President of the Medical Board of Bombay. His proposal was to supplement the salary of those masters who reached a certain professional standard, in return for waiving fees for twenty-five pupils, selected as deserving cases by the Kirk Session. The initial intention had been to extend the opportunities for a good elementary education to the most impoverished pupils, but the underlying importance of high academic qualification was also upheld: by 1864, the award had come to be reserved for university graduates.

The provision of Latin was crucial. Without access to the subject, even the brightest scholar would be effectively debarred from the annual bursary competition examinations run by King's and Marischal Colleges (united in 1860 to form Aberdeen University) and thus from any opportunity to win sufficient funds to underwrite a degree course. By the mid-century, the Aberdeen bursary contests had developed into an object of competitive prestige. These were open to all and yielded lists of merit which were published in full; an individual's success was seen as conferring honour on the local community which had reared such a champion.[5] The widespread availability of university trained schoolmasters in North-East schools, able to prepare candidates for this annual trial, rapidly became viewed as a defining virtue. They were the means by which the region became supreme in its ability to fulfil the democratic promise inherent to the

Scottish parochial system: that no lad, from however humble a background, should be denied the chance to ascend the ladder of academic opportunity to the heights merited by his native wit and application.

The impact of this funding, and the rigorous professional stipulations which attended it, was judged to be considerable. When the government carried out its next comprehensive investigation into Scotland's schooling, the Argyll report, published in 1866–7, it was able to report that 'the teachers are more highly educated and the whole tone of parochial schools is higher in those counties where the [Dick] Bequest applies than in any other part of Scotland'.[6]

The annual Reports to the Bequest trustees express a similar satisfaction and frequently do so in terms which relate scholastic progress to wider social developments:

> science and industry have wrought a marvellous change during the last twenty years, covering a rude and sterile surface with verdure and plenty. It has been a delightful duty in the application of this Bequest to second the benevolent and enlightened efforts of ministers and heritors in imparting to the hardy tenants of the soil in such localities the blessing of a high moral and intellectual culture.[7]

These claims, written in the 1850s, point to a second influential factor in the ascendancy of North-East schools: the dramatic improvements to the agrarian economy since the beginning of the century, a time when visitors to the North-East were writing its landscape down as a backward waste of peaty bogs, of stone-strewn, unenclosed fields and straggling heath-choked vistas, dotted with the miserable hovels of a benighted peasantry.[8] In the span of those fifty years a great work of agricultural progress had taken place, partly through the patronage of 'improving landlords' like Grant of Monymusk, but mostly through the endeavour of a multitude of labourers who had been clearing, enclosing, draining and ditching, and then applying the latest methods of fertilisers and stockbreeding, and doing so to such an extent that they succeeded in transforming the North-East into one of Britain's most advanced agrarian economies.

A number of studies, pre-eminently by the then Aberdeen University sociologist Ian Carter,[9] have explored these developments as an interaction with the structures and attitudes which became prevalent in North-East rural communities. Using the subtitle 'The Poor Man's Country', Carter documents a land where the largest farms were usually of no more than medium size and where there were real opportunities for 'the poor man' to move up the socio-economic scale, from crofter to tenant to the well-acred 'muckle farmer', all through his own skilful industriousness. Living standards were visibly improving. As Ian Simpson concludes in his *Education in Aberdeenshire before 1872*, the county 'had ceased to be a miser's pensioner'.[10]

This sense of having the means for self-improvement in their own hands bred an aspirational culture which was conducive to the acquisition of education, to 'getting on', in the classroom and in the fields which surrounded it. The local school came to be valued both as a source of the basic reading, writing and

counting so useful to the planning and implementation of new farming techniques and also by the brightest sons of the North-East soil as the gateway into
the socially prestigious posts of church minister or school dominie.

Parish Schooling and the North-East

The 'hardy tenants of the soil', the blessing 'of a high moral and intellectual culture', the opposition of 'rude and sterile' lands to those of 'verdure and plenty' –
the language of Allan Menzies, professor of conveyancing at the University of
Edinburgh and, here, reporter to the trustees of the Dick Bequest, takes us beyond
the soberly factual and into the register of literary embellishment. But already,
by the time of its composition, it had become common to employ such charged
description, loaded with moralistic valuations, when writing of the schools of the
North-East.

It was this combination of authoritative reportage and evocative acclama-
tion which made this model so irresistible to a work which appeared seventy-five
years later, in 1925: William Barclay's *The Schools and Schoolmasters of Banffshire*.
Produced for the county's branch of the Educational Institute of Scotland, the
intention was to document the achievements of Banffshire schools from the
earliest sixteenth century Reformation records to the latest era of county-wide
education authorities, as established by the national 1918 Act. Although it is full
of lists, dates and diligently assembled events, the factual account is swelled by
passages from local histories, extracts of public speeches, sketches of exemplary
careers, individual reminiscences and contemporary press cuttings.

Citing Menzies' comments in his 'Introduction', Barclay uses them as the
first steps on a romantic historical journey. They are a fitting curtain raiser to
the pageant which follows as, parish by parish, Barclay sweeps us through his
county's chronicle, each page peopled by a succession of golden scholar heroes
and their magisterial dominies. There are the Ogilvies,[11] that 'quintet of famous
educationists' reared as a tenant farmer's sons, who each marched forth from the
little school at Milltown of Rothiemay to make his mark upon the intellectual
life of the country, as a spread of headmasters, school inspectors and, in Joseph,
the very first principal of the teachers' training college at Aberdeen. Then there
is Ramsay MacDonald, Britain's first ever Labour Prime Minister but, beyond all,
a Lossiemouth loon taught at the feet of his namesake John Macdonald, where,
in the tiny school of Drainie, he tells us in his rhapsodic tribute: 'The machinery
was as old as Knox; the education was the best ever given to the sons and daughters of men'.[12] Or the young George Stephen who set out on life as a humble 'herd
laddie' on the glebe at the manse of Mortlach, but who, given his learning by
John Macpherson – a 'man of outstanding abilities', yet content to devote thirty
years to the service of the parochial school – grew up to become Lord Mount
Stephen, founder of the Canadian Pacific Railway and noted philanthropist.[13]

This stirring human drama is played out before an emblematically grand
background. In the Preface, the author informs us that his is 'a county that may
be taken as representative of conditions throughout Scotland'.[14] This is, on the

face of it, an improbably bold claim to make of a tapering finger of territory, almost exclusively wild upland and agricultural lowland, over 150 miles north of the industrialised Central Belt, where the majority of the country's population actually live and find their work.

That, however, is to miss the point. Barclay's Banffshire might be a small and sparsely populated land mass but it is one that stretches into a varied hinterland of 'field, pasture, glen, moor, and forest and abundance of running water', up to the Cairngorms, 'the greatest mountainous area of Scotland'. Barclay's school-masters stride out over a land marked by the elemental symbolism of a country which, historically, has preferred to seek its soul within its rural and, therefore, more 'natural' past, away from the factories and the conurbations that have lately troubled its countenance in less favoured, more southerly spots.

By the time Barclay came to compile his opus, a whole century's worth of similar writing lay behind him. Ninety years beforehand, the *Aberdeen Magazine* had hymned its readers with these 'Remarks on Parochial Education in Scotland':

> It is a system of which Scotland has just reason to be proud . . . Of silver and gold, she has ever but possessed a trifling share; nor has nature bestowed upon her the warmth of unclouded sun and rich products of luxuriant soil . . . yet her moral atmosphere has been generally serene and unclouded. While the benefits of knowledge in other countries have been, comparatively speaking, locked up from all those whose fortunes have not raised them above the lower or even middling ranks of life, the son of the most humble peasant in our native land has it in his power to approach the fountain of learning and to drink unmolested from its pure and invigorating and ennobling stream.[15]

It is a mix of romanticised landscape portrayal, sententious moralising and aca-demic chauvinism that is as much concerned to establish a compelling myth as it is to record a sociological truth. Appearing in 1834, it set weaving a rich pattern of evocative writing that was to be much copied in the biographies, the poetry, the local histories and the journalistic comment that were to follow over the next hundred years.

By the time that Walter Gregor produced his 1874 *Echo of the Olden Times in the North of Scotland*, the tradition had ripened into an almost folkloric intensity. In a series of 'education' chapters,[16] Gregor orchestrates the stages by which his archetypal 'anxious boy' wins his way towards his destiny by striving upwards from industrious poverty to occupy, first, the position of parochial schoolmaster at his very own native parish, and then to enter its pulpit.

It is 'that platform of equality', 'the Parish School', where, 'at a cost of less than twenty shillings a-year such an education was furnished as fitted the scholar for entering university', which sets him on his way. Ultimate success is depicted as a perfect native collaboration of academic system, individual will, communal support and moral strength. The school both feeds his hunger for knowledge and tests his character. Hours at the desk have to be intertwined with duties on the farm, the threshing flail in hand, his Latin grammar propped up before him, his diet that of oatmeal porridge – 'Scotland's halesome food'. His years at the college in the distant city are a round of unremitting study sustained by no more than the sack of meal, the small box of butter, a few eggs and the yellow haddock he takes from home.

The eventual success is a fitting personal reward but it is more than just an individual triumph. All through his journey, Gregor's hero is depicted as the representative of his parish, the unnamed generic 'he' who, by enacting the virtues of his people, becomes the champion of the tribe. The setting is firmly bucolic; its values are those of thrift, piety, work and gritty, self-sacrificing discipline. When the whole parish gathers to send him off on his trek to the city for the bursary competition, they are demonstrating that he is carrying more than their simple best hopes: he is the bearer of the very qualities they steer their own lives by. And when the news comes through of his victory, it is felt as one that belongs to them all, 'for was he not an honour to the parish?'

The interaction between the nation's school system and North-East values is promoted as the perfect match. This was a marriage celebrated by a succession of writers in the years leading up to Barclay's book of 1925. In the local histories which began to appear of districts as far-flung as Laurencekirk and Fettercairn in the south and Glass and Aberlour to the north, a chapter on 'School and Schoolmasters', to be followed by one on the 'Eminent Men' thus fashioned, appears as an automatic inclusion. In verse collections such as 'Under the Crusie'[17] and 'Wylans frae my Wallet',[18] the iconic title, the 'Dominie', becomes a standard item.

When Elsie Rae came to brandish Sir Henry Craik's accolade before the reader, she could do so with the confidence that it would command instant recognition. Her *A Waff o' Win fae Bennachie* is written to constitute a definitive guide to her region. In her chapter 'North East Folk', she steers us through the full range of topographical and historical features but her key statement comes when she announces: 'If I were asked what was the most outstanding thing about the people of the North east, I would say, without hesitation, their love of learning'.[19]

The claim is encased in the same binding that Gregor employs: there is the 'frugal' life, the 'plain' behaviours, the stinting and the starving to ensure a full education for the bairns; there are tales of a daily ten-mile slog over steep heather-clad slopes by infant feet, intent on the schooling which will win them through to the University of Aberdeen, 'the university of the working man's family'. And overarching all is the repeated assertion that this is 'Scotland', or rather, Scotland purged of its more recent degenerative and urbanised pretension: 'The folk of the North east are apt to be judged thus because what are common Scottish characteristics are in them more obvious, more intense'.[20]

Challenging the 'North-East Tradition'

Mythologised history of the kind offered by Barclay, Rae and Gregor seeks to imbue the current scene with the inherited properties of an idealised past and thus turn chronicle into tradition. It is by this process that the human elements

Figure 10.1 A Primary 5–6 class gather around their teacher, Mrs McDonald, at
Aberlour High School, 1951. Copyright the author.

take on iconic status: village teachers become 'dominies'; their prize pupils are
'lads o' pairts'(they are the sons of pious 'peasant folk'); the parochial establishment is the dear remembered 'skweel'; the scholars' progress is a precious morality
tale. The appeal to the reader's self-identification as a proud Scot is overpowering.

Despite, or because of, the implied invitation to suspend critical judgment,
it is important to consider those other commentators who have approached the
hallowed North-East story as one in need of demystification. In 1952, at the same
period Joan Stewart was settling into her Corgarff idyll, John R. Allan, noted
North-East author and farmer, published a work which came to be widely considered as the definitive study of its subject: *The North-East Lowlands of Scotland*. He
regarded his chapter on education 'to be an indispensable key' to the culture and
history of his region for, as he tells us, 'Education is a chief industry of the north'.
Its title is 'The Lad o' Pairts'.[21]

Allan begins with the familiar set of inherited ingredients: the native pride
in fashioning a system superior to anything 'the rich' English had managed to put
together; the ladder of opportunity erected by John Knox's reformers; the image
of the clever lad proceeding to university, his bag of oatmeal on his shoulder,
the prayers of his self-sacrificing parents ringing in his ears, there to subsist in
some mean lodging on a diet of salt herring, Livy, Xenophon and the occasional
luxurious egg. Then there are the anecdotes: the old man who was forced to leave
school at the age of twelve to support his impoverished family by working at a
farm for £4 a year but, at the end of each twelve-hour day, reporting back to his

old dominie, there to be coached in the Classics that, finally, in his mid-twenties, enabled him to win his bursary and, four hard years later, a glorious MA.

But then comes another story, that of an 'old gentleman' who, describing his parish schoolmaster, offers this wry summing up: 'Aa he taught me was the weight o the tawse'. And from this point onwards, the anticipated rehearsal of virtues gives way to a critique which is more concerned to conduct clear-eyed enquiry than to rehearse the customary homage. Blending personal recall with historical evidence, Allan explores a system which, he concludes, is designed to serve the ambitions of a small minority of star pupils and is content to treat the 'ordinary unacademic child' as a by-product. All are pushed onto the same assembly line of memorised facts and precepts, so that the few who have the capacity to endure the process may be moulded into the approved scholastic shape. And even those who may be reckoned the victors in this evolutionary scramble are ill-served, for, by 'moulding', Allan means that the 'pairts' are squeezed and trammelled until all that is left of the individual's 'mind and spirit' is the faculty of mechanical repetition of imprinted abstraction. The lads o' pairts emerge from this 'indoctrination into dullness' as 'machines, cautious, unemotional, unimaginative'.

By the 1950s, Allan had built up a canon of commentary on his North-East world, one which played over the scene with a taut mix of lyrical appreciation and sceptical interrogation. But if his was a distinctive voice, his confrontation of the shibboleths of his people was not an unprecedented one. A century before, another – and, for his own era, equally influential – presence was at work with enquiries into the sociology of rural Aberdeenshire. This was William Alexander who, in 1869, embarked on a serialisation in the *Aberdeen Free Press* of what was to be a masterpiece of Victorian Scottish fiction: *Johnny Gibb of Gushetneuk*.[22] It is an ambitiously epic novel, one which, by bringing together the tensions which existed between the interests of lairds and muckle farmers on the one side, and cottars and tenants on the other, seeks to provide a comprehensive rendering of the socio-economic forces within his region.

Education is shown to occupy a significant position in this conflict. In the chapter 'Pedagogical',[23] Alexander sets up a pair of contrasting schools to serve his typical parish of Pyketillim, the first of which is the public establishment run by the appropriately named Reverend Jonathan Tawse, widely considered to be 'a superior educationist'. The fact that he conforms to eponym means, however, that he runs a classroom which is designed to subdue the youthful spirits of the sons and daughters of the soil entrusted to his parochial care. He rules them through a regime of leather strap, outbursts of ferocious temper and a syllabus of catechism, 'Gray's Arithmetic' and rote-learned alphabet. That is the fare prescribed for the peasant masses; 'democratic' opportunity is served by his willingness to take on the very occasional client for Latin – in this case the natural son of a local laird and Benjie, the son of a muckle farmer whose push towards social advancement demands this extra scholastic gloss.

The results are predictably farcical. At the end of one session the wretched Benjie, having stumbled through the mystifying pages of *Ruddiman's Rudiments* can just about manage to blurt out 'amo, amas, amat' without, however, 'the remotest conception of what it was all about'. It is the second school, the unofficial private one run by Sandy Peterkin, which attracts Alexander's favour. No Latin here but, instead, the sort of practical skills in land surveying, everyday calculation and an imaginative introduction to geography that are designed to engage the interests of his farmers' offspring. The contrast that it forms with Johnny Tawse's parochial school is designed to lay bare the values that inform the official system as being inimical to the culture and needs of Aberdeenshire children.

Alexander's was far from being the only critical voice. Since the seminal work of William Donaldson began to appear,[24] it has become impossible to ignore the extent to which a persistent strain of criticism became a staple feature in the local newspapers and magazines that flourished at that time. Donaldson has shown how the columns of, for example, the *Peterhead Sentinel* and the *Aberdeen Weekly Press* acted as a platform for irreverent observation on such pillars of Victorian parish life as council officials, landlords and the kirk, the very agencies which continued to be so influential in overseeing the conduct of parochial schooling even into the post-1872 era of elected school boards. Popular columnists like William Latto and 'Jeems Kaye' were weekly at work, puncturing the pretensions of the self-regarding 'democratic' schooling of the era. Significantly, in pieces such as Archie Tait's 'Eddicashin an' Teachers',[25] the criticism is couched in the everyday Doric which was excluded from the classroom, a usage which carried a pungent riposte to the manner in which the contemporary school system deliberately excluded the vigorous oral culture of its communities.

Indeed, the extent to which the North-East's schools sought to supplant the language of the home with an inculcation into a standardised form – though a process common to most European systems – was a particular source of tension in nineteenth-century North-East Scotland, whose 'Doric' persisted as a markedly distinct dialect. As much of its intensely physical vocabulary and intonations were expressive of the region's predominantly agricultural way of life, the official drive to enhance social mobility and a modernising outlook with an insistence on linguistic uniformity meant that the local school was liable to be experienced as an unsympathetically alien presence within the community that it purported to serve.

Tait was writing in the 1890s, at a time when a considerable body of criticism lay behind him. Even the rapid spread of the adult 'mutual instruction' movement by which agricultural workers banded together, though often presented as yet another tribute to the ingrained North-East hunger for education, can be seen as evidence of dissatisfaction with the official school system. Robert Smith, who composed *An Aberdeenshire Village Propaganda* in 1889[26] as a celebration of the energy with which the 'Aberdeen and Banffshire Mutual Instruction Union' spread from its Rhynie origins in 1846 to generate fifteen such organisations within five years, tells us that one of the major thrusts behind its growth was the need 'to remedy the lamentable deficiency in elementary education' of the day.[27] His book gives an insight into an alternative self-help tradition whose communitarian values of mutual assistance, of evening classes and subscription libraries stood as a popular alternative to the individualistic outlook practised by the selective academicism of the village school.

Throughout these years and into the following century, a powerful body of writing accumulated into what amounted to a denunciation of the inherited Scottish system. There is the work of George MacDonald who, before he went on to become a noted writer of children's stories based in the south of England, had to endure his own school days in Huntly, an experience which gave him the material for his novel *Alec Forbes of Howglen*. His character Murdoch Malison offers us a portrait of a schoolmaster whose 'savage sense of duty' impels him to thrash his young charges into penitential submission.[28] Yet he is not cruel by nature and, out of school, behaves with gentle benevolence. The brutality he daily assumes is a culturally determined role which he feels he must adopt if he is to act as a credible dominie.

Seventy years later, another prominent North-East novelist, Lewis Grassic Gibbon, shows that while the harsh Calvinistic judgementalism that MacDonald pillories may have eased, the school system remains a repressive force. In his pair of novels, *The Thirteenth Disciple*[29] and the unfinished *The Speak of the Mearns*,[30] he uses his ability for sharp irony and critical dramatisation to show how, in its Kincardineshire setting, the local school acts as an alien presence, the high-spirited, whooping activities of the playground a rebuke to the dull, unimaginative routines within.

Of the region's notable poets, Charles Murray's 'It wasna his wyte' (1929) remains a potent evocation of the destructive way in which a North-East education can confront the country child's own natural environment with an obscurantist regime of adult externalities.[31] And, after the war, the work of John C. Milne offers a sustained critique of the daily struggle the schoolmaster must wage to yoke his rural 'scholars' to the plough of academic learning, when the abundant life of the countryside calls them. Milne was himself a brilliant lad o' pairts who took three first-class honours degrees and then, in the 1950s, served as Master of Method at Aberdeen College of Education. In poem after poem, he builds up a series of sardonically knowing observations of North-East life and the formative role entrusted to its parish schools. A phrase from his 'skweelin' sums it all up: 'Fut's a' yon skweelin for?'[32]

Tradition and Reality

Against the established story of the North-East's parish school education it is possible to range a powerful revisionist account, one which opposes the lustrous tales of striving cottar loons and selfless graduate masters, of socially inclusive classrooms and the ladder of opportunity firmly planted down in each little local schoolroom, with a counter-claim which presents us with a system that is preoccupied with the forced feeding of the occasional bright lad and is content to impose upon the rest a diet of dry academicism and pietistic subjugation, policed by the swinging tawse and the bitter lash of the sermonising tongue.

To put the history this way is, however, simply to set one tradition of stylised renditions against another: an anti-myth to replace the officially cherished one. Given the polarisation of viewpoints it would be useful, in so far as we can, to examine some hard evidence as to the effective function of the parochial system in providing 'democratic' opportunities to the North-East community. This would mean fixing on not only the rate of bursary wins but also the literacy and attendance rates it generated among the general population. Here we could begin by taking another look at the raw data supplied by that 1834 survey which features Joan Stewart's Strathdon parish. The range of subjects on offer there is sound and does include the all-important Latin but while the assurance that 'none in the parish above fifteen years of age . . . are unable to write' is impressive, a closer examination reveals a less solid state of affairs. We are informed, for example, that while the total school roll is ninety-six, actual attendance normally dips to only half that. We are also told that this number represents not much more than one-third of the relevant age group in the parish since no fewer than 283 pupils do not attend the official establishment at all but are enrolled into one or other of the six dame or venture schools dotted across the community.[33]

Indeed, if we read further into the 1834 data, it becomes clear that, although the principle of a public school to every parish holds, it had to be supplemented by myriad private institutions. The summary figures that are attached to the Aberdeenshire section tell the story: in the county as a whole, there are 440 schools listed but 347 of them were 'non-parochial'; 9,926 pupils went to these and only 5,410 to the 'public' remainder.[34] Attendance figures, moreover, reveal that 'going to school' in these agricultural areas tended to be a seasonal matter for most families, whose younger members took large chunks of time off to act as cheap farm labour – in the case of Strathdon usually 'to herd the family cow'. Latin was confined to the parochial schools, which the large majority did not attend; the lists of subjects there seem imposing but they had to be delivered by one master to all-age classes of up to eighty pupils. As for uptake, while the returns for North-East schools are indeed superior to the rest of the country, the figures yielded by the later Argyll report put the tales of bursary winners into raw perspective: the Report states that in the North-East counties the proportion of pupils learning Latin and Greek was certainly greater than elsewhere – but that this only meant 6.7 per cent compared to 4 per cent and 1.5 per cent against 0.5 per cent.[35]

Even more delimiting is the fact that half of the region's population could, by virtue of their sex, never even dream of becoming a 'lad o' pairts'. It was not until the 1890s that Aberdeen University, following the Universities (Scotland) Act of 1889, permitted the entrance of its first female students and while, following the Act of 1872, the great expansion of the national system had to be resourced by an influx of training centre female teachers, the male bias was perpetuated by the general practice of confining the instruction of senior classes and the promotion to headships to men, a practice which lingered on into the late twentieth century.

A 'tradition', however, cannot simply be washed away on a flow of data. The perception of 'North-East' education as archetypically, democratically 'Scottish' is more a matter of emotional engagement than it is of dry statistical measurement. The real problem in knowing how to respond to the narrative invitations of such as Barclay, Rae and Stewart on the one side, and the fictive exposures of MacDonald, Alexander and Gibbon on the other, is not that they tell us stories but that these are only stories of a certain kind, focusing as they do on the exceptionally dramatic. The biographies of outstanding careers, the celebratory parish histories proudly garnered by local scribes, the intensely rendered social criticisms of novelists and poets, are all alike in their generic lack of interest in the prosaic round of the average daily experience.

If we are to recover a properly balanced appreciation of the ways in which the famed/notorious North-East educational system satisfied the aspirations of the unheard North-East majority, then we will need recourse to testimony of a more basic kind. It is here that the particulars dutifully recorded in the individual school log books point to a more day-to-day reality. The school records deposited in the Aberdeenshire county archive[36] reveal a series of preoccupations that take us well away from the world of Latin conjugations and Greek aphorisms. The struggle to achieve a passable attendance rate in the face of the vagaries of the weather and of inaccessible cross-country tracks; the visitations of scarletina, diphtheria and the measles; the indifference of parents more concerned with their offspring's potential as agricultural labourers than with their schooling; absences due to days at the hairst (harvest); and the attritional daily battle for order over 100 or so country children that was waged by a solitary dominie and his young female assistant teacher – these were the daily realities of North-East educational life. Here, going to local parish school is revealed to be just that: a fact of life, like the weather and the state of the soil, a matter neither for glorification nor for rebellion, but simply a phase of life to be got through, part of the immemorial North-East lot.

Education and Community in the Modern North-East

Within a fifteen-minute drive from where this piece is being written it is possible to count some fifty buildings which, at one time or another, have borne the title 'school'. Now, despite a vastly expanded population, there are no more than a dozen. The place is Muchalls, a small village ten miles to the south of Aberdeen. Forty years ago, its children still walked the mile down the tracks and across the then single carriageway A90 road, to the homely two-teacher place that was tucked away round the corner among the beech trees at the Bridge of Muchalls. Today, their own offspring are bussed to the sleekly modern primary school which is set among the multiplying streets of the neighbouring commuter settlement of Newtonhill. The A90 is now a dual carriageway, and further housing and commercial development is planned on 4,000 acres of agricultural land.

What has happened in this small wedge of the North-East stands for the region as a whole. The shift from an economy grounded on the land to one based

Figure 10.2 The passing of age: the interior of the Bridge of Muchalls School, Kincardineshire, taken a couple of years before its closure as an outmoded rural school in 1969. Copyright the author.

on light commerce, oil-related employment in the city, a career in the service industries and the ubiquitous car, has brought about a creeping suburbanisation which, coupled with the related social and geographical mobility, has eroded the contours of older life patterns. And with it has come the corresponding regrouping of schools into ever larger centralised units, with the result that the experience of 'going to school' has been utterly transformed.

At the beginning of the twentieth century official returns listed over 300 North-East educational establishments in receipt of public funding;[37] 100 years later that figure has fallen to little more than one-third. The bare statistic conceals a further radical shift. When, in 1965, the county's Director of Education reported on Aberdeenshire's plans for comprehensivisation, he could number forty-three schools that sustained a secondary department;[38] that figure has now shrunk to fewer than a quarter. When Joan Stewart enjoyed her spell in the upper years at Towie School, most of that village's population would have completed their entire education at the one local school; today, after the age of twelve, their descendants are transported to Alford Academy, ten miles distant.

If the process of centralisation has rapidly accelerated since that date, it is one whose transformations may be traced back to the early Victorian era when the government began to intrude its bureaucratic systems into the organisation of Scotland's education and initiated the series of Acts and regulations which moved its maintenance from a purely local, parish-based concern to a nationally accountable enterprise.

It is no accident that the upsurge of writing that celebrated the 'North-East tradition' surfaced in the 1920s, a few years after the 1918 Act swept away the old parish board system and replaced it with the larger unit of the county. In the strongholds of rural education this development was interpreted by Barclay, for example, as yet another hostile step in the movement by the Edinburgh- and London-based Scottish Education Department (SED) towards the concentration of secondary-level work into burgh centres, and away from all the little places – the Ordiquhills, the Bogmuchals, the Longmanhills – where generations of dominies had given each local lad the chance, in his own birthplace, to imbibe the higher learning that would propel him upwards to university and into the professions.

Barclay's side could muster up the forces of deep-set imagery and native romance: 'under the old and well tried regime, sons of the county were so trained in the classics as in homely moralities that in after life Banffshire was proud to acclaim them as her children'.[39] But against this charging rhetoric the civil servants of the SED – whatever the worthiness of their aim to widen opportunity through the provision of larger, more centralised schools – could be depicted as ranging the weaponry of modernisation and a bloodless efficiency.

Eighty years on, it is now clear which side has prevailed in that particular battle. Nor is it simply that a steamrolling economic force has won the day, for the icons themselves have crumbled since the 1920s. The kirk, and the binding piety that sustained it, has dwindled to become just one of a range of social agencies hopefully attempting to reach out to the young; it is now pointless to speak with proprietorial intensity of 'lads o' pairts' when upwards of 40 per cent are expected to move onto higher education, the majority of them female; poverty is no longer justified as a character-forming essential; farming, and the communal structures which served it, is increasingly peripheral; and it is now thirty years since the region's teacher education institution had a Latin graduate on its roll.

Above all, it has become increasingly clear that the hallowed North-East conceit that its schools were providing the nation's shining example of its claim to equality of opportunity has rested upon a concept of democracy which was rooted in outmoded assumptions as to what constitutes true social justice. A system that operated a harshly narrow selection procedure based upon trial by academic rigour – as defined by mastery of the intricacies of a Classical language – and by an heroic capacity to overcome the exigencies of poverty and social derogation can, in retrospect, only be viewed as one that works in a narrowly competitive rather than any openly enabling fashion. The North-East version, like the national system it so proudly epitomised, was essentially meritocratic, not inclusive, one that worked through the deliberate exclusion of the great majority in the interests of sifting out the tiny elite necessary to fill the few professional offices required for efficient parochial organisation. For the rest – the extensive work force of artisans and agricultural labour – an elementary education would suffice.

In the revisionist light cast by late-twentieth-century educational sociologists,[40] it is tempting to see all that lustrous imagery of lads o' pairts, of paternalistic dominies, of socially mixed classrooms and the soaring ladder of opportunity as justification by myth of a form of social control, one which was designed to serve the conservative interests of a pre-First World War sexist and semi-feudal agricultural community where the requirement was for plentiful manual labour, topped by a small elite of professional male leaders. In ethos too, the insistence on punitive discipline and repetitive effort was useful preparation for a pre-mechanised agricultural industry which was ruled by hierarchical order and strict adherence to laborious procedure.

In the network of farming communities invoked by Barclay, Rae and Bruce, life was experienced as a strictly local affair, one that was necessarily centred on the parish and where allegiances were forged through the daily familiarity with the commonly held landmarks of kirk, village hall, local shop, a scattering of fermtouns and the parochial school that generation succeeding generation attended and by which their values were formed.

That society and the value systems which fed it are now no more. In that sense the very notion of there being a 'North-East tradition' has receded into an object of historical recovery rather than holding current value. And yet the memories and the stories survive. Since 1990, for example, the development of desktop publishing has generated an outpouring of books and booklets which invite the reader to share the sense of fond recognition that springs from retracing the 'old days', when life was, somehow, simpler, more boldly patterned, more humanly nourishing. And in each of them, the days at the little local school play a centrally formative role.

If the line of sterling qualities traditionally proclaimed as defining the North-East – piety, the work ethic, parental sacrifice, 'getting on' and a landscape so saturated in education that each tiny parish must have its own academy of learning – are now sufficiently dated as to require revision, respect for those ingredients remains. The process of mixing together specific incident and the emotive, retrospective response in order to replicate the myth of tribal identity, goes on. To offer some quick examples: the lovingly detailed evocation of infant schooling at Cairnorrie, by which, in her autobiography *Good Vibrations*,[41] the internationally renowned percussionist Evelyn Glennie reaffirms her Aberdeenshire roots; the glowing portraits of mental arithmetic sessions and annual prizegivings recreated in Winnie Carnegie's reminiscences of early days at Tortoston School;[42] and the sections of personal recall garnered in local histories and school centenary booklets such as Richard Bennett's *Elgin Academy 1801–2001*[43] and Alisoun Nicol's history of Dunottar School, Stonehaven, entitled *Tak Tent o' Lear*.[44]

The urge to celebrate the small local school as the continuing repository of the age-old national tradition has survived the more recent moves towards the institution of centralised comprehensive schooling. When, in 1999, the popular *Aberdeen Press and Journal* contributor Norman Harper devoted one of his weekly columns to a eulogy for the thoroughgoing education he had received at Alford in the 1970s – 'an average village in an average part of Scotland'[45] – and set that against his sense of subsequent decline, he received his largest ever postbag of shared reminiscence and sorrowful agreement.[46]

As that last instance reminds us, the literature of school reminiscence has frequently been one of nostalgia in which the experience of the school has become wrapped up in the gratefully embroidered recreation of identity invoking influences and the personal laying down of roots. The 'North-East tradition' is, inevitably, a backward-looking construct, a narrative of faded glories and regretfully superseded models. Given the seriousness of the issues implicated – individual and communal social control, individual opportunity, gender politics, the reconciliation of personal with communal interests – the soundest course might be to do a debunk, that is to rein in the memories and trust the analysts and the policy makers to fix their attention on the proper actualities.

However, the tales of the past are still able to enact a present meaning. *The Schools and Schoolmasters of Banffshire* opens with a set scene.[47] It is of a graveside in a country churchyard where, in November 1921, there are gathered the sons of Charles Mair, for more than thirty years grocer and farmer in the remote moorland parish of Grange. Unknown beyond his native North-East, he has nevertheless been a man of considerable stature: well-read, an expert in his county's place names, faithful Sunday school teacher and kirk elder. But what is really remarkable is his lineage: father of the magical number of seven sons who ascended from the local school to the University of Aberdeen, each of them there to win first-class honours in the Classics. They had then gone on to become headmasters, to occupy church and legal positions, to take up a chair in Greek or, equally honoured, had stayed behind to build up the cattle business of their own region.

It is still difficult to resist the spell of a scene which is at once recognisably domestic and grandly heroic. The glimpse of those seven brothers, whose talents had flung them apart but who are now reunited in the black uniform of their common homage, is a reminder that the stories people tell of their social experience compel the imagination and engage our sense of common identity in a way that the bureaucratic systems-speak of Curriculum for Excellence and Higher Still can never do.

How we respond to the role played by the school in the formation of our localised character within the framework of 'Scotland' remains a live issue. The cultivation of a critical attitude towards the North-East educational tradition, and the larger national virtues which it claims to have in its safe keeping, is essential. But, to be sensitively informed, it must also take note of the experiences of the past, of the texts and the lore which have enshrined them, and of the ways in which any community, however 'modern' and multiculturally diverse it may appear to have become, instinctively shares and debates its educational ideals.

And if the central question is, as ever, 'what is education for?', then, if we are to understand the mix of personal experience and received valuations by which people commonly respond to it, we must be prepared to ask it with a local as well as the standard accent. 'What is education for?' – or, once more, as the poet and educationist J. C. Milne puts it, 'Fut's a' yon skweelin for?'[48]

Notes

1. Rae, Elsie, *A Waff o' Win fae Bennachie: Country Cameos in Prose and Verse* (Bisset, 1930). See also W. S. Bruce, *The Nor'east* (Bisset, 1922), p. 13.
2. Joan Cantlie Stewart, *Pine Trees and the Sky* (Scottish Cultural Press, 1998), pp. 55–63.
3. Here, 'the North-East' is to be understood as referring to the predominantly rural counties of Aberdeenshire, Banffshire, Kincardineshire and Moray. The city of Aberdeen is to be excluded: it is a populous urban area whose history and educational arrangements have followed their own, largely separate, history.
4. HCPP 1837, 133, *Parochial Education Enquiry: Abstract of Answers and Returns Made Pursuant to an Address of the House of Commons, dated 9 July, 1834*, pp. 1288 and 1294.
5. For a contemporary account of the role that the Aberdeen bursary competitions played in the popular North-East imagination, see Norman Maclean, *Life at a Northern University*, ed. W. K. Leask (Rosemount Press, 1906 [1874]).
6. *Education Commission (Scotland): Report on the State of Education in the Country Districts of Scotland* (HMSO, 1866), p. 141.
7. Cited in William Barclay, *The Schools and Schoolmasters of Banffshire* (Banffshire Journal, 1925), p. 10.
8. See, for example, John Middleton, 'Mr Middleton's tour of the North', *Monthly Magazine* (1820), 514–16.
9. Ian Carter, *Farm Life in North East Scotland 1840–1914: The Poor Man's Country* (John Donald, 1979).
10. Ian Simpson, *Education in Aberdeenshire before 1872* (University of London, 1947), p. 216.
11. Barclay, *Schools and Schoolmasters*, pp. 291–305.
12. Ibid., pp. 306–8. Drainie was actually in the adjacent county of Moray.
13. Ibid., p. 136.
14. Ibid., p. vii.
15. 'Remarks on parochial education', *Aberdeen Magazine* (1832), 5.
16. Walter Gregor, *An Echo of the Olden Times in the North of Scotland* (Menzies, 1874), pp. 41–57.
17. Alexander Gibson, *Under the Crusie* (Wylie, 1916), p. 58.
18. George Abel, *Wylans fae my Wallet* (Gardner, 1916), p. 30.
19. Rae, *A Waff o' Win*, p. 70.
20. Ibid., p. 68.
21. John R. Allan, *The North East Lowlands of Scotland* (Hale, 1974 [1952]), pp. 228–46.
22. William Alexander, *Johnny Gibb of Gushetneuk* (Tuckwell Press, 1995 [1871]).
23. Ibid., pp. 51–7.
24. William Donaldson, *Popular Literature in Victorian Scotland: Language, Fiction and the Press* (Aberdeen University Press, 1986).
25. Ibid., pp. 209–11.
26. Robert H. Smith, *An Aberdeenshire Village Propaganda Forty Years Ago* (Douglas, 1889).

27. Ibid., p. 36.
28. George MacDonald, *Alec Forbes of Howglen* (Hurst and Blackett, 1865), pp. 30–1.
29. Lewis Grassic Gibbon, *The Thirteenth Disciple: Being Portrait and Saga of Malcolm Maudsley in his Adventures through the Dark Corridor* (Jarrold, 1931).
30. Lewis Grassic Gibbon, *The Speak of the Mearns: With Selected Short Stories and Essays* [unfinished] (Polygon, 1994 [1931]).
31. Charles Murray, 'It wasna his wyte', in Charles Murray, *Hamewith. Charles Murray: Collected Poems*, ed. Colin Milton (Alden Press, 2008 [1930]), pp. 115–17.
32. John C. Milne, *Poems* (Aberdeen University Press, 1963), p. 82.
33. HCPP 1837, 133, *Education Enquiry*, pp. 1288 and 1294.
34. Ibid., p. 63.
35. *Education Commission (Scotland)*, p. 680.
36. Aberdeen City and Aberdeenshire Archives. Available at www.aberdeencity.gov.uk/archives (accessed 21 July 2014).
37. *Report of the Committee of Council on Education in Scotland* (HMSO, 1906), pp. 354–517.
38. Alexander Young, 'Comprehensive education in Aberdeenshire', *Education in the North* 6 (1966), 57–60.
39. Barclay, *Schools and Schoolmasters*, p. 2.
40. See, for example, Andrew McPherson and Charles Raab, *Governing Education: A Sociology of Policy Since 1945* (Edinburgh University Press, 1988).
41. Evelyn Glennie, *Good Vibrations: My Autobiography* (Hutchinson, 1990).
42. Winnie Carnegie, *Ugie Pearls and Other Stories* (Carnugie, 2000).
43. Richard Bennett, *Elgin Academy 1801–2001* (Moravian Press, 2001).
44. Alisoun Nicol, *Tak Tent o' Lear: A History of Dunnottar School, Stonehaven* (Dunnottar School, 1990).
45. Norman Harper, 'Scotland spirals down to blissful ignorance', *Press and Journal*, 28 July 1999.
46. As related to the author during an interview, 16 January 2002.
47. Barclay, *Schools and Schoolmasters*, p. 1.
48. Milne, *Poems*, p. 81.

Bibliography

Allan, John R., *The North East Lowlands of Scotland* (Hale, 1974 [1952]).
Barclay, William, *The Schools and Schoolmasters of Banffshire* (Banffshire Journal, 1925).
Carter, Ian, *Farm Life in North East Scotland 1840–1914. The Poor Man's Country* (John Donald, 1979).
Donaldson, William, *Popular Literature in Victorian Scotland: Language, Fiction and Press* (Aberdeen University Press, 1986).
Gregor, Walter, *An Echo of the Olden Times from the North of Scotland* (Menzies, 1874).
Milne, John C., *Poems* (Aberdeen University Press, 1963).
Northcroft David (ed.), *North-East Identities and Scottish Schooling. The Relationship of the Scottish Education System to the Culture of the North-East of Scotland* (The Elphinstone Institute, Aberdeen University, 2005).
Northcroft, David, *Grampian Lives. Eyewitness Accounts of Growing Up in the Townships of North-East Scotland, Volume 1, 1900–1950* (Leopard Press, 2010).
Rae, Elsie, *A Waff o' Win fae Bennachie: Country Cameos in Prose and Verse* (Bisset, 1930).
Simpson, Ian, *Education in Aberdeenshire before 1872* (University of London, 1947).

11

Education and Society in the Era of the School Boards, 1872–1918

Jane McDermid

On the centenary of the 1872 Education (Scotland) Act the journal *Scottish Educational Studies* featured a debate over whether, as argued by J. D. Myers, the Act had dealt a death blow to the educational tradition by introducing English practices or, as countered by Donald Withrington, it had simply adapted some aspects of the 1870 Elementary Education Act for England and Wales, including the establishment of school boards.[1] Thirty years later, Lindsay Paterson recognised the influence of the Presbyterian Reformation while paying particular attention to the institutional legacy of the 1872 Act.[2] This examination of a sample of urban and rural, Highland and Lowland school board records confirms that the Act may indeed be seen as an attempt to revive the Presbyterian educational tradition by seeking to ensure common provision across the country.[3] According to the tradition, the parochial schoolmaster – the dominie – and the heritors and Kirk Sessions played the key role in determining educational policy and practice, but changing economic and social conditions from the later eighteenth century had threatened the centrality of the parish school, while demographic and urban growth brought fears for the social stability which it was believed the parish school had underpinned. Educational debate and investigation, notably between the 1830s and 1860s, convinced many in Scotland that the continuation of common provision was essential for the social order.

The 1872 Act and the School Boards

Historically, then, the system of school boards, of which 987 were established by the 1872 Act, had its roots in the parish schools associated with the Reformation and legislation of the late seventeenth century, notably the 1696 Act for the Settling of Schools. Certainly, there were English influences as well as economic and social pressures on school boards while more immediately, the boards were a response to legislation in England and Wales, but this did not mean passively following English policy and practice. Rather, as James Scotland has observed, there was a general feeling in Scotland that the proposed education Bill should not simply be an extension of the 1870 Act: the Scottish system was influenced by England, but during the lifetime of the boards this was more through reaction than imitation.[4]

The 1870 Act allowed voluntary schools in England and Wales to continue, limiting school boards to filling the gaps in provision. The 1872 Act was more ambitious and the boards it established had more powers than those in England. Firstly, school boards in Scotland were to serve the local community and establish a national, unified system. Secondly, while the Presbyterian basis of the tradition meant the continuing involvement of the Church of Scotland and its offshoots through membership of school boards, the secular authorities had a central role to play in providing education and through it promoting a common culture. Thirdly, the belief in the 'democratic intellect', represented by the 'lad o' parts' and university-educated dominie, meant that the boards aimed to establish schools open to all social classes (at least in theory). They would also (again in theory) not be limited to an elementary education as the 1870 Act decreed for England and Wales, but would continue the parochial tradition of promoting the educational and social mobility of the talented but poor scholar. The notion of the democratic intellect was highly idealised, as Robert Anderson has shown, but it informed both the debates over the 1872 Act and the working of the school boards after they had been set up. Thus, the *Educational News* (3 March 1900) quoted Flora Stevenson, a member of the Edinburgh School Board: 'We in Scotland have not been brought up to measure out our education to suit the requirements of any particular class or community'.[5] Whereas in England the schooling of the poor was held in low social esteem, in Scotland it was seen as a key means of cementing the national community, thereby preserving not only social harmony but also its identity within the Union.

The restricted nature of the 1870 Act meant that school boards in England suffered from persistent tension with the voluntary sector, the Church of England in particular obstructing their work. In contrast, those in Scotland established a national system which lasted until the Education Act of 1918. Scottish boards were charged with absorbing parish, burgh, voluntary and religious schools, with the exception of those run by the Catholic and Episcopalian churches which opted to remain outside the national system. The boards were to be elected every three years, starting in 1873; those eligible to vote and to stand were owners or occupiers, female as well as male, of property above £4 annual rental; each had as many votes as the board had members (generally from five to fifteen). A House of Lords amendment, however, barred serving teachers from standing for election.

Another contrast to the 1870 Act was that the 1872 Act established compulsory education. Hence a key function of the boards from the start was to ensure attendance (raised to fourteen by the Education (Scotland) Act of 1883, but not free until 1890). Their immediate duties were to conduct an educational census of children aged between five and thirteen – though in practice boards accepted that children in Scotland were often not sent to school until six or even seven – as well as school accommodation. Compulsory attendance also applied to denominational schools so that, though not part of the system, these had to report absentees to the boards. Boards soon offered prizes for good attendance, such as medals or money: thus the Fala board in Midlothian offered ten shillings to the boy or girl attending most regularly during the school year 1886–7. Incentives, however, confirmed that absenteeism and early school-leaving persisted.

Given the widespread poverty, the need to contribute to family income militated against most working-class children staying on at school longer than the minimum period required. Even when school fees were removed, boards recorded that many children still left for work as soon as possible. Moreover, school board minute books for areas such as the Borders and the Highlands show that into the twentieth century there was continuing dependence of farming on child labour, female as much as male, as well as on adult women, the latter similar to North Wales but in contrast to England.[6] Nor were urban boards free of the attractions of seasonal agricultural work: throughout the existence of the Glasgow school board its attendance committee noted the absence of boys and girls during the potato harvest. Still, whereas irregular attendance was a concern for all school boards, it appears to have been a particular problem in the Highlands. There, although boards summoned parents to explain their children's absence, they seem to have accepted that families needed their children, and their mothers, to work either on the croft or in seasonal employment, so that the pre-1872 practice of winter attendance persisted. Thus, in contrast to the Glasgow board, rural and especially Highland boards did not pursue defaulters vigorously. Indeed, in Sutherland the Kildonan board received a letter from the Scotch Education Department (SED) at the beginning of 1892 complaining of persistently low attendance, while Creich board was castigated in a report by Her Majesty's Inspectorate (HMI) of August 1896 for not making a serious effort to improve attendance at Bonar Bridge public school. Again, there were exceptions: Nairn board took a much sterner line, seen for example in 1876 when it threatened to prosecute a father whose daughter was absent herding her grandfather's cow if she did not return to school within a week.

Besides irregular attendance, some school boards had to deal with the half-time system. This was more common in England (especially in the north, but also in some southern counties such as Bedfordshire, related to the local economy) than in Scotland where most boards resisted it. By the late Victorian period, half-timers in Scotland were mostly found in textile regions. They were employed in the mills either for ten hours every other day, with alternate days in school, or at work each morning, with the afternoon in school. The Dundee school board in particular was heavily influenced by mill-owners, granting many more school exemptions for child labour than boards elsewhere in Scotland. Indeed, the *Dundee Advertiser* (1 April 1889) argued that half-time education was beneficial because it kept children, especially girls, in state-inspected schools; but in half-time schools the curriculum was very basic and only a tiny minority of children under the Dundee board received more than elementary education. In contrast, the Glasgow board was very energetic in seeking to enforce full-time attendance. Besides the necessity of children earning wages, boards also had to contend with juvenile delinquency. Again the Glasgow board was in the forefront. Under the chairmanship of William Mitchell, the attendance committee took a cue from the English day industrial school system (introduced by an Act of 1876): the city's Juvenile Delinquency Prevention and Repression Act of 1878 pre-dated the introduction of such schools across Scotland by fifteen years.

Still, school board minutes show improved attendance, especially among girls, by the later nineteenth century and growing opportunities in rural areas for a 'lass o' parts', though not on the scale offered in Glasgow, Edinburgh or Aberdeen. Thus, as my research has shown, by the 1890s increasing numbers of girls in the Lothians were taking higher subjects, including Latin and mathematics.[7] In 1892, a Merit Certificate was introduced to encourage pupils to complete Standard V, and most girls who were awarded it seemed destined for teacher training and employment by the school boards.

Boards also had to account for the expenditure of grants to the London-based SED, whose subordination to the Committee of Council on Education caused such great resentment in Scotland that the House of Commons accepted an amendment to the 1872 Bill by the Lords which set up a Board of Education in Edinburgh. However, as James Scotland pointed out in his centennial appraisal of the Act, this amounted to an executive commission to oversee the administrative parts of the Act, while the Commons insisted it was a temporary body, for three years in the first instance, and a maximum of five; it ceased to function in 1878.[8] This meant a stronger degree of centralisation than in England as well as the influence of English educational policy, both reflected in the SED's first Code enforcing the principle of 'payment by results': introduced into England and Wales in 1862, it doled out school grants from government according to pupils' success in examinations as judged by the HMI. Prior to the 1872 Act, this had been resisted and thereafter it was resented by teachers in Scotland.

Despite the centralising forces represented by the SED and HMI, the board system ensured a limited yet still significant degree of local democracy. Indeed, though based in London the SED successfully resisted attempts to abolish the boards in Scotland, as was done in England and Wales in 1902. Moreover, while teachers and their professional association, the Educational Institute of Scotland (EIS), worried that locally elected board members would see their role as keeping expenditure (including salaries) low even as they looked after the interests of their own constituency (representing religious, economic and political interests or worse, in the view of the *Educational News*, organ of the EIS, 'cranks' and 'faddists'), in practice it accepted that most boards were reasonable. Indeed, the impression from board minutes is that those returned were determined to continue the educational ideal. Hence, as will be discussed below, although secondary education was not to be funded by the rates, even under the smallest boards there were efforts to offer more than the basics of reading, writing and arithmetic, plus sewing for girls. Thus, in February 1886, the Kingussie board resolved to offer English literature and Latin to boys and English literature and domestic economy to girls in the higher standards, as well as science to boys who stayed on after the sixth standard; and in August 1894, the Creich board resolved to approach the Kincardine board in Easter Ross with a view to working together for the promotion of secondary education.

Since the new boards found that existing provision was inadequate, a great era of school building began almost immediately, not only in the large cities but also in small towns. Whereas Glasgow was dealing with the construction of schools to accommodate thousands of pupils, which, as Sarah Hamilton has shown, left the city a rich architectural legacy, smaller boards were looking to provide for around a tenth of that number.[9] All boards had to purchase land and negotiate with banks as well as architects, solicitors, builders and tradesmen (joiners, masons, plasterers, plumbers and slaters are often itemised in board minutes). Boards depended heavily on their (part-time) clerks and treasurers (in the smaller boards one man usually took on both roles). Occasionally, there were disagreements both within a board and between boards over the chosen site for a school. An example of the former was the dispute in Dumfries in 1874 where there were allegations that a board member would benefit from building the school on a particular site. An example of the latter was the dispute, which simmered into the second term of office, between the Laggan and Kingussie boards, with the latter complaining to the SED in December 1875 that the former planned to build too close to the homes of children of school age who would come under the Kingussie board.

School Board Membership

The composition of the boards reflected the local social hierarchy. The majority were middle class, though in some rural areas the board might be chaired by the local laird or his agent. In 1873, Lord Lovat was elected to two boards, Kilmorack and Kiltarlity, on his estate in Inverness-shire, the first of which he chaired for two consecutive terms and the second for five until his death in 1887. Factors to the Earl of Cawdor chaired the Nairn and Ardersier boards. More commonly, the chairman was a minister either of the Established or Free Church, a businessman, professional or farmer.

According to Robert Anderson, in the first elections in 1873 a quarter of the successful candidates were ministers of religion, though these were more influential in the east of the country while businessmen were more to the fore in the west.[10] For example, the first Aberdeen school board consisted of six members of the Free Church, five of the Established Church, one Catholic and one Episcopalian. The first Glasgow election returned five businessmen, seven clerics (two Church of Scotland, two Free Church, one Latter Day Saints, two Catholic priests), one Unitarian on a secularist platform and an anti-Catholic missionary. However, all the businessmen were deeply religious philanthropists. For example, Michael Connal, a merchant prominent in the tea and tobacco trade, was a member of the Free Church of Scotland. Active in educational philanthropy long before 1872, he founded a Bible institute in which he taught for nearly four decades, and from 1873 until his death twenty years later served on the Glasgow school board which he chaired for three terms (1876–82). Whereas many members served only one or two terms, a significant number sat on between three and eight boards. A few served even longer: William Mitchell in Glasgow was first elected in 1873, winning a seat on each successive board until he retired in 1905; similarly, Flora Stevenson in Edinburgh also won eleven consecutive elections, serving until her death in 1905.

Since Scotland did not have a government separate from Westminster, local politics played the biggest part in the lives of most people and local newspaper reports of board elections reveal that campaigns were often lively affairs. They also show that smaller boards were sometimes returned without a contest: for example, the Kells board, Kirkcudbright, between 1889 and 1909. Membership across Scotland was remarkably stable in social and political terms though at the turn of the century it broadened to a limited degree with the election of Labour candidates, more so in industrial regions and mostly male but with some women, such as Clarice McNab on the Leith board in 1912. She had taught music and by the turn of the century a few retired teachers were standing for the boards. For example, the *Educational News* (13 May 1903) reported that an EIS fellow, Miss J. Stuart Airlie, had been elected to the Paisley board after a long career in teaching (ill-health, however, prevented her from serving).

One factor in the debates over educational reform in the 1860s was the extension of the parliamentary franchise (1867 in England and Wales, 1868 in Scotland and Ireland) to considerable numbers of working-class men, notably in urban areas. Educational reform was to imbue conservative values, including loyalty to family, monarchy, state and empire. John Stuart Mill had lost the amendment to include women in the electorate on the same basis as men, but in the educational acts of 1870 and 1872, it was achieved. This reflected the view that the education of young children was the first responsibility of mothers, as well as the long established philanthropic work of women in setting up, teaching in and inspecting schools for the poor. Throughout Britain, education was a key area where women could achieve a measure of status and authority, and the work they did on school boards set an important precedent for women holding public office. Ladies who stood for election often had organised support: thus, the 'ladies' platforms' in both Glasgow and Edinburgh were supported by the Association for Promoting Lady Candidates at School Board and Parochial Elections, which included male professionals, members of the clergy and businessmen. As my research has shown, it took longer for women to break through in small towns. Here they relied on the support of local individuals. This was the case in Ardrossan where in 1888 Jessie Moffat, daughter of a prominent local industrialist, was the first woman to stand and be elected to the seven-member board.[11]

Female board members regularly visited schools, inspecting the girls' industrial work, while middle-class women continued to serve as unpaid school visitors with a particular interest in infants and the domestic education of girls. The Edinburgh school board set great store by female visitors who were deemed 'lady managers'. Jane Arthur of the Paisley board urged the appointment of lady managers on the Edinburgh model, who were introduced in 1879; and in 1899, Mrs McNab, first elected to the Perth board in 1894, submitted a list of ladies to report on cookery and laundry. Though fewer, there were also male visitors: from the 1880s, for example, the Dumfries board appointed gentlemen visitors with the power to order repairs and furnishings at a cost of up to £2, a practice which continued up to the First World War.

Membership of a school board was seen by the middle classes as a phil-anthropic and civic duty, while it also confirmed the local standing of those elected. For example, William Mitchell, businessman, Free Church member and JP, took a keen interest in destitute, delinquent and disabled children. Likewise, the women who stood for election were already involved in a wide range of social and charitable activities. Yet whereas Andrew Bain has examined women's role on small boards in east central Scotland, they are missing from James Roxburgh's history of the largest board, Glasgow, which was responsible for about a fifth of all schoolchildren in the country.[12] Few of the smallest boards had female members, and fewer women still were elected in the tiny parishes of the Highlands, though there were exceptions: Mrs Ellice served on the Glengarry board in Inverness-shire from 1888 until 1903. Even on the larger boards of Dundee and Aberdeen, the first woman was returned two decades after the first election. Large boards generally had only two women members, though five were returned in 1914 in Glasgow when the board had been expanded to twenty-five, reflecting the growth of Britain's second city of empire.

Whereas the Catholic and Episcopalian churches remained outside the national system until 1918, the cumulative voting system allowed them – indeed, Robert Anderson suggests that it may have been designed to do so – to partici-pate in local politics, with representatives standing for election to the boards to safeguard their interests since they not only had to fund their own schools but were ratepayers.[13] When Catholics stood, generally in west and central Scotland where most Irish migrants were found, they regularly had two or three candidates elected. Indeed, the system achieved more results for Catholic candidates (all male and usually priests) representing an impoverished community than for the well-off ladies (none of whom were Catholic).

However, while religious beliefs often lay behind standing for the school board, such motivation was explicitly associated in election campaigns more with male candidates than female. Thus, in 1876 the *Ardrossan & Saltcoats Herald* (25 March) welcomed the female candidate as a non-sectarian balance to the churches. In 1879, concern was expressed in the *Scotsman* (7 April) that if the ladies were defeated, the Edinburgh board would be composed 'of ministers and men who are ready to do what the ministers bid them to do', while in 1885 the *Glasgow Herald* (18 April) reported on a meeting in support of the two lady can-didates in Govan at which the Reverend Robert Howe declared that their lack of 'selfish or sectarian aims' meant they would represent the whole community.

Helen Corr has shown that it was female board members who championed the domestic education of working-class girls (in which they were strongly supported by the Catholic Church) and insisted on the need for ladies to oversee it, a discourse which highlighted the social differences between women.[14] Whereas some female members, notably Flora Stevenson and Mary Burton in Edinburgh and Isabella Pearce in Cathcart, worried over this emphasis on the domestic education of girls, Grace Paterson's twenty-one-year career on the Glasgow school board reflects the more common position outlined by Corr. Still, as my research has also shown, Paterson did not limit her work to domestic subjects but was a member of a wide range of committees, including physical education.[15] She was, however, never a member of the finance committee, which was generally chaired by a man, exceptions being Flora Stevenson in Edinburgh and Isabella Pearce in Cathcart during the second of her two terms (1893–1900).

Teachers and the School Boards

The 1872 Act followed the 1870 Act in not stipulating that all teachers had to be trained. However, as Marjorie Cruickshank has shown, in contrast to England school boards in Scotland required that teachers be certificated.[16] Hence by 1914, the majority of teachers employed by boards in Scotland held certificates from training colleges, compared with less than half of those working for school boards in England.

T. R. Bone pointed out that the 1872 Act withdrew the dominie's security of tenure, but noted that this attack on the profession was rectified, to a considerable degree, in 1882 with the Public Schools (Scotland) Teachers Act, by which no certificated teacher was to be dismissed without due notice to the teacher and due deliberation by the board, while the 1908 Education Act gave teachers the right to appeal against dismissal by a board.[17] It did not end dismissals, but these Acts were a concession to the professional status of teachers in Scotland, another contrast with England (though not Wales) where elementary teachers were held in relatively low esteem.

An earlier English influence, the pupil-teacher system (introduced in Scotland as well as England and Wales in 1846), had also been seen as a threat to the status of the dominie and the link between parish school and the universities. Not only did school boards come to depend on pupil teachers but, as Helen Corr has shown, the system opened up the male-dominated teaching profession in Scotland to women.[18] Yet although by 1911 women teachers were numerically dominant, just as they were in England and Wales, Scottish boards ensured that men continued to monopolise senior positions in their schools. Indeed, whereas it would appear that the easiest way to reduce the rates was to dismiss a male teacher and employ a female one, most boards continued to advertise for headmasters, always certificated and in the larger boards preferably with a university education. The Glasgow board in particular encouraged its schoolmasters to supplement their training with university courses (usually in the morning), with no loss of pay. By the late 1890s, this also applied to board mistresses, though not to the same extent due to boards' continuing preference for male headteachers.

The treasured parish school dominie did not always accept the decrees of the boards; nor were boards always able to rid themselves of troublesome teachers. Thus, in 1873 the Ardersier board inherited Mr Gray who resisted all efforts to undermine his position. He complained about the collection of fees, took arbitrary decisions to close the school and in 1876 took the board to court over the loss of his potato plot to the new school building, for which he eventually, in February 1879, received compensation of £3. He even wrote to the *Inverness Advertiser* in July 1879 criticising the board's 'suicidal policy' of trying to reduce the teacher's salary and alleging religious discrimination (he was a member of the Church of Scotland and the board was dominated by the Free Church). Yet despite complaints by successive assistant mistresses about his interfering, autocratic ways, the board felt that the headmaster should be 'king' in his school and accepted the eventual resignation of all those aggrieved women. Not only did he remain in post until he retired in 1905, but in 1894 his son was taken on by the board as a monitor with a view to becoming a pupil-teacher. This case was not unique, though few headmasters prevailed as Gray did. Nor were his female assistants exceptional in complaining to the board, but as in this case the authority of the master was generally confirmed.

Whereas the EIS considered the boards harsh employers, many school board women declared themselves guardians of the interests of female teachers. There is no evidence in school board records, however, that they, or indeed the schoolmistresses, sought equal pay with men. Some women protested against their low salary by resigning, and the impression from board minutes is of a considerable turnover of female staff. Most boards simply advertised for a replacement, but some regretted the loss, or inconvenience: thus, the Sanquhar board asked the mistress who resigned in April 1874 if the reason was her salary, offering her an extra £5 a year if she would continue in post; she agreed but only until the summer. Boards often increased the headmaster's earnings indirectly by granting them a house and appointing family members to the same school. For example they took on wives, daughters and sisters to teach sewing, as the Assynt board did in December 1873 to Elphine school (daughter) and Assynt school (wife), both at £11 per annum. The master's children were also employed as pupil-teachers: Nairn board agreed in January 1883 to Mr Penny's request that his second daughter Jeannie replace his eldest daughter Aggie as pupil-teacher. Especially under smaller boards, a husband-and-wife or brother-and-sister 'team' were appointed. In August 1873, the Dumfriesshire school board of Westerkirk discussed salaries for a new schoolmaster and mistress, proposing £60 for the former, with the addition of a house and the school fees, and £20 for the latter if a wife or relative lived in the same house. It recognised that if no such schoolmistress could be found, 'a much larger sum' would be required for her salary. While the board did appoint a married couple, there had been some negotiation: Mr Rogers accepted the post for £65 per annum, his wife for £27 10s. Of course, boards held the upper hand in such dealings, but by the early twentieth century they were contributing to the superannuation fund.

Not only was there no single standard of pay for teachers under the boards but many in the small boards never had their salary raised. Teachers had to apply to their board for an increase in salary, and even where this was agreed once that teacher resigned or retired smaller boards often advertised for a replacement at a lower rate. This was not always a penny-pinching exercise. Between 1886 and 1893, the Carrington school board in Midlothian had to deal with complaints from a headmaster that his assistant mistress acted 'as if entirely independent of my control' and her counter-accusation that he was domineering and disrespectful. The board agreed there were faults on both sides and hoped for 'more mutual forbearance', but resolved that she must recognise him as her superior. Her response was to resign, and the board replaced her with an ex-pupil teacher who was not only cheaper to employ (at £35 to her £45), but also in a more subordinate position than a certificated mistress. Although boards consistently paid women teachers less than men, where a school was run by a woman they might be offered a house and where one was not available, as in 1874 in Dalry, Galloway, the board agreed to an addition of £5 to her salary. Similarly, in Highland boards where schools were in villages which lacked appropriate rented accommodation, salaries might be raised to compensate for the teacher having to commute, as in the case of Miss Squair, assistant at Culloden public school, who travelled by train from Nairn: the board raised her annual salary by £10 in October 1893.

Schoolmistresses, however, were in a weak bargaining position. Few professions other than teaching were open to women in this period, reflected in the practice of even the smallest board to cast its net widely and advertise posts in the regional press (usually the *Glasgow Herald* and *Scotsman*), not just the local press, as well as in the response. For example, of the nine women who replied to the Balmaclellan (Castle Douglas) school board's advertisement for a certificated schoolmistress, there was only one local applicant; the rest wrote from Fife, Perthshire, Aberdeenshire, Glasgow, Cumbria and Yorkshire.

Since school boards preferred men as headteachers, the earnings of the dominie outstripped those of the schoolmistress so that in 1878 the average female salary was scarcely more than half that of the male. Indeed, under the boards the gap widened: in 1899, the average male teacher's salary was just under £144; the average female salary was just under £70.[19] When setting up a secondary department at Fort William public school in February 1893, the school board for Kilmallie advertised for a male assistant who was both a university graduate and a certificated teacher at £120 per annum, and a female certificated assistant who also had a university education at £80 per annum. Although women had only recently gained entry to the universities by law, some had taken extra-mural courses or gained the St Andrews Lady Literate in Arts (LLA) certificate.[20]

School boards also had to deal with parents' complaints, notably of corporal punishment. Again they tended to side with their employees, except in the most serious cases. Thus when a father remonstrated in March 1895 against the excessive punishment of his son, whose left leg was black and blue from hip to ankle, the Kingussie board put this incident into the wider context of two complaints

made in the previous two years, pointing out to the headmaster that the consequence of three consecutive assistants inflicting such severe beatings was 'an
injurious effect on the tone of the school'. The board decreed that if any pupil
merited punishment the headmaster alone could wield the tawse. School boards
nevertheless agreed that corporal punishment was necessary. Roseneath school
board in Dunbartonshire took the headmaster to task in November 1896 only
after sixteen years of complaints from parents of his cruelty, both physical and
verbal, towards their children; but although the board asked for his resignation
it was due for election the following March and could not enforce it. Indeed, he
remained in post until retiring in 1902.

Curriculum

School boards saw it as their duty to preserve the meritocratic tradition by providing a liberal education and a uniform curriculum taught by qualified teachers. At
the core of this curriculum was literacy in English, confirming the Lowland basis
of the tradition and the bias of the 1872 Act which made no provision for Gaelic.
Lindsay Paterson has noted that although there was some financial support for
the inclusion of Gaelic in the curriculum from the late 1870s, the national system
set up by the 1872 Act aimed to make children literate in English: the school
boards had a modernising agenda.[21] Gaelic was to be used in board schools as a
medium of teaching where it would benefit learning English. Thus, in August
1876 the Assynt school board recorded that, following an SED circular, it would
apply for a grant to provide instruction in the reading and spelling of Gaelic for
an hour a week to children entering the fourth standard whose first language was
Gaelic.

The Scottish belief in the superiority of a broad academic curriculum
throughout the system not only masked the tendency of boards to focus on
elementary education but also resulted in neglect of vocational and technical
education. Boards offered continuation classes to school leavers, but these often
consisted of subjects taught in their day schools, and while an Act of 1887
authorised boards to maintain technical schools, no additional funding was allocated. Moreover, although boards provided a wider range of vocational subjects
for boys than girls in their schools, these were all generally taught at basic levels
and tended to be some form of manual training, often depending on the local
economy. Thus the Fala board in Midlothian offered agriculture to boys in 1891,
while the Applecross board in Wester Ross offered woodwork and gardening to
boys in 1911.

Cookery schools (first established in London in 1873 and soon after in the
major cities of Scotland as well as England) were independent of the SED and
the boards. While board schoolmistresses were expected to teach sewing and
domestic economy, once cooking was introduced (in Glasgow from around 1880)
school boards were strenuously lobbied to employ trained cookery teachers. As
Tom Begg has shown, Christian Guthrie Wright did this in Edinburgh while
Willie Thompson and Carole McCallum have shown Grace Paterson did the

same in Glasgow.[22] Honorary secretary of the Glasgow School of Cookery for thirty years since its establishment in 1876 and member of the Glasgow school board between 1885 and 1906, Paterson pushed for centres for cookery, since not all schools had the facilities to teach it. She persuaded the board to refurbish a disused school as a district centre for teaching housewifery, cookery and laundry work, which opened in May 1899 with lessons given by specialist teachers. Paterson also played a part in negotiations to establish the regulations for training schoolteachers in cookery and laundry work, in anticipation of the SED taking control of the cookery schools in 1908.

Only a few large boards had the resources to provide such an expensive subject in terms of equipment, accommodation, ingredients and the specialist teacher. Miss Penny told the Nairn board in November 1893 that while she was willing to qualify for a diploma in cooking the number of girls in the higher standards was so small she thought it best to defer introducing the subject. In some areas, boards did not supply cooking directly but agreed to the request from Mrs Black of the West End School of Cookery in Glasgow to supply a peripatetic teacher of evening classes, as the Dumfries burgh school board did in July 1882, asking three of the mistresses it employed if they would attend her classes. Mrs Black provided cookery classes to boards across the country, from Dumfries to Inverness, while some boards paid for a mistress to attend classes in her Glasgow school. Again, it was more difficult in the Highlands to provide cookery classes. In 1903, the Applecross board, covering a thinly populated, very poor district, was unable to offer secondary education and particularly regretted it was no longer able to offer cookery classes. It felt that, 'as part of the nation', it should get some financial help to resume cookery at least.

Whereas school boards in Scotland, in contrast to England, preferred co- (or mixed-sex) education over single-sex schooling, great efforts were made – as in England – to ensure a gendered curriculum. Over the period of the school boards, gender-specific subjects took up increasing space on the curriculum. Girls' industrial training consisted of sewing (compulsory) and domestic economy, enlarged by subjects such as cookery, laundry and, in the early twentieth century, care of infants and basic health and hygiene. The emphasis was first on equipping a girl for her assumed future as a wife and mother rather than for working in service. Thus, the Applecross board which was unable to offer cookery classes in 1903 recorded that while most girls in its schools did indeed go into service, members felt that cookery and washing classes would be most useful to them in their 'after life'. Boards in Scotland came up against parental resistance to such an emphasis on domestic subjects: one headmaster even complained to the Ardersier board in 1880 and 1881 that some parents forbade their daughters from attending the compulsory sewing class on which the school grant depended. As Lindy Moore has shown, parents saw board schools as being for 'book-learning' for girls as well as for boys.[23] Board minutes also show parental suspicions that daughters were being used as unpaid servants by the teacher.

Besides board members' expectations that the curriculum should reflect the different gender roles expected of boys and girls, increasing social stratification in Scotland put pressure on boards to draw clearer distinctions between elementary and secondary education as was done in England. Nevertheless, the tradition of common provision and the notion of a democratic intellect had a continuing influence as even in small towns and rural areas boards sought to provide the 'higher' work which had been found in parish schools. Thus, the Crossmichael board offered mathematics, English literature, Latin, French, physical geography and domestic economy in 1883. Certainly, the notion of 'democratic' was limited by the belief in a meritocracy, poverty and gender expectations, but at least there was, by the end of the century, the opportunity of social advancement through board schools for a few, and for girls now as well as boys, though still with nar-rower employment opportunities for the former. Yet while members of boards across Scotland believed that their schools should impart more advanced learn-ing than the minimum requirements of the 3Rs, there was no agreement on what constituted secondary education, apart from subjects other than, and knowledge above, the basics as the Crossmichael and earlier Kingussie examples show. The parochial tradition persisted through such 'specific subjects' as English literature, ancient and modern languages, mathematics and a variety of science subjects being taught in the higher standards of board schools from the first Scotch Code of 1873 until the end of the century; but few pupils completed all three stages, while some (for example scientific subjects and domestic economy) were rather basic at all levels. Moreover, boards' control over the curriculum was constrained since only subjects recognised by the SED could earn a grant, which subjects were taught depended on what the teachers could offer, most pupils took only one or two and domestic economy was compulsory for girls. In the early 1890s, sec-ondary education committees, with membership drawn from school boards and local authorities, were set up in Scotland, mainly in larger urban centres. This meant that school boards were not the sole source of funding or administration for secondary education, while the historical link between the parish school and university was being undermined by the gradual reorganisation of the system into a sequence of end-on stages.

Although there were similar developments in school board provision of higher classes and higher grade schools in the major cities of England and Wales after the 1870 Act, there was still strong resistance in England to broadening the elementary curriculum for the poor, whereas the parochial tradition encouraged boards to include university subjects in schools across Scotland. At the same time, this attachment to the democratic tradition in education obscured the widespread social inequalities in Scotland which were compounded by geogra-phy, with small, rural and especially Highland boards having much less scope in what they could provide than large urban centres. As in the rest of Scotland, when secondary departments and schools were established in the Highlands it was in towns: as the example above shows, the Kilmallie board established a secondary department at Fort William public school.

Twentieth-century Challenges

The 1872 Act had represented a significant increase of state intervention in society, and this grew as government anxiety over the health of the imperial 'race' in the late nineteenth century led to school boards taking on responsibilities for public health and wellbeing. This was reflected in the introduction into the curriculum of physical education, notably drill, both military and musical: in 1892, the Dumfries board procured a piano for drill classes in the mixed department of Noblehill public school, and in 1894 the Borgue board (Kirkcudbright) considered that 'in teaching military drill it would be a great advantage to the boys to have imitation guns and to the girls to have bar-bells', ordering two dozen of each. As Robert Anderson has shown, however, the emphasis was not militarisation but fitness and the inculcation of self-discipline, reflected in the deliberations of the Royal Commission on Physical Training (Scotland) which reported in 1903.[24] There was a shortage of playgrounds and playing fields as well as trained teachers, but by the beginning of the twentieth century physical education in the larger urban centres included swimming lessons: in May 1902, for example, the clerk to the Maryhill board reported that a swimming class for girls in Gairbraid school was under the charge of Miss Margaret Cameron who was paid at the rate of 3s for the one-hour lesson, whereas a teacher for the boys could not be got for less than 7s 6d.

The development of the domestic curriculum for girls beyond sewing, cleaning, cooking and to cover hygiene, nutrition, health and welfare, was also a response to fears for 'national efficiency'. Scotland temporarily lagged behind England and Wales where the 1906 Education (Provision of Meals) Act allowed (but did not require) local authorities to provide needy children with school meals, and the 1907 Education (Administrative Provisions) Act introduced medical inspection and the appointment of medical officers and school nurses. Both measures were introduced by the 1908 Education (Scotland) Act which went further than the English legislation in that school boards were required to investigate cases of 'neglected' children and provide clothing as well as food. Some of the bigger boards already did this: for example, the seventh triennial report of the proceedings of the Edinburgh board (1894) recorded that Flora Stevenson was secretary and treasurer of the committee for feeding and clothing neglected and destitute children. Whereas there was an upper limit set on the amount which could be spent in England and Wales, this was not the case in Scotland. The Education Act of 1913 added dental health to boards' responsibilities. These developments were largely, but not exclusively, confined to the towns: Applecross board began providing dental care in 1913.

Growth in the Scottish economy in the second half of the nineteenth century had been narrowly based on the predominantly male sector of heavy industry (coal, iron and steel, shipbuilding and heavy engineering), and was very dependent on world markets. Given the curriculum favoured by the boards, their schools were not specifically geared towards the needs of the economy, reflected in neglect of vocational and technical education. Another factor highlighted by the discussion on cookery lessons was the limited catchment area of many boards where economies of scale made it difficult to offer technical education. Boards at least tried to respond to the growing commercial sector, introducing commercial subjects for both sexes in the higher standards as well as in evening schools: for example, Perth school board offered book-keeping in evening classes at Perth Academy in September 1895 while the Gretna board offered continuation classes in shorthand and typing in 1915–16. Government preoccupation, however, was with industrial and imperial challenges. International competition in the late nineteenth and early twentieth centuries led to fears in Britain that a poorly educated working class could not compete industrially, prompted not least by the key role in education taken by the recently (1871) unified German state. Such concerns do not find much expression in the minutes of school boards. True, board members believed strongly in the central importance of education: Flora Stevenson was reported in the *Evening News* (7 March 1903) to have claimed that education was 'quite as important as the other great Departments of Imperial Administration'. Yet whatever the appeal to and of empire, the focus of boards across Scotland was domestic and social rather than political or economic.

The First World War brought additional duties and problems for school boards. Some schools or parts of schools were requisitioned: the army took over the Noblehill school kitchen early in 1915. Some boards adapted the curriculum: classes on war cookery were offered in Dumfries board schools in 1916. There was considerable turnover of staff, with some masters joining up and asking the board to keep their places open for them, while some board members also volunteered: Reverend Gilchrist of the Applegarth board went to the front as a chaplain. Boards were lobbied by the EIS and feminist organisations to increase teachers' salaries in recognition of the rising cost of living due to the war. Rural boards allowed exemptions from attendance for children to perform agricultural work due to the shortage of adult male labourers, but followed a Ministry of Food circular that children could gather brambles for payment only after school hours.

The end of the war saw the end of the school boards. Still, despite English influences, the Scottish belief in a distinctive educational tradition and local control had helped ensure that school boards continued to run popular education sixteen years after they were abolished in England and Wales; and although the 1918 Act seemed to bring Scotland into line with England and Wales by replacing boards with larger local education authorities, this was only partial as the authorities in Scotland were, like school boards, elected until the 1929 Local Government Act.

Since the first election in 1873, the larger school boards had developed a corporate identity through correspondence and conferences: for example, in February 1898, representatives from the boards of Aberdeen, Dundee, Edinburgh, Glasgow, Govan, Leith, Old Monkland and Paisley met in Edinburgh to discuss the early age at which children still left school, even where, as in Edinburgh, there were many bursaries to encourage children to stay on. Above all, school boards were rooted in their communities. They employed local people, notably janitors (invariably men) and cleaners (both men and women, the latter in the majority and generally married). They worked with local organisations as well as businesses and tradesmen. They allowed concerts and club meetings on their premises and, in the case of Glasgow, opened penny banks in some schools in the 1870s. English influences, government centralisation and international pressures notwithstanding, the boards played a central role in local society for forty-five years and their meetings were regularly reported in the local press. The preamble to the 1872 Act stated that the purpose of school boards was to ensure that 'efficient education for their children may be furnished and made available to the whole people of Scotland' and, as James Roxburgh observed of the Glasgow board, this they did.[25]

Of course, Glasgow was not representative of Scotland, but this study of school boards across the country suggests that all sought to fulfil that purpose as far as possible and while their remit was the local community, taken as whole they constituted a truly national system of education. Indeed, in contrast to the tensions between school boards and voluntary schools in England, in Scotland the boards brought the denominations together, if not always in harmony. Initially, some Protestants, notably evangelicals, objected to Catholic membership and some refused to help the poorer Catholic schools, for example with free book distribution: allowed by the Education Act of 1908, this was furiously debated in the 1909 election to the Edinburgh school board. Negotiations to bring Catholic schools into the national system were slow, beginning in the 1890s, and James Conroy has shown that the relationship between the secular authorities and the Catholic church remained uneasy. Nevertheless, the decision of the Catholic as well as the Episcopalian churches to enter the national system in the 1918 Education Act was partly based on the churches' largely positive experience of working with the school boards.[26]

Notes

1. J. D. Myers, 'Scottish nationalism and the antecedents of the 1872 Education Act', *Scottish Educational Studies* 4(2) (1972), 76–92; Donald J. Withrington, 'Towards a national system, 1866–72: The last years in the struggle for a Scottish Education Act', *Scottish Educational Studies* 4(2) (1972), 107–24.
2. Lindsay Paterson, *Scottish Education in the Twentieth Century* (Edinburgh University Press, 2003), pp. 37–40.
3. School board minute books cited in this chapter were found in the following archives and libraries: Aberdeen City and Aberdeenshire Archives; Ayrshire Archives Centre; Ewart Library, Dumfries (Dumfriesshire and Kirkcudbright); Glasgow City Archives (Cathcart, Dumbarton, Glasgow, Lanark, Maryhill, Renfrew); Dundee City Archives; Edinburgh Central Library; Highland Council Archives (Argyll, Inverness, Nairn County, Ross and Cromarty, Sutherland); Perth and Kinross Council Archives; Stirling Council Archives; West Register House, Edinburgh (the Lothians). I wish to acknowledge the award of a British Academy/Leverhulme Small Grant which made possible visits to these archives.

4. James Scotland, *The History of Scottish Education*, 2 vols (London University Press, 1969), vol. I, p. 363; vol. II, p. 262.
5. Robert Anderson, 'In search of the "lad of parts": The mythical history of Scottish education', *History Workshop* 19 (spring 1985), 82–104.
6. L. J. Williams and Dot Jones, 'Women at work in nineteenth-century Wales', *Llafur: The Journal of the Society of Welsh Labour History* 3(3) (1983), 20–32; Nicola Verdon, 'The employment of women and children in agriculture: A reassessment of agricultural gangs in nineteenth-century Norfolk', *Agricultural History Review* 49 (2001), 41–55.
7. Jane McDermid, *The Schooling of Working-Class Girls in Victorian Scotland: Gender, Education and Identity* (Routledge, 2005), p. 93.
8. James Scotland, 'The centenary of the Education (Scotland) Act of 1872', *British Journal of Educational Studies* 20 (1972), 121–36.
9. Sarah L. Hamilton, 'The architecture and impact of the school boards in Glasgow', *Architectural Heritage* 22(1) (November 2011), 115–36.
10. R. D. Anderson, *Education and the Scottish People 1750–1918* (Clarendon Press, 1995), p. 107.
11. Jane McDermid, 'Blurring the boundaries: School board women in Scotland 1873–1919', *Women's History Review* 19 (2010), 357–73.
12. Andrew Bain, 'The beginnings of democratic control of local education in Scotland', *Scottish Economic and Social History* 23 (2003), 7–25; James Roxburgh, *The School Board of Glasgow 1873–1919* (University of London Press, 1973).
13. Anderson, *Education and the Scottish People*, p. 166.
14. Helen Corr, 'Home-rule in Scotland: The teaching of housework in schools 1872–1914', in Fiona M. S. Paterson and Judith Fewell (eds), *Girls in Their Prime: Scottish Education Revisited* (Scottish Academic Press, 1990), pp. 38–53.
15. Jane McDermid, 'Place the book in their hands: Grace Paterson's contribution to the health and welfare policies of the School Board of Glasgow, 1885–1906', *History of Education* 36 (2007), 697–713.
16. Marjorie Cruickshank, *A History of the Training of Teachers in Scotland* (University of London Press, 1970).
17. T. R. Bone, 'Teachers and security of tenure 1872–1908', in Thomas R. Bone (ed.), *Studies in the History of Scottish Education 1872–1939* (University of London Press, 1967), pp. 71–135.
18. Helen Corr, 'Teachers and gender: Debating the myths of equal opportunities in Scottish education 1800–1914', *Cambridge Journal of Education* 27 (1997), 355–63.
19. *Report of the Committee of Council on Education* (1878–9), p. xviii; (1900), pp. xxiv, 44.
20. Lesley A. Orr Macdonald renders LLA as 'Lady Literate in Arts': *A Unique and Glorious Mission: Women and Presbyterianism in Scotland 1830–1930* (John Donald, 2000), p. 277; the second 'L' is also referred to as 'Licentiate': Robert Bell and Malcolm Tight, *Open Universities: A British Tradition* (Open University Press, 1993), p. 78. See also Elisabeth Smith, 'To walk upon the grass: The impact of the University of St Andrews Lady Literate in Arts 1877–1892' (unpublished PhD dissertation, University of St Andrews, 2014).
21. Paterson, *Scottish Education in the Twentieth Century*, p. 45.
22. Tom Begg, *The Excellent Women: The Origins and History of Queen Margaret College* (John Donald, 1994); Willie Thompson and Carole McCallum, *Glasgow Caledonian University: Its Origins and Evolution* (Tuckwell Press, 1998).
23. Lindy Moore, 'Educating for the "woman's sphere": Domestic training versus

intellectual discipline', in Esther Breitenbach and Eleanor Gordon (eds), *Out of Bounds: Women in Scottish Society* (Edinburgh University Press, 1992), p. 25.

24. Robert Anderson, 'Secondary schools and Scottish society in the nineteenth century', *Past and Present* 109 (1985), 199.

25. Roxburgh, *School Board of Glasgow*, p. 225.

26. James Conroy, 'A very Scottish affair: Catholic education and the state', *Oxford Review of Education* 27 (2001), 548.

Bibliography

Anderson, R. D., *Education and Opportunity in Victorian Scotland* (Clarendon Press, 1983).

Bain, Andrew, *Three Into One: Significant Changes in Representation and Leadership Related to the Amalgamation of the School Boards of Bothkennar, Polmont and Grangemouth* (Falkirk Council Education Services, 2003).

Bain, Andrew, *Ancient and Modern. A Comparison of the Social Composition of the Burgh School Boards of Stirling and Falkirk from 1873 to 1919* (Falkirk Council Education Services, 2006).

Bryce, T. G. K. and W. M. Humes (eds), *Scottish Education* (Edinburgh University Press, 1999).

Holmes, Heather (ed.), *Institutions of Scotland: Education*, Scottish Life and Society: A Compendium of Scottish Ethnology, vol. 11 (Tuckwell Press, 2000).

Humes, Walter M. and Hamish M. Paterson (eds), *Scottish Culture and Scottish Education 1800–1980* (John Donald, 1983).

McDermid, Jane, 'School board women and active citizenship in Scotland 1873–1919', *History of Education* 38 (2009), 33–47.

Paterson, Lindsay, *Scottish Education in the Twentieth Century* (Edinburgh University Press, 2003).

Roxburgh, James, *The School Board of Glasgow 1873–1919* (University of London Press, 1973).

Withrington, Donald J., 'The 1872 Education Act – a centenary retrospect', *Education in the North* 9 (1972), 5–9.

12

Schoolteachers and Professionalism, 1696–1906

Christopher R. Bischof

In the 1990s, a descendant of the Highlands schoolmaster William Campbell typed up the diary this teacher had kept for more than thirty years and deposited it at the Highlands Archive and Registration Centre. He affixed to the beginning a brief sketch of Campbell's life. Campbell was born in 1867 in Durness, the illegitimate son of a twenty-year-old domestic servant and an unknown man. Cast out of his grandparents' home along with his mother, he appeared to have poor prospects in life. According to his descendant, such a birth 'marked him as a boy and man who would only succeed through his own merits and determination'. But succeed he did. The biographical sketch tells us that 'A local Schoolmaster befriended him, and recognised his winning character. As a result, William Campbell found himself rescued from rejection and some obscure living, and made his way to professional life.' After completing school, he first became a pupil-teacher, then attended the Free Church Normal School at Moray House in Edinburgh on a scholarship from 1890 to 1893 and finally taught at the schools in Nethybridge and Rogart. He married, started a family, spent his evenings and weekends studying languages and philosophy (becoming proficient in five languages) and turned his school in Rogart into a local museum and soup kitchen when not in use for classes.[1]

His descendant's biographical sketch locates Campbell's life firmly within the 'lad o' parts' tradition whereby a poor but clever and hard-working boy could effect his own upward social mobility by means of an open education system. Part myth and part reality, the idea of the 'lad o' parts' has long had enormous political potency through its appeal to a sense of social justice through education that is distinctly Scottish. Yet Campbell was born at a moment when the teaching profession – the agents, beneficiaries and embodiment of meritocratic uplift – was in the midst of an upheaval that seemed to threaten the social and cultural opportunities which it had traditionally offered.

Scholarship on the history of Scottish teachers has situated their story within three main areas of inquiry. First, the question of Scottish distinctiveness: how did Scotland's relationship to England change in the wake of the Union?

Historians' attempts to answer this question have led them to explore the lad o' parts myth which emerged in the late nineteenth century. They have not only examined the gap between myth and reality, but have asked how, when and why that myth came into being.[2] The question of Scottish distinctiveness is closely related to a second major concern: the role teachers played in social relations. Were they agents and embodiments of social meritocracy or social control? Did they remain relics of an earlier, paternalistic era or did they become part of the new, increasingly depersonalised industrial order? On the whole, historians have moved towards a moderate consensus on these questions, locating teachers within a tradition of both social control and social mobility, paternalism and impersonal bureaucracy.[3] Historians of women and gender have opened up a third major area of inquiry. Telling the story of women teachers and unpacking the ideas about gender which structured the development of the teaching profession has also resulted in fresh perspectives on the history of Scottish national identity and social relations.[4]

This chapter explores the teaching profession in the comparatively stable eighteenth and the tumultuous nineteenth centuries. It situates changes to teaching, teacher training and teachers' professionalism within the context of broader social, cultural and political upheavals. Though the teaching profession did not have quite such a hallowed position in Scottish society in 1893, when Campbell graduated from training college and began his career, as it had a century earlier, it was in many ways more dynamic, democratic and self-conscious.

Teachers, particularly those working in parochial and, later, board schools, often strove to present a professional front in their periodicals, lobbying and institutions. Though they had a strong claim to professional status in many ways, theirs was nonetheless a tenuous professionalism. Even before the wave of Victorian policy changes emphasising classroom management and teaching the basics to all students, teachers faced criticism of their lack of specialised pedagogical training, the priority they gave to boys over girls and their preference for teaching advanced subjects to a few students rather than teaching the basics to the many.[5] Teachers also recognised and sometimes chafed at the limits of their own autonomy in the form of interference from ministers, local notables, parents and pupils, and presbytery policies. Finally, even in around 1800 parochial schoolmasters with a university education were substantially outnumbered by teachers in the Society in Scotland for the Promotion of Christian Knowledge (SSPCK) and so-called 'dame' and 'adventure' schools, groups that often enjoyed little education or prestige. The best-educated teachers – nine-tenths of the famous Dick Bequest teachers in the North-East – expressed a desire to become ministers, according to one 1865 report.[6] Clearly not all the professions were equal. The story of teachers and professionalism is, then, quite complex; we cannot write about teachers' 'professionalisation' with the straightforward narrative from a body of amateurs to a body of professionals that that implies, nor can we write about the decline of professionalism from the eighteenth to the nineteenth centuries. The story of teachers and professionalism between 1696 and

1906 is one of both continuity and rupture, but most of all it involved redefining teachers' professionalism to emphasise pedagogical expertise, thoroughly grounding all students in the basics, and the inclusion of women within the profession, albeit not as equals.

Chronologically, the history of teachers' relationship to professionalism in the eighteenth and nineteenth centuries falls into three periods. First, the period from 1696, when parish schools with their tenured schoolmasters were brought into existence by law, until roughly the 1820s, when Scottish reformers began to seriously criticise the state of education, including the teaching force. Second, a period of transition between the 1820s and 1846. This was a time of social upheavals that saw experimentation with new pedagogies and the foundation of institutions that were to evolve into teacher training colleges. Third, the period from 1846 to 1906 during which a series of policies and laws emanating in good part from London – though less so after the creation of the Scotch Education Department (SED) under Henry Craik in 1885 – created a new system of teacher training and certification, subjected them to an array of supervisory and disciplinary mechanisms on the job and ushered in an era of universal schooling. The Education (Scotland) Act 1872 was a major landmark during this period, creating a system of state schools managed by locally elected school boards. The schools in this new system included former parish and burgh schools, transferred by law to school board control. By 1906, the SED had taken over the Presbyterian teacher training colleges and was beginning to eliminate regulations that allowed for untrained teachers. Universities had also begun to open their doors more fully to teachers, renewing a relationship that had never disappeared but which had faded in the mid-Victorian years. By this time secondary school teachers were also coming to take the place of social and cultural prominence that teachers in parochial and board schools had once occupied.

Teachers and School Systems, 1696–c. 1820

At the heart of Scotland's distinctive education system were the parish schools and their teachers. A 1696 law required the heritors (major local landowners) in every rural parish to build and maintain a school as well as to support a schoolmaster. The law entitled schoolmasters to a minimum base salary of £5 11s and a maximum of £11 2s (plus whatever they collected in fees, usually in the £4–£8 range), a house with a garden and tenure for life. A respectable enough salary in the early and mid-eighteenth century, inflation had so devalued it by the 1790s that some teachers suffered a 'sort of genteel starving', in the words of one minister.[7] The ideal parochial schoolmaster had attended university for a time on a church bursary or through the patronage of a local elite, perhaps even graduating. Such an education would enable them to teach a range of liberal subjects, including Latin, advanced mathematics, history – even Greek, French or German. The intent of parish schools was to create an educational system that served the children of the poor and the well-to-do, boys and girls, Highlands and Lowlands, bringing them all together in a common national culture and giving them access to the full range of the liberal curriculum. Parish schools in the Lowlands came closer to securing a teacher who met the high standards of this ideal than in the Highlands, where poverty and geography presented numerous challenges.[8] Though outside the scope of the 1696 law, urban areas operated burgh schools for middle-class pupils and church-controlled sessional schools for the upper working classes. Parochial and burgh schoolmasters enjoyed roughly similar levels of public status and generally felt themselves to be members of the same profession, as is evident from their co-operation during the early years of the Educational Institute of Scotland (EIS) in the late 1840s and 1850s.

Parochial schoolmasters enjoyed something like professional social status in the eighteenth century, though that status did not manifest as a movement to create a professional association to set standards and secure teachers' autonomy. To some extent, schoolmasters controlled access to their profession. They singled out promising young men, gave them special instruction in the subjects that they would need for university and helped them to navigate the process of applying for a bursary or finding a patron to sponsor their attendance. It was to this process that 'lad o' parts' came to refer. Amongst the often impoverished communities of eighteenth-century Scotland's countryside, teachers enjoyed a great deal of respect and prestige thanks to their learning, job security, and solid salary and housing. An 1803 Act of Parliament helped to bring the position of the parochial schoolmaster up to date for the early nineteenth century by doubling the maximum base salary and mandating that teachers' gratis housing have two rooms and a garden. Though he was doubtless looking back with nostalgia, there is some truth to the observation W. Milligan made in 1857 that the parochial schoolmasters of yesteryear had been

> spirited old men whose native force of character and talent had never known a check; who amidst the undeniable degradation of the schools in many parts of the country, lent such a lustre to the profession that all men spoke well of it.[9]

However, it is easy to exaggerate the 'lustre' of life as an eighteenth-century parochial schoolmaster. Teachers' salaries dropped precipitously when student fees dried up during the harvest season and inflation chipped away at the buying power of their salary. Parochial schoolmasters also worked within a system of supervision and patronage by the church and local elites. Their appointments were not purely meritocratic, but rather the result of a selection process by the heritors and minister that could be nepotistic or otherwise biased. Once appointed, parochial schoolmasters could end up doing a great deal of side work for the local minister and the church, including clerking for Kirk Sessions, leading the singing at church on Sundays and keeping marriage and baptism records for the parish. Such side work could be welcome when it was optional and came with supplemental pay, but when it was forced on them without compensation it was a bitter pill to swallow. The problem of ministers coercing teachers into undertaking side work afflicted teachers in schools with many different religious affiliations on both sides of the Tweed until the era of school boards.[10] Some schoolmasters aspired to become ministers themselves – including a few men who had attended university and were fully qualified in divinity, but who had failed to attain a parish. It was a phenomenon common enough that some advertisements for parish schoolmasters declared that 'applicants must not have the kirk in view'.[11] A very few eventually attained a parish, but it seems that it was more common for a teacher to desire and intend to use teaching as a stepping stone to the ministry than to actually succeed in doing so. Investigations into the state of the parish school system also reported concerns that girls' education was neglected. This neglect was in part because of girls' importance to the family economy, but in part because some schoolmasters allegedly relished and devoted a disproportionate amount of time to teaching advanced subjects to boys. However, girls who did attend regularly at a school with a dedicated teacher could and did receive a thorough grounding in Latin, advanced mathematics and other subjects.[12]

Parochial schoolmasters regarded tenure as among their most cherished rights, a privilege which gave them social status, helped them to weather economic downturns and granted them some measure of immunity from the tribulations of local politics. The looming threat of the loss of tenure followed by its actual abolition in 1872 led to major professional agitation. However, tenure also had its limits. Technically, teachers' tenure was *ad vitam aut culpam* ('for life or until fault'). That second clause – 'until fault' – meant that schoolmasters never had total immunity from sacking: they could be and regularly were dismissed for gross misconduct. Between 1793 and 1853, heritors formally brought 139 cases against teachers, resulting in 106 teachers vacating their office. Probably more teachers resigned under threat of being charged or as a result of other informal pressure from the heritors and/or the community in instances where they were no longer wanted.[13] Teachers' job security and autonomy was never total even with tenure.

By the early nineteenth century, Scotland had a substantial network of private, burgh and sessional schools. According to an 1818 investigation, Scotland had 3,633 day schools, of which only 942 were parish schools.[14] Private schools filled in the many gaps left by parish schools in rural areas, where some parishes were so large that children would have had to walk a dozen or more miles a day to go to school. In towns and cities a growing population was filling up the burgh and sessional schools that served the middle- and working-class urban populations, respectively. In the urban areas where parental demand combined with the financial capacity to pay the fees, teachers could make a good living – especially in the burgh schools serving the children of the middle class. In rural areas, however, the majority of private schools were individual, haphazard affairs that opened and closed their doors as demand waxed and waned. The major exception to this pattern was the SSPCK, which acquired a royal charter in 1709 and immediately began founding and supporting schools. By 1800, the SSPCK had opened more than 150 schools, most located in the Highlands but subsidised by donations from the Lowlands. The foremost concern in SSPCK schools was to teach

Christianity and inculcate morality – though in the Protestant tradition teaching reading was an important part of that process. The final type of non-parochial schools were day schools which operated on the monitorial system. Developed by Andrew Bell and Joseph Lancaster, this system allowed one teacher to instruct simultaneously up to 1,000 pupils through the use of older children known as monitors. Monitorial school societies were founded in Glasgow, Edinburgh and Aberdeen between 1810 and 1815, though the monitorial system never caught on as widely in Scotland as it did in England and Wales.

The intellectual abilities of and instruction given by teachers in all but the burgh schools was typically limited compared to parochial schoolmasters, though it varied enormously. In SSPCK schools, teachers ranged from the parish schoolmaster's daughter to men and women whose own poor education made it a struggle to teach the 3Rs and who lived in houses which, according to a report, 'had got into great disrepair'. Between 1818 and 1820, the SSPCK undertook a reformation of the teacher hiring process. They began requiring candidates to appear in Edinburgh for an exam in 'reading, spelling, definition and explanation of words and terms, grammar including parsing, the leading facts of the Old Testament history and gospels, the shorter catechism with proofs, geography . . . writing, arithmetic, [and] history', as well as an interview with the SSPCK's Committee of Directors.[15] In rural areas in the Lowlands and Highlands alike middling farmers could band together to hire a teacher on a temporary basis; often during the winter season children were not needed for work. The qualifications of such teachers ranged from university-educated men experienced in teaching, to men who struggled to read. Robert Burns, son of a struggling farmer, received part of his education at the hands of one of the more gifted of these peripatetic pedagogues. Teachers in monitorial schools were often adept disciplinarians and not ineffective at imparting basic literacy and numeracy. However, the very premise of the monitorial system precluded both a close, nurturing relationship with individual students and the teaching of advanced subjects. Teachers in this system did not need to be either skilled in child-centred pedagogy or particularly learned in the liberal curriculum. Information about the teachers in the 'dame' and 'adventure' schools is hard to come by, but the accounts we do have suggest that the quality of instruction and status of the teachers was quite low.[16] Teachers often set up these schools as a side business or to help them in their old age, acting as childminders as much as pedagogues. Yet with their extremely low fees, convenience and many teachers' success in teaching the very basics of reading, arithmetic and Christianity, these schools met the needs of many poor families.

Social and Pedagogical Upheavals, c. 1820–1846

By the beginning of the Victorian period reformers had begun to call for more and better teachers to cope with a society that looked very different from how it had when the parish school system got its start. Changes to the population distribution, religious beliefs and the nature of work that had been underway for at least half a century were gathering pace by the late 1820s. Social reformers, educationalists and men of the cloth grappled with these changes to the social landscape. Fears and anxieties about these upheavals created the context within which changes to teachers' education, work, and the enactment of their professionalism unfolded in the Victorian period.

Perhaps the most striking and troubling change of all was urbanisation. The rapid growth of cities left churches, schools and philanthropic institutions straining to keep pace with the population boom. The nature of urban work and living also led to the fraying of the bonds of community and allowed for the possibility of anonymity, a seemingly startling and worrying change to the social landscape compared to the rural past. In this context, in 1834 George Lewis, editor of the *Scottish Guardian*, published a ninety-five-page pamphlet entitled *Scotland a Half-Educated Nation, Both in the Quantity and Quality of her Educational Institutions*. Lewis may have been the author of the pamphlet, but the ideas in it had been articulated by MPs in speeches on the education question in the 1820s and 1830s, by reformers speaking at the meetings of the recently founded Glasgow Education Association, and in the *Scottish Guardian* itself. The general thrust of the reform movement encapsulated in *Scotland a Half-Educated Nation* was twofold. First, that Scotland lacked the schools and teachers to educate its population, particularly in its cities. Second, that those schools which Scotland did have in urban areas were 'almost entirely in the hands of private schoolmasters' rather than parochial schoolmasters educated at universities and affiliated with and supervised by the church. As a result, MP J. C. Colquhoun argued in the House of Commons, the proportion of Scottish children receiving an education had fallen precipitously compared to their counterparts in Prussia, Holland and parts of the United States. Coloquhoun proposed a Bill on 17 June 1834 to expand Scotland's vaunted parochial school system, but the £60,000 a year price tag and the imperative that would have accompanied it to undertake a comparable – and far more costly – expansion of education in England and Wales resulted in the Bill's demise.[17]

Although *Scotland a Half-Educated Nation* and the reform movement of which it was a part glorified parochial schoolmasters and sought to make them the role models for whatever expanded educational system was to come, even those hallowed pedagogues were not immune from critical scrutiny. The 1820s and 1830s saw growing concerns about parochial schoolmasters' lack of specialised training in pedagogy, part of a wider critique of their teaching methods. Given the public discussion about the sorry state of popular education and the quality of many teachers, coupled with the difficulty of getting parliament to take action, the professional reputation of teachers arguably approached a low point in the early 1830s.

However, the social and educational anxieties of this period did give rise to private reform efforts. At the forefront of this effort were John Wood, active in Edinburgh, and David Stow, who worked primarily in Glasgow. Stow became the better known of these two leading educationalists. The son of a Paisley merchant, he concentrated particularly on teacher training in the 1820s. Though he participated in the meetings of the Glasgow Education Association, which saw parochial schools and schoolmasters as role models, Stow worked outside the parochial school system. In 1836, he opened a Glaswegian model school where teachers came to train and subsequently published *The Training System*, as he called his method. He took as his students and audience men and, crucially, *women* interested in working in schools of all kinds, though particularly with infants and young children from poor families. Influenced by pedagogical methods developing on the continent (and, in turn, himself influential on the continent) as well as the social context of Scotland, Stow stressed the need for the teacher to treat each child as an individual and to develop their character as a whole. So important was the need to develop children's morality in the context of this new urban life that Stow declared the main goal of his pedagogy to be 'to supply an actual deficiency in the moral economy of large towns'.[18] Stow's method constituted a break from earlier methods of teaching through its emphasis on individuality, cultivating curiosity and carefully guiding moral development rather than the rote learning, disconnected attempts at social control, moralising and intellectual instruction which he felt characterised some parish, SSPCK, burgh and other schools.

Despite all the anxiety and innovation in the 1820s and 1830s, the tradition of the university-educated parochial schoolmaster gained force in at least part of Scotland thanks to the Dick Bequest, an 1828 endowment by a Scottish merchant who had made good in the West Indies.[19] The Dick Bequest offered a substantial addition to the base salary of parochial schoolmasters in Aberdeen, Moray and Banff who passed a rigorous initial test of their own learning and a biennial inspection of their teaching. The vast majority of these schoolmasters were university graduates – indeed, in 1875 Her Majesty's Inspector John Kerr estimated that 130 out of 150 schoolmasters in the bequest area had an MA. The Dick Bequest did not simply preserve the tradition of the well-educated parochial schoolmaster, however. Its trustees also helped to reform the parochial school system. They offered monetary assistance and incentives for giving all pupils a solid foundation in the basics and for getting as many pupils as possible – boys and girls alike – to attend regularly and to go on to advanced subjects. The trustees also used a carrot-and-stick approach to encourage teachers who were no longer effective to retire. For learned but pedagogically ineffective teachers still in their prime, the trustees arranged and paid for short visits to a training college to acquire the professional skills which they increasingly felt were a necessary adjunct to liberal knowledge.[20] Thus teachers' professionalism had begun to place a greater emphasis on pedagogy even in an area which the support of the Dick Bequest seemed to render a stronghold of tradition.

On the eve of the Victorian period, teaching as a profession in Scotland was in a state of flux. Through their longing glances to the parochial schools of the contemporary North-East and the rural past, the reformers of this period began the process of inscribing the socially meritocratic, intellectually redoubtable parochial schoolmaster into the heart of Scottish culture – a process which would culminate in the final decades of the nineteenth century with the famous coinage 'lad o' parts'. Yet even as this idea became part of Scottish culture reformers began to explore how to adapt it to an urban setting and integrate it with emerging theories about pedagogy. Teachers' professionalism on the eve of the Victorian period's major changes to the educational landscape was dynamic, yet rooted in tradition.

The Minutes of 1846 and the Formation of the EIS

Reformers came to feel during the Victorian period that the state should take on a much larger role in the provision and regulation of education. There were always myriad motives behind this sentiment, ranging from humanitarianism and Christian duty on the one hand to ideas about national culture, an educated citizenry and national strength on the other. In the words of one pamphlet written on the eve of the Victorian period by an educational society active in the Highlands, 'the might of the Government only . . . can send forth the means effectually to enlighten the dark glens of our mountain land'.[21] S. S. Laurie, arguably mid-Victorian Scotland's leading educationalist and the professor of education at Edinburgh from 1876, staunchly defended the parochial tradition of schooling with liberally educated schoolmasters who could exert an uplifting influence on the population. Taking a more utilitarian view of education at times, he also believed that educational opportunities (including becoming a teacher) 'makes the clever poor contented, and thus saps the foundations of Socialism'.[22] Later in the century national efficiency and competitiveness became a factor. As scientist and educationalist turned MP Lyon Playfair put it in his 1889 book *Subjects of Social Welfare*, 'In the competition of nations, both in war and in peace, their position for the future will depend upon the education of their peoples'.[23] Though there was a general enthusiasm about the growth of state involvement in popular education that spanned the whole of the Victorian period, the devil was in the details. Particularly when it came to teachers – the figures who embodied the Scottish ideal of education – the actual reforms appeared threatening to many in Scotland.

The first truly major change of the Victorian period was the 1846 Minutes of the Committee of Council on Education (CCE), which ushered in a new era in teacher training and teaching itself. The CCE was a London-based governmental body created in 1839 to provide government oversight for the growing sum of money which the state awarded each year in grants. Most of this grant money went to denominational schools and teacher training colleges, effectively giving rise to hundreds of denominational schools which stood alongside the parish school system. The 1846 Minutes marked one of the first major interventions into Scottish educational policy from south of the Tweed.

The 1846 Minutes had the biggest impact on the recruitment and training of teachers in the growing number of state-aided schools. The path to becoming a teacher now began at age thirteen with the formal apprenticeship of promising students for five years as 'pupil-teachers'. They earned a small salary and received daily private lessons from the teacher in exchange for assistance giving lessons and keeping discipline among the younger children. At the end of this apprenticeship they sat for an exam and competed for admission for a two-year course at one of Scotland's teacher training colleges. Particularly as the century wore on, many won a Queen's Scholarship on the basis of their exam results and had most of their fees paid by the state. At the end of college students took a certification exam, their score in which played a major role in their desirability as applicants for teaching positions. For instance, by the 1870s a first-class certificate was virtually required to get a first posting under the large, wealthy Glasgow School Board.

In the face of the 1846 Minutes schoolmasters working in parish, burgh, academy and other schools of a similar calibre banded together to form the EIS in 1847, a union-like association dedicated to the protection of its own vision of professionalism. Central to the EIS understanding of professionalism was the link between schools and universities. In an open letter to Viscount Melgund read before the EIS in 1851 and later published, James Bryce expounded on the idea that

> the schools and universities of Scotland form one structure, whose parts are beautifully adapted to one another, – and here lies the great beauty and excellence of her educational system, – the vital principle which, despite the incubus of sectarian exclusiveness, makes it at this moment the best in the world.[24]

Many speeches at and publications by the EIS similarly called for high standards of education, pay and status for teachers. The EIS instituted its own certification system based on a challenging exam, focusing largely on traditional liberal subjects. It was designed to supplant the government-regulated certificates created with the 1846 Minutes which had a more pedagogical focus. Campaigning for government recognition of the EIS certificate became an important purpose of the organisation in its first decades.[25] While the Education Department stressed mastery of pedagogical techniques, in its early years the EIS conceived of teachers' professionalism more broadly. It emphasised teachers' historical social status and their share in the liberal spirit of the universities.

Although it had a traditional vision of professionalism, the EIS also had a progressive streak. Tellingly, Bryce's defence of the traditional link between parish schools and universities was embedded within a call for reform – in this case, to open up parish schoolmaster positions to applicants of all Protestant denominations, which happened in 1861. In 1872, the EIS finally admitted women, perhaps in part because it was clear that the huge new demand for teachers which the Act of that year had created would be filled largely by women, as indeed was the case. EIS publications and annual meetings also served as spaces for the discussion of other reform proposals and new pedagogical techniques.

The Revised Code of 1862 and the Education Act of 1872

In addition to the Minutes of 1846, other policy changes emanating from south of the Tweed also seemed to threaten Scotland's education system and teaching profession. Created in the wake of the Newcastle Commission's investigation of popular education in England and Wales, the Revised Code – the set of regulations which controlled state grants to schools – alarmed Scottish teachers with its declared intent to slash government grants for schools and teacher training colleges; narrow the curriculum by emphasising the 3Rs; and institute new disciplinary and supervisory measures which would make teachers more directly accountable to the state. On no issue were Scottish teachers more vocal than the Revised Code. Teachers spearheaded the publicity campaign against the Revised Code, which they felt to be a serious and unwise reversal of the Scottish tradition of education. However, it never achieved full force in Scotland as it did in England and Wales. The Revised Code was suspended in Scotland within six weeks of its initial implementation. Over the next ten years only some of its measures were implemented. The petitions, pamphlets and lobbying which teachers used to express their discontent and the harm that they believed the Code would do to Scotland seemed to have succeeded.

The 1872 Education Act (Scotland) and the Codes that followed it did bring teachers more fully under the supervision of the state, but otherwise it generally represented a move away from the agenda of the Revised Code. Jane McDermid explores the effect of the 1872 Act in depth in her contribution to this volume, but important for the teaching profession were three developments. First, it created a system of elected school boards to which teachers had to answer. Second, and related, it brought all parish schools under the auspices of the school boards and created conditions which made it desirable for many managers of state-aided denominational schools to hand their schools over to school boards as well. This might be said to have, in a sense, restored the national system of education. Third and finally, the 1872 Act created a huge demand for new teachers. The number of teachers in publicly supported schools in Scotland rose from 5,713 in 1870 to 16,858 in 1899.[26]

To help meet this demand the state made it easier for teachers who had not attended a training college to get a certificate and allowed former pupil-teachers to stay on as staff in the capacity of 'ex pupil-teachers' without acquiring a certificate. Many of these new teachers had not attended a training college let alone university, were women, or both. Whereas women made up one-third of teachers in publicly supported schools in 1870, by the end of the century they made up two-thirds.[27] School boards were keen to hire female teachers, who could be paid as little as half of what their male counterparts could command. In 1873, the average salary for a male certificated teacher was £110 per year compared to £58 per year for women.[28]

To some educationalists and teachers, these developments seemed to threaten the exclusivity, intellectualism and overall prestige of the teaching profession. In 1894, a male certificated assistant teacher complained at a teachers' conference that 'the downward tendency in wages' had occurred as a result of the turn to 'unskilled [female and untrained] labour . . . in practically unlimited quantities'. He concluded that 'The profession as a means of earning a livelihood is falling into comparative disrepute', leading 'men of ability' to undertake 'other and more profitable work'.[29] Scottish communities also believed an educated male teacher to be important to their prestige. For example, following the departure of a 'gentle young woman who taught in a small school on the shore of a loch in Wester Ross', the parents of the community sent a deputation to the school board to argue 'that better discipline would be maintained, and consequently better results secured, were a man appointed to fill the vacancy. They also alleged that the dignity of their township would be enhanced through such an appointment.'[30] Together the Revised Code and the 1872 Act seemed to threaten teachers' autonomy and the status of the profession as a whole.

The growing number of women teachers may have been perceived as a threat to the Scottish tradition of education, but in some ways they were emblematic of that tradition. Women teachers sought out training and formal credentials to improve their skill in the classroom, further their general education and gain publicly recognised qualification for their work. The entry of a growing number of women into the profession extended the tradition of social meritocracy to gender. However, women still faced a culture within the profession and an occupational structure set up by school board officials and Education Department bureaucrats that kept the upper echelons of teaching and access to universities a largely male preserve until the very end of the century. Male head teachers and educationalists tended to write about women assistant teachers as junior partners.[31] Helen Corr has suggested that Scottish women teachers did not press for equal (or near-equal, at least) pay and prestige with the same energy and spirit as their counterparts in England and Wales.[32] Still, acknowledging the limits of women's inroads should not blind us to the extent to which the Victorian period saw the expansion of the openness and meritocracy at the heart of Scotland's system of popular education.

In practice, the effects of the educational policies of the mid- and late-Victorian years on teachers did not prove quite so revolutionary as they at first appeared. In some ways these developments actually benefited teachers' quest for professional recognition and autonomy as well as their commitment to meritocratic advancement for themselves and their pupils.

Teacher Training Colleges

Created in the 1830s but expanded dramatically thanks to funding from the 1846 Minutes, Scotland's teacher training colleges were key sites in the making of teachers' professional identity. They were hybrid institutions supported by funding from both the state and a religious educational organisation (the educational wings of the Free Church and the Established Church being the most important). Glasgow, Edinburgh and eventually Aberdeen each supported two colleges. By the 1850s, the colleges collectively had about 500 students at any given time, two-thirds of them men. The ratio of men to women quickly changed after the Education Act of 1872 with its demand for huge numbers of teachers, particularly women. By 1899, training colleges collectively had 1,112 students,

72 per cent of them women.[33] Despite the growing number of places for women, a significantly higher proportion of women than men applied relative to the places available, probably because of women's difficulty finding lower-middle-class work other than teaching compared to men. In their early years, the colleges took in some students who only spoke Gaelic and lodged them specially in the college, though the numbers of such students dwindled in the wake of the Revised Code. Geographically, students came from all over Scotland and upon graduation more often than not took postings in a different county than that from which they had come.[34] Training colleges offered a point of entry into the teaching profession that cut across the lines of gender, geography and language, at least to a degree.

The training college curriculum combined a pedagogical training with a more liberal curriculum including Latin, mathematics, science and music. The majority of time was dedicated to the teachers' education rather than their 'training', with just five to ten hours a week allotted to pedagogy and actual teaching.[35] Teachers-in-training enjoyed a rich intellectual and cultural life outside the college as well. They formed literary and debating societies, wrote poetry and regularly organised picnics. Young men in training colleges also enjoyed more liberty than their counterparts south of the Tweed since Scottish training colleges were non-residential for them, allowing the men to board with families near the college (women, by contrast, lived on the college premises). Though college officials had to approve the young men's boarding situation and reserved the right to make unannounced inspections, this paled in comparison to the disciplinary aspirations of English training colleges with their in-college sleeping cubicles supervised by a staff member even at night.[36] Whatever their limitations, training colleges fostered intellectualism, professional skills and collegiality.

The link between teachers and the universities survived the rise of training colleges. It waned from 1846 to the 1870s, but even then teachers in Dick Bequest schools and some training college graduates pursued a university education. By the 1880s, training colleges had forged a more formal connection to the universities, arranging for many of the most promising male students to take classes while at college. In 1889, the Education Department began to pay 75 per cent of the fees for such students to pursue a 'third' year of their course primarily or entirely at university. By this point it was not uncommon for male teachers to earn a university degree within a short time of graduating from training college. By 1893, 62 per cent of the male teachers under the Glasgow Board had attended or currently were attending university classes.[37] Some even worked at their MA, attending classes for several hours in the morning and then working at their school for the rest of the day. In 1895, the state began to offer bursaries for prospective teachers – male and female – to enrol directly at universities under the Queen's Studentship scheme (though Edinburgh University did not participate). There, much like at training colleges, they would receive both a liberal and a professional, pedagogical education resulting in a diploma that was officially recognised as a qualification for teaching.[38] In a move that substantially pre-dated their English counterparts, Scottish universities themselves also promoted the study of pedagogy. In 1869, Alexander Bain, professor of logic at the University of Aberdeen, published *Education as a Science*, a landmark contribution to the formal study of pedagogy. Seven years later, the first chairs in education were created at Edinburgh at St Andrews, though these chairs played no direct role in teacher training.[39]

Professional Changes and Continuities

Although the changes to the school curriculum – the subjects teachers taught – during the Victorian period have traditionally been seen as imperilling teachers' professionalism, they can also be understood as part of a reworking of that professionalism to accommodate the needs and values of a changing society. Policies and funding mechanisms may have emphasised the 3Rs, but teachers continued to offer advanced classes in specific subjects. By the late 1870s, teachers received a small grant for each student who passed an exam in one of the subjects recognised by the ever-changing Code. This included established liberal subjects such as Latin, Greek, advanced mathematics, French, German and English Literature, as well as domestic economy (for girls), botany, physical geography, mechanics, animal physiology, chemistry, light and heat, and magnetism and electricity. Though most of these advanced curricular opportunities were open to boys and girls alike, there arose some gender-specific divisions in practice. Greek and some of the advanced branches of science and mathematics became largely the province of boys working under male teachers, while girls spent upwards of a dozen hours a week on cookery, needlework and botany under the supervision of female teachers. Women teachers resisted the emergence of these curricular differences, particularly what they felt to be the unduly prominent position given to needlework and the sheer amount of time it took up. Though needlework remained a cornerstone of the girls' curriculum, female teachers were at least relatively successful in fending off the efforts of solidly middle-class women educationalists and school board members to secure professional status for domestic economy teachers. The struggle reflected women teachers' desire to relegate moral and domestic education to only a small corner of their professionalism.[40]

Many of the same Victorian-era educational policy shifts designed to bring teachers more closely under the thumb of educational policy makers and bureaucrats also contributed to the growth of professional organisations, a corporate identity among teachers and a sense of being part of a national system of education. For one thing, it pushed teachers to join the EIS, which had nearly 2,000 members across sixty-five local associations by 1852. The potential threat of state encroachment brought together a diverse body of teachers from parochial, burgh, denominational and even secondary schools. Working within a substantially similar system as English and Welsh teachers after 1872, Scottish teachers also came to join the National Union of (Elementary) Teachers, which had been founded in 1870. Though at the national level it was far more concerned with England and Wales than Scotland, occasional articles in *The Schoolmaster*, its weekly periodical, did proudly emphasise the Scottish tradition of education. It even went so far as to urge English and Welsh teachers to look to their Scottish counterparts' everyday pedagogy and efforts to professionalise as an example: 'by following Scotch examples, [we] may realise a union of a practical character from which at no distant date there may arise unmeasured good'.[41]

Despite the increasing role national associations, unions and state structures played in teachers' lives, local economies and cultures continued to exert a substantial influence on the everyday experience of teaching. In Dundee, for instance, the textile industry's insatiable demand for female workers left teachers with a serious truancy problem among their girls, who absented themselves to assist with childminding and other household tasks while their mothers were away at work. In Glasgow and Edinburgh, by contrast, fewer women worked and there was a sizable stratum within the working class that could afford to keep their daughters in school, apprentice them as pupil-teachers and see them become teachers in their own right. Even in the days of secular school boards, teachers everywhere – but especially in the Highlands – had to contend with three-way religious tensions between parents, pupils and school board officials who were members of the Catholic Church, Free Church and Church of Scotland. And of course a dictatorial headteacher, rude colleagues and interfering parents could still make work challenging – just as a supportive community of parents and officials could make a teacher's work exponentially easier and more effective. On an everyday level, the extent to which teachers garnered respect and had control over their work depended as much on the local community as it did the high politics of education policy and teachers' national campaign to enact and defend their professionalism.

Conclusion

'I refuse to believe those who prate about marriage as emancipation for a woman. Marriage is a prison.'[42] This was only one of A. S. Neill's many rather radical views about class, gender, politics and pedagogy. He recorded them in a journal-like notebook in 1915 which he published in a serialised format in the *Scottish Educational News* the next year to both approbation and controversy. Neill's views and generally truculent attitude were still probably the exception rather than the rule at the time he wrote.[43] Teaching as a profession still had a staunchly conservative streak. Nonetheless, the Victorian years saw the teaching profession become more open to women and those of both sexes who had not necessarily won the patronage of local notables. Though a training college education increasingly became the norm, many teachers – Neill included – continued to attend university. Once on the job these teachers found in their unions and sometimes even their school boards a means to redress grievances that they had largely lacked a century earlier. Associations, unions and periodicals – such as the one in which Neill published his *Log* – offered a strong sense of identity and community among teachers.

Even Neill's cutting assessment of the state of the teaching profession in 1915 suggests how much the ideal of professionalism had shifted in the past century:

I blame the teachers for their low social status. To-day they have no idea of corporate action. They pay their subscriptions to their Institute, and for the most part talk of stopping them on the grounds that it is money wasted. The authorities of the Institute try to work for a better union, but they try clumsily and stodgily.[44]

The sort of corporatism and unionisation promoted by the EIS had – for Neill, at least – largely supplanted the individualist idea of the lad o'parts as the heart of teachers' professionalism. However, in moving beyond the ideal of the lad o' parts teachers did not turn their back on the ideas at its heart: providing and taking advantage of opportunities for upward social mobility; securing a high degree of education; and acting as part of a national system of schooling. From this perspective it is possible to say that the teaching profession modernised in the Victorian period by reworking and updating the tradition established in the long eighteenth century.

Notes

1. 'Diary of a Highland school master, 1899–1930', Highland Archive and Registration Centre, Inverness (HARC), HCA/D423/2/1, pp. 1–4.
2. H. M. Knox, *Two Hundred and Fifty Years of Scottish Education 1696–1946* (Oliver and Boyd, 1953); Douglas Myers, 'Scottish schoolmasters in the nineteenth century', in Walter M. Humes and Hamish M. Paterson (eds), *Scottish Culture and Scottish Education 1800–1980* (John Donald, 1983), pp. 75–92; James Scotland, *The History of Scottish Education*, 2 vols (London, 1969); Thomas Wilson, 'A reinterpretation of "payment by results" in Scotland, 1861–1872', in Humes and Paterson (eds), *Scottish Culture and Scottish Education*, pp. 93–114; Donald Withrington, 'Towards a national system, 1867–72: The last years in the struggle for a Scottish Education Act', *Scottish Educational Review* 4 (1972), 107–24; R. D. Anderson, 'In search of the "lad of parts": The mythical history of Scottish education', *History Workshop* 19 (1985), 82–104; R. D. Anderson, *Education and the Scottish People 1750–1918* (Clarendon Press, 1995).
3. All the works in the previous note take up these issues. For historians who have moved towards a moderate consensus, see Anderson, *Education and the Scottish People*; Jane McDermid, *The Schooling of Working-Class Girls in Victorian Scotland: Gender, Education, and Identity* (Routledge, 2005); David Limond, 'Locality, education and authority in Scotland 1902–2002 (via 1872)', *Oxford Review of Education* 28 (2002), 359–71.
4. McDermid, *Schooling of Working-Class Girls*; Fiona M. S. Paterson and Judith Fewell (eds), *Girls in Their Prime: Scottish Education Revisited* (Falmer Press, 1991); Lindy Moore, 'Invisible scholars: Girls learning Latin and mathematics in the elementary public schools of Scotland before 1872', *History of Education* 13 (1984), 121–37.
5. McDermid, *Schooling of Working-Class Girls*, pp. 35–52.
6. See Anderson, *Education and the Scottish People*, pp. 11, 75.
7. Quoted in ibid., p. 30.
8. Ibid., pp. 3–10.
9. Quoted in Myers, 'Scottish schoolmasters', p. 80. On the social status and working conditions of eighteenth-century schoolmasters, see ibid., pp. 76–80; Anderson,

Education and Opportunity in Victorian Scotland: Schools and Universities (Clarendon Press, 1983), pp. 3–6; Anderson, *Education and the Scottish People*, pp. 3–14.

10. Marjorie Cruickshank, *A History of the Training of Teachers in Scotland* (University of London Press, 1970), pp. 17–18; Anderson, *Education and the Scottish People*, pp. 9, 4–5; John Smith, 'A Victorian Class Conflict?' Schoolteaching and the Parson, Priest and Minister, 1837–1902 (Sussex Academic Press, 2009), pp. 47–69.

11. Quoted in Cruickshank, *History of the Training of Teachers*, p. 19.

12. McDermid, *Schooling of Working-Class Girls*, p. 36; Moore, 'Invisible scholars'.

13. Myers, 'Scottish schoolmasters', p. 78. For a fuller treatment of the limits of tenure in the face of serious offences, see Andrew Bain, *Patterns of Error: The Teacher and External Authority in Central Scotland, 1581–1861* (Moubray House Publishing, 1989).

14. Anderson, *Education and the Scottish People*, p. 75.

15. HARC SSPCK report series, D/124/1. For examples and quotations, see D/124/1/56, p. xli; D/124/1/56, p. xlvi.

16. See Anderson, *Education and the Scottish People*, Chapter 4.

17. Donald Withrington, '"Scotland a half-educated nation" in 1834? Reliable critique or persuasive polemic?', in Humes and Paterson (eds), *Scottish Culture and Scottish Education*, pp. 55–74.

18. David Stow, *The Training System Established in the Glasgow Normal Seminary and its Model Schools* (Blackie and Son, 1840), p. vii.

19. On the Dick Bequest, see also David Northcroft's chapter in this volume.

20. Cruickshank, 'The Dick Bequest: The effect of a famous nineteenth-century endowment on parish schools of north east Scotland', *History of Education Quarterly* 5 (1965), 157–8.

21. Quoted in Anderson, *Education and the Scottish People*, p. 35.

22. Quoted in Anderson, *Education and Opportunity*, p. 235.

23. Quoted in Anderson, *Education and the Scottish People*, p. 69.

24. James Bryce, *Practical Suggestions for Reforming the Educational Institutions of Scotland* (William Oliphant and Sons, 1852), p. 5.

25. Myers, 'Scottish schoolmasters', pp. 83–8.

26. Anderson, *Education and the Scottish People*, p. 177.

27. Ibid., p. 177.

28. Cruickshank, *History of the Training of Teachers*, p. 234.

29. Quoted in Helen Corr, 'The sexual division of labour in the Scottish teaching profession, 1872–1914', in Humes and Paterson (eds), *Scottish Culture and Scottish Education*, p. 146.

30. John Wilson, *Tales and Travels of a School Inspector* (Jackson, Wylie & Co., 1928), p. 108.

31. McDermid, *Schooling of Working-Class Girls*, pp. 120–1.

32. Helen Corr, *Changes in Educational Policies in Britain, 1800–1920: How Gender Inequalities Reshaped the Teaching Profession* (Edwin Mellen Press, 2008), pp. 132–6. For an account of English women teachers, see Dina Copelman, *London's Women Teachers: Gender, Class and Feminism 1870–1930* (Routledge, 1996).

33. Corr, 'Sexual division of labour', p. 140; Anderson, *Education and the Scottish People*, p. 177; Cruickshank, *History of the Training of Teachers*, pp. 61–2.

34. Peter Hill, 'The church period, 1843–1904', in Margaret Harrison and Willis Marker (eds), *The History of Jordanhill College of Education 1828–1993* (John Donald, 1996), pp. 18–21; Cruickshank, *History of the Training of Teachers*, pp. 77–8.

35. Cruickshank, *History of the Training of Teachers*, p. 58.

36. On the disciplinary aspirations of English training colleges, see Marianne Larsen,

The Making and Shaping of the Victorian Teacher: A Comparative New Cultural History (Palgrave Macmillan, 2011). On some of the gaps between aspirations and reality, see Christopher Robert Bischof, '"A home for poets": The liberal curriculum in Victorian Britain's teacher training colleges', *History of Education Quarterly* 54(1) (2014), 42–69.

37. Cruickshank, *History of the Training of Teachers*, pp. 113–18; James Roxburgh, *The School Board of Glasgow 1873–1919* (University of London Press, 1971), p. 50.
38. Cruickshank, *History of the Training of Teachers*, p. 119.
39. On the study of education at the university level, see Brian Simon, 'The study of education as a university subject in Britain', *Studies in Higher Education* 8 (1983), 1–13.
40. McDermid, *Schooling of Working-Class Girls*, Chapter 5.
41. 'An Anglo-Scotch alliance', *The Schoolmaster*, 25 May 1872, 228.
42. A. S. Neill, *A Dominie's Log* (Herbert Jenkins Ltd, 1985 [1916]), p. 155.
43. On the reception of A. S. Neill's publications among Scottish teachers, see David Limond, '"[A]ll our Scotch education is in vain": The construction of Scottish national identity in and by the early Dominie books of A. S. Neill', *History of Education* 28 (1999), 297–312.
44. Neill, *A Dominie's Log*, p. 125.

Bibliography

Anderson, R. D., 'In search of the "lad of parts": The mythical history of Scottish education', *History Workshop* 19 (1985), 82–104.

Anderson, R. D., *Education and the Scottish People 1750–1918* (Clarendon Press, 1995).

Bain, Andrew, *From Church to State: The Significance of the Education Act of 1861 in East Central Scotland* (Stevenson Printers Ltd, 1993).

Corr, Helen, 'The schoolgirls' curriculum and the ideology of the home 1870–1914', in Glasgow Women's Studies Group (eds), *Uncharted Lives: Extracts from Scottish Women's Experiences, 1850–1982* (Pressgang, 1983), pp. 74–97.

Cruickshank, Marjorie, 'The Dick Bequest: The effect of a famous nineteenth-century endowment on parish schools of north east Scotland', *History of Education Quarterly* 5(3) (1965), 153–65.

Cruickshank, Marjorie, *A History of the Training of Teachers in Scotland* (University of London Press, 1970).

Humes, Walter M. and Hamish M. Paterson (eds), *Scottish Culture and Scottish Education 1800–1980* (John Donald, 1983).

McDermid, Jane, *The Schooling of Working-Class Girls in Victorian Scotland: Gender, Education, and Identity* (Routledge, 2005).

Moore, Lindy, 'Invisible scholars: Girls learning Latin and mathematics in the elementary public schools of Scotland before 1872', *History of Education* 13 (1984), 121–37.

Roxburgh, James M., *The School Board of Glasgow 1873–1919* (University of London Press, 1971).

13

Democracy or Intellect: The Scottish Educational Dilemma of the Twentieth Century

Lindsay Paterson

Introduction

It is half a century since the publication of the book that has done more to shape debate about Scottish education than any other (except ultimately the *First Book of Discipline*). When George Davie's *The Democratic Intellect* appeared in 1961, its meaning would probably have been more widely evident than it has been since.[1] The essential problem of interpretation may be summed up tritely as one of where to put the stress. Is Scottish education characterised by democracy, to which the intellect contributes, or is it shaped by the intellect, enjoining it to behave in democratic ways? Walter Elliot, from whom Davie borrowed his title, would have had no doubt that it was the latter. 'Democratic intellectualism', which is the term that Elliot actually coined in 1932, is not in any doubt that the emphasis is to be on the character of the mind, and Elliot defined it thus:

> it is a heritage wherein discipline is rigidly and ruthlessly enforced, but where criticism and attack are unflinching, continuous, and salt with a bitter and jealous humour. It is a heritage wherein intellect, speech and, above all, argument are the passports to the highest eminence in the land.[2]

The competitiveness and exclusion inherent in such an image then have provoked the main counter-story to that told by Davie – the claim that Scottish education is inherently hierarchical, unequal and destructive of spontaneity and creativity.

This is no mere terminological quibble, or device of rhetoric, because whether 'democracy' or 'intellect' is to have primacy determines not only education itself but also how we interpret the Scottish experience of the twentieth century generally, not only in education. The significance is greater still, indeed, because it raises questions of social order and good government. Again in Davie's words:

> The words 'democratic intellect' offer a twentieth-century formulation of an old problem. Does the control of a group . . . belong, as of right, to the few

(the experts) exclusively, and not at all to the ignorant many? Or are the many entitled to share the control, because the limited knowledge of the many, when it is pooled and critically restated through mutual discussion, provides a lay consensus capable of revealing certain of the limitations of interest in the experts' point of view? Or thirdly it may be held that this consensus knowledge of the many entitles them to have full control, excluding the experts.[3]

Davie's dilemma is thus between expertise and populism. To him, any kind of deliberate radicalism was a 'short-cut to a material utopia',[4] a mechanical response where what was needed was the wide diffusion of moral responsibility trained through the intellect:

a polity which postpones the spiritual or cultural problems of society in favour of an unrestricted material advance based on intensive specialisation produces the dangerous consequences of an intellectual atomisation of society.[5]

The dilemma that he outlines is also the dilemma of Scottish education: he did not invent the problem (as indeed his citation of Elliot and Elliot's contemporaries such as Herbert Grierson and Hugh MacDiarmid makes clear). Those who have governed and sought to reform the system have recurrently tried to reconcile these two poles of intellect and democracy, selection and access, knowledge from a tradition and practical utility.[6] The purpose of this chapter is to examine not their intentions so much as the outcomes of what they tried to do.

The chapter is mainly concerned with developments in secondary schooling, not only because, until the very last decade of the century, that was the sector where by far the most change was happening,[7] but also because Davie mostly ignores its fundamental importance. Within the story of the development of secondary schooling, the curriculum matters as much as school structures, because the meaning of the twentieth-century educational experience lies in the ideas that have been offered to young people rather than merely in their opportunities to move through institutions or to acquire credentials. Attempting to cover the whole century in one chapter is of course too ambitious, and many of the details inevitably will be lost; but something like this sweep is necessary to understand the long-term consequences of educational reform. The guiding questions here, then, are: is the twentieth-century story really one of decline from the intellectual distinction of the old university curriculum, as Davie would allege? Or is it, by contrast, a process of heroically asserting a humane educational practice against the sort of competitive ethos that Elliot celebrated? Or is neither of these competing stories subtle enough to capture what actually happened?[8]

The Beginnings of Reform: Secondary Schooling in the 1920s and 1930s

Development of secondary schooling to the 1930s

Nevertheless, however important the curriculum is, the developing structures of schooling matter because they shape the opportunity to learn anything important. The starting point to understanding how secondary education developed in

Scotland in the twentieth century, and how it related to inherited ideas about a worthwhile curriculum, is that it barely existed previously. The country did have a long tradition of providing higher education in parish schools, the advanced classes where the mythological tradition of open access to higher learning was located, but the concept of a properly secondary sector did not emerge coherently until the last part of the nineteenth century. There were then some fifty-six proper secondary schools, many of ancient lineage and most surviving on the basis of endowments. Within that group, there were schools which the 1872 Education (Scotland) Act designated as 'Higher Class' schools, the rather token recognition which that legislation gave to the older parochial tradition. Their number rose from a dozen to around twenty by the beginning of the new century, but their development was restricted because the school boards (also set up by the Act) were not permitted to use public money to support them, as Jane McDermid explains in her chapter in this book.

The real expansion of secondary education then happened in the two decades 1900–20, and the important first move came in 1899, when the Scotch Education Department (SED) recognised a category of Higher Grade school. These were, at first, intended to be specialist scientific schools, like the schools of that name which were emerging in parts of England.[9] But, whereas in England such schools were restricted from the first decade of the century to low-level technical instruction, in Scotland the Department under Henry Craik and then John Struthers permitted them to move in quite the opposite direction. From 1903, they could provide the same kinds of course as the Higher Class and endowed schools, and after 1908 they could extend this to the full five years of secondary education. Thereafter a Higher Grade school which had been recognised for this purpose was, in an administrative sense, the same as an older full secondary school. The number of Higher Grade schools grew rapidly, from seventy-five in 1903–4, through 164 in 1906–7 to 196 by 1918–19; at that time, they contained 60 per cent of the pupils on publicly financed secondary courses.[10]

The Higher Grade schools served districts populated mainly by the lower middle class and the skilled working class, and mostly were free or charged only low fees.[11] In fact, they were rarely wholly new foundations, often being built up from parish schools that had a tradition of providing higher subjects: they thus became the main twentieth-century carrier of that tradition. The SED's rationale for all this was that the country would benefit from encouraging the education of talented young people wherever they might be found. In Struthers' words when he was still assistant secretary of the SED, writing in 1903 to an inspector in Fife: 'if there is [in a neighbourhood] any considerable body of pupils who may be expected to remain on at school till 15 or 16 then there is a *prima facie* case for the recognition of a Higher Grade department'.[12]

The structure of the courses offered in this secondary system was also such as to encourage opportunity. The content of the courses will be considered below, but the main organisational feature, from 1912, was that secondary education was officially in two progressive parts: a three-year 'intermediate' stage and a further two years beyond that which would lead to the Leaving Certificate. Inaugurated in 1888, the Leaving Certificate marked the end of a full secondary course, analogously to the contemporary development of such assessment in other countries – the *baccalauréat* in francophone countries, the *Abitur* in the German-speaking ones.[13] This two-stage Scottish structure encouraged access to secondary schooling because pupils whose parents could not afford to keep them at school for five years could follow a well-constructed course over a shorter period. The most able of these pupils could then be encouraged by bursaries to stay on for five years, especially after provision for these was made more systematic in the Education (Scotland) Act of 1918. Also encouraging participation was the provision for schools to be recognised as 'Intermediate', for the provision of the three-year course only. Some of them were subsequently upgraded, but, even when they were not, they represented a further way in which the tradition of providing higher subjects in the public schools was continued.

The momentum of this expansion was abruptly halted by SED restrictions imposed from 1925, outlined in a circular issued in 1921 that subsequently has become infamous.[14] The important point about this controversial episode was that the two-stage system was now officially discouraged, thus requiring pupils to commit themselves to a full five years of secondary education with all the expense and forgoing of earnings which that entailed. This was undoubtedly a serious shift of policy, but it was not a complete reversal, because most of the former Higher Grade schools now were recognised as full secondaries. The secondary sector thus consisted of approximately 250 schools by the 1930s, some four times more numerous than in 1900 (even though the size of the relevant age groups had risen by no more than about 5 per cent),[15] indicating that a great deal of the expansion of the earlier decades had been maintained. By the 1930s, moreover, about one third of the age group was entering full secondary courses, and, although only one in twenty completed them in the sense of taking the examinations for the Leaving Certificate, that reach was quite high by wider European standards.[16] From the 1920s, new teachers of secondary subjects had to possess a relevant degree from a university or a central institution (the higher technological colleges which the SED had established in each region of the country),[17] so that by the 1930s some two-thirds of teachers were graduates.[18] After 1923, all heads of subject department had to have a relevant honours degree.

In short, the post-primary-school system from 1924 was in four broad segments: the old secondaries; the pioneering secondaries that had started as Higher Grade schools and that had achieved secondary status by 1923; the newer secondaries created after that; and the remainder, which were elementary schools providing some two years of modestly advanced classes to around two-thirds of the pupil population. Allocation between the senior-secondary courses, which were in principle five years long, and the shorter courses was mainly by tests of general intelligence taken in the final year of primary school.

Leaving Certificate

What, then, was taught in these courses – what opportunities to acquire significant culture were offered or restricted by these new structures? The five-year courses were intended to lead to the Leaving Certificate,[19] the SED's means of defining and regulating the curriculum of secondary education. So to understand that curriculum, and to understand the model of a proper secondary education which it embodied, it is to the Leaving Certificate that we must turn. By the 1920s, the Leaving Certificate had become the normal route of entry to the universities, to the advanced courses of the central institutions or directly to the training courses of the professions.

Subjects in the curriculum were assessed individually, mostly by written examination (although with the significant exception of science, where laboratory work was tested directly by school inspectors). In most subjects in this period, these examinations took place at two levels, Higher and Lower. However, the SED came to believe that a wholly open choice of subjects was fragmenting pupils' learning, and so, from 1902, a Group Certificate was offered, this becoming, in effect, mandatory from 1908: according to it, a Certificate would be awarded only if certain officially recognised combinations of subjects had been passed. The curriculum of full secondary pupils was strongly shaped by the grouping requirements. These rules were complicated, and underwent several changes, but two consistent principles were that English was compulsory and that some degree of breadth was enforced (requiring candidates to take both a language and either mathematics or a science).

In essence, therefore, the curricular principles governing the Leaving Certificate reflected the shift to the schools of the old principles of liberal education, and thus also the old principles of the undergraduate degree. Accompanying that shift, three significant changes had taken place, representing a modernisation of the principle of curricular breadth and thus a modernisation of the meaning of a liberal education. These changes involved, first, the rise to prominence of English over Latin and its assuming something of the place that moral philosophy used to have in the undergraduate programme. The view taken of the place of English at that time may be summed up by a comment in 1910 from A. M. Williams, who was head of the Glasgow centre for training teachers: 'the place of literature in moral education', he argued, was to make people after Milton's ideal, 'fitted to perform justly, skilfully, and magnanimously all the offices, both private and public, of peace and war'.[20] As it was put in 1899 by Simon Laurie (first holder of the chair of education at Edinburgh University), the study of literature is 'the making of a good citizen',[21] because appreciating the beauty of a great literary work will tend to improve the reader's character. John Strong, rector of the high school in Edinburgh, argued in 1919 that the study of literature encouraged the 'constant exercise of the judgement, and ever present appeal to wider and deeper sympathies, and a gradual development of the sense of harmony and beauty'.[22] Indeed, at the 1918 annual meeting of the English

Association (a professional grouping of teachers of English at both secondary and university level), Charles Herford, professor of English literature at Manchester University, argued that literary studies could take on the cultural role played by philosophy at the Scottish universities.[23]

The second change also involved Latin – the emergence of French alongside it, representing an attempt to make liberal education of contemporary relevance, as in fact had recurrently happened to liberal education since its invention during the European Renaissance.[24] John Burnet – professor of Greek at St Andrews – proposed in an essay in 1910 that, at secondary level, any language would confer the intellectual benefits which Latin was commonly supposed to offer, although he would prefer if all students arriving at university had a 'simple working knowledge of two languages in addition to real attainment in the two languages or the scientific subjects which form the main work of the pupil'.[25] The headmistress of St Leonard's School for girls, Mary Bentinck Smith, argued likewise for the relevance to young lives of modern languages in a speech to the Classical Association in 1913: although she did not doubt that girls were as capable as boys of learning Latin, 'the spirit of the more modern literatures being more akin to the spirit of the age kindles more readily in the average mind, more especially the young mind, that spark of intellectual sympathy which is necessary for comprehension'.[26]

The third shift was an even clearer instance of modernisation – the serious treatment of science. The general principle came from T. H. Huxley, who, in his address upon being elected Rector of Aberdeen University in 1874, had made the point rhetorically by substituting the word 'science' for 'the ancient languages' in a passage from John Stuart Mill's rectorial address at St Andrews University in 1867: 'in cultivating . . . science as an essential ingredient in education, we are all the while laying an admirable foundation for ethical and philosophical culture'.[27] Mathematics in Scotland was always treated in this liberal fashion. For example, the requirement for Higher Grade mathematics in 1922 stipulated that the goal should be to 'encourage thought on the part of the pupils . . . and maintain the feeling of unity between the different branches of Mathematical study'.[28] The same was argued for science by people who helped to develop the syllabus for the Leaving Certificate. For example, in 1919, J. Arthur Thomson, professor of natural history in Aberdeen, argued that 'men should seek after science primarily in the hope of clearer vision, not because of expected miracles of loaves and fishes'.[29]

Thus the general intention of embedding a liberal curriculum in the Leaving Certificate may be summed up by a comment on Latin in 1922, by W. King Gillies, rector of the Royal High School of Edinburgh. The comment also shows the inclination to interpret the changes as modernising the tradition rather than usurping it: 'in Scotland, [Latin] was never the hall-mark of a social class, but we must prevent it becoming such now, and provide it for every genuine secondary pupil'.

Moreover, if these were the intentions, then the practice by the 1930s was not so invidious or restrictive as has often been claimed. Even though the pupils entering the five-year courses were in a minority, and even though the proportion completing them by gaining the Leaving Certificate was tiny by later standards, nevertheless the key point is that the liberal curriculum was not differentiated between old and new sectors, and thus became available as the model on which subsequent expansion for the next half century took place. In fact, just over one half of all candidates for the Leaving Certificate came from the former Higher Grade schools.

More light can be cast on how the new system widened access to a liberal curriculum for this highly selected but symbolically important group of pupils. The National Archives of Scotland hold detailed evidence on presentations for and passing of the Leaving Certificate, and hold also comments by school inspectors on schools and on syllabuses.[30] In broad summary, we can say that:

- English played the same core moral philosophical role in the old sectors as in the new.
- English displaced Latin in the old sectors as in the new: there was no sense in Scotland of English being a 'poor man's Latin' as it has been claimed to have been in England, where Latin continued to dominate the curriculum of the public schools, and where Latin continued to lie at the heart of the highest-status curricula in the grammar schools.[31]
- French rose to prominence in the old schools as well as in the new.
- Nevertheless, Latin did not vanish in this period, and nor did it survive merely at the top end of a social hierarchy: it was taken in the new schools by much the same proportions of Leaving Certificate candidates as in the old.
- And science also grew in the old as much as – in fact rather more than – in the new: there was no sense that science was of lesser significance in training the mind than the humanities. The influence of scientists such as J. Arthur Thomson was profound: science was an intellectual discipline that required both theory and rigorous attention to empirical facts, and served the nation not only through its economic uses but also through its place in liberal culture. Scotland was thus a rather more faithful heir to the approach pioneered by T. H. Huxley in the previous century than was England.

Because the new schools served the lower middle and upper working classes, we can conclude that there was no class distinction between the kinds of secondary education offered, although there continued to be large class differences in the chances of taking part in it, despite the partial democratisation represented by the expansion of the secondary system. So not only did Scottish policy eschew the officially differentiated tracks found in France and Germany; Scotland also avoided de facto differentiation of the kind that was found in England: the SED's aim of having a common system of advanced secondary schooling for the academically able was realised. It remained far more difficult for a working-class pupil than for a middle-class pupil to enter and survive in a full secondary course, but, once there, all pupils were treated more or less equally.

By the 1930s, there was also an equalising of access to the liberal curriculum in relation to gender and religion. Girls' participation in the full liberal curriculum came to be similar to that of boys, with the important exception of science (though they did have equal participation in mathematics): in the 1930s, no more than about a quarter of Leaving Certificate candidates taking Higher science were female, whereas girls made up around 40 per cent of all candidates. One of the reasons for the limited advance in female science at this time may have been the growth of girls' schools, because girls there were less likely to take science in the Leaving Certificate than girls in mixed schools.

The impact on opportunities for Catholics was even more striking. In the nineteenth century (as Stevenson explains in his chapter in this book), Catholic schools struggled to match the standards of the public schools, mainly because of lack of educational resources of various kinds: buildings were poor, teachers more often than in the public schools did not have adequate training and the generally low social status of the large majority of Catholics (having come as migrant labour from Ireland and elsewhere in Europe) deprived children of much in the way of educational stimulation outside the school. The educational problems of Catholics were thus the problems of education in industrial capitalism concentrated into one community. The church did manage to build up a system of elementary schools, an effort which the inspectors praised, but declined to transfer them to the school boards after 1872 for fear of Protestant domination (despite evidence in the Argyll report of the 1860s that public schools catered well for Catholics in those areas where there was no Catholic school; see also Stevenson's chapter).[32] The church also established a Catholic teacher training college in Glasgow in 1895; a second was opened in Edinburgh in 1918–20.[33] Nevertheless the challenge of next having to set up a Catholic secondary school system was daunting, and so the church agreed to SED proposals that the 1918 Act would allow for the transfer of its schools to the boards, in return for being funded on the same basis as non-denominational schools and for continuing Catholic influence over the appointment of teachers and over aspects of the curriculum that pertained to church doctrine. Nearly all Catholic primary schools were transferred by the early 1920s (as were the small number of Episcopal (Anglican) schools). Several legal cases in the 1920s established, moreover, that the boards were obliged to found and fund new Catholic schools wherever the church deemed there to be sufficient need. Thereafter, Catholic and non-denominational secondary schooling expanded in the same way, using the same curriculum, the same Leaving Certificate courses, the same universities for specialist teachers – since Scotland never had any denominational universities – and, despite the distinct Catholic training colleges, essentially the same curriculum of teacher education.[34] By the 1930s, religion as such was probably no longer a barrier to obtaining a full secondary education: the continuing educational disadvantage of the Catholic community was because the Catholic population remained more working-class than the population as a whole. The Catholic schools served essentially secular purposes, especially for the most able children who could use the Leaving

Certificate to gain access to the universities and the professions: the proportion of pupils from Catholic schools among candidates for the Leaving Certificate rose from 4 per cent in 1911 to 11 per cent in 1935, while the proportion of Catholics in the age-17 group remained approximately stable at around 11–13 per cent.[35]

In summing up this first period of reform, to the 1930s, we can draw more complex conclusions than is common. It is true that, as is usually pointed out, secondary schooling remained sharply divided: it was still the case that the full liberal education was experienced only by a minority, and indeed a very small minority if we take the most restrictive definition of that curriculum, the actual passing of the Leaving Certificate. Nevertheless, there was significant extension of access, in that the new schools provided a liberal curriculum to the most able children in areas populated mainly by lower-middle-class and skilled-working-class families. The most important point for the rest of the century was thus that the principle was being established that a proper secondary education had to rest on a modernised liberal education, transferring to the senior years of the secondary school the principles of breadth, rigour and, through literary studies, reflection on human existence that previously had been a characteristic of the undergraduate curriculum at university.

The Consolidation of Reform: 1950s

We jump forward now for our next body of evidence to examine this new system as it stabilised after the Second World War. There are three reasons to look at the 1950s and early 1960s in more detail. The first is pragmatic: for the first time, survey data is available. Whereas the information on which the discussion of the 1920s and 1930s was based came from the National Archives and published sources, and thus related almost entirely to institutions rather than individuals, the 1947 Scottish Mental Survey allows us to trace the experience of individual pupils while still setting that in the context of the institutional changes from earlier in the century.[36] The survey covered a representative sample of around 1,200 pupils who were born in 1936, who thus transferred to secondary school mainly in 1947 and left school mainly between 1950 and 1953, re-interviewing them annually until 1963; it collected information about education after school, about entry to employment and about their home life. The project was conducted by the Scottish Council for Research in Education as part of its programme of research that is discussed by Lawn and Deary in their chapter in this volume. Detailed information was collected in the survey about the schools which the sample members attended, and so we can relate the experience of the respondents to the history of the secondary schools that we have been considering.

That pragmatic methodological point is not the sole reason to look at this period, because the experience of the 1950s was the source of pressure for the radical reforms that came next: that is, the pressure for comprehensive secondary schooling – the ending of all selection for secondary school in the public sector – and also the beginnings of fundamental change to the curriculum. A third reason to look at the 1950s is that they formed the immediate background to Davie's own writing, a point to which we will return at the end of the chapter.

The secondary school system of the 1950s was the consolidated version of the system that was put in place by the end of the 1930s. Formally, it consisted of two kinds of courses, senior and junior secondary. In practice, that became in the urban areas senior and junior secondary schools, the latter offering only three-year courses that did not lead to national certification, the former offering five-year courses and, in the majority of cases, three-year courses as well. But the schools and courses that were defined administratively in that way were the heirs to the process of reform earlier in the century that we have looked at. So for this period, too, we can investigate whether the earlier reforms – the new schools – were providing opportunities to wider groups of pupils who were not served well by the oldest schools whose founding pre-dated the reforms.

The Leaving Certificate stopped being a group certificate after 1950, so that pupils could gain evidence that recorded the results of examination in individual subjects. But the character of these subjects, and the overall philosophy of the courses, had barely changed: it remained the core of a liberal education extended to senior school pupils. Moreover, the highest status was accorded to combinations of subjects that would have obtained a Group Award before 1951. Thus the curricular philosophy of the Leaving Certificate remained as it had been established in the 1920s, summed up for example in the SED guidelines for teaching English literature: 'the main aim . . . is not so much the imparting of information as the inculcation of a liberal culture'.[37]

The analysis of this 1950s evidence reaches similar conclusions to those for the 1930s, and thus suggests that the contemporary and subsequent pessimism about the operation of the selective system in the 1950s was somewhat excessive. In brief, four points may be made about the 1950s. First, the 1950s data confirms that the reforms of the first four decades of the century were continuing to provide to much wider segments of the population a model of secondary schooling that had previously been confined mainly to the children of the professional classes. The offering of selective opportunities to all classes was particularly evident in the newer sectors of senior secondary school, notably the former Higher Grade schools. In the 1950s, the distribution of social classes within these newer secondary schools was close to the distribution across the national sample as a whole. If the former Higher Grade schools, and other secondary schools founded in the 1920s and 1930s, had not offered these opportunities, then the proportion of able lower-status pupils who would have had access to senior secondary courses would have been about a quarter less than it actually was; in the lowest class of all, the fall would have been over one half. A similar point was specifically true of Catholic schools: by the 1950s, there were no directly denominational differences in opportunities to enter academic courses, as opposed to differences associated with socio-economic status (which in turn was still associated with denomination), and progress in these courses depended on pupils' measured intelligence in the same way in the Catholic as in the non-denominational sectors.[38]

Second, social class and ability were related to progress and attainment in the newer schools in the same way as in the older ones. The effect of social class on progress towards the Leaving Certificate examinations, and attainment in them, operated within schools and was not exhausted by the process of allocating children to schools. The same was true of ability. Nevertheless, there was no evidence that class operated differently in schools of different kinds. Moreover, although there was a class segmentation between sectors, the old, highest-status schools did not exclude the lowest-status classes, and there was a significant presence of working-class pupils in all sectors, whether new or ancient.

Third, girls gained unprecedented opportunities as well, and except in science had the same opportunities as boys. With that exception, girls were participating in Leaving Certificate courses in similar proportions to boys, maintaining in the post-war world the gains they had made in the 1920s and 1930s. Even in science, around one-third of candidates for examination were female, probably somewhat higher than in the 1930s.

Thus the reforms of the first few decades of the twentieth century had widened opportunity. It is true that the selective system of the 1950s did not operate in a fully merit-selective fashion in its allocation of pupils to courses: social class influenced children's progress even once they had been allocated to schools and courses.[39] However, that was probably a consequence of the relationship between educability and the wider social structure rather than of any failure of the reformers' intent. It is likely that class operated in ways that did not stop when a child was sent to secondary school: lack of financial resources, lack of social and cultural capital, and lack of aspirations by both the family and the child would have restricted children's development after the age of twelve just as effectively as they did at earlier ages, even among children with high measured intelligence at age twelve.[40] The main point, however, is that if being working class was a disadvantage in being allocated to five-year courses and in making progress on them, it was no greater or lesser a disadvantage in the newer sectors than in the older. The uniformity of the class effects across sector might indicate the limits of reform to the school system in overcoming structural inequalities in society, but it might also illustrate that the reforms successfully extended an older model of schooling to a much wider population.

So the conclusions to be drawn from this period in the middle of the century are, as with the conclusions for the earlier period, more complex than has often been claimed. The advantage of placing the 1950s experience in the longer perspective of schooling reform going back half a century is that it forces us to view the 1950s dynamically. Seen in isolation, as they were by contemporaries, they appeared as a period of stasis; and on the whole that static view is how they have been seen ever since. But seen as the period when half a century of cautious reform came to fruition, they appear in a much more favourable light as offering to working-class children, girls and Catholics opportunities that, without these earlier reforms, they would have been denied. The worst that can be said about the reforms of the 1920s and earlier was that they were not strong enough to overcome the effects of social structure: they were specifically educational reforms, not social reforms.

The Extension of Reform

From the 1960s onwards, however, educational policy and practice came to be expected to do a lot more than operate on education itself: it would henceforth have to overcome the effects of social structure. This change in expectation came about for two main reasons. One was political ambition allied with political caution: politicians still wanted to overcome social ills, but were not so willing as in 1945 to engage in large-scale redistribution of wealth and income. So they tried to use education as a lever to bring about equality. The second reason we will come to shortly.

The central policy was the ending of selection into different kinds of secondary course in the public sector. The new comprehensive schools were accepted so swiftly and so relatively uncontroversially in Scotland – by the mid-1970s – that the country did not in fact call any of its secondary schools 'comprehensive': there are no 'comprehensive' schools, only 'schools' (usually called 'high schools' or 'academies', terms that themselves indicate allegiance to older traditions).

The structural reform was followed by reforms to curriculum and to examinations to cater adequately for the vastly expanded and more diverse population of pupils. These changes started just before the ending of selection, with the creation of the Ordinary Grade in 1962, providing fourth-year pupils of moderate ability with a ladder towards Highers in fifth year. Then this principle was taken further: in the reforms that eventually led to the Standard Grade courses by the mid-1980s, proper courses were planned for the whole range of ability. The intention of this reform was firmly in the tradition of widening access to a modernised version of the liberal curriculum. Conceived out of Paul Hirst's analysis of the nature of knowledge,[41] and his conclusion that, for the purposes of the school curriculum, knowledge may be organised into about eight modes of thought, the report that led to the introduction of Standard Grade proposed that all pupils should engage in all these modes of study – for example, linguistic, literary, mathematical, scientific and so on. For pupils in their mid-teenage years, this was firmly in line with the whole inherited tradition – not only with the ideas which had led to the Highers, but also with the philosophy which had in turn shaped these, from the old undergraduate curriculum. The proposals expressed goals for the curriculum that came straight out of that same tradition, for example asserting that 'socially relevant issues can[not] really be explored without making use of the insights provided by the various traditions of intellectual enquiry' and that 'there are many activities and experiences which do not seem to have any direct bearing on the social realities of pupils' lives, but which none the less have a profoundly liberating effect'.[42]

The evidence on the effects of all these reforms is rich and complex because of the existence of the series of surveys of Scottish school leavers, starting in effect in 1962–3, and then continuing biennially from 1971 until after the end of the century. This series allows the same kind of detailed analysis as the 1947 survey which gave us evidence about the 1950s, presented in the subtle and extensive programme of evaluation that was conducted by the Centre for Educational Sociology at Edinburgh University led by Andrew McPherson.[43]

The research showed that the structural reform itself had some of the intended effect, in that social-class differences in attainment by the end of schooling were narrowed somewhat, and that girls' average attainment rose to match and then overtake that of boys. Attainment of pupils in Catholic schools rose particularly strongly because of the effect on the social-class differences. Because the remaining educational disadvantage of the Catholic population in the 1950s had been due to social disadvantage, a reform that extended opportunities for a full secondary education to all social-class groups had a disproportionate effect on Catholics. The result was that, by the 1980s, the attainment of pupils in Catholic schools was better than would have been expected from their social status alone.[44] The long-term consequences of the several phases of denominational reform that ultimately were due to the 1918 Act was that Catholics came to have equal access to the professions and to full citizenship.[45]

The structural reforms to secondary schooling were part of wider reforms that included also post-school education – the expansion of higher education from the 1960s, accelerating from the 1980s, and an expansion of adult education to serve a different kind of purpose from when it was mainly to compensate for lost opportunities in the inadequate old school system. Both these changes were offered as educational routes to the deepening of citizenship – in the Robbins report of 1963 which inaugurated half a century of higher-education expansion (across the UK), and in the Alexander report of 1975 which argued for a modernised adult education in Scotland on the grounds that 'it is only where people have developed their own unique individualities that social ideals of the highest order emerge'.[46]

The changes to the school curriculum did extend access to a broad programme of liberal study, especially for working-class children and girls. Indeed, the low female participation in science that we have noted from early in the century to the 1950s was finally ended. Nevertheless, the most effective of the new schools in narrowing social-class differences in attainment were not on the whole the new comprehensive schools created afresh in the 1960s and 1970s but rather those older schools that served a whole community, dating mostly from the earlier reforms which we have been looking at here. The old omnibus school which was attended by most children in the community had been, before the 1960s, internally selective, but made the transition to a less-selective era fairly smoothly. In the words of Gray, McPherson and Raffe in their definitive account of these changes published in 1983, 'the form of comprehensive education that sustains' the claims made by its advocates 'is not the one introduced by the post-1965 reorganisation, but one arising out of an older and traditional form in Scottish education, the omnibus school'.[47]

What happened next would take us into current policy, and away from history, but we may note that the conclusions that were drawn after the 1970s from the only partial success of the comprehensive reforms have disrupted the inherited debate about the curriculum for the first time.[48] Until Standard Grade, it was taken as given that the purpose of a liberal education was to give access to the best that has been thought and said: the curriculum, as in Hirst's analysis, was defined by the structure of knowledge. By the 1970s, the view emerging in the new sociology of the curriculum – pioneered in Britain by Basil Bernstein and colleagues at the London Institute of Education, and associated internationally with Pierre Bourdieu – was that the problem of access lay precisely in such inherited cultural structures. That was the second reason for the emergence of the belief that reform to education should be expected to overcome the effects of social structure – the view that a major reason for social inequalities of outcome in education was the education process itself. In particular, Bourdieu, Bernstein and their followers argued, the curriculum of liberal education was itself alienating of children who were not from the core middle-class and English-speaking segments of society.

This belief was slower coming to Scotland than to other places, but it has dominated debate about the curriculum since the 1980s. Simplifying enormously, we can say that from this line of thinking has come the questioning of subjects as the components out of which the whole curriculum is built, the defining of the purpose of the curriculum as being to enable the pupil to enjoy learning and the notion that all learning has to be judged by its practical utility. Indeed, so hegemonic have these ideas become in the past quarter of a century that it is sometimes difficult to think of them as being historically contingent. But they would certainly not have been self-evident to most of the reformers who created the Scottish secondary system that we have been looking at in this chapter.

Conclusion

There are four points to be made in conclusion of this sketch of a history. First, from the beginning of the century until a generation after the ending of selection among schools in the public sector, the aim of reforming policy was to widen access to a liberal curriculum that was a recurrently modernised version of the old undergraduate curriculum which Davie said died with late-nineteenth-century reforms.

The second point is that, in having this reforming aim as a strong strand within its developing policy on education, Scotland was absolutely normal. As the main goal of reforming educational policy, that widening of access to a liberal curriculum was a common theme throughout Europe and North America until the 1950s. However, elsewhere too, and rather earlier than in Scotland, scepticism about the inherited form of liberal education gradually permeated all curriculum planning. Liberal education came to be seen not as a universal prize to be aimed for, but as itself the reason why children from outside the dominant culture were less likely to succeed in education than children who had acquired that culture from their families. Eventually, Scotland too has come round to this point of view, with gradual and now fundamental reforms to the school curriculum; that is no longer history, but current politics.

Third, these specific conclusions then lead to a methodological one. To judge whether any particular period is radical or conservative, it is not enough to take the opinions of contemporaries on it. Neither is it enough to evaluate only what was deliberately attempted in that period and what the outcome was within that period. Put differently: the 1930s or the 1950s or the 1970s ought not to be judged on their own if we want to reach a proper understanding of the scope for reform. The 1930s, despite the policy restrictions of the 1920s, saw the stabilising of reforms that had been inaugurated at the very beginning of the century. The SED restricted expansion after 1924, but did not reverse what had previously been put in place. The effects of these previous reforms were still being worked through in the 1920s and 1930s.

The 1950s, likewise, was a period of consolidating the older reforms – the 1930s stabilisation of the pre-1920s expansion. Again we were able to conclude that the opportunities available to working-class children (and girls and Catholics) were much greater than they would have been without these earlier reforms. A reform – the creation of the Higher Grade schools after 1903 – was still achieving marked effects half a century later. Sir Henry Craik and Sir John Struthers were more radical than they imagined or than their critics have ever allowed. Without them there would not have been the senior secondary sector serving some four out of ten pupils in the 1950s that could become the model on which the non-selective schools could be created after the 1960s. Conservative though they were in many respects, Craik and Struthers had created the defining institutions and the defining liberal curriculum of a core element of social democratic policy. But maybe the political conundrum is not so great if we allow ourselves also to accept that Tory unionism was, when they were operating, still a remarkably creative force. Nevertheless, if Craik and Struthers set the process in motion, their successors were responsible for maintaining it. It is anachronistic to suppose that being radical entails doing something new: it can equally well be allowing the radical potential of inherited structures to be realised. A structure once created can then be used by a later generation to do things that its originators would never have envisaged. Up to the 1950s, that is broadly what happened to the system bequeathed by the pre-First World War changes. In Alasdair MacIntyre's words, 'an adequate sense of tradition manifests itself in a grasp of those future possibilities which the past has made available to the present'.[49]

We finish back with Davie, as one always does, infuriatingly but in tribute to his wayward genius. He was wrong in many fundamental respects. He did not see that to understand the influence of education on Scotland from the late nineteenth century to the 1980s, at least, the university curriculum was less immediately relevant than what was taught at secondary school. Davie's evident lack of interest in sociology here has its most deleterious effect: he simply failed to notice that, in the first few decades of the twentieth century, secondary schools were taking over the traditional role of the elementary years of the universities, or that the nineteenth-century universities in Scotland had played a role that in England, France and Prussia had been taken by early forms of secondary schooling.

Davie was thus also wrong about the Scottish Education Department. It was not the unimaginative bureaucracy that he portrayed it as being: in the new system of secondary schools that in the 1920s was formed from the Higher Grade schools, it transformed the extent of secondary schooling in a manner that remained attached to inherited structures of knowledge through the Leaving Certificate. Indeed, insofar as most of the Higher Grade schools had themselves been created out of a tradition of parish schools where higher subjects had been taught, even the structural changes were firmly in keeping with the older practices. He was wrong too in his view that radical ideas were always merely mechanical and never consistent with tradition: the subtle interplay of even the most radical of reforming ideas with tradition is evident only if a more historically accurate approach to the evidence is taken than he ever did. The point is that the SED was both deeply conservative and also gradually persuaded of the virtue of widening access to the inherited curriculum; and by being conservative it also was able to ground the extended school system in a cultural tradition that a sharper kind of radical break would never have achieved. Unless we – unlike Davie – can find a way of understanding that, we will never grasp properly the nature of change in Scottish education or in Scotland generally.

But that then also allows us to say that, in a much deeper sense than concerns the ephemeral politics of successive moments in the process of change, Davie was right. Without fully appreciating why, he correctly pointed out the centrality of the liberal curriculum to the Scottish tradition, and the central importance of democratising access to it in the nation's educational politics. He was also right in an important sense that has not yet been resolved in policy or in democratic practice. If the central educational problem for democracy, as Davie suggested, is how to ensure sufficient expertise and wisdom in our rulers, then it matters profoundly whether a liberal curriculum can be made democratically available without diluting its intellectual rigour. That is the important essence of the Scottish dilemma. The real context of Davie's writing was not the late-nineteenth-century university reforms, nor even, really, the Scottish Education Department's policies on teaching in the 1920s. The actual context is his own time – the ending of selection for secondary school and the first stages in the massive expansion of higher education. The question for his time was whether these bold changes would undermine the tradition. He feared they might, but was caught in the dilemma of knowing that the populist appeal of widening access was irresistible. The answer until the 1980s still seemed to be that the dilemma could be evaded – that democratisation and the maintenance of the old standards were compatible with each other. That that no longer seems to be widely accepted, and that populism seems to be more powerful than standards, is why we still have to return repeatedly to Davie's dilemmas.

Notes

1. George Elder Davie, *The Democratic Intellect* (Edinburgh University Press, 1961).
2. W. Elliot, 'The Scottish heritage in politics', in Atholl et al., *A Scotsman's Heritage* (Alexander Maclehose and Co., 1932), p. 64.
3. George Elder Davie, *The Crisis of the Democratic Intellect* (Polygon, 1986), p. 262.
4. George Elder Davie, 'The social significance of the Scottish philosophy of common sense', in George Elder Davie, *The Scottish Enlightenment and other Essays* (Polygon, 1991), p. 57.
5. Ibid., pp. 57–8.
6. This argument is developed in L. Paterson, 'Does Scottish education need traditions?', *Discourse: Studies in the Cultural Politics of Education* 30 (2009), 253–68; and L. Paterson, 'Competitive opportunity and liberal culture: The significance of Scottish education in the twentieth century', *British Educational Research Journal* (2013).
7. R. D. Anderson, *Education and Opportunity in Victorian Scotland* (Edinburgh University Press, 1983); R. D. Anderson, 'Education and society in modern Scotland: A comparative perspective', *History of Education Quarterly* 25 (1985), 459–81; R.D. Anderson, 'Secondary schools and Scottish society in the nineteenth century', *Past and Present* 109 (1985), 176–203; R. D. Anderson, *Education and the Scottish People, 1750–1918* (Oxford University Press, 1995); A. McPherson, 'Schooling', in A. Dickson and J. H. Treble (eds), *People and Society in Scotland, 1914–1990* (John Donald, 1992), pp. 80–107; G. S. Osborne, *Scottish and English Schools: A Comparative Survey of the Past Fifty Years* (University of Pittsburgh Press, 1966); J. Stocks, 'The people versus the department: The case of circular 44', *Scottish Educational Review* 27 (1995), 48–60; J. Stocks, 'Social class and the secondary school in 1930s Scotland', *Scottish Educational Review* 34 (2002), 26–39.
8. Expansion of some of the argument in this chapter is in L. Paterson, *Scottish Education in the Twentieth Century* (Edinburgh University Press, 2003); L. Paterson, 'The modernising of the democratic intellect: The role of English in Scottish secondary education, 1900–1939', *Journal of Scottish Historical Studies* 24 (2004), 45–79; L. Paterson, 'The reinvention of Scottish liberal education: Secondary schooling, 1900–1939', *Scottish Historical Review* 90 (2011), 96–130; L. Paterson, 'George Davie', in Gordon Graham (ed.), *Oxford History of Scottish Philosophy* (Oxford University Press, forthcoming); Lindsay Paterson, Alison Pattie and Ian Deary, 'Post-school education and social class destinations in Scotland in the 1950s', *Longitudinal and Life Course Studies* 1 (2010), 371–93; Lindsay Paterson, Alison Pattie and Ian Deary, 'Social class, gender and secondary education in Scotland in the 1950s', *Oxford Review of Education* 37 (2011), 383–401.
9. John Lawson and Harold Silver, *A Social History of Education in England* (Methuen, 1973).
10. Anderson, *Education and the Scottish People*, p. 310; published lists of Higher Grade schools were provided periodically by the SED in their annual reports from 1906–7 onwards; for a full (unpublished) list in 1903–4, see National Archives of Scotland [henceforth: NAS], Higher Grade Schools 1903–8, ED7/1/24.
11. Anderson, *Education and Opportunity*, p. 243.
12. NAS, Higher Grade Schools 1903–8, ED7/1/24, Struthers to HMI Dr [George] Dunn, 2 May 1903.
13. Detlef K. Müller, Fritz Ringer and Brian Simon (eds), *The Rise of the Modern Educational System: Structural Change and Social Reproduction, 1870–1920* (Cambridge

University Press, 1987); Fritz Ringer, *Education and Society in Modern Europe* (Indiana University Press, 1979).

14. Paterson, *Scottish Education in the Twentieth Century*, pp. 60–7; Stocks, 'The people versus the department', 48–60.
15. Paterson, 'The modernising of the democratic intellect', 56.
16. Anderson, 'Education and society'; Paterson, 'The modernising of the democratic intellect', 70–1.
17. Anderson, *Education and the Scottish People*, pp. 274–8; Paterson, *Scottish Education in the Twentieth Century*, pp. 81 and 91–2.
18. Paterson, 'The modernising of the democratic intellect', 49.
19. Henry L. Philip, *The Higher Tradition* (Scottish Examination Board, 1992); Paterson, 'The modernising of the democratic intellect', 52–4.
20. Paterson, 'The modernising of the democratic intellect', 52.
21. S. S. Laurie, *Lectures on Language and Linguistic Method in the School* (Oliver and Boyd, 1889), p. 3.
22. J. Strong, 'Moral and religious elements in the school', in John Clarke (ed.), *Problems of National Education* (Macmillan, 1919), pp. 141–2.
23. *Bulletin of the English Association* 35 (September 1918), 7.
24. Sheldon Rothblatt, *Tradition and Change in English Liberal Education* (Faber, 1976).
25. J. Burnet, 'Languages in secondary schools', *Secondary School Journal* III (May 1910), 37–8.
26. National Library of Scotland (1913), *Proceedings of the Classical Association of Scotland*.
27. T. H. Huxley, 'Universities: Actual and ideal', in T. H. Huxley, *Collected Essays Vol. III* (Macmillan, 1874), pp. 189–233.
28. Philip, *The Higher Tradition*, p. 271.
29. J. A. Thomson, 'The place and function of science', in Clarke (ed.), *Problems of National Education*, pp. 205–40.
30. Paterson, 'The modernising of the democratic intellect'; Paterson, 'The reinvention of Scottish liberal education'.
31. Brian Doyle, 'The hidden history of English studies', in Peter Widdowson (ed.), *Re-Reading English* (Methuen, 1982), pp. 17–31; Brian Doyle, 'The invention of English', in Robert Colls and Philip Dodd (eds), *Englishness: Politics and Culture 1880–1920* (Croom Helm, 1986), pp. 89–115.
32. Paterson, *Scottish Education*, pp. 40–1, 57–60.
33. Marjorie Cruikshank, *History of the Training of Teachers in Scotland* (University of London Press, 1970), p. 162.
34. Ibid., pp. 160–85.
35. Paterson, 'The modernising of the democratic intellect', 64–5; Paterson, 'The reinvention of Scottish liberal education', 122–4.
36. Paterson et al., 'Post-school education and social class'; Paterson et al., 'Social class, gender and secondary education'.
37. Scottish Education Department, *English in Secondary Schools* (HMSO, 1952), p. 24.
38. Lindsay Paterson, C. Calvin and I. J. Deary, 'Education, employment and school religious denomination in Scotland in the 1950s', *Oxford Review of Education* (2015).
39. J. W. B. Douglas, J. M. Ross, S. M. M. Maxwell and D. A. Walker, 'Differences in test score and in the gaining of selective places for Scottish children and those in England and Wales', *British Journal of Educational Psychology* 36 (1966), 150–7; J. Gray, A. McPherson and D. Raffe, *Reconstructions of Secondary Education: Theory, Myth and Practice since the War* (Routledge and Kegan Paul, 1983); Keith Hope, *As*

Others See Us: Schooling and Social Mobility in Scotland and the United States (Cambridge University Press, 1984); John S. Macpherson, *Eleven-Year-Olds Grow Up* (University of London Press, 1958).

40. J. W. B. Douglas, *The Home and the School* (Macgibbon and Kee, 1964), pp. 40–5; Hope, *As Others See Us*, pp. 137–64.

41. Paul H. Hirst, *Knowledge and the Curriculum* (Routledge and Kegan Paul, 1975).

42. Scottish Education Department, *The Structure of the Curriculum in the Third and Fourth Years of the Scottish Secondary School* (HMSO, 1977), p. 17.

43. Some of the major works in this series are: Gray et al., *Reconstructions of Secondary Education*; A. McPherson, 'Schooling'; A. McPherson and J. D. Willms, 'Certification, class conflict, religion, and community: A socio-historical explanation of the effectiveness of contemporary schools', in Alan C. Kerckhoff (ed.), *Research in Sociology of Education and Socialization*, Vol. 6 (JAI Press, 1986), pp. 227–302; A. McPherson and J. D. Willms, 'Equalisation and improvement: Some effects of comprehensive reorganisation in Scotland', *Sociology* 21 (1987), 509–39; A. Gamoran, 'Curriculum standardisation and equality of opportunity in Scottish secondary education, 1984–1990', *Sociology of Education* 69 (1995), 1–21; L. Croxford, 'Equal opportunities in the secondary school curriculum in Scotland', *British Educational Research Journal* 20 (1994), 371–91.

44. McPherson and Willms, 'Certification'; McPherson and Willms, 'Equalisation'; Lindsay Paterson, 'Trends in attainment in Scottish secondary schools', in Steven W. Raudenbush and J. Douglas Willms (eds), *Schools, Classrooms, and Pupils* (Academic Press, 1991), pp. 85–100.

45. Lindsay Paterson and Cristina Iannelli, 'Religion, social mobility and education in Scotland', *British Journal of Sociology* 57 (2006), 353–77.

46. Scottish Education Department, *Adult Education: The Challenge of Change* (HMSO, 1975), p. 35.

47. Gray et al., *Reconstructions of Secondary Education*, p. 266.

48. Paterson, 'Competitive opportunity and liberal culture'; and the chapter by Humes in the present volume.

49. Alasdair MacIntyre, *After Virtue* (Duckworth, 1981), p. 223.

Bibliography

Anderson, R. D., 'Education and society in modern Scotland: A comparative perspective', *History of Education Quarterly* 25 (1985), 459–81.

Anderson, R. D., *Education and the Scottish People, 1750–1918* (Oxford University Press, 1995).

Davie, George Elder, *The Democratic Intellect* (Edinburgh University Press, 1961).

Davie, George Elder, *The Crisis of the Democratic Intellect* (Polygon, 1986).

Davie, George Elder, 'The social significance of the Scottish philosophy of common sense', in Davie, George Elder *The Scottish Enlightenment and other Essays* (Polygon, 1991), pp. 51–85.

Gray, J., A. F. McPherson and D. Raffe, *Reconstructions of Secondary Education: Theory, Myth and Practice since the War* (Routledge and Kegan Paul, 1983).

McPherson, A., 'Schooling', in A. Dickson and J. H. Treble (eds), *People and Society in Scotland, 1914–1990* (John Donald, 1992), pp. 80–107.

Paterson, Lindsay, *Scottish Education in the Twentieth Century* (Edinburgh University Press, 2003).

Paterson, Lindsay, 'Competitive opportunity and liberal culture: The significance of Scottish education in the twentieth century', *British Educational Research Journal* 40 (2014), 397–416.

Paterson, Lindsay, 'George Davie', in Gordon Graham (ed.), *Oxford History of Scottish Philosophy* (Oxford University Press, forthcoming).

14

Adult Education, c. 1750–1950: A Distinctive Mission?

Douglas Sutherland

Adult learning has a rather peripheral position in the historiography of Scottish education. In part, this may stem from the relative elasticity of the concept of adulthood: this was particularly the case in the first hundred years or so of the period considered in this chapter, when initial schooling in Scotland was not yet universal and the necessity of work encroached significantly into the lives of so many children. A second factor is the sheer diversity of what adult education entails: during our period this ranges across a wide spectrum of educational provision, from basic literacy and numeracy to higher, university-level education, and from a narrow utilitarian focus on vocational training to the more holistic emphasis of a liberal arts tradition. These considerations have implications for research on the history of adult education across Britain, but a third complication is more particular to Scotland and emerges from the pervasive, and sometimes controversial, place of tradition in its educational culture. Historically, adult education has largely been concerned with addressing inequalities in access to formal learning; but in Scotland the historical openness of its education system – often lauded as providing a ladder of opportunity from the parochial schools to its universities – may, from this perspective, be viewed as a counterweight to the need for some forms of adult education. Of course, the extent to which the much-vaunted openness of Scottish education is in fact a myth has been the subject of some debate,[1] but, as Paterson argues, the power and influence of tradition is not always contingent upon its truth: the fact that those involved in shaping educational provision were influenced by it may be as significant as the tradition's accuracy or overall truth.[2] Thus, for instance, the administrators of Scottish education in the early twentieth century were perhaps persuaded by the prevailing belief that the nation's education system was comparatively open and meritocratic, and their policy decisions may reflect the associated assumption that the need for adult education provision was less pressing or, at least, required a response which took full account of the distinctive characteristics of Scottish education.

It is only comparatively recently that this dearth of research on the history of adult education in Scotland – a dearth highlighted by the particularly rich seam of work on elementary, secondary and higher education – has begun to be addressed by a growing body of research into various aspects of adult education, and by the 2006 publication of Anthony Cooke's comprehensive history of adult education in modern Scotland, the first extensive synthesis of research in this area.[3] This chapter sets out to survey the expanding historiography of adult education in Scotland, and considers the distinctiveness of its mission. For clarity, its discussion is organised around three phases of development in adult education; but it is important to stress that these phases are not discrete, either chronologically or in terms of the forms of educational activity highlighted: the autodidactic or self-taught tradition (central to the education of many gifted working men, like the labour movement leader, Keir Hardie), for instance, has an important place in adult education for most of this period. The first phase – the age of 'popular enlightenment' in the eighteenth and early nineteenth centuries – was characterised by the growth of autodidactic learning and the extension of universities' engagement with their wider communities. At the same time, the quest for increased access to education led to the foundation of philosophical, literary and scientific societies, libraries, mechanics' institutes and early mutual improvement societies. During the second phase, there was a growing alignment between adult education and the amelioration of the social, economic and political problems associated with the spread of industrialisation and urbanisation, and this led to the involvement of Owenites, Chartists and co-operative societies in educational projects. The third phase saw the campaign for women's access to higher education achieve a critical mass which by the end of the nineteenth century had at least breached the walls of academia. In addition, this period witnessed growing demand for working-class access to higher education, and, early in the new century, the Workers' Educational Association was founded and helped to initiate the tutorial class movement that provided opportunities for university-level education to significant numbers of adults in England. In the face of official indifference and the fervent opposition of independent working-class education, the tutorial class movement failed to take root in Scotland. Nonetheless, several Scottish universities continued to develop their provision of extra-mural education, and by the end of our period the levels of such provision across the United Kingdom as a whole had largely converged.

The Age of Popular Enlightenment

During the eighteenth century teaching in the five Scottish universities had passed from the hands of regents – who had traditionally taught the whole university curriculum, in Latin – to new specialist lecturers who taught increasingly large classes, in English. In addition to the longstanding Master of Arts degree which was largely a preparation for the Presbyterian ministry or a teaching career, specific medical and legal education began to be offered, particularly by Edinburgh and Glasgow Universities.[4] At the same time, the intellectual climate that was being cultivated within these two universities contributed significantly

to the European Enlightenment. Despite their place at the heart of developments in Enlightenment thought, the Scottish universities were comparatively
poor institutions, and far less well endowed than Oxford and Cambridge. One
important consequence of this was that lecturers came to depend on the fees paid
directly to them by individual students. Their lectures were open to students who
were not 'gowned' (matriculated) and – subject to the fee being paid – students
of a wide range of ages and backgrounds could attend as regularly as they wished.
(These eighteenth-century developments are examined fully by Allan in his
chapter in this book.)

In Glasgow, one of the first open courses – 'a course of philosophical lectures and experiments' – taught by Robert Dick, the university's professor of
natural philosophy, was advertised in the Glasgow Press in 1756. The following year, John Anderson succeeded Dick to the chair of natural philosophy and
continued to develop the range of such classes offered by the university, switch-
ing the emphasis from theory to practical demonstration earning himself – as a
result of his employment of explosives in his lectures – the affectionate sobriquet
Jolly Jack Phosphorus. A colourful and controversial figure, he demonstrated a
strong commitment to extending the benefits of higher education to the wider
population and the terms of his will provided for the proposed foundation of
a new university which would provide both vocational and popular academic
education – 'useful knowledge' – to women and working-class men. The relatively
modest value of Anderson's estate meant that the initial foundation in 1796
could only afford the services of a single professor of natural philosophy, and the
executors of his will chose wisely to name the nascent university 'Anderson's
Institution'. Despite its comparatively humble beginnings, the institution experienced a high level of interest in the courses delivered by its first professor,
Thomas Garnett. After Garnett's departure in 1799, his place in the institution
was taken by George Birkbeck, a Yorkshire Quaker and recent medical graduate of Edinburgh University. Birkbeck's courses continued to meet the growing
demand for scientific and technical education and became particularly popular
with mechanics and instrument makers: the free course on popular science he
provided for them recruited an annual audience of around 500.[5] After he left in
1804, he was replaced by Dr Andrew Ure, whose approach to adult education was
rather different: a passionate advocate of industrial capitalism and laissez-faire
economics, the future author of The Philosophy of Manufactures (1835) exhibited
little genuine commitment to proletarian education and targeted his classes at a
more middle-class audience. Ure's relations with the mechanics of Glasgow were
far from amicable and his introduction of charges for the classes Birkbeck had
pioneered provoked outrage. Matters came to a head in 1823 when the mechanics
broke away from Anderson's to found their own Glasgow Mechanics' Institution.

Outwith the university walls and often outwith their urban settings,
some working-class adults were taking charge of their own learning; as Rose
observes, autodidactic learning was particularly common amongst the weavers of
eighteenth-century Scotland.[6] These skilled workers whose craft prospered in the

early stages of the industrialisation of textile manufacture, but suffered terribly as mechanisation steadily reduced the market value of their skills, were renowned for their enjoyment of reading while working at the loom. Initially, much of their appetite for reading was related to religious commitment but, as their economic and social circumstances declined, weavers became widely noted for their radical tendencies, not least in Paisley which became a fount of radical poetry. As the eighteenth century progressed, the autodidactic tradition became widely established across a broad range of Scottish communities and the *Statistical Account of Scotland*, conducted in the 1790s, notes that in Wigtown:

> Servility of mind, the natural consequence of poverty and oppression, has lost much of its hold here ... An attention to publick affairs, a thing commonly unknown among the lower ranks, pretty generally prevails now. Not only the farmers, but many of the tradesmen, read the newspapers and take an interest in the measures of government.[7]

Autodidactic learning – although it evokes the image of dedicated learners toiling over their books by candlelight, often after a hard day's work – frequently had a social dimension, and many of its practitioners shared their books and ideas, sometimes informally, but often in more formal, organised settings. The latter form of activity was exemplified by the mutual improvement societies, of which the earliest known example is the poet Allan Ramsay's Easy Club, founded in Edinburgh in 1727. Similar clubs were founded across Scotland in the eighteenth century; among them, Robert Burns' Bachelors' Clubs in Tarbolton and Mauchline. Although some of these clubs were paragons of mutuality, the associated conviviality – frequently lubricated by heavy drinking – gives some of them a somewhat tenuous place in the history of adult education. Rather more consistently earnest were the reading societies and libraries which, Rose argues, represent the most important early expressions of the mutual improvement ethos in Scotland. In 1769–97, there were thirty-five reading societies around Glasgow and Paisley, many of them located in weaving communities; and by 1822, there were fifty-one working-class lending libraries in Scotland which charged annual subscriptions of sixpence or less and were run democratically by their members. These were all in town of less than 10,000, and three, in the remote mining communities of Leadhills (founded in 1741), Wanlockhead (1756) and Westerkirk (1792), were the first working-class libraries in Britain.[8] Another interesting development that helped to widen working-class access to literature was Samuel Brown's 'itinerating libraries scheme' in East Lothian. By 1836, there were thirty-six library branches with around 2,380 books, most on moral and religious subjects but with some on travel, popular science and agriculture.[9] Although Brown's experiment was not extended across Scotland, it enjoyed considerable success in East Lothian and offered a clear indication of the growing demand for access to literature – a demand that was eventually addressed by the foundation of public lending libraries later in the nineteenth century. These formal endeavours, added to the countless informal networks through which books, newspapers, periodicals, pamphlets and ideas were shared, helped to nourish the 'cult' of self-improvement in Scotland, and it is hardly surprising that the particular philosophy of 'self-help', proselytised in the best-selling book of that name by the Scottish doctor Samuel Smiles, emerged from this milieu.

At this time, there were also a number of philosophical, literary and scientific societies established which aimed their provision at a more affluent and, in their view, sufficiently educated audience. Fieldhouse suggests that there was sometimes an element of concern that the admission of a working-class audience to the lectures such bodies organised would lead to an increased emphasis on entertainment inimical to the seriousness of their intellectual endeavour.[10] This reflects a long-held belief, still evident in the early nineteenth century, particularly amongst the traditional Tory elite, that educating all but the most gifted of the working class beyond a basic level was potentially dangerous and might weaken the lower orders' acceptance of their place in society. However, as the nineteenth century progressed and the symbiotic processes of industrialisation and urbanisation steadily transformed Scotland, this uncompromising stance faced a growing challenge from new, radical schools of philosophical and political thought. Utilitarian philosophy and its direct political offshoot, philosophical radicalism, argued that universal education was an essential prerequisite of harmony in a rapidly changing society – a harmony that, in part, depended on the enculturation of the working classes in the values of the modern capitalist economy. The *Edinburgh Review*, founded in 1801, became an important conduit for the dissemination of philosophical radicalism: one of its founders and most influential contributors was Henry Brougham, who later rose to prominence in the Whig government. His pamphlet entitled *Practical Observations on the Education of the People* (1825) outlined three stages of educational provision: nursery schools, elementary schools and adult education. In relation to adults, the pamphlet did not advocate any formal state provision as Brougham felt this might undermine civil liberty, but emphasised the central importance of private reading. Confirming his radical credentials, he suggested rather provocatively that the government's stamp duty (intended to silence the radical press) was 'a tax on knowledge', and he cited Samuel Brown's East Lothian itinerating library scheme as an exemplar of an effective vehicle for promoting *appropriate* working-class learning. He also acknowledged the value of mutual improvement societies and the expanding range of opportunities for adults to attend lectures in Scotland's larger towns and cities. The pamphlet was highly influential and some of its ideas underpinned the activities of the Society for the Diffusion of Useful Knowledge (SDUK) and the establishment of mechanics' institutes across the United Kingdom.

The SDUK was founded in 1826 with Brougham as its chair and Lord John Russell – another eminent Whig and future prime minister – its vice president; the society's stated aim was the dissemination of 'useful information to all classes of the community, particularly such as are unable to avail themselves of experienced teachers, or may prefer learning by themselves'[11] – an aim which clearly signalled its faith in the utility of autodidactic learning. To support this, its activities were centred on the provision of 'useful' and appropriate reading materials. Its *Library of Useful Knowledge* produced 158 booklets on a wide range of subjects including science, art, philosophy and history, and it published a monthly *Penny Cyclopedia* and weekly *Penny Magazine*. Although both publications enjoyed impressive early circulation levels, interest in them declined drastically in the early 1840s and they experienced substantial financial difficulties, as did the society itself which was wound up in 1846. It is difficult to assess the overall impact the SDUK had on adult education, but the levels of criticism and satirical comment it engendered at least suggest that it caught the public's imagination. It was humorously depicted as the Steam Intellect Society (an allusion to the trains delivering SDUK publications across Britain) in Thomas Love Peacock's satirical novel *Crotchet Castle* (1831), and – on a more serious level – incurred the wrath of conservative commentators, notably in Blackwood's *Edinburgh Magazine*, who warned of the dire consequences of educating 'the working adults of a great nation'.[12] At the opposite end of the political spectrum, more radical commentators like William Cobbett argued that the aims of the society were far too narrow and ill-judged in that they epitomised a belief that education could – almost single-handedly – alleviate the problems of British society. Johnson has suggested that the central weakness of 'useful knowledge' was that it largely marginalised political considerations in the forms of education it sought to promote; in other words it encouraged workers to gain an education to better equip them for participation in an economic and political system that largely failed to serve their interests. In was only when these political, social and economic considerations entered the mix – and the working classes began to take more responsibility for their own learning – that education became a source of 'really useful knowledge'.[13]

The second aspect of adult education particularly influenced by Brougham and philosophical radicalism was the foundation of numerous mechanics' institutes and similar bodies across Britain in the mid-nineteenth century. Although education explicitly targeted at skilled artisans is particularly associated with the work of Birkbeck in Glasgow and London, the first mechanics' institute in Britain was actually the Edinburgh School of Arts, founded in 1821. Demonstrating its clear links to the educational principles of philosophical radicalism, the School of Arts was founded by Leonard Horner, a close associate of Brougham and one of the co-founders of the *Edinburgh Review*. Its principal aim was to provide skilled artisans with a sound knowledge of scientific principles that would build upon their existing skills and, potentially, enhance their contribution to technological progress. The shining example of James Watt, the Glasgow instrument maker whose refinement of the steam engine had been, and continued to be, so central to industrial development, provided the inspiration behind the foundation of many institutes and helps to explain why many members of the ruling elite supported this particular form of education. George IV became the School of Arts' patron, six of its early presidents were members of the nobility and the board of directors was drawn entirely from its principal financial supporters, effectively ensuring that no students were involved in its management. Considerable care was taken to avoid the intrusion of controversial subjects – such as politics or any economic or social criticism – that might undermine the purity of the school's technological curriculum. In its first year the Edinburgh society had 482 members who paid the comparatively high annual membership fee of fifteen shillings.[14] In 1823, the year Glasgow mechanics founded their institution, the Haddington Mutual Improvement Society was transformed into the Haddington School of Arts under the leadership of Samuel Brown (aforementioned founder of the itin-erating library scheme) and, within a few years, mechanics' institutes were estab-lished in major towns and cities across Scotland, including Aberdeen, Dundee, Kilmarnock, Greenock and Dumfries. Most of them were open to women and – building on John Anderson's legacy – their participation was particularly encour-aged in Glasgow. Interest in the mechanics' institutes went through several peaks and troughs, often related to trade cycles: the depression of 1842–3 had a par-ticularly severe impact on membership levels; this was followed by a period of recovery and reorganisation after 1844. By 1850, Scotland had fifty-five mechan-ics' institutes with around 12,500 members while England had 610 institutes and around 102,000 members; their level of activity probably peaked around 1860 and declined fairly rapidly thereafter as much of their role was taken over by nationally organised Science and Art Department classes aimed at improving technical and vocational education.[15]

The extent to which the mechanics' institutes of the mid-nineteenth cen-tury opened access to higher learning has been questioned by historians of adult education. In relation to their contribution across the United Kingdom gener-ally, Royle argues that:

> They failed to become all that they might have been, they failed to be what they were thought to have been, and they failed to live up to the expectations of their patrons. They did not attract the majority of working men, and they did not teach science.[16]

As Royle acknowledges, however, there was considerable local variation in the nature of the institutes: in how they were established; how they were governed; who attended their classes; and what subjects were taught. One of the most repeated criticisms is that the mechanics' institutes provide a clear example of top-down provision of adult education; that is an education whose organisation and curricula were 'imposed' on a working-class audience by higher levels of the contemporary social strata. The founding principles of the Edinburgh School of Arts, considered above, would appear to support this interpretation, and it is undoubtedly the case that the majority of the institutes founded in Scotland had a distinctly middle-class tenor. Although most of the institutes that lasted more than a few years maintained an explicit adherence to serious scientific lec-tures – on subjects such as natural philosophy, chemistry, physiology, botany and astronomy – there was also a gradual infiltration of some of their programmes by fashionable, sometimes quasi-scientific subjects like phrenology and mesmerism –

changes symptomatic of an increasing focus on education as a leisure pursuit for a largely middle-class audience. High levels of middle-class attendance tended to act as a deterrent to working-class participation, as did the fact that many of the lectures were delivered at a time too early in the evening for a working-class audience, many of whom worked twelve-hour days.

Whilst acknowledging that Scottish institutes were generally as subject to middle-class influence as their English counterparts, Kelly suggests that, within fairly narrow utilitarian limits, they were able to remain more true to their founding principles and made a more substantive contribution to scientific education. This, he argues, was a result of the wider availability of secondary education in Scotland's parochial school system and the higher proportion of adults educated beyond a basic level, and was underpinned by the Protestant work ethic and emphasis on serious discourse that parish schools cultivated.[17] However, what this interpretation fails to take account of is that many of the institutes in Scotland were located in rapidly expanding and industrialising cities like Glasgow and Dundee where access to parochial schools, where it existed, was rapidly breaking down. A contemporary commentator, who had been the director of the Watt Institution in Dundee, argued that 'the failure of the Mechanics' Institutions generally has arisen from a mistaken idea that mechanics were better educated than they really are'.[18] Thus, after 1850, many mechanics' institutes in Scotland began to offer more basic classes in literacy, handwriting, grammar and arithmetic; in other words, to provide a remedial education to meet an increasing demand for clerks and shopkeepers, an educational gap that was simultaneously being addressed by the proliferation of evening schools for adults. Whilst acknowledging the importance of this caveat, there can though be little doubt that – with some institutional and regional variation – Scotland's mechanics' institutes did provide some scientific education to a substantial number of adults; but the prevailing insistence on an uncontroversial, insulated curriculum, largely devoid of any consideration of political and economic conditions, seems to have undermined their appeal to many of the very people they sought to serve: skilled men who certainly valued knowledge of science and technology, but often sought to contextualise that knowledge within a deeper understanding of the rapid social and economic changes they were experiencing. Despite their limitations, as Fieldhouse argues, mechanics' institutes 'significantly extended the coverage of adult education in the nineteenth century'[19] and helped to lay the groundwork for the pursuit and provision of a less constrained education by organisations more closely attuned to its wider social significance and value.

Challenging the Status Quo – the Radical Turn

Whilst the tradition of autodidactic learning was eminently compatible with the ethos of economic individualism and self-improvement so enthusiastically proselytised by Edinburgh's philosophical radicals and the acolytes of Samuel Smiles' cult of self-help, it has an alternative place in the history of adult education. The very same tradition of working-class self-education underpinned the development of distinctly collectivist British radical thought in the eighteenth and nineteenth centuries. Amongst its most influential figures were Tom Paine, author of *The Rights of Man*, and Thomas Spence, an early advocate of socialism, both self-taught men. Indeed, the history of radical thought and popular agitation in this period is peppered with the names of leading figures who were largely self-educated: men like Thomas Hardy, one of the founders of the London Corresponding Society, the Chartists Francis Place and William Lovett, and James Wilson the Strathaven weaver who was hanged and beheaded on Glasgow Green in 1820 for his part in a relatively minor insurrection.

Although the radical tradition has deep historical roots – for instance, precedents of eighteenth-century radical thought are evident in ideas advanced by the Levellers in the Putney Debates during the English Civil War – it gained fresh momentum in reaction to the French Revolution and the economic and social changes that were beginning to gather pace across Britain at this time. Tom Paine's *Rights of Man*, written in answer to Edmund Burke's denunciation of the French Revolution, condemned hereditary government and called for universal male suffrage. It is estimated to have sold as many as one million copies and provided inspiration to new reformist organisations, notably the Corresponding Societies where radical ideas – particularly parliamentary reform – were articulated and exchanged. These bodies focused on education as a means of both spreading their message and preparing the working classes for their eventual role in an extended democracy and, to this end, produced and disseminated a range of radical pamphlets and periodicals. In Scotland, Paine's influence was also apparent in the establishment of a similar reform society, the Friends of the People; founded in Edinburgh in 1792, it quickly established branches in several major Scottish towns. The activities of the Friends were controversial enough to attract the attention of the Scottish establishment, particularly the church which signalled its concern by emphasising the role its parochial schools should play in discouraging and discrediting radical thought. As Cooke suggests, such concerns also stimulated the proliferation of evening classes and the extended provision of access to literature – carefully chosen by those responsible for such schemes – that would steer the working classes of Scotland away from ideas that questioned and challenged the status quo. However, such local measures were soon surpassed by the repressive actions of the British government which, to quell the perceived threat of internal radicalism, suspended habeas corpus, banned seditious meetings (a ban applied to reform societies) and prohibited workers' combination in trade unions. Although the radical tradition was far from extinguished by these measures, it was effectively driven underground and would not resurface fully until the end of the Napoleonic Wars in 1815. After this period of suppression, its emphasis on education was even more pronounced, and particularly evident in the rapid growth of the radical press, whose publications included Cobbett's *Political Register*, Wooler's *Black Dwarf* and Hetherington's *Poor Man's Guardian*. Radical newspapers mounted a sustained attack on 'old corruption' and proselytised radical solutions to political, economic and social ills. Adding very significantly to their circulation figures, many of them were shared or read aloud in clubs, pubs, coffee houses, workplaces and homes, and this revitalised wave of radical thought provided much of the ideological inspiration behind the formation of the mass Chartist movement of the mid-nineteenth century; a movement which – not least in Scotland – highlighted the centrality of education to political and social progress.

An explicit recognition of the wider social value of education was also evident in the philosophy and experiments in communitarian living of Robert Owen. Owen is perhaps best known as the joint owner of New Lanark cotton mill in the Clyde Valley, a humane but rather paternalistic establishment where workers' families were provided with decent homes and access to progressive educational facilities. Owen's social vision drew on Adam Smith's concept of enlightened self-interest and utilitarianism's focus on the integral links between individual and communal happiness. Individual character, he argued, was shaped by the social environment and improving that environment had the potential to promote the health, temperance, manners and industriousness of the working class.[20] Children in New Lanark did not start work in the mill until they reached the age of ten, and prior to that received a good education in New Lanark's school, rather grandiosely named the Institution for the Formation of Character. Owen was also an early advocate of the concept of lifelong learning, involving children from a very early age to adults whose education – Owen maintained – would enable them to help their children to develop into 'rational beings'. Thus the Institute was open in the evening to provide education to young employees between the ages of ten and twenty, and there were adult classes – in chemistry and mechanics, and less serious pursuits like music and dancing – paid for by a levy on wages.

Although Owen is a rather controversial figure, whose espousal of utopian socialism is occasionally contrasted unfavourably with the realities of working-class life in the benevolent but authoritarian community he created in New Lanark, the extent of his influence on the development of left-wing popular movements in mid-Victorian Britain is widely acknowledged. Owen's work raised issues of social justice, tolerance and humanity and, unlike the ascendant prophets of laissez-faire social and economic policy, he advanced the case that something more proactive could be done to foreground these issues. Some of his ideas were impractical, even naïve, but the sheer optimism of his vision inspired a generation of followers who developed and implemented his ideas. Silver argues that these 'Owenites' were particularly important pioneers of organised radical adult education:

> They established schools and ran lecture courses on political, social and scientific subjects; they gave rise to private ventures in education and wrote educational aims into the constitutions of trade unions and co-operative societies; they planned infant and adult education; they issued cheap publications and taught masses of people to analyse economic and social issues; they made ideas a real tool in the work of social reformation. All this was in a real sense education from below.[21]

Owenite 'Halls of Science' – intended to develop and disseminate the new 'science of society' – were established in cities across Britain, including Glasgow. Although less widespread than mechanics' institutes, they created important new opportunities for working-class people to participate in the generation of knowledge by asking their own questions about social and economic issues, thus developing a more 'democratic epistemology' to challenge the imposition of education from above.[22] Owenism also filtered into the early co-operative movement which sought to promote the Owenite ideals of co-operation and brotherhood. Education was viewed as the best way of encouraging people to adopt these ideals and early societies established schools, libraries and reading rooms, and organised a range of educational activities. When the Rochdale Equitable Pioneers' Society was founded in 1844, it assigned a percentage of its profits to educational provision. Cooke indentifies an interesting link between prominent figures in the Scottish Co-operative Movement and the influence of Owen: some of the founders of the Lanark Provident Society, a co-operative society, had attended 'Owen's school' and two early-twentieth-century Labour MPs, Robert Murray and Neil Maclean, both prominent in the Co-operative Movement, were the sons of women raised and educated in New Lanark.[23]

The alignment of adult education with a radical political agenda gained considerable impetus in the Chartist movement of the 1830s and 40s – the first truly mass working-class political movement in British history. Indeed its influence on working-class radical education is arguably one of the most tangible aspects of Chartism's legacy. The origins of this complex movement lie in the economic conditions of the time and the groundswell of working-class disenchantment with the policies of the Whig government. Demonstrating that it also had firm roots in the radical tradition, the essence of its agenda was extensive parliamentary reform, outlined in the six points of the People's Charter, the most 'revolutionary' of which was universal manhood suffrage. Education was central to the Chartists' overall strategy for achieving political reform: they campaigned for the abolition of the stamp duty – which had troubled but not silenced the radical press – and for secular education for children and adults. Like the Whiggish philosophical radicals before them – some of whom appeared to have lost their appetite for democracy on gaining political office – they viewed education as an essential preparation for the extension of the franchise to the working classes. In addition to seeking improvements to existing schools, they sought to create opportunities for independent education free from the influence of the state, the church, middle-class conservatism and other taints of the establishment. By 1838, there were around 200 local Chartist associations in Scotland, many of them in weaving communities blighted by the effects of industrialisation. In addition to their overtly political activities, these associations had a clear social and cultural dimension, partly to raise essential funds for their campaign, but also to enhance solidarity and provide the working classes with access to forms of culture from which they had so often been excluded. Thus the Chartist associations of Glasgow, Greenock and Cumnock held social meetings and concerts on a regular basis and – in addition to politics – their educational activities included classes and discussions on science, theology, philosophy, literature and poetry. As Rose argues, an engagement with literature could fuel indignation against social injustice far more effectively than dry political texts or discourse.[24] These local cultural trends reflected what was happening in the Chartist press where literary extracts were increasingly published alongside political articles. In part, this was to maintain circulation levels at a time when there was growing competition for working-class readers from cheap mass-circulation general-interest periodicals like the *Penny Magazine* and *Chambers's Edinburgh Journal*. The most widely read Chartist newspaper, the *Northern Star*, published Fenimore Cooper and Charlotte Bronte, and others published lengthy extracts from the established canon of Western poetry and philosophy. In 1841, the *Chartist Circular*, published in Glasgow, staked a bold claim to that heritage when it suggested that 'Homer, Aesop, Socrates, Shakespeare, Milton, Defoe and Dr Johnson were all sons of the proletariat'.[25] Although it occasionally veered towards political invective, the general cultural standard of the Chartist press was consistently high, as was the quality of much of its journalism: the *Northern Star*'s editorial policy acknowledged the value of open-minded debate, and regularly published letters from those who questioned or opposed Chartist aims.

In Scotland, the Chartists added to the existing network of Halls of Science and established a number of schools for adults and children. The movement thrived in areas which had a strong radical tradition, often associated with religious dissent. As a result it had a distinctive religious dimension and many of these schools were attached to Chartist churches in places like Arbroath, Greenock, Hamilton and the Gorbals. Education was a major concern for the Scottish Chartists; the *Chartist Circular* called for the establishment of normal schools to improve teacher training and championed more equal access to education for women to help them to pass on an understanding of politics and philosophy to their children. There is little doubt that Chartist educational activities – the mass meetings, debates, lectures, reading groups, libraries and tradesmen reading aloud in the workplace – combined with the actual experience of political campaigning contributed to both the nascent democratic epistemology, alluded to above, and the development of working-class political consciousness. The Chartist movement rapidly declined after the rejection of its last great petition in 1848, but huge numbers of working-class people had been immersed in education in politics, economics and history for the first time, and this engagement did not simply end in 1848: many of those who had received a firm educational grounding through Chartism continued to participate in and facilitate working-class learning in some trade unions and in co-operative, mutual improvement and temperance societies, suggesting that the movement's educational legacy played a part in the formation of the labour movement later in the century.

Opening the Doors of Higher Education

The growing – but far from universal – access to various forms of adult education considered thus far had signally failed to address the most glaring manifestation of educational inequality: women's limited access to education in general, and higher education in particular. The mechanics' institutes were widely open to women but, in a patriarchal society that increasingly espoused the Victorian domestic ideology and frowned upon women's participation in the public sphere of employment and politics, many of the courses aimed specifically at women had an inclination towards leisure rather than serious study. At the same time, women were denied admission to Scotland's five universities and Oxford and Cambridge. In Glasgow, Anderson's Institution became Anderson's University in 1828 and, reflecting its founding principles, continued to promote women's access to higher education: in the 1830s and 40s, women outnumbered men in some of its classes. The first institution dedicated to providing higher education to women – Queen's College, Glasgow – was founded as early as 1842 and provided full-time access to a broad range of sciences as well as languages, literature and theology.[26] In 1845, Professor Hutton Balfour of Glasgow University organised that institution's first systematic course of lectures for women, on botany. These developments reflected a growing rejection of the gender stereotyping which underpinned the belief that women had neither the abilities nor the temperament to benefit from advanced education. In the vanguard of this challenge to the educational status quo were progressive young academics like Edward Caird of Glasgow University. In 1874, he and his brother John – by then principal of the university – were the only members of the University Senate who opposed its decision to petition parliament against a Bill calling for the admission of women to Scottish universities. Across Scotland, similarly enlightened academics organised a number of classes for women, and were clearly tapping into a major seam of demand for such provision. Their working alliance with female campaigners for access led to the establishment of formal associations for women's higher education, in Edinburgh in 1876 and Glasgow in 1877. In Glasgow, the courses organised by its association had comparatively high fees: the charge was one guinea for a course of twelve lectures, although – acknowledging the increased demand for teachers created by the 1872 Education Act – students preparing for the 'profession of education' were offered discounts of 50 per cent. High fees had the twin effects of encouraging serious study and – although a few bursaries were available to gifted students – giving the association a distinctly middle-class character. Within a few years its mission attracted substantial endowments and led to the establishment of Queen Margaret College, a women-only institution that mirrored much of Glasgow University's curriculum but was not permitted to award degrees until after the full admission of women to Scottish universities in 1892.

Several of the academics who sought to address gender inequities in access to higher education were also concerned with facilitating greater working-class access. Anderson has shown how the Scottish universities were more open to working-class students than their English counterparts: this stemmed primarily from their urban location, comparatively low fees and the fact that until late in the nineteenth century matriculation was not compulsory. However, as Anderson also points out, many of these students were from the upper echelons of the working class, very often the sons of well-paid, skilled artisans. In an example of an attempt to reach further into the heart of the proletariat, William Smart, president of the Glasgow Ruskin Society, tried to arrange a series of lectures for workers in Bridgeton Cross Hall but found that most of his audience were proponents of land nationalisation who came to teach him.[27] These two challenging aspects of nineteenth-century access to higher education – gender and class – led to the birth of the university extension movement, a model of educational provision particularly associated with the universities of Oxford, Cambridge and London. Responding primarily to a groundswell of interest in women's education, the movement effectively began in 1873 when James Stuart, a Scottish-born Cambridge don who had experimented in extension in the north of England, was appointed as the first secretary of Cambridge's Local Lectures Syndicate. Extension involved universities sending out peripatetic lecturers to deliver lectures – at a similar level to higher education – in systematic courses organised by local associations. In England, the movement remained active until the early twentieth century and, although it generally failed to reach the working classes, it is credited with extending some important educational opportunities to women, particularly young teachers. A similar movement was founded in Scotland but lasted for only a few years, a failure that has been attributed to the more democratic nature of Scotland's universities and a resulting lack of demand. However, recent research has suggested that extension did not fail simply because of lack of interest but, rather, because of a combination of factors including limited university resources and the complete failure of the institutions involved to co-operate with one another.[28] There was, in fact, significant demand for extension courses – an interpretation supported by the Educational Institute of Scotland's explicit endorsement of extension as a vehicle for delivering education to young pupil-teachers in more remote areas, and by high levels of initial interest, notably in Perth, where more than 600 students attended it first four courses in 1887–8.[29] The extent of demand for extra-mural higher education is also evidenced by the success and international renown of Patrick Geddes's summer schools in Edinburgh, and the remarkable popularity and longevity of St Andrews University's LLA (Lady Literate in Arts) university-level distance-learning scheme.[30] Rather than lack of demand, the problems extension faced in Scotland were actually very similar to those the English movement encountered. First, whilst the educational value of many extension courses was certainly high, their credential worth was tenuous. In England, successful completion of certain extension courses led to Queen's Scholarships for teacher training, but although this was called for in Scotland, no similar opportunity was provided. The universities were largely responsible for this: they refused to give the extension courses explicit recognition and insisted that they were only university courses 'by asso-ciation'. Second, extension faced difficulties with the continuity of its courses; it was often very difficult to provide successive courses that were linked to and built upon each other. Thus Perth's Co-operative members – who had donated £20 to the establishment of the Perth University Education Society – were able to study political economy during the first session but quickly lost interest as succeeding courses offered in the 'non-science' strand favoured literary subjects, and pre-sented little opportunity to develop their interests. Third, extension encountered a plethora of organisational and administrative difficulties, not least the recruit-ment and retention of appropriate talented lecturers. The range of problems was similar in England, but the movement there was sustained by small but effective administrative structures – such as the Cambridge Syndicate – established by Cambridge, Oxford and London Universities. In 1887, a General Committee for the Extension of University Teaching in Scotland was established in Edinburgh, largely through the efforts of Patrick Geddes, and might have provided such vital administrative support to extension in Scotland. Although it took part in the meeting, Glasgow University quickly signalled that it wished to play little part in any such national body, and for the next few years it and St Andrews, the two universities most heavily involved in extension, disagreed over territorial boundaries for course provision and ignored pleas from advocates of extension for them to work together. Undoubtedly, Scotland's universities were under very significant financial and administrative pressure at this time, but their myopia in relation to national organisation and co-operation – developments that would have enabled them to pool their limited financial resources and share their most talented and committed lecturers – substantially undermined Scottish extension and is, therefore, one of the most significant reasons for its early demise.[31]

In the early twentieth century disenchantment with the overall failure of university extension to reach the working classes led to the foundation of the Workers' Educational Association (WEA). Following the recommendations of the 1908 Report on Oxford and Working-Class Education, and in direct partner-ship with the universities (notably Oxford), the WEA began to deliver intensive three-year courses of study targeted explicitly at working-class adult students. This 'tutorial class movement' provided access to university-level study to a sig-nificant number of able working-class students, several of whom became impor-tant figures within the Labour party. Though certainly not without its ideological critics, it arguably represented the apogee of the direct relationship between universities and working-class adult education, an association Harold Wiltshire famously described as 'The Great Tradition'. However, the WEA struggled to gain a foothold in Scotland where, as Turner suggests, it faced three particular difficulties.[32]

First, working-class access to university education in Scotland was rather less restricted than in England, and was enhanced by the provision of Carnegie scholarships to able students after 1904. Second, while the WEA and its univer-sity partners in England gained direct government funding for tutorial classes through the award of 'Responsible Body Status', no such early recognition and support was given to the Scottish WEA. In reluctant evidence given to the 1919 Ministry of Reconstruction committee, the Scottish Education Department (SED) signalled a belief – arguably rooted in the pervasive myth of egalitarian education mentioned above – that such provision was wholly unnecessary in Scotland and the WEA received no direct funding from the SED until 1952. A third impediment the WEA faced in Scotland was the opposition of a strong tradition of independent working-class education. The project of working-class educational provision inspired by the Owenite and Chartist movements of the mid-nineteenth century was taken up by a number of small secular bodies like the Eclectic Society in Glasgow and – most significantly – by the rapidly growing co-operative societies many of which set aside funds for educational provision. Towards the end of the century, new socialist organisations – notably the Social Democratic Federation (SDF) – provided opportunities for workers to study economics and history from a predominantly Marxist perspective and were particularly active in the industrial west of Scotland and the mining heartland of Fife. It was from this milieu that a particularly radical strand of independent proletarian education was to emerge: it reached its zenith during and immediately after the First World War and is particularly associated with the work of John Maclean. Maclean, a graduate of Glasgow University, began to teach economics for the SDF in 1906 and became increasingly radicalised by the wave of industrial unrest in the years immediately preceding the war, by the nature of war itself and by the acrimonious character of industrial relations on Clydeside at its end. Maclean proved to be an inspirational teacher and regularly attracted large audiences to his lectures on Marxist economics; he established a residential Scottish Labour College in Glasgow in 1919. To Maclean and others involved in independent education, the WEA represented an educational arm of the status quo, whose avowed co-operation with universities and the establishment could only serve to provide an ideological counter to socialism. Although, in the immediate post-war period, independent working-class education in Scotland certainly appeared to be more popular than the liberal education offered by the WEA, it would be simplistic to argue that this suggests there was little demand for less politically orientated education in Scotland; it is arguably the case that the WEA was rather more significantly undermined by the absence of direct funding. In the 1920s, the growing involvement of Scottish universities in adult education pointed to the existence of significant demand for liberal adult education and, at the same time, offered an important lifeline to the WEA. Under the auspices of A. D. Lindsay, Glasgow University established an extra-mural committee in 1924, and Edinburgh University followed suit in 1929. In the subsequent decades, often working closely with the WEA, the universities' extra-mural committees steadily developed their provision of non-vocational adult education.

Another experiment in adult education, one of whose explicit aims was to steer working men away from socialism, was the residential college at Newbattle Abbey founded by the Liberal peer Lord Lothian in 1937. Inspired by Grundtvig's

Danish Folk Schools and Harlech College in Wales, and under the guidance of its first warden, the Reverend Alexander Fraser, the college had a distinctly religious agenda and focused on turning young working-class men and women into well-rounded citizens. It struggled financially and had some difficulty attracting appropriate working-class students, some of whom were deterred by the college's opposition to socialism and its religious character.[33] As it was beginning to make some important steps in the development of interactive adult education practice, it was given over to military use at the outbreak of war in 1939 and did not return to its normal role until 1950. The war also saw the involvement of the WEA in educational provision for the armed forces as a partner in the Central Advisory Council and this contributed to the movement away from tutorial classes towards short courses. Founded in 1949, the Scottish Institute of Adult of Education continued to forge links between the universities, the WEA, trade unions, churches and local government. Thus by the end of our period there was arguably a growing element of homogeneity in the characteristics of adult education provision across the United Kingdom: in both England and Scotland, higher 'liberal arts' classes were almost exclusively provided by university extra-mural departments, often in close collaboration with WEA branches, while technical and further education colleges focused primarily on vocational and recreational education.

A Distinctive Mission?

This brief overview of two centuries of adult education shows that there were strong parallels between the forms of provision in Scotland and the rest of Britain, and this might initially seem to undermine the case for it having a particularly distinctive mission. However, if viewed from the slightly different perspective of the extent of Scotland's influence on adult education elsewhere, a stronger case for a distinctive mission – or approach – can be made. Autodidactic learning and culture – which provided so many working-class adults with a first glimpse of what they were excluded from both educationally and in terms of social justice – has been central to the development of adult education and, as Rose points out, particularly flourished during the eighteenth century in the Scottish Lowlands, an area which had one of the highest literacy rates in the world. Mutual improvement added a social and collective dimension to autodidactic learning and, for Rose, it is 'hardly surprising' that it originated in Scotland.[34] As adult education began to enter more formal settings, Scottish influence was also clearly evident: Birkbeck took his Scottish model for mechanics' institutes to England, and James Stuart, pioneer of university extension, asserted that one of his aims was to introduce some of the openness of the Scottish higher education system to England. Edward Caird, who had vigorously championed women's access to higher education in Scotland, became master of Balliol College, Oxford in 1893 and continued to build the college's links with the wider society. Balliol was at the heart of the partnership between Oxford and the WEA that led to the creation of the tutorial class movement, and the college's connection with Scottish higher education was further reinforced when A. D. Lindsay – a passionate supporter of adult education who, during his time in Glasgow, had delivered lectures on political economy to militant Clyde shipyard workers – became its master in 1924.

Despite some romantic exaggeration of the prevalence of the ladder of opportunity Scotland's schools offered the nation's children, and George Davie's contested elegy for the lost 'democratic intellect' of its nineteenth-century universities, there can be little doubt that Scottish education in this period had characteristics that distinguished it significantly from education elsewhere in the United Kingdom. The educational culture these characteristics shaped gave adult education in Scotland a distinctive mission, a mission that was clearly mirrored in developments in England. Here, as in several other contemporary aspects of Scotland's international influence, it was largely through the diaspora of its people that this mission was carried beyond its borders.

Notes

1. See, for example, Robert Anderson, 'In search of the "lad of parts": The mythical history of Scottish education', in A. Cooke, I. Donnachie, A. McSween and C. A. Whatley (eds), *Modern Scottish History 1707 to the Present, Volume 4: Readings 1850 to the Present* (Tuckwell Press, 1998), pp. 271–81.
2. Lindsay Paterson, *Scottish Education in the Twentieth Century* (Edinburgh University Press, 2003), pp. 5–7.
3. Anthony Cooke, *From Popular Enlightenment to Lifelong Learning: A History of Adult education in Scotland 1707–2005* (NIACE, 2006).
4. R. D. Anderson, 'Scottish universities', in Heather Holmes (ed.), *Institutions of Scotland: Education*, Scottish Life and Society: A Compendium of Scottish Ethnology, vol. 11 (Tuckwell Press, 2000), pp. 157–8.
5. Cooke, *From Popular Enlightenment*, p. 51.
6. Jonathan Rose, *The Intellectual Life of the British Working Classes*, 2nd edn (Yale University Press, 2010), p. 16.
7. John Sinclair, *The Statistical Account of Scotland*, 21 vols (William Creech, 1791–9), vol. 3, pp. 597–600.
8. Rose, *Intellectual Life*, p. 59.
9. Cooke, *From Popular Enlightenment*, p. 45.
10. Roger Fieldhouse and Associates, *A History of Modern British Adult Education* (NIACE, 1996), pp. 11–12.
11. Harold Silver, *The Concept of Popular Education: A Study of Ideas and Social Movements in the Early Nineteenth Century* (Macgibbon and Kee, 1965), p. 211.
12. Ibid., p. 212.
13. Richard Johnson, 'Really useful knowledge 1790–1850: Memories for education in the 1980s', in T. Lovett (ed.), *Radical Approaches to Adult Education* (Routledge, 1988).
14. Cooke, *From Popular Enlightenment*, p. 52.
15. Ibid., p. 58.
16. Edward Royle, 'Mechanics' Institutes and the working classes 1840–1860', *Historical Journal* 14(2) (1971), 320.
17. Thomas Kelly, *A History of Adult Education in Britain*, 3rd eds (Liverpool University Press, 1992), p. 120.
18. Cooke, *From Popular Enlightenment*, p. 58.

19. Fieldhouse, *A History*, p. 29.
20. Ibid., p. 48.
21. Silver, *The Concept of Popular Education*, p. 203.
22. Jean Barr, *The Stranger Within: On the Idea of an Educated Public* (Sense Publishers, 2008), p. 94.
23. Cooke, *From Popular Enlightenment*, p. 50.
24. Rose, *Intellectual Life*, pp. 36–7.
25. Ibid., p. 36.
26. Sarah J. Smith, 'Retaking the register: Women's higher education in Glasgow and beyond, c. 1796–1845', *Gender and History* 12 (2000), 321–5.
27. Douglas Sutherland, 'University extension in Scotland c.1886–96' (unpublished MPhil dissertation, University of Glasgow, 2007), 36–7.
28. Ibid., 74–89.
29. Ibid, 68.
30. On the LLA see Elisabeth Smith, 'To walk upon the grass: The impact of the University of St Andrews Lady Literate in Arts 1877–1892' (unpublished PhD dissertation, University of St Andrews, 2014).
31. Sutherland, 'University extension', 74–89.
32. Robert Turner, 'Workers' Educational Association tutorial classes and citizenship in Scotland, 1907–1939', *History of Education* 38(3) (2009), 375–9.
33. Cooke, *From Popular Enlightenment*, p. 146.
34. Rose, *Intellectual Life*, pp. 16, 59.

Bibliography

Anderson, R. D., *Education and Opportunity in Victorian Scotland* (Clarendon Press, 1983).

Anderson, R. D., 'Scottish universities', in Heather Holmes (ed.), *Institutions of Scotland: Education*, Scottish Life and Society: A Compendium of Scottish Ethnology, vol. 11 (Tuckwell Press, 2000), pp. 154–74.

Barr, Jean, *The Stranger Within: On the Idea of an Educated Public* (Sense Publishers, 2008).

Cooke, Anthony, *From Popular Enlightenment to Lifelong Learning: A History of Adult Education in Scotland 1707–2005* (NIACE, 2005).

Fieldhouse, Roger and Associates, *A History of Modern British Adult Education* (NIACE, 1996).

Paterson, Lindsay, *Scottish Education in the Twentieth Century* (Edinburgh University Press, 2003).

Rose, Jonathan, *The Intellectual Life of the British Working Classes*, 2nd edn (Yale University Press, 2010).

Silver, Harold, *The Concept of Popular Education: A Study of Ideas and Social Movements in the Early Nineteenth Century* (Macgibbon and Kee, 1965).

15

The Universities and National Identity in the Long Nineteenth Century, c. 1830–1914

Robert Anderson and Stuart Wallace

Introduction

I should like to point out the difference between the Scotch and English
Universities and the importance of trying to get hold of the Universities
in the national spirit in which they are viewed in Scotland. The English
Universities . . . may be roughly said to teach men how to spend 1,000 a year
with dignity and intelligence while the Scotch Universities teach them how to
make 1,000 a year with dignity and intelligence. That has been the success of
the Scotch Universities. The teaching Universities in England have one student
to every 3,500 of the population; in Ireland there is one student to 2,040 of the
population; while in Scotland there is one University student to 580 of the
population. Therefore, the roots of University education have gone wider and
broader among the people of Scotland than they have done either in England
or in Ireland. The object has always been to try and evolve brain power from all
capable citizens, and it is this which has made Scotland what it is. Every man
in Scotland knows that by the numerous bursaries and scholarships that are
provided he can, if he has any brain power at all, get a University to develop
it; and . . . this has done more to make Scotland peaceable and prosperous and
the Scotch citizens successful in every part of the world than anything else in
connection with our history.[1]

These were the words of the scientist and politician Lyon Playfair, speaking in
the House of Commons in 1889. Playfair used themes that were constantly
repeated when nineteenth-century Scots discussed their universities.[2] They were
seen as national and 'popular' institutions, serving the whole community, without
religious tests for students, and open to talent wherever it might be found. They
were part of a national educational system, linked directly with the parish schools
which had provided opportunities for social mobility as well as widespread literacy since the seventeenth century. Their influence percolated throughout the
country, with a university-trained minister and a teacher capable of preparing

boys for university entry in every parish. Unlike Oxford and Cambridge, they gave effective professional training in law, medicine and divinity, combining this with a broad general education and preparing Scots for successful careers outside as well as within Scotland. They were public not private institutions, and were supported financially by the state;[3] fees were charged – traditionally three guineas a year for non-medical courses – but living expenses were modest because the universities were urban and non-residential. In 1854, a German observer estimated the cost of studying at Edinburgh at about £100 a year, higher than at Glasgow (£70), St Andrews or Aberdeen (both £50), but only half the cost of Cambridge (£200) and one-third the cost of Oxford (£300).[4]

These features were recognised by both English and continental observers as characteristic of the institutional identity of the Scottish universities, and seen by educated Scots as clear evidence of their superiority, not simply in making higher instruction accessible and cheap, but also in following the historic model of the European university, from which Oxford and Cambridge had departed. It was with the English universities – expensive, restricted to Anglicans and largely the preserve of the aristocratic and wealthy – that the Scottish universities were most obviously contrasted.

National Identity and National Character

The nineteenth century was the age of nationalism in Europe, and education was commonly used to create and strengthen national loyalties, whether in newly united countries like Germany and Italy, or among peoples striving for independence. In many parts of Europe contests over the control of universities, or the language in which they should teach, were at the heart of nationalist campaigns. Some subjects, notably history and the study of modern literature, were subordinated to patriotic ends.[5] But the patterns characteristic of small nations throughout Europe are difficult to apply to Scotland. Ethnic and linguistic factors, often taken as the defining characteristics of a nation, did not clearly distinguish Scotland from England, and most Scots were content with the Union of 1707; political loyalties were focused on Britain and its constitution, and beyond that on the 'greater Britain' of the empire in which Scotland was a partner. The universities were safeguarded in the Act of Union, and were part of the complex of institutions – church, law and education – which remained under local control. Through this autonomy, said the historian Richard Lodge in 1898, 'Scotland has retained its national existence and its national identity in spite of the Union'.[6] Modern historians and sociologists, who have made national identity a central interpretative concept since the 1980s, have agreed that in Scotland's case, in the absence of political nationalism, this rested primarily on the nation's culture and institutions.

Lodge's use of the phrase 'national identity' was unusual, but the terms 'nationality' and, even more, 'national character' were commonplace. The idea of national character lent itself to ahistorical stereotypes, and the universities were linked with two common ideas of the Scottish character, found time and again in celebratory speeches and in literary accounts of Scottish life. The first was the stereotype of the enterprising, practical, thrifty, hard-headed Scot. Scottish students worked hard, lived frugally and had their eyes fixed on a career. 'In the history of the University of Edinburgh, we may clearly trace the national character of Scotland', William Gladstone noted in his rectorial address in 1860:

> we find there all that hardy energy, that gift of extracting much from little, and husbanding every available provision – of supplying the defects of external appliances and means from within by the augmented effort and courage of man, that power to make an ungenial climate smile, and a hungry soil teem with all the bounties of Providence, which have given to Scotland a place and a name among men so far beyond what was due to her geographical extent or to her natural resources.[7]

Ten years later, at the opening of Glasgow University's new buildings, the theologian John Caird was equally florid. Glasgow University

> has struck its roots deep into the soil of our national life, and with the other and kindred educational institutions has rendered Scotland, long one of the poorest of European nations in material wealth, one of the foremost in intelligence and civilisation, an institution which has contributed to the formation of that type of character, that sobriety of mind, reasonableness, steadiness, sagacity, sturdy independence, self-reliance, not unrelieved by quiet humour or ungraced by the love of poetry and song – that peculiar combination of qualities, intellectual and moral, which renders the typical Scotchman remarkable all over the world.[8]

The quintessence of this type was the 'lad o' parts', the boy from a relatively obscure background who rose through education to professional success. This was one of those powerful and enduring images which turn complex realities into national myths. The 'lad o' parts' was in part a literary construction, and the term itself did not appear until 1894, but the idea was an old one.[9] It was a very masculine ideal, and also a very Protestant one, seeing the Reformation as the source of modern Scotland's vigour and identity.

Calvinism also lay behind the second stereotype, the 'metaphysical' Scot, a lover of argument and speculation, always inclined to see issues in terms of abstract principle. The Edinburgh lawyer and university reformer James Lorimer, in an 1860 article on Scottish nationality, contrasted English empiricism with the 'more general thoughtfulness of the Scotch as a nation'. 'The Scotchman is more conscious and less spontaneous than the Englishman', and has

> a tendency to run into logical extremes, and to carry out principles with a rigour and exclusiveness which shut out many of the incidental considerations which come to be important in shaping a course of action. This tendency, which is thoroughly un-English, constituted the chief point of resemblance between the Scotch and their ancient allies the French. It exhibits itself both in politics and religion.[10]

For Lorimer and others, the preservation of this distinctive intellectual tradition depended on the university arts curriculum, whose philosophical and general-ised emphasis was contrasted with the more specialised studies of Oxford and Cambridge.

The Early Nineteenth Century

After 1707 the Scottish universities developed along their own lines without intervention from the state. As David Allan's chapter shows, the new professorial system enabled them to expand their teaching to appeal to a wide clientele, and was the basis of their role in the Scottish Enlightenment. Edinburgh and Glasgow also developed medical schools of international renown, and for many years the only effective medical degrees in Britain were those of the Scottish universities. Chairs of chemistry, originally introduced to serve medicine, now contributed to Scotland's agricultural and industrial progress. Edinburgh had a chair of agricul-ture as early as 1790, and Glasgow a chair of engineering from 1840.

The universities continued to train the Presbyterian clergy, and for students aiming at a clerical career there was a prescribed four-year curriculum based on six subjects: Latin, Greek, mathematics, logic, moral philosophy and natural philosophy (roughly equivalent to physics, but with a mathematical rather than experimental emphasis). Completing the course was enough, and formal gradu-ation in arts became unusual. The lecture system – fees were paid separately for each course, and collected directly by the professors – allowed students to pick and choose, and part-time and occasional students were numerous, with a wide range of ages. Sixteen or seventeen was the typical age of entry by the 1860s, though younger boys might come direct from parish schools (Thomas Carlyle entered Edinburgh aged thirteen in 1809, and William Thomson, the future scientist Lord Kelvin, matriculated at Glasgow aged ten in 1834, but these were untypical cases). There were older men catching up with an interrupted educa-tion, and many who attended individual courses to suit their own purposes. At Glasgow and Edinburgh, there were young men in offices fitting lectures around their work, the sons of businessmen sent for a year or two of general education with no intention of taking a degree and members of the general public attracted by the reputation of individual professors. At Aberdeen and St Andrews, the standard curriculum was more regularly enforced, but it was widely agreed that the openness of the universities to all citizens was a national principle to be valued and defended.

Thus although the professorial system was a recent innovation, it soon came to be treated as part of an institutional identity which had always been rooted in Scottish soil. The Edinburgh philosopher William Hamilton contrasted it favour-ably, in a series of articles in the 1830s in the *Edinburgh Review*, with the closed collegiate systems of Oxford and Cambridge. The Scottish lecture system was in line with European traditions, and became a model, along with Germany, for new colleges elsewhere, notably University College London, founded in 1828 (as the 'University of London') by two Scots, Thomas Campbell and Henry Brougham, with the assistance of a third, Joseph Hume. In the English provinces, Owens College was founded at Manchester in 1851, and set the pattern for what would later be called the 'civic' universities, on a secular, urban, professorial and non-collegiate model.

Pressures for Reform

These new foundations, though perhaps a tribute to the Scottish universities, also threatened their educational dominance. Many students had come from outside Scotland, including Nonconformists from England and Wales and Irish Presbyterians, but these now had opportunities nearer home. In the golden age of the Scottish Enlightenment, Oxford and Cambridge had been intellectually stagnant, but were now reinvigorated by the stimulus of competitive honours examinations; by the 1850s, demands for modernisation were leading them to introduce new subjects, and parliamentary intervention opened them to non-Anglican students. The creation of three non-denominational university colleges in Ireland, federated as the Queen's University in 1850, removed another traditional source of recruitment. In London, University College had a rival in the Anglican King's College (1830), and from 1836 there was a University of London empowered to award degrees to these and other affiliated colleges. Most of these new colleges taught modern subjects still neglected in Scotland. At the same time, the development of medical schools based on the great London hospitals and leading to University of London medical degrees, and of similar schools in the English provinces and Ireland, seriously threatened Scotland's medical monopoly.

By the 1820s there were about 4,250 students in the Scottish universities, a very high figure for the time in relation to population.[11] But the picture also had a negative side. In 1826, a royal commission was appointed to investigate constitutional weaknesses and abuses which had long gone unreformed and which were increasingly targeted by critics. These included the financial control of Edinburgh University by the town council; the existence of two competing colleges at Aberdeen, Marischal and King's, each with degree-awarding status (so that Scotland could claim five universities); the precarious existence of St Andrews, which had fewer than 300 students; and the narrowly local and often nepotistic basis on which professors were appointed. The 1826 commission made radical proposals for overhauling the universities and imposing greater national uniformity, but no legislation followed, and these problems persisted until the Universities (Scotland) Act of 1858, the key measure of Victorian reform.

Pressures for change came from various quarters. In many respects the universities were still rooted in a rural Scotland now being overtaken by industrialisation and urbanisation. Situated in large cities (except for St Andrews), the Scottish universities were less insulated from these pressures than Oxford or Cambridge. Other trends included professionalisation, as careers in the expanding middle class came to depend on examinations and formal qualifications, and secularisation. Secularisation meant, in general terms, the decline of religious control of such areas of life as education, with the state moving in to supplement or replace the churches. In Scotland, the Disruption of 1843, the split in the Church of Scotland which led to the formation of the rival Free Church, had a direct impact on the universities. Divinity professors who joined the Free Church had to give up their university posts, and the new church founded its own divinity colleges in Edinburgh, Glasgow and Aberdeen. The religious test for lay professors, though it had never been strictly enforced, now became a political issue, and was abolished in 1853. The close relationship between the universities and the church, the institution which had perhaps been the dominant expression of Scottish national identity, was thus shaken.

The convergence of these pressures made the 1850s a period of intense debate on university issues. Change was necessary, on both institutional and intellectual fronts, but could it follow and develop Scottish traditions, and if so how? For many critics, Scots had become complacent about their educational superiority. Thomas Carlyle wrote to John Stuart Blackie in 1855, thanking him for his pamphlet *On the Advancement of Learning in Scotland*:

> You have told the poor Public there a good few home truths, such as they are not nearly often enough in the habit of hearing, – nay have not heard at all for a couple of generations back; the more is their misfortune, poor pot-bellied blockheads, drinking 'the Cause of Education' at public dinners, and asking all men, 'Did you ever know such a country for Education?' In a way disgusting to behold.[12]

In this pamphlet and other polemical writings Blackie, who was professor of Greek at Edinburgh, attacked the low intellectual level and neglect of scholarship in the Scottish universities. Blackie was typical of university reformers in focusing on the inadequate preparation and immaturity of students. For high student numbers reflected the fact that the Scottish universities performed functions filled by secondary schools in other countries. Students from rural parish schools knew some Latin, but otherwise their knowledge was rudimentary and for their benefit university lectures had to begin at a low level. Professorial lectures provided a general survey of their subjects, but specialised or advanced work was excluded from the official curriculum: as a university professor of Greek, Blackie had to begin with the alphabet.

Blackie was not alone in thinking that Scotland was falling woefully behind other countries in its contribution to science and scholarship. The other main reformer of the 1850s, James Lorimer, was the driving force behind the Association for the Improvement and Extension of the Scottish Universities, which did much to bring about legislation in 1858, and he wrote its manifesto *Scottish Universities Past, Present and Possible* (1853). Lorimer's particular aim was to expand the number of university chairs and to encourage 'learning' and specialised scholarship, with Germany as the model. Reformers had a consistent programme, first set out by the 1826 commission and not finally achieved until the 1890s. The key to progress was to raise the age of entry to seventeen or eighteen, with an entrance examination to test students' prior knowledge. University courses could then begin at a more appropriate level, and proceed to greater specialisation later. In effect, one or two years would be removed from the beginning of the university curriculum and transferred to secondary schools, and a year or two added at the end to allow more advanced work. The development of secondary education was thus an integral part of the reform programme. The proposed compulsory entrance examination was particularly controversial, because it was feared that breaking the direct link with parish schools and excluding younger (and older) students would limit the openness to all seen as central to the Scottish tradition. Greater specialisation was also resisted as a threat to the general, philosophical nature of the Scottish arts curriculum.

University Reform and 'Nationality'

Many of those who wrote about university reform at this time also reflected on Scottish 'nationality'. Competition with England was one spur to reform, but equally important was the influence of Germany. The German secondary school, the *Gymnasium*, and the school-leaving examination essential for university entry, the *Abitur*, were the models. German universities were now setting the pace in science and scholarship for the whole of Europe, and an increasing number of Scottish academics spent a period of study there – notably in classics, theology, medicine and the natural sciences.[13] They began to absorb the principle, laid down by the founder of Berlin University Wilhelm Humboldt, that a true university must not simply award qualifications or prepare for careers, but combine teaching and research in the advancement of knowledge. Blackie studied in Göttingen and Berlin in his youth, and became a passionate Germanophile. Lorimer had studied in Bonn and Berlin, as well as (more unusually) Geneva. Lyon Playfair was a chemist who studied at Giessen under the celebrated Justus Liebig, and was a champion of German-style technical education before becoming professor at Edinburgh and then, in 1868, MP for a Scottish university seat.

Familiarity with Germany encouraged Scots to think about how their own universities were distinctive, but also about their deficiencies. They were aware of the criticisms of experts like V. A. Huber and L. A. Wiese, both much cited by Blackie, whose reports on British universities were translated into English in 1843 and 1854 respectively. They admired the financial support given by the state in Germany, especially in Prussia, to science and higher education. More generally, they were influenced by the emphasis in German idealist thought on the 'organic' nature of nations and their historical embodiment in ancient but continually evolving institutions and traditions. Thus for Alexander Campbell Fraser, professor of moral philosophy at Edinburgh, 'the university is the nation or the community operating in and through its highest appropriate organ of self-culture'. Fraser admired Germany as 'the brain of Europe'.[14] Such ideas were familiar to a later generation of Germanophiles including James Donaldson, a powerful figure in the university world as principal of St Andrews between 1886 and 1915 and a champion of the positive role of the state, and the Liberal politician Richard Haldane, a pupil of Fraser at Edinburgh, and deeply involved in university reform in England and Wales. 'It is in the Universities, with their power over the mind . . . that we see how the soul of a people at its highest mirrors itself', Haldane declared in 1910.[15]

For Lorimer, nationality was 'not political, or even institutional, but social, and, above all, intellectual'. It followed that if Scotland was to retain 'a distinctive and individual position amongst the nations of Europe' it was on the 'educational institutions of Scotland . . . that Scottish nationality, if it is to be intellectual, must be mainly dependent for its life'.[16] University reform should not mean assimilation to the English pattern – though, unusually, Lorimer was keen to introduce residential colleges and personal tuition to supplement professorial lectures – but a renewal of Scottish traditions. William Brown, professor of divinity at St Andrews, also called for more generous financial treatment by the state, and argued in 1855 that only as public establishments could universities be effective in 'training the national mind. Guaranteed in their permanence and independence, the life within them grows in its native soil, breathes its own native atmosphere', and shapes 'the distinctive features of our national character, its intellectuality, its high moral tone, its thoughtfulness, its discreet soberness, its utter abhorrence of fanatical extravagance'.[17] 'Perhaps the Scottish universities', said Campbell Fraser,

> from their genius and history, are fitted to keep a place intermediate between the ancient universities of England and the modern universities of Protestant Germany. Like those of England, they have a history of their own, which binds them to the past; while the practical character of the people and their own, saves them from becoming mere manufacturers of intellect, and enables them to blend . . . with the active and political life of the nation.

Like other reformers, Fraser thought it essential to encourage graduation and give graduates a say in university government, so that alumni would identify permanently with their universities; with this involvement of the educated public, the universities would 'recover their place as centres of national unity, that Scotland may, through them, preserve her intellectual distinction in Europe'.[18]

The Universities Act of 1858

When legislation came about in 1858, therefore, there was widespread expectation that it would provide a Scottish solution. The Universities (Scotland) Act was prepared by the Liberal lord advocate James Moncreiff and put through by his Conservative successor John Inglis. It thus represented a Scottish consensus. In 1857, Inglis had stressed that reform should be in the hands of 'those who know the Scottish Universities experimentally, and who are fully alive to both the existence and the value of the peculiarities which distinguish them from those of other countries',[19] and he chaired the temporary executive commission, drawn from the Scottish legal and political establishment, which implemented the act in detail. Many aspects of their work stood the test of time. Constitutional powers were now divided between the Court, the ultimate governing body representing various university interests and chaired by the student-elected rector, and the Senate, responsible for strictly academic matters. The Court included representatives of the General Council, theoretically composed of all graduates, though in practice the council meetings became a forum for local activists.

The act ended the control of Edinburgh University by the town council, and created a united University of Aberdeen. A striking feature of the reforms was the imposition of uniformity, in both constitutions and curricula, reflecting the idea that the universities formed a single national system, each serving its own city and region rather than competing with the others. The act even contained a clause supported by Gladstone envisaging a National University of Scotland, of which the four universities would become colleges. This depended on their consent, which made it a non-starter, but there was quite wide support for a national examining board to ensure common standards, and Playfair later suggested a General University Court, where university delegates would meet to discuss national policy.[20]

One successful achievement was the commission's overhaul of the professional faculties of divinity, law and medicine. Medical education expanded rapidly, and dominated the Scottish universities in the late nineteenth century more than before or since. In 1861, the universities had 3,399 students, of whom 986 were in medicine (29 per cent). By 1889, there were 6,854 students, of whom 3,239 were in medicine (47 per cent); at Edinburgh, 56 per cent of the students were medical.[21] Medical education in Scotland relied more on professorial lectures than the English hospital schools, and the Scottish-trained doctor remained a recognisable social type. Medicine was also the main attraction for overseas students, most of whom now came from countries in the 'white' British empire.

Arthur Conan Doyle, an Edinburgh medical graduate of 1881, pictured his alma mater in an early novel as

> a great unsympathetic machine, taking in a stream of raw-boned cartilaginous youths at one end, and turning them out at the other as learned divines, astute lawyers, and skilful medical men. Of every thousand of the raw material about six hundred emerge at the other side. The remainder are broken in the process.[22]

Yet the university was, he later recalled, a practical preparation for life, since

> there is none of the atmosphere of an enlarged public school, as is the case in English Universities, but the student lives a free man in his own rooms with no restrictions of any sort. It ruins some and makes strong men of many.[23]

But this was to change soon after Doyle's years with the growth of 'corporate' student life, discussed in Catriona Macdonald's chapter: Students' Representative Councils, student unions, organised sport, student clubs and magazines, were innovations which influenced the growing English civic universities. Like them, the Scottish universities remained non-residential – there were a few not very successful experiments with halls of residence – but corporate life brought students out of their homes and lodgings into the mainstream of urban life.

Indeed, the period after 1858 saw a strengthening of the universities' links with their local communities, partly through the General Councils, partly through the emphasis on professional education. In the Scottish cities, unlike most English ones, professional and business elites commonly attended their local university, and took a close interest in its affairs. They had usually been to local schools as well, since the Scottish middle classes preferred day schools to boarding, and the development of secondary education forged close links between the universities of Edinburgh, Glasgow and Aberdeen and the leading schools of those cities. The universities demonstrated and celebrated their civic connections in the elaborate centenary ceremonies held by all four between 1884 and 1911.[24] Thus they combined a regional and civic identity with their common national role.

The Problem of the Arts Curriculum

On two related issues, the 1858 commission took decisions which were conservative and designed to preserve Scottish traditions, but which proved controversial. These were the nature of the arts curriculum, and the rejection of an entrance examination in order to preserve the link with the parish schools. Succeeding decades saw continual controversy between those who defended traditional practices against what was sometimes stigmatised as 'anglicisation', and those who argued that the Scottish universities must be modernised if they were to retain their reputation and compete both within Britain and internationally.

The uniformity of the MA curriculum was now reasserted. In the preceding years, curricula had diverged quite widely; at Glasgow, for example, a BA degree had been developed to attract students who did not wish to go through the full curriculum. Graduation in arts had become uncommon, and flexibility had been seen as a virtue. Now such local divergences were banned, and formal graduation was encouraged. English Literature was added to the standard subjects, making seven rather than six. Latin, Greek and mathematics were still to be taught in both first and second years, to keep the universities accessible to students with little advance preparation. There was a cautious move towards specialisation, as students who completed the curriculum could also take honours in one of four schools – classics, philosophy, mathematics or natural science. But even though the universities had chairs of botany, chemistry and natural history (mainly zoology, but covering geology until separate chairs were created), none of these sciences was included in the general curriculum, except at Aberdeen, where natural history made an eighth subject.

Inglis and his colleagues believed they were restating and clarifying the Scottish tradition. Several clear principles appear in their work. Teaching rather than research was seen as the main business of the university, and Lorimer's ambitious plans for new chairs were rejected. The 1858 Act was accompanied by increased state funding, but this was allocated to meet teaching

Figure 15.1 Degree-giving ceremony at Glasgow Jubilee, 1901. With permission of SCRAN.

needs. In Inglis's words, 'the pursuit of scientific research, and the cultivation of the highest scholarship' would be desirable if resources were available, but the great principle behind 'every sound theory of University education in this country' was that the universities existed for the students, not the professors. [25] The purpose of the MA was to give a general liberal education, complete in itself but also as a foundation for the professional faculties of law and divinity. Its aim

> is not the acquisition of knowledge for its own sake. It is the development and purification of the moral nature, the training and strengthening and energising of the intellectual powers; or, in other words, the formation of the character and the culture of the mind. [26]

For this the classics, philosophy and other tried and tested subjects were the best instruments. In the commissioners' thinking, the MA covered three types of study, each indispensable to a rounded education – classics, philosophy and science. This encyclopedic form of liberal education distinguished Scotland from Oxford and Cambridge, where classics and mathematics respectively were still the main basis of study. Philosophy was especially emphasised, as

> the long and successful cultivation of this branch of learning by the Scotch Universities has not only had the effect of producing those great metaphysical writers, whose European reputation has reflected the highest honour on Scotland, but has also exercised a special and most beneficial influence on the national character. [27]

In encouraging graduation, the 1858 commission was in line with the reform party, and the proportion of students graduating began to rise. But the inflexibility of the new MA curriculum soon came under attack. While Latin and Greek were still compulsory, other developing disciplines such as history, modern languages and economics were excluded. Training secondary teachers was an obvious role for the arts faculties, yet leading school subjects were not taught. Despite the distinction of many scientific professors, the natural sciences had only a marginal position. The universities responded to this by developing separate BSc degrees, but this fell short of giving science equal status. There was a telling contrast with medicine, where the Scottish universities had to compete internationally and could not ignore the latest scientific developments. They kept up by creating new chairs and lectureships, recognising new specialities, and building expensive laboratories and teaching facilities. In the arts degree, there was less competition, and resistance to change was easier.

From the 1860s to the 1880s, there were numerous proposals for introducing new subjects and allowing students some freedom of choice within a framework which would still preserve the traditional general approach. [28] A royal commission appointed in 1876 made radical proposals on these lines, but they were resisted by conservatives who argued for the unique virtues of the single curriculum. Yet as in the 1850s, reformers could argue that Scotland was being outpaced by England. Playfair, a member of the 1876 commission, told the House of Commons in 1889 that

> the English universities have adapted themselves largely to the changed condition of the world, and . . . in this respect the Scotch Universities remain much behind. The lion rampant of Scotland has been standing on its hind legs pawing the air, while the lion passant of England with its four feet on the ground has been going ahead.[29]

To retain their position the universities must extend their training to new professions, and the preparatory MA must be modernised accordingly. The civic colleges in England, expanding rapidly in the 1870s and 1880s, taught many practical and vocational subjects, and university colleges like Leeds, Sheffield or Birmingham had close links with local industry and business. But in Scotland various branches of applied science, along with subjects like art and commerce, developed outside the universities, and from 1900 selected technical and vocational colleges (which achieved university status later in the twentieth century) were financed as 'central institutions' by the Scotch Education Department (SED). The ancient universities began to seem old-fashioned, too narrowly focused on careers in the 'learned' professions, teaching and public service.

The response to several decades of criticism of the arts degree was a set of reforms following the Universities (Scotland) Act of 1889. The limited honours system of 1858 was replaced by the distinction between ordinary and honours degrees, with two years of common preparation, which remains familiar. New subjects were introduced, with corresponding chairs and lectureships, and though no single subject was now compulsory, the arts curriculum was structured so that students still normally took a language, a philosophy course and mathematics or science. Separate science faculties and degrees were created to give full scope to scientific subjects. The revised curriculum was generally thought to satisfy the Scottish principle of breadth of study, while allowing new disciplines to expand, though there were academic conservatives who regretted the abandonment of the old MA and the common culture which it embodied. For Herbert Grierson, professor of English at Aberdeen then Edinburgh, the dominating influence in 1889 'was that of men who were not deeply imbued with the spirit of the Scottish universities, and had no adequate faith in their capacity for development on the lines of the past'. He recalled his student days at Aberdeen, when everyone went through the curriculum as a 'single class'.[30] Grierson, writing in 1919, could romanticise the old curriculum once the practical problems it encountered had been remedied, just as nostalgia for dominies and lads o' parts had appeared only as the rural parish school passed into history.

Universities, Schools and Opportunity

The reform of the universities in 1858 came before the rapid development of schools which followed the Education (Scotland) Act of 1872. Controversies over school policy interacted with those over universities, and for a time the centrality of the universities to the national educational system seemed threat-ened. The new SED had no jurisdiction over universities, and gave priority to the expansion of elementary schools. Needing to recruit large numbers of modestly paid teachers (of whom a majority were now women), the SED preferred to concentrate their training in the colleges which it controlled, and refused a role to the chairs of education founded in 1876 at Edinburgh and St Andrews. There were also controversies, especially in the early years after 1872, over the teaching of Latin. Latin was traditionally seen as the link between school and university, and a key to social mobility. In other countries, the classics were the preserve of the social elite; in Scotland they were open to the people. The disappearance of the parish school as a distinct institution ended this tradition, which was always stronger in some areas – like the North-East – than others, but critics of the SED's utilitarianism continued to argue that elementary education needed an infusion of the liberal spirit of the university.

The trend, however, was to separate elementary and secondary education, and the latter greatly expanded, at first through the reform of endowed schools, mainly in the cities, then through state grants from 1892, and after 1899 by the SED's encouragement of 'higher grade' schools, which included both schools in smaller towns, and new urban schools linked to the elementary sector. The outcome of these changes was that instead of passing direct to the university, poor but promising pupils were transferred to secondary schools, and scholar-ships or free places replaced the previously rather haphazard chances offered to lads o' parts. As secondary schools developed their advanced teaching, the school leaving age rose steadily, and this made possible the enforcement of a university entrance examination in 1892. It corresponded to the School Leaving Certificate, usually taken at the age of seventeen, which the SED introduced in 1888. Few now entered the universities before that age, and full-time study for a degree became the norm.

In 1858, the admission of women to universities had not been on the agenda, and the question played no part in early debates on university reform. But from the 1870s there were girls' schools giving a full academic education, and univer-sity entrance seemed the next step. University-level lectures given by sympathetic professors began at the end of the 1860s, but legal obstacles delayed the admis-sion of women on equal terms until 1892. Even then prejudice against mixed classes allowed the Edinburgh medical school to exclude them. But after 1900 the number of women students rose significantly, and compensated for the loss of occasional and part-time students caused by the new entrance examination. In 1891, there were 6,604 students, all male; by 1913 there were 7,776 – 6,025 men and 1,751 women (23 per cent).[31] The admission of women, the expanded cur-riculum and changes in teacher training which encouraged prospective teachers to take degrees created a surge of students into the arts and science faculties, and brought schools and universities together again.

Defenders of national tradition sometimes claimed that these changes cut off opportunities for the talented poor. The evidence suggests there was some truth in this in the early years after 1872, but that by the early twentieth century democratic opportunity had been restored in a new form. University education was an elite experience, as it always had been, only reaching about 3 per cent of the age group, but data about the social backgrounds of students show that talented individuals could still climb the educational ladder.[32] Official apologists like John Struthers, secretary of the SED, claimed that in Scotland equality of opportunity was complete: 'It has been a tradition in Scotland from time immemorial ... that, to put it in the broadest way, no boy of ability should be deprived of an opportunity of making the best of his talents so far as circumstances admitted', and the new structure of secondary schools and scholarships, according to Struthers, was faithful to this tradition.[33] For the Scottish-American philanthropist Andrew Carnegie, whose Carnegie Trust paid university fees for Scottish students, 'No better reason than this can be given for the position which Scotland has attained among nations than that the aspiration of Knox has been fulfilled, and we have become beyond other nations an educated people'. Knox 'made Scotland a democracy while England remains a nation of caste'.[34]

British Dimensions

We have argued that the Scottish universities responded, as was inevitable, to the multiple pressures for change of the nineteenth century. Whether these responses were 'on the lines of the past' (Grierson) was something about which Scots could disagree. The extent of change was disguised by institutional continuity, which made it easier to see the Scottish universities as a single national system with its roots deep in history. There were four (or five) universities in 1800 and four in 1900 (or five: University College at Dundee was founded in 1883, but was soon 'affiliated' to St Andrews), and student numbers were already high in the early nineteenth century. In England, the foundation of new universities and a rapid increase of student numbers after 1870 made change more striking.

The themes illustrated in this chapter – universities as national institutions, democratic opportunity, the organic unity of Scottish education – remained the staples of debate in the early twentieth century. But in the 1850s, the universities still had a self-contained life, with only Oxford and Cambridge (and Germany) for contrast. By 1914, this uniqueness was diluted, as the Scottish universities became just one group – along with Oxbridge, London, the civic universities, Wales and Ireland – in a British system. There were influences in both directions, and Scotland was still the chief model for the professorial, non-residential university. But academics, like middle-class families planning careers, thought in British as well as Scottish terms. Most students were still born in Scotland and attended Scottish schools, but professorial chairs – except in law and divinity, which remained Scottish preserves – became part of a wider academic market. The growth of research as a university function encouraged academics to think in national or international terms, with loyalty to their discipline as much as their university.

Those disciplines themselves became less characteristically Scottish. This was clearest in the case of philosophy, where the intuitionist or 'common sense' school developed in eighteenth-century Scotland still had exponents until the 1890s but was superseded by influences with continental roots – the positivism of Comte, the idealism of Kant and Hegel. This did not take place without a struggle, and contests over appointments sometimes invoked patriotic arguments and appeals to the 'metaphysical' stereotype of national character.[35] Many university subjects, of course, had no national angle, especially in science and medicine, though there could be distinctive teaching traditions. As a classicist, Blackie included the traditional Scottish pronunciation of Latin and Greek among his many causes. More significantly, he took up the cause of the Highlands, and campaigned successfully to raise money for a chair of Celtic at Edinburgh, which was founded in 1882. Glasgow established a visiting lectureship in 1900, and a permanent one in 1906. But these posts concentrated on Gaelic scholarship and did not play a political role, unlike Celtic studies in Ireland.[36] There was a revival of interest in Celtic Scotland and its culture in the late nineteenth century, but it took place largely outside the universities. Besides, at a time when racial thinking was widespread, Lowland Scots often saw themselves as 'Teutons' and part of the Anglo-Saxon world, rather than as Celts.[37]

The British dimension was especially clear in history, which became a full subject in 1892, though constitutional history had been taught at Edinburgh with law since 1862. The new professors at Glasgow, Edinburgh and Aberdeen were Englishmen educated at Oxford or Cambridge, and brought with them the established orthodoxy of the discipline, which stressed the long-term development of the British state and constitution. Scotland had a role in this story, and history courses provided a scholarly rationale for unionism, but Scottish history was not given independent status until a chair was founded by endowment at Edinburgh in 1901. This was filled by Peter Hume Brown, who concentrated on careful scholarship, no doubt in reaction against the sentimental popular history of the time, and did not challenge the unionist consensus.[38]

In Glasgow a chair of Scottish history and literature was founded in 1913, but a historian, not a literary expert, was appointed to it. Edinburgh had had a chair of 'rhetoric' since 1762, and Scotland pioneered the teaching of English when neither Oxford nor Cambridge taught the subject. English literature became part of the MA curriculum after 1858, and an honours subject in 1892; but Scottish writers had only a marginal place in the literary syllabus, and there was no sense of Scottish literature as a connected tradition. Like the British constitution, the canon of English literature was seen as the common heritage of Scots and English, and as with history this idea was diffused widely through graduate schoolteachers. University English, it has been said, 'was tied to the maintenance and development of a national, Scoto-British ethos'. It was British with a 'Scottish inflection'.[39]

The Imperial Dimension

From the 1880s, a new imperialism was apparent in British politics, and became inseparable from the sense of British identity, giving Scots a special status as partners in the imperial enterprise. Imperial awareness was strong among students, not least for career reasons. The Scottish universities always produced more graduates than Scotland could absorb. Many students were interested in the Indian civil service and other branches of overseas service, and many more became doctors, ministers, missionaries, teachers, scientists, engineers or businessmen in the white 'dominions' or in Asia and Africa. The presence of students from those countries in the Scottish universities made the relationship reciprocal. The subject has been studied in detail only for Aberdeen, where it is estimated that over the period 1860–1925 at least a quarter of all graduates worked overseas.[40] At Edinburgh, an analysis of 19,501 graduates in 1933 showed that only 56 per cent lived in Scotland, 28 per cent in the rest of Britain and 17 per cent overseas, the largest contingents being in India and South Africa.[41] Expatriate alumni could join local graduates' associations, attend celebratory dinners and read news from their alma mater in the *Aberdeen University Review* (1913) or the *University of Edinburgh Journal* (1925). When they thought of the home country, their student days and the physical setting of their university evoked nostalgic memories. The universities thus contributed to 'diaspora' Scottish identity, as well as being part of the complex of cultural ties which held together the greater British world.

A barometer of student opinion was the triennial election of a rector. Elections were usually conducted on party lines, and most rectors were national politicians who confined their duties to an inaugural lecture. From 1880, imperial and proconsular figures became popular, including the Scottish-Canadian tycoon Lord Strathcona at Aberdeen, Haldane, Joseph Chamberlain, George Curzon and Winston Churchill. The Liberal imperialist Lord Rosebery achieved the unique feat of election at all four universities. Rectorial addresses often celebrated a British and imperial rather than Scottish identity, and stressed citizenship, duty and public service. Lord Balfour of Burleigh, Conservative Secretary for Scotland, entitled his address at Edinburgh in 1899 'University Training and National Character'. National character, he said, was more than the product of race or inherited tradition. It was 'a matter of intellectual and moral discipline', directly shaped by education. 'The Universities are really shrines, which the slow-working wisdom of the nation, and the long experience of the centuries, have established to be the guiding lights of intellectual progress.' They were 'nurseries of national spirit', and 'with the Scottish universities sooner than any others, the bond between them and the national life became a real and an active one'. University training, he told students, would help them to understand their duties and responsibilities as citizens, and to meet them

> with a national character strengthened, developed, and buttressed by intellectual training . . . Will you not be enabled to rise to the vast burdens of Empire,

Figure 15.2 Edinburgh University rifle volunteers around 1880. With permission of SCRAN.

to feel its grandeur, to rise to new enthusiasm for its great possibilities, and to new devotion to its service?[42]

Soon after Balfour of Burleigh's address, Britain went to war in South Africa, and Rosebery's rectorial at Glasgow in 1900 was an impassioned appeal for university graduates to work for the future of the empire.[43]

If called on to serve, said the Aberdeen student magazine, 'the sons of our Alma Mater will acquit themselves in a manner worthy both of British subjects and Scottish gentlemen'.[44] Few actually served in that war, but military 'volunteering' had been a popular student activity since the 1860s, and after 1908 most volunteer units became Officers' Training Corps. When the call did come in 1914, the universities were denuded of young men. August 1914, wrote the Edinburgh student magazine, would 'be hailed as a great month in our nation's great history, the month which issued in a new era of national development and national consciousness'. The British people were now 'knit together in a great project of sacrifice', a war 'for the vindication of abstract principles, for the preservation of national traditions, national honour and national ideals'.[45]

Conclusion

In the nineteenth century, 'national character' was a popular idea, but an oversimplified one which assumed that a single set of characteristics applied to all members of the nation. The modern concept of national identity is more useful because it allows for multiple, concentric and overlapping identities. Individuals could define their identity in relation to a city, a region such as the North-East, Scotland, Great Britain or the British empire, and universities as educational institutions could reflect and reinforce any or all of these. Moreover, as Lorimer perceived when writing about 'nationality' in 1860, the sense of national identity could take varying political, social, religious and cultural forms. This allowed the Scottish universities to develop on authentically national lines within the unionist political system. The compromises worked out in 1858 and 1889 lasted broadly until the 1960s, when the era of social democracy and the move from elite to mass higher education brought an entirely new set of pressures.

Notes

1. *Parliamentary Debates*, House of Commons, 20 June 1889, cols 381–2. Playfair's figures somewhat overstated the 'backwardness' of England.
2. Lindsay Paterson, 'Traditions of Scottish education', in Heather Holmes (ed.), *Institutions of Scotland: Education*, Scottish Life and Society: A Compendium of Scottish Ethnology, vol. 11 (Tuckwell Press, 2000), pp. 21–43; Donald Withrington, 'Scotland: A national educational system and ideals of citizenship', *Paedagogica Historica* 29 (1993), 699–710.
3. Robert Anderson, 'The state and university finance in modern Scotland', *Scottish Affairs* 85 (autumn 2013), 29–41.
4. L. A. Wiese, *German Letters on English Education* (Longmans, 1854), p. 131.

5. Robert Anderson, *European Universities from the Enlightenment to 1914* (Oxford University Press, 2004), esp. pp. 225–40.
6. Richard Lodge, *Some Problems of Scottish History* (Aird and Coghill, 1898), p. 17.
7. Archibald Stodart-Walker (ed.), *Rectorial Addresses Delivered Before the University of Edinburgh, 1859–1899* (Grant Richards, 1900), pp. 17–18.
8. *Introductory Addresses Delivered at the Opening of the University of Glasgow, Session 1870–71. With a Prefatory Notice of the New Buildings by Professor Allen Thomson, M.D.*(Blackwood, 1870), p. 15.
9. Robert Anderson, 'In search of the "lad of parts": The mythical history of Scottish education', *History Workshop* 19 (1985), 82–104.
10. [J. Lorimer], 'Scottish nationality – social and intellectual', *North British Review* 33(65) (1860), 71.
11. Robert D. Anderson, *Education and Opportunity in Victorian Scotland: Schools and Universities* (Clarendon Press, 1983), p. 347.
12. Stuart Wallace, *John Stuart Blackie, Scottish Scholar and Patriot* (Edinburgh University Press, 2006), pp. 223–4.
13. Stuart Wallace, 'The university and national identity: Scottish academics and German universities', in Martin Hewitt (ed.), *Scholarship in Victorian Britain* (Leeds Centre for Victorian Studies, 1998), pp. 14–26; Stuart Wallace, 'Scottish university men and German universities before 1914', in R. Muhs, J. Paulmann and W. Steinmetz (eds), *Aneignung und Abwehr. Interkultureller Transfer zwischen Deutschland und Grossbritannien im 19. Jahrhundert* (Philo, 1998), pp. 227–61.
14. [A. C. Fraser], 'The British universities and academical polity', *North British Review* 35(69) (1861), 4–5.
15. R. B. Haldane, *Universities and National Life: Three Addresses to Students* (John Murray, 1910), p. 31 (speech at Aberystwyth).
16. Lorimer, 'Scottish nationality', 57, 76.
17. William Brown, *The Scientific Character of the Scottish Universities, Viewed in Connection with Religious Belief and their Educational Use* (A. and C. Black, 1856), pp. 38–9.
18. Fraser, 'British universities', 12.
19. J. Inglis, *Inaugural Discourse Delivered to the Graduates of King's College, Aberdeen, on his Installation as Lord Rector, October 14, 1857* (Blackwood, 1857), p. 10.
20. Donald Withrington, 'The idea of a national university in Scotland, c. 1820–c. 1870', in Jennifer J. Carter and Donald J. Withrington (eds), *Scottish Universities: Distinctiveness and Diversity* (John Donald, 1992), pp. 40–55.
21. Anderson, *Education and Opportunity*, pp. 347–51.
22. Arthur Conan Doyle, *The Firm of Girdlestone: a Romance of the Unromantic*, new edn (Chatto and Windus, 1899 [1890]), p. 33.
23. Arthur Conan Doyle, *Memories and Adventures* (Hodder and Stoughton, 1924), pp. 23–4.
24. Robert Anderson, 'University centenary ceremonies in Scotland, 1884–1911', in P. Dhondt (ed.), *National, Nordic or European? Nineteenth-century University Jubilees and Nordic Cooperation* (Brill, 2011), pp. 241–64.
25. John Inglis, *Inaugural Address Delivered to the University of Edinburgh on his Installation as Chancellor, April 21, 1869* (Blackwood, 1869), p. 5.
26. John Inglis, *Inaugural Address Delivered to the University of Glasgow on his Installation as Lord Rector, March 22, 1866* (Blackwood, 1866), p. 27.
27. Parliamentary Papers 1863 XVI, *General Report of the Commissioners under the Universities (Scotland) Act, 1858*, p. xxix.
28. For a full account, see Anderson, *Education and Opportunity*, Chapters 3 and 7.

29. *Parliamentary Debates*, House of Commons, 20 June 1889, col. 383.
30. Herbert Grierson, 'The Scottish universities', in John Clarke (ed.), *Problems of National Education, by Twelve Scottish Educationists* (Macmillan, 1919), pp. 314, 317. Cf. Anderson, *Education and Opportunity*, pp. 282–3.
31. Anderson, *Education and Opportunity*, pp. 352–7.
32. Ibid., pp. 294–335.
33. Parliamentary Papers 1913 XVIII, *Royal Commission on the Civil Service: Appendix to Third Report*, p. 168.
34. *Educational News*, 5 September 1903 (speech at Kilmarnock).
35. The classic account is George Elder Davie, *The Democratic Intellect: Scotland and her Universities in the Nineteenth Century*, 2nd edn (Edinburgh University Press, 1964).
36. Donald E. Meek, 'From Magnus MacLean to Angus Matheson: Glasgow and the making of Celtic studies in Scotland'. Available at http://meekwrite.blogspot.co.uk/2013/03/celtic-studies-glasgow-and-making-of.html (accessed 21 September 2013).
37. Colin Kidd, 'Race, empire, and the limits of nineteenth-century Scottish nationhood', *Historical Journal* 46 (2003), 873–92.
38. Bruce P. Lenman, 'The teaching of Scottish history in the Scottish universities', *Scottish Historical Review* 52 (1973), 165–90; Robert Anderson, 'University history teaching, national identity and unionism in Scotland, 1862–1914', *Scottish Historical Review* 91 (2012), 1–41.
39. Robert Crawford, 'Scottish literature and English studies', in Robert Crawford (ed.), *The Scottish Invention of English Literature* (Cambridge University Press, 1998), p. 232.
40. John D. Hargreaves, *Academe and Empire: Some Overseas Connections of Aberdeen University, 1860–1970* (Aberdeen University Press, 1994), pp. 120–1.
41. Arthur L. Turner (ed.), *History of the University of Edinburgh, 1883–1933* (Oliver and Boyd, 1933), pp. 427–8.
42. Walker (ed.), *Rectorial Addresses*, pp. 328–30, 332.
43. Lord Rosebery, *Questions of Empire* (A. L. Humphreys, 1900).
44. *Alma Mater*, 7 February 1900.
45. D. P. Blades, 'Editorial', *The Student* 12(1) (1914), 3–4.

Bibliography

Anderson, R. D., *Education and Opportunity in Victorian Scotland* (Clarendon Press, 1983).
Anderson, R. D., 'In search of the "lad of parts": The mythical history of Scottish education', *History Workshop* 19 (1985), 82–104.
Carter, Jennifer J. and Donald J. Withrington (eds), *Scottish Universities: Distinctiveness and Diversity* (John Donald, 1992).
Davie, George Elder, *The Democratic Intellect: Scotland and her Universities in the Nineteenth Century*, 2nd edn (Edinburgh University Press, 1964).
Wallace, Stuart, 'National identity and the idea of the university in 19th-century Scotland', *Higher Education Perspectives* 2(1) (2006), 125–45.
Withrington, Donald J., 'Scotland: A national educational system and ideals of citizenship', *Paedagogica Historica* 29 (1993), 699–710.
Withrington, D., 'The Scottish universities: Living traditions? Old problems renewed?', in Lindsay Paterson and David McCrone (eds), *The Scottish Government Yearbook 1992* (Unit for the Study of Government in Scotland, 1992), pp. 131–41.

16

Alba Mater: Scottish University Students, 1889–1945

Catriona M. M. Macdonald

> The universities in Scotland do not fulfil the function of universities in other territories. They do not present Scotland to the world, nor the world to Scotland. They have nothing universal about them, they are mere provincial variants of the Anglocentric culture.
>
> Douglas Young, 'The Young idea', *Alba Mater*[1]

In the year that Aberdeen students voted the nationalist Eric Linklater their rector, Douglas Young demanded that Scottish universities ought to become 'truly Scottish and increasingly universal'.[2] The office of the rector has long been considered a barometer of student political opinion (the opportunity of this most unruly constituency to express a view on the world outwith the classroom), and yet the vote for Linklater ought not to be read necessarily as the endorsement by the student body of Young's fears of Anglicisation.[3] Linklater's 'old-boy' status at Aberdeen University and his reputation as a popular writer were significant. The very fact that his tenure followed that of a Labour politician (Stafford Cripps) and was followed by that of a Unionist peer (John Norman Stuart Buchan, the Second Baron Tweedsmuir) surely points to the fact that rectorial elections fail to point to a singular narrative in the politics of Scottish students. Over the years, prominent politicians have occupied the office in one or more of Scotland's universities: Glasgow alone boasted prime ministers Gladstone, Rosebery, Asquith, Bonar Law and Stanley Baldwin, while more recent generations of Edinburgh students elected Jo Grimond, David Steel and Tam Dalyell. The rectorship is thus an important means through which students contribute to the civic life of Scotland. That said, Scottish students have also used the office to confirm celebrity of another kind: St Andrews university students in the 1970s and 80s returned comedy actor John Cleese, satirist Alan Coren, comedy writer Frank Muir and comedian Tim Brooke-Taylor. To fully appreciate the meaning of these elections (if indeed there always is one beyond the logic – or whimsy – of the moment) it makes sense to view these choices as expressive of something in the lived experience of students, rather than as subtle (or less than subtle) indicators of the priorities of the next generation of the political elite. One ought to be wary of resting too much on universals that fail to acknowledge the transience of the student body and the inherent contradictions in its voice(s).

Democratic Intellect?

So it is with one of the central features of the myth of Scottish education – the 'democratic intellect'. For those intent on sustaining the belief that the Knoxian settlement of a school in every parish betokened an inclusive vision of education at the heart of the Scottish psyche, George Elder Davie's publication in 1961, *The Democratic Intellect: Scotland and her Universities in the Nineteenth Century*, appeared to offer the evidential base on which to ground claims of Scottish distinctiveness and the erosion in the late nineteenth century of core values – the casualties of a process of Anglicisation exemplified in the Scottish universities. His prose was forthright. According to Davie, Scots in this period 'looked up to England as the model in most departments of life', and 'despite certain grave misgivings, abandoned the attempt to regulate the higher education of their country according to their own ideals'.[4] In particular, Davie highlighted the diminished role that philosophy was to have in the arts curriculum that emerged in the last decade of the century, and proposed that this was symptomatic of 'assimilationist' tendencies in Scotland that undervalued the teaching approaches of the universities in the north and their characteristic products – 'the soberly intellectual but very adaptable Scot who made so big a mark at home and overseas in the age of reform'.[5] That Davie was writing in a period alert to the rhetoric of nationalist claims is important: between 1959 and 1970 the Scottish National Party share of the parliamentary vote grew from 0.8 per cent to 11.4 per cent at the same time as – following the Robbins report (1963) – the number of students in UK universities rose dramatically. If it had not been before, Scottish higher education was now a political issue.[6]

Yet Davie's focus was essentially on the arts curriculum of the universities rather than the composition of their intake: his emphasis fell on the intellect rather than the democracy of the institutions. Few commentators who make use of Davie's analysis, however, adopt such a narrow interpretation of the 'democratic intellect'. According to Chris Harvie, for example, the phrase 'meant the recruitment of a discursive elite from the widest social catchment area, through a widely diffused and open intellectual system, combining methodological rigour with an openness of agenda'.[7] In contrast, in 2000 Michael Gove, a decade before his appointment as England's Secretary of State for Education, suggested that the 'democratic intellect' was a contradictory Enlightenment principle encompassing both 'the belief that educational achievement is a surer sign of merit than any other badge of rank, and the feeling that the drawing of distinction, or creation of elites, is invidious'.[8] In part the conflation of these issues in popular readings of Davie's volume can be explained by his own misappropriation of a phrase – 'democratic intellectualism' – used by Walter Elliot, a long-serving

Scottish Unionist MP, who had coined it in a short essay in 1932.[9] Elliot's use of the term in 'The Scottish heritage in politics' – which is almost wholly about Scottish Presbyterianism – is contested, making (by association) Davie's use of it somewhat opaque. Elliot points to church government, not the universities, as illustrative of 'a fierce egalitarianism and a respect for intellectual pre-eminence, and a lust for argument on abstract issues'.[10] Indeed, Elliot's essay does not make one reference to the Scottish universities and is so replete with metaphors as to make his meaning at times obscure.

One of the most important consequences of this state of affairs has been the understandable tendency of scholars who, while claiming to respond to Davie, have tended to challenge a broader myth of educational inclusivity itself rather than simply Davie's specific philosophical points. For all that, however, the ensuing debate has had a transformative effect on our understanding of Scottish university education in the period 1889–1963. The work of R. D. Anderson and Lindsay Paterson in particular exemplifies the rigour of recent research on Scottish higher education in these years that has, in turn, cast new light on the polemical and (oftentimes) ahistorical quality of Davie's iconic text.[11]

Contemporary evidence would suggest that they have a point: opinion at the time of the 1889 Universities (Scotland) Act was far less complimentary of the Scottish universities than Davie, when he was writing some seventy years later.[12] A contributor to the *Cornhill Magazine* in 1878 commented critically on the short university sessions of five months' duration, while a year later a column in *All the Year Round* suggested that many thought of the Scottish university as little more than 'an unruly day school'.[13] While insensitive comparison with Oxford and Cambridge colleges may have been at the root of such criticism, others with a more intimate knowledge of the Scottish system were just as unforgiving. The merits of the pre-reform arts curriculum celebrated by Davie were caricatured in the 1880s by W. J. Douglas in his memories of his years at the University of Glasgow:

> For three guineas I shall learn logic, and that will teach me how to dissever truth from error. At the same moderate price I shall be taught philosophy, and then I shall be quite certain that I am I and nobody else. Three guineas will unlock for me the palaces of Greece, and other three the fortresses of Rome. For sixty-three shillings, paid in advance, I shall be shown how to become an orator like Burke, and a writer like Ruskin. For these few coins, too, I shall be taught the mathematics, and thus I will be able to measure the church spire without climbing to the top of it.[14]

The experience of students in these years seems to challenge Davie's defence of Scottish 'tradition'. In a series of pamphlets published between 1882 and 1883, Glasgow students complained how the amount of work demanded in the mathematics class offered 'few opportunities for the development of individual peculiarities'; compared the reading room to 'something between a Lancashire skittle-alley and a high-class bear garden'; and complained of the 'tyrannical power of the professors' and their own 'training in servility'.[15] Describing the Scottish university system as being in a state of 'senile decay', they reflected:

> Our Universities have forgotten the purpose for which they exist. They are not now places of education. They are not now national institutions existing for the benefit of the people. They are private shops, where professors indulge a lucrative trade.[16]

Clearly, in reality the universities fell short of the democratic ideals of future commentators, and feelings were also growing that they were simply unfit for purpose. In 1886, Douglas suggested that

> Until very lately the Scottish Universities cared nothing for modern languages. French, in their opinion, was only fit for dancing-masters; Italian for opera singers; and German for pedants; while English was a little useful as a medium for grammars and lexicons. History began with the politics of Troy, and ended with the fall of Constantinople. And just as Conservatives always try to prove themselves Democrats, and Democrats assert that they are the only true Conservatives, so the Professors of these studies assumed that only these studies were 'useful'.[17]

In contrast to Davie's assessment of the Universities (Scotland) Act, John Kirkpatrick, writing in the *Juridical Review* of 1889, suggested that, after years of debate, the Act of that year was 'pregnant with promises' and would give a fresh impetus to that higher education, which is 'the greatest of Scottish industries'.[18]

Anderson and Paterson follow in the wake of such contemporary commentators who – far from appreciating reform merely in the context of the emulation of English ideals – identified a need in these years for the modernisation of the Scottish universities, not at the expense of Scottish traditions, but in part in order that such traditions might survive the very assaults on the 'democratic intellect' that Walter Elliot identified in modernity. By critically examining the class, gender and regional composition of the student body and the persistence of generalism in Scottish curricula, Anderson and Paterson have variously shown how, long after 1889, many of the distinctive features of the Scottish universities survived, and the 'democracy' of Scottish education was actually enhanced.[19] Their views might now be taken for the new orthodoxy.

Yet what of Scottish students themselves? Building on this historiographical legacy, the claim being made here is that a still more nuanced appreciation of debates surrounding the 'democratic intellect' is possible if we follow student careers beyond matriculation and into the corporate life of the universities.[20] In so doing, it is apparent that the history of student life throws light upon the contested and contradictory ethos at the heart of education in Scotland and the inadequacy of the paradigms that to date have dominated the historiography. In this endeavour this piece echoes the call of Jean Barr in 2006 for 'an alternative democratic epistemology' – in this instance, one that is alert to the tensions and paradoxes of the student state.[21]

The Student Body Politic

The 'democracy' – whether philosophical or material – of any system which condemned many of its students to penury whilst at the same time lauding its own inclusivity is open to question. The fact that – in comparison to its near neighbour – the social diversity of the Scottish student body was more apparent does not seem to excuse such manifest hypocrisy, particularly when one appreciates that (leaving to one side the female students) even in 1914 only 2 per cent of young males in Scotland attended one of the four Scottish universities.[22] In 1870, according to Paterson, 14 per cent of male students at the University of Glasgow were from working-class backgrounds, and a decade later only around 10 per cent of Aberdeen graduates shared such humble beginnings.[23] These statistics serve to put in context claims familiar at the time and since, in both history and literature, of the mixed intake in Scotland's lecture halls and the opportunities Scottish universities accorded talented Scots of all classes. Examples in real life of students such as 'Stanhope' in Norman Fraser's semi-fictional *Student Life at Edinburgh University* (1884) – a lad who went to 'the weaving every summer . . . to pay my class fees for the winter session' – were the exception.[24] Bursaries certainly made entry easier for some, but until the charity of Andrew Carnegie paid the fees of most Scots-born students after 1901, and until the state acknowledged its own obligations in this regard, these were limited and were not necessarily awarded simply on the merit (or the need) of the candidates involved. In 1883, Thomas Baynes, professor of logic and English literature at the University of St Andrews, emphasised that, particularly at Aberdeen and St Andrews, 'the number of bursaries virtually, and as a rule, determines the average number of students in the faculty of arts'. At this time, the faculty of arts at Aberdeen had 242 bursaries and eight scholarships, while the St Andrews arts faculty boasted just ninety-three bursaries and eight scholarships.[25] Aberdeen and St Andrews remained the smallest universities in Scotland during these years (and beyond). Looking at the bursary regulations at the University of Glasgow in 1912 throws further light on the qualifications required – beyond aptitude – of those who sat some bursary exams. Thus, to qualify for the Brown-Paton bursary (amounting to £17 for three years), preference was given to natives of Loudon or Galston, whom failing, to natives of any other part of Ayrshire. In similar fashion, while students of the name Mitchell or Lochhead were preferred for the Lochhead and Mitchell bursary (amounting to £34 for four years), an unambiguous requirement was that their parents had to be members of the Established Church of Scotland.[26] For some Scottish students, little had apparently changed since the 1880s, when Glasgow students satirised the bursary system:

> it is evident that it thoroughly upholds our proverbial Scottish clannishness, and our devotion to religious sect . . . To obtain an Arts Bursary at the University of Glasgow it is of paramount consequence to cringe to a sporting Peer, to be the son of a tanner in a country town, to be the offspring of a certain Freemason, or

to rejoice in such patronymics as Duncan, Stewart or Simpson! It is comparatively small importance to possess skill in classics, mathematics and English.[27]

By 1913, the total number of students across all four Scottish universities was
7,776, the vast majority of them at the universities of Glasgow (2,916) and
Edinburgh (3,283) – some 80 per cent.[28] And by the 1920s, 37 per cent of male
students and 35 per cent of female students at the University of Glasgow were
from working-class households. This suggests that if Scottish education has ever
been democratic in a socio-economic sense, it was more democratic in the inter-
war years than it had ever been in the halcyon days of the 'democratic intellect'.
Local authority grants from 1946, then state grants from 1962, served to develop
this tendency into the later twentieth century.

The entry of more working-class Scots into higher education, however, did
not necessarily guarantee an equivalent experience of university life across all
classes. In 1904, W. McQuilliam, writing his 'Recollections of a St Andrews
man', emphasised the lack of snobbery in the Scottish student body: 'There is no
one whom a distinguished air leaves more entirely unimpressed than a Scottish
student.'[29] Yet inequalities were still evident. O. H. Mavor, an active student politician at the University of Glasgow in the years preceding the Great War – before
becoming better known as the playwright James Bridie – emphasised throughout
his autobiography the dominance of Glasgow's private schools in many areas of
the corporate life of the university.[30] At much the same time, L. J. Russell – later
chair of philosophy at Birmingham University from 1925 – remembered how,
in contrast, he could simply not afford the 7s 6d required to join the Glasgow
University Union.[31] He, like many others, was a 'quad boy' – a student who
could not pay for the shelter far less the delights of the common room. Money,
however, was not the only barrier to participation.

The year 1892 is widely accepted as a turning point in the history of women
in higher education in Scotland as it was from this year onwards that women
were allowed to matriculate in the Scottish universities, although it was some
time before they could graduate in all subjects in all the Scottish universities, and
they were for some time educated separately from male students in a variety of
subjects. By the 1920s, however, women made up about a third of the students
in Scotland's universities – their route to higher education considerably eased by
the gender neutral terms of Carnegie bursaries. St Andrews University in particular was notable for its high percentage of female students, amounting to some
43 per cent in 1913.[32] Yet what of their reception in these erstwhile bastions of
male privilege?

The evidence is contradictory. The annual report of the University of
Aberdeen Students' Representative Council (SRC) in 1892 supported women's
right to graduate, but – despite the SRC's boasting a women's committee from
1900 – the first female office bearer only appeared in the Aberdeen SRC in
November 1916 (when the number of male students had been depleted by the
war).[33] Women appear to have been active in the Edinburgh SRC from 1894,

and were on its executive committee from session 1895–6. In 1915, however, a motion in support of female graduation in medicine was rejected by the SRC, and as late as 1923 it was emphasised that women ought only to participate in torchlight processions from the safe sanctuary of decorated lorries, not on foot.[34] By 1905, a representative of Queen Margaret College – the women's college of the University of Glasgow – had acquired a position on the executive committee of the Glasgow SRC, but two years later, in response to increased pressure of numbers in lecture halls, the SRC carried a motion in support of restricting the number of female students to ease congestion.[35] Its ambivalent attitude was proved again in 1910 when, having passed a motion reprimanding Aberdeen University students for voting against all motions in favour of women at a recent inter-varsity conference, the Glasgow SRC rescinded the motion a week later.[36] In St Andrews, meanwhile, women featured surprisingly little in the activities of the SRC: while entrusted with the quality and styling of gowns in March 1907, as late as 1923 the SRC rejected an inter-varsity motion for the award of the parliamentary franchise to women on the same terms as men.[37] The matriculation of women as students in Scotland's universities was clearly only the beginning of a far longer struggle for equality in a system that was far from democratic.

The contrasting gender histories across the four Scottish universities speaks to a further feature of the composition of the Scottish student population: its regionalism. The Aberdeen University magazine recorded as early as 1897 the contrasting student 'types' attending the Scottish universities when a writer reflected on the participants of a recent inter-varsity conference in these terms: 'the bantam-like pugnacity of the Clyde, the classic superciliousness of the modern Athens, the impecunious wails of St Andrews, and the granite persistence of Aberdeen'.[38] As both Anderson and Paterson have noted, university students in Scotland in these years were overwhelmingly Scottish, and tended to matriculate as students in their local university. As late as the 1930s, over 70 per cent of students from the University of Glasgow came from within a thirty-mile radius of the university, and at the other Scottish universities the proportion of students from equivalent hinterland areas was still over 50 per cent.[39] Indeed, after 1889 one could make a convincing case for the regional Scottish identity of the Scottish universities being enhanced rather than eroded – General Councils developed as the effective organ for communicating the views of alumni, many of whom lived locally even after graduation; the inter-war years found students more heavily involved than ever before in charity activities in Scotland's university neighbourhoods; and from 1868 Scottish graduates – like their English counterparts – had a second parliamentary vote for the university constituencies, thus enhancing the voice of uniquely Scottish institutions at Westminster.[40] Whether or not Davie is right about the erosion of a Scottish educational tradition with respect to the arts curriculum – and Paterson in particular makes a strong case for the continued popularity of the Ordinary degree speaking to the persistence of a generalist dynamic in Scotland's arts faculties despite growing specialisation – it is clear that in the post-1889 world there were more avenues through which that which was distinctive about Scotland's university traditions (broadly conceived) could be articulated.[41]

But what of Douglas Young's counter-claim in 1948 that such nationalism also required an international reach? Scottish students had been familiar scholars in continental Europe since medieval times, and Scotland's universities had recruited students from other nations for generations. In 1910, the proportion of first entrants to Scotland's universities born outwith the UK was 5 per cent (Aberdeen), 20 per cent (Edinburgh), 12 per cent (Glasgow) and 5 per cent (St Andrews), and at this time Scottish universities boasted a disproportionate number of students from the Indian subcontinent in comparison with other UK institutions.[42] The mere presence of international students within Scotland, however, is not proof of a sensitivity to international stimuli. While research into university curricula is one means by which an intellectual internationalism might be gauged, another is to consider the international perspectives of Scottish students themselves.[43] Such a study reveals that students in the early twentieth century were far more inclined than previous generations to consider themselves part of a worldwide community of scholars and more apt to take action in pursuit of international understanding in this regard. Early signs of this were evident in Edinburgh in the 1880s and 1890s when students – funded by the university Senate and representing their university – attended university celebrations in Bologna, Dublin and Montpellier, and in 1892 formed the International Academic Committee which by 1905 was representing all the Scottish universities in international liaison activities.[44] By the first decades of the twentieth century, students in Scotland had clearly taken at least some aspects of international engagement into their own hands.[45] While ambivalent about the utility of the British Student Congresses held at the turn of the century, Scotland's SRCs, working together, were early members of the Confédération Internationale des Etudiants (CIE), sending delegates to conferences in Warsaw, Copenhagen, Prague and Budapest in the 1920s.[46] Throughout, Scottish students insisted on representing Scotland and refused to condone joint UK membership. Their membership, however, was pragmatic, and regular debates questioned what Scottish students were getting in return for the work and money they devoted to the CIE.[47] Nevertheless, in 1941 the Scottish National Union of Students reaffirmed their desire to promote international understanding at the war's end.[48] This would be expressed in Scotland's membership of the International Union of Students (IUS) from 1946, although pragmatic concerns would be replaced by political anxieties when Soviet influence in the ICS became evident, and in 1952 the Scots withdrew.[49]

As Anderson and Paterson have shown, the class, gender, regional and international composition of Scottish students in the first years of the twentieth century suggest that after 1889 access to a university education in Scotland became wider. The experiences of these students, however, retained distinct features that in part were still determined by their class, gender and geographical origins. This is not surprising: matriculation did not dissolve inequalities and differences, and could actually enhance these. In what follows, the extent to which a democratic imperative was articulated within university structures in Scotland will be considered, identifying the contexts of student liberties, university discipline, student influence and the emergence of a corporate student identity as fundamental features in any consideration of the influence of democratic intellectualism.

The Right to Make a Noise

In 1907, four Edinburgh University graduates would reflect that students at their alma mater still retained the 'inalienable right to make a noise'.[50] This comment is characteristic of a conventional appreciation of the Scottish student as enjoying liberties unknown at the same time to students in Oxford and Cambridge, where residence in college typically meant that student lifestyles were more constrained and controlled. This comparison, however, is misleading and at best faintly sentimental. After all, Scottish students who could reside at home during their studies tended to do so: this amounted to 42 per cent of male students and 49 per cent of female students in 1918.[51] O. H. Mavor recorded how in 1904 'at the age of sixteen I stopped being a school-boy and became a student. I was given a latchkey and a small allowance'.[52] The extent to which such residential arrangements in general were conducive of 'liberty' is, to say the least, debatable.

Other Scottish students, however, bought such liberties at a high price. Familiar tales of Victorian Scottish students surviving winter terms on a sack of oatmeal and the light of a handful of candles romanticise student poverty and ignore the implications such conditions had for student health. The career of Lewis Morrison Grant (1872–93) is a case in point.[53] After two attempts at the bursary examinations at the University of Aberdeen, Grant – a gifted young poet from Banffshire[54] – came 57th out of 245 candidates in 1890 to secure a stipend of £10 that had to be supplemented by his family. As he noted in correspondence, 'the best bursaries went to the seminaries in Aberdeen, who were better acquainted with what was going on in professional minds'.[55] Within three years, after recurring bouts of ill health – friends spoke of a 'strange depression' – Grant was dead. Despite the youth of Scottish students, ill health was a familiar feature of university life. In 1861, a contributor to the *Scottish Review* wrote of the 'seeds of disease' that regularly ripened into 'lingering consumption'.[56] Others found little to commend in the lodgings or 'digs' (known as 'bunks' in St Andrews) in which many students lived: hence, one of the first activities of the infant SRCs was the creation of a lodgings register, and university-sponsored student residences were increasingly identified as fundamental to better student welfare.[57] In Edinburgh, for example, Patrick Geddes sought to invigorate rather than undermine student liberties by placing the administration of University Hall – the largest hall of residence in the country in 1905 – firmly in student hands.[58] D. B. Keith – a student at Edinburgh between 1908 and 1914, and a resident of St Giles House (part of the all-male University Hall) – reflected on the serious consequences that participatory democracy brought to residential life:

We started as 'Junior Residents' and after a period of probation could be elected 'Senior Residents' when we had full voting power and security of tenure. If unlucky or unpopular at the Election we would be blackballed and put out.[59]

The number of residences across Scotland, however, remained small (and they were typically governed by wardens rather than students). Again, the relative liberty of Scottish students in comparison to their Oxbridge peers ought not to blind us to the extent to which university discipline remained a powerful force in the lives of many students. Disciplinary issues ranged from the mundane to the serious. Academic staff across Scotland regularly had cause to chastise students following disturbances at rectorial installations and graduation ceremonies.[60] But periodically university authorities could come close to usurping the statutory duty of the SRCs, as recognised in law, to represent the interests of students. During the Second World War, for example, officials and students at the University of St Andrews clashed over a range of issues, leading to allegations from students of 'autocratic' rule. Controversy grew following the authorities' ban, then conditional re-instatement, of Raisin Monday (a student celebration that ended in a 'battle' in St Salvator's quadrangle), allegations of censorship relating to student publications and the curtailment of late-night dances. In the end the SRC acknowledged in 1940 that a 'spirit of antagonism' had grown between it and the university, but were forced to 'admit that the Senatus by its constitution has full disciplinary powers over the students; that it has a legal right to quash any recommendations the SRC may make'. It concluded that the 'only answer . . . would appear to be a greater measure of co-operation between the SRC and the authorities'. A year later, the SRC stepped back from further antagonism following a warning from Court members that it would be 'a grave mistake' if it were to revisit the issue of late dances. That November the SRC conspired with the Senate to restrict Raisin weekend celebrations as rumours circulated that Senate had threatened a total ban of the event had the restrictions not been accepted.[61] SRC reliance on university funding gave added weight to the threats of university officials. From its foundation in 1884, for example, Edinburgh University had granted funds to the SRC: by the inter-war years this amounted to an annual payment of about £300. The possibility that such funds could be cut or withdrawn was always to the fore for SRC members who realised how precarious their finances could be: for example, student magazines often ran at a loss – a loss SRCs were often called on to make up.[62]

The Scottish SRCs, however, were the principal vehicles of student democracy and could, on occasion, carry real weight with university authorities. During the period when Davie's 'democratic intellect' had appeared relatively secure, it had failed to create an environment conducive to student participation in the decision-making processes of the universities. In 1858 the Associated Societies at the University of Edinburgh ('the aristocrats among University societies'[63]) had unsuccessfully campaigned for official recognition. It would not be until 1884 that the first SRC would be established at Edinburgh. Within two years, however, all four Scottish universities boasted their own SRCs, and these would gain statutory authority through the 1889 Universities (Scotland) Act – the legislation much maligned by Davie. By 1912, these student bodies had become 'a recognised and useful part of University machinery'.[64] Criticised by some as the 'transient potentates of the University polity',[65] divided into cliques, with 'no sense of humour' and 'too great a sense of their own importance', SRC members were also said to evoke 'the Scots' passion for democracy'.[66] Amongst many things, SRCs proved themselves to be anxious for greater influence and pushed for direct representation on both Senate and Court; they regularly opposed fines imposed on students by university authorities; and they contributed to discussions on the development of curricula.[67] In this last aspect, we alight upon a direct challenge to Davie's paradigm: after 1889, students had a right to be heard on matters affecting what they were taught. So, for example, Aberdeen agriculture students pushed for a compulsory practical element in their curriculum in 1912; Edinburgh students spoke up in favour of coursework counting towards their overall marks as early as 1931; and St Andrews medics dominated intervarsity discussions in 1905–6 with motions relating to their curriculum.[68]

Acting in concert, first as the Students' Representative Councils for Scotland (SRCS), then, from 1935, as the Scottish National Union of Students (SNUS) and finally as the Scottish Union of Students (SUS, est. 1946), Scotland's SRCs paralleled the attempts of academics across the Scottish universities to present a united front to university commissioners and governments that were taking an increasingly interventionist role in the Scottish universities.[69] In so doing they formed 'the first national forum for corporate opinion among students in Britain' and it was through such bodies that Scottish students were represented in the CIE and later in the IUS.[70] The extent to which the SRCs ought to be considered representative of a democratic impulse in the student body in Scotland, however, must be qualified. Interest waxed and waned from one session to the next: SRC elections at the University of St Andrews in 1931–2, for example, attracted just a 33 per cent turnout, but this rose to 58 per cent the following year.[71] Regularly across Scotland SRC offices were unfilled. At a national level, the limits of SRC inclusivity were also made starkly apparent immediately following peace in 1945 when there were debates as to whether extra-mural college students ought to be incorporated into the SNUS. On the surface this was a discussion about whether the inclusion of bodies not blessed with legislative sanction would undermine the authority of the SRCs operating in concert, but it is difficult not to see this as a screen behind which lurked academic and class snobbery.[72] The academic environment had changed dramatically: by 1908, Scotland boasted sixteen central institutions and by 1938 around 2,500 students in colleges such as these (of which there were by then nineteen) were working at university level.[73] Paterson pushes the point home: 'university-type education was not less open in the 1930s than in the period before the 1889 reforms'.[74]

Yet clearly the advantages of post-secondary education were not equitably shared. Until 1948 graduates of Scotland's four universities elected first two, then – after 1918 – three university MPs. The General Councils were resolute in the defence of this privilege, and contributed to seeing off a Labour challenge in 1931.[75] In 1948, however, despite continued General Council opposition, Clement Attlee secured what Ramsay MacDonald (MP for the Combined Scottish Universities, 1936–7) had failed to do seventeen years earlier.[76] Change was afoot in the post-war world: when a motion to reintroduce the university seats was put to a student parliament in Aberdeen in 1949, celebrating a hundred years of the university's debating society, it was rejected. Half in jest, a female delegate led the opposition:

> She . . . claimed that if a University degree merited an additional vote, a Higher Leaving Certificate should command half a vote, two degrees two votes and *pro rata ad absurdum*. She ended with the categorical statement that no-one should have more than one vote, and called on the members to strike a blow for real democracy . . .[77]

By 1948, democracy came at the cost of privilege.

The development of a corporate life in the Scottish universities also had a price. In December 1889, the 'editorial' of the *Glasgow University Students Union Bazaar News* emphasised a familiar complaint about a lack of sociability that the new Union building would address:

> It has long been felt to be a great defect in our Scottish University system that it affords little or no opportunity for a common or corporate life among the students. In the Colleges of the great English Universities the students live together, and association with each other, not merely within the walls of the class-rooms, but in their common pursuits and recreations, has always been recognised as an important element in their University life.[78]

Until this period only irregular breakfast parties with obliging professors and periodic rectorial contests seemed to suggest the existence of a corporate spirit in the Scottish student body.[79] J. M. Barrie's recollections of Edinburgh University, for example, focused on the professors, with the only corporate colour afforded by his memory of throwing a clod of earth at Lord Rosebery. ('He was a peer; those were my politics.'[80]) From the 1890s, however, aided by the generosity of benefactors and successful fundraising, Scotland's universities came to boast unions, sports fields and a vibrant societal culture. By the turn of the new century, such facilities had been around long enough to sustain more than one generation of perpetual students – or 'chronics' as they were known – who seemed to have taken root in Scotland's university unions. In 1939, the Glasgow University Union alone (now occupying new premises and its older building home to the ladies of the Queen Margaret Union) had 1,464 student members.[81] By this time, all Scottish universities boasted student newspapers, magazines and journals (often short-lived) and a tradition of literary pursuits. Edinburgh University students peopled over sixty clubs and associations[82] in the inter-war years, and across Scotland student rag weeks raised thousands of pounds for Scottish charities.[83] Glasgow students alone raised £26,000 in 1947.[84]

Fissures in the student body still remained, however. Political affiliations energised periodic rectorial campaigns, despite recurrent calls for a 'non-political working rector', and political clubs and societies regularly challenged the authority of the SRCs as the principal voice of the student body.[85] Magazine editors were often at loggerheads with SRC officials who bore the brunt of official complaints about literary bad taste and could see their funding affected as a consequence, and similar disputes often benighted SRC executive relationships with their amusements committees.[86] Some societies were more alive on paper than in real life: the Aberdeen Conservative Club, for example, was in the doldrums in 1891, attracting fewer than five members to its meetings, and in 1899 only 30 per cent of St Andrews students were buying copies of *College Echoes*.[87] Throughout these years SRCs often found themselves in the role of unpopular disciplinarian when students failed to toe the corporate line, and – as has been shown – female students were often only reluctantly accommodated (and usually at one remove) in activities generally dominated by male students.[88]

Conclusion

The foreword to an edited collection of pieces that had first appeared in the *Glasgow University Magazine* between the wars recorded that 'During these two decades the complexion of student thought has changed considerably; the twenties were usually more "literary" and detached, the thirties more obsessed with social and political questions'.[89] In similar fashion, in his introduction to a collected volume of student verse published by the Scottish Union of Students in 1948, Eric Linklater, erstwhile rector of the University of Aberdeen, would reflect: 'There is a maturity in this new anthology . . . The newest poets in the Scottish universities have not shrugged off their experience of war, but kept it to live with'. He went on to comment upon 'the maturity of apprehension and the governed emotion of the better pieces'. Here, he noted, are 'adult voices, speaking not of the class-room but of the world; not of their youth but of our stern age'.[90]

The experience of two world wars meant demobbed servicemen and women and conscripted workers took their places in Scotland's university classrooms in the first half of the twentieth century alongside scholars whom a new age would call 'teenagers'. National crises rather than university admissions criteria had, for the most part, delayed or interrupted their studies, and the gratitude of a nation more alive to the fragility and value of youthful talent (rather than the largesse of philanthropists) increasingly funded their studies. These students emerged into adulthood at a time before youth had been constructed as a group, before the Cold War had frozen the age of empire and before the need for a 'New Left' to shake the 'Old' out of its lethargy.[91] These students attended Scotland's universities at a transitional stage in their development, when the elitism of the 'democratic intellect' felt the full force of democracy in real time and not in the abstract: in 1947, students, contributing to a national debate through the Scottish Union of Students, announced their first priority to be to ensure that 'ability and not financial means should be qualification for entry into universities'.[92]

To read forward from this a narrative of student radicalism into the 1960s and beyond is as foolish as to read backwards a tale of a lost ethos, more evident with hindsight than in history. Student days are contradictory and contested, framed by power relations that shift and change, and are moulded by circumstances that few can control. Divisions shape the expression of the student voice as much as periodic unity, and narrative threads across decades are gossamer-like when student days are transitory. Looking afresh at the meaning of rectorial office and the paradigm of the 'democratic intellect' from the student perspective makes one question more than both politics and the paradigm itself; it makes one alive to the inadequacy of all such paradigms to capture the protean nature of student lives.

Notes

1. Douglas Young, 'The Young idea', *Alba Mater* (Aberdeen University Scottish Nationalist Association, November 1945), 4.
2. Ibid., 4.
3. Rectors are elected student representatives who chair the university courts of the four 'ancient' Scottish universities (Aberdeen, Edinburgh, Glasgow and St Andrews). It was a position revived and consolidated by the 1889 Universities (Scotland) Act.
4. George Davie, *The Democratic Intellect: Scotland and her Universities in the Nineteenth Century*, 2nd edn (Edinburgh University Press, 1964), pp. 5, 7.
5. Ibid., pp. 8, 13–16, 19. One aspect, according to Davie, of the timing of the crisis in nineteenth-century Scottish higher education was changes made to the Indian civil service examinations which tended to favour the 'Oxbridge' colleges. This is discussed – though not conclusively – in David Limond, 'An educational crisis in Scotland: The democratic intellect revisited', *Scottish Educational Review* 36(1) (2004), 58–65.
6. 'The *Democratic Intellect* does read more like a period piece than it did in the 1970s or even in the run-up to Scotland's restored Parliament when it was regularly cited', Brian Morton, 'Democratic intellectual: Remembering George Elder Davie', *Scottish Review of Books*, 8(1) (2 March 2012). Available at www.scottishreviewofbooks. org/index.php/back-issues/volume-8-2012/volume-seven-issue-four/457-democratic-intellectual-remembering-george-elder-davie-brian-morton (accessed 20 October 2014).
7. Chris Harvie, 'The democratic intellectual: George Elder Davie', *Open Democracy* (11 April 2007). Available at www.opendemocracy.net/node/4517 (accessed 18 October 2014).
8. Michael Gove, 'What is clever Gordon's game plan?', *The Times*, 30 May 2000.
9. Andrew McPherson, 'An angle on the geist: Persistence and change in the Scottish educational tradition', in Walter M. Humes and Hamish M. Paterson (eds), *Scottish Culture and Scottish Education 1800–1980* (John Donald, 1983), pp. 216–43.
10. Walter Elliot, 'The Scottish heritage in politics', in His Grace the Duke of Atholl (ed.), *A Scotsman's Heritage* (A. Maclehose, 1932), pp. 53–65.
11. See in particular R. D. Anderson, *Education and Opportunity in Victorian Scotland* (Clarendon Press, 1983); Lindsay Paterson, *Scottish Education in the Twentieth Century* (Edinburgh University Press, 2003).

12. The 1889 Universities (Scotland) Act marks a crucial stage in the modernisation of the corporate and academic life of the Scottish universities. Formalising the rights and responsibilities of the Court, Senate and General Council, and stipulating the powers of the SRCs and the university commissioners, thereafter Scottish universities shared very similar governance structures and would closely collaborate in the standardisation of curricula.

13. Anon, 'North country students', *The Cornhill Magazine* 37(220) (April 1878), 452–67; Anon, 'Scottish university students', *All the Year Round* 24(577) (20 December 1879), 80–2.

14. W. J. Douglas, 'Glasgow students I', *The Celtic Magazine* 11(132) (1 October 1886), 557–65.

15. M. A., 'Personal experiences II', *University Pamphlets* (n.p., 1882), pp. 47, 41; M. A. and Others, 'Personal experiences III', *University Pamphlets* (Glasgow, 1883), p. vii.

16. MEDICUS, 'Conclusion V', *University Pamphlets* (Glasgow, 1883), p. 10; Anon., 'Considerations by the way IV', *University Pamphlets* (Glasgow, 1883), p. 23.

17. W. J. Douglas, 'Glasgow students II', *The Celtic Magazine* (1 November 1886), 29–37.

18. John Kirkpatrick, 'Universities (Scotland) Act, 1889', *Juridical Review* 1(4) (1889), 344–351.

19. Addressing more recent history, see Lindsay Paterson, 'The survival of the democratic intellect: Academic values in Scotland and England', *Higher Education Quarterly* 57(1) (2003), 67–93.

20. By far the most comprehensive study of student life in any Scottish university is that offered by Robert Anderson in *The Student Community at Aberdeen, 1860–1939* (Aberdeen University Press, 1988).

21. Jean Barr, 'Re-framing the democratic intellect', *Scottish Affairs* 55 (2006), 23–46.

22. R. D. Anderson, 'Scottish universities', in Heather Holmes (ed.), *Institutions of Scotland: Education*, Scottish Life and Society: A Compendium of Scottish Ethnology, vol. 11 (Tuckwell Press, 2000), pp. 154–74.

23. Paterson, *Scottish Education in the Twentieth Century*, pp. 79–80.

24. Norman Fraser, *Student Life at Edinburgh University* (J. & R. Parlane, 1884), p. 64.

25. Thomas Spencer Baynes, *The Bursary System in Relation Especially to the Universities of St Andrews and Aberdeen* (F. Murray, 1883), pp. 7, 11.

26. University of Glasgow Special Collections, Maclehose 847, *University of Glasgow, Bursaries Competition, June 1912*, p. 3.

27. M.A. and Others, 'Personal experiences III', 8.

28. Anderson, *Education and Opportunity*, pp. 352–7.

29. W. McQuilliam, 'Recollections of a St Andrews man', *MacMillan's Magazine* 91(541) (1 November 1904), 20–8.

30. James Bridie, *One Way of Living* (Constable & Co, 1939).

31. Anon., *The Curious Diversity: Glasgow University on Gilmorehill – the First Hundred Years* (University of Glasgow, 1970), p. 54.

32. Anderson, *Education and Opportunity*, pp. 352–7.

33. University of Aberdeen, Special Libraries and Archives [henceforth: AU], SRC Minutes, 11 November 1916. The first Students' Representative Council was founded in Edinburgh in 1884 and was modelled on the *Student Ausschuss* at the University of Strasbourg. The status of the Scottish SRCs as the voice of the student body in the corporate life of the universities was confirmed in statute in 1889.

34. University of Edinburgh, Archives [henceforth: EU], SRC Minutes, 31 October 1923.

35. University of Glasgow, Archives [henceforth: GU], SRC Minutes, 22 November 1905.

36. GU, SRC Minutes, 2 December 1909, 24 January 1910, 7 February 1910.
37. University of St Andrews, Archives [henceforth: StAU], SRC Minutes, 30 April 1923.
38. AU, *Alma Mater*, 27 January 1897.
39. Paterson, *Scottish Education in the Twentieth Century*, p. 77.
40. Instituted by the 1858 Universities (Scotland) Act, the General Council of an 'ancient' university in Scotland is the body that represents graduates in the life of the institution.
41. Paterson, *Scottish Education in the Twentieth Century*, p. 162. It is also important to note that the Junior classes survived for some time after the 1889 legislation. See G. S. Osborne, *Change in Scottish Education* (Longmans, 1968), p. 12.
42. Anderson, *Education and Opportunity*, pp. 296–8. See also Bashir Maan, *The Thistle and the Crescent* (Argyll Publishing, 2008), pp. 195–6.
43. Anderson has examined the extent to which the history curriculum in Scotland's universities responded to contrasting approaches on continental Europe and in England. See Robert Anderson, 'University history teaching, national identity and Unionism in Scotland, 1862–1914', *Scottish Historical Review* 91 (2012), 1–41.
44. EU, SRC Executive Minutes, 13 May 1888, 16 June 1892; SRC Minutes, 19 June 1890; George Foulkes (ed.), *Eighty Years On: A Chronicle of Student Activity in the University of Edinburgh During the Eighty Years of the Existence of the Students' Representative Council* (University of Edinburgh SRC, 1964), pp. 12–13.
45. The Edinburgh SRC showed sensitivity to racial discrimination against Indian students during World War One, and boycotted local cafés in 1931 that had discriminated against Indian students. EU, SRC Minutes, 25 February 1915, 28 April 1931, 19 May 1931, 26 May 1931; *Student*, 26 May 1931.
46. EU, SRC Minutes, 7 February 1912, 30 October 1924, 17 June 1925, 28 June 1926, 30 October 1929; StAU, SRC Minutes, 11 March 1908. See also Eric Ashby and Mary Anderson, *The Rise of the Student Estate in Britain* (Macmillan, 1970), p. 58.
47. Catriona M. M. Macdonald, '"To form citizens": Scottish students, governance and politics, 1884–1948', *History of Education* 38 (2009), 383–402. For England and Wales, see Brian Simon, 'The student movement in England and Wales during the 1930s', *History of Education* 16 (1987), 189–203.
48. EU, SRC Minutes, 2 May 1944, 20 February 1945.
49. *The Times*, 25 February 1952. The National Union of Students had disaffiliated the year before.
50. Four Graduates, *The Old Quadrangle: Edinburgh University 1900–1905* (William J. Hay, 1907), p. 5.
51. Paterson, *Scottish Education in the Twentieth Century*, p. 77.
52. James Bridie, 'The Glasgow undergraduate', in Iain R. Hamilton (ed.), *The Five Hundred Year Book; to Commemorate the Fifth Centenary of the University of Glasgow* (Students' Fifth Centenary Committee, 1951), pp. 10–17.
53. Isabella Fyvie Mayo, 'An Aberdeen student of today', *The Leisure Hour* (January 1894), 150–7.
54. Lewis Morrison Grant, *Protomantis and Other Poems* (A. Gardner, 1892).
55. Jessie Annie Anderson, *Lewis Morrison-Grant: His Life, Letters and Last Poems* (A. Gardner, 1894), p. 106.
56. Anon., 'Scottish student life', *Scottish Review* (July 1861), 261.
57. The provision of health services was an important aspect of this. See Keith Vernon, 'The health and welfare of university students in Britain, 1920–1939', *History of Education* 37 (2008), 227–52. Anderson has also identified a growing interest among

university office holders in the organisation of sports at this time. See Anderson, 'Sport in the Scottish universities, 1860–1939', *International Journal of the History of Sport* 4 (1987), 177–88.

58. Ashby and Anderson, *The Rise of the Student Estate*, p. 59. Residences were only one element of Geddes' radical approach to Scottish higher education. See Douglas Sutherland, 'Education as an agent of social evolution: The educational projects of Patrick Geddes in late-Victorian Scotland', *History of Education* 38 (2009), 349–65.

59. Sheriff D. B. Keith, *Bygone Days at Edinburgh University* (reprinted from the *University of Edinburgh Journal*, spring 1965), p. 59.

60. Catriona M. M. Macdonald, 'Rhetoric, place and performance: Students and the heritage of Scottish universities', in Iain J. M. Robertson (ed.), *Heritage from Below* (Basingstoke, 2012), pp. 59–74.

61. StAU, SRC Minutes, 15 October 1940, 29 January 1941.

62. EU, SRC Minutes, 25 May 1926, 29 April 1930, 29 May 1930.

63. J. H. Burns and S. Sutherland Graeme, *Scottish University* (Darien Press, 1944), p. 31. Combining for the first time in 1834, these were the Dialectic, Scots Law, Diagnostic, Hunterian Medican and Plinian Societies.

64. W. J. Gibson, *Education in Scotland: A Sketch of the Past and Present* (Longmans, 1912), pp. 117–18.

65. Four Graduates, *The Old Quadrangle*, p. 100.

66. Burns and Graeme, *Scottish University*, pp. 81–2.

67. EU, SRC Minutes, 15 February 1922; AU, SRC Minutes, 12 January 1929.

68. AU, SRC Minutes, 3 February 1912; EU, SRC Minutes, 24 February 1931; StAU, SRC Minutes, volume 1892–1909.

69. I. G. C. Hutchison, 'The Scottish Office and the Scottish universities, c. 1930–1960', in Jennifer J. Carter and Donald J. Withrington (eds), *Scottish Universities: Distinctiveness and Diversity* (John Donald, 1992), pp. 56–78. After 1889, the Scottish University Commissioners issued 169 ordinances. See H.M. Knox, *Two Hundred and Fifty Years of Scottish Education, 1696–1946* (Oliver and Boyd, 1953), p. 158.

70. Eric Ashby, 'The student movement', in Roy Lowe (ed.), *The History of Higher Education, Volume 5: Major Themes in Education* (Routledge, 2009), pp. 273–85.

71. StAU, SRC Minutes, 22 November 1932.

72. Macdonald, '"To form citizens"', 397.

73. Paterson, *Scottish Education in the Twentieth Century*, p. 81.

74. Ibid., p. 81.

75. *Aberdeen University Review* (1931).

76. EU, Edinburgh General Council Minutes, 1948.

77. *Gaudie*, 4 May 1949.

78. *Glasgow University Students Union Bazaar News*, 18 December 1889.

79. J. Leys, 'Life at the Scottish universities', *National Review* 8(46) (December 1886), 533–41. See also *Chambers's Journal* 11(560) (22 September 1894), 593–6.

80. J. M. Barrie, *An Edinburgh Eleven: Pencil Portraits from College Life* (Hodder and Stoughton, 1889), p. 1.

81. C. A. Oakley, *Union Ygorra: The Story of the Glasgow University Student over the Last Sixty Years* (Committee of Management, Glasgow University Union, 1950–1), p. 47.

82. James Scotland, *The History of Scottish Education, Volume 2: From 1872 to the Present Day* (University of London Press, 1969), p. 157.

83. Students were also central figures in the university settlement movement in Scotland. See L. Bruce, 'Scottish settlement houses from 1886–1934' (unpublished PhD dissertation, University of Glasgow, 2012).

84. C. A. Oakley, 'The students', in Hamilton (ed.), *The Five Hundred Year Book*, pp. 113–23.
85. See Macdonald, 'Rhetoric, place and performance', pp. 59–74.
86. Edinburgh SRC took issue on a number of occasions with the editorial policies of the *Student*. See EU, SRC Minutes, 15 March 1932, 13 November 1945.
87. *Alma Mater*, 28 January 1891. *College Echoes* was a major source of financial anxiety for the St Andrews SRC.
88. GU, SRC, Executive Minutes, 15 May 1924.
89. J. Welsh and H. H. Munro (eds), *The G.U.M. Between Wars* (R. Maclehose and Co., 1940), p. 5.
90. Eric Linklater, 'Introduction', in Ian F. Holroyd (ed.), *Scottish Student Verse, 1937–1947* (Ettrick Press, 1948), pp. xi–xii.
91. These are all criteria used by Caroline Hoefferle to define the parameters within which the students' movement of the 1960s emerged. See Hoeefferle, *British Student Activism in the Long Sixties* (Routledge, 2013), Chapter 1.
92. EU, SRC Minutes, 29 April 1947.

Bibliography

Anderson, R. D., 'Scottish universities', in Heather Holmes (ed.), *Institutions of Scotland: Education*, Scottish Life and Society: A Compendium of Scottish Ethnology, vol. 11 (Tuckwell Press, 2000).

Anderson, R. D., *The Student Community at Aberdeen, 1860–1939* (Aberdeen University Press, 1988).

Anderson, R. D., *Education and Opportunity in Victorian Scotland* (Clarendon Press, 1983).

Carter, Jennifer J. and Donald J. Withrington (eds), *Scottish Universities: Distinctiveness and Diversity* (John Donald, 1992).

Davie, George, *The Democratic Intellect: Scotland and her Universities in the Nineteenth Century*, 2nd edn (Edinburgh University Press, 1964).

Humes, Walter M. and Hamish M. Paterson (eds), *Scottish Culture and Scottish Education 1800–1980* (John Donald, 1983).

Macdonald, Catriona M. M., '"To form citizens": Scottish students, governance and politics, 1884–1948', *History of Education* 38 (2009), 383–402.

Macdonald, Catriona M.M., 'Rhetoric, place and performance: Students and the heritage of Scottish universities', in Iain J. M. Robertson (ed.), *Heritage from Below* (Ashgate, 2012), pp. 59–74.

Paterson, Lindsay, *Scottish Education in the Twentieth Century* (Edinburgh University Press, 2003).

Scotland, James, *The History of Scottish Education, Volume 2: From 1872 to the Present Day* (University of London Press, 1969).

17

Gaelic Education since 1872

Fiona O'Hanlon and Lindsay Paterson

The Education (Scotland) Act 1872 aimed to 'provide elementary education in reading, writing and arithmetic' for all children aged five to twelve,[1] but did not specify the language in which literacy skills should be developed. There was a general assumption that this was to be English.[2] The lack of mention of Gaelic in the Act was perceived to be a 'disastrous omission' by MacLeod which ignored the effective pedagogical uses of Gaelic in the nineteenth century (see Cameron, this volume), both in facilitating Gaelic-speaking pupils' acquisition of English and as an appropriate education for Gaelic-speaking pupils living in the Highlands and Islands.[3] MacLeod's view has been followed by many campaigners for Gaelic in the twentieth century.[4] However, others, such as Withers and Smout, present the linguistic provisions in the Act in terms of pupils' geographical destination, rather than pupils' home community, and emphasise the 'widespread assumption that the purpose of education for Highlanders was to facilitate their advancement in an English-speaking world'.[5] Giving priority in education to the state language was the standard practice throughout Europe at the time, on the classic republican grounds of creating common citizenship and what would later be called equal opportunities.[6]

The implementation of the Act in Gaelic-speaking areas thus raised key questions regarding the civic purposes of schooling, the relationship between the school and the local community, and effective practice in second language acquisition – questions that have continued to mark the debates regarding the use of Gaelic in education ever since. This chapter outlines associated ideas and developments from 1872 to the present. It is in two chronological sections, before and after 1980, since around 1980 provision through the medium of Gaelic broadened from being primarily intended for Gaelic-speaking pupils in Highland areas to include pupils whose first language was English from across Scotland. It then also became increasingly a matter of cultural maintenance, seeking to sustain Gaelic not only through ensuring its survival among the now much smaller group of children for whom it was their first language but also through creating new speakers.

Gaelic in Education (1872–1980): From Social Mobility to Child-centredness

In 1865, MacKay estimated there to be 300,876 Gaelic speakers living within 135 parishes in the north-west of Scotland. In island areas, he estimated only 2 per cent of the population to be able to speak English.[7] The Gaelic Society of London had approached the Lord Advocate in 1871, during the preparation of the 1872 Education (Scotland) Act, to emphasise the 'necessity' of the Act's recognising the Gaelic language as an instrument of school instruction in Gaelic-speaking Highland regions. Despite being sympathetic to the views of the deputation, the Lord Advocate argued that the place of Gaelic in Highland education would be more effectively addressed in regulatory guidance, because of the 'inflexible nature' of legislation.[8] The question of Gaelic in Highland education thus fell to the Board of Education for Scotland, the temporary body charged with facilitating the implementation of the Act, and with providing advice to the Scotch Education Department (SED) on amendments to the Scotch Education Code (the regulatory guidance of which the Lord Advocate spoke). In their 1873 report to the Department, the Board thought it premature to specify 'the arrangements which would be most suitable for these wild and sparsely-populated districts', and proposed waiting for a year or two before doing so.[9] MacLeod notes the challenge of making provision for Highland education to be a combination of social, economic and linguistic factors, for example the rural nature of much of the Highlands, the paucity of suitable school buildings and the linguistic demographics of the region.[10] However, in 1873 the Board did propose to restore an entry which had disappeared from the Scotch Code in 1860–1,[11] namely that first-language Gaelic-speaking children in the middle primary-school stages (Standards II and III) be asked to explain a passage of English reading in Gaelic after reading it aloud, to show comprehension of their early English literacy.[12] Durkacz notes that the incorporation of this provision into the Scotch Code of 1873 'tacitly admitted the principle that the use of the mother tongue in the early stages [of schooling] was educationally desirable'.[13]

Following petitioning by the Gaelic Society of Inverness and the Gaelic School Society – which argued that teaching Gaelic reading for an hour or two per week to Gaelic-speaking pupils would increase the pupils' achievements in English reading – the Department distributed a questionnaire to 103 school boards within Gaelic-speaking areas of Argyll, Caithness, Inverness, Perth, Ross and Cromarty, and Sutherland in May 1876 to seek their views on the teaching of Gaelic. Ninety replies were received, with sixty-five in favour of providing Gaelic-language teaching, and fifty of these additionally reporting the local availability of suitable teaching staff. Amongst these fifty school boards, the projected take-up of Gaelic provision was at least 14,606 children across 188 public schools, with the potential reach being 16,331 pupils across 208 schools if staffing could be found for the additional fifteen interested school boards.[14] The Board of Education was by then also advocating the teaching of Gaelic reading to Gaelic-speaking Highland pupils.[15] However, not all school inspectors agreed, and some advocated the teaching of Gaelic as a specific subject in upper elementary school, but not at the lower stages, where they felt that the focus should be the acquisition of English. William Jolly, for example – the inspector for Inverness, the Western Isles, Nairn and Elgin who was sympathetic to Gaelic – acknowledged the 'theoretic grounds for learning to read the native language before a foreign one' but perceived this to be an 'idea entertained only by a few enthusiasts' and believed that Gaelic-speaking pupils ought rather to have the maximum available school time to develop English literacy.[16] The Department relaxed the School Code to allow Gaelic to be taught as a subject in 1878, but this was not widely implemented as the Department was not willing to provide funds to employ additional Gaelic-speaking teachers.[17]

The main change in views about Gaelic was provoked by the report in 1884 of the Royal Commission chaired by Lord Napier, the purpose of which was to investigate the position of the crofters in response to the growing political success of the Highland Land League and the Crofters' Party.[18] The result, as in other areas of policy, was greater state involvement, including increased state funding. To the private chagrin of the Education Department, the Commission strayed beyond its remit to condemn the 'discouragement and neglect of the native language in the education of Gaelic-speaking children',[19] and recommended that Gaelic be used in the early education of all Gaelic-speaking pupils and be offered as a specific subject at the middle and upper elementary school stages, with appropriate centrally provided funding. Although the Commission had not sought views about Gaelic in education from more than a handful of its witnesses (15 out of 775), and although only a third of these had been favourable to teaching Gaelic, the SED did respond.[20] Henry Craik – a senior examiner in the Department, who became its Secretary the following year – was sent to the Highlands to investigate educational issues relating to Gaelic. His report of 1884 'admitted that some Gaelic teaching is likely to be of great benefit' to Highland pupils' acquisition of English. Craik thus recommended that there be SED grants to employ Gaelic-speaking pupil-teachers to support Gaelic-speaking pupils' learning at the infant and early elementary school stages, and that Gaelic also be recognised as a specific subject at the middle and upper elementary school stages in Gaelic-speaking areas.[21] (As explained by Bischof in his chapter in this book, pupil-teachers were assistants in training, complementing the main class teacher.) Craik's report did not, however, accept the Napier Commission's recommendation that reading be introduced in Gaelic, reporting this to be an 'extreme view' for which there was no support amongst the school inspectors, school boards, ministers, teachers and parents with whom he had consulted.[22]

Craik's recommended provisions were incorporated into the 1886 Scotch Code, but were implementable only in the counties of Inverness, Argyll, Ross, Sutherland, Caithness, Orkney and Shetland.[23] These 'specified counties' had been identified as those in which 'exceptionally large expenditure . . . has been or will be incurred in providing efficient education', and it was acknowledged that 'benefit would result from additional provision being made for teaching Gaelic in certain of these counties'.[24] The SED thus did not attempt to delineate Gaelic-speaking areas, following Craik's advice that 'a Gaelic-speaking district is not easily defined'.[25] However, the restriction of the Gaelic provisions in the 1886 Scotch Code to the 'specified counties' meant in practice that Gaelic could be taught as a subject in Shetland – where twelve people (0.04 per cent of the population) reported themselves to be Gaelic speakers in the 1881 Census – but not in Perth, an area which had been included in the Department's 1876 survey of Gaelic-speaking areas and where 14,537 people (11 per cent of the population) reported themselves to be Gaelic speakers in the 1881 Census.[26]

The uptake of the Gaelic aspects of the new Code is difficult to ascertain, as no comprehensive county-level information is available. However, in 1901 the SED reported the overall provisions made by 683 schools in the 'specified counties' inspected during the first nine months of 1900. Out of the 503 schools in Argyll, Inverness, Ross and Sutherland, 1,979 infant pupils (6.4 per cent) were being partly taught by Gaelic-speaking pupil-teachers, but no pupils were receiving such initial Gaelic-medium instruction in Caithness, Orkney or Shetland.[27] National records show 286 pupils to have been examined in Gaelic as a specific subject in 1898–9, compared with 424 for Greek, 2,995 for German and 22,188 for French.[28] Such statistics do not include the use of Gaelic as a medium of instruction by Gaelic-speaking certified teachers in the Highlands, but in 1888 the Scottish Education Inquiry Committee noted there to be 'scarcely any' Gaelic-speaking students on teacher training courses because poor levels of education in the Highlands made it difficult for such students to pass the appropriate entrance examination.[29]

Dissatisfaction with Highland school boards' progress in implementing the optional provisions for Gaelic within the School Code led An Comunn Gàidhealach and the Gaelic Society of Inverness to approach parliament on the issue of Gaelic in Scottish education – in a delegation in 1897, and subsequently in the debate leading to the 1908 Education (Scotland) Act where An Comunn requested an amendment to the Bill to make Gaelic a compulsory subject in the education of Gaelic-speaking children in Highland districts, in day schools and in evening continuation classes. Such a request for compulsion was counter to the long-standing approach of the Department in leaving the school boards to decide on language provision (see the chapters by Cameron and by McDermid in this volume). An amendment that enabled, but did not compel, school boards to provide 'instruction in the Gaelic language and literature' to students in evening continuation classes in 'Gaelic-speaking districts' was incorporated into the 1908 Act, but the analogous provision for day schools suggested by John Sinclair (the Scottish Secretary) was defeated. The provision was incorporated into the subsequent 1918 Education Act, however, following further campaigning including a petition organised by An Comunn Gàidhealach, which attracted at least 12,000 signatures.[30] The 1918 Act required education authorities to ensure 'adequate provision . . . of all forms of primary, intermediate and secondary education in day schools (including the adequate provision for teaching Gaelic in Gaelic-speaking areas)', with the Scottish Secretary accepting compulsion for the school boards in this regard on account of the precedent for this in Wales,[31] where, for example, the Welsh Board of Education stated in the Education Code of 1907: 'Provision for the teaching of the Welsh Language and Literature should be made in districts where Welsh is spoken'.[32] However, the Scottish provision was not as strong as its Welsh counterpart, as no additional finance was made available. Moreover, the phrases 'adequate provision' and 'Gaelic-speaking areas' were not defined in the 1918 Act, and thus the latter presumed Craik's definition in the Code of 1886.

The long-term effect of the Act and of other developments since the 1886 Scotch Code – for example, the incorporation of Gaelic in the School Leaving Certificate at the Lower Grade in 1905 and at the Higher Grade in 1915 – was measured by An Comunn Gàidhealach in 1935–6 through a survey of Highland schools' use of Gaelic. The results showed that 7,129 elementary pupils were being taught Gaelic as a subject, within 284 schools in Inverness-shire, Ross, Argyll and Sutherland (approximately 20 per cent of elementary pupils in these areas). This provision was typically for native speakers of the language. At the secondary school stage, the survey found 864 pupils to be studying Gaelic as a subject, for an average of 3.75 hours a week, within twenty-two schools in Inverness-shire, Ross and Argyll. This was mostly for native speakers of Gaelic, but the county of Argyll additionally made provision for pupils whose parents wished them to learn the language. On the basis of this evidence, An Comunn recommended the extension of the teaching of Gaelic as a subject in primary and secondary schools across Scotland.[33]

Further indication of the generally more sympathetic official view of Gaelic after 1918 may be detected in An Comunn's finding that Gaelic was 'very generally' used as a medium of instruction in the infant department, and as a medium of instruction of subjects such as 'nature study, geography, gardening, music and history' in primary schools in which pupils were native Gaelic speakers.[34] This use of Gaelic to provide a link between the child's home and school environments constituted a form of child-centred education, as had been developing in Scotland since the early 1920s.[35] Thus, as respect for the child continued to grow in policy after 1945, so too did official acceptance of Gaelic as part of some children's identity. In 1946, the Advisory Council on Education in Scotland – in its generally child-centred report on primary education – recommended Gaelic lessons for pupils in Gaelic-speaking areas, and in 1947 the Council similarly accepted the cultural value of school-based tuition in Gaelic language and literature at the secondary school stage for Gaelic-speaking pupils in the Highlands, and for pupils of 'Celtic origin' living outwith the Highlands.[36] They argued that the study of Gaelic was the 'best linguistic training that can be offered' to Gaelic-speaking pupils at secondary school, with Gaelic literature having 'an intimacy of appeal no other [literature] could rival, since it enshrines the experience of their own race'.[37] That such Gaelic language provision was intended to be a form of child-centred education is underlined by the Council's rejection of An Comunn Gàidhealach's recommendation that Gaelic should be offered as a secondary-school subject to all pupils in Scotland. Indeed, the Council argued that for pupils not of Celtic origin, Gaelic was difficult to learn, lacked utility value and did not have a literature of the 'sustained greatness' and the 'immense range and volume' of its European counterparts.[38]

Outwith the Highlands, there was the beginning of local interest in teaching Gaelic. The developments were summed up by the SED slightly later, when they noted that demand for Gaelic as a secondary subject had developed in 'some Lowland towns with a strong Gaelic speaking population'.[39] Two secondary schools in Glasgow began teaching Gaelic to learners in 1946, and in 1958 new provision for teaching Gaelic was made in Greenock and Edinburgh. The rationale for the provision had also begun to anticipate later aims of reviving the language, not just catering in a child-centred way for existing speakers: thus, according to a survey by the Scottish Council for Research in Education (SCRE) in 1959, amongst the eighty-nine first-year secondary pupils studying Gaelic within these four Lowland secondary schools, fifty-six pupils reported that neither of their parents spoke Gaelic.[40]

The emergence of such a dual role for Gaelic in education (child-centredness and Gaelic language maintenance) was acknowledged by the SED in its memoranda on primary and junior secondary education (published in 1950 and 1955 respectively). These reports recommended the incorporation of Gaelic language and literature into the education of Gaelic-speaking pupils from Gaelic-speaking areas, and also recommended the use of Gaelic in social subjects (such as local geography and history, music, nature study, rural subjects, homecraft, games and religious education). The aims of such provision were primarily child-centred – that the curriculum 'be properly related to the language and culture of the community to which these [Gaelic-speaking] pupils belong' and in which 'many pupils . . . are likely to remain'. The linguistic aim was 'to make the pupils completely bilingual'.[41] However, the 1955 report also suggested a role for the school in Gaelic-language maintenance, the first SED publication to do so. It noted the role of Gaelic teachers in encouraging pupils 'to regard their own language with respect, to find its study satisfying and rewarding, and to continue its use in the future' and the importance of Gaelic-speaking parents 'co-operating with the schools in their efforts to preserve the language'.[42] The SED's recommendations were formalised in the 1956 Schools (Scotland) Code:

> In Gaelic-speaking areas . . . reasonable provision shall be made in schemes of work for the instruction of Gaelic-speaking pupils in the Gaelic language and literature, and the Gaelic language shall be used where appropriate for instructing Gaelic-speaking pupils in other subjects.[43]

The effects of these post-war changes were measured by a SCRE survey in 1957 of Argyll, Inverness, Ross and Sutherland. Gaelic was found to be taught as a subject to 4,848 primary pupils within 211 schools (19 per cent of the primary school population in these areas), with 1,257 pupils also being taught other subjects through the medium of Gaelic. Of all the pupils in these areas, 3,829 had Gaelic as a first language – here defined in a rather more child-centred way than in such reports previously (which had normally referred to the language of the home): it was 'the language in which the child is more at ease and the one which he or she tends to use first in conversation'.[44] At the secondary school stage in 1959, 1,941 pupils (18 per cent of the secondary school population in these districts) were studying Gaelic as a school subject, with twenty-seven pupils presented at the Lower Grade of the Leaving Certificate, and sixty-two at the Higher Grade.[45]

A Gaelic Education Scheme was launched in the bilingual areas of Inverness-shire in 1960 as a response to the permissive policy context created by the 1956 Schools Code.[46] The scheme proposed a focus on oral immersion in Gaelic at the early primary school stage, the introduction of reading in Gaelic for monolingual Gaelic speakers, the teaching of Gaelic as a subject through the medium of Gaelic and the use of Gaelic in history, geography, nature study, physical education, art and scripture. Such a pedagogical approach was informed by research evidence from 1948 on the benefits of postponing the teaching of English to first-language Gaelic primary pupils, and with experience of using Welsh in the education of first-language Welsh pupils in Wales.[47] The aim of the pedagogical approach adopted by the Inverness-shire scheme was to give pupils a 'reasonable fluency in oral expression, reading and writing [in Gaelic], at the end of the primary school course'.[48]

This scheme also strengthened the emerging theme of using education to help maintain the Gaelic language. This more overtly political purpose was to become the dominant rationale in the development of Gaelic education later in the century. The Inverness-shire scheme claimed that it would contribute to the perpetuation of Gaelic as a spoken language by 'promoting the prestige of Gaelic as the community language', as had been recommended by the Welsh Board of Education in relation to Welsh in 1927.[49] Awareness amongst Scottish educationalists that Welsh-medium education had successfully increased both the levels of Welsh language competence amongst children and the prestige of Welsh as a community language is suggested by the attendance by representatives of the Welsh Department of the Ministry of Education at a conference on Gaelic in education in 1956,[50] and by explicit acknowledgement of such success by the SCRE in 1961: 'in Wales . . . the schools, backed by the Welsh-speaking communities are being used . . . as a conscious instrument for the preservation of the Welsh language . . . and the result of all this effort is that the Welsh language is holding its own'.[51]

Such language maintenance rationales came at a time when census figures had shown a decrease in the number of Gaelic speakers from 136,135 in 1931 to 80,978 in 1961, and the study conducted by SCRE in 1958 had shown the proportion of first-language Gaelic speakers in Argyll, Inverness-shire, and Ross and Cromarty to decrease from 17.7 per cent of Primary 7 pupils to 13.7 per cent of Primary 1 pupils.[52] Evidence provided by the SCRE regarding the linguistic background of the first-year secondary school pupils studying Gaelic as a subject in these counties showed that one-third of pupils reported 'usually' speaking English at home.[53] One consequence of the emergence of secondary pupils' studying Gaelic who were not already Gaelic speakers was a need for a properly devised course for Gaelic learners (analogously to other languages). Inspectors' reports from the mid-1950s noted the different performance of the two groups of pupils, 'native speaking candidates' having 'a distinct advantage over those whose first language is English'.[54] In 1960, the decision was thus taken to differentiate between the two groups, and to introduce 'learners' and 'native speakers' examinations in Gaelic in the Ordinary Grade when it was launched in 1962. A learners' Higher Grade examination in Gaelic was introduced in 1968. (We return towards the end of the chapter to the question of Gaelic learners in this sense.)

The culmination of the child-centred developments, and thus the immediate background to the much firmer growth of the language-maintenance rationale, was the Scottish Education Department's *Primary Education in Scotland* report of 1965 – the 'Primary Memorandum' that continued to shape Scottish education in child-centred ways for the next half-century.[55] It acknowledged the decline in Gaelic use amongst school-aged children in Gaelic-speaking areas, but did not suggest including first-language English speakers in Gaelic education: the aim was still to meet the needs of first-language Gaelic pupils by using Gaelic in the initial primary school stages, teaching Gaelic as a subject and also, where resources allowed, using Gaelic as a medium of instruction for other subjects.[56] For the first time in any official report, there was also some recognition of the pedagogical benefits of introducing reading in Gaelic: Gaelic-speaking pupils 'readily go on to master the mechanics of reading in English, and both languages can be used to support each other in enabling the pupils to understand the content of their reading'.[57] The report additionally reiterated the role of the school in Gaelic language maintenance, first acknowledged by the SED in 1955.[58]

State support for Gaelic educational developments was also evidenced in the SED's contribution to the funding of the 1975 Bilingual Education Project established by the new all-purpose local authority Comhairle nan Eilean (Western Isles Council). The Council covered the outer island areas of the former counties of Ross and Cromarty and Inverness and was the most strongly Gaelic-speaking local government area (with 82 per cent of the population reporting themselves to be Gaelic speakers in the 1971 Census). However, there was evidence of a decline in Gaelic speaking amongst the young in the new Council's area: research conducted in 1974 showed the proportion of fluent Gaelic-speaking pupils to decrease from 78 per cent amongst the Primary 7s to 61 per cent amongst the Primary 1s in the fifty-six primary schools in the Gaelic-speaking areas.[59]

The Bilingual Education Project, like the Inverness-shire scheme, aimed to develop bilingual education for pupils from Gaelic-speaking areas which developed links between the pupils' community context and the school. Following the Primary Memorandum, the project intended that reading be introduced in

Gaelic to Gaelic-speaking pupils, and otherwise, in the words of the project director John Murray, that Gaelic 'flow across the curriculum', primarily by bilingual teaching of the multi-disciplinary curricular area Environmental Studies. The project began with the development of bilingual teaching materials for the lower primary school stages of twenty schools in which approximately 90 per cent of pupils and teachers were Gaelic speakers, and extended throughout the primary school stages of these schools by 1978. By 1981, the scheme was operating within thirty-four of the authority's sixty primary schools. The aim was to make all Gaelic-speaking pupils equally fluent and literate in Gaelic and English by the end of primary school and to enable English-speaking pupils in infant classes to learn Gaelic if their parents so wished. [60] However, despite such enthusiasm for Gaelic from the local council, MacLeod noted in 1976 that attitudes to Gaelic amongst many parents within Gaelic-speaking areas of the Highlands and Islands remained ambivalent,[61] still holding that Gaelic could be an impediment to social mobility.

The Bilingual Education Project was successful in providing a curriculum which related to the local community, and indeed was reported to have gradually overcome parental scepticism (rather in the manner that child-centred education was gradually accepted in Scottish education by the early 1980s).[62] In the second phase of the project (1978–81), it was noted that 'almost all [Gaelic-speaking] parents who choose to speak English in the home wish their children to become skilled in Gaelic through the school. Also, almost all non-Gaelic speaking parents . . . are very eager for their children to learn Gaelic in school'.[63] At the end of the SED-funded period of the project (1981), Comhairle nan Eilean thus decided to establish a Bilingual Curriculum Development Unit to continue the work of the Bilingual Education Project at the primary school stage, and to extend the project to the secondary school stage 'in selected schools and involving a restricted range of subjects'.[64] A bilingual secondary pilot project was launched in 1983 in which pupils in two small junior secondaries in Lewis were taught social subjects through Gaelic. The Scottish Office's evaluation of the Bilingual Education Project at the primary school stage, published in 1987, perceived it to be a good example of both child-centred and bilingual education, but expressed reservations about the future efficacy of the bilingual language model in making pupils as competent in Gaelic as they were in English in communities where there was a language shift to English.[65]

Such concerns had been voiced by parents, educationalists and language activists since the early 1980s in relation both to the Bilingual Education Project and to a similar scheme that had been launched in five primary schools on Skye, within Highland Region, in 1978.[66] Awareness of research which indicated that the early years were the 'critical period' for language learning,[67] together with knowledge of the efficacy of the early total immersion approach employed in Anglicised areas of Wales (where pupils had their nursery and early primary education entirely through the medium of Welsh), prompted the establishment of four Gaelic-medium playgroups in Edinburgh, Pitlochry, Oban and Sleat (on Skye) in 1980. Like the Welsh-medium playgroups, these would accept pupils from both Celtic-language-speaking and non-Celtic-language-speaking backgrounds. By 1990, there were seventy-six such Gaelic-medium playgroups with 1,200 children, organised under a national Gaelic playgroup association – Comhairle nan Sgoiltean Àraich.

Gaelic in Education (1980–2013): Child-centred Language Maintenance

Parental demand for Gaelic-medium early-total-immersion primary education in the 1980s developed from such Gaelic-immersion playgroups, and was facilitated by a policy context of increased parental choice in education. The 1980 Education (Scotland) Act reiterated the stipulation (established in 1918) that local authorities were to make 'adequate provision' for 'the teaching of Gaelic in Gaelic-speaking areas', and the 1981 Education (Scotland) Act extended provision for parental choice in education (established in the 1945 Act) to enable parents to request that their child attend a particular school. Parental choice rapidly became an accepted principle throughout Scottish education (despite the origins of the policy with the increasingly unpopular Conservative government).[68] A study of Gaelic-speaking and English-speaking parents conducted by Grant in 1983 explored the rationales underpinning parental preference for Gaelic-medium primary education, finding it typically to be associated with a wish to continue a tradition of Gaelic speaking (at a family, community or national level) and with a wish to realise the advantages of bilingualism, for example the easier acquisition of subsequent languages.[69] The conversion of such parental views into Gaelic-medium primary provision was supported by recently established local and national administrative structures for Gaelic, such as Highland Regional Council's working party on Gaelic (established in 1982), and Comunn na Gàidhlig, a government-funded national development body established in 1984 charged with co-ordinating pre-school and primary education developments. The first Gaelic-medium primary provision was set up in 1985 within John Maxwell Primary School in Glasgow and Central Primary School in Inverness. Such schools became 'dual-stream' schools, meaning that they provided both Gaelic-medium and English-medium education.

These pioneering developments became the beginnings of a national movement when the Scottish Office was converted to supporting the cause, a means by which the embattled Conservative administration could emphasise its Scottish credentials and could draw upon a political consensus towards Gaelic that has persisted to the present. (It was for similar reasons that the government also invested in Gaelic-medium broadcasting.[70]) The financial mechanism for the new education developments, established in 1986, was the Grants for Gaelic Language Education (Scotland) Regulations which enabled local authorities to apply for funding for 'the teaching of the Gaelic language or the teaching in that language of other subjects'. The grant allocated £250,000 in its first year. Crucially, the money was additional to general local authority grants (attractive at a time of persisting financial stringency) and was ring-fenced, thus enabling language campaigners locally to insist that the money be spent as intended.

The distinguishing feature of Gaelic-medium education, as compared with earlier bilingual education, was the emphasis on immersion in Gaelic. The model used is known in the international bilingual education literature as 'early total immersion', and typically involves 100 per cent immersion in the second language for the first two or three years of primary schooling, with the second language used as the main medium of instruction in middle and upper primary.[71] The model used in the Bilingual Education Project in the Western Isles was an example of 'partial immersion' – where the language is used for up to 50 per cent of curricular instruction throughout primary schooling. The shift towards early total immersion emerged from local experience of the shortcomings of the bilingual education model in fostering equal competence in Gaelic and English, and from the emergence of research from Canada illustrating the effectiveness of early total immersion.[72]

Wider curricular developments in Scotland in the early 1990s enabled an unprecedented degree of standardisation in the definition of Gaelic education. As part of the 5–14 programme – new curricular guidance covering the primary and early secondary school stages – Gaelic 5–14 was published in 1993, and provided recommendations for both the language model to be used in Gaelic-medium education, and for the teaching of Gaelic as a subject within English-medium education. For Gaelic-medium education, the guidelines recommended an 'initial [Gaelic] immersion phase of at least two years' duration', that literacy be introduced in Gaelic and that Gaelic remain the 'predominant teaching medium throughout the primary stages'.[73] By this time, a total of forty-five Gaelic-medium primary providers teaching 1,080 pupils existed within six local authorities. The Specific Grants allocated £1.72 million in the 1992–3 academic year.

The growth in Gaelic-medium primary education continued in the 1990s. Studies show parental rationales for choice at this time still to relate to a wish to preserve cultural heritage and to the benefits of bilingualism, but also to relate to a belief that Gaelic-medium education provided a strong pedagogical context for pupils (small class sizes, a good ethos and high-quality teaching).[74] The rationale for the choice of Gaelic-medium education had thus become what might be termed child-centred language maintenance. By 1999, there were a total of fifty-nine Gaelic-medium primary providers, teaching 1,831 pupils within twelve local authorities. However, growth of Gaelic-medium education has slowed since 1999. In the 2013–14 school year, Gaelic-medium primary provision was still available in fifty-nine schools, although the number of pupils taught within these had increased to 2,652. The provision is made across fourteen local authorities, with children from thirteen of the remaining eighteen local authority areas in Scotland able to access Gaelic-medium education through cross-boundary agreements between local authorities.

The lack of increase in the number of Gaelic-medium primary providers between 1999 and 2013, despite policy support for the expansion of such provision in the early years of political devolution in Scotland, is mainly due to a shortage of Gaelic-speaking primary teachers.[75] This shortage is related to the precarious position of the language itself, with only 58,652 speakers (or 1.2 per cent of the Scottish population) at the 2001 Census. Thus, the Standards in Scotland's Schools etc. Act 2000, which required local authorities to report annually on their present and planned provision for Gaelic-medium education, and the Gaelic (Language) Scotland Act 2005 – which established Bòrd na Gàidhlig as a body charged with promoting Gaelic language, culture and education – have mostly helped to expand pupil numbers within existing Gaelic-medium primary provision, rather than establish new provision. Such an increase in capacity has been partly enabled by the conversion of three dual-stream schools into free-standing (that is, wholly Gaelic) schools – in Glasgow in 1999, Inverness in 2007 and Edinburgh in 2013. In the 2013–14 school year these urban free-standing schools had an average of 288 Gaelic-medium pupils per school, compared with an average of thirty-two per dual-stream school.

Such Gaelic-medium primary education is available in a range of community-level linguistic contexts, and is usually associated with a Gaelic-medium nursery (of which there were fifty-eight, with 985 pupils, in 2013–14). Figure 17.1 shows the location of Gaelic-medium primary providers in 2013–14 alongside the population density of Gaelic-speakers (civil parish level) at the 2011 Census.

Most of this Gaelic-medium primary education is in the north-west, with Highland Council making provision within twenty-two schools, Comhairle nan Eilean Siar (Western Isles Council) in nineteen and Argyll and Bute in six. Ten local authorities in the Lowlands offer Gaelic-medium provision within one school in the authority, whilst Perth and Kinross offer it within two. In total, 0.7 per cent of the Scottish primary-school population is educated in Gaelic-medium education; the proportion of Gaelic-medium pupils within a local authority ranging from 30.9 per cent in Comhairle nan Eilean Siar to 0.12 per cent in Perth and Kinross in 2013–14. Gaelic language use in the community surrounding Gaelic-medium provision is particularly important in the context of the Curriculum for Excellence, a 3–18 curriculum launched in 2010 (see the chapters by Humes and by Paterson in the present volume). This follows the early-total-immersion language model outlined in Gaelic 5–14, but additionally emphasises the importance of pupils using their Gaelic language skills both 'within and beyond' their place of learning.[76]

Developments in Gaelic-medium secondary education have been more limited. Only fifteen of the thirty-three secondary schools into which the Gaelic-medium primary schools feed provide any subjects through the medium of Gaelic in addition to Gaelic as a subject for fluent speakers of the language. Four of these fifteen secondaries provide six or more subjects through the medium of Gaelic; the other eleven offer an average of three subjects per school (usually including history and geography).[77] There is only one wholly Gaelic-medium secondary school, established in 2006 in Glasgow. The consequence is that, amongst all secondary schools making provision for pupils who have attended Gaelic-medium

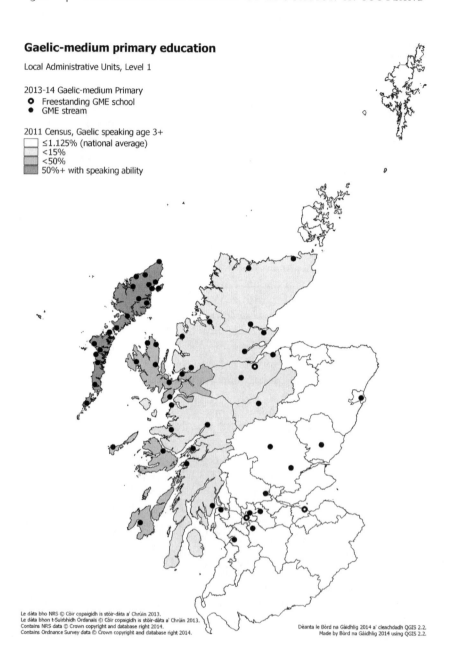

Gaelic-medium primary education

Local Administrative Units, Level 1

2013-14 Gaelic-medium Primary
- ○ Freestanding GME school
- ● GME stream

2011 Census, Gaelic speaking age 3+
- ≤1.125% (national average)
- <15%
- <50%
- 50%+ with speaking ability

Le dàta bho NRS © Còir copaigidh is stòir-dàta a' Chrùin 2013.
Le dàta bhon t-Suirbhidh Òrdanais © Còir copaigidh is stòir-dàta a' Chrùin 2013.
Contains NRS data © Crown copyright and database right 2014.
Contains Ordnance Survey data © Crown copyright and database right 2014.

Dèanta le Bòrd na Gàidhlig 2014 a' cleachdadh QGIS 2.2.
Made by Bòrd na Gàidhlig 2014 using QGIS 2.2.

Figure 17.1 Location of Gaelic-medium primary education, 2013–14.
Copyright Bòrd na Gàidhlig.

primary education, the average teaching time conducted through the medium of Gaelic is 17 per cent in the first year of secondary school. This compares with a national average of 70 per cent in the final year of Gaelic-medium primary schooling.[78] Provision reduces further at the middle to upper secondary school stages – with only geography and history provided through the medium of Gaelic in at least four secondary schools in Scotland in the third and fourth years of secondary school stages, and only Gaelic as a subject taught through the medium of Gaelic in at least four secondary schools in the fifth and sixth years of secondary school.[79] In the new Scottish national examination system inaugurated in 2014, Gaelic language examinations were available for Gaelic, geography, history, modern studies and mathematics.

The most apparent reason for such a weak pattern of provision for Gaelic-medium secondary education is in policy. In 1994 – a decade after the appearance of Gaelic-medium primary schooling – Her Majesty's Inspectors still had doubts about Gaelic-medium secondary education. They noted existing secondary provision to be 'fragmented and incidental' because it was determined by the availability of Gaelic-speaking subject specialists who were also literate in Gaelic. The inspectorate expressed concern that small year cohorts of Gaelic-medium pupils could not sustain a varied and stimulating learning environment, and would be isolated from the 'main school'.[80] The inspectorate concluded that such Gaelic-medium secondary provision was 'neither desirable nor feasible' and instead recommended that pupils from Gaelic-medium primary education be offered Gaelic language and literature as a secondary school subject, and a Gaelic-medium course in Gaelic culture – which was to include 'aspects of Gaelic culture, including elements from History, Geography, Music, Art and Drama'.[81] The Scottish Office adopted the inspectorate's recommendations in April 1996 (announced in the Williamson lecture by Secretary of State for Scotland Michael Forsyth), but revised their position in June 1997, when Brian Wilson MP, Minister of State at the Scottish Office with special responsibility for Gaelic, announced that the inspectors and Education Department officials had been asked to 'enter into discussions with local authorities about ways in which [Gaelic-speaking] secondary subject teachers . . . might be given additional training to allow them to use [their] Gaelic as the medium of the classroom in S1/S2'.[82] By 2005, in the next official HMI report on Gaelic education, the inspectorate's position had shifted from that expressed in 1994. In 2005, they argued 'a single Gaelic course' to be 'insufficient' to maintain and develop the Gaelic language competencies of pupils educated in Gaelic-medium primary education, and rather advocated the further development of Gaelic-medium provision at the secondary-school level.[83]

There are also two other explanations for the current situation in secondary schools. One, noted by the General Teaching Council for Scotland in 1999, and by the inspectors in 2005 and 2011, is the shortage of teacher supply.[84] The other reason may be a persistence of the sense among parents – despite the much-changed attitudes to Gaelic – that English is of paramout importance for educational success in further and tertiary education, and still the main means of occupational success later.[85] There exist limited opportunities to undertake tertiary education through the medium of Gaelic – with 240 students studying for degrees through the medium of Gaelic in the 2013–14 academic year within the University of the Highlands and Islands (at Sabhal Mòr Ostaig on Skye and Lews Castle College in Lewis) – 0.15 per cent of the total undergraduate population in Scotland.[86] Students may also study through the medium of Gaelic as part of degrees in Celtic at the Universities of Aberdeen, Edinburgh and Glasgow, and as part of initial and postgraduate Gaelic-medium teacher education at the Universities of the Highlands and Islands, Aberdeen and Strathclyde. Opportunities for Gaelic-medium employment are currently limited, with posts typically within the education, media and public administration sectors.[87]

The two national language plans that have been published for Gaelic by Bòrd na Gàidhlig (2007–12 and 2012–17) both emphasise language acquisition through Celtic-medium pre-school and primary education and the continued development of Gaelic amongst such pupils in adolescence and adulthood as crucial elements of the maintenance of Gaelic. Results from research into the attainment of Gaelic-medium primary pupils conducted using data from 1996–9 and from 2006–9 showed Primary 7 pupils to be attaining the expected curricular levels in Gaelic for their school stage; indeed, Gaelic-medium pupils were doing as well in Gaelic as English-medium pupils do in English, and additionally Gaelic-medium pupils outperform English-medium pupils in English reading, whilst performing as well as their English-medium counterparts in English writing, mathematics and science.[88] Such Gaelic-language attainment is notable, given that a maximum of 17 per cent of Gaelic-medium pupils have Gaelic as their 'main home language'.[89] The bilingual competencies of Gaelic-medium primary pupils have also recently been shown to be associated with the cognitive benefits of bilingualism.[90] However, if the impact of Gaelic-medium education is measured by the use of Gaelic in everyday communication, the conclusion is much more uncertain, especially after early childhood. For example, it was reported by teachers in a survey in 2011 that, in secondary schools which provide some Gaelic-medium education, only about 12 per cent of Gaelic-speaking pupils actually used Gaelic for more than half the time outwith the classroom even when speaking to each other.[91]

Nevertheless, there is evidence that the growth of Gaelic-medium education may indeed have started to fulfil the policy makers' goals of reversing the decline in Gaelic-speaker numbers. The 17 per cent decrease between 1981 and 1991 reduced to 11 per cent between 1991 and 2001 and to 2 per cent between 2001 and 2011. The impact of education on the percentage decrease is suggested by there being an increase in the proportion of three to four, five to fourteen and fifteen to nineteen year olds who speak Gaelic in 2011, as compared with 2001, but a decrease in all older age groups.[92]

The final part of the story concerns recent developments in Gaelic for learners, in the sense of Gaelic provided as a subject like any other additional language in the curriculum. Opportunities for English-medium primary pupils to learn

Gaelic as a school subject have developed independently from Gaelic-medium education. Comhairle nan Eilean Siar pledged to offer Gaelic as a school subject to all primary and early secondary school pupils in 1980, and in 2000 a pilot scheme entitled Gaelic Language in the Primary School was undertaken in Argyll and Bute and in Highland. The latter provision was similar to that for other languages under the heading of 'Modern Languages in the Primary School', which had been launched in 1989. The Gaelic provision differs in that it typically starts in the middle, rather than the upper, primary school stages. All such language teaching is provided by the class teacher, who receives training for this purpose, and the Gaelic scheme is usually provided in addition to its modern foreign languages counterpart. The expansion of Gaelic as a primary school subject is difficult to track as annual figures on the number of pupils studying Gaelic at primary school within English-medium education were only incorporated into the Government's annual reporting in 2005, when 5,019 pupils were reported to be receiving Gaelic learners' provision.[93] A study conducted by Bòrd na Gàidhlig in 2009–10 showed there to be 5,500 pupils learning Gaelic in 113 schools within eight local authority areas.[94] Gaelic as a subject was thus taught to 1.5 per cent of the primary school population, in around 5 per cent of all primary schools in 2009–10. Governmental records from the 2013–14 school year report the number of pupils receiving Gaelic for learners in English-medium education to be 3,389.[95] Gaelic as a subject is also offered to learners of the language in thirty-one secondary schools, mostly the same as offer Gaelic as a subject for fluent speakers. In 2013–14, Gaelic was taught to 3,431 learner pupils within these secondary schools.[96]

Conclusions

Attitudes to Gaelic in education since 1872 have been shaped by changes of two quite different kinds. One is the specific instance of Gaelic within the much more general growth of child-centredness in Scottish education. That helps to explain the increasingly favourable official attitudes from the first decade of the century onwards – symbolised most influentially in the Gaelic passages in the 1918 Education (Scotland) Act. Even though the main aim still was to render Gaelic-speaking children fluent in English, the new international ideas of the time encouraged policy makers to understand that effective teaching had to pay attention to the child's world. Where that world was still predominantly Gaelic, recognising the language and cultural context of the child's home community was to be inferred from these new pedagogical principles. But alongside this has been the slow growth of a different motive, that education be used to maintain the Gaelic language and culture. This approach emerged alongside the child-centred rationale in the 1950s and continued to run in parallel up to the early 1980s when language-planning aims came to the fore. At this time, there emerged a wish to use Gaelic-medium education both to develop the Gaelic-language abilities of Gaelic-speaking pupils, and to enable the acquisition of Gaelic by English-speaking pupils. The provision of Gaelic as a subject in English-medium

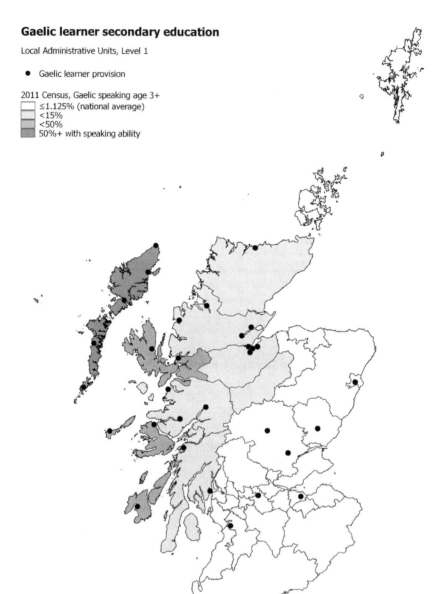

Gaelic learner secondary education

Local Administrative Units, Level 1

● Gaelic learner provision

2011 Census, Gaelic speaking age 3+
- ≤1.125% (national average)
- <15%
- <50%
- 50%+ with speaking ability

Le dàta bho NRS © Còir copaigidh is stòir-dàta a' Chrùin 2013.
Le dàta bhon t-Suirbhidh Òrdanais © Còir copaigidh is stòir-dàta a' Chrùin 2013.
Contains NRS data © Crown copyright and database right 2014.
Contains Ordnance Survey data © Crown copyright and database right 2014.

Dèanta le Bòrd na Gàidhlig 2014 a' cleachdadh QGIS 2.2.
Made by Bòrd na Gàidhlig 2014 using QGIS 2.2.

Figure 17.2 Location of Gaelic-learner secondary education, 2013–14.
Copyright Bòrd na Gàidhlig.

education has been shaped by similar influences. Provision made in the Lowlands in the 1940s was recommended only for those of Celtic origin, following a child-centred rationale, and the development of Gaelic in primary education from the 1980s initially focused on Highland regions. Indeed, Gaelic as a subject for learners at the secondary-school stage is still predominantly offered within the north-west of Scotland, as Figure 17.2 highlights.

The main outcome of the history outlined in this chapter is a form of Gaelic-medium education which has been shown to be an effective model of fostering bilingualism and its associated benefits amongst both its Gaelic-first language and English-first language pupils. Provision has also developed for a small proportion of English-medium pupils to learn Gaelic. The immediate challenge facing Gaelic in education is now staffing – particularly for the planned expansion of Gaelic-medium primary education and the extension of such provision to secondary and tertiary education. The next few decades will also reveal whether the development of Gaelic in education since the 1980s does achieve the political goal of safegarding the future of the language itself.

Notes

1. *Education (Scotland) Act 1872* (John Menzies & Co., 1872).
2. Alexander Thomson, 'Introduction', in *Education (Scotland) Act 1872*, p. 5.
3. Murdo MacLeod, 'Gaelic in Highland education', *Transactions of the Gaelic Society of Inverness* 43 (1963), 320.
4. Kenneth MacKinnon, 'Education and social control: The case of Gaelic Scotland', *Scottish Educational Studies* 4 (1972), 130–1; Matthew MacIver, 'Gaelic medium education. Is it really a 20th century phenomenon?' Conference presentation at Rannsachadh na Gàidhlig 6, 24 August 2010.
5. Charles Withers, 'Education and the Gaelic language', in Heather Holmes (ed.), *Institutions of Scotland: Education*, Scottish Life and Society: A Compendium of Scottish Ethnology, vol. 11 (Tuckwell Press, 2000), p. 403; T. C. Smout, *A Century of the Scottish People* (Collins, 1986), p. 83; John Lorne Campbell, *Gaelic in Scottish Education and Life: Past, Present and Future* (W. & A. K. Johnston., 1945), p. 62; John A. Smith, 'The 1872 Education (Scotland) Act and Gaelic education', *Transactions of the Gaelic Society of Inverness* 51 (1978–80), 8.
6. Eugen Weber, *Peasants into Frenchmen: The Modernisation of Rural France, 1870–1914* (Chatto and Windus, 1977); Ernest Gellner, *Nations and Nationalism* (Blackwell, 1983); John Edwards, *Language and Identity* (Cambridge University Press, 2009), Chapter 10.
7. George D. Campbell, James Greig, Thomas Harvey, Charles F. Maxwell, A. Nicolson, A. C. Sellar, *Education Commission (Scotland)* (HMSO, 1866), PP vols XXV and XXVI, p. 968; Education Commission (Scotland), First Report by Her Majesty's Commissioners appointed to inquire into the Schools in Scotland. (HMSO, 1865), PP vol. XVII, p. 372.
8. John Forbes, 'Letter from the Gaelic Society of London to the Secretary of the Board of Education for Scotland', *The Highlander*, 2 May 1874, p. 5.
9. Scotch Education Department, *Minute of the Board of Education for Scotland submitting draft articles of a code for that country* (HMSO, 1873), PP vol. LII, p. 504.

10. Mary K. MacLeod, 'The interaction of Scottish educational developments and socio-economic factors on Gaelic education in Gaelic-speaking areas, with particular reference to the period 1872–1918' (unpublished PhD dissertation, University of Edinburgh, 1981), 11, 60–1.
11. Smith, 'The 1872 Education (Scotland) Act', 37.
12. Scotch Education Department, *Minute of the Board of Education*, p. 13.
13. Victor E. Durkacz, *The Decline of the Celtic Languages* (John Donald, 1996), p. 179.
14. Scotch Education Department, *Return, in the Form annexed, of the Names of the School Boards in certain parts of Scotland to which the Circular of the Education Department regarding Instruction in the Gaelic Language, dated the 17th day of May 1876, was addressed; together with the replies from the Boards* (HMSO,1877), PP vol. LXVII, pp. 803–10.
15. Board of Education for Scotland, *Third Annual Report of the Board of Education for Scotland* (HMSO, 1876), PP vol. XXV, p. 308.
16. Committee of Council on Education in Scotland, *Report of the Committee of Council on Education in Scotland 1877–78* (HMSO, 1878), PP vol. XXXI, p. 170. For a less supportive view of Gaelic in education, see Committee of Council on Education in Scotland, *Report of the Committee of Council on Education in Scotland 1878–79* (HMSO, 1879), PP vol. XXV p. 248.
17. Scotch Education Department, *Code of Regulations* (HMSO, 1878), PP vol. LX, pp. 527–8; Smith, 'The 1872 Education (Scotland) Act', p. 50.
18. Ewen A. Cameron, *Land for the People? The British Government and the Scottish Highlands, c. 1880–1925* (Tuckwell Press, 1996).
19. Francis Napier, *Report of Her Majesty's Commissioners of Inquiry into the Condition of the Crofters and Cottars in the Highlands and Islands of Scotland* (HMSO, 1884), PP vol. XXXII, p. 81.
20. Smith, 'The 1872 Education (Scotland) Act', 46.
21. Henry Craik, *Report on Highland Schools*, vol. XXVI (HMSO, 1884), p. 534.
22. Ibid., p. 530.
23. Scotch Education Department, *Code of Regulations* (HMSO, 1886), PP vol. LI, pp. 686, 730.
24. Committee of Council on Education in Scotland, *Report of the Committee of Council on Education in Scotland 1885–86* (HMSO, 1886), PP vol. XXVII, p. 516.
25. Craik, *Report on Highland Schools*, p. 8.
26. *Gaelic Census (Scotland)* (HMSO, 1882), PP vol. L, pp. 857–9.
27. Scotch Education Department, *Scotch Education Department Return* (HMSO, 1901), PP vol. LVII, p. 288.
28. Committee of Council on Education in Scotland, *Report of the Committee of Council on Education in Scotland* (HMSO, 1899), PP vol. XXVI, p. 97.
29. Charles S. Parker, *Third Report of the Committee appointed to inquire into certain questions relating to Education in Scotland* (HMSO, 1888), PP vol. XLI, p. 689.
30. For details on the processes surrounding the incorporation of Gaelic into the 1908 and 1918 Education Acts, see MacLeod, 'The interaction of Scottish educational developments', pp. 313–42.
31. Ibid., p. 341.
32. Board of Education, Welsh Department, *Code of Regulations for Public Elementary Schools in Wales* (HMSO, 1907), PP vol. LXII, p. 85.
33. An Comunn Gàidhealach, *Report of the Special Committee on the Teaching of Gaelic in Schools and Colleges* (An Commun Gàidhealach, 1936), p. 10.
34. Ibid., pp. 6, 12.

35. Lindsay Paterson, *Scottish Education in the Twentieth Century* (Edinburgh University Press, 2003), pp. 46–50.
36. Scottish Education Department, *Primary Education: A Report of the Advisory Council on Education in Scotland.* (HMSO, 1946), PP vol. XI, p.105. Scottish Education Department, *Secondary Education: A Report of the Advisory Council on Education in Scotland.* (HMSO, 1947), p. 271.
37. Scottish Education Department, *Secondary Education*, p. 271.
38. Ibid., p. 271.
39. Scottish Education Department. *Education in Scotland in 1960. A Report of the Secretary of State for Scotland* (HMSO, 1961), PP vol. XIII, p. 927.
40. Scottish Council for Research in Education [henceforth: SCRE], *Gaelic-speaking Children in Highland Schools* (University of London Press, 1961), p. 76.
41. Scottish Education Department, *Junior Secondary Education* (HMSO, 1955), p. 274. See also Scottish Education Department, *The Primary School in Scotland.* (HMSO, 1950).
42. Scottish Education Department, *Junior Secondary Education*, p. 275.
43. MacLeod, 'Gaelic in Highland education', 325.
44. SCRE, *Gaelic-speaking Children*, pp. 26, 68, 74.
45. SCRE, *Gaelic-speaking Children*, pp. 74–5.
46. MacLeod, 'Gaelic in Highland education', 326.
47. Christina A. Smith and Derrick N. Lawley, *Mental Testing of Hebridean Children in Gaelic and English* (University of London Press, 1948); G. E. Marjoribanks and A. MacLeod 'Report on visit to Wales', in An Comunn Gàidhealach, *Report*, pp. 18–19.
48. Inverness County Council Education Committee, *Scheme of Instruction in Gaelic* (Inverness County Council, 1964), p. 3.
49. Ibid., p. 3. See also Welsh Board of Education, *Welsh in Education and Life* (HMSO, 1927).
50. Scottish Education Department, *Education in Scotland in 1956* (HMSO, 1957), PP vol. X, p. 1198.
51. SCRE, *Gaelic-speaking Children*, p. 64.
52. Ibid., p. 35.
53. Ibid., p. 49.
54. Scottish Education Department, *Education in Scotland in 1956*, p. 1176.
55. Paterson, *Scottish Education*, pp. 114–18.
56. Scottish Education Department, *Primary Education in Scotland* (HMSO, 1965), p. 201.
57. Ibid., p. 199.
58. Ibid., p. 201.
59. M. MacLeod, *Scottish Gaelic: Its Roles and Functions Within and Outside the Curriculum* (Sabhal Mòr Ostaig, 1976), p. 2.
60. John Murray and Catherine Morrison, *Bilingual Primary Education in the Western Isles, Scotland. Report of the Bilingual Education Project 1975–81* (Acair, 1984), pp. 5, 80, 161.
61. MacLeod, *Scottish Gaelic*, p. 3.
62. Paterson, *Scottish Education*, pp. 118–27.
63. Murray and Morrison, *Bilingual Primary Education in the Western Isles*, p. 148.
64. 'Bilingual policy for secondary pupils adopted [in Comhairle nan Eilean Siar]', *Stornoway Gazette*, 30 August 1980.
65. Rosamond Mitchell, Donald McIntyre, Morag MacDonald and Joan McLennan, *Report of an Independent Evaluation of the Western Isles' Bilingual Education Project* (University of Stirling, 1987), pp. 190–9.

66. Boyd Robertson, 'Gaelic education', in T. G. K. Bryce and W. M. Humes (eds), *Scottish Education, Second Edition* (Edinburgh University Press, 2003), p. 251.
67. Murray and Morrison, *Bilingual Primary Education in the Western Isles*, p. 158.
68. Paterson, *Scottish Education*, p. 140.
69. James H. Grant, 'An investigation into the feasibility of establishing Gaelic/English bilingual schools on the mainland of Scotland' (unpublished MPhil dissertation, University of Glasgow, 1983).
70. Alastair Moffat, *Dreams and Deconstructions: The Sabhal Mòr Lecture 1995* (Sabhal Mòr Ostaig, 1995), p. 14.
71. Colin Baker, *Foundations of Bilingual Education and Bilingualism*, 4th edn (Multilingual Matters, 2006), p. 245.
72. Wallace E. Lambert and G. Richard Tucker, *Bilingual Education of Children. The St. Lambert Experiment* (Newbury House, 1972); Merrill Swain and Sharon Lapkin, *Evaluating Bilingual Education: A Canadian Case Study* (Multilingual Matters, 1980).
73. Scottish Office Education Department, *National Guidelines for Curriculum and Assessment in Scotland: Gaelic 5–14* (HMSO, 1993), p. 9.
74. Alistair Roberts, 'Parental attitudes to Gaelic-medium education in the Western Isles of Scotland', *Journal of Multilingual and Multicultural Development* 12(4) (1991), 253–69; Morag MacNeil, *Parental Experience of Gaelic-Medium Schooling: Final Report* (Lèirsinn Research Centre, 1993); Richard Johnstone, Wynne Harlen, Morag MacNeil, Bob Stradling and Graham Thorpe, *The Attainments of Pupils Receiving Gaelic-medium Primary Education in Scotland* (Scottish Centre for Information on Language Teaching, 1999).
75. General Teaching Council for Scotland, *Teaching in Gaelic-medium Education: Recommendations for Change* (GTCS, 1999), pp. 5–6; Her Majesty's Inspectors of Education, *Improving Achievement in Gaelic* (HMIe, 2005), p. 34.
76. Scottish Government, HMIe, SQA and LTS, *Curriculum for Excellence: Literacy and Gàidhlig* (Scottish Government, 2010), p. 4.
77. John Galloway, *Gaelic Education Data 2013–14* (Bòrd na Gàidhlig, 2014).
78. Fiona O'Hanlon, Lindsay Paterson and Wilson McLeod (2012), *Language Models in Gaelic-medium Pre-school, Primary and Secondary Education* (University of Edinburgh, 2012), pp. 32, 59.
79. Galloway, *Gaelic Education Data*; O'Hanlon et al., *Language Models*.
80. Her Majesty's Inspectors of Schools, *Provision for Gaelic Education in Scotland: A Report by HM Inspectors of Schools* (Scottish Office Education Department, 1994).
81. Ibid., p. 3.
82. Scottish Office, 'News release: Three-point boost for Gaelic education announced by Brian Wilson', Scottish Office Information Directorate, 19 June 1997.
83. Her Majesty's Inspector of Education, *Improving Achievement in Gaelic* (HMIe, 2005).
84. Ibid., p. 37. General Teaching Council for Scotland, *Teaching in Gaelic-medium Education* (GTCS, 1999), pp. 5–6. Her Majesty's Inspectors of Education, *Gaelic Education: Building on the Successes, Addressing the Barriers* (HMIe, 2011), p. 14.
85. Fiona O'Hanlon, Wilson McLeod and Lindsay Paterson, *Gaelic-medium Education in Scotland: Choice and Attainment at the Primary and Early Secondary School Stages* (Bòrd na Gàidhlig, 2010), pp. 72–7.
86. John Norman MacLeod, personal communication, 18 May 2014.
87. Iain Campbell, Marsaili MacLeod, Michael Danson and Douglas Chalmers, *Measuring the Gaelic Labour Market: Current and Future Potential. Final Report – Stage 2* (HECLA Consulting, 2008), pp. 7, 11.
88. O'Hanlon et al., *Gaelic-medium Education*, pp. 20–39; Fiona O'Hanlon, Lindsay

Paterson and Wilson McLeod, 'The attainment of pupils in Gaelic-medium primary education in Scotland', *International Journal of Bilingual Education and Bilingualism* 16(6) (2013), 707–29; Johnstone et al., *The Attainments of Pupils*.

89. Scottish Government, *Pupil Census 2012 Supplementary Data* (Scottish Government, 2013).

90. Fraser Lachlan, Marinella Parisi and Roberta Fadda, 'Bilingualism in Sardinia and Scotland: Exploring the cognitive benefits of speaking a "minority" language', *International Journal of Bilingualism* 17(1) (2013), 43–56.

91. O'Hanlon et al., *Language Models*, p. 62.

92. Registrar General for Scotland, *Census 1981: Gaelic Report* (HMSO, 1981); General Register Office for Scotland, *1991 Census: Report for Scotland* (HMSO,1991); Registrar General for Scotland, *Scotland's Census 2001: Gaelic Report* (GROS, 2005); National Records of Scotland, *2011 Census – Release 2A* (NRS, 2013), p. 27. See also Kenneth MacKinnon, 'Reversing language shift: Celtic languages today: any evidence?', *Journal of Celtic Linguistics* 8 (2004), 109–32.

93. Scottish Government, *Pupils in Scotland 2006* (Scottish Government, 2006), Table 1.14.

94. Bòrd na Gàidhlig, *Gaelic Learners in the Primary School* (Bòrd na Gàidhlig, 2010).

95. Scottish Government, *Pupils in Scotland 2013, Supplementary Data* (Scottish Government, 2013), Table 6.16.

96. John Galloway, *Gaelic Education Data 2013–14* (Bòrd na Gàidhlig, 2014).

Bibliography

Campbell, John Lorne, *Gaelic in Scottish Education and Life: Past, Present and Future* (W. & A. K. Johnston, 1945).

Durkacz, Victor E. *The Decline of the Celtic Languages* (John Donald, 1996).

MacLeod, Donald J., 'An historical overview', in Margaret Nicolson and Matthew MacIver (eds), *Gaelic Medium Education* (Dunedin Academic Press, 2003)

MacLeod, Murdo, 'Gaelic in Highland education', *Transactions of the Gaelic Society of Inverness* 43 (1963), 305–34.

Robertson, Boyd, 'Gaelic education', in T. G. K. Bryce, W. M. Humes, D. Gillies and A. Kennedy (eds), *Scottish Education*, 4th edn (Edinburgh University Press, 2013), pp. 274–85.

Withers, Charles W.J., 'Education and the Gaelic language', in Heather Holmes (ed.), *Institutions of Scotland: Education*, Scottish Life and Society: A Compendium of Scottish Ethnology, vol. 11 (Tuckwell Press, 2000).

18

Inventing a Scottish School of Educational Research, 1920–1950

Martin Lawn and Ian J. Deary

Introduction: Scotland in 1920

The idea of a Scottish School of Educational Research[1] was created to capture a unique phenomenon which occurred in Scotland in the middle decades of the twentieth century, in which networks of teachers and experts came together to investigate schooling and intelligence in search of improvement and fairness. What distinguishes Scottish education research at this time is its scale, its organisation and its ambition. The range of organised inquiries was undertaken by a collection of disciplined professionals and students, working on a voluntary basis, spread across the years. The research accumulated techniques and knowledge, produced regular research reports and developed into a coherent infrastructure of research support and strategy. This was very unusual compared to European and American developments at the time, which were more commonly based on a single expert researcher, sometimes a professor, in a small university department. From our researches and inquiries, there was nothing like this Scottish experience in its scale, ambition and quality.

However, key questions relating to Scotland's capacity to create and maintain networks, to educate and train researchers, to spread widely the value of testing and to assume the mantle of necessity in its role as a leading education nation, still need answers. The ambition to investigate the nation and its intelligence, through large-scale and extended mass inquiry, was not echoed at the time elsewhere nor could it have been learnt by precedent. The ready willingness by well-educated teachers to participate in researching their classrooms, and by university and training college academics to support them, is highly unusual both in the UK and elsewhere in Europe.

In the year 1919, the challenge to Scotland's perceived role as a leading education nation was recognised; the urgency of action to reform its institutions and to test its citizens was strong and appears to have been common currency among its leading educators. The president of the Educational Institute of Scotland

(EIS), Duncan MacGillivray, led the call for renewal in Scottish education and tried to mobilise the teachers in their annual assembly:

> It must frankly be admitted that here Scotland lags seriously behind (i.e, in all that concerns the science and art of our profession). The tremendous educational ferment that is at present stirring scholastic circles in England has absolutely no counterpart with us. We are in some respects professionally dead. We are not thinking enough about our profession. We are making no experiments. We have in our Universities and Training Colleges no great Departments of Education in any way comparable to those of England and America. We have, so far as we are aware, no Child Study Association, no Parents' Association, no Pedagogical Clubs, no Pedagogical Magazines, no Educational Reading Circles . . . At present the whole American continent is swept by two great movements. One has for its aim the measurement of educational results by objective instead of subjective methods. The other movement is concerned with what are known as educational surveys . . .[2]

This sense of threat and of acute urgency was still present a few years later in 1925 when Dr John Morgan retired from his post as director of studies at Moray House, and again there was talk of Scotland's supremacy in education being challenged. In fact, his retirement dinner introduced Professor Godfrey Thomson, who was not only the new director of studies (or principal) at Moray House but also the head of department at the university. Thomson's new position confirmed a radical departure: the close collaboration of the two institutions, sharing staff and mission, something for which Morgan had been arguing for some time, and a sign that Scotland was organising anew in education. Robert Rusk, a leading Scottish writer and researcher in education, argued contrarily that the conditions for the development of research were good, but, in fact, he was describing the new, modern version of research – empirical or experimental psychology – that was becoming influential in Scotland.

> From the first decade of the century training college students were familiarized with the procedures and made acquainted with the results of research and thus a supply of qualified workers in research was provided, and an influx of teachers favourably disposed to research was annually entering schools.[3]

It can clearly be seen here that the common understanding about the crisis in education progress was that the teachers in classrooms and in training were a major solution to it, and that new research perspectives and associations were necessary.

By 1920, events and ideas were emerging which would shape the next thirty years of Scottish education research. The catalytic energy of William Boyd at the University of Glasgow and his ideas for strengthening the teaching profession included the idea of self–government, a graduate profession and the development of expertise, especially research training and inquiry. His ideas about what was possible in Scotland depended upon the high skills and motivation

Figure 18.1 William Boyd, 1940s. Photograph in the possession of the authors.

of the teachers and their central position in the system. The new Edinburgh postgraduate BEd and the Glasgow EdB, with their in-depth training in theory and research training, had just begun and it was expected that teachers' greater involvement in research would have the dual result of increasing their knowledge and expertise as well as enabling them to improve their teaching methods and techniques. Boyd was working with the grain of teacher education in Scotland, where half the men were graduates by 1920[4] (rising to 70 per cent and 30 per cent for women in 1938, compared to figures in the mid-teens in England) and were to establish a strong reputation in education at home and abroad.

Boyd was deeply involved with the EIS in its determination to use its professional power to assist teachers in improving the education system by researching it. The *Scottish Educational Journal* was a weekly publication sent to all EIS members and from 1919 it ran regular articles about education research, often written by Boyd, encouraging teachers and providing support for co-operative projects through the new EIS Research Committee. Boyd made an appeal to all Scottish teachers to get involved in this work:

> If every teacher is ready to do his or her bit, in the way of providing the material and service required, even at considerable personal trouble, if, further, those with the capacity and leisure for research are ready to develop and apply their talents in work for the Committee, there is no reason why the Institute should not in course of time make a substantial contribution to the sum of assured knowledge about education.[5]

A series of projects then began and continued into the mid-1920s, with the *Journal* as their main public forum. From this work in the 1920s came the gradual realisation of a research foundation for Scotland built on co-operation between the EIS, some of the new directors of education, university professors and staff in the teacher training colleges. In this network, called the Scottish Council for Research in Education (SCRE), each of the partners had a role through his or her expertise, contacts, volunteering and interest. Starting in 1928, the SCRE ran projects on a local and national scale, worked with international partners and gradually organised a broader research infrastructure, which closely linked Scottish resources. Within this network, there was a great deal of experience and expertise in testing and surveying in the field of education research, based on advanced education study or visits to the US, and through the influence of texts.

One of the advanced institutions in education, created in 1924 on a single site, was that created through the merger of the University of Edinburgh's department of education and the Moray House teacher training college, although they continued to be independently financially managed. Under Professor Godfrey Thomson, the model of the Teachers College, Columbia University, the leading American teacher education and graduate school, was used as the archetype for change in Edinburgh. The model of America, or at least the Teachers College, was in the air in Scotland in two ways, first as a great institution in education, and second as the home for innovative thinkers and scientists in education, such as Edward Thorndike and John Dewey. Alexander Darroch, then occupying the Bell chair of education in Edinburgh, had argued in his 1907 book on educational problems that the German and American model of universities as 'great national laboratories for the extension of knowledge and the betterment of practice' and an 'intimate union of scientific investigation and professional instruction' [6] was the model Scotland should follow. In 1912, James Drever set up a pedagogical laboratory in the new Moray House building; in effect, it was a research lab for educational psychology, a first step in the move to an experiment-based education. Bell had argued that the establishment of the 1917 University Ordinance or regulation combined a new university influence in the professional training of teachers with the advanced study of education and scientific investigation of educational problems (the new BEd).[7] Lying behind these reforms was the thought that what Darroch and others intended already existed in America. There was constant reference to the Teachers College as their symbol of success: it appeared to represent what Scotland wanted to do in the future. It had 'managed to integrate not only the various contributing disciplines but also scholarship and the teachers' professional training in a way that had so far eluded the Scottish centres'.[8] Roman, in his survey of new education in Europe, had said that 'in no country in Europe does the American investigator of schools find himself more at home than in Scotland'.[9]

The organisation of this chapter will follow these linked actors and organisations, which made up what was referred to as the distinctive Scottish School of Educational Research in the early to mid-twentieth century.

The EIS Research Committee

Boyd's 1919 manifesto for educational research in Scotland was ambitious and represented the spirit of the time. His ideas, which must have been discussed at length in the EIS Council, foreshadowed the way in which Scotland organised its research activity over the next thirty years. The manifesto begins by noting the lack of funds for its operation, a regular theme in the coming years, and then emphasises the role of willing volunteers, the teachers. Among the tasks the Research Committee set itself were the following: publishing the results of its education experiments and collecting articles and books from other countries; starting a summer school; acting as an information hub for teachers about their inquiries; and compiling a list of the most important books on educational research. David Kennedy-Fraser, another member of the Committee, who had trained at Edinburgh, Leipzig and Cornell Universities, supported Boyd but also advocated a role for psychological investigations and research centres. The centres should be aware of work in other countries, offer fruitful lines of research, create parallel work in schools to justify generalised deductions, produce standardised scales and train teachers in experimental education methods. Although he had a greater sense of a directing and supporting centre than Boyd, viewing it like an army HQ, he too argued that the work would depend on volunteers working co-operatively. In this way the idea of a large co-operative organisation, informally managed through the EIS, started out, with Boyd writing about clearing houses, collation machinery and a collective energy of progress.

The Research Committee immediately set to work on several rather ambitious projects. It had identified as being of primary importance the creation of standards which teachers could use to compare their pupils in order to see how they were performing. Following the abolition of fixed standards in the elementary schools of Scotland in the 1890s, the Qualifying Examination was instituted to identify potential students for the secondary schools. Although the higher authorities dictated the general requirements, the decision as to the suitability of individual pupils for secondary education was largely in the hands of their teachers. The existence of standards by which to compare pupils with the general population would be of great benefit to teachers. Three core subjects of the school curriculum were decided upon for research: composition, spelling and arithmetic. These investigations involved the Research Committee's identifying suitable tasks for schoolchildren to complete and relied heavily on individual teachers volunteering to give their classes these tasks under controlled conditions. For example, three titles and precise instructions for the administration and scoring of the compositions were published in an article in the *Scottish Educational Journal* of 27 February 1920. Teachers were implored to follow the instructions precisely in order to ensure as complete uniformity of conditions as possible and were asked to send all compositions, along with details of when the class would be or had been presented for the Qualifying Examination, directly to Boyd. The response was both enthusiastic and impressive. A total of 4,284 essays were sent to Boyd from 128 different schools across Scotland. Boyd and his team selected one in five of the essays submitted by each teacher, in rough proportion to the number of essays assigned by the teachers to each mark. The resulting 400 papers were then thoroughly mixed and made up into eight bundles of fifty. Each bundle was then given to a teacher who undertook to mark his or her own bundle before asking four other teachers of the qualifying stage to give an independent assessment. At this stage, teachers were asked to assign marks based on a normal distribution, assuming that most pupils would achieve a grade of 'satisfactory' with smaller numbers in the highest and lowest categories. Boyd then chose only essays written under one title – 'A Day at the Seaside' – as this was by far the most popular and the best- performing of the titles given, and chose first those essays where there was consensus between the five markers on the mark given, and then those where there was the most disagreement. The resulting twenty-six essays were then printed in the *Journal* in June 1920 and teachers were asked to mark them on a seven-point scale and return their answers on a postcard directly to Boyd. A total of 271 postcards were received, 83 per cent of them from teachers of pupils at the qualifying stage or teachers with an intimate knowledge of qualifying work. The results were presented in the *Journal* in August 1920, followed by sample essays from each category and a commentary on why the essay deserved the mark given. Boyd concluded his series of articles by describing the difficulties presented in applying the scale produced to the classroom. Although only a few individuals from within the Research Committee undertook the planning, execution and analysis of the study, it achieved its aim of giving teachers participation in and control over assessment standards through the sharing of professional expertise.

Boyd and his colleagues then turned their attention to spelling, aiming to create a definitive list of words which children at the qualifying stage should, in the opinion of the teachers, be able to spell. The contribution of teachers was therefore crucial and instrumental to the success of the investigation into spelling. A similar exhaustive process was followed in this study and, after a series of revisions, use of American research and classroom testing, the complete list of 750 words was published in the *Journal* in January 1921. By 1926, a Standard Spelling List and a Longer Spelling List had been published. The Spelling Lists, published by the EIS and compiled by Boyd, sold upwards of a million copies – mostly in Scotland but many further afield – and remained profitable for twenty years. Boyd brought out a Revised List in 1946, and this was equally profitable. The Spelling Lists enabled him, in 1925, to establish an EIS essay prize for teachers and students in training. The Committee received a large number of essays on education history or classroom inquiry, from teachers and students alike, and the prize-winners received a standing ovation at the EIS's Annual General Meeting in June 1926. The following year, the essay competition topic for teachers was 'Economy of Time in School Work'. The essay competition continued for many years, funded by the Council of the EIS after the first couple of years, directly involving and rewarding teachers and students in research work.

Although Boyd's reputation flourished, and he had invitations to speak or study in the USA, there was some disquiet about how the teacher research movement was working out. Critics of the Research Committee's approach argued that teachers were ill-equipped to ensure the adequate provision of experimental conditions within their classrooms, meaning that their research might not be generalisable across schools.

Scottish Council for Research in Education

Partly funded by the EIS from teachers' annual subscriptions, the founding of the SCRE in 1928 was the culmination of months of negotiation and collaboration between the EIS, the Association of Education Authorities, the Association of Directors of Education in Scotland, the National Committee for the Training of Teachers, the training centres and colleges, university education departments and the British Psychological Society (Scottish Branch). Right from the start, the SCRE was able to conduct research the breadth of which Boyd and his Committee could barely have hoped for, and its arrival was welcomed by its partners. The aims of the SCRE closely matched those of the EIS's Research Committee: it would negotiate and control investigations, receive suggestions for research, allocate problems to investigators and publish results and recommendations. Unlike the Research Committee, however, the SCRE intended to finance research investigations and their publication. It was the first research institute of education in the United Kingdom and so had a symbolic value as well as a growing scientific output. The SCRE was formed with one part-time director, Dr Robert Rusk (who held the post from 1928 to 1958), a secretarial assistant and a clerk. Although the Research Council produced a series of publications and major projects, it was an organising hub, a nodal point in a network of teachers and academic workers. It had no research workers or statisticians of its own, although it had close support from its two founding associations in voluntary service, and flourished because of its networks.

> a number of teachers, head teachers mostly, some directors of education, some university people, but very largely people from [the four] training colleges – in Jordanhill, Moray House, Aberdeen and Dundee. Although we tend to think of universities as the bases for educational research, the real strength of educational research in Scotland, in the early days, in the 30s, came from the training colleges.[10]

Until the late 1940s, the Council was dependent on financial contributions from the EIS and the education authorities. Although it had great expertise in the area, it did not publish tests. Without subventions from outside sources the major projects of the Council could not have been financed. From 1931 to 1941 significant grants were received from the Carnegie Foundation in New York and later from the Population Investigation Committee (founded by the Eugenics Society and based at the London School of Economics).

Within three years, from 1930, the Council had produced ten free short research reports on subjects like individual differences, reading comprehension, arithmetic in school, pupil attainment and school leaving. It had a lending library with technical journals for researchers; it compiled lists of Scottish theses in education, and tried to assemble a master file of mental and scholastic tests. It managed major investigations on optimal school size, comparisons with US children (using American tests), distribution of intelligence and time allocation to school subjects. It began a process of classifying pupils, conceptually refining pupil categories and even influencing class nomenclature (proposing standard names for Scottish classes). Data flowed out of Scottish schools about how their selection processes worked, how much time was spent teaching subjects and how to understand the 'ability' of the pupil. This information was to be used in the school system and, indeed, formed the system as it began to shape its key categories – pupils, ability, time and organisation. Although this had cumulative policy effects in the system, through its close and practical relations with the teacher union and the local education directors, it is worth noting that, in the formal sense, the Scottish Education Department did not enter into this innovative relation between professional experts and the effective government of schooling.

Significantly, the SCRE acted as the leading edge of the developing expertise about testing, and as early as 1931 the Council determined to devise tests for types of ability to 'enable pupils to be directed into the appropriate secondary school course'; it did so for English, modern languages, mathematics, engineering, science and technical subjects. By 1936, the Council had, through extensive testing of ability and attainment, been able to promote 'the best combination' of intelligence tests, examinations and teacher assessment of pupil ability to standardise the forecasting of the post-primary course best suited to the individual pupil. This voluntary partnership was ambitious for results and for Scottish education. In its 2nd Annual Report, its inquiries produced, applied and analysed thousands of tests, designed and piloted a new pupil progress card and began a long-term project on the effects of environment and mentality. In 1930, a huge Curriculum Inquiry was undertaken, involving sixty subject panel meetings, which delivered ninety draft reports in 1931. Its base was still the voluntary participation of many educationalists and experts which it supported by subsidising investigations and publishing results.

The 1932 Mental Survey of the intelligence of Scottish children was a considerable achievement of the young research institute, a model of extensive fieldwork, a research partnership with teachers and an exemplar of policy-focused research work. Many of the key researchers in testing in Scotland were involved with the SCRE – for example, Drever[11], Thomson, Philip Vernon[12] in Glasgow and William McClelland[13] in Dundee. The survey was based on a Moray House test produced by Thomson, and almost all pupils born in Scotland in 1921 – 87,498 pupils in education authority, grant-aided or independent schools or 'institutions' – were tested on 1 June 1932. This was a remarkable logistical feat, undertaken by a neophyte Council with its new network of voluntary support from the teachers and local authorities. The tests were administered and marked by the teachers. The whole exercise created a standard in education research for 'sheer hard thinking, lucidity of research design, and credibility of findings'.[14] Testing was still new in classroom practices and great efforts had to be made to work across the time and space of Scottish schools. The Mental Survey affected every school in the land. Tests had to be administered, practice facilitated and marking organised. This was a major insertion of new practices into schooling, involving new skills, training and the management of space and time. The test itself occupied only a small part of the effect, the organisation of the test the major part. The development of the manual of instructions for the Moray House test used in the Mental Survey shows how this process of ordering grew out of the logic of the test and the experience of its use over time: 'It cannot be too strongly emphasised that the instructions which are set out in the following must be adhered to exactly'. The test had to enter schools ordered in their own or local ways, or in which headteacher judgement or teacher classroom autonomy may have allowed discretionary action and local work habits. Now teachers needed 'watches with second hands' and if a stopwatch was used, its accuracy had to be checked. Precision in time and behaviour was required. In the instructions produced in 1932, timings of '4, 5 or 7 minutes (precise to the second) are to be allowed':

> Note that the 4 or 7 minutes allowed include the time for reading the short instruction at the head of each Test (not of course the front page instruction) as well as the time for working the Test itself. The supervisor therefore should

commence to read these instructions punctually to the second, and then through without delay (there should be no pause and no preliminary comments).

Teachers and pupils had to learn what a test was, how to behave, what to use and what to do. Through this process, the child was becoming testable. Becoming alert to the new conditions of schoolwork, pupils learned new rules on time and motion, the order of things, the individualisation of work and the exact specification of work. Pencils were crucial; each pupil should have two sharpened pencils and if they broke, the pupil had to raise his or her hand. Pupils should not have 'rulers, India-rubbers, scribbling paper and pens'. They were unable to ask questions. Their invigilators were under instruction to answer 'no question whatever'. In this huge undertaking, precision and standardisation were absolutely necessary in the production of the data.

Consequently the SCRE became a major source of expertise on mental testing and promoted its use in the training of teachers, in the armed forces and in the empire (where its expertise was recognised and in demand). In fact, it was an early scientific knowledge network in the field of education, linking together professional and lay expertise across the country in such a way that it acted as a single consistent, disciplined force.

In 1935, the SCRE began a focused study on assessment in Dundee, based on the relative value of examinations, intelligence tests, scholastic tests and teacher estimates of pupils' ability, their best combination, their weighting and the comparability of teachers' marks. In addition, teachers and headteachers, with the help of the School Medical Officer, produced a rating card for each pupil; this had data on health, talents, attainments, home conditions and qualities. As the pupils moved through the secondary course, a new record booklet was created, containing every mark the pupil obtained in all subjects and an average term mark. The study took place over six years, with 3,000 pupils taking part.

In Dundee, a triumvirate of Professor McClelland, Margaret Young, lecturer in experimental education at Dundee Training College, and Douglas Macintosh, assistant to the director of education, county of Fife, undertook a major study on entry examinations to secondary school. They organised a large group of people to carry out this research: around 400 students from the college and eighty teachers in local schools, six local headmasters and fourteen college staff. In total these people voluntarily gave approximately 13,000 hours of labour. At Dundee Training College, a research room was set up. Known as the Inquiry Room, it contained the numerous documents collected, requiring a 'rather intricate system of filing and storing', and it was 'furnished with tables, shelves, cupboards, bookcases etc annexed by Miss Young from other departments'. A full-time clerical assistant managed the documents, sorting and lending them out for operations. As later reported, an assistant 'mastered the whole plan of the investigation, and in addition to the laborious clerical work, . . . supervised groups of calculators . . . [and helped] the voluntary workers with even the most difficult statistical techniques used in working up the results'.[15]

Figure 18.2 Conference on examinations, Eastbourne, 23–5 May 1931. Back row: Rusk (7th from left), Hepburn (10th from left), Thomson (12th from left). Front row: Smith (6th from left). Photograph in the possession of the authors.

It was a huge and complex organisation of many part-time volunteers, each of whom was assigned a task when he or she arrived and then trained, or was trained by, his or her colleagues. The project had three main categories of researcher and research assistant: the correctors and computers; the trainers and group leaders; and the special researchers. The first group comprised the wide range of volunteers from the schools and the college. Macintosh and Young trained most of them but a group emerged from among the more skilled workers, who then in turn acted as team leaders and trainers. A list of nine leaders, instructors or assistants in advanced statistical methods (six men and three women) was given at the front of the report; local teachers who assisted in the 'Correction of Tests, Tabulation and Calculations' (eight men and twenty-nine women) were also listed. The third group were graduate students undertaking special studies; each year, the students were introduced to the project and a list of problems was submitted from which those interested could make their choice – there was no lack of volunteers for these investigations. Students were encouraged to familiarise themselves with the plan of research so that they understood how their own contribution fitted into the whole.

It is worth quoting the report in which their organisation was described:

Throughout the sessions 1936–7 and 1937–8 this group met one or two evenings a week from 6 to 9pm. Practically all members have helped with the investigation from the start, and they have become highly skilled workers who can handle most of the essential techniques involved. They have been a most faithful and reliable group, whose only reward, apart from their keen interest in the research, has been a cup of tea in the middle of the evening's work . . . A large amount of the grid making and other mechanical parts of the working up of the results was undertaken by large groups of students who gave us their help in free periods during the college session . . . Many of them have become interested in special aspects of the investigation and have undertaken to work up the results of these independently.[16]

The collection of data could also be arduous. A proposal to test a sample of pupils, within an individually administered testing process, was submitted to the third International Examinations Inquiry (IEI) Folkestone Conference in 1935. After devising a way of randomising the sample, the children were to be found throughout Scotland, both in the cities and across the country. The process of locating the children was a complicated affair. It needed a set of permissions, complex transport arrangements and intricate work plans. Letters were sent out explaining the necessity of the sampling process, how it would work and its confidential nature. Across the country the members of the thirty-four education committees received the request and, in each case, after deliberation, gave assent. Although the cities supplied the majority of pupils, some counties supplied only a single boy and girl. The tester prepared a testing programme and communicated by letter with the headteachers regarding suitable days and times of testing. In all the IEI reports, the description of the sheer physical effort involved in this research process in Scotland stands out, and indeed the lyrical nature of the description is unusual:

Such field work as this survey necessitated the use of a car, and by the end of the survey this car did indeed know its Scotland – main roads, side roads, winding hill roads, leading from valley to valley, lonely moor roads, and even such roads as one in a certain part of Scotland that, degenerating into a mere track among turnip fields, did at length lead to a school. One day it travelled 200 miles over Sutherland roads through country lonely, wild, and unbelievably beautiful, to a little school perched on the very edge of the world. It sought out children in the Black Isle and in wooded Highland country. It got to know the gracious beauty of Moray and Speyside, the windswept stretches of Buchan, the placid beauty of more Lowland Perthshire. It found its way through sheltered and winding roads to schools in the Solway country. On its last journey of the survey it nosed its way over Border hill country in the wind and driving rain to a little school up in the hills where a shepherd's child was to be tested.

The Scottish air services were the means of saving much precious time and much travel-weariness, when, in spite of gales and fog, it was possible to adhere to a prearranged programme in Caithness, the Orkney Islands and Shetland.

In such a way, too, it was possible to leave Edinburgh in the morning and put in a day's testing in the south of Kintyre, then in the evening fly over in 35 minutes to Islay, ready to test there the next morning. Some experiences are happier in retrospect – a stormy sea journey to Barra in the Outer Hebrides and an overnight gale when sailing from Barra up to Harris; but then followed the recompense of the amazing beauty of Harris under a morning sky swept clear by the storm, as one travelled 26 miles south to the edge of the Sound of Harris to test two children there. This field aspect leaves memories of timetables, maps, roads, weather and much planning.[17]

From the moment of its inception, it is clear that the SCRE became part of an international network of institutes and an international movement of scientific testing and survey research. Part of its stability and growth was its involvement in international research studies with private funding from the Carnegie Foundation. Within a year of its creation, the Council was invited to join the IEI by Professor Paul Monroe at the International Institute, Teachers College. The IEI membership was used to develop a range of Scottish studies and was essential to the 1932 Mental Survey and the 1935–7 survey of assessment in Dundee. The International Inquiry was to involve key experts over a ten-year period from at least ten countries, all of which, apart from the US, were in Europe – Switzerland, Germany, France, England, Scotland, Finland, Sweden, Norway and Holland. Key SCRE members like Rusk, Kennedy-Fraser, W. A. F. Hepburn (Director of Education, Ayrshire), Boyd, McClelland and Thomson met and talked with major researchers from other countries, for example Michael Sadler (in Oxford); Edward Thorndike; Paul Monroe and Isaac Kandel (both at the International Institute at Teachers College, Columbia University); and Pierre Buvet (in Geneva). The SCRE began to establish the dominance of a Scottish tradition of experimental investigation in education: it viewed research as a specialised activity, based largely on psychology and statistical analysis, requiring extended training and producing findings which were supposed to tell teachers and policy makers what to do.

The SCRE was the source of data about the Scottish system of education and about a specific problem, the demand for secondary education. The way it began to conceptualise this problem – as a question of intelligence – was a modern idea. The SCRE produced more than a series of research reports in the 1930s and 1940s (and beyond); the effect of working in this close partnership of actors with different responsibilities and skills was that it built a Scottish research infrastructure around itself. For example, in 1946, several of the key members of the International Inquiry in Scotland, acting as heads of university departments, met under the auspices of the SCRE to co-ordinate the research undertaken by their students for the new degree in education. In reality, they were establishing a national agreement between the main providers about the nature and content of research training in education. The Research Council would list 'suitable' research topics, and this research was made available for access. In this way, the

Council established a vetting system for educational research in Scotland and, with light steering, guaranteed research results on required topics. The Council prepared a Guide, which acted as a 'list of works', a bibliography and a source book in which support for this planned research could be found. They were more than suggestions; they had become the recommended tools for a supported, managed and networked Scottish research system. They were a key element in a process of approval and licence, which ranged from agreed topics for study, head of department consent and Committee endorsement. The research reading list had the power of an official (and Scottish) permit to research, in which the researcher entered into an agreed set of tasks. The list itself was a mixture of American, Scottish and English sources, with a strong experimental, statistical and measurement perspective, mainly drawn from the still-new field of educational psychology. It reflected the interests of the Scottish network in the International Inquiry, which in turn followed the emerging and distinctive way that the subject, the network and the science had developed in Scotland from the 1920s. The Guide shows the influence of American empirical and measurement-based research, which had gradually established itself as a support for the early move into intelligence testing in Scotland in the 1920s, and was then gradually consolidated within the work of the SCRE and the IEI.

A crucial part of this regime of research governance in Scotland, the heterogeneous research network, was its progress in producing advanced study in education, based upon the BEd (the equivalent of a Masters degree in England) which was undertaken mainly in the Universities of Glasgow and Edinburgh and was the joint responsibility of the education and psychology departments.

In Edinburgh, this was a full-time course but in Glasgow (and in Aberdeen, which also had a small number of BEd students) part-time attendance was permitted; classes operated after 4.30 on weekdays and on Saturday mornings. The BEd was a rigorous degree and could be up to nine times longer than its English counterpart, the MEd course.[18] Using the list of theses, it is possible to analyse the scale and type of research work undertaken under Professor Godfrey Thomson's guidance at Edinburgh. The lists of theses covered the UK and Ireland, and the first volume was partly based on material published in the *British Journal of Educational Psychology* in the war years. All theses are included – at BEd, Masters and doctoral level. Each volume of the list is divided into two main parts, Educational Psychology and Education. Each part is then subdivided; the Educational Psychology part comprises sections entitled Mental Development, Sense and Sense Perception, Executive Functions, Higher Mental Processes, Special Mental Conditions and Abnormal Psychology. The main section, Mental Development (in the first volume this took up forty-three pages out of a total of sixty pages), has three sections, Mental Characteristics, Psychology of Types (and Individuals) and Intelligence and Mental Tests. In the first volume, this last section on Intelligence Tests is thirty pages long. So, by far the largest section in the Educational Psychology part, over half the pages overall, is that on Intelligence and Mental Tests. Its equivalent section in the Education subsection

Table 18.1 Edinburgh BEd Theses, 1918–51

	1918–27		1928–37		1938–47		1948–51	
Subject	N	%	N	%	N	%	N	%
Psychology and experimental	88	38	325	49	354	55	373	69
Historical and comparative	74	32	199	30	156	24	82	15
Method	27	12	71	11	53	8	58	11
Philosophy and principles	46	20	75	11	77	12	32	6
Total	235	100	670	100	640	100	545	100
Average number per year	23.5		67.0		64.0		136.3	

Table 18.2 Theses produced at Edinburgh and London Universities in 'Educational Psychology: Intelligence and Tests', 1918–48

	Edinburgh	London
BEd (Ed.) or MA (Lond.)	102	83
PhD	10	57

Sources for Tables 18.1 and 18.2: Blackwell, A. M. List of researches in education and educational psychology presented for higher degrees in the universities of the United Kingdom, Northern Ireland, and the Irish Republic from 1918 to 1948 NFER (Additional Supplements 1948–55).

is that on Education; in the first volume, this is twenty-seven pages long. Other sections are entitled Teachers, Schools, Adult Education, Curriculum, Women, Colleges and Universities, and The State and Education. For over thirty years, psychological and experimental research dominated thesis output and increased proportionately over time.

The growing dominance of Intelligence and Tests at Edinburgh can be seen in Table 18.1, as can, in Table 18.2, the strength of its researcher output at Masters level against London.

It was not just the output of these postgraduate researchers that was significant; they were expected to create the next stage in the Scottish research network and thus a national register of researchers, their specialisms and their willingness to assist was developed.

Thomson and the University

As we have seen in Dundee, the shift into a research culture linked to teaching changed the institution. This was also the case in a more powerful institution, the redesigned Moray House, a partnership between the Provincial Training Board (for teachers) and the University of Edinburgh. Since his appointment in 1925, fresh from his year at Columbia Teachers College, Godfrey Thomson intended to produce a model school of education, institutionalised in a combined university department and teacher training college, which would have a research laboratory and offer an advanced research degree. This new institution was modelled on the

Columbia Teachers College, and was driven by a strong demand in Scotland for advanced practice in education. The radical new step of combining a university department and a teacher training college interested Thomson greatly: it permitted 'the possibility of a real amalgamation of the two. This amalgamation I took to be my task. For I could not resist this post.'[19]

Teachers College, Columbia was constantly used as a symbol of success: it appeared to represent what Scotland wanted to do in the future. Thomson said it had 'managed to integrate not only the various contributing disciplines but also scholarship and the teachers' professional training in a way that had so far eluded the Scottish centres'.[20] For Thomson, this American model of a university – a degree-granting institution which had developed a large postgraduate section – was the best model for a powerful, integrated educational institution and 'his central enterprise – the development of a school of educational research'.[21]

Constant reference to developments in the US, and particularly New York, was not accidental. In 1927, two years after Thomson had been there, Teachers College had become the largest school of education in the world, with a growing international reputation. For Scottish scholars like Thomson, part of a generation which took advanced degrees in Germany, it had become a major influence in education, and even more so when Professor John Dewey left Chicago for Columbia. Only American elite universities had begun to develop graduate schools of education. They were distinguished from the normal teacher education colleges by their admission policy of recruiting graduates. They soon began to limit their recruitment to high school teacher training and designed advanced degree and certificate programmes in emerging specialisations for experienced professionals. Research became a feature of these professional schools, and thus of their faculty on appointment. William Russell, Dean of Teachers College, wrote that a union of systematic research and controlled observation would define research in education as it did in the new professional schools in medicine and engineering. Thomson's attempt over the next twenty-five years to try to recreate a Teachers College in the much smaller country of Scotland was to be recognised later:

> the close links between the University department and Moray House gave rise to a great school of education, which deployed a common staff in teaching and research and from which there came a steady stream of Bachelors of Education, trained educationists, who made their mark in the teachers' centres, in educational guidance and in administration.[22]

The new institution combined teacher education with advanced or more disciplinary-based work in education studies, and, in addition, the research laboratory (the testing laboratory), the advanced research degree and the experimental school. Although each activity existed within its own areas, there was some integration of staff and practice across the site. For the first time, nursery and primary education, experimental education, research training and advanced research work took place in a single university-based site – an integrated organisation – and was directed by a leading research scholar and teacher.

In 1938, Thorndike had successfully recommended Thomson for a grant from Carnegie, which was one of the first individual educational research grants in the UK, and Thomson wrote to Keppel, who managed the Carnegie Foundation in New York: the letter was on headed notepaper with 'Department of Education' on the left, 'Moray House' on the right and 'University of Edinburgh' in the middle. In the letter, he described his new institution:

> I hold a joint post, namely i) Professor of Education and head of the Education Department of Edinburgh University and ii) Director of Studies of the Edinburgh Provincial Training College for Teachers ie what in America would be called Dean of a Teachers College. My salary of £1400 is paid half by the University, half by the National Committee for the Training of Teachers ie in effect by the nation. All the work is carried on in one building (Moray House) and my task during the past decade has been largely that of amalgamating into one what were formerly two institutions. I have an efficient Depute Director (salary £1050) and seven clerks to do all the routine administration, a staff of about forty lecturers, about 700 students and a Demonstration School with 560 children and a separate staff of 20 teachers.

In addition, there was a small group of highly specialised research staff working on test production in a laboratory (Room 70). Soon after arriving at Moray House Thomson had set up a research fund, based on the growing income from the sale of Mental Tests. Reporting in 1934 to his board, Thomson said that the fund was

> used in the main for subsidising research into the preparation of (the) tests, and into other educational problems, and the surplus had been expended in giving prizes to students, in paying the expenses of visiting lecturers, in purchasing specially expensive books, and in various other ways of helping the students in the college.

Thomson described how he saw this modest source of funds as enabling the essentials of a research culture to be funded in Moray House, and eventually to endow a lectureship in experimental education. The laboratory not only produced tests but engaged in frequent correspondence on the reliability and validity of test results with their contracted local education authorities, and Inglis wrote that 'by the end of his tenure [the tests] were being sold at the rate of almost one and a half millions per year and they continued to increase thereafter'.[23]

So not only was Room 70 well known but so was the involvement of student teachers and the postgraduate (BEd) research students in testing and, according to Cruikshank,

> Room 70 . . . became famous as the centre of experimental and statistical investigation in which successive teams of young men and women, students for the

degree of Bachelor of Education, were engaged. Their work in practical testing and mental measurement became famous throughout the world.[24]

In addition, teaching and research were linked. Indeed, in 1946, the post-war Scottish Advisory Council on Education, in its *Training of Teachers*, suggested that Scottish teacher education centres should have a nursery and demonstration school and it

> should be in the van of educational advance. It should therefore, in co-operation with the SCRE, be a centre for educational research in all its branches, training research workers and organizing large scale investigations carried with the co-operation of teachers in the province.[25]

This had been Thomson's desire too, ever since he had worked in Columbia, and during his time in office, Moray House became the exemplar for the new Scottish vision for teaching and research in education.

Conclusions

The idea of a Scottish School of Educational Research is an imaginative and credible way to understand what appear to be independent phenomena and actors operating in the same space and time. Their ideas and practices continue the Scottish Enlightenment concern for empirical investigation in one of the few areas left undiscovered. They all shared, in their different ways, a concern for investigation and for educational improvement, using the potential of the new technology of testing. They were not only Scottish researchers but are also researchers on Scotland, that is, it is Scotland and its education that was the subject of study. They investigated many aspects of Scottish education, and always with ambitions to widen their scope of inquiry. This is especially so in the national survey of 1932, but also within many regional studies and specialist investigations. Boyd's appeals to Scottish teachers, the partnership between actors across the education system and the links forged between theory and practice announced the creation and development of a distinctively Scottish institutionalism. This took the form of parallel studies, networked activities, collaborative work and shared planning. As it grew organically in the 1920s and 1930s, it established permanent arrangements and consistent plans, of which the SCRE was the most visible.

Strong Scottish traditions of empirical investigation readily absorbed new twentieth-century ideas about intelligence and testing and produced a cadre which translated, used and developed the concepts and the practices of this new field. This meant that the advances made in America, especially at Teachers College, Columbia University, influenced them and they read US psychological and education journals, used their textbooks and travelled across the Atlantic if they could. They were heavily involved with the IEI in the 1930s, which brought them closer to leading American and European actors in education and psychological testing. A distinctive element of this Scottish school was its use of tests to understand Scotland and to improve its education, which meant tests were used mainly as a research tool and not, as in England, mainly as a selection device. These researchers acted as a scientific community and as a policy community, in a period when a professional class of experts and teachers could operate as if they represented Scotland and had direct responsibility for it.

It has become clear that what happened between 1920 and 1950 in Scotland as a national and international phenomenon in education research was unusual and dissimilar to a more standard pattern of university-led research across Europe. The idea of a network, working across a community and in extended expert and voluntary partnership, was not present elsewhere at the time, and has apparently not been replicated since, even in modern-day Scotland.

Notes

1. The evidence and argument in this paper are based upon a three-year research project at the University of Edinburgh entitled 'Reconstructing a Scottish School of Educational Research 1925–1950', UK ESRC grant no. RES-000-23-1246.
2. Educational Institute of Scotland Conference Minutes 1919, quoted in R. E. Bell, 'Godfrey Thomson and Scottish education', British Educational Research Association Seminar, 1975.
3. R. R. Rusk, 'National Research Centres 11 – Scottish Council for Research in Education', British Journal of Educational Studies 1 (1952), 39–42.
4. Rosemary Wake, 'Research as the hallmark of the professional: Scottish teachers and research in the early 1920s', Scottish Educational Review 20 (1988), 42–51.
5. William Boyd, 'Educational research', Scottish Educational Journal 2 (November 1919), 14.
6. A. Darroch, The Children – Some Educational Problems (T. C. and E. C. Jack, 1907), p. 7.
7. R. E. Bell, 'Educational studies in the Scottish universities, 1870–1970' (unpublished PhD dissertation, Open University, 1986), 277.
8. Ibid., 238.
9. Frederick W. Roman, The New Education in Europe (Routledge, 1930), p. 277.
10. John Nisbet, interview, Banchory, Scotland (13 March 2003). Nisbet was editor of the British Journal of Educational Psychology, chair of the Scottish Council for Research in Education, first president of the British Educational Research Association and chair of the Education Research Board of the Social Science Research Council
11. Drever was a leading experimental psychologist and 1931 became the first professor of psychology in a Scottish university, in Edinburgh.
12. Vernon was head of the psychology department at Jordanhill Training Centre, and then at the University of Glasgow (appointed 1938), psychological research adviser to the Admiralty and War Office during the Second World War and professor of educational psychology at the University of London Institute of Education from 1946 until 1968.
13. William McClelland was appointed to the Bell Chair at St Andrews University and its associated directorship of studies at Dundee Training Centre in 1925.
14. Keith Hope, 'The SCRE and the teacher', in Scottish Council for Research in Education 50th Anniversary 1928–1978 (SCRE, 1978), p. 24.
15. SCRE, 'Qualifying examination inquiry – IEI meeting, Dinard', IEI internal report (1938), 16.

16. Ibid., 12.
17. A. M. Macmeeken, *The Intelligence of a Representative Group of Scottish Children* (SCRE Publications XV, University of London Press, 1939), pp. 8–9.
18. Stephen Wiseman, 'Higher degrees in education in British education', *British Journal of Educational Studies* 2 (1953), 55.
19. G. Thomson, *Autobiography* (University of Edinburgh Library Special Collections, c. 1950s), Chapter 12, p. 2.
20. Bell, 'Educational studies in the Scottish universities', 283.
21 21. W. B. Inglis, 'Edinburgh and Moray House', in Godfrey Thomson, *The Education of an Englishman. An Autobiography* (Moray House Publications, 1969), p. 117.
22. Marjorie Cruickshank, *A History of the Training of Teachers in Scotland* (University of London Press, 1970), p. 183.
23 23. Inglis, 'Edinburgh and Moray House', p. 120.
24. Cruickshank, *History of the Training of Teachers in Scotland*, p. 183.
25. Advisory Council on Education in Scotland, *Training of Teachers* [McClelland Report] (Scottish Education Department, 1946), paragraph 215.

Bibliography

Brett, Caroline E., Martin Lawn, David J. Bartholomew and Ian J. Deary, 'Help will be welcomed from every quarter: The work of William Boyd and the Educational Institute of Scotland's Research Committee in the 1920s', *History of Education* 39(5) (2010), 589–611.

Deary, Ian J., Lawrence. J. Whalley and John M. Starr, *A Lifetime of Intelligence: Follow Up Studies of the Scottish Mental Surveys of 1932 and 1947* (American Psychological Association, 2009), Chapter 1.

Inglis, W. B., 'Edinburgh and Moray House', in Godfrey Thomson, *The Education of an Englishman. An Autobiography* (Moray House Publications, 1969).

Lawn, Martin, 'The institute as network: The Scottish Council for Research in Education as a local and international phenomenon in the 1930s', *Paedagogica Historica* 40 (2004), 719–32.

Lawn, Martin (ed.), *An Atlantic Crossing? The Work of the International Examination Inquiry, its Researchers, Methods and Influence* (Comparative Histories of Education – Symposium Books, 2008).

Lawn, Martin, 'Godfrey Thomson and the rise of university pedagogical study: A recorded lecture delivered at the University of Edinburgh in November 1950 by Godfrey H. Thomson: A transcript with commentary', *History of Education: Sources and Interpretations* 38 (2009), 565–85.

Lawn, Martin and Ian Deary, 'The new model school of education: Thomson, Moray House and Teachers College, Columbia', *Paedagogica Historica* 50 (2014), 301–19.

Lawn, Martin, Ian J. Deary, David Bartholomew and Caroline Brett, 'Embedding the new science of research: The organised culture of Scottish educational research in the mid-twentieth century', *Paedagogica Historica* 46 (2010), 357–81.

Sutherland, Gillian, *Ability, Merit and Measurement: Mental Testing and English Education 1880–1940* (Clarendon Press, 1984).

19

Scottish Education in the Twenty-first Century: Continuities, Aspirations and Challenges

Walter Humes

Introduction

By the end of the twentieth century, the distinctive character of Scottish education, developed in the centuries following the Reformation, was well established. Indeed, the educational system, together with Scots law and Presbyterian religion, was regarded as a powerful expression of the country's national identity and cultural values. Its distinctiveness from the rest of the UK was evident in several ways: in the political, legal and institutional framework which produced policies and sought to influence practice; in its separate curriculum and examination system; in the training of teachers and provision for their professional development; and in the official narratives that described the aims and aspirations of Scottish education.[1]

At the same time, Scotland was subject to similar pressures to those affecting other developed countries, deriving from the combined effects of economic globalisation, information technology, demographic mobility and the expansion of knowledge. These forces prompted questioning of the adequacy of existing educational systems and gave impetus to what has been called a Global Education Reform Movement driving educational policies in many countries in uniform directions. Traditional conceptions of learning were seen as too narrow and rigid to cope with the demands of rapidly changing work environments: it was argued that more emphasis should be given to a range of social and vocational skills, of the kind that would have utility value beyond the classroom. The globalisation argument can, however, be overstated: although regularly invoked by policy makers at a rhetorical level, it is often subject to a process of domestication in which national assumptions and values remain dominant.[2] In the Scottish context, a similar tension between rhetoric and practice can be seen in relation to another set of pressures – the case for a reconfiguration of the relationship between the private and public sector. Some of the operational principles of the former, it was argued, should be introduced into the latter, including competition, value for money, measurable targets and clear lines of accountability. The challenge for Scottish education was to remain true to its cherished values of democracy, equality and social unity – as set out, for example, in James Scotland's two-volume *History of Scottish Education* – while at the same time responding to external forces that carried the possibility of putting those values at risk.

The account that follows attempts to trace some of the ways in which policy makers responded to this situation, both in terms of the discourse they employed and the reforms they introduced. The main focus is on primary and secondary schooling, but some reference will also be made to further and higher education, and to developments outside the mainstream which cast interesting light on the formal system.[3] In the present chapter, particular attention is given to Curriculum for Excellence (CfE), a major programme to reform the 3–18 curriculum, begun in 2004 and still in the process of implementation. CfE has involved an attempt to reshape the Scottish teaching profession, and the form this has taken, and the intentions behind the process, are examined. The relationship between education and the economy also features prominently in the discussion. First, however, some brief observations on the overall political context are required.[4]

The devolution settlement, leading in 1999 to the re-establishment of a Scottish Parliament in Edinburgh after nearly 300 years, led to the expectation that divergence from the rest of the UK in educational provision would become more marked. As will be shown, to some extent that has been the case but the point requires careful qualification. In the first place, Scottish education in the pre-devolution period already enjoyed a substantial measure of autonomy, with legislation and policy proposals being developed in Edinburgh rather than London. Although there was some attempt in the 1980s to introduce policies consistent with measures in England (e.g. the right of schools to opt out of local authority control), these were subject to resistance and nothing as prescriptive as the Education Reform Act of 1988, which applied to England and Wales, was attempted in Scotland. What did happen was that some of the language associated with the New Right appeared in Scottish policy documents, emphasising 'consumer' rights, targets, accountability and performance indicators, and became part of professional discourse, particularly among those who held, or aspired to, positions of responsibility. It is doubtful, however, whether the impact on Scottish teachers' thinking and their everyday classroom practice was as great as the politicians driving the changes (most notably, Michael Forsyth) had hoped.[5]

As devolution approached, hopes were high that a new political order would more fully represent the democratic ideals of Scottish society. It was said that the Scottish Parliament 'should be accessible, open, responsive and develop procedures which make possible a participative approach to the development, consideration and scrutiny of policy and legislation'.[6] The first major piece of legislation following devolution, the Standards in Scotland's Schools etc. Act of 2000, did indeed involve an extensive consultation exercise, but one study suggested that responses led to very few changes in the draft legislation. It concluded that the process was of more value to the politicians 'in terms of policy promotion, public relations and political campaigning' than an example of genuine democratic participation which made a difference.[7] Nevertheless, among politicians, much was made of their stated desire to achieve 'consensus' and to work in 'partnership' with other stakeholders.

An early test of the effectiveness of the parliament came in the form of the examinations crisis of 2000. This occurred when the Scottish Qualifications Authority (SQA), the national body responsible for running the examination system, failed to produce results for a significant number of candidates in an efficient and timely manner. As well as senior staff within SQA itself, other members of the Scottish policy community, including the inspectorate, were seen as bearing some responsibility for what had happened. The episode attracted a substantial amount of adverse publicity and led to swift ministerial intervention, resulting in the departure of the chief executive and reconstitution of the SQA board. It also opened up a broader debate about the fundamental aims of the educational system and led to the Scottish Parliament's Inquiry into the Purpose of Scottish Education (2002–3). More immediately, it provided an opportunity for parliamentary committees to question key figures, including senior members of the civil service, who were subject to an uncomfortable grilling. One consequence was that the role of the inspectorate was, for a time at least, redefined in ways that limited its input into the policy process.[8]

The SQA crisis was a difficult period for Scottish education, challenging as it did the self-image of educational leaders as trusted stewards who could be relied upon to ensure quality and high standards. Other developments presented a more positive picture. In December 2000, five national priorities for education were approved under the following headings: Achievement and Attainment; Framework for Learning; Inclusion and Equality; Values and Citizenship; Learning for Life. Furthermore, an enquiry into the future of the teaching profession was commissioned by the Labour/Liberal Democrat administration. The recommendations of the enquiry report, A Teaching Profession for the 21st Century, formed the basis of the McCrone settlement of 2001, covering salaries, promotion, staff development and conditions of service. In March 2002, a national debate was launched to canvass public views on future policy, the responses to which indicated a fair degree of public confidence in existing provision: the title of the Scottish Executive's response to the debate introduced the word 'excellence', which was to become so significant in the following decade, into official discourse.[9] These developments served as the backdrop to the work of the review group set up to consider the form and content of the Scottish curriculum.

Curriculum for Excellence

One of the lessons of the pre-devolution period was that managing change in Scottish education is a slow and difficult process. As the end of the twentieth century approached, it was apparent that it had taken twenty-five years to introduce relatively modest reforms into the school curriculum. This could be defended as sensible evolution and seen as evidence of an educational system grounded in, and constrained by, tradition. But it could also be seen as evidence of a system run by conservative professionals who were resistant to social, political and economic pressures to rethink the priorities of education. The experience of earlier attempts to reshape Scottish education was mixed. The progressive 1947 Advisory Council Report on Secondary Education was widely applauded as offering an impressive vision of the democratic purposes of education but its impact on practice, certainly in the short term, was extremely limited. By contrast, the 'child-centred' philosophy of the 1965 Primary Memorandum did lead to significant changes in curriculum and teaching methods, perhaps reflecting the liberal social attitudes of that decade.

The reforms that are most relevant to an understanding of CfE started with the setting up of the Munn committee in 1974 (whose 1977 report entitled *The Structure of the Curriculum in the Third and Fourth Years of the Scottish Secondary School* led to the introduction of Standard Grade, sat by students in the fourth year of secondary school), followed by the 1987 document, *Curriculum and Assessment in the 1990s: A Policy for the 1990s*, which introduced the 5–14 programme, covering the whole of primary school and the first two years of secondary, and concluded with Higher Still (later National Qualifications), partly based on the Howie report of 1992 (*Upper Secondary Education in Scotland*), which focused on the fifth and sixth years. It was felt that the piecemeal nature of these reforms had created problems of progression and continuity between the different stages, which lacked a common set of concepts and principles running through the whole experience of schooling and underpinning pedagogic practice. A more comprehensive approach to the curriculum as a whole was required, one which would enable changes to be put in place more swiftly and which would make Scottish education better able to respond to the social and economic challenges of the twenty-first century.

A curriculum review group was established in 2003 to address these issues and produced its report the following year: this marked the formal beginning of the CfE programme. Members of the group were appointed on the traditional (pre-devolution) patronage model used to control entry to the Scottish policy community, a well-established system of recruitment to public service in Scotland.[10] The group was asked to identify the purposes of education from 3 to 18 and the principles for the design of the curriculum, taking account of the views expressed during the national debate, evidence from research and international comparisons. Their report argued for a curriculum that would:

- make learning active, challenging and enjoyable
- not be too fragmented or over-crowded in content
- connect the various stages of learning from 3 to 18
- encourage the development of high levels of accomplishment and intellectual skill

- include a wide range of experiences and achieve a suitable blend of what has traditionally been seen as 'academic' and 'vocational'
- give opportunities for children to make appropriate choices to meet their individual interests and needs, while ensuring that these choices lead to successful outcomes
- ensure that assessment supports learning[11]

The main reason offered for listing these particular features was that 'we need a curriculum which will enable all young people to understand the world they are living in, reach the highest possible levels of achievement, and equip them for work and learning throughout their lives'.[12] Towards this end, four key 'capacities' were identified: young people should become 'successful learners', 'confident individuals', 'effective contributors' and 'responsible citizens'. These terms quickly became part of professional discourse and were not subject to much critical scrutiny. Some commentators saw this as symptomatic of weak conceptualisation in the report as a whole. Gillies criticised the failure to define excellence adequately.[13] Priestley and Humes commented on an uneasy drift between different models of curriculum (curriculum as content, as process and as product).[14] And an important collection of papers published in 2013 offered a critical analysis of each of the four capacities, as well as questioning CfE's understanding of what might be required for teachers to become effective agents of change.[15]

After the initial set of proposals, there followed a lengthy, and at times fraught, process of development designed to translate the broad principles of the 2004 report into a carefully structured programme setting out the knowledge and skills that learners should acquire, the expectations for different stages of development and the 'experiences and outcomes' with which they should engage. In some respects what emerged was not strikingly new. For example, although detailed content was not prescribed – the intention being to give teachers more autonomy in deciding what to teach – the basic structure of the curriculum was framed around eight familiar curricular areas: expressive arts, health and wellbeing, languages, mathematics, religious and moral education, sciences, social studies and technologies. This was balanced by an encouragement to engage in interdisciplinary work, and to use progressive pedagogic approaches (such as 'active learning'), as well as the stipulation that all teachers had a responsibility for pupils' 'wellbeing'. In promoting the new curriculum there was sometimes a tension between the message that what was proposed was exciting, radical and new and the reassurance that good teachers were already doing much of what was being recommended. Not everyone was convinced. As late as 2011 a former headteacher of Kilmarnock Academy, who was also a former president of School Leaders Scotland, complained about 'the gulf in opinion between the educational establishment and the professionals on the ground' with regard to the success of the initiative. She cited 'poor management' and 'poor communication' as features of the way the development was promoted and posed the question: 'Where is the solid evidential and intellectual basis for CfE developments?'

Questioning the enthusiasm for interdisciplinary learning, as well as doubting the wisdom of giving so much weight to 'confident individuals' as one of the key capacities, she claimed that 'much of CfE runs counter to teachers' experience, training and intuition'.[16]

Reference here to 'poor management' and 'poor communication' brings into focus the relationship between the various agencies that were charged with developing CfE. Initially this was the responsibility of Learning and Teaching Scotland (LTS), the national advisory body on the curriculum. However, LTS was going through a major exercise of internal restructuring, with staff changes at senior level, and both civil servants from Scottish Government and representatives from Her Majesty's Inspectorate of Education (HMIE) were closely involved in the process. The steering of the reform was subject to some public criticism, including from people who had been members of the original review group, and the Cabinet Secretary for Education had to give a number of assurances that the programme was proceeding as planned. Against this background, it came as no great surprise when, in 2011, LTS and HMIE were brought together in a single organisation, Education Scotland (ES), with combined responsibilities for inspection and review, curricular reform and teacher development. The rehabilitation of the inspectorate at the centre of the policy process, a decade after the SQA episode of 2000, was complete.

By this time, the implementation of CfE was well underway and there was no going back. A suite of New National Qualifications had been developed, designed to reflect the curricular and pedagogic changes. It will be some time before the extent to which this has been achieved can be properly assessed, but teachers have raised concerns about what has been proposed for a number of specific subjects and about what they perceive as restricted subject options compared to Standard Grades. Ironically, the intention was to reduce prescription and to offer more personalisation and choice to learners: for some qualifications this meant giving more weight to coursework and less to final examinations. CfE had become a 'high stakes' policy in the sense that the reputation of Scottish education – as well as the reputation of the individuals and organisations who had been involved in its development – now depended on it being perceived as at least reasonably successful. Political considerations came into play. Calls for a fully independent study of the CfE programme were resisted by government until September 2013, when it was announced that the Organisation for Economic Co-operation and Development would carry out an evaluation, reporting in 2015. Research studies suggested a mixed picture, with general support from teachers for the broad principles of the reform but uncertainties, particularly in secondary schools, about their state of readiness.[17]

Reshaping the Teaching Profession

The introduction of a new school curriculum meant that the role of teachers had to be re-assessed. Throughout the 1980s and 1990s there had been a concern, not only in Scotland but internationally, that governments had become too prescriptive in their expectations for educational systems, evident in tight inspection regimes, testing in core subjects at specified ages and demands that standards of achievement should show steady improvement. The result was that the work of teachers had been laid down in a fair amount of detail, leaving them little scope for the exercise of their professional judgement, or imaginative approaches that strayed beyond what was contained in official policy documents. Although in Scotland this had not taken the form of statutory regulation, in practice most teachers regarded curricular 'guidelines' as mandatory. This led some commentators to speak of the 'deskilling' or 'deprofessionalisation' of teachers, turning them into unreflective technicians implementing instructions laid down from above.[18]

Soon after devolution a committee was set up to look at how Scottish teachers' 'pay, promotion structures and conditions of service should be changed in order to secure a committed, professional and flexible teaching force'.[19] The title of their report, A Teaching Profession for the 21st Century, signalled the importance attached to making teaching an attractive career, geared to the country's aspirations and offering opportunities for professional development. It led in 2001 to the McCrone Agreement which the then Minister for Education, Peter Peacock, later said was much more than a pay deal:

> it is a comprehensive and radical programme to help build the profession as a basis for giving it the trust and the freedoms that are necessary in schools and classrooms to drive the continuous improvement that we want to see and to which we are committed.[20]

Substantially improved salaries ensured that the deal was acceptable but there were conditions attached that subsequently proved problematic: in particular, a 'job sizing' exercise which affected many principal teachers in secondary schools and led to the introduction of faculty structures, combining departments that had previously operated as separate units. The 'flexible teaching force' envisaged by McCrone did not appeal to everyone. Another feature which produced a mixed response was the introduction of the new role of Chartered Teacher (CT), which was designed to recognise and reward experienced teachers who wanted to remain in the classroom rather than seek a management position. Although both 'professional' and 'academic' routes to CT status were offered, initial take-up was rather disappointing and, as will be seen shortly, the programme was discontinued after a few years.

The debate about the new curriculum requiring teachers to be less dependent on central direction and more willing to exercise independent judgement also led to a reassessment of existing provision for pre-service and in-service training. It was felt that a co-ordinated programme of professional development, starting from initial training and extending to the various stages of a teacher's career, was required. In 2009, the former Senior Chief Inspector of Education, Graham Donaldson, was asked to carry out a review with the remit: 'To consider the best arrangements for the full continuum of teacher education in primary and secondary schools in Scotland. The review should consider initial teacher education, induction and professional development and the interaction between them'.[21] Evidence was taken from a wide range of individuals and organisations, a literature review was commissioned, a teacher survey carried out and stakeholder meetings held in different locations. A total of fifty recommendations were made covering entry qualifications for teaching; the professional standards laid down by the General Teaching Council for Scotland (GTCS); partnerships between teacher education institutions, schools and local authorities; the quality of school-based placements; the evaluation of continuing professional development activities; and pathways to leadership positions. Perhaps the most important recommendation sought to address concerns that some existing courses were too narrowly focused on pedagogy, offering insufficient scope for the wider education of students. It was proposed, therefore, that the traditional four-year BEd degree, which had been the main route into primary teaching, should be phased out: it was to be replaced by 'degrees which combine in-depth academic study in areas beyond education with professional studies and development'.[22] The overall intention was to create 'a reinvigorated approach to 21st century teacher professionalism'.[23]

The aim of reshaping the professional profile of Scottish teachers was also apparent in the McCormac review of the 2001 agreement on teachers' pay and conditions, reported in a 2011 document entitled *Advancing Professionalism in Teaching*. Its recommendations included control of the number and grade of promoted posts in schools, no increase in teachers' class contact time but greater flexibility in the use of non-contact time and the ending of the CT scheme, which was felt not to have produced measurable benefits. This last recommendation was subject to strong criticism, not only from Chartered Teachers themselves, but also from those who felt that some headteachers had shown a lack of imagination in the deployment of Chartered Teachers, and that local authorities were principally motivated by a desire to reduce salary costs. Another area of criticism was a perceived reduction in teachers' conditions of service, implying a lack of trust in their professional commitment. Notwithstanding the criticisms, the Cabinet Secretary for Education and Lifelong Learning announced in February 2012 that the CT scheme would be discontinued. However, he stated that the Scottish Government was strongly committed to improved professional learning opportunities for teachers, supporting the vision of a masters-level profession.

One of the conclusions to be drawn from the reception of the McCrone, Donaldson and McCormac reports by Scottish teachers (and consistent with some of their reactions to the CfE programme) is that they are somewhat ambivalent towards their own professionalism.[24] They want to be accorded professional status and have their expertise as practitioners recognised, which includes giving them a fair degree of autonomy to decide what and how to teach. At the same time, they want the reassurance of a curriculum that offers a clear framework, backed by resources developed by local authorities and ES. Furthermore, they may say that they value the insights that educational research can offer but are more likely to rely on 'good practice' than engage in a re-examination of educational principles. Whereas, in the period between 1920 and 1940, Scottish teachers, through their main professional body, the Educational Institute of Scotland, were partners in national educational research projects, this is rarely the case today. (See the chapter by Lawn and Deary in the present volume.) The decision to discontinue the CT programme might even be seen as an example of an anti-intellectual attitude, not by any means confined to classroom teachers but also evident among some headteachers, inspectors and policy makers.

Viewed from this perspective, the reshaping of the Scottish teaching profession may still have some way to go. In 2012, the GTCS introduced a new suite of professional standards designed to offer a framework for teachers at different stages of development – from initial registration, through career-long professional learning, to leadership and management. This took place at the same time as the GTCS changed from being an advisory non-departmental public body to a fully independent self-regulatory body under the Public Services Reform (General Teaching Council for Scotland) Order 2011. The enhanced status can be regarded as evidence of the relative standing of teaching as a profession in Scotland compared to England. Whereas the Scottish GTC had been in existence since 1965, an English GTC was not established until 1998, with significantly weaker powers. Its composition led to inter-union rivalries and criticisms that it was over-bureaucratic and weak in dealing with underperforming teachers. It only lasted until March 2012, following a decision by the UK Conservative–Liberal Democrat coalition to abolish it.

Education and the Economy

A recurring theme of many policy documents in the post-devolution period has been the importance of education to the Scottish economy. The strategic goals of ES, as set out in its website, are explicitly linked to the Scottish Government's National Performance Framework, a central element of which is sustainable growth. A particular pressure on the SNP government in the run-up to the 2014 referendum was the need to convince voters that an independent Scotland would have the economic strength to survive in a competitive international environment, particularly given the decline of traditional heavy industries and the proportion of people employed in the public sector (some 23 per cent of the total workforce according to Scottish Government figures issued in 2013). This line of thinking has led to the perception, particularly among employers, that conventional ways of structuring and assessing knowledge are too narrow to cope with the demands of rapidly changing work environments. What is needed, they believe, is the development of generic skills, such as flexibility and teamwork. In one of the CfE documents, *Building the Curriculum 3*, the focus is on three types of skill – skills for learning, skills for life and skills for work. A skill is defined as

> the ability, competency, proficiency or dexterity to carry out tasks that come from education, training, practice or experience. It can enable the practical application of theoretical knowledge to particular tasks or situations. 'Skill' is

also applied more broadly to include behaviours, attitudes and personal attributes that make individuals more effective in particular contexts such as education and training, employment and social engagement.[25]

One of the 'personal attributes' that has been particularly promoted is 'enterprise'. Throughout the post-devolution period, under both the Labour–Liberal
Democrat coalition which governed until 2007 and the SNP administrations
thereafter, there has been a strong focus on the promotion of enterprise as an individual and collective value.[26] The concept can be traced through several official
publications including *Determined to Succeed: A Review of Enterprise in Education*
(2002), *Ambitious, Excellent Schools* (2004), *A Smart, Successful Scotland* (2006)
and *Employability and Skills: Taking Forward our National Conversation* (2009). In
each case a clear link is made between the confidence and aspirations of individuals, the skills and attitudes they need in order to succeed in the world of work and
the future economic prospects for Scotland, whether as a part of the UK or as an
independent nation.

At one level, the emphasis on enterprise can be seen as evidence of 'market'
thinking making inroads into the educational system. But has this amounted to
more than the invocation of currently fashionable discourse? It is striking that
the basic framework of Scottish schooling – with some 95 per cent of pupils
attending state schools run by local authorities and, in the case of secondary
schools, structured on non-selective 'comprehensive' lines – has remained unal-
tered since the 1960s.[27] This can be contrasted with the situation in England
where the effects of the market are more visible. Types of school and the way they
are run are much more diversified. They include sixth-form colleges and some
selective grammar schools, as well as the more recent arrivals of 'free schools' and
'academies'. In July 2013, there was a report that Michael Gove, the Education
Secretary in England, was considering a proposal that free schools and academies
could become profit-making businesses using venture capitalists to raise funds.
At present it is inconceivable that such an idea would get off the ground in
Scotland, indicating a clear difference in the extent to which market thinking has penetrated the education systems in the two countries. Ever since the
Education (Scotland) Act of 1872, there has been a general acceptance of the
idea that the prime responsibility for the provision of Scottish education should
lie with the state.[28]

Nevertheless, the discourse of the market (ambition, competition, targets,
growth) does feature quite strongly in debates about the direction in which
Scottish education should be going. A positive 'can do' attitude is seen by politicians and employers as desirable at all stages of education, but it becomes particularly important in the post-16 stage, when students are preparing for examinations,
seeking work or moving on to college or university. Scottish further education
(FE) colleges have a long history of offering courses leading to vocational qualifications, developed in association with employers and often involving periods
spent in a workplace environment.[29] As patterns of employment have changed,

with the decline of manufacturing and shipbuilding, so the balance of course provision has shifted, with an increase in courses preparing students for work in the fields of health and social care, sport and recreation, catering and hospitality, computing and design. More traditional fields such as construction and engineering are still strongly represented and the Modern Apprenticeships scheme aims to offer 25,000 young people each year the opportunity to gain qualifications while in paid employment. The scheme is run by Skills Development Scotland, a national body, established in 2008, bringing together provision for careers and training, and working with local and national partners to enhance employability.

The FE sector has long regarded itself as the 'Cinderella' service of Scottish education which, despite making a vital contribution to learning provision for both young people and adults of all ages, has traditionally been accorded lower status than universities and even, to some extent, to academic pathways in the upper secondary school. That perception is beginning to change, albeit slowly. Many FE colleges have informal or formal partnership agreements with schools and universities. In the case of the former, school students may attend certain courses at their local college. In the case of the latter, it is possible for college students to gain advanced entry to degree-level courses at universities on the basis of qualifications gained at college. It has been estimated that roughly one-quarter of college work is at 'higher' rather than 'further' education level, as judged by the Scottish Qualifications and Credit Framework. This means that they should be regarded as comprehensive providers of lifelong learning rather than simply institutions which offer a limited vocational alternative to 'academic' education.

However, some tensions between the sectors undoubtedly remain. When it comes to budget allocations by the Scottish Funding Council, FE colleges feel that the system favours universities. In 2012–13 this problem was exacerbated by a Scottish Government programme of major restructuring within the college sector, involving a transition from forty-one individual colleges to thirteen college regions. This involved mergers, cutting courses (to avoid duplication), staff retirements and job losses. These changes were given statutory force in the Post-16 Education (Scotland) Act, approved in the summer of 2013. It is somewhat ironic that a sector which has been given a crucial role in helping the economy to grow should itself be subject to stringent savings and economies.

Scottish universities too face stiff economic challenges, not least because of the differential fee regimes which operate north and south of the border. Whereas English universities can charge up to £9,000 a year, financed through student loans and repayable after graduation, the Scottish Government has pledged that a similar charge will not be introduced in Scotland, on the grounds that access to higher education should not be dependent on ability to pay but on the capacity to benefit from the educational experiences on offer. This position is in line with the liberal values associated with George Davie's 'democratic intellect',[30] which promotes a generalist conception of education embracing philosophical, scientific and humanistic dimensions, linked to a vision of the good society, but there is evidence to suggest that the proportion of students going on to university from socially disadvantaged areas is small (particularly at St Andrews and Edinburgh). Moreover, it is doubtful whether the 'no fees' for home-based students policy can be sustained without placing Scottish institutions at a serious disadvantage compared with their English counterparts. Scotland also faces the problem of a relatively high drop-out rate among first-year students at some of the newer universities (23 per cent at the University of the West of Scotland in 2013, compared with less than 4 per cent at St Andrews), to which it is easier to gain entry than at older institutions.

Judging from the 'mission statements' set out on their websites, all universities (including those which would describe themselves as 'research intensive') are keen to shed the 'ivory tower' image which has sometimes been attached to them. They stress their contributions to economic growth and to national strategic goals. These take a variety of forms: collaborative working with public and private sector partners, sometimes under the heading of 'knowledge exchange'; various forms of community engagement; enhancing the student experience beyond the formal content of their courses; and encouraging enterprise and entrepreneurship. These measures are designed to improve the employability of graduates. As universities have expanded, and to the extent that they depend heavily on public resources, so government demands that they should demonstrate the contribution they make to national economic and social priorities have increased. The freedoms that universities have enjoyed in the past have come under pressure, evident for example in the setting up of a review of university governance in 2012.[31] The recommendations of this review sought to increase the democratic accountability of university management by defining the powers of principals and university courts and increasing the transparency of decision-making. What has emerged as a code of governance falls short of what was proposed and the suspicion is that behind-the-scenes lobbying by Universities Scotland, the body which represents the collective interests of Scottish university principals, has led to a watered-down set of proposals.

One underlying problem associated with budgetary cutbacks, whether at school, FE or HE levels, is that the number of people who have a good understanding of the economics of Scottish education is small. There is no Centre for the Study of the Economics of Education, such as there is at the London School of Economics (with links to the London Institute of Education). This means that there is a limited constituency of informed opinion which might be able to contribute to debates about shifting resources from one sector to another (say from higher education to pre-school education) or about the capacity of local authorities to meet their statutory obligations under a tight financial regime.[32] University schools of education in Scotland have tended to focus their research enquiries on matters of curriculum, assessment and pedagogy rather than on the wider political and economic context. Arguably, this intellectual caution has not served the system well at a time when hard choices have to be made. In the absence of academic input, the way is left open for politicians to make decisions that may be influenced by short-term expediency rather than by long-term strategic thinking.

Voices from the Margins

Most descriptions of Scottish education are 'insider' accounts, in the sense that they are written by people who work within the mainstream system and who enjoy considerable powers of narrative privilege; that is, they are able to construct versions of events that convey a fairly positive picture of what happens. This is particularly true of official organisations, such as ES and the GTC, which have a vested interest in promoting the message that their efforts ensure that Scottish education is proceeding along the right lines. However, in seeking to understand not just the surface configurations but also the subterranean movements in Scottish education, it is important to pay attention to developments outside the mainstream. These take a number of forms.

Firstly, there is what might be called the radical tradition of Scottish education. During the twentieth century there were a number of significant figures who developed an educational philosophy that ran counter to the dominant values of state schooling; it included people such as Patrick Geddes (1854–1932), A. S. Neill (1883–1973), John Aitkenhead (1910–98) and R. F. Mackenzie (1910–87). They saw conventional schooling as narrow, authoritarian and lacking in freedom: the approach they favoured was progressive and child-centred, committed to creativity and self-expression, and not confined to the classroom. Compared to the mainstream of educational provision, the radical approach was always a minor tradition, often regarded as unrealistic and occasionally as dangerously subversive.

But it has been significant in at least three ways. Firstly, it was a reaction against what was perceived as the harsh authoritarianism of conventional Scottish schools, quick to pass negative judgement on pupils and to impose physical punishment. Secondly, it raised important questions about a number of fundamental issues, including the nature of childhood and the rights of children, the ways in which schools should operate and the personal and social aims which should inform the whole enterprise. And thirdly, although the philosophy underlying the radical tradition, particularly as expressed in the writings of Neill and Mackenzie, was often dismissed as romantic idealism, over time it did help to bring about change within the state system: schools are much more enlightened places than they used to be, with greater concern for the welfare of children, including those with various forms of learning disability, and a widespread acceptance that worthwhile learning and development require much more than the formal teaching of a limited body of knowledge. Mackenzie may never have achieved the fundamental change of direction that he hoped for, but he would certainly have been encouraged by the current emphasis on citizenship and well-being and by the introduction of Scottish Studies into the curriculum. It remains true, however, that there is still a high measure of uniformity within the mainstream state system and there is no figure comparable to Mackenzie currently making a case for an 'educational revolution'.[33]

For something genuinely different, and more in line with the vision of the radicals, it is necessary to look to the independent Steiner schools and the small, but increasing, numbers of parents who take their children out of school altogether and educate them at home. The inspiration for Steiner schools was the work of the Austrian Rudolf Steiner (1861–1925) and there are currently four in Scotland (in Edinburgh, Glasgow, Aberdeen and Forres). They seek to take account of the whole needs of the child (academic, physical, emotional, cultural and spiritual), informed by understanding of the various phases of child development. Artistic activity is regarded as integral to learning, encouraging creativity and imagination.

Parents have a legal duty to ensure that their children are educated but they are not obliged to fulfil this duty by sending them to school. They can choose to educate them at home and do not require to have obtained teaching qualifications in order to do so. It is difficult to obtain exact figures for the number of children being educated in this way. A Scottish Government estimate in 2009 suggested that there were only about 755 home-educated children but Helen Lees has argued that this is likely to be a significant under-estimate as parents are not obliged to inform their local authority of their intention.[34] The reasons for the choice are varied. Parents may feel that the local school cannot provide for the particular needs of their child; or that the school has failed to deal satisfactorily with episodes of bullying; or that the curriculum and examination system are too inflexible. The nature of home education can be immensely varied but it tends to be informal, integrated with everyday family activities and more concerned with individual fulfilment than group conformity.[35] Support groups enable home educators to share ideas and an independent organisation, Schoolhouse Scotland, has a website with links to various resources.

There are other sources of ideas from outside the mainstream which, though less fundamentally divergent from orthodox thinking than the radical tradition, are worthy of note. In 2013, two independent (i.e. not government-sponsored) reports on the future direction of Scottish education were published. These were the work of 'think tanks' and, although they did not receive wholehearted endorsement from the educational community, they did attract some attention. 'Think tanks' have been influential in shaping policy south of the border, but debate in Scotland has been dominated by official agencies and professional voices. The first report contained the findings of the Commission on School Reform, produced jointly by Reform Scotland and the Centre for Scottish Public Policy.[36] Its starting point was the belief that, while Scotland's educational system had achieved a great deal, it was no longer among the world's best. The difficult question of precisely when, and in what respects, Scottish education could once have been regarded as among the best, is not explored. It is simply asserted that it had been slow to change and, in particular, had failed 'to tackle successfully the educational consequences of social and economic disadvantage'.[37] The main reason for this, the report claimed, was excessive uniformity and a culture which discouraged diversity and innovation. Schools should be given more autonomy and encouraged to take initiatives without having to gain approval from a hierarchical bureaucracy. Unsurprisingly, the Commission's recommendations, which would have reduced the role of local government education authorities, were not met with enthusiasm by the Convention of Scottish Local Authorities. One conclusion that might be drawn from this is that a major obstacle to change is the entrenched bureaucratic structure of the educational system itself: established institutions are reluctant to embark on anything that might reduce their power and influence, even if the case for benefits to learners is strong.

The second report was a study by Scotland's Futures Forum, in partnership with the Goodison Group in Scotland, which looked to the year 2025 and considered possible future scenarios.[38] It identifies two fundamental 'drivers' which will shape society and learning – increased globalisation and greater social inequality – and goes on to sketch alternative ways in which educational provision might evolve. Four scenarios of possible futures are described, each of which represents a different set of responses to the two key 'drivers'. The first scenario is a 'Market Driven Learning Society' in which Scotland has embraced globalisation: there will be winners and losers, with the leading universities emerging as powerful players. This contrasts with the second scenario, a 'Local Learning Society', in which the principles of equality and social justice influence policy to a greater extent than international pressures. The third scenario is the 'Global Learning Society', in which government (not the private sector) takes the lead in promoting learning and skills as instruments of growth and marketable exports to other countries. The final scenario is the 'Divided Learning Society', in which the gap between the rich and the poor, the educated and the uneducated, has intensified: this leads to social unrest, fuelled by the stark contrast between areas of extreme deprivation and the gated communities of the wealthy.

The appearance of these think tank reports may signal reduced trust in the formal agencies which run Scottish education and a feeling that other voices need to be listened to in the framing of educational policy. But the impact and significance of the development should not be overstated. Some of those involved are (or were) very much part of the current system and seek to build on existing practices rather than replace them with something totally new. The bureaucratic structures of Scottish education – represented by bodies such as ES, the SQA and the GTC – remain firmly in place, with strong lines of communication to Scottish Government. Likewise, although there have been some changes to the composition of the policy community, with wider representation beyond education professionals and senior civil servants, the processes of policy conception and development are still subject to strong political direction from the centre. There are no indications that a major shift of approach, in a more radical direction, is likely to happen soon.

Conclusion

Scottish education in the post-devolution period has sought to balance a number of aspirations: to build on the reputation and achievements of the Scottish educational tradition; to use the powers of the Scottish Parliament to consolidate the distinctiveness of education north of the border; to modernise the curriculum in response to economic pressures and new patterns of employment; to take account of international developments, including demographic shifts and the promotion of global citizenship[39] as an ideal. These multiple influences have led to some interesting tensions in the policy discourse that has been employed and in the mechanisms that have been used to try to drive the agenda for change. Moreover, although there has been some restructuring of the institutional framework of Scottish education, there has been substantial continuity in the composition of the policy community entrusted to implement the reform programme. It is a story of continuity and change, convergence and divergence, ambition and consolidation.

What of Scotland's long-standing reputation as a country where education is greatly valued and standards are high? Throughout the post-devolution period, politicians of all parties, as well as the general public, have been in agreement that education is one of the most important policy priorities: the evidence for this can be found in successive election manifestos and in the findings of the regular Scottish Social Attitudes Surveys. Naturally, however, there have been differences about how resources should be allocated and the best means of achieving objectives. In some areas, Scotland can justly claim that its provision has made significant progress, perhaps particularly in relation to children with various forms of additional support needs. The question of overall standards remains highly contentious and occasionally allegations of 'dumbing down' are made – such as happened in relation to the Higher Mathematics exam in 2013. In international comparisons, such as those carried out by the Organisation for Economic Co-operation and Development (OECD), Scotland performs fairly well, but levels of achievement are uneven, leading one commentator to question the 'myth' that Scotland is 'better than England' in attainment and in attitudes.[40] The same writer called for more research data and offered two challenging hypotheses for investigation: that 'competition and diversity are quite compatible with high standards'; and that 'equal opportunities don't require uniformity of structures'.[41] There was no real engagement with these challenges by the Scottish educational establishment, a response that suggests a worrying degree of denial among policy makers and senior education professionals.

In 2007, the OECD produced a report entitled *Quality and Equity of Schooling in Scotland*. Although the report found much to commend it also identified a number of challenges, most notably the need to reduce the achievement gap that opens up from about Primary 5 onwards: 'Children from poorer communities and low socio-economic status homes are more likely than others to underachieve, while the gap associated with poverty and deprivation in local government areas appears to be very wide.'[42] The extent to which schools, on their own, can compensate for these disadvantages is limited, leading the report to assert that 'Who you are in Scotland is far more important than what school you attend, so far as achievement differences on international tests are concerned'.[43] The comprehensive system, which in many respects has served

Scotland well, enabling many more pupils to gain qualifications than the previous selective system, has found it difficult to make significant inroads into the underachieving minority who fail to engage with what schools have to offer. There is no easy answer to this problem as it calls for a co-ordinated approach across many areas of public policy (health, housing, employment and planning, as well as education). Although successive governments have expressed a commitment to 'joined-up thinking' in developing policies, in practice this has been difficult to achieve. What tends to happen is that ameliorative efforts are introduced for a limited period but that as soon as resources are withdrawn any improvements cannot be sustained.

In September 2014 a majority of people in Scotland rejected the option of becoming a completely independent nation and voted in favour of remaining part of the United Kingdom. For the immediate future, therefore, educational policy will continue on its current trajectory. In any case, as was noted at the outset, Scottish education in the pre-devolution period already enjoyed a fair measure of freedom within the UK. However, it is likely that economic conditions will restrict education budgets and set limits to new initiatives. The subject of student fees may have to be revisited and the continuing viability of thirty-two local authorities, each providing education services, may be called into question. Already there are a few cases of authorities entering into agreements to provide shared services.

Nevertheless, although education was not the most contentious issue during the debate about independence, it was not without significance. Arnott and Ozga, in their study of educational policy in the period after the SNP came to power, first as a minority administration and later as a government with an overall majority, offer an account that helps to explain some of the tensions at work. They say that nationalism was 'used as a discursive resource' to persuade Scots that they 'could safely aspire to independence'.[44] This involved an appeal to traditional conceptions of education as a vital component of national identity, expressive of a commitment to equality and social justice. Running alongside this, however, have been global pressures for a 'knowledge economy', pursuing an agenda of 'competitiveness, skill development and employability'. This, they suggest, limits the extent to which a highly distinctive educational policy can be pursued. Although it is not difficult to portray recent developments in Scottish education as quite different from those in England,[45] there are nonetheless convergent tendencies deriving from economic objectives being driven by a number of trans-national organisations (such as the European Union and the OECD). Thus in the run-up to the referendum vote in 2014, it remained important for the Scottish Government to invoke the appeal of Scottish distinctiveness, while responding to the wider external context. This involved 'crafting the narrative' to accommodate both Davie's 'democratic intellect' and the strategic aim of creating a 'smarter Scotland'.[46]

Notes

1. Walter Humes and Tom Bryce, 'The distinctiveness of Scottish education', in T. G. K. Bryce and W. M. Humes (eds), *Scottish Education, 3rd edition, Beyond Devolution* (Edinburgh University Press, 2008), pp. 98–110.
2. See Jenny Ozga and Bob Lingard, 'Globalisation, education policy and politics', in Jenny Ozga and Bob Lingard (eds), *The RoutledgeFalmer Reader in Education Policy and Politics* (Routledge, 2007), pp. 65–82.
3. More comprehensive coverage of the period under review can be found in T. G. K. Bryce and W. M. Humes (eds), *Scottish Education*, 1st, 2nd and 3rd edns (Edinburgh University Press, 1999, 2003, 2008) and in T. G. K. Bryce, W. M. Humes, D. Gillies and A. Kennedy (eds), *Scottish Education*, 4th edn (Edinburgh University Press, 2013).
4. See also Lindsay Paterson, *Education and the Scottish Parliament* (Dunedin Academic Press, 2000) and Willis Pickard and John Dobie, *The Political Context of Education after Devolution* (Dunedin Academic Press, 2003).
5. Walter Humes, 'The significance of Michael Forsyth in Scottish education', *Scottish Affairs* 11 (1995), 112–30.
6. Scottish Office, *Shaping Scotland's Parliament* (The Stationery Office, 1998), p. 3.
7. Donald J. Gillies, 'The Scottish Parliament and educational policy making' (unpublished MEd dissertation, University of Strathclyde, 2001).
8. Lindsay Paterson, *Crisis in the Classroom* (Mainstream, 2000).
9. Scottish Executive, *Educating for Excellence: Choice and Opportunity* (Scottish Executive, 2003).
10. On the composition of the Scottish educational policy community, and the use of patronage to control entry to it, see Walter Humes, *The Leadership Class in Scottish Education* (John Donald, 1986) and Andrew McPherson and Charles D. Raab, *Governing Education: A Sociology of Policy since 1945* (Edinburgh University Press, 1988).
11. Scottish Executive, *A Curriculum for Excellence: The Curriculum Review Group* (Scottish Executive, 2004), p. 10.
12. Ibid., p. 10.
13. Donald Gillies, 'Curriculum for Excellence: A question of values', *Scottish Educational Review* 38 (2006), 25–36.
14. Mark Priestley and Walter Humes, 'The development of Scotland's Curriculum for Excellence: Amnesia and déjà vu', *Oxford Review of Education* 36 (2010), 345–61.
15. Mark Priestley and Gert Biesta (eds), *Reinventing the Curriculum: New Trends in Curriculum Policy and Practice* (Bloomsbury, 2013).
16. Carol Ford, 'The trouble and truth about Curriculum for Excellence', *Times Educational Supplement Scotland*, 16 December 2011, 35–6.
17. See Mark Priestley and Sarah Minty, 'Curriculum for Excellence: "A brilliant idea, but . . ."', *Scottish Educational Review* 45 (2013), 39–52.
18. One powerful expression of this argument, quite influential in Scotland, was a book by an Australian academic, Judyth Sachs, *The Activist Teaching Profession* (Open University Press, 2003).
19. Scottish Executive Education Department, *A Teaching Profession for the 21st Century: Report of the Committee of Enquiry into Professional Conditions of Service for Teachers* (HMSO, 2000), p. 1.
20. Peter Peacock, *Official Report of the Scottish Parliament*, 22 January 2004, col. 5126. Available at www.scottish.parliament.uk/parliamentarybusiness/28862.aspx?r=4488 &mode=pdf (accessed 1 June 2014).

21. Scottish Government, *Teaching Scotland's Future: Report of a Review of Teacher Education in Scotland* (Scottish Government, 2011), p. 106.
22. Ibid., p. 88.
23. Ibid., p. 84.
24. See Walter Humes, 'Conditions for professional development', *Scottish Educational Review* 23 (2001), 6–17.
25. Scottish Government, *Building the Curriculum 3: A Framework for Learning and Teaching* (Scottish Government, 2008), p. 31.
26. For a study of the relationship between enterprise and citizenship, both of which feature prominently in Scottish policy discourse, see Ross Deuchar, *Citizenship, Enterprise and Learning: Harmonising Competing Educational Agendas* (Trentham Books, 2007).
27. The chapter on secondary education in Lindsay Paterson's *Scottish Education in the Twentieth Century* (Edinburgh University Press, 2003) offers a good account of the ending of selection and the switch to a comprehensive system.
28. See Walter Humes, 'State: The governance of Scottish education 1872–2000', in Heather Holmes (ed.), *Institutions of Scotland: Education*, Scottish Life and Society: A Compendium of Scottish Ethnology, vol. 11 (Tuckwell Press, 2000), pp. 84–105.
29. See Craig Thomson, 'Scottish Further Education', in T. G. K. Bryce, W. M. Humes, D. Gillies and A. Kennedy (eds), *Scottish Education*, 4th edn (Edinburgh University Press, 2013), pp. 76–87.
30. George Davie, *The Democratic Intellect: Scotland and her Universities in the Nineteenth Century* (Edinburgh University Press, 1961).
31. Scottish Government, *Report of the Review of Higher Education Governance in Scotland* (Scottish Government, 2012).
32. A recent, and very welcome, contribution to our understanding of the economics of Scottish education is David Bell's chapter, 'The funding of Scottish education', in Bryce et al., *Scottish Education*, 4th edn, pp. 987–1002.
33. See Walter Humes, 'R. F. Mackenzie's "Manifesto for an educational revolution"', *Scottish Educational Review* 43 (2011), 56–72.
34. Bryce et al., *Scottish Education*, 4th edn, p. 135.
35. See Helen E. Lees, 'Alternative forms of schooling', in Bryce et al., *Scottish Education*, 4th edn, pp. 129–37.
36. Reform Scotland/Centre for Scottish Public Policy, *By Diverse Means: Improving Scottish Education*, Final Report of the Commission on School Reform (Reform Scotland/CSPP, 2013).
37. Ibid., p. 5.
38. Scotland's Futures Forum/Goodison Group in Scotland, *By 2025, Scotland will be Regarded as a World-leading Learning nation: Scenarios for the Future* (SFF/GGiS, 2013).
39. The emphasis on 'responsible citizenship' as one of the key capacities of Curriculum for Excellence has sometimes been promoted as a global, not just a national, aspiration. See T. L. K. Wisely, I. M. Barr, A. Britton and B. King (eds), *Education in a Global Space* (IDEAS, 2010).
40. Lindsay Paterson, 'English schools are the best in the UK', *Times Educational Supplement Scotland*, 3 July 2009.
41. Ibid.
42. Organisation for Economic Co-operation and Development, *Quality and Equity of Schooling in Scotland* (OECD, 2007), p. 15.
43. Ibid., p. 15. For a useful discussion of the report's findings and conclusions, see David Raffe, 'As others see us: A commentary on the OECD review of the quality and equity of schooling in Scotland', *Scottish Educational Review* 40 (2008), 22–36.

44. Margaret Arnott and Jenny Ozga, 'Education and nationalism: The discourse of educational policy in Scotland', *Discourse* 31 (2010), 347.
45. See Margaret Arnott and Ian Menter, 'The same but different? Post-devolution regulation and control in Scotland and England', *European Educational Research Journal* 6 (2007), 250–65.
46. Arnott and Ozga, 'Education and nationalism', 335.

Bibliography

Bryce, T. G. K. and W. M. Humes (eds), *Scottish Education*, 1st, 2nd and 3rd edns (Edinburgh University Press, 1999, 2003, 2008).
Bryce, T. G. K., W. M. Humes, D. Gillies and A. Kennedy (eds), *Scottish Education*, 4th edn (Edinburgh University Press, 2013).
Humes, Walter, 'State: The governance of Scottish education 1872–2000', in Heather Holmes (ed.), *Institutions of Scotland: Education*, Scottish Life and Society: A Compendium of Scottish Ethnology, vol. 11 (Tuckwell Press, 2000), pp. 84–105.
Paterson, Lindsay, *Education and the Scottish Parliament* (Dunedin Academic Press, 2000).
Pickard, Willis and John Dobie, *The Political Context of Education after Devolution* (Dunedin Academic Press, 2003).
Priestley, Mark and Gert Biesta (eds), *Reinventing the Curriculum: New Trends in Curriculum Policy and Practice* (Bloomsbury, 2013).
Scotland, James, *The History of Scottish Education*, 2 vols (University of London Press, 1969).
Scottish Executive, *A Curriculum for Excellence: The Curriculum Review Group* (Scottish Executive, 2004).
Scottish Executive, *A Teaching Profession for the 21st Century* (the McCrone Report) (Scottish Executive, 2000).

Notes on the Contributors

David Allan is a Reader in Scottish History at the University of St Andrews. He has published widely in Scottish and British history between the sixteenth and the twentieth centuries, with particular interest in cultural and intellectual history, historiography, book history and the history of ideas and of political thought.

Robert Anderson is Professor Emeritus of Modern History, University of Edinburgh. He has written extensively on the history of education in Scotland, Britain and Europe. His current interests include the history of history as a university subject, and the relation between education and modern nationalism.

Christopher R. Bischof is Assistant Professor of History at the University of Richmond. His research interests include the history of elementary teachers in Victorian Britain, particularly their role in debates about social mobility, gender, the nature of childhood and the role of the state.

Ewen A. Cameron is Sir William Fraser Professor of Scottish History and Palaeography at the University of Edinburgh. His research interests are in the history of the Scottish Highlands, Scottish political history and the history of Scottish universities.

Kimm Curran is an Affiliate Researcher at the University of Glasgow in Theology and Religious Studies. Her research interests include medieval monasticism from 1100 to 1600 in Britain and Ireland, the prosopography of monastic men and women, and monastic houses in medieval and modern landscapes.

Ian J. Deary is Professor of Differential Psychology at the University of Edinburgh, and Director of the MRC-BBSRC Centre for Cognitive Ageing and Cognitive Epidemiology. He directs the Lothian Birth Cohorts of 1921 and 1936. His research aims to discover the causes of people's differences in cognitive and brain ageing.

Elizabeth Ewan is University Research Chair and Professor, Department of History, University of Guelph. Her research interests include medieval and early modern Scotland, Scottish urban history, the history of crime in medieval and early modern Scotland, and Scottish women's history.

John Finlay is Professor of Scots Law at the University of Glasgow. His research specialism is legal history and he has a particular interest in the history of the legal professions of Europe.

Mark Freeman is a Senior Lecturer at the UCL Institute of Education, University College London. He is co-editor of the journal *History of Education*.

Matthew Hammond is a Research Associate in History in the School of Humanities, University of Glasgow. He has research interests in all aspects of the history of Britain and Ireland in the period between about 1050 and 1350, including digital humanities and prosopography, national identities and historiographical narratives.

Stephen Mark Holmes is an Honorary Fellow in the School of Divinity at the University of Edinburgh and Associate Rector of St John's Episcopal Church, Edinburgh. He is the author of books on late medieval Scottish church furnishings and Basil of Caesarea, as well as many articles on church history. His research interests include Reformation studies, liturgical studies and the history of Renaissance Scotland.

Walter Humes is a Visiting Professor in the School of Education at the University of Stirling. He has long-term research interests in teacher education, educational leadership and management, the history of education and policy studies.

Martin Lawn is an Honorary Research Fellow in the Department of Education at the University of Oxford. His research interests are in the European policy space in education – its conceptualisation, development and practices – and the sociology and history of the education sciences.

Catriona M. M. Macdonald is a Reader in Late-Modern Scottish History at the University of Glasgow. Her research interests include the socio-political and cultural history of Scotland from 1832, and interdisciplinary studies of late-modern Scottish society and culture (principally literature).

Jane McDermid is a Reader in History at the University of Southampton. Her current research interests lie in late-eighteenth- and nineteenth-century British women's history. She has a long-term interest in nineteenth- and twentieth-century Britain and Russia, and specifically in gender history.

Lindy Moore is an independent researcher and former librarian. She has published widely on the history of girls' and women's education in Scotland, particularly in the eighteenth and nineteenth centuries.

David Northcroft is a Research Associate of the Elphinstone Institute, University of Aberdeen, and was formerly Vice-Principal, Northern College, Aberdeen and

Dundee. His research interests include the relationship between education and identity in North-East Scotland.

Fiona O'Hanlon is a Chancellor's Fellow in the School of Education at the University of Edinburgh. Her research interests include bilingual education, languages education, attitudes to language and language policy.

Lindsay Paterson is Professor of Educational Policy, School of Social and Political Science, University of Edinburgh. His academic interests include the relationship of education to civic engagement and political attitudes.

John Stevenson is a retired Church of Scotland minister who served in the parish ministry before being appointed as General Secretary of the church's Department of Education. In 2000, he was made an Honorary Fellow of the Educational Institute of Scotland (FEIS) in recognition of his services to school education. He was awarded a PhD by the University of Edinburgh in 2005 for his research into the historical role of the Church of Scotland in school education.

Douglas Sutherland is a Tutor in the University of Glasgow's Centre for Open Studies. His research interests are in contemporary adult education and its recent history, particularly the nature and course of the relationship between higher and adult education in the nineteenth and early twentieth centuries.

Stuart Wallace was a Lecturer in History at Newbattle Abbey College (1985–9) and at the Centre for Continuing Education at the University of Edinburgh (1991–2001). He is the author of *War and the Image of Germany: British Academics 1914–1918* (John Donald, 1988) and *John Stuart Blackie: Scottish Scholar and Patriot* (Edinburgh University Press, 2006).

Index

Note: page numbers in **bold** refer to figures and those in *italics* refer to tables